MAIMONIDES THE UNIVERSALIST

THE LITTMAN LIBRARY OF
JEWISH CIVILIZATION

Life Patron
COLETTE LITTMAN

Dedicated to the memory of
LOUIS THOMAS SIDNEY LITTMAN
who founded the Littman Library for the love of God
and as an act of charity in memory of his father
JOSEPH AARON LITTMAN
and to the memory of
ROBERT JOSEPH LITTMAN
who continued what his father Louis had begun

יהא זכרם ברוך

'Get wisdom, get understanding:
Forsake her not and she shall preserve thee'

PROV. 4:5

The Littman Library of Jewish Civilization is a registered UK charity
Registered charity no. 1000784

MAIMONIDES THE UNIVERSALIST

The Ethical Horizons of the Mishneh Torah

◆

MENACHEM KELLNER
AND
DAVID GILLIS

London
The Littman Library of Jewish Civilization
in association with Liverpool University Press

The Littman Library of Jewish Civilization
Registered office: 14th floor, 33 Cavendish Square, London W1G 0PW

in association with Liverpool University Press
4 Cambridge Street, Liverpool L69 7ZU, UK
www.liverpooluniversitypress.co.uk/littman

Managing Editor: Connie Webber

Distributed in North America by Longleaf Services
116 S Boundary St, Chapel Hill, NY 27514, USA

First published in hardback 2020
First published in paperback 2025

© Menachem Kellner and David Gillis 2020

All rights reserved.
No part of this publication may be reproduced,
stored in a retrieval system, or transmitted, in any form or
by any means, without the prior permission in writing of
the Littman Library of Jewish Civilization

This book is sold subject to the condition that it shall not, by way
of trade or otherwise, be lent, re-sold, hired out or otherwise circulated
without the publisher's prior consent in any form of binding or cover
other than that in which it is published and without a similar condition
including this condition being imposed on the subsequent purchaser

Catalogue records for this book are available from the
British Library and the Library of Congress

ISBN 978–1–802078–92–3

Publishing co-ordinator: Janet Moth
Copy-editing: Lindsey Taylor-Guthartz
Proof-reading: Mark Newby
Indexing: Shoshana Hurwitz
Designed and typeset by Pete Russell, Faringdon, Oxon.

The manufacturer's authorised representative in the EU for product safety is:
Easy Access System Europe, Mustamäe tee 50, 10621 Tallinn, Estonia
https://easproject.com (gpsr.requests@easproject.com)

'His mercy is over all His works'
PSALM 145: 9

Acknowledgements

WE THANK our wives, Jolene Kellner and Sally Gillis, for their support in the pleasurable task we undertook in writing this book, and the many other members of our families, and the friends and colleagues, who have enriched our understanding of Maimonides over the years. We also thank each other for the enjoyable and rewarding experience of working together. Thanks too to Seth Kadish, who gave valuable advice on the manuscript, to Shoshana Hurwitz for her pinpoint indexing, and to Lindsey Taylor-Guthartz, Janet Moth, Pete Russell, and all concerned at the Littman Library for their skill and dedication in bringing the book to publication.

Contents

Note on Transliteration	x
INTRODUCTION	1
1. *Knowledge*: To Know Is To Love	14
2. *Love*: Abraham, Moses, and the Meaning of Circumcision	40
3. *Seasons*: Hanukah and Purim Reconfigured	73
4. *Women*: Marital and Universal Peace	82
5. *Holiness*: Commandments as Instruments	90
6. *Asseverations*: Social Responsibility and Sanctifying God's Name	106
7. *Agriculture*: Sanctifying All Human Beings	129
8. *Temple Service*: The Divinity of the Commandments	144
9. *Offerings*: The Morality of the Commandments	173
10. *Ritual Purity*: Intellectual and Moral Purity	183
11. *Damages*: Who Is a Jew?	221
12. *Acquisition*: Slavery versus Universal Humanity	235
13. *Civil Laws*: God of Aristotle in the God of Abraham	267
14. *Judges*: Messianic Universalism	277
CONCLUSION	302
APPENDIX: Maimonides' Cosmic Paradigm	321
Bibliography	339
Index of Citations	355
Index of Subjects	363

Note on Transliteration

◆

THE TRANSLITERATION of Hebrew in this book reflects consideration of the type of book it is, in terms of its content, purpose, and readership. The system adopted therefore reflects a broad approach to transcription, rather than the narrower approaches found in the *Encyclopaedia Judaica* or other systems developed for text-based or linguistic studies. The aim has been to reflect the pronunciation prescribed for modern Hebrew, rather than the spelling or Hebrew word structure, and to do so using conventions that are generally familiar to the English-speaking reader.

In accordance with this approach, no attempt is made to indicate the distinctions between *alef* and *ayin*, *tet* and *taf*, *kaf* and *kuf*, *sin* and *samekh*, since these are not relevant to pronunciation; likewise, the *dagesh* is not indicated except where it affects pronunciation. Following the principle of using conventions familiar to the majority of readers, however, transcriptions that are well established have been retained even when they are not fully consistent with the transliteration system adopted. On similar grounds, the *tsadi* is rendered by 'tz' in such familiar words as barmitzvah. Likewise, the distinction between *ḥet* and *khaf* has been retained, using *ḥ* for the former and *kh* for the latter; the associated forms are generally familiar to readers, even if the distinction is not actually borne out in pronunciation, and for the same reason the final *heh* is indicated too. As in Hebrew, no capital letters are used, except that an initial capital has been retained in transliterating titles of published works (for example, *Shulḥan arukh*).

Since no distinction is made between *alef* and *ayin*, they are indicated by an apostrophe only in intervocalic positions where a failure to do so could lead an English-speaking reader to pronounce the vowel cluster as a diphthong—as, for example, in *ha'ir*—or otherwise mispronounce the word. An apostrophe is also used, for the same reason, to disambiguate the pronunciation of other English vowel clusters, as for example in *mizbe'aḥ*.

The *sheva na* is indicated by an *e*—*perikat ol*, *reshut*—except, again, when established convention dictates otherwise.

The *yod* is represented by *i* when it occurs as a vowel (*bereshit*), by *y* when it occurs as a consonant (*yesodot*), and by *yi* when it occurs as both (*yisra'el*).

Names have generally been left in their familiar forms, even when this is inconsistent with the overall system.

INTRODUCTION

What Is a 'Universalist'?

Often, at the end of a section of the *Mishneh torah*, Maimonides steps back from the textual grindstone of halakhah and surveys broader horizons. Eloquent codas expressing philosophical and moral ideas, rather than halakhah proper, are a feature of the *Mishneh torah* throughout, but are particularly marked at the end of each of the fourteen books into which it is divided.[1] In the present study we treat those book endings as a distinct Maimonidean genre. We examine each of them, in an attempt to assemble a picture of what Maimonides sees when he lifts his gaze from the technical details of halakhah and seems to ask himself, 'What is the point of all this?'

We maintain that, for all that the *Mishneh torah* is a code of Jewish law, the vision that Maimonides sees is universalist. It behoves us (as Shlomo Pines' Maimonides likes to say) to explain what we mean by that term. One may speak of weak universalism and strong universalism. Weak universalism would be to say that Maimonides sees the commandments of the Torah as a particular means to a universal end, which is the position advanced in several of the chapters in this book. The universal end is that of Torah in the larger sense, which, according to Maimonides, encompasses the universal disciplines of physics and metaphysics. They are in fact the acme of Torah study, representing the content of what the rabbis called *ma'aseh bereshit* and *ma'aseh merkavah*, or collectively, *pardes*.[2] Maimonides refers to as this as the

---

[1] This feature of the *Mishneh torah* has long been recognized. It is noted by the translators of at least two of the work's volumes in the Yale Judaica series. Isaac Klein, *The Book of Acquisition*, p. xiv, writes: 'Finally, Book XII fully confirms the often made observation to the effect that Maimonides tends to detect a moral-ethical point of view even in laws that at first sight seem to be of purely civic and ritual nature.' Similarly, Jacob J. Rabinowitz, *The Book of Civil Laws*, p. xx, notes: 'In three of the five treatises of our book (i, iv, v) the last section represents a sort of peroration, with an appropriate passage from Scripture skillfully woven into the text. These perorations, which are also found in many of the other treatises of the Code, reveal a depth of feeling and beauty of style rarely matched in Halakhaic [sic] literature.'

[2] See 'Laws of Torah Study', 1: 12.

'great thing', whereas the details of halakhah are a 'small thing'.³ The 'small thing' is particular; the 'great thing' is universal.

Strong universalism would be to say that the commandments of the Torah are themselves also universal. We suggest below that Maimonides might have believed that all of humanity will keep all of the commandments in the days of the messiah—this despite the commandments' historical and geographical references. If this is the case, then Maimonidean Judaism is weakly universalist in the pre-messianic era, and strongly universalist in the messianic world.

Any claim of Judaic universalism must take into account the fact that Judaism has limited elasticity. Crudely speaking, it can be vertically universal, or populist, like hasidism, granting immortality to the pious but ignorant as much as, or maybe even more than, to the learned, as long as they are Jewish; or it can be horizontally universal, or elitist, and grant the possibility of immortality to all irrespective of ethnicity, as long as they reach enlightenment.

To what sort of universalism did Maimonides subscribe? It is very much of the horizontal kind. This finds expression in many different ways, but they may be summarized as follows: all human beings are equally created in the image of God, Jews as such are in no way different from or superior to non-Jews as such, any nation could have received the Torah, and in the end of days some form of Abrahamic monotheistic universalism will hold sway. Related issues include Maimonides' attempt to turn Judaism into what might be called a community of true believers (in which theology trumps biology), and the idea that halakhah establishes social realities as opposed to reflecting what might be called antecedent supernatural realities—we maintain instead that Maimonides sees the laws of nature as the model for the individual and social perfection that halakhah promotes, as will shortly be explained.

Restating these claims, we maintain that Maimonides held the following:

- All human beings are created in the image of God, with no ifs, buts, or wherefores.

- The notion of the chosen people, therefore, carries with it no sense that Jews are in any sense inherently superior to non-Jews.

---

³ After BT *Suk.* 28a. *Ma'aseh bereshit* is the account of Creation. *Ma'aseh merkavah* is the account of Ezekiel's vision of the heavenly chariot. These are associated with physics and metaphysics in 'Laws of the Foundations of the Torah', 4: 13. For discussion and sources, see Twersky, *Introduction to the Code*, 493–4. In his introduction to the *Guide of the Perplexed*, Maimonides similarly distinguishes the 'legalistic study of the Torah' from 'the science of the Torah in its true sense' (p. 5). For more on *ma'aseh bereshit* and *ma'aseh merkavah*, see Ch. 1.

- Connected to this is the idea that the Torah is ultimately directed at all human beings, given to the Jews in the expectation that it would ultimately be accepted by all humanity in one way or another.

Going into more detail at this point would be to put the cart before the horse. In our conclusion we will show how these ideas, and, it will turn out, many others, reflect the universal horizons of the *Mishneh torah*.[4]

It also makes sense to explain what we do *not* mean by universalism. We certainly do not mean that Maimonides was either a relativist or a pluralist. By 'relativism' we understand (following the *American Heritage Dictionary*) the view that holds 'that conceptions of truth and moral values are not absolute but are relative to the persons or groups holding them'. Like almost all medievals, Maimonides held truth to be one, objective, and unchanging—no matter from which perspective one looked at it. Moral values, on the other hand, were not absolute, but, despite that, were largely shared by the societies with which Maimonides was familiar. By 'religious pluralism' we understand the normative (as opposed to simply descriptive) claim that different religions make equally correct truth-claims, which are equally acceptable. Maimonides held Islam to be truly monotheist, but aside from that, had little good to say about it. Christianity he held to be a form of idolatry. Thus, universalism as understood here is actually the *opposite* of pluralism. Like medieval Muslims and Christians, Maimonides was convinced that only his religion was absolutely true. But, unlike Muslims and Christians, Maimonides saw no need to force Judaism on non-Jews (outside a Jewish state).

Thus, Maimonides allowed plural means to what we might call a universal end: one did not need to be Jewish to achieve a share in the world to come (what Christianity would call 'salvation' and what the philosopher Gersonides (1288–1384) would call *hatslaḥah*). But the end is still single. Maimonides does not allow a multiplicity of equally valid, self-determined (or at least self-selected) goals of human life, or no goal at all.

Maimonidean universalism is also not egalitarianism: Maimonides was a strict intellectual elitist. Also, while he clearly held that women could, in principle, be taught, and could achieve high levels of intellectual (i.e. human) perfection, he appears to have been untroubled by the fact that few women were given the opportunity to fulfil their human potential, and even made

---

[4] Relevant here is Maimonides' claim in his introduction to *Perek ḥelek* (Mishnah *San.*, ch. 10) that by examining the *ḥukim* (laws ordinarily thought—but not by Maimonides!—to have no rational explanation), non-Jews will be brought to see the wisdom of the Torah (see Maimonides, *Hakdamot*). For details and discussion, see Twersky, *Introduction to the Code*, 386–7. On *ḥukim* in the *Mishneh torah* see below, Chs. 8–10.

legal rulings to make that less likely to happen. Nor did he have any apparent reservations concerning laws discriminating against non-Jews. And why should he have? Halakhah, most emphatically including Maimonidean halakhah, discriminates against non-Jews, but then every legal system distinguishes between citizens and aliens, to the detriment of the latter (thus, for example, one of the authors of this book could in principle be elected president of the USA while the other could not).

Maimonidean universalism should not be confused with toleration. For most medievals, including Maimonides, tolerating evil was unacceptable, and even tolerating error was wrong. Further, much of the halakhah that Maimonides faithfully records is highly intolerant.

Maimonidean universalism should also not be confused with humanism, which places the human being at the centre. For Maimonides God must be at the centre—the extent to which people are worthy to be called 'human' is the extent to which they imitate God and thus (and only thus) actualize their humanity. At the same time, his brand of universalism goes with a profound humanity. There is a tension here that is characteristic of several of the 'endings' of the *Mishneh torah*, the subject matter of this book.

We also do not subscribe to the interpretation of Maimonidean universalism held by the philosopher Hermann Cohen (1842–1918), to the effect that an ethics which admits no morally relevant difference among human beings is (along with belief in God) the highest possible level of human attainment. We would agree that Maimonides considered all human beings to be morally equal, but Maimonidean halakhah, as mentioned, grants advantages to Jewish 'citizens'. Further, Maimonides clearly and explicitly held that moral perfection is only the second-highest species of human perfection, being a prerequisite for and stepping-stone towards the highest form, that of the intellect.[5] Nor did he believe every individual to be constitutionally capable of reaching this perfection, although in this respect Jews are not more favoured than non-Jews.[6]

Another tension that we explore is that between the individual and the collective. Maimonides clearly held that the Torah applied to all Jews, but he acknowledged that its laws might actually be harmful in some cases.[7] Similarly, he held the Torah to be applicable without variation in all times and places.[8] A uniform code of law, universally applicable to the whole community at all times, was simply a political necessity to him. Nevertheless, he did

---

[5] *Guide* iii. 54 (p. 634). For Cohen's views, see Bruckstein, *Hermann Cohen on 'Maimonides' Ethics'*. For further discussion, see Kellner, *Maimonides on Human Perfection*.
[6] See Freudenthal, 'Biological Limitations'.   [7] See *Guide* iii. 34 (pp. 534–5).   [8] Ibid.

suggest ways in which the individual might find meaning in the commandments for himself or herself.⁹ Moreover, Maimonides' universalism is really based upon individualism, on the idea that individuals pursue their own perfection rather than seeking salvation through tribe, class, nation, or church, whereas the Torah appears to be very much a collectivist creed.¹⁰ These tensions too find expression in the *Mishneh torah*'s book endings.

The universalism of the *Mishneh torah* is also not of a deracinated kind. Quite the contrary: much of its force derives from the way in which it emerges from the specifically Jewish. The work's commitment to Jewish law is of course its *raison d'être*, but it is also represents an aspect of Maimonides' deep concern for the integrity and morale of the Jewish people as demonstrated by the *Epistle to Yemen*, for example. Writing to his favourite pupil, Joseph ben Judah, the addressee of the *Guide*, he says that part of his motivation for composing the *Mishneh torah* was that 'I saw a nation without a genuinely comprehensive code of law, and without true and exact doctrines.'¹¹ The work also displays Maimonides' intense feeling towards the Land of Israel, exceeding the bounds of halakhic obligation,¹² and his vivid sense of Jewish history and destiny. It is no part of our enterprise to downplay these sentiments towards nation and land. We only seek, where necessary, to put them in the context of Maimonides' world outlook as we understand it.

Obviously, Maimonides never used the term 'universalism' (in any language).¹³ One might even think that he was unaware of the universalist implications of his positions. Given the evidence adduced in this volume, we find that unlikely.

The *Mishneh Torah*'s Philosophical Basis

Having settled these matters, we may now turn to the question of how we plan to examine the *Mishneh torah* and show that the views we attribute to Maimonides here, which are easily found in his *Guide of the Perplexed*, also find expression in his legal code.

The authors of this book have devoted considerable attention to what

---

⁹ See *Guide* iii. 51 (pp. 622–4).
¹⁰ For an account of the reaction of a collectivist, R. Naftali Tsevi Yehudah Berlin (Netsiv), that brings Maimonides' individualism into sharp focus, see Diamond, *Maimonides and the Shaping of the Jewish Canon*, 205–30.   ¹¹ *Igerot harambam* (trans. Shailat), i. 1, 300–1.
¹² See e.g. 'Laws of Kings and their Wars', 5: 9–12, and the motto of the *Book of Temple Service*: 'Pray for the well-being of Jerusalem; may those who love you be at peace' (Ps. 122: 6).
¹³ The term itself derives from Christian debates over whether or not there can be salvation outside the Church.

Isadore Twersky called the 'non-halakic aspects of the *Mishneh Torah*'.[14] In *Reading Maimonides' Mishneh Torah*, David Gillis showed that Maimonides modelled the structure of the work on his cosmology. By this device, he placed the 'small thing' (halakhah) in the setting of the 'great thing' (physics and metaphysics), or, to put it another way, he cast the *Mishneh torah*'s (mostly) particularist content in a universal form. Gillis interprets this as a means of relating the commandments of the Torah and the idea of Jewish destiny culminating in the messiah (the theme on which the *Mishneh torah* ends) to the philosophical ideal of the pursuit of the knowledge of God within a stable and just society.[15] The *Mishneh torah*'s microcosmic form suggests that the cosmos is a paradigm of perfection for all human individuals and societies that the Torah converts into a law adapted to the situation of a particular people (see Appendix).

Menachem Kellner's writing has also focused on the combination of halakhah, Aristotelian science, history, and messianism in Maimonidean thought. In a series of studies, he has sought to show that Maimonides is a consistent universalist.[16] In *Maimonides on Human Perfection*, in particular, he shows that the *Guide of the Perplexed* is meant to lead appropriate readers from a view of God as transcendent intellect alone, to a connection with God as the object of worship and the model for imitation. Kellner's reading of the *Guide* is paralleled in precisely the kind of development that Gillis finds in the *Mishneh torah*.

Our joint endeavour in this book may thus be seen as a mutual continuation of our work. Gillis's earlier book shows that while the major content of the *Mishneh torah* is commandments, the book has a philosophical message expressed in its structure. Here we show that that the philosophical message is also adumbrated in the statements closing each book of the work. Kellner's studies have demonstrated that halakhah is a tool, not an end in and of itself, for Maimonides, and that the *Mishneh torah* should therefore be understood as a tool whose purpose is better expressed in the closing statements of many sections and of each book than in the halakhic meat and potatoes of the work itself.

---

[14] See Twersky, 'Some Non-Halakic Aspects'. Twersky expanded his discussion dramatically in his *Introduction to the Code*, 356–507.

[15] As far as Maimonides is concerned, God's existence is rationally necessary, and recognition of that is a matter of knowledge, not belief, hence the knowledge of God is a philosophical goal. For confirmation of this one need go no further than the very first *halakhah* of the *Mishneh torah* itself. See below, Ch. 1.

[16] Kellner, *Maimonides on Judaism*; id., *Maimonides' Confrontation*; id., *They, Too, Are Called Human* (Heb.).

The *Mishneh torah* states, in chapter 8 of 'Laws of the Foundations of the Torah', that the truth of the Torah is guaranteed by the fact that the entire Jewish people were witness to the revelation at Sinai and could attest to the genuineness of the prophecy of Moses; that is to say, it is guaranteed by tradition, the faithful transmission down the generations of the record of an incontrovertibly real historical event. At the same time, the message that emerges from the *Mishneh torah*'s microcosmic form is that the Torah is eternally and universally true because it faithfully reflects the eternal laws of nature, independently of history and tradition.[17] The Torah may have been revealed to a particular people in a unique historical nexus of the human and the divine, but its basis is universal. In our examination of the endings of the books of the *Mishneh torah*, we have frequently found that these endings work in tandem with the general structure to establish that universalism as not only the basis of the Torah, but also its tendency and final vision.

The Model of the Mishnah

Maimonides took Rabbi Judah the Prince, editor of the Mishnah, as one of his models.[18] It has been observed that the Mishnah itself contains a coda expressing moral and religious ideas with almost no reference to halakhah per se: tractate *Avot*. Robert Travers Herford suggested that *Avot* was meant to express Rabbi Judah's judgement on the whole mishnaic project.[19] This suggestion gains added credence when we recall that *Avot* originally may have been the last tractate in the Mishnah. Furthermore, there are individual tractates that end with matters not wholly halakhic.[20] Thus, in composing codas to each of the books of the *Mishneh torah*, Maimonides may well have been following in the footsteps of his role model, Rabbi Judah the Prince. It will be argued below that this is certainly the case with respect to the closing, messianic chapters of the work as a whole. Vis-à-vis these matters, note Maimonides' closing words in his commentary on tractate *Berakhot*, to the effect that in his commentary on *Avot* he would indicate how the views of the Sages and of the 'greatest among the philosophers' were compatible. The closing

---

[17] There is a complication here in that, in *Guide* ii. 25 (p. 329), Maimonides declares the validity of the Torah to be *dependent* on the doctrine of Creation, but that is not what seems to be implied in the *Mishneh torah*.   [18] Twersky, *Introduction to the Code*, 64–5.

[19] Herford, *The Ethics of the Talmud*, 1. See Epstein, *Mavo lenusaḥ hamishnah*, ii. 980–1.

[20] Epstein, *Mavo lenusaḥ hamishnah*, ii. 980–1. Many mishnaic tractates (and not a few talmudic tractates) end with aggadic (non-halakhic) material: *Berakhot, Pe'ah, Yoma, Sotah, Bava batra*, and *Uktsin* come to mind. For Maimonides aggadah is much more than simply stories. Compare Twersky, *Introduction to the Code*, 150–3.

codas of the parts of the *Mishneh torah* may be further way of fulfilling that promise.

His promise should not be surprising. For Maimonides, after all, halakhah is a divinely ordained instrument for the attainment of a high level of moral and social perfection, but it does not in and of itself lead to true human fulfilment; that can only be accomplished through knowledge of scientific/philosophical truth. It should surprise no one, therefore, that Maimonides injects into the dry halakhic material of the *Mishneh torah* indications of what he takes to be God's broader agenda.

Halakhah or Meta-Halakhah?

Maimonides' penchant for attaching moral and philosophical codas to the sections of the *Mishneh torah* is recognized by prominent rabbinic students of the text. Thus, we find Rabbi Isaac Shailat, a leading contemporary translator and interpreter of Maimonides, noting (with reference to one of the highly contested codas we will examine, namely 'Laws of the Sabbatical Year and the Jubilee', 13: 13): 'These are general matters of thought and morality, as is customary in the conclusions of the volumes of the *Mishneh torah*, and not matters of halakhah.'[21] In his magisterial *Introduction to the Code of Maimonides*, Isadore Twersky writes of 'frequent ethical digressions and interpolations ... These extra-halakic motifs are deftly sprinkled throughout all the fourteen books in prolegomena and perorations, in exegetical comments and interpretive embellishments, parenthetic explanations, and assorted pretexts'.[22] Despite such recognition, there are formidable students of Maimonides who reject this claim, prominent among them both the late Lubavitcher Rebbe, Menachem Mendel Schneersohn, and, perhaps, the late Rabbi Joseph Soloveitchik.[23] Both claimed that Maimonides' aim in the *Mishneh torah* was purely halakhic.

Shailat in effect dismisses the texts at the heart of this study, presenting them as at best ancillary to the true purpose of the *Mishneh torah*. Schneer-

---

[21] In his edition and Hebrew translation of Maimonides, *Commentary on Avot* (Heb.), 75. One wonders if there an expression of ambivalence here, in that the *Mishneh torah* is really meant to be about halakhah.

[22] pp. 371–2. But see p. 257: 'The ruling passion of Maimonides' life was order, system, conceptualization, and generalization.' This being the case, is it possible that the closing passages in so many parts of the *Mishneh torah* have no significance?

[23] For R. Schneersohn, see his *Maimonidean Rules* (Heb.), 39–40: every part of the *Mishneh torah* (including section titles) is halakhah and every passage in the text has halakhic significance. For R. Soloveitchik the situation is more complex. While very much aware of

sohn and Soloveitchik, on the other hand, absorb these texts back into the work's halakhic matter. In our view, both of these approaches are mistaken: the passages at the heart of this study are not just attractive moral sermonettes, digressions, or interpolations, nor are they simply part of halakhah. They are, rather, expressions of a fundamental theme in the *Mishneh torah*.[24] And what is that theme? That the Torah is ultimately aimed at human beings generally, and not just at Jews: the Torah is ultimately meant to be adopted by *kol ba'ei olam*, all those who have come into the world.[25] It is our aim to bring these universalist horizons of the *Mishneh torah* into full view.

Maimonides is notorious for having stated the following at the end of his introduction to the *Mishneh torah*:

> On these grounds I, Moses, the son of Maimon, the Sefardi, bestirred myself, and, relying on the help of God, blessed be He, intently studied all these works [Mishnah, Talmud, Midrash, geonic literature], with the view of putting together the results obtained from them in regard to what is forbidden or permitted, ritually pure or impure, and the other rules of the Torah—all in plain language and terse style, so that thus the entire Oral Torah might become systematically known to all . . . [and so] that all the rules shall be accessible to young and old . . . so that no other work should be needed for ascertaining any of the laws of Israel, but that this work might serve as a compendium of the entire Oral Torah . . . Hence, I have entitled this work *Mishneh torah* (*Second Torah*),[26] for the reason that a person who first reads the Written Torah and then this compilation, will know from it the whole of the Oral Torah, without having occasion to consult any other book between them.[27]

Assuming that Maimonides meant what he said about his work serving 'as a

how much he himself differs from Maimonides on important matters, he still seems to want to present him as an exemplar of Halakhic Man, for whom what is not rooted in halakhah is not Judaism. On R. Soloveitchik on Maimonides, see Diamond and Kellner, *Reinventing Maimonides*, ch. 1, and Kaplan (ed.), *Maimonides: Between Philosophy and Halakhah*. See also below, Ch. 10.

[24] It is more than likely that Maimonides had several objectives for the *Mishneh torah*, and that the one we focus on here is one of many. For an account of the many different theories about why Maimonides wrote the book, see Twersky, 'The *Mishneh Torah* of Maimonides'.

[25] On the expression used here, and the rabbinic debates about it, see Hirshman, 'Rabbinic Universalism'. This article is based on Hirshman, *Torah for All Human Beings* (Heb.).

[26] The term derives from Deut. 17: 18 and became the common rabbinic appellation for the book of Deuteronomy (and the source of that Greek name). Given that the term means a recapitulation of the Torah, Maimonides' choice of it reflects his ambitions for the book and, it is likely, constitutes the reason for the resistance in rabbinic circles for using that name. In such circles the book has for centuries been called *Yad haḥazakah*, 'the strong hand' (Deut. 7: 19 and 34: 12), itself quite a compliment, and a play on the book's fourteen volumes (*yad* = 14 when letters are understood as numbers).

[27] *Book of Knowledge*, trans. Moses Hyamson, 4*b*.

compendium of the entire Oral Torah' such that 'no other work should be needed',[28] many of his readers concluded that this revision (and reduction) of the traditional curriculum was designed to make room for the study of physics and metaphysics.[29] Reading him in this fashion strengthens our claim that the codas scattered throughout the work, and especially at the end of sections and books, are neither purely halakhic nor mere flourishes.

The Science of the Torah

The formal parallel between the *Mishneh torah* and the cosmos suggests that there is a science of the Torah analogous to natural science. In his introduction to the *Guide*, Maimonides states that it is about just such a science—not 'the legalistic study of the Law', but 'the science of the Law in its true sense'.[30] The abstraction of general principles from the halakhic data, and the understanding of relationships between the halakhic phenomena, will then give access to the commandments not just as a body of law, but as a body of knowledge, the study of which is conducive to the love of God in the same way as is the study of nature. Systemization of the commandments leads to conceptualization of the commandments, which is their ultimate fulfilment (this without detracting in the least from the need for 'legalistic study' and observance of halakhah in all its details, as Maimonides demands both action and abstraction).[31] The human mind suffers from the same severe limitations in under-

---

[28] Which is something that many of his students have been unwilling to do. For details, see the studies cited in Kellner, '*Mishneh Torah*: Why?' (Heb.).   [29] Ibid.

[30] *Guide*, Introduction to the First Part (p. 5). We take Maimonides to mean by this everything that the *Guide* covers: God, the cosmos, prophecy, the proper way of reading the Bible, culminating in the reasons for the commandments. See also the parable of the palace in *Guide* iii. 51 (pp. 618–20), in which 'ignoramuses who observe the commandments' and 'the jurists' are ranked below 'Those who have plunged into speculation concerning the fundamental principles of religion'; see Strauss, 'How to Begin to Study the *Guide of the Perplexed*', p. xiv. In 'Laws of the Foundations of the Torah', 2: 2, Maimonides states that the way to the love of God is through contemplation of the natural world, and cites the Sages as saying 'For through that, you recognize the one who spoke and the world was.' The reference appears to be to *Sifrei* on Deut. 6: 6, but that *midrash* advocates contemplation of the commandments, not of nature, as the way to such recognition. In the *Book of the Commandments* (positive commandment 3) Maimonides cites *Sifrei* in its original sense. This has been seen as a minor crux (e.g. Kreisel, *Maimonides' Political Thought*, 117–18), but it is explicable if we acknowledge that, for Maimonides, contemplation of nature and contemplation of the commandments amount to the same thing. See further discussion of this point below, Ch. 1.

[31] See for example the regret that Maimonides expresses in the introduction to his commentary on Mishnah *Zev.* that the demise of sacrifices means that the systematic study of their laws is neglected. This is discussed further in Ch. 10 below.

standing some of the commandments as it does in understanding nature, particularly superlunary nature,[32] but that is no excuse for not making the attempt.[33]

In tandem with the structural hints, the *Mishneh torah*'s book endings do just this, distilling essential principles and directing our attention towards 'the science of the Law in its true sense'. The *Mishneh torah* is thus at the same time an exposition of the Torah and a meditation upon it. The book endings meditate out loud, while the cosmic structure does so silently, but, as mentioned, the two must often be considered in combination in order to catch the full message.

The upshot is that the conventional notion of the *Mishneh torah* as a work of halakhah supplemented by philosophical introductory material and some scattered philosophical reflections needs to be replaced with a notion of it as a work of philosophy through and through. The relationship between the 'small thing' and the 'great thing' is not just a matter of graduating from one to the other; as stressed already, the former is a model of the latter.[34] This can be seen as reflecting the view of Islamic philosophers that religion is philosophy in popular guise.[35] It can also be seen as imbuing the commandments of the Torah with a universalism that, perhaps paradoxically, is more radical than that of the *Guide*. Rather than demonstrating, as does the *Guide*, that the commandments are compatible with certain external, universally recognized principles, in the *Mishneh torah*'s presentation such principles are immanent within the commandments, and emerge organically from contemplation of them. If the commandments are particular means to universal ends, then in the *Guide*, means and ends are largely separate, whereas in the *Mishneh torah* they are integrated.

This brings us close to Maimonides' famous two-layered approach to the interpretation of biblical and rabbinic parables: the idea of an external meaning that 'contains wisdom that is useful in many respects, among which is the

---

[32] See *Guide* ii. 24 (p. 326).

[33] This is a theme of the endings of Books 8 and 9; see Chs. 8 and 9 below.

[34] Cf. Twersky's remark that for Maimonides '*yesodot* are the theological foundations and premises of practical laws, their invisible core' (*Introduction to the Code*, 361).

[35] See Berman, 'Ethical Views'; Pessin, 'The Influence of Islamic Thought on Maimonides'. The ostensible difference between Maimonides and the philosophers is over the doctrine of Creation. We say 'ostensible' because Maimonides' true position on this question is the subject of a controversy that we will not survey here. For what it is worth, our view is that when Maimonides says that he believes in Creation and not in Aristotle's theory of a universe that has always existed, he means it; see *Guide* ii. 6 (p. 265). The precise content of that belief and its implications are beyond the scope of the present study.

welfare of human societies' and an internal meaning that contains 'wisdom that is useful for beliefs concerned with the truth as it is'. As law, the commandments have the first, political utility. As knowledge, they have the second, philosophical kind. Both layers, of course, relate to universal values, but the second does so in a most profound way. This idea of the commandments as parables in the *Mishneh torah* is used in later chapters of this book.[36]

The consequence of all this for an assessment of the book endings in the *Mishneh torah*, where a large part of the work's philosophical reflections is to be found, is to make it highly likely that they are not floating islands of philosophy, but protrusions from a submerged philosophical continent. This vindicates their systematic study. It also vindicates an esoteric approach to their interpretation. The universalism of the *Mishneh torah* is sometimes only hinted at, or even disguised (although in some places, notably the opening and the close, it is fairly explicit). Our purpose is to amplify the hints and remove the disguises, in what we hope is a responsible manner, and thereby reveal that the underlying meaning follows what we see as the work's general drift, and is in harmony with the universalist subtext embodied in its form.

Here too, we can distinguish a weak universalism and a strong universalism. Weak universalism has one foot in each camp, asserting that Judaism is compatible with general morality and culture, that one can appreciate both the Talmud and Schiller. Strong universalism is the Maimonidean position just outlined, that Judaism and philosophy are parallel, if not almost identical.[37] In the universalism of the *Mishneh torah* there is no compromise or apology.

Universalism Prevails

At the endings of the books of the *Mishneh torah*, Maimonides confronts difficulties arising from the law and from the very idea of a divine law. In almost every case some tension is resolved, or a misconception that might arise from too literal or narrow a construal of the law is removed—generally not by pronouncement but through persuasion. Ritual obligation is balanced against social obligation, legalism is balanced against piety, reason is bal-

---

[36] For the application of the idea to the *Guide*, see J. Stern, *Problems and Parables*.

[37] Apropos Schiller, the irony is that the poets are liable to find themselves ousted from the Maimonidean state, not for being un-Jewish, but for being unphilosophical, concerned with imagination rather than truth; see Gillis, *Reading Maimonides' Mishneh Torah*, 20–5. Actually, Maimonides was accused of wishing to dispense with study of the Talmud as well, but that is another story.

anced against revelation. Maimonides takes us from the level of law to the level of values, and the weighing of values; from conformity to responsibility.

Two of the tools of persuasion that he employs are logical argument and citation of biblical verses expressing some transcendent or overriding concept (every book except the first ends with such a citation). The *Mishneh torah*'s microcosmic form represents another means of establishing priorities. Maimonides' universe is a hierarchy, in which goodness, originating in God, flows from high to low, in a version of the Neoplatonic idea of emanation. This hierarchy is reflected in the order of the *Mishneh torah*'s books (see Appendix), establishing a scale of value in which, we argue, the universal ranks above the particular. Such prioritization of the commandments, and, what is more, prioritization according to a philosophical principle, is in our view one of Maimonides' boldest moves in the *Mishneh torah*.

The *Mishneh torah* may have universal horizons, but before one reaches them there is much territory that is not universal at all. In this vast area there is blatant discrimination between Jew and non-Jew, in ways that affect not just citizenship rights but human rights as well, and all is faithfully recorded. How are these things to be reconciled? Each point must be individually argued, but in general the scale of values implied by the *Mishneh torah*'s hierarchical structure determines that, in cases of conflict between universal values and particularist ones, the higher universal values prevail.

A powerful example of this is found in Chapter 12, where we deal with Book 12, the *Book of Acquisition*, the last *halakhah* of which concerns the humane treatment of a non-Jewish slave, and cites the verse, 'And His mercy is over all His works'.[38] Understanding the symbolic, cosmic form of the *Mishneh torah* allows us to see how this is not just the expression of a pious sentiment. Behind Maimonides' deployment of this verse is the force of his entire system, so that it encapsulates his radical universalism. For this reason, we have chosen it as the motto for our book.

---

[38] Ps. 145: 9. The same verse is cited in 'Laws of Kings and their Wars', 10: 12, which similarly concerns relations between Jews and non-Jews.

ONE

KNOWLEDGE
To Know Is To Love

Introduction

In many ways the *Book of Knowledge* is the most unusual of all fourteen books of the *Mishneh torah*. More than any other book, it contains materials not ordinarily found in halakhic works. It also makes a series of claims that have aroused confusion and consternation. While this chapter seeks to analyse the closing paragraph of the *Book of Knowledge*, that analysis will require digressions to the opening paragraphs of the *Mishneh torah*, to passages in Maimonides' *Book of Commandments*, and to his discussions of love and knowledge of God, and of the patriarch Abraham.

What Is the *Book of Knowledge*?

Unusually for what purports to be a compendium of laws, Maimonides opens his *Mishneh torah* with *Sefer hamada*, the *Book of Knowledge*. What sort of knowledge is taught in this book? Maimonides explains that the *Book of Knowledge* teaches that which one must know in order to make possible the fulfilment of the Torah's commandments. Thus in his introduction to the *Mishneh torah* Maimonides writes, concerning this book, 'I will include in it all the commandments which are the root [*ikar*][1] of the religion [*dat*][2] of Moses our Master; one must know them before everything, such as, the unity of His name, blessed be He, and the prohibition of idolatry [*avodah zarah*].[3] I have called this book *Sefer hamada*.'[4]

---

[1] On Maimonides' use of this term, often translated as 'principle', see Kellner, *Dogma in Medieval Jewish Thought*, 17–21, and id., *They, Too, Are Called Human* (Heb.), 89–91.

[2] Maimonides may have been the first Jewish authority to use the term *dat* as meaning something close to the modern word 'religion'. See Kellner, *They, Too, Are Called Human* (Heb.), 60–2 (and in the index, s.v. *dat*), and, more generally, Melamed, *'Religion': From Law to Religion* (Heb.). [3] On Maimonides on idolatry, see Seeskin, *No Other Gods*.

[4] On Maimonides' use of the term *mada*, see Septimus, 'What Did Maimonides Mean by Madda?' Septimus argues that Maimonides' use of the word *mada*, as in *Sefer hamada* (the

Sefer hamada contains five sections. Two of them were alluded to in this passage by Maimonides (namely 'Laws of the Foundations of the Torah' and 'Laws of Idolatry'), and they are surely relevant to an exposition of what must be known so that the commandments of the Torah may be properly obeyed. The other three sections are: 'Laws of Moral Qualities',[5] 'Laws of Torah Study', and 'Laws of Repentance'.

'Laws of Moral Qualities' contains chapters on walking in God's ways, cleaving to those who know God, loving one's neighbour (*re'a*),[6] loving proselytes, not hating fellow Jews (*aḥim*), remonstrating (where appropriate), not causing embarrassment, not persecuting the downtrodden, not being a talebearer, not taking revenge, and not holding a grudge. In fact, much of the section is given over to issues of healthy living, both psychologically and physically. In Maimonides' holistic approach, psychic and physical health are interconnected, and both are intimately connected to what we might call moral health. Since, according to Maimonides (and all of his fellow philosophers in the medieval Aristotelian tradition), intellectual perfection depends upon antecedent moral perfection, it is perfectly clear why this section should appear in a book devoted to that which must be known.

'Laws of Torah Study' concerns itself with the obligation to study the Torah and to respect those who teach it, and those who know it. Since for Maimonides the Torah guides those who study it *properly* not only concerning right behaviour, but also concerning right thought, the seven chapters of this section are surely at home in *Sefer hamada*.

In the ten chapters of 'Laws of Repentance' Maimonides deals with many topics other than repentance, including freedom of the will (without which there can be no observance of the commandments, no reward and punishment, and certainly no repentance), the messianic era, and the world to come. Since no one actually manages to keep entirely free from sin, the message that repentance is possible, and the commandment to do it, clearly fall under the rubric of that which must be known in order to fulfil the commandments

Book of Knowledge), refers to 'a property of mind' rather than to a body of learning, and comments, 'In *Mishneh Torah*, *yada* means both "to know" and "to come to know"' (p. 86). For more on the *Book of Knowledge*, see S. Harvey, 'Alghazali and Maimonides and their Books of Knowledge' and Kraemer, 'Alfarabi's *Opinions of the Virtuous City* and Maimonides' *Foundations of the Law*'. On *Sefer hamada* itself, see Maimonides, *Guide* iii. 36 (pp. 538–9).

[5] *Hilkhot de'ot*; in his characterization of this text in the *Guide* (iii. 35 (p. 535)), Maimonides says that it deals with the improvement of *al-ahlaq*, a term which Pines there translates as 'moral qualities'. In light of this, it is surprising that Pines translates *Hilkhot de'ot* (clearly incorrectly) as 'Laws of Opinions'. Schwarz translates it as *tikun hamidot*.

[6] On Maimonides on love of neighbour (*re'a*) see *Book of the Commandments*, positive commandment 206 and Rosenberg, 'You Shall Walk in His Ways'.

of the Torah. Maimonides himself points this out in the *Guide*. Prophecy too is an indispensable basis for the commandments. The discussions of the messiah and the world to come are stepping stones to the idea of performing the commandments out of love.[7]

Like Beethoven, Maimonides apparently liked false climaxes, since it would seem that chapter 9 in 'Laws of Repentance' should be the climax of the *Book of Knowledge* (just as its subject matter, messianism, is the climax of the *Mishneh torah* as a whole).[8] But actually, from Maimonides' perspective, the climax should be chapter 8, since the point of the messianic era is to make the achievement of the world to come possible for more people. Despite this, Maimonides chooses to end the book with chapter 10, concerning the love of God.[9] Perhaps this is because not everyone will live to see the messianic era and, according to Maimonides, very few people will actually reach the hereafter.[10] But all Jews, at least, are commanded to love God, and, to some extent, others can achieve that love too.[11] Maimonides would not have agreed with Kant's repeated assertion that ought implies can,[12] but held that love of God is a state towards which all ought to strive, even if not all can actually achieve it. It will become clear during the course of our discussions that love of God is indeed a state towards which *all*, women and non-Jews included, ought to strive.[13] Even if someone is confident of reaching the hereafter, that should not be their motivation. For the state, the ultimate perfection is the messianic era, but for the individual it is love of God without regard for reward or punishment.

[7] Guide, iii. 36 (p. 540). On 'Laws of Repentance' see Kadari, *Studies in Repentance* (Heb.).

[8] Another example: *Guide* iii. 50 (pp. 613–17), which, according to Maimonides' own testimony (iii. 51, beginning (p. 618)), was meant to end the book.

[9] For the significance of the different numbers of chapters in the various sections, see Gillis, *Reading Maimonides' Mishneh Torah*, 248–50. See also ibid. 66–7 for a discussion of the fact that the *Book of Knowledge* has no real mishnaic parallel or model. On the structure of the *Book of Knowledge* as a whole, see ibid. 243–50.

[10] We ignore the scholarly debate concerning Maimonides' real views on whether or not anyone actually achieves immortality in any sense whatsoever. For discussion and references to many relevant studies, see J. Stern, *Matter and Form*, 132–4.

[11] The question of how many Jews in particular and humans in general can achieve that love remains a vexed issue, which need not detain us here.

[12] This is so since all are commanded to know God, but not many achieve that knowledge. In this Maimonides may be contrasted with Rabenu Bahya Ibn Pakuda (early 11th cent.), who, in *Ḥovot halevavot*, also held knowing God to be a commandment, but may have been more indulgent than was Maimonides towards those who lacked the requisite ability or circumstances. See Kasher, 'Does "Ought" Imply "Can"?' (Heb.).

[13] With respect to non-Jews, see Kellner, *They, Too, Are Called Human* (Heb.), and our discussion below in this chapter; with respect to women, see below, n. 22.

Chapter 10 should be understood as a fitting end, not just to 'Laws of Repentance', but to the whole *Book of Knowledge* and, in fact, as an appropriate transition to the second book of the *Mishneh torah*, the *Book of Love*. Indeed, in the final paragraph of the book, Maimonides explicitly refers us back to the beginning of the *Book of Knowledge* and also forces our attention forwards, towards the *Book of Love*, and its first section, 'Laws of the Recitation of the Shema'.[14] He does this by quoting from the Shema: '[Love the Lord your God] with all your heart and all your soul.'[15] The nature of the love of God commanded by this verse is elucidated in 'Laws of Repentance', chapter 10 and in 'Laws of the Foundations of the Torah', chapters 1–2. By sending his readers back to the beginning of 'Laws of the Foundations of the Torah', Maimonides indicates that perfect love of God involves the apprehension of the truth spoken of there.[16] In that passage Maimonides cites Jeremiah 10: 10, and parses it to refer to a truth beyond good and evil and beyond reward and punishment; indeed, in one sense a truth unrelated to the created world. This is implied by his citation there of Deuteronomy 4: 35: 'It has been clearly demonstrated to you that the Lord alone is God; there is none beside Him.'

Unpacking this complex of claims is important for us in our attempt to understand the message of the last paragraph (*halakhah*) in the *Book of Knowledge*. Maimonides, to the continuing surprise of many of his readers, devotes the first four chapters of the 'Laws of the Foundations of the Torah' (which are the first chapters of the *Book of Knowledge* and therefore the first four chapters of the *Mishneh torah* as a whole) to matters that are not usually considered halakhic.[17] Instead, these chapters deal with what the Sages called *ma'aseh bereshit* (the account of the beginning)[18] and *ma'aseh merkavah* (the account of the chariot).[19] As far as Maimonides is concerned, these subjects are the content of Jewish esoteric lore. In his earlier *Commentary on the Mishnah*, he had already identified one branch of that lore, *ma'aseh bereshit*, with physics, and the other, *ma'aseh merkavah*, with metaphysics.[20]

---

[14] Maimonides places these laws at the start of the book, before 'Laws of Prayer and the Priestly Blessing'. The recitation of the Shema should be a consequence of the mind-set created by 'Laws of Repentance' and 'Laws of the Foundations of the Torah' and should serve as a foundation for prayer.   [15] Deut. 6: 5.   [16] i: 4.

[17] So much so that references to these chapters barely appear in the Bar Ilan Global Jewish Database ('Responsa Project') and in the many commentaries written on the *Mishneh torah*.

[18] i.e. the exposition of the Creation stories in Genesis.

[19] i.e. the exposition of the visions in Ezek. 1 and 10.

[20] The identification is made in the *Commentary on the Mishnah*, Ḥag. 2: 1. This *mishnah* places restrictions on the teaching of *ma'aseh bereshit* and *ma'aseh merkavah*. See also *Guide* i, Introd. (p. 6). For a translation and analysis of the *Ḥagigah* commentary see Kellner, 'Maimonides' Commentary on Mishnah Hagigah II.1'. In the *Mishneh torah* the first two chapters

'Laws of Repentance', Chapter 10

Let us now look further into these matters. In order to understand the final *halakhah* of the *Book of Knowledge* it will be useful to look at the entire tenth and final chapter:[21]

1. One ought not to say: 'I will perform the Torah's commandments and engage in its wisdom to secure the blessings indited in the Torah', or 'to attain to the life of the world to come'. 'And I will forbear from the transgressions proscribed by the Torah to be spared the curses indited in the Torah', or 'so as not to be excised from the life of the world to come'. It is not fitting to serve God in that way. For one who serves in that way is a servant for fear, which is not the rank of prophets or [even] of sages: None serve God in that way save the ignorant, women, and children, who are trained to serve out of fear, till their understanding increases and they can serve out of love.[22]

2. The servant from love engages in the Torah and the commandments and follows the paths of wisdom, without any [extraneous] motive whatever—neither fear of harm, nor to inherit the good: he rather does what is true because it is true, and the good ultimately comes implicit in it.[23] This is a rank of the utmost nobility: not every sage attains to it. It is the rank of Our Father, Abraham, whom the Holy One

---

of 'Laws of the Foundations of the Torah', concerning God and the angels, are summed up as being about *ma'aseh merkavah* (2: 11), while the next two chapters, concerning the heavenly spheres and the elements, are stated to be about *ma'aseh bereshit* (4: 10). In 'Laws of the Foundations of the Torah', 4: 13, Maimonides describes the arcane, theoretical subjects of *ma'aseh bereshit* and *ma'aseh merkavah* (collectively known as *pardes*) as 'a great thing', and halakhah, the practical side of Torah which is understandable by all, as 'a small thing'. This is based on BT *Suk.* 28a. Twersky, *Introduction to the Code*, 494, notes that Maimonides is unusual in taking this text 'with crushing literalism'.

[21] We cite Bernard Septimus's translation from his forthcoming translation of the *Book of Knowledge* for the Yale Judaica series. We have eliminated almost all of Professor Septimus's extremely learned notes and slightly modified some of his translations. It is our pleasant duty to thank him here for his kindness in furnishing us with an advance copy of his translation. His notes will be identified by '[S]'.

[22] While this is not our issue here, it is important to point out that in this sentence Maimonides indicates two things about women. On one hand, women (in his day) are uneducated, like 'the ignorant' and 'children'. But on the other hand, they are educable and can be brought to serve God out of love. For discussion and references to related studies, see Kellner, 'Misogyny'.

[23] *Vesof hatovah lavo bikhlal* (MS Huntington 80); a variation on the similar phrase in BT *Ned.* 62a. The addition of *bikhlal* indicates that we are dealing with a reward which is a natural consequence of virtue, not one that is externally bestowed [S]. For a detailed discussion of Maimonides on reward as consequence and not response, see Kellner, *Must a Jew Believe Anything?*, 149–63.

(blessed be He) called 'my lover' [Isa. 41: 8], because he served solely from love.[24] It is the rank to which the Holy One (blessed be He) exhorted us, through Moses our Master; for it is said, 'And you shall love the Lord your God' [Deut. 6: 5]—and when one loves God rightly, he will straightaway fulfil all the commandments out of love.[25]

3. And what *is* the right love? To have a love of God so great, abundant, plenteous and intense,[26] that one's soul is bound up with it, and one is constantly enthralled by it[27]—like the lovesick, whose minds are never free of love for the woman who always enthrals them, whether they are sitting, standing, eating, or drinking. Greater yet should be the love of God in the hearts of His lovers, always enthralling them, as He charged us: 'With all your heart, all your soul, and all your might' [Deut. 6: 5]. That is what Solomon meant when he said, in figurative mode: 'For I am sick with love' [S. of S. 2: 5]. Indeed, the entire Song of Songs is a figure for this idea.[28]

4. The ancient sages said: 'Lest you think to say, "I'll study Torah so I'll be rich," "so I'll be addressed, 'my master',", [or] "so I'll receive reward in the world to come", Scripture instructs: "[If you obey my commands] . . . to love the Lord" [Deut. 11: 13]—whatever you do, do only from love.'[29] The sages further observed '[Scripture says of the God-fearing person], "In His commandments, he greatly delights" [Ps. 112: 1]—in His *commandments*, not the reward of His commandments.'[30] So too would the pre-eminent sages instruct their most understanding and discerning students in private: 'Be not like servants who serve their master expecting to receive some good [in return]; be rather like servants who serve their master expecting to receive nothing,[31] but [do so nevertheless] because he is the master [and] ought, [therefore], to be served', which is to say: serve from love!

5. Whoever engages in Torah to reap reward or keep punishment at bay, does so, 'not for its own sake'. Whoever engages it, not out of fear or for reward, but out of love for the Lord of all the Earth who commanded it—does so 'for its own sake'. The

---

[24] Abraham's love of God is here connected to his apprehension of abstract truth, the truth spoken of in 'Laws of the Foundations of the Torah', 1: 4, and, at least at this point, not connected in any way to fulfilment of commandments or attachment to a particular people.

[25] This clause completes the argument: Deut 6: 5, which urges a fitting love of God, can also be said to urge disinterested service because a fitting love of God *necessarily* entails disinterested service; the idea of necessary and natural causality is expressed here by *miyad* (straightaway) [S].

[26] See S. of S. 8: 6. [27] The language is borrowed from Prov. 5: 19.

[28] On Maimonides' understanding of Song of Songs, see Gersonides, *Commentary on Song of Songs*, pp. xv–xvi.

[29] *Sifrei Deut.* (no. 41, p. 87), cited by Maimonides in *Perek ḥelek* (see Maimonides, *Hakdamot*, 132). [30] BT *AZ* 19a. [31] See Mishnah *Avot* 1: 3.

Sages said: 'One should by all means engage in Torah[32] even [if it is] not for its own sake; for through [service that is] not for its own sake, comes [service] that *is* for its own sake.' So when teaching children, women, and the run of the ignorant, [at first] one only teaches them to serve from fear and for reward, till their knowledge grows and they acquire ample wisdom, whereupon one reveals this mystery to them by degrees and accustoms them to the idea gently, till[33] they grasp it fully and serve from love.[34]

6. It is plainly known that love of the Holy One (blessed be He) becomes bound up in one's heart (so that he is always enthralled by it as he should be, forsaking all else, as He charged, '[Love the Lord your God] with all your heart and all your soul' [Deut. 6: 5]), only through the knowledge he attains of Him. As is one's knowledge [*de'ah*] so is his love: if [the one be] little, [the other will be] little, if [the one be] great, [the other will be] great. One must, therefore, be single-minded in studying and reflecting on the disciplines and sciences that give him such knowledge of his Master as humans can understand and apprehend,[35] as we have explained in 'Laws of the Foundations of the Torah.'[36]

Quite a few issues in this chapter demand attention; prominent among them for our purposes is the relationship between knowledge of God and love of God. But before turning to that, a number of other points beg to be taken up. Maimonides ends his *Book of Knowledge* with an encomium on the proper love of God, suggesting, as adumbrated above, that the sort of love of God to which he alludes here is the point of the next book, namely, *Sefer ahavah*, the *Book of Love*. That book contains six sections and the text of the prayerbook

---

[32] *batorah*; the printed texts of BT *Pes.* 50b (and *Sot.* 22b, 47a) read: *batorah uvamitsvot*. Maimonides follows a Spanish textual tradition that omits *uvamitsvot*; see *Talmud bavli im shinuyei nushaot: Sotah*, ad loc., and *Perek helek* (Maimonides, *Hakdamot*, 133) [S]. This point is of cardinal importance, given Maimonides' distinction between the 'legalistic study of the Law [*al-shari'a*]' and 'the science of the Law [*al-shari'a*] in its true sense' on the very first page of the *Guide* (Introd. (p. 5)). On Maimonides' use of the term *al-shari'a*, where we would expect to find him using *al-torah*, see Diamond and Kellner, *Reinventing Maimonides in Contemporary Jewish Thought*, ch. 5, n. 59, and the literature cited there.   [33] Or: 'so that'.

[34] Concerning the implication of this sentence, that women can achieve worship of God out of love, and not only out of fear, see above, n. 22.

[35] *Kefi ko'ah sheyesh ba'adam lehavin ulehasig*; refers to the limited capacity of all humans to know God (as opposed to that of the individual student, who is mentioned at the beginning of the sentence and would take a pronoun if intended here) [S]. Note should be taken of the way that this paragraph focuses on human beings (and not specifically on Jews) and on the importance of knowledge. There is much foreshadowing here of the very last paragraph of the *Mishneh torah*, to be taken up below in Ch. 14. The universalism of the two passages is quite striking.

[36] In this *halakhah*, Maimonides is not talking about the intensity of love itself, but about how to reach the required intensity, namely through knowledge.

as an appendix. The six sections concern (1) the recitation of the Shema, (2) prayer and the priestly blessing, (3) tefillin, mezuzah, and Torah scroll, (4) fringes (*tsitsit*), (5) blessings, and (6) circumcision. Maimonides seems to be telling us that even these fairly technical matters of halakhah are connected to the love of God as taught in the *Book of Knowledge* and are thus particular means to a universal end.[37]

Love of God

What sort of love of God is commanded, and who can love God in that fashion? Maimonides answers these questions in the very last sentence of the chapter, the very last sentence of the first book of the *Mishneh torah* as a whole. He does this by sending us back to 'Laws of the Foundations of the Torah'. But in the very same sentence he also sends us to the end of the entire *Mishneh torah*, one of the most clearly universalist texts in the entire canon of Judaism (and which makes it, as we will argue below in Chapter 14, the *end* of the *Mishneh torah*, in the sense of its goal). The expression used here, *kefi ko'aḥ sheyesh ba'adam*, appears only one other time in the *Mishneh Torah*, in its very last paragraph.[38] There are other relevant allusions here. The word translated 'his Master' here is *kono*, a word which sends us back to Maimonides' commentary on Mishnah Ḥagigah 2: 1.[39] Further, in our text from 'Laws of Repentance', chapter 10, Maimonides informs us that it was Abraham who best exemplified love of God. It therefore behoves us to spend some time examining how Maimonides presents the figure of Abraham.[40] But before doing that,

---

[37] One wonders if there is a further hint here: the prayers of Jews are commanded, those of non-Jews, welcome.   [38] The precise expression there is *kefi ko'aḥ ha'adam*.

[39] In his *Commentary* on Mishnah Ḥag. 2: 1, on the term *kevod kono* ('honour of his Master'), Maimonides writes:

> Examine this wonderful expression, said with divine help, 'All who are not protective of the *kavod* of their master', the meaning of this being, all who are not protective of their intellects, for the intellect is the *kavod* of the Lord. Since he does not know the value of this matter which was given him, he is abandoned into the hands of his desires, and becomes like an animal. Thus, they said, 'Who is he who is not protective of the honour of his Master?—he who transgresses secretly.' They said elsewhere, 'Adulterers do not commit adultery until the spirit of madness enters them.' This is the truth, for while one craves any of the desires, the intellect is not perfected.

The complete text, with detailed explanatory notes, may be found in Kellner, 'Maimonides' Commentary on *Mishnah Hagigah* II.1'. For the use of *kavod* in this passage, see the illuminating comments of Diamond, 'Failed Theodicy', revised in Diamond, *Converts, Heretics, and Lepers*, 369. For further discussion, see Kellner, *Maimonides' Confrontation*, ch. 6.

[40] On which see Gillis, *Reading Maimonides Mishneh Torah*, 146–8, below, Ch. 2, and our Conclusion.

let us anticipate the answers to the questions posed at the beginning of this paragraph: the love of God commanded in Deuteronomy 6: 5 is intellectual and is, in principle, something which all humans can achieve, men and women, Jews and non-Jews.

'Laws of the Foundations of the Torah', 1: 1 and 2: 1–2

To understand this, we must look at the text to which Maimonides explicitly sends us, 'Laws of the Foundations of the Torah'. That text begins with the following passage:

The foundation of all foundations and the pillar of all sciences is to realize that there is a First Being who brings every existing thing into being. All existing things, whether celestial, terrestrial, or belonging to an intermediate class, exist only through His true existence. If it could be supposed that He did not exist, it would follow that nothing else could possibly exist. If, however, it were supposed that all other beings were non-existent, He alone would still exist. Their non-existence would not involve His non-existence. For all beings are in need of Him; but He, blessed be He, is not in need of them nor of any of them. Hence, His real essence is unlike that of any of them. This is what the prophet means when he says 'But the Eternal is the true God' [Jer. 10: 10]; that is, He alone is real, and nothing else has reality like His reality. The same thought the Torah expresses in the text: 'There is none else besides Him' [Deut. 4: 3]; that is: there is no being besides Him, that is really like Him. This being is the God of the Universe, the Lord of all the Earth. And He it is, who controls the sphere with a power that is without end or limit; with a power that is never intermitted. For the sphere is always revolving; and it is impossible for it to revolve without someone making it revolve. God, blessed be He, it is, who, without hand or body, causes it to revolve. Knowing this thing is an affirmative precept, as it is said, 'I am the Lord, thy God' [Exod. 20: 2; Deut. 5: 6]. And whoever permits the thought to enter his mind that there is another deity besides this God, violates a prohibition; as it is said 'Thou shalt have no other gods before me' [Exod. 20: 3; Deut. 5: 7], and denies the essential principle [*ikar*]—this being the great principle on which everything depends.[41]

[41] Maimonides teaches that there is a commandment to *know* that God exists ('Laws of the Foundations of the Torah', 1: 1–6). This is often taken to mean (correctly in our eyes) that in order to fulfil this commandment in the best possible way, one must study *ma'aseh bereshit* and *ma'aseh merkavah*, i.e. physics and metaphysics (as understood by Maimonides). The commandment, in other words, relates to knowledge, not to belief or trust. Joseph Soloveitchik denied that Maimonides here meant to distinguish knowledge from belief. In this he opposes his teacher, Hayim Heller. Septimus, in turn, possibly influenced by *his* teacher, R. Soloveitchik, holds that Maimonides here means knowledge gained by tradition, not necessarily by intellection. On the distinction between knowledge and belief in this context, see Kellner, *Must a Jew Believe Anything?* For Soloveitchik's comment, see *On Repen-*

The rest of the chapter is given over to a discussion of God's unity and incorporeality, a discussion in which a variety of biblical verses are deployed to provide textual support for claims about God which are unprecedented in the Jewish tradition before Sa'adyah Gaon (882–942).

With respect to the opening sentence of 'Laws of the Foundations of the Torah' 1: 1 (*yesod hayesodot ve'amud haḥokhmot leida sheyesh sham matsui rishon*), it has long been noted that the initial letters of the first four words spell out the Tetragrammaton.[42] The 'melody' behind the words is clearly biblical.[43] Maimonides is trying to put his traditionalist readers at ease.[44] The text itself, however, is hardly traditional. This point was emphasized by Isaac Abravanel (1437–1508) who, in his *Principles of Faith*, objected:

Why in the *Book of Knowledge* did Maimonides write of the first principle that it was 'the foundation of all foundations and the pillar of the sciences', when he should have said, 'one of the foundations', not 'the foundation of foundations'? Of what concern is it of ours whether or not this foundation is the pillar of Gentile sciences, 'which are not of the children of Israel' [1 Kgs. 9: 20]?[45]

Abravanel asks two questions here: first, why in 'Laws of the Foundations of the Torah' does Maimonides call knowledge of the existence of the First Being the foundation of all the foundations? After all, Abravanel implies, it is no more important than the other foundations of the Torah. Second, why does Maimonides teach that this religious principle is equivalent to what we can call the axiom of all the sciences, the existence of God? This second question clearly vexed Abravanel as it is based upon the unspoken (and for Abravanel unacceptable) notion that the Torah and the sciences share the same structure (and method): just as the sciences have axioms, so does the Torah[46]— and it is to the refutation of that claim that Abravanel devotes *Principles of*

tance, 130. For discussion of this text, see ch. 2 in Diamond and Kellner, *Reinventing Maimonides*. Heller comments on the know/believe dichotomy in the first footnote of his edition of Maimonides' *Sefer hamitsvot*. Septimus raises the issue in 'What Did Maimonides Mean by *Madda?*', 90–1. See further below, n. 49. On the issues raised in this footnote, see also *Guide* i. 34 (pp. 74–6).

[42] Joel Kraemer has noted that the poem opening the *Guide* has precisely twenty-six words, 26 being the numerical value of the Tetragrammaton. See Kraemer, 'Maimonides, the Great Healer', 9 n. 25.

[43] Expressions like 'Song of Songs' come to mind immediately; for other examples of this biblical usage, see Gen. 9: 25; 1 Kgs. 8: 27; Ezek. 17: 7; and 2 Chron. 6: 18.

[44] See Kellner, 'Literary Character', and, in greater detail, id., *They, Too, Are Called Human* (Heb.), ch. 2.

[45] The first part of the verse is instructive: 'All the people that were left of the Amorites, Hittites, and Perrizites'; Abravanel, *Principles of Faith*, ch. 5, p. 76.

[46] See Kellner, 'The Conception of the Torah'.

Faith. Perhaps even more troubling, the God whose existence can be understood as the pillar of the non-Jewish sciences (in the sense of final cause) is most assuredly the God of the philosophers, not the God of the Patriarchs and Matriarchs.

Chapter 1 of 'Laws of the Foundations of the Torah' presents further evidence to the effect that Abravanel understood Maimonides correctly. In our passage, Maimonides writes:

> This being is the God of the Universe, the Lord of all the Earth. And He it is, who controls the sphere with a power that is without end or limit; with a power that is never intermitted. For the sphere is always revolving; and it is impossible for it to revolve without someone making it revolve.

This is a proof for God's existence based upon the unceasing and eternal motion of the outermost sphere, which, in the medieval model of the universe, controls the motions of the system of earth-centred spheres containing the stars and planets. By 'always revolving' Maimonides indicates here that the spheres are uncreated, as he himself makes clear in the *Guide of the Perplexed*:

> Thus it has become manifest to you that the proofs for the existence and the oneness of the deity and of His not being a body ought to be procured from the starting point afforded by the supposition of the eternity of the world, for in this way the demonstration will be perfect, both if the world is eternal, and if it is created in time. For this reason you will always find that whenever, in what I have written in the book of jurisprudence, I happen to mention the foundations and start upon establishing the existence of the deity, I establish it by discourses that adopt the way of the doctrine of the eternity of the world. The reason is not that I believe in the eternity of the world, but that I wish to establish in our belief the existence of God, may He be exalted, through a demonstrative method as to which there is no disagreement in any respect. Thus we shall not cause the true opinion, which is of immense importance, to be supported by a foundation that everyone can shake and wish to destroy, while other men think that it has never been constructed.[47]

Thus, in his legal writings, wherever Maimonides sought to prove the existence of God, he used proofs based upon the assumption that the cosmos is uncreated. Abravanel had good reason to be concerned.[48]

---

[47] *Guide*, i. 71 (pp. 181–2). See also the addition to the fourth of Maimonides' 'Thirteen Principles'. For details, see Kellner, *Dogma in Medieval Judaism*, 54. This issue will come up again below, in Ch. 2.

[48] We have no commentary by Abravanel on this chapter of the *Guide*, but he hints at this concern in *Principles of Faith*, ch. 5 (p. 77).

There are other issues raised here which Abravanel does not address. Among these are the following:

- that the Torah has foundations of an intellectual nature;
- that there are commandments to *know* things (as opposed to simply believing them);[49]
- that what is commanded to be known here is that there exists a 'First Being' or 'Prime Existent' (*matsui rishon*);
- that all that exists does so by virtue of the truth of God's *existence*, as opposed to by virtue of God's willed *creation*.

Maimonides helps his more narrowly traditionalist readers avoid apoplexy by using the expression 'blessed be He' (*barukh hu*) after several of his references to the deity here, but that hardly changes the content, thrust, and tone of the passage as a whole.

None of this is meant to imply that in our view Maimonides is a thoroughgoing follower of Aristotle as he understood him (or that he was a follower of Leo Strauss, for that matter).[50] However, the lover of God described in the last chapter of 'Laws of Repentance' is still (or can be) a philosopher (who need not be Jewish). This approach is strengthened by the opening of chapter 2 of 'Laws of the Foundations of the Torah' and by Maimonides' account of Abraham, the lover of God, in 'Laws of Idolatry', which we will address below.

Maimonides opens the second chapter of 'Laws of the Foundations of the Torah' with the following passage:

This God, honoured and revered, it is a commandment to love and fear; as it is said 'Love the Lord your God' [Deut. 6: 5], and it is further said 'Thou shalt fear the Lord, thy God' [Deut. 6: 13]. And what is the way that will lead to the love of Him and the fear of Him? When a person contemplates His great and wondrous works and creatures and from them obtains a glimpse of His wisdom which is incomparable and infinite, he will straightway love Him, praise Him, glorify Him, and long with an exceeding longing to know His great Name; even as David said 'My soul thirsts for God, for the living God' [Ps. 42: 3]. And when he ponders these matters, he will

---

[49] Much has been written concerning knowledge versus belief in Maimonides. For entry into the discussion, see Nuriel, 'The Concept "Faith" in Maimonides' (Heb.) and Rosenberg, 'The Concept of "Emunah" in Post-Maimonidean Jewish Philosophy'. Cf. n. 41 above.

[50] Strauss's many writings on Maimonides are now conveniently available in Green (ed.), *Leo Strauss on Maimonides*. Green analyses Strauss's contributions to the study of Maimonides (in a remarkably sympathetic fashion) in *Leo Strauss and the Rediscovery of Maimonides*.

recoil affrighted, and realize that he is a small creature, lowly and obscure, endowed with slight and slender intelligence, standing in the presence of Him who is perfect in knowledge. And so David said 'When I consider Thy heavens, the work of Thy fingers—what is man that Thou art mindful of Him?' [Ps. 8: 4–5]. In harmony with these sentiments, I shall explain some large, general aspects of the works of the Sovereign of the Universe, that they may serve the intelligent individual as a door to the love of God, even as our sages have remarked in connection with the theme of the love of God, 'and from this,[51] you will come to know Him Who spoke and the world was.'[52]

This passage and the previous one, with which Maimonides chose to open the first two chapters of the *Mishneh torah*,[53] invite a multitude of questions, among them: What does it mean for something to be the 'foundation of

---

[51] To what does the word 'this' (*kakh*) refer? Shmuel Tanhum Rubenstein, the editor of the Mosad Harav Kook's *Rambam le'am* edition of the *Mishneh torah*, thinks it refers to God's Torah and its commandments, quoting as a source *Sifrei Deut.*, 'Va'ethanan' (i. 33). On the face of it, this is absurd, since the reference is clearly to God's 'great and wondrous works and creatures'. This is the view of both Joseph Kafih and Nachum Rabinovitch in their commentaries ad loc. But Rubenstein's gloss is not as absurd as it appears at first glance, since in his *Book of Commandments*, positive commandment 3 (to which we shall return below), Maimonides cites *Sifrei* to the effect that study of God's words (*vehayu hadevarim ha'eleh*) brings one 'to know Him Who spoke and the world was'. In his responsa, however, Maimonides says that it is an examination of God's Creation which brings one 'to know Him Who spoke and the world was' (*Teshuvot harambam*, i, no. 150). As is his wont, Maimonides is writing for different audiences at the same time; but, as we shall see below, the story may be more complicated than that.

[52] We do not accept an interpretation of 'Laws of the Foundations of the Torah', 2: 2, as being about knowledge necessarily leading to love. Our interpretation depends on understanding *sheyitbonen* to mean 'to gaze intently' rather than to 'to try to understand'. At this point Maimonides is talking about a love at first sight, an awareness that the universe hangs together beautifully. This sparks a desire for knowledge, which will in turn lead to a firmer and deeper kind of love. The initial access of love is unstable—it immediately gives way to fear. This love is not the product of a steady course of instruction in logic, mathematics, and astronomy. Thereafter, love is consolidated by study of nature, which Maimonides immediately commences, while fear is consolidated, and channelled, through observance of the commandments, which Maimonides proceeds to set out. In 'Laws of Repentance' the process is reversed, for love has been betrayed and a way back needs to be found. Thus 'Laws of Repentance' starts with the kind of self-consciousness that fear consists of in 'Laws of the Foundations of the Torah' 2: 2, with self-examination and confession, and climbs back to love via knowledge.

[53] Despite which they have been almost entirely ignored by the thousands of rabbinic scholars who have commented on or alluded to the *Mishneh torah* in the eight centuries since it was written. Note, for example, the almost total lack of commentaries on these chapters in the standard printed editions of the *Mishneh torah*; indeed, the commentary that is often printed is anonymous! See Metzger, 'The "Commentator" on Maimonides' "Laws of the Foundations of the Torah"' (Heb.). Note also the almost total lack of links from these chapters

all foundations'? What does it mean for that something also to be the 'pillar of all sciences', and what is the relation between them? What or Who is the 'First Being', *knowledge* of the existence of which is not only the 'foundation of all foundations' and also the 'pillar of all the sciences', but is also the first commandment of the Torah and 'the great principle on which everything depends'? What is the significance of the fact that knowledge of the Deity's necessary existence (such knowledge being a 'foundation', 'pillar', commandment, and 'great principle') is gained through an argument which, as we have seen, presupposes the eternity of the cosmos *a parte ante*? Does Maimonides really mean to teach that the study of science and philosophy (and not the fulfilment of the commandments) leads to love and fear of God?

These two passages lead to the following conclusions: the Deity (and we use the word advisedly), knowledge of the existence of which is a 'foundation', 'pillar', commandment, and 'great principle', is the God of (a Neoplatonized) Aristotle, as opposed to the God of Abraham, Isaac, and Jacob. This is not to say, we hasten to emphasize, that Maimonides rejected the God of Abraham, Isaac, and Jacob in favour of the God of Aristotle (Neoplatonized or not). God (of Abraham, Isaac, and Jacob) forbid! Rather, it means that it is enough *to know that the God of the philosophers exists* in order *to observe the first commandment of the Torah, and to arrive at love of God*, as expressed both in the opening paragraphs of chapter 2 of 'Laws of Foundations of the Torah' and in the passage from 'Laws of Repentance' with which we began this discussion. This is not to imply that for Maimonides fulfilling the commandment in this fashion is the best way to do it. As Jolene S. Kellner likes to remind people, Maimonides was 'also' a rabbi and took seriously the idea that contemplation of the commandments (not to mention fulfilling them *properly*) leads to love of God.[54] It must be remembered that for Maimonides, love of God does not remain purely in the contemplative realm. This is surely the burden of *Guide* iii. 54.[55]

One wonders, of course, what sort of love it is that one can have for a being as impersonal as Aristotle's God—a point to which we shall have to return below—but it can be no surprise that many have seen in Maimonides a source for Spinoza's notion of *amor Dei intellectualis*, the intellectual love of God.[56]

to rabbinic literature in the Bar Ilan Global Jewish Database ('Responsa Project'). Compare above, n. 17.

[54] On contemplation of the commandments, see Gillis, *Reading Maimonides' Mishneh Torah*, 317–18, and below in this chapter.   [55] See Kellner, *Maimonides on Human Perfection*.
[56] See the essays by Steven Frankel, Warren Zev Harvey, and Kenneth Seeskin in Nadler (ed.), *Spinoza and Medieval Jewish Philosophy*.

As we have seen, Maimonides opens chapter 2 of 'Laws of the Foundations of the Torah' by citing commandments to love and fear God. In silent acknowledgement of the difficulties involved in commanding love and fear, he asks, 'And what is the way that will lead to the love of Him and the fear of Him?' The answer that Maimonides gives is that contemplation of God's works and creatures offers a glimpse of God's incomparable and infinite wisdom. Having had this glimpse, one 'will straightway love Him, praise Him, glorify Him, and long with an exceeding longing to know His great Name'. It is for that reason, Maimonides goes on to explain, that he will spend the coming three chapters of 'Laws of the Foundations of the Torah' explaining 'some large, general aspects of the works of the Sovereign of the Universe, that they may serve the intelligent individual as a door to the love of God'. As noted above, and as Maimonides himself tells us at the end of chapter 4, the subjects covered in these chapters are those which the Sages called *ma'aseh bereshit* and *ma'aseh merkavah*. In this paragraph Maimonides cites verses from Psalms and a statement of the talmudic Sages, clearly seeking to convey the impression that David, king of Israel, and the talmudic Sages are in agreement with Maimonides' position as sketched out here.

Book of Commandments, Positive Commandment 3

So far we have seen that in order to fulfil the commandment 'Love the Lord your God' (Deut. 6: 5), one must study physics and metaphysics, according to Maimonides. Implied, but not actually stated, is the affirmation that the philosopher loves God more than does the philosophically illiterate rabbi.[57]

In his *Book of the Commandments* Maimonides counts love of God as the

---

[57] See Diamond and Kellner, *Reinventing Maimonides*, ch. 5. To be fair, the status of a saintly and philosophically accomplished non-Jew relative to that of a saintly but philosophically ignorant Jew may not have interested Maimonides all that much. Still, one wonders what he thought of the moral status of many of the philosophically sophisticated Muslims he encountered in the circle of his friend and patron al-Fadil. See Kraemer, 'Maimonides' Intellectual Milieu in Cairo'. In general, since Maimonides held moral perfection to be a prerequisite of intellectual perfection, philosophically sophisticated but morally corrupt individuals (such as Martin Heidegger) would present him with a problem. We know of no place where he addresses the question directly. Many readers of the parable of the palace in *Guide* iii. 51 (p. 618) (such as Shem Tov ibn Shem Tov ad loc.) thought that Maimonides placed non-Jewish experts in physics and metaphysics on a higher level than talmudists, implying that such non-Jews were of high moral character (since otherwise they could not have advanced so far in physics and metaphysics). In *Maimonides on Human Perfection*, ch. 3, Kellner argues that Maimonides meant to compare philosophically erudite talmudists to talmudists without such erudition, and that non-Jews are not part of that particular discussion at all.

third of the positive commandments. At first glance, it appears that the position enunciated there differs from the one we have seen so far:[58]

By this injunction we are commanded to love God (exalted be He); that is to say, to dwell upon and contemplate His commandments, His injunctions, and His works, so that we may obtain a conception of Him; and in conceiving Him attain absolute joy. This constitutes the love of God, and is obligatory. As the Sifri says: 'Since it is said [Deut. 6: 5], "And thou shalt love the Lord thy God", the question arises, how is one to manifest his love for the Lord? Scripture therefore says [Deut. 6: 6] "And these words which I command thee this day, shall be upon thy heart", for through this [i.e. the contemplation of God's words] you will learn to discern Him whose word called the Universe into existence.'[59] We have thus made it clear to you that through this act of contemplation you will attain a conception of God and reach that stage of joy in which love of Him will follow of necessity. The Sages say that this commandment also includes an obligation to call upon all mankind to serve Him (exalted be He), and to have faith in Him. For just as you praise and extol anybody whom you love, and call upon others also to love him, so, if you love the Lord to the extent of the conception of His true nature to which you have attained, you will undoubtedly call upon the foolish and ignorant to seek knowledge of the Truth which you have already acquired. As the Sifri says: '"And thou shalt love the Lord thy God": this means that you should make Him beloved of man as Abraham your father did, as it is said [Gen. 13: 5]: "And the souls they had gotten in Haran"'—that is to say, just as Abraham, being a lover of the Lord—as Scripture testifies [Isa. 41: 8], 'Abraham My lover'—by the power of his conception of God, and out of his great love for Him, summoned mankind to believe, you too must so love Him as to summon mankind unto Him.[60]

---

[58] A number of scholars have pointed out that in this text Maimonides seems to differ from the position found in 'Laws of the Foundations of the Torah', 2: 1 (and throughout his writings), to wit, that it is also contemplation of the commandments, and not just study of creation, which leads to love of God. See e.g. Lamm, 'Maimonides on the Love of God'. Lamm solves the discrepancy by maintaining that the *Book of the Commandments* is aimed at a more popular audience than is the *Mishneh torah*. Baris, 'Limited Knowledge, Unlimited Love', notes the discrepancy but does not explain it. The most extensive discussions of the text are to be found in Seeman, 'Reasons for the Commandments' (esp. pp. 302–5), and in Gillis, *Reading Maimonides' Mishneh Torah*, 317–19. Seeman construes our passage as relating to the study of the reasons for the commandments. Gillis sees the passage as foreshadowing the *Mishneh torah*'s concern to show the commandments as an object of contemplation.

[59] *Sifrei* on Deut. 6: 6. Note here the very insightful discussion of Don Seeman (see previous note). He convincingly construes Maimonides to mean here the contemplation of the *reasons* for the commandments, such contemplation leading to further appreciation of God's wisdom, which, in turn, leads to love of God. See Chs. 8 and 9 below on the importance of understanding the wisdom of the commandments.

[60] We cite the translation of Charles Chavel. For a very useful analysis of this commandment, see Feintuch, *Maimonides' Book of Commandments with the Commentary* Pikudei yesharim (Heb.), 125–9, and, especially on linguistic issues, Seeman (above, n. 58).

On the face of it, this text appears to be less clearly philosophical (and hence less clearly universalist) than 'Laws of the Foundations of the Torah', 2: 1–2, since contemplation of the commandments is listed before contemplation of the divine works (i.e. the cosmos) as leading to a conception of God. Non-Jewish philosophers can contemplate God's works, and thus be led to knowledge and love of God, while only Jews contemplate the commandments. But as the passage continues, we discover that the point of the contemplation of the commandments is to achieve a conception of God. In this we must follow Abraham, the only person in the entire Torah who is called a *lover* of God.

We must immediately ask: what is it that brought Abraham to the love of God? Was it contemplation of the commandments? Obviously not![61] In a long passage in 'Laws of Idolatry', worth citing in full due to its importance for our argument (in this chapter and throughout this book), Maimonides tells us:

> In the days of Enosh [Gen. 4: 26; 5: 7–11] mankind fell into grave error; the wise of that generation turned brutish in counsel; and Enosh himself was among the errant. Their fallacy was to say as follows: 'Since God created the stars and spheres to govern the world, set them on high, and granted them honor, and [since] they are ministers who serve Him, they deserve to be praised, extolled, and honored. Indeed, it is the will of God (blessed be He) that [we] magnify and honor those whom He has magnified and honored, just as a king wants his servants and attendants to be honored—for this redounds to the honor of the king.' Once this notion got into their heads, they began to build temples to the stars, offer them sacrifices, praise and extol them verbally, and bow down toward them, in order to win divine favor, by their corrupt lights. That was the root of alien worship.[62]

---

[61] The rabbinic legend that the patriarchs fulfilled the commandments is precisely that: a legend, and one that Maimonides never mentions and could hardly accept. A letter attributed to Maimonides in which this idea is expressly rejected is of doubtful provenance (see *Igerot harambam* (trans. Shailat), ii. 673–84), but it is clear from his writings that in his view observance of the 613 commandments began only with Moses (see 'Laws of Idolatry', 1: 3; *Guide* ii. 39 (pp. 378–81)). The comment of Abraham Maimonides on Gen. 35: 4, to the effect that the actions of Abraham, Isaac, and Jacob were in the spirit of the commandments but they did not actually observe them, perhaps reflects his father's way of reading the *midrashim* in question. For more on the patriarchs' alleged observance of the commandments, see Kellner, *Maimonides' Confrontation*, 76–7. Gerald Blidstein also claims that according to Maimonides, Abraham did not actually observe the commandments. See his 'R. Menahem Ha-Me'iri: Aspects of an Intellectual Profile', 65.

[62] 'Laws of Idolatry', 1: 1. We again cite Bernard Septimus's translation from his forthcoming translation of the *Book of Knowledge* for the Yale Judaica series. We have again eliminated Professor Septimus's extremely learned notes.

Having explained the origin of idolatry,[63] Maimonides describes Abraham's rebellion against it:

After much time had passed, false prophets arose among the human race, claiming that God had commanded them: 'Worship such and such a star (or all the stars): offer it these sacrifices and libations; build it a temple; and fashion its image' . . . Thus it was that they began to make images in temples, under trees, atop mountains and on hills. They would come together, bow down to them, and tell the whole populace: 'This image can help or harm, and ought to be worshiped and feared.' The priests would then tell them: 'Through this worship you will multiply and prosper: do such and such; don't do such and such.'[64] . . . It thus became the universal practice to worship the [various] images with distinct rites, and to sacrifice and bow down to them. With the passage of time, the Honored and Revered Name sank [into oblivion, fading] from the mouths and minds of all beings: they recognized it not. So all the commoners, women, and children, knew nothing but the wood or stone image and fabricated temple that they were brought up from childhood to bow down to, worship, and swear by. The wise among them—priests and the like— imagined there was no deity save the stars and spheres, for which those images had been made as [symbolic] representations. But as to the Eternal Rock [*tsur olamim*], none recognized or knew Him save singular individuals like Enoch, Methuselah, Noah, Shem, and Eber. Thus the world was declining by degrees, till the World's Pillar, our Father Abraham, was born. No sooner was this hero weaned than he began to ponder, though but a child, and to meditate day and night, wondering: 'How can the Sphere forever follow its course with none to conduct it? Who causes it to rotate? For it cannot possibly cause *itself* to rotate?' He had no one to teach or instruct him in anything, but was immersed in [the culture of] Ur of the Chaldees among the foolish adherents of alien worship. His father, mother, and the entire populace worshiped alien deities, and he worshiped along with them, while his mind was searching and seeking to understand—till he grasped the true way and understood the right course of his own sound reason: He realized that: there is a single God, He conducts the Sphere, He created the universe, and, in all that exists, there is no god but He. And he realized that all the people were in error, and [that] what had caused them to err was worshiping the stars and images for so long that the truth [of God's existence] was lost to their minds. It was at age forty[65] that Abraham recognized his Creator.[66]

---

[63] *Avodah zarah*; Septimus translates this more literally as 'alien worship'.

[64] This is very telling. Idolatry can only mean fear of punishment and hope of reward, so that such fear and hope smack of idolatry even when directed towards God. Genuine love and genuine knowledge can only be of the genuine God.

[65] When he had reached intellectual maturity, and not at the age of 3, as *Gen. Rabbah* 95 has it. See Abraham ben David's gloss here, and Kellner, *Maimonides' Confrontation*, 79.

[66] 'Laws of Idolatry', 1: 2–3. On this text, see below in Ch. 2.

Maimonides goes on to describe how Abraham then engaged Ur's inhabitants in argument, refuted their beliefs, broke their images, and began instructing them in the truth. After he convinced his fellow-countrymen (thus apparently upsetting the traditional order), the king sought to kill him. He was miraculously saved, whereupon he emigrated and 'began to call out loudly to all the people, teaching them that the world has [but] one God, who [alone] ought to be worshiped'. He travelled from city to city and from kingdom to kingdom, teaching this truth which he had discovered. Arriving in the land of Canaan, he proclaimed his message, instructed the inhabitants, implanted truth in their hearts, composed books on it, and taught it to his son Isaac.[67]

Prominent in these texts is the emphasis on the activity of Abraham. God is entirely absent from this account as anything but the object of philosophical speculation. In this account, God does not even issue the command which opens the Abraham story in the Torah, 'Get thee hence . . .'.[68] Even the (midrashically based) miracle by which Abraham was saved from the king of Ur is presented without directly and clearly involving God—the text literally says: 'a miracle was performed for him' (*na'asah lo nes*).[69] Throughout these passages it is Abraham, and not God, who is the subject of active verbs: Abraham meditated, pondered, wondered, searched, grasped, understood, realized, recognized, argued, refuted, broke images, convinced, emigrated, proclaimed, travelled, taught, instructed, implanted, and composed.[70] God is cognized, according to this account, but does not act.[71]

---

[67] Compare Maimonides' account in *Guide* iii. 29 (p. 516):

However, when the Pillar of the World grew up and it became clear to him that there is a separate deity that is neither a body nor a force in a body and that all the stars and the spheres were made by Him, and he understood that the fables upon which he was brought up were absurd, he began to refute their doctrine and show up their opinions as false; he publicly manifested his disagreement with them and called 'in the name of the Lord, God of the world' [Gen. 21: 33]—both the existence of the deity and the creation of the world in time by that deity being comprised in that call.

For other parallels in the *Guide*, see ii. 39 (p. 379) and iii. 24 (p. 502).   [68] Gen. 12: 1.

[69] BT *Pes.* 118a. The Talmud here has God insisting on saving Abraham himself (the angel Gabriel had sought the assignment); Maimonides clearly presents the story in an entirely different light. See also *Gen. Rabbah* 39: 3.

[70] We owe this point to Zev Harvey.

[71] The God described here is the 'God of the philosophers'. Compare Kreisel, *Maimonides' Political Thought*, 43: 'What is crucial to stress in this context is that Abraham is depicted by Maimonides as an Aristotelian philosopher. His deduction that God "created" everything as depicted in Laws Concerning Idolatry, I. 3, is in reality the Aristotelian view that God is the First Cause of all existence.'

The upshot of all this is that Abraham discovered God on his own, so to speak.[72] God did not choose Abraham, God did not seek him out; God did not make himself known to Abraham. God waited till someone discovered the truth about him; that someone happened to be Abraham, progenitor of the Jews.[73]

We can now return to positive commandment 3. The citation of Abraham as the ultimate exemplar of the lover of God teaches us that the claim there that the route to love of God is the contemplation of the commandments must be seen as an example of Maimonides' 'art of writing', both because Maimonides' Abraham certainly did not contemplate the commandments and because Maimonides tells us explicitly that Abraham came to knowledge of God through contemplation of the physical world.

For Maimonides, love of God is consequent upon knowledge of God, such knowledge, in turn, being consequent upon study of the Torah (in its fullest sense). But here we must be careful. Non-Jewish philosophers (such as Abraham) can achieve this knowledge and hence come to love God. Jews, however, have several advantages over non-Jews. One of them is that the study of Torah includes what we today would call science. Maimonides, in his capacity as halakhic decisor, makes the study of science (philosophy) a religious obligation.[74] Averroes may have tried to do this for Muslims,[75] but he never achieved the level of authority to which Maimonides aspired and actually achieved. Further, David Gillis has shown that the *Mishneh torah* was structured so that contemplation of its overall construction, and the relation of its parts to each other, lead one to knowledge of God's wisdom, implying that contemplation of God's works and contemplation of his commandments amount to the same thing. Non-Jewish philosophers have one route to come

---

[72] In other words, Abraham discovered God through *hekhra hada'at*, reasoned conviction. He also brought his contemporaries (Noahides in the most literal sense of the term) to acceptance of monotheism through *hekhra hada'at*. It is a safe assumption that, according to Maimonides' view, Abraham himself and those whom he brought near to God achieved a share in the world to come; that being the case, the standard reading of 'Laws of Kings and their Wars', 8: 11 (according to which Maimonides denies the world to come to non-Jews), cannot be correct. For discussion, see Kellner, *Maimonides' Confrontation*, 241–7. The classic study of the reception of 'Laws of Kings', 8: 11, in early modern and modern Judaism remains that of Schwarzschild, 'Do Noachites Have to Believe in Revelation?' See further Katz, 'The Vicissitudes of Three Apologetic Statements' (Heb.) and Korn, 'Gentiles, the World to Come and Judaism'.

[73] For elaboration on this point, see Kellner, *Maimonides' Confrontation*, 77–83.

[74] See Davidson, 'The Study of Philosophy as a Religious Obligation', and W. Z. Harvey, 'Averroes, Maimonides, and the Virtuous State' (Heb.).

[75] Averroes, *On the Harmony of Religion and Philosophy*.

to an appreciation of God's wisdom (and hence to come to love God); Jewish philosophers have two. An examination of this point brings us (finally) to our long-delayed discussion of the relation between knowledge of God and love of God.

Love and Knowledge of God—Again

Let us review. All Jews are commanded to love God: 'You shall love the Lord your God with all your heart and with all your soul and with all your might' (Deut. 6: 5). But what is the nature of this love? As we have seen, Maimonides consistently connects love of God to knowledge of God, making love depend upon knowledge, but without reducing the former entirely to the latter. As we have seen, he raises the issue explicitly first in 'Laws of the Foundations of the Torah':

And what is the way that will lead to the love of Him and the fear of Him? When a person contemplates His great and wondrous works and creatures and from them obtains a glimpse of His wisdom which is incomparable and infinite, he will straightway love Him, praise Him, glorify Him, and long with an exceeding longing to know His great Name.[76]

Maimonides tells us here that love of God is dependent upon knowledge of God. The more knowledge, the more love; as we have also seen:

It is plainly known that love of the Holy One (blessed be He) becomes bound up in one's heart (so that he is always enthralled by it as he should be, forsaking all else, as He charged, '[Love the Lord your God] with all your heart and all your soul' [Deut. 6: 5]), only through the knowledge he attains of Him. As is one's knowledge [*de'ah*] so is his love: if [the one be] little, [the other will be] little, if [the one be] great, [the other will be] great.[77]

Might it not appear from this that love of God and knowledge of God are the same thing, as Spinoza was later to claim?

A passage in the *Guide of the Perplexed* seems to support both possibilities:

As for the dictum of Scripture: 'And thou shalt love the Lord with all thy heart' [Deut. 6: 5]—in my opinion its interpretation is: with all the forces of your heart; I mean to say, with all the forces of the body, for the principle of all of them derives from the heart. Accordingly the intended meaning is . . . that you should make His apprehension the end of all your actions.[78]

On the one hand, we are told that in order to fulfil the scriptural command to

---

[76] 2: 1.   [77] 'Laws of Repentance', 10: 6.   [78] *Guide* i. 39 (p. 89).

love the Lord, one must use all the forces of one's body. On the other hand, we are further told that the goal of using all the forces of one's body to love the Lord is to make knowledge of God the end of all our actions. Everything we do should serve the end of furthering our knowledge of God.[79] The points made here are expressed again in the *Guide*: '"with all thy heart, and with all thy soul, and with all thy might" [Deut. 6: 5]. We have already explained ... that this love becomes valid only through the apprehension of the whole of being as it is and through the consideration of His wisdom as it is manifested in it.'[80] In this passage, Maimonides seems to present love of God as a consequence of knowledge of God, and not as identical with it.

Near the end of the *Guide*, Maimonides reiterates the relationship of dependence between love and knowledge: 'Now we have made it clear several times that love is proportionate to apprehension.'[81] The more we know God, the more we love God.

What is the nature of this love we are commanded to have for God? Maimonides tells us:

And what *is* the right love? To have a love of God so great, abundant, plenteous and intense, that one's soul is bound up with it, and one is constantly enthralled by it—like the lovesick, whose minds are never free of love for the woman who always enthrals them, whether they are sitting, standing, eating, or drinking. Greater yet should be the love of God in the hearts of His lovers, always enthralling them.[82]

Maimonides reiterates the point made in the passage quoted above from later in the same chapter, making clear the sort of love expected from one who loves God.

He makes much the same claim in some passages in the *Guide*, defining the passionate love of God (Arabic: *ishq*) as 'an excess of love, so that no thought remains that is directed toward a thing other than the Beloved'.[83]

Let us now look at the last passage in the *Guide* in which the issue comes up explicitly:

You know to what extent the Torah lays stress upon love: 'With all thy heart, and with all thy soul, and with all thy might' [Deut. 6: 5]. For these two ends, namely love and fear, are achieved through two things: love, through the opinions taught by the Law, which include the apprehension of His Being as He, may He be exalted, is in truth; while fear is achieved by means of all actions prescribed by the Law, as we have explained.[84]

[79] See further 'Laws of Moral Qualities', 3: 2.
[80] *Guide* iii. 28 (pp. 512–13).
[81] *Guide* iii. 51 (p. 621).
[82] 'Laws of Repentance', 10: 3.
[83] *Guide* iii. 51 (p. 627); see S. Harvey, 'The Meaning of Terms Designating Love'.
[84] *Guide* iii. 52 (p. 630).

Maimonides' position here is tolerably clear: we achieve love of God through the apprehension of God's being to the greatest extent possible for humans.

All this may help us to understand why the *Book of Love* follows the *Book of Knowledge* in the *Mishneh torah*: love of God is dependent upon and follows from knowledge of God. Indeed, as we have seen, 'Laws of Repentance', the last section of the *Book of Knowledge*, which is the object of our concern in this chapter, ends with a chapter devoted to love of God, providing an elegant transition to the *Book of Love*. As we understand him, Maimonides holds that knowledge (and hence love) of God alone does not constitute the highest possible form of human perfection. The *vita contemplativa* must be completed in the *vita activa*, and the one who truly knows and loves God will seek to imitate God, 'Who acts with loving-kindness, justice, and righteousness in the world [Jer. 9: 23]'. Knowledge of God must be followed by love of God, which, if true, finds expression in behaviour ('the obligatory observance of the commandments in general', as above).

With all this in mind, let us look at *Book of Commandments*, positive commandment 3 again:

> By this injunction we are commanded to love God (exalted be He); that is to say, to dwell upon and contemplate His commandments, His injunctions, and His works, so that we may obtain a conception of Him; and in conceiving Him attain absolute joy. This constitutes the love of God, and is obligatory. As the Sifri says: 'Since it is said [Deut. 6: 5], "Love the Lord your God", the question arises, how is one to manifest his love for the Lord? Scripture therefore says [Deut. 6: 6], "And these words which I command thee this day, shall be upon thy heart", for through this [i.e. the contemplation of God's words] you will learn to discern Him whose word called the Universe into existence.' We have thus made it clear to you that through this act of contemplation you will attain a conception of God and reach that stage of joy in which love of Him will follow of necessity. The Sages say that this commandment also includes an obligation to call upon all mankind to serve Him (exalted be He), and to have faith in Him. For just as you praise and extol anybody whom you love, and call upon others also to love him, so, if you love the Lord to the extent of the conception of His true nature to which you have attained, you will undoubtedly call upon the foolish and ignorant to seek knowledge of the Truth which you have already acquired. As the *Sifrei* says: '"Love the Lord your God": this means that you should make Him beloved of man as Abraham your father did, as it is said [Gen. 13: 5]: "And the souls they had gotten in Haran"—that is to say, just as Abraham, being a lover of the Lord—as Scripture testifies [Isa. 41: 8], 'Abraham My lover'—by the power of his conception of God, and out of his great love for Him, summoned mankind to believe, you too must so love Him as to summon mankind unto Him.

We are told in this passage that love of God involves the following:

- Dwelling upon and contemplating God's commandments and works;
- Which will lead to a conception of God which leads to absolute joy;
- These two things make *possible* the love of God. Having achieved such knowledge and love, one will seek to follow in the footsteps of Abraham, who, out of his knowledge of God (not of God's commandments!) and consequent love for God, summoned all humanity to acknowledge God. So too, must we also learn to love God, and summon all humankind to acknowledge God and love God. The fulfilment of this mission is what Maimonides calls the messianic age (to which we will return in Chapter 14 below).

It would thus appear that knowledge of God's existence derived from proofs for the existence of the 'God of the philosophers' is enough to satisfy the demands of positive commandments 1 and 2 in *Sefer hamitsvot* and of the first two chapters of the *Mishneh torah*. One who knows God in this fashion is the true lover of God described with such pathos in 'Laws of Repentance', chapter 10. But, and this is an important 'but', the entire chapter is about how to fulfil God's commandments, not about how to be a philosopher. Thus it would appear that the point Maimonides is concerned with at the end (and beginning) of the *Book of Knowledge* is that the perfected Jewish life involves fulfilment of the commandments *after* having achieved a sophisticated philosophical understanding of God. This is the burden also of Maimonides' famous parable of the palace in the *Guide*.[85]

Conclusions

Our discussion appears to lead to the following conclusions:

- In order to love God, one must know as much about God as possible.
- Knowledge of God depends upon study of God's 'two books': the book of Torah and the book of nature. Further along in the passage we are told that the joy mentioned here leads *necessarily* to the love of God.
- Contemplation of God's commandments, the Sages teach, leads to a conception of God. The commandment to love God includes an obligation to call upon all humanity to acknowledge God. This Maimonides explains as follows: love of God is proportionate to the extent of one's understanding of God's true nature.

---

[85] *Guide* iii. 51 (pp. 618–19) and iii. 54 (pp. 636–8); as argued by Kellner, *Maimonides on Human Perfection*.

- Jews who study and obey the Torah in the proper manner have three advantages over non-Jews:
    1. Obedience to the commandments leads one to moral perfection, a prerequisite for intellectual perfection; without Torah it is harder (but not impossible) for non-Jews to perfect their morals
    2. Contemplation of the commandments leads to deeper appreciation of God's wisdom
    3. The Torah itself teaches metaphysical truths
- Unlike non-Jews, Jews who have achieved a high level of intellectual perfection are *commanded* 'to call upon all mankind to serve Him (exalted be He), and to have faith in Him'.

Can non-Jews, who only know God through the study of nature and philosophy, love God? The answer for Maimonides is obvious, since Abraham, the pre-eminent lover of God, achieved that love without benefit of Torah and commandments. It is the great boon given to Abraham's descendants that their path is made so much easier.

This being the case, with respect to questions of their essential humanity, and their ability in principle to achieve human perfection (which in turn leads to providence, prophecy, and immortality), non-Jews are the same as Jews.

It is no surprise that Maimonides held that the Torah, which commands Jews to love God, gives them the tools to do so. It may be surprising that he held that non-Jewish philosophers, such as Abraham and Aristotle, could love God no less than Jews. But, of course, since Maimonides took seriously the biblical claim that God created all humanity in the divine image, this should really not be surprising, any more than it should be surprising that the final paragraph of the *Book of Knowledge* implicitly refers to human beings generally, and not just Jews.

Summary

In this chapter we have addressed the last paragraph in the *Book of Knowledge*, in 'Laws of Repentance'. In order to do so, we looked at the *Book of Knowledge* as a whole, and, following indications in the text itself, connected our paragraph back to the book's opening ('Laws of the Foundations of the Torah') and forward to the next book of the *Mishneh torah*, the *Book of Love*. Looking back at the opening paragraphs of the *Book of Knowledge*, we found a text clearly addressed to human beings as such. Looking forwards, we addressed the issue of love of God: what it is, and by whom it can be achieved. This involved a discussion of Abraham, the first non-Jewish philosopher to discover God and come to love him, and the nature of that love. Along the way we examined the third positive commandment in the *Book of Commandments*, a text which we showed did not contradict the universalist thrust of the opening and closing passages in the *Book of Knowledge*.

TWO

LOVE
Abraham, Moses, and the Meaning of Circumcision

Introduction

The theme of the *Book of Love* (*Sefer ahavah*) is constant awareness of God. In his introduction to the *Mishneh torah* Maimonides writes of this book, 'I include in it all the precepts which are to be continuously observed, and which we have been bidden to keep, in order that we may always love God and be ever mindful of Him.' It thus gives practical expression to the ideal of the unceasing love of God that appears at the end of the previous book, the *Book of Knowledge*.

The book has six sections. The first is 'Laws of Recitation of the Shema', about the obligation to recite three passages from the Torah (Deut. 6: 4–10; Deut. 11: 13–21; Num. 15: 37–41) with their accompanying blessings every morning and evening. These passages are collectively known by the first word of the first one, *shema*, meaning 'hear'. The first two verses are 'Hear, O Israel: the Lord our God, the Lord is one. And thou shalt love the Lord thy God with all thy heart, and with all thy soul, and with all thy might.' This forms a twice-daily meditation on the doctrines of the existence and unity of God and the duty to love him as expounded in the *Book of Knowledge*, while the main subject of the rest of the recitation is the study and performance of the commandments.

The second section, 'Laws of Prayer and the Priestly Blessing', is chiefly about the three daily prayer services and the special services on the New Moon and festivals. In the first chapter, Maimonides stresses that the original obligation enjoined by the Torah was a single extempore prayer each day, but that this was later regularized into set prayers at set times. The section also covers synagogues, the cycle of readings from the Torah and the Prophets, and the bestowal of blessing by the priests, consisting of the verses Numbers 6: 24–6.

Section 3, 'Laws of Tefillin, Mezuzah, and Torah Scroll', is about the leather cubic boxes containing parchments inscribed with the first two passages of the Shema and additional passages and generally worn during weekday morning prayer; the *mezuzah*, which is the parchment inscribed with the first two passages of the Shema that is affixed to doorposts; and the preparation and writing of a Torah scroll.

Section 4 is 'Laws of Fringes', about the threads, four white and one blue, attached to the corners of a four-cornered garment, prescribed in the third passage of the Shema as a reminder of the commandments. The fifth section, 'Laws of Blessings', is about the Torah commandment to recite a blessing after meals, and other blessings instituted by the rabbis.

The sixth and last section is 'Laws of Circumcision'. This is about the commandment to circumcise a male child on the eighth day after his birth if he is healthy enough, or later if he is not. This commandment is exceptional in the context of the *Book of Love* in that it is not something constant or regular like the other commandments in the book. In the introduction to the *Mishneh torah*, Maimonides justifies its inclusion in the *Book of Love*: 'Included in this group is the rite of circumcision, because this is a sign in our flesh, serving as a constant reminder, even when tefillin and fringes of the garment, etc. are not being worn.' In other words, circumcision is only performed once in a lifetime, but its effect is always observable and so it serves a purpose similar to that of commandments performed regularly.

'Laws of Circumcision' ends as follows:

8. The foreskin is disgusting, since the wicked[1] are defamed with reference to it, as it says, 'For all these nations are uncircumcised' [Jer. 9: 25]. Great is circumcision, since Abraham our father was not called 'perfect' until he was circumcised, as it says, 'Walk in My ways and be blameless. I will establish my covenant between Me and you' [Gen. 17: 1–2]. Anyone who violates the covenant of Abraham our Father and does not remove his foreskin or pulls it,[2] has no share in the world to come, even if he has performed many other good deeds.

---

[1] The Vilna edition has 'The foreskin is disgusting, since *the nations [hagoyim]* are defamed with reference to it' (emphasis added), which does have support in a variant reading of the main text on which our *halakhot* are based (BT *Ned.* 31b–32a, discussed further below), but the Bodleian Libraries Huntington 80 MS <http://maimonides.bodleian.ox.ac.uk/viewer/> and the Makbili edition, which we consider the best text of the *Mishneh torah* available, have 'since the wicked' (*haresha'im*) as given above.

[2] 'So that even though he is circumcised he appears to be uncircumcised' (translator's note).

9. Come and see how serious a matter circumcision is, since Moses our Teacher was given no respite from performing it, even though he was travelling. There were only three covenants made for all the other commandments of the Torah, as it says, 'These are the terms of the covenant which the Lord commanded Moses to conclude with the Israelites in the land of Moab, in addition to the covenant He had made with them at Horeb' [Deut. 28: 69]; there also he said, 'You stand this day . . . to enter into the covenant of the Lord your God' [Deut. 29: 9]—this comes to three covenants. But concerning circumcision, thirteen covenants were made with Abraham our Father, as it says: 'I will establish My covenant between Me and you' [Gen 17: 2], 'As for Me, this is my covenant with you' [Gen. 17: 4], 'I will maintain my covenant between Me and you' [Gen. 17: 7], 'as an everlasting covenant throughout the ages' [Gen. 17: 7], 'you and your offspring to come throughout the ages shall keep My covenant' [Gen. 17: 9], 'Such shall be the covenant' [Gen. 17: 10], 'and that shall be the sign of the covenant' [Gen. 17: 10], 'Thus shall My covenant' [Gen 17: 13], 'an everlasting pact' [Gen: 17: 13], 'he has broken My covenant' [Gen: 17: 14], 'I will maintain My covenant with him' [Gen: 17: 19], 'an everlasting covenant' [Gen. 17: 19], 'But My covenant I will maintain with Isaac' [Gen. 17: 21].³

In relation to the theme of universalism, the endings of the books of the *Mishneh torah* are broadly of two types. In some, as in the *Book of Knowledge*, the universalist message is unambiguous and fairly clear. In others, it is disguised, with Maimonides deploying particularist rhetoric in order to discourage transgression while undercutting that rhetoric in order to convey his true position.⁴

The ending of the *Book of Love* is of the second type.⁵ The object appears to be to appeal to the sense of tribal belonging and to religious fears in order to ensure that Jews will carry out the difficult procedure of circumcision, distressing for all concerned and 'a very, very hard thing',⁶ on their male babies. 'Do not think that circumcision is repugnant', is the message of the opening words of our *halakhah*, 'for a foreskin is more so'.

Once the rhetorical wave has washed over us, however, the questions rise

---

³ 'Laws of Circumcision', 3: 8–9. Maimonides appends his version of the prayer book to the *Book of Love*, but this is the end of the book proper.

⁴ That Maimonides sometimes writes on more than one level in the *Mishneh torah* is well established—see Kellner, 'Literary Character', 54. For example, Maimonides himself states in *Guide* i. 71 (p. 182) that he based his proof of God's existence in the *Mishneh torah* on the doctrine of the eternity of the world rather than on the doctrine of Creation, something that will elude most readers. Cf. above, Ch. 1, n. 51. On the distinction between descriptive and persuasive writing in Maimonides, see Kellner, *They, Too, Are Called Human* (Heb.), ch. 8.

⁵ This chapter discusses the universalism of circumcision in Maimonides from a theoretical point of view. Another important aspect is the historical, social one, which is discussed in Kasher, 'Maimonides' View of Circumcision'. ⁶ *Guide* iii. 49 (p. 610).

to the surface. Maimonides is flatly dogmatic about the importance of circumcision, offering no explanation of wherein the importance lies, other than castigation of uncircumcised non-Jews as 'wicked'. What is bad about a foreskin? What was imperfect about Abraham before he was circumcised, and how did circumcision perfect him? According to the *Mishneh torah*, the world to come is a disembodied experience of contemplation of God, attained through intellectual development, the 'acquired intellect' being what survives after death.[7] What has that to do with the condition of a man's penis? Moreover, the world to come is not supposed to be exclusive to Jews,[8] yet circumcision is not one of the seven Noahide commandments considered incumbent upon non-Jews.[9] How then do otherwise qualified non-Jews gain admission? Alternatively, is it not unfair if Jews have to undergo circumcision in order to reach the world to come while non-Jews do not? Lastly, what substantive idea, if any, lies behind the numerical comparison of expressions of covenant that exalts circumcision above all the other commandments of the Torah? (All this is without even starting to consider how women might fit into the picture).

Circumcision in the *Guide*

The treatment of circumcision in the *Guide* gives an entirely different impression from the one created by our *halakhot*. In the first place, it turns out that there is nothing bad about a foreskin; on the contrary, like everything else in creation, the human male reproductive organ is perfectly adapted to its purpose, foreskin and all. In the context of a discussion of commandments that according to Maimonides are meant to quell sexual excitement, we read:

It has been thought that circumcision perfects what is defective congenitally. This gave the possibility to everyone to raise an objection and to say: How can natural things be defective so that they need to be perfected from the outside, all the more because we know how useful the foreskin is for that member? In fact this *commandment* has not been prescribed with a view to perfecting what is defective congenitally, but to perfecting what is defective morally.[10]

The perfection of 'natural things' is something that Maimonides frequently stresses. In the *Guide*, apropos the eternity of the world post-Creation, he states:

---

[7] See 'Laws of Repentance', 8: 2.
[8] See 'Laws of Kings and their Wars', 8: 11. [9] Ibid. 9: 1.
[10] *Guide* iii. 49 (p. 609). This is *contra* Sa'adiah Gaon, *Book of Beliefs and Opinions*, iii. 10 (trans. Samuel Rosenblatt, 177).

Now the works of the deity are most perfect, and with regard to them there is no possibility of an excess or a deficiency... the Master of those who know had already clearly stated this, saying: 'The Rock, His work is perfect'.[11] He means that all His works—I mean to say His creatures—are most perfect, that no deficiency at all is commingled with them, that there is no superfluity in them and nothing that is not needed.[12]

If there is no excess or deficiency in nature, taking away the foreskin can only make the body less perfect, not more so. Moreover, the belief that the foreskin is not superfluous or a blemish is not just a matter of faith in the perfection of God's creation; we actually know 'how useful the foreskin is for that member'. There is nothing to cause disgust. The problem is that human beings find it hard to control their sexual drives, and one of the purposes of circumcision, Maimonides argues, is to reduce desire: 'with regard to circumcision, one of the reasons for it is, in my opinion, the wish to bring about a decrease in sexual intercourse and a weakening of the organ in question, so that this activity be diminished and the organ be in as quiet a state as possible.'[13]

This in itself requires clarification. If creation is entirely perfect, how does moral imperfection arise? How can the perfect body be the cause of a defect in the mind? The short answer is that the body is not a cause of imperfection, but rather the mind is its own cause: it chooses its orientation, whether towards matter, in which case it betrays its own nature, or towards God and knowledge, in which case it fulfils itself.[14] Maimonides stresses that this ability to choose on the part of human beings is actually an aspect of the perfection of nature as much as are the motions of the elements and the spheres.[15]

Ideally, then, Jewish males would leave their penises intact. The Torah intervenes, however, to aid the mind in making a correct choice.[16] The moral

---

[11] Deut. 32: 4.   [12] *Guide* ii. 28 (pp. 335–6).   [13] Ibid.

[14] There is ambivalence in Maimonides' attitude to the human body: on the one hand, appreciation of what he saw as the perfection of the body's design, and, on the other, the disgust at bodily functions he expresses in *Guide* iii. 8 (pp. 430–6). Moreover, however well-adapted the body may be to its purpose, material existence remains an impediment to intellectual apprehension—see *Guide* iii. 9 (pp. 436–7). Even so, in these chapters of the *Guide* the emphasis is still on the choice between matter and intellect, and Maimonides does posit an individual in whom 'the matter of a man is excellent, and suitable, neither dominating him nor corrupting his constitution'. The perfection in question is, then, a perfection of the species; for individuals, the degree of choice depends on their precise material composition. See Freudenthal, 'Biological Limitations'.

[15] See 'Laws of Repentance', 5: 4, and also *Guide* iii. 49 (p. 609), where it is explained that even angels and heavenly spheres have free choice, 'but always do that which is good'.

[16] As explained in *Eight Chapters*, ch. 4.

ideal is the middle path, with no excess or deficiency in respect of any moral trait. Courage, for example, represents the middle path between the excess of recklessness and the deficiency of timidity. The middle path is the way of nature itself, in which, as we saw above, 'there is no possibility of an excess or a deficiency'. It is advisable, however, for most people, to tilt slightly towards the ascetic extreme, because of the lure of matter. This is the function of the commandments of the Torah. Sexual desire is particularly difficult to master, and the commandment of circumcision is accordingly an intervention in nature that lessens desire without eliminating it.

The restraint of desire is one of the general reasons for the commandments listed in the *Guide*, where Maimonides expounds on the evils that follow from unbridled lusts as follows:

This is what destroys man's last perfection, what harms him also in his first perfection, and what corrupts most of the circumstances of the citizens and of people engaged in domestic governance. For when only the desires are followed, as is done by the ignorant, the longing for speculation is abolished, the body is corrupted, and the man to whom this happens perishes before this is required by his natural term of life; thus cares and sorrows multiply, mutual envy, hatred, and strife aiming at taking away what the other has, multiply.[17]

'Last perfection' and 'first perfection' refer to what Maimonides has already explained,[18] that 'man has two perfections: a first perfection, which is the perfection of the body, and an ultimate perfection, which is the perfection of the soul', the latter consisting in 'knowing everything concerning all the beings that it is within the capacity of man to know'. This passage thus tells us that uncontrolled desire is physically, morally, intellectually, and socially corrosive. On that basis, circumcision is a rational measure in any society that values harmony and the pursuit of moral and intellectual perfection, with no particularly Jewish significance.[19]

Circumcision as a Sign

The *Guide* goes on to provide a second reason for circumcision:[20] it serves as a sign uniting those who believe in the unity of God and distinguishing them from unbelievers, and thereby promotes 'mutual love and mutual help' in the community of believers, and 'forms for them a sort of covenant and alliance'.

---

[17] *Guide* iii. 33 (p. 532). [18] *Guide* iii. 27 (p. 511).
[19] Compare *Kuzari* iii. 7, where Judah Halevi describes circumcision as opposed to reason and of no social utility; it is rather a direct means of connecting Israel to the divine. Our thanks to Professor Barry Kogan for his kindness in providing us with an advance copy of his forthcoming translation of the *Kuzari*. [20] *Guide* iii. 49 (p. 610).

Again, though, the Jewish aspect is downplayed. The basis of admission to this covenant is ethical and ideological, not ethnic, and moreover it is presented not as a covenant made directly between God and a person or a people (a highly problematic notion for Maimonides), but as one made between people, committing them to a certain ideology: 'Circumcision is a covenant made by Abraham our Father with a view to the belief in the unity of God. Thus everyone who is circumcised joins Abraham's covenant. This covenant imposes the obligation to believe in the unity of God: "To be a God unto thee and to thy seed after thee."'[21]

Abraham is referred to as 'Abraham our Father', and the covenant is with 'thy seed after thee', but we know from the 'Letter to Obadiah the Proselyte' that Maimonides did not regard these phrases as having biological significance. Obadiah is told that although not born a Jew he may pray along with the synagogue congregation using the terms 'our God' and 'God of our fathers' because 'Abraham our Father, peace be with him, is the father of his pious posterity who keep his ways, and the father of his disciples and of all proselytes who adopt Judaism'.[22] A disciple of Abraham is anyone who believes in the unity of God, while even those born Jewish are to be regarded as Abraham's 'seed' only insofar as they 'keep his ways'.[23]

Some may regard Maimonides' kind letter to Obadiah as less than persuasive evidence (although it results in a halakhic ruling, which is not something that Maimonides would have taken lightly), but in fact his reassurance to the troubled convert that he has equal standing in the community has deep philosophical foundations. An aspect of the perfection of natural things is a basic equality, such that there is no essential difference between members of the same species. Differences that do exist are due to the vagaries of matter, but have nothing to do with essential form.

Regarding manifestations of His justice, may He be exalted, and of the equality established by Him between them, they are very evident. . . . There in no way exists a relation of superiority and inferiority between individuals conforming to the course of nature except that which follows necessarily from the differences in the disposition of the various kinds of matter . . . He makes individuals of the same species equal at their creation. With a view to this true consideration, the Master of those who know says: 'For all His ways are judgement'.[24]

---

[21] Ibid. The verse quoted here is Gen. 17: 7.

[22] *Igerot harambam* (trans. Shailat), i. 231; English trans. from Twersky, *A Maimonides Reader*, 476.

[23] See also 'Laws of Idolatry', 2: 5. For an analysis of the 'Letter to Obadiah', see Diamond, *Converts, Heretics, and Lepers*, 11–32.   [24] *Guide* iii. 12 (p. 447).

'For all His ways are judgement' is the continuation of the verse that begins 'The Rock, His work is perfect', which we saw cited above in support of the idea of the perfection of creation. The verse, as read by Maimonides, states that the world is perfect, and that this perfection entails justice, such that God does not discriminate in any essential way between individuals of the same species. The implication is that neither should we. This stance of Maimonides is opposed to that of Judah Halevi, according to whom converts can never attain the same status as Jews in relation to the divine,[25] for in this respect Jews are in effect a separate, superior species.[26] There is no trace of such a notion in Maimonides.

As for the positive idea that a convert can identify as a descendant of Abraham, this is anchored in the *Mishneh torah* through the famous ruling that a convert who fulfils the commandment of bringing first fruits to the Temple also makes the prescribed accompanying declaration that states, among other things, 'I am come unto the country which the Lord swore unto our fathers to give us.'[27] The grounds given for this ruling are that 'Abraham was told, "The father of a multitude of nations have I made thee" [Gen. 17: 5], implying that he is the father of everyone who enters under the wings of the Presence; and the Lord's oath was given first to Abraham that his children shall inherit the Land.'[28] In other words, a convert has a stake in the Land of Israel by virtue of being a spiritual descendant of Abraham.

A Comprehensive Commandment

To sum up, circumcision has a universal orientation in both functions assigned to it in the *Guide*, that is, both as a restraint on sexual desire and as a unifying sign for the community of believers in the unity of God. This is underwritten by the doctrine that the human form is the same for all human beings, who share the same purposes, which are to attain moral and intellectual virtue, even if individual capacities vary. Such equality is a matter of divine justice, which is part of the perfection of creation. This complex of ideas is represented in the verse 'The Rock, His work is perfect, for all His ways are judgement.'

Corresponding to this is the idea that, from the human side, the apprehension of the world's perfection must lead to doing justice. This, we argue in this chapter, is what circumcision ultimately signifies for Maimonides, in the *Mishneh torah* as well as in the *Guide*. For the time being, let us simply note that circumcision spans all three of the main aims of the Torah, as

[25] See *Kuzari* i. 27 and 115. [26] See *Kuzari* i. 31.
[27] See Deut. 26: 1–11. [28] 'Laws of First Fruits and Other Priestly Offerings', 4: 3.

Maimonides understands them.[29] As a sign of belief in the unity of God, which is a foundation of intellectual virtue,[30] it stands for 'the welfare of the soul'; as a means of promoting 'mutual love and mutual help' among the believers in God's unity it stands for 'the welfare of the body' or moral virtue (which extends from physical health to the social and political virtues and the just state); and it restrains desire.[31] At the same time, circumcision is not presented in the *Guide* as in itself making a human being perfect; certainly not intellectually or physically, and not even morally—it is at most an aid in the process of moral perfection.

Contrast with the *Book of Love*

By contrast with what we have seen from the *Guide*, the emphasis at the end of the *Book of Love* appears to be upon a distinction between Jews and the rest of humanity that originates with 'Abraham our father'. The foreskin is declared to be disgusting—inherently, essentially so, it would seem; the uncircumcised nations are wicked—again, apparently inherently so; circumcision somehow perfected Abraham, on the face of it by removing this inborn defect, and it presumably also perfects his descendants who continue the practice; the world to come is only for the circumcised; circumcision outweighs the rest of the Torah by thirteen covenants to three. Completely absent from 'Laws of Circumcision' is the *Guide*'s idea of circumcision as a retardant of sexuality.

The universalistic approach to circumcision in the *Guide* is no surprise. That is the approach to all the commandments in that work, as Maimonides goes about demonstrating that they promote the universally acknowledged benefits of the welfare of the body and the welfare of the soul. The apparent contrast with the ending of the *Book of Love* means, however, that we have here a test of Maimonides' universalism. Is it that the apparent particularism, if not obscurantism, of the *Book of Love* represents the real meat of Judaism while the *Guide* apologetically serves philosophy's insipid fare? Or is the latter's universalism to be taken as authentically Jewish, so that the ending of the *Book of Love* should be read in a way that is consistent with it?

It is not difficult to construct a reading of the ending of the *Book of Love* that removes the contradictions. The statement in 'Laws of Circumcision'

---

[29] On this see Gross, 'Reasons for Circumcision' (Heb.), 27.

[30] See 'Laws of the Foundations of the Torah', 1: 7.

[31] See *Guide* iii. 33 (p. 532): 'To the totality of the purposes of the perfect Law there belong the abandonment, depreciation, and restraint of desires in so far as is possible, so that these should be satisfied only in so far as this is necessary.'

that 'The foreskin is disgusting, since the wicked are defamed with reference to it',[32] can certainly be taken to mean that circumcision repairs a moral defect rather than a physical or mystically essential one. The sense is then that those who are uncircumcised are wicked in that they permit themselves sexual licence, which is what 'the nations' do, whereas the Jews have the Torah to rescue them from such degradation, with no implication of any inherent difference between the two groups. The circumcision of Abraham can be understood as a sign, not a cause, of his perfection, since after all he found God and truth well before he was circumcised at the age of 99,[33] while his chastity is established in the *Guide* through citation of the *midrash* about his imperviousness to his wife's beauty, in an episode that took place long before he was commanded about circumcision.[34] Failure to be circumcised can be seen as an opting out of the community of believers in the unity of God, an intellectual rather than an ethnic or religious betrayal, a consequence of which could be loss of the world to come.

This is indeed the general direction we propose to take, but, as outlined, this reading suffers from at least two deficiencies. Firstly, it rather begs the question, in that it assumes that the *Mishneh torah* really ought to be read in the light of the *Guide*. It would provide greater confidence if we could find support for it within the *Mishneh torah* itself. Secondly, it ignores the challenge that the ending of the *Book of Love* presents to explore some key themes in Maimonides' thought.

We therefore propose to examine the following themes in Maimonides, not in full, but as they bear on 'Laws of Circumcision', 3: 8–9:

- The relationship between Abraham and Moses, and between the Abrahamic and Mosaic covenants
- Perfection
- Circumcision and the values that it expresses

In general, we shall argue that the underlying idea of the *Book of Love's* ending is that Moses was the lawgiver, but that Abraham personifies the perfection at which the Torah aims. Circumcision, which is a commandment of the law and was also performed by Abraham, serves as a link between the two, a point of comparison and contrast. These *halakahot* also point to a certain tension that exists between the idea of perfection and that of covenant.

---

[32] 'Laws of Circumcision', 3: 8.   [33] See Gen. 17: 24.
[34] See *Guide* iii. 49 (p. 609). Maimonides' source for the *midrash*, on Gen. 12: 11, is probably BT *BB* 17b.

As a basis for the human relationship with God, perfection has at least the possible connotation of the fulfilment of an inner potential inherent in all people, whereas a covenant connotes a convergence of interests (compliance with God's rules in return for God's favour and protection) rather than the cultivation of inward qualities, and is limited to the covenantal partners.[35] In our exploration of the *halakahot* we seek to resolve this tension.

How Maimonides Moulds His Source

In attempting to clarify the intent of a difficult passage of the *Mishneh torah*, it can often be helpful to compare it with its sources in the Talmud and elsewhere, to see which ideas Maimonides has emphasized and which he has downplayed or discarded altogether. 'Laws of Circumcision', 3: 8–9 is mainly based upon Mishnah *Nedarim* 3: 11.[36] This *mishnah* states, inter alia:

Rabbi Eleazar ben Azariah said: The foreskin is loathsome, since it is a term of opprobrium for the wicked, as it is written, 'For all the nations are uncircumcised'. Rabbi Ishmael said, Great is [the precept] of circumcision, since thirteen covenants were made thereon. Rabbi Jose said, Circumcision is a great precept, for it overrides [the severity of] the sabbath. Great is [the precept of] circumcision, for [neglecting] which Moses did not have [his punishment] suspended even for a single hour . . . Rabbi said, Great is circumcision, for [notwithstanding] all the precepts which Abraham fulfilled, he was not designated perfect until he circumcised himself, as it is written, 'Walk before me, and be thou perfect.' Another explanation: Great is circumcision, since but for that, the Holy One, blessed be He, would not have created the universe, as it is written, 'But for my covenant by day and night, I would not have appointed the ordinances of heaven and earth'.[37]

A number of modifications made by Maimonides stand out:

- He abbreviates 'great is circumcision, for [notwithstanding] all the precepts which Abraham fulfilled he was not designated perfect until he circumcised himself' to 'since Abraham our father was not called "perfect" until he was circumcised', omitting Abraham's observance of the commandments, presumably because he did not subscribe to the midrashic idea that Abraham, Isaac, and Jacob observed all the commandments, even the rabbinic ones.[38]

---

[35] It is worth noting, however, that the first covenant recorded in the Bible is between God and Noah (Gen. 9: 8–17), and thus with the entire human race.

[36] See also *Mekhilta*, 'Yitro' on Exod. 18: 3.

[37] Translation by Rabbi Dr R. H. Freedman, from the Soncino Babylonian Talmud, *Ned.* 31b.

[38] See above, Ch. 1, n. 61.

- He inverts the order in which the *mishnah* mentions Moses and Abraham, putting Abraham first.
- He omits the idea that circumcision overrides sabbatical prohibitions.
- He rearranges the placement of 'Great is [the precept] of circumcision, since thirteen covenants were made thereon', placing it at the end of the discussion instead of at the beginning. The numerical comparison with the three covenants relating to the Torah is taken from elsewhere,[39] but the Gemara on this *mishnah* does make the general statement 'Great is circumcision, for it counterbalances all the [other] precepts of the Torah.'[40]
- He omits the statement in the *mishnah*, 'Great is circumcision, since but for that, the Holy One, blessed be He, would not have created the universe, as it is written, "But for my covenant by day and night, I would not have appointed the ordinances of heaven and earth,"' again very likely on doctrinal grounds: Maimonides did not consider that the Torah and its commandments in any way preceded creation.[41]

Some of these modifications are discussed later in this chapter, but their general effect, besides stripping the rabbinic source of doctrinally repugnant ideas, is to align a comparison between circumcision and the other commandments of the Torah with a comparison between Abraham and Moses, intensifying and personifying—one could almost say dramatizing—the contrasts drawn.

The Pillars of the World

As far as Maimonides is concerned, Abraham and Moses are the outstanding figures not just in Judaism but in the history of the world.[42] They are 'the two prophets who are the pillars of the well-being of the human species'.[43] Both, then, are of universal significance. They are constantly paired in Maimonides' writings. Their roles, though, are different.

---

[39] See BT *Ber.* 45b; BT *Pes.* 69b.   [40] BT *Ned.* 32a.
[41] See Kellner, *Maimonides' Confrontation*, 68–77. This statement is included in the blessings prescribed in 'Laws of Circumcision', 3: 4–5, to be said when converts and slaves are circumcised, following BT *Shab.* 137b.   [42] See Turner, 'The Patriarch Abraham'.
[43] *Guide* ii. 23 (p. 321). The two prophets are not actually named at this point, but their identities are clear from the invocation of Abraham and Moses at the end of the previous chapter as authorities for the doctrine of the creation of the world in time, to which the current statement refers back.

Abraham in the *Book of Knowledge*

We have already seen Abraham portrayed in the *Guide* as a philosopher and teacher, but not as a lawgiver. In the *Mishneh torah*, the clearest definition of the different missions of Abraham and Moses is in the narrative at the beginning of 'Laws of Idolatry',[44] where Abraham is described as having discovered the one God though observation of natural phenomena, and as setting out to convert the world to belief in him. Moses enters the story when Abraham's descendants are on the point of completely forgetting their ancestor's legacy, which he restores through the commandments. So Abraham, as in the *Guide*, is a seer who sets out to impart universal truths through persuasion and personal example to all who will attend, whereas Moses is a legislator and enforcer who enshrines those truths in a particular, binding law for a particular nation.[45]

The account of Abraham's career in 'Laws of Idolatry' is almost entirely based on midrashic material.[46] The scriptural Abraham barely features. There is no mention of circumcision, or the binding of Isaac, or any other of the 'ten trials' that Abraham underwent, apart from his departure from Haran.[47] A good reason for this is that at this point Maimonides is seeking to portray Abraham in the role of liberator from the delusions of idol worship in courageous defiance of a regime for which idolatry is a prop of its power, a portrayal for which there is little scriptural basis. All the same, the very casting of Abraham in this role suggests that, in Maimonides' view, circumcision and the rest of his trials did not make Abraham what he was and do not define his significance; rather they are subordinate to his character and his intellectual journey.

In the *Guide*, circumcision and the other trials that Abraham underwent are presented as demonstrations for the benefit of others, rather than as advancing him either morally or intellectually: 'Know that the aim and mean-

---

[44] See above, Ch. 1.

[45] See Kaplan, 'Maimonides on the Singularity of the Jewish People'. Note that this does not imply that Abraham was somehow a greater prophet than Moses. Abraham reached the highest measurable ranks of prophecy (see *Guide* ii. 45 (pp. 401–2)), but the prophecy of Moses was unique, off the 'normal' prophetic scale ('Laws of the Foundations of the Torah', 7: 6–7). Not even the messiah will quite reach his level ('Laws of Repentance', 9: 2). Moses' prophecy produced a perfect, eternal law, that no subsequent prophet may alter ('Laws of the Foundations of the Torah', ch. 9), whereas Abraham's legacy proved ephemeral. Nevertheless, despite Moses' unique status, or perhaps because of it, Maimonides consistently presents Abraham rather than Moses as the ideal.

[46] Chiefly *Gen. Rabbah* 38, but see Alex P. Jassen, 'Reading Midrash with Maimonides'.

[47] See Mishnah *Avot* 5: 3 and Maimonides' commentary there.

ing of all the trials mentioned in the Torah is to let people know what they ought to do or what they must believe. Accordingly the notion of a trial consists as it were in a certain act being done, the purpose being not the accomplishment of that particular act, but the latter's being a model to be imitated and followed.'[48] The lack of any mention of circumcision and the other trials in the biographical sketch in 'Laws of Idolatry' can be taken as reflecting the same view. This tends to justify reading 'Laws of Circumcision', 3: 8 in the light of the *Guide*, and interpreting 'Abraham our father was not called "perfect" until he was circumcised' as meaning not that circumcision perfected Abraham—much less effected a connection with the supernatural 'divine matter' that he and his descendants were uniquely, genetically predisposed to receive, as Judah Halevi would have it[49]—but rather that Abraham gained moral and intellectual perfection through years of intense thought about his observations of nature, and that circumcision is a sign that communicates this process.

The narrative in 'Laws of Idolatry' also downplays the dynastic aspect of the story of Abraham, who arrives in Canaan not as someone leaving behind security and ease at God's command in order to found a nation, but as an émigré dissident intellectual who has been hounded in his home country.[50] The legacy to his son and grandson is an ideological one. Maimonides does not of course deny the importance of Abraham as ancestor of the Jewish people, but here, in the *Book of Knowledge*, the conceptual fountainhead of the *Mishneh torah*, the intellectual, universalist aspect prevails. As mentioned, particularism enters only with Moses.

Earlier in the same book, in 'Laws of Moral Qualities', Abraham is said to have taught the doctrine of the middle path as 'the way of God': 'and this is what the patriarch Abraham taught his children, as it is said "For I love him, because he will charge his children and his household after him, that they may keep the way of the Lord" [Gen. 18: 19].'[51] This doctrine is imposed by the commandment 'and [you shall] walk in His ways',[52] the keynote commandment of this section of the *Book of Knowledge*. Again, Abraham bequeaths a philosophical/ethical legacy rather than a national one, and again, Mosaic legislation subsequently embodies Abrahamic teaching, although Moses is not mentioned here by name.

---

[48] *Guide* iii. 24 (p. 498).   [49] See above, n. 19.
[50] See Aviezer Ravitzky, 'The Binding of Isaac' (Heb.), 14. Ravitzky points out that, in the *Guide*, the binding of Isaac is similarly treated as an event in the history of the spread of monotheism rather than as a formative event in the history of the Jewish people.
[51] 'Laws of Moral Qualities', 1: 7.   [52] Deut. 28: 9.

A similar relationship is described towards the end of the *Book of Knowledge*, where Maimonides extols the service of God out of love, and writes, 'And this virtue is a very high virtue, and not every philosopher attains to it. It is the rank of Our Father, Abraham, whom the Holy One (blessed be He) called "my lover" [Isa. 41: 8], because he served solely from love. It is the rank to which the Holy One (blessed be He) exhorted us, through Moses our Master; for it is said, "And you shall love the Lord your God" [Deut. 6: 5].' The Abrahamic value of love becomes an institution of Mosaic law.

Abraham is thus a motif that appears in the *Book of Knowledge* in all three phases of the human relationship with God: the ethical phase, or moral science, in 'Laws of Moral Qualities'; the cognitive phase, which is the study of natural science, in 'Laws of Idolatry', 1: 3, where he is described as having apprehended the existence of the one incorporeal God through his cogitations on the observable movements of the stars; and the metaphysical phase, which is the study of divine science, expressed in the *Guide* in the doctrine of negative attributes of God, but in the *Mishneh torah* in the incessant, all-consuming love of God. It seems to have been very important to Maimonides to project onto Abraham all the values that the Torah of Moses represents. Circumcision, too, as we have said, runs the entire gamut of these values, and in that sense it balances the entire Torah. It is this connection between Abraham and circumcision—Abraham as the all-embracing exemplar, and circumcision as the all-embracing commandment—that Maimonides is anxious to make at the end of the *Book of Love*.

Abraham as Patron of the *Book of Love*

In several ways, the *Book of Love* is the book of Abraham. The end of the *Book of Knowledge*, with its depiction of Abraham as the unremitting lover of God, is a kind of overture to it, heralding the theme of commandments that 'we were commanded in order to love God and remember him always'. The Mosaic commandment that is a vessel for that love, 'And thou shalt love the Lord thy God', is from the first passage of the Shema recital, which, as already mentioned, is the first commandment in the *Book of Love*. But 'Laws of the Recitation of the Shema', 1: 4 connects the Shema recital directly to Abraham, for it relates the *midrash* that, on his deathbed, Jacob (also called Israel), concerned that his sons might have idolatrous tendencies, exhorted them to 'take particular care concerning correct belief in God's unity and not to stray from the path of God, on which his fathers Abraham and Isaac had walked', to which the sons responded 'Hear, O Israel! the Lord is our God, the Lord alone',[53] which is the first line of the Shema. Maimonides is selective, often creative, and always pointed in his use of Midrash. In this case, he associates Abraham with the declaration of the unity of God and of loyalty to the way of God with which the *Book of Love* begins, namely the Shema, as well as with the badge of that belief and loyalty with which it ends, namely circumcision. Moreover, Maimonides compares Jacob's misgiving with that of Moses about the continued fidelity of the children of Israel to the laws of the Torah: 'as Moses our master said to us, "Perchance there is among you man or woman"'.[54] The weighing of the covenant of Abraham against the covenant of Moses is there from the start of the *Book of Love*.[55]

Prayer, the next subject of the *Book of Love* after the Shema, is also associated with Abraham, for he initiated regular morning prayer, while his son and grandson, Isaac and Jacob, who are portrayed in the *Mishneh torah* as essentially preserving Abraham's legacy, initiated the afternoon and evening prayers.[56] Again, this is a midrashic legend, and one that is actually somewhat at odds with the account of the origin of regular thrice-daily prayer in the first chapter of 'Laws of Prayer and the Priestly Blessing', which associates it with the Temple ritual. It serves, though, to give additional Abrahamic colouring to the *Book of Love*. The book's theme of love, and several of the acts of love that it prescribes, are thus traced to 'Abraham our father'.

In sum, Maimonides' Abraham is very much a universalistic figure who preached a universal religion (if what he taught can be called 'religion'), and his presence pervades the *Book of Love*. It seems unreasonable then to view his appearance at the end of that book in an ethnocentric light. This lends further credence to the universalistic reading of 'Laws of Circumcision', 3: 8–9.

Circumcision of the Heart

In the tenth and final chapter of 'Laws of Repentance', reference is repeatedly made to the verse 'And thou shalt love the Lord thy God with all thy heart, and with all thy soul, and with all thy might',[57] which for Jews is most familiar as

---

[53] See *Gen. Rabbah* 98: 4; *Deut. Rabbah* 2: 25. The mention of Abraham and Isaac seems to be Maimonides' embellishment; at least, there is no such mention in these sources.

[54] Deut. 29: 17. In full the verse reads: 'Lest there should be among you man, or woman, or family, or tribe, whose heart turneth away this day from the Lord our God, to go to serve the gods of those nations; lest there should be among you a root that beareth gall and wormwood.'

[55] The motif that runs through these phases in the *Guide* is the verse from the Shema: 'And thou shalt love the Lord thy God with all thy soul and all thy heart and all thy might.' See Gillis, *Reading Maimonides' Mishneh Torah*, 139–42.

[56] See 'Laws of Kings and their Wars', 9: 1; BT *Ber.* 26b.   [57] Deut. 6: 5.

the second verse of the Shema recital, so that the references provide a further link to the following book where, as we have noted, the Shema is the opening topic. At least, that appears to be the reference, but the verse is not actually cited in full, and the phrases that are cited could refer to other verses. In 'Laws of Repentance', 10: 2, the citation is 'And thou shalt love the Lord thy God', which could also be a reference to the verse 'Therefore thou shalt love the Lord thy God, and keep His charge, and His statutes, and His ordinances, and His commandments, always.'[58] In the following *halakhah* and in *halakhah* 6 of the same chapter, the phrase cited is 'with all thy heart and with all thy soul', which, besides the verse in the Shema, could also refer to the verse 'And now, Israel, what doth the Lord thy God require of thee, but to fear the Lord thy God, to walk in all His ways, and to love Him, and to serve the Lord thy God *with all thy heart and with all thy soul*',[59] which clearly brings in the fear of God as well as love, and, with the phrase 'to walk in all His ways', also evokes 'Laws of Moral Qualities', of which the keynote commandment is to walk in God's ways, albeit on the basis of a slightly different phrase from another verse.[60] It is possible, then, although the main theme of the chapter is the love of God, and although readers will most readily link these biblical phrases to the Shema, that by making only partial references Maimonides is artfully introducing undertones of other aspects of the human being–God relationship—the aspects of fear and moral virtue—bringing them all together at the climax of the *Book of Knowledge*, in which that relationship is the central theme.

Most intriguingly, one possible reference of the phrase 'with all thy heart and with all thy soul' is the verse 'And the Lord thy God will circumcise thy heart, and the heart of thy seed, to love the Lord thy God with all thy heart, and with all thy soul, that thou mayest live.'[61] The final chapter of 'Laws of Repentance' may thus allude to the last topic of the *Book of Love* as well as the first. That may seem over-subtle, but in the *Guide*, where Maimonides discusses 'the abandonment, depreciation, and restraint of desires' as one of the main purposes of the commandments,[62] he refers explicitly to circumcision of the heart:

Similarly to the totality of intentions of the Law there belong gentleness and docility; man should not be hard and rough, but responsive, obedient, acquiescent, and docile. You know already His commandment, may He be exalted: 'Circumcise

---

[58] Deut. 11: 1.   [59] Deut. 10: 12.
[60] The phrasing in 'Laws of Moral Qualities', 1: 6, is 'and thou shalt walk in His ways', which is from Deut. 28: 9.   [61] Deut. 30: 6.   [62] *Guide* iii. 33 (p. 532).

therefore the foreskin of your heart, and be no more stiffnecked.'[63] 'Be silent, and hearken, O Israel.'[64] With regard to docility in accepting what ought to be accepted, it is said: 'And we will hear it, and do it.'[65]

The word indicating an attitude of docility and acquiescence in the verses cited in this passage is 'hear', or 'hearken'—in Hebrew, *shema*.

There can be no certainty that Maimonides intends any of these allusions. All the same, a consistent picture is starting to form. It must always be borne in mind that the common purpose of the commandments in the *Book of Love*, as defined by Maimonides in his introduction to the *Mishneh torah*, is 'to love God and remember him always'. The most direct expression of this purpose is the recital of the Shema, which begins 'Hear, O Israel' and continues with the commandment 'And thou shalt love the Lord thy God'. If 'to hear' is associated with the circumcision of the heart, we may conclude that the way in which circumcision expresses the love of God is as an outward sign of this inward disposition, so that the commandment of circumcision at the end of the *Book of Love* embodies (quite literally) the spirit of the commandment of the Shema recital at the beginning.

Furthermore, just a little earlier in the same chapter of the *Guide*, where the discussion is of the socially disruptive effect of the pursuit of desire, Maimonides states: 'Therefore God, may His name be held sublime, employed a gracious ruse through giving us certain laws that destroy this end and turn thought away from it in every way.'[66] Circumcision is probably the prime example of such a law. In other words, it is not just a sign of docility but a cause of it, and the ruse, we may speculate, consists in presenting it as a matter of tribal loyalty and belonging, and as in itself a passport to the world to come, while the true purpose is to lessen desire as a necessary preliminary to the attainment of moral perfection and then intellectual perfection, which is the only real entrée to the world to come.[67]

Thus not only is the universalistic reading of 'Laws of Circumcision', 3: 8–9 the more reasonable one in the light of the characterization of Abraham elsewhere in the *Mishneh torah* and in Maimonides' writings generally, but we also have a reason that Maimonides should have disguised his universalism at that point. Had he written 'Great is circumcision, for it lowers your libido' it might not have had the desired effect, but he certainly held that the diminution of physical love is the way to enhance the love of God.[68]

---

[63] Deut. 10: 16.   [64] Deut. 27: 9.   [65] Deut. 5: 24.   [66] *Guide* iii. 33 (p. 532).
[67] Josef Stern sees the restraint of desire as the inner, philosophical significance of circumcision. See his *Problems and Parables*, 103–4.
[68] See *Guide* iii. 8–9 (pp. 430–6). On the positioning of 'Laws of Circumcision' in relation

The Covenant of Love and the Covenant of Law

We have understood that Abraham and Moses had different missions, the one universal, the other particular, but how exactly is the relationship between them to be defined?

Maimonides expresses himself clearly on this point in his *Commentary on the Mishnah*:

> And note this great principle expressed in this *mishnah* in the statement 'it was forbidden from Sinai', namely that you must realize that everything that is prohibited to us or that we do today, we do not observe other than because of God's commandments through Moses, and not because God thus commanded the prophets who preceded him. For example, we do not eat a limb torn from a living animal, not because God forbade a limb torn from a living animal to Noah's descendants, but because Moses forbade us a limb torn from a living animal in what he was commanded at Sinai, that a limb from a living animal should remain forbidden. Similarly, we circumcise, not because Abraham circumcised himself and the males of his household, but because God commanded us through Moses to be circumcised as Abraham, peace be upon him, circumcised. Similarly, in the case of the thigh tendon, we do not follow the prohibition of Jacob our father but the commandments of Moses our teacher.
>
> Compare the statement of the sages that 613 commandments were communicated to Moses at Sinai[69]—all these are among those commandments.[70]

This trenchant statement that there is no continuity between pre-Torah commandments and Torah commandments is borne out in the *Mishneh torah* by the ruling that those who observe the seven Noahide commandments incumbent on all mankind are considered to be 'of the pious of the nations of the world' only if they accept these commandments on the authority of the Torah of Moses, even though, as their name implies, they originated with Noah, the progenitor of mankind after the Flood.[71] That is to say, Mai-

---

to the explanations of circumcision in the *Guide*, see Gillis, *Reading Maimonides' Mishneh Torah*, 217.

[69] See BT *Mak.* 23*b*.

[70] *Commentary on the Mishnah*, *Ḥul.* 7: 6; our English translation is based on the Hebrew translation by J. Kafih, p. 140.

[71] See 'Laws of Kings and their Wars', 8: 11. This does not appear to be entirely consistent with the language of 'Laws of Kings and their Wars', 9: 1, where, having enumerated commandments originating with Adam, Noah, Abraham, Isaac, Jacob, and Amram, Maimonides writes 'until Moses our teacher came and the Torah was completed through him', as though Moses supplemented existing commandments rather than replacing them with a new, comprehensive set. It is perhaps necessary to distinguish between the substance of a commandment, which may predate the Torah, and its authority, which is from the Torah alone.

monides does not seem to have changed his mind on this question: the Torah is a complete restart as far as divine legislation is concerned.

In the light of that, the way that the *Book of the Commandments* introduces the commandment of circumcision may seem puzzling: 'The commandment that we were commanded to circumcise, and He, may He be exalted, stated it to Abraham: "Every male among you shall be circumcised".[72] And the Torah explicitly prescribed *karet* [excision] for he who omits to perform this positive commandment, as He, may He be exalted, said, "And the uncircumcised male who is not circumcised in the flesh of his foreskin, that soul shall be cut off from his people, etc."'[73]

The explanation is given in one of Maimonides' letters, in which he states that we only know about Abraham's history and his being commanded to circumcise (along with other pre-Sinaitic legislation) because these matters are recorded in the Torah of Moses, and so the current authority of the commandment of circumcision derives from the Torah, and not from the historical event.[74] This may look like a demotion of Abraham, but in fact we shall see that, in the way that Maimonides handles the relationship between the two great prophets, it is a way of reversing the view of this relationship that might emerge from a simple reading of the biblical narrative. Instead of Abraham being a precursor to Moses and to the covenant that establishes Abraham's descendants as a people with its own law and state, the law and the state become the means of fulfilling the more ideal covenant with Abraham.

In the listing of the commandments in the introduction to the *Mishneh torah*, the basis given for circumcision is the obvious verse from Leviticus: 'To circumcise the son, as it says, "And in the eighth day the flesh of his foreskin shall be circumcised."'[75] At the opening of 'Laws of Circumcision', however, the first biblical text cited is God's warning to Abraham that the consequence of failing to be circumcised is that 'that soul shall be cut off from his people' (the verse cited in the *Book of the Commandments*). Maimonides frequently introduces a commandment with a mention of the penalty for breach of it, but it is noteworthy that this important detail of the commandment of circumcision derives from the command to Abraham, even though that is not the basis for the current practice. In 'Laws of Circumcision', the verse 'And in the eighth day the flesh of his foreskin shall be circumcised' is

---

[72] Gen. 17: 10.
[73] *Book of the Commandments*, positive commandment 215. The verse quoted is Gen. 17: 14.   [74] 'Letter to Joseph Ibn Jabbir', *Igerot harambam* (trans. Shailat), i. 410–11.
[75] *Mishneh torah*, introd., positive commandment 215. The verse quoted is Lev. 21: 3.

used only as proof for the rule that circumcision must be performed by day and not by night.[76]

A possible reason for this is that what Maimonides seeks to stress in 'Laws of Circumcision' is not the once in a lifetime act of circumcision, but the lifelong fact of being circumcised, in accordance with the stated theme of the *Book of Love*, namely that it concerns commandments instituted 'that we may always love God and be ever mindful of Him'. Failure to be circumcised is a continual omission that entails the lack of this constant reminder. Hence Maimonides begins 'Laws of Circumcision' with the penalty for not being circumcised, namely *karet* (literally 'being cut off'), which he interprets as deprivation of the world to come,[77] that is, intellectual extinction. On a philosophical level, such a fate is not a punishment for this or that sin but a consequence of failure to cultivate love and mindfulness of God through intellectual attainment, which commandments such as circumcision (and ultimately all the commandments) assist.

Be that as it may, the way in which the Torah narrates God's command to Abraham presents some difficulty to Maimonides' thesis that Jews circumcise because of Moses and not because of Abraham, since it is clearly stated that circumcision is mandated for all time as part of the Abrahamic covenant itself:

This is My covenant, which ye shall keep, between Me and you and thy seed after thee: every male among you shall be circumcised. And ye shall be circumcised in the flesh of your foreskin; and it shall be a token of a covenant betwixt Me and you. And he that is eight days old shall be circumcised among you, every male throughout your generations.[78]

The answer that suggests itself from a reading of the historical account in 'Laws of Idolatry' is that this was indeed the original intention,[79] but that the moral and intellectual decline of Abraham's descendants required intervention that gave circumcision the force of law, along with the other 612 commandments of the Torah. The reconciliation of the texts may not be entirely smooth, but at any rate there is evidently a delicate relationship between circumcision as practised by Abraham and circumcision as commanded by

---

[76] See 'Laws of Circumcision', 1: 8.

[77] See 'Laws of Repentance', 8: 1 and 5; *Commentary on the Mishnah*, 'Introduction to *Perek ḥelek*'. *Karet* is an unusual punishment for breach of a positive commandment; the only omission to which it applies besides failure to be circumcised is failure to make the paschal offering. These two commandments are closely connected both legally, in that an uncircumcised male may not partake of the paschal offering, and historically; see *Guide* iii. 46 (p. 585).

[78] Gen. 17: 10–12.   [79] See 'Laws of Idolatry', 1: 2–3.

Moses. This is reflected in the language of the *Commentary on the Mishnah* cited above: 'God commanded us through Moses to be circumcised as Abraham, peace be upon him, circumcised.' Circumcision is a Mosaic commandment, but it retains the connection to the circumcision of Abraham that it evokes. This could be regarded as of purely legal significance, as meaning that the commandment given to Moses incorporates the terms of the commandment given to Abraham. But we should note the phrasing of the end of 'Laws of Idolatry', 1: 3:

> The doctrine implanted by Abraham would, in a very short time, have been uprooted, and Jacob's descendants would have relapsed into the error and perversities universally prevalent. But because of God's love for us and because He kept the oath made to our ancestor Abraham, He appointed Moses to be our teacher and the teacher of all the prophets, and charged him with his mission.[80]

'The oath made to our ancestor Abraham' is 'the covenant between the pieces', in which Abraham was promised that his descendants would suffer but would become a great nation and inherit the Land of Israel.[81] Neither in that covenant nor in the subsequent covenant of circumcision[82] is any mention made of sending a prophet who, as this passage goes on to express it, 'crowned them with precepts'.[83] In Genesis, the substance of the covenant is the land. Maimonides' narrative changes the perspective. It presents God's 'oath to Abraham' as a promise that his doctrine will be given a political framework, in the form of the constitution of his descendants as a nation with its own land, in order to preserve it. Rather than adherence to the 'doctrine implanted by Abraham' being a condition for Abraham's descendants retaining the land, inheritance of the land becomes a means of retaining the doctrine. Moreover, and as has frequently been observed, in this account the commandments are contingent: the strong implication is that had the doctrine not been at risk of being forgotten, they would have not have been required. Rather than a culmination, the advent of Moses and the law is actually presented as a rescue operation. In short, the commandments of Moses exist for the sake of the Abrahamic doctrine.

The connection between God and Abraham's descendants was almost lost, but not quite; the love survived. We may speak of two covenants: the covenant of love with Abraham and the covenant of law made through Moses, but they are not entirely separate, for the law was given out of love, as we have

---

[80] Kellner points out that this is the only reference in Maimonides to God's love for Israel, or indeed for anyone; see Kellner, *Maimonides' Confrontation*, 104 n. 55.

[81] See Gen. 15.   [82] See Gen. 17: 1–14.   [83] 'Laws of Idolatry', 1: 3.

just seen, and love is commanded by the law:

And this degree is a very high degree and not every sage attains it. And this is the degree of Abraham our father whom the Holy One Blessed be He called his lover because he served only out of love. It is the standard which God, through Moses, bid us achieve, as it is said, "And thou shalt love the Lord thy God" [Deut. 6: 5].[84]

This may be what is expressed by Maimonides' rearrangement and condensation of his rabbinic material, noted above. It results in a chiastic structure. In the course of the two final *halakhot* of 'Laws of Circumcision' we first meet Abraham and circumcision as perfection, then Moses and failure to circumcise as grounds for punishment, followed by Moses again and the covenant of law, before the discussion is capped by a reversion to Abraham and the covenant of love.

The covenant of love was never abrogated; it only took a different form. Some will remain with the form, performing the commandments out of hope of reward and fear of punishment. A few will transcend the form, the covenant of law, and reach the covenant of love, 'And when a person loves God with the worthiest love, he will immediately perform all the commandments out of love.'[85] Rather than dissolving the covenant of law, the covenant of love transfigures it. We may discern a Neoplatonic dynamic here: the covenant of law emanates from the covenant of love and desires to return to it.

Perfection and Covenant

We turn to the question of what Maimonides means by perfection in 'Laws of Circumcision', and how, if at all, the concepts of perfection and of covenant are related.

To remind ourselves, 'Laws of Circumcision' states: 'Abraham our father was not called "perfect" until he was circumcised, as it says, "Walk in My ways and be blameless. I will establish my covenant between Me and you" [Gen. 17: 1–2].'[86] The Hebrew word *shalem*, translated as 'perfect' here, is probably more accurately rendered as 'complete', which of course is ironic: that which made Abraham incomplete physically was a sign of his moral and intellectual completeness. But that is a side point. The main thing to note is that the word in the verse translated as 'blameless' is *tamim*. This is the same as the word for 'perfect' in the verse 'The Rock, His work is perfect; for all His ways are judgement.'

As we have seen, this is the verse upon which Maimonides hangs the

---

[84] 'Laws of Repentance', 10: 2. [85] Ibid. [86] 'Laws of Circumcision', 3: 8.

idea of the perfection of the world and the divine justice that flows from that perfection. Human perfection is a reflection of this divine perfection. Maimonides compares the perfection of the Torah to the perfection of nature, using the same verse: 'It says: "The Rock, His work is perfect; for all His ways are judgement." It says that just as the things made by Him are consummately perfect, so are His commandments consummately just.'[87] In other words, the perfection of the law given by Moses mirrors the perfection of nature, and thus the law can perfect human beings (see the outline of the *Mishneh torah*'s structure in the Appendix).

It becomes tempting to use the *tamim* in 'The Rock, His work is perfect', quasi-midrashically, to gloss the *tamim* in 'Walk in My ways and be blameless', and to conclude that 'Laws of Circumcision', 3: 8 implies that the perfection of Abraham similarly mirrors the perfection of the world, and that this is the point of comparison between him and Moses. We have already seen that the idea that Abraham attained perfection through contemplation of nature underlies the narrative in the first chapter of 'Laws of Idolatry'. If we bear in mind the Aristotelian theory that to know something means to become like it, we can understand that, implicit in Abraham's realization of how nature works and how it derives from God, is that he became assimilated to these natural structures, or in other words he personified 'The Rock, His work is perfect; for all His ways are judgement.'

Meaning of 'the Rock'

Support for this can be found in the *Guide*, in which Maimonides assigns a special meaning to the word 'rock'.[88] He notes that 'rock' can mean a quarry, and hence metaphorically 'the root and principle of everything', as in Isaiah 51: 1–2: 'Look unto the rock whence ye were hewn, and to the hole of the pit whence ye were digged. Look unto Abraham your father, and unto Sarah that bore you.' From this he derives the meaning of 'rock' when applied to God as 'the principle and the efficient cause of all things other than Himself'. As an example, he cites 'The Rock, His work is perfect.'

The conclusion of this passage from the *Guide* is, in essence, that Moses firmly grasped this notion of God. From this intellectual supremacy came his supreme law. Intriguingly, though, when he cites the verses from Isaiah, Maimonides somewhat digresses from his ostensible philological mission to define 'rock' and expatiates on the subject of Abraham. Scripture here, he

---

[87] *Guide* iii. 49 (pp. 605–6).
[88] *Guide* i. 16 (p. 42). We hope to present a detailed analysis of this passage elsewhere. See also *Guide* i. 54 (pp. 123–8) and Kasher, 'Maimonides' Interpretations'.

says, gives 'an interpretation according to which the "rock whence ye were hewn" is "Abraham your father". Tread therefore in his footsteps, adhere to his religion, and acquire his character, inasmuch as the nature of a quarry ought to be found in what is hewn from it.'[89] In short, we see again that Abraham personified what Moses legislated (albeit from a stance of intellectual superiority), and it is Abraham that we should emulate.

The divine perfection that Abraham's perfection reflects is not only a matter of God being the first principle and the cause of the world's existence, that is, not just the first half of the verse 'The Rock, His work is perfect', but also the continuation 'for all His ways are justice; a God of faithfulness and without iniquity, just and right is He'. This latter half of the verse is cited in various places in the *Guide* where the context is God's justice and benevolence: in the essential equality of creatures of the same species and the provision of their basic needs;[90] in granting free will, such that punishment for offences is not undeserved;[91] in exercising providence;[92] in not inflicting undeserved suffering simply as a trial of faith;[93] in showing 'mercy towards the weak'.[94] In the *Mishneh torah*, Abraham is frequently invoked as the exemplar of such virtues. He stands for forgiveness (*meḥilah*),[95] charity (*tsedakah*),[96] compassion (*raḥamim*),[97] and, perhaps above all, loving-kindness (*ḥesed*).[98]

El Olam

'The Rock, His work is perfect' is not cited anywhere in the *Mishneh torah*, but a very similar verse (at least in Maimonides' reading of it) is not only cited, but is made the motto verse of the *Mishneh torah* as a whole and of every single book within it (as well as of the *Guide*). The verse is 'In the name of the Lord, God of the world', from the verse 'And Abraham planted a tamarisk-tree in Beer-sheba, and called there on the name of the Lord, God of the world.'[99]

It is of course immediately apparent that there is a discrepancy between the motto and the translation presented here of the verse from which it is taken.[100] The way that Maimonides reads the verse is clear from 'Laws of Idolatry', where it is cited as evidence that Abraham called on people to recognize the one God as creator of the world,[101] and from a similar account of Abraham's confrontation with idolaters in the *Guide*: 'he publicly manifested his

---

[89] *Guide* i. 16 (p. 42). [90] *Guide* iii. 12 (p. 448). [91] *Guide* iii. 17 (p. 469).
[92] Ibid. (p. 471). [93] *Guide* iii. 24 (p. 498). [94] *Guide* iii. 53 (p. 632).
[95] 'Laws of Moral Qualities', 6: 6. [96] 'Laws of Gifts to the Poor', 10: 1.
[97] 'Laws of Slaves', 9: 8. [98] 'Laws of Mourning', 14: 2. [99] Gen. 21: 33.
[100] The version here is taken from the New Jewish Publication Society translation (NJPS).
[101] 'Laws of Idolatry', 1: 2.

disagreement with them and called "in the name of the Lord, God of the world"—both the existence of the deity and the creation of the world in time being comprised in that call.'[102]

There are at least two objections to Maimonides' reading. Firstly, the Hebrew *vayikra sham beshem adonai* is better translated 'and called there *on* the name of the Lord' than 'and called there *in* the name of the Lord'; the more likely meaning is that Abraham invoked the Lord, not that he issued a call to all and sundry concerning the Lord[103] Secondly, as Maimonides must surely have been aware, in the Hebrew Bible the word *olam*, as in *el olam* ('the Everlasting God' in the NJPS version), means 'eternity', not 'world'.[104] The latter meaning emerges only in mishnaic Hebrew.[105]

What is clear, though, is that this reading makes the verse equivalent to 'The Rock, His work is perfect'.[106] Remembering that 'the Lord' (*adonai*, as the word formed by the Hebrew letters *yod, heh, vav, heh* is pronounced) is the name of God that indicates his unknowable essence, whereas 'God' (*el*) is one of the names that is 'derived from terms signifying actions the like of which ... exist as our own actions',[107] we can see that, for Maimonides, 'In the name of the Lord, God of the world' expresses God's simultaneous separation from the world and unfathomability, and his presence in the world, understood through the study of his works.

The very fact that this verse forms the motto of the *Mishneh torah* and its

---

[102] *Guide* iii. 29 (p. 516).

[103] The NJPS translation in fact has 'and invoked there the name of the Lord, the Everlasting God'. Compare Gen. 12: 8, 13: 4, 26: 25; Exod. 34: 5.

[104] Of 436 occurrences of *olam* (in its various forms) recorded by Even-Shoshan, *A New Concordance of the Bible* (Heb.), 841–2, just two (Ps. 89: 3 and Eccles. 3: 11) are listed under the meaning 'the world and its contents' (*tevel umelo'ah*), and even those are indicated as doubtful. All the rest are listed as expressions of time: either eternity, or a remote past or future time.

[105] J. B. Soloveitchik comments on this at length, and makes an attempt at reconciliation through the observation that Maimonides regarded time as a property of the created, physical world. See Kaplan (ed.), *Maimonides: Between Philosophy and Halakhah*, 75–87. See also Schwarz's note 14 on *Guide* ii. 13 (pp. 298–9). The King James translation of the phrase *ad olemei-ad* in Isa. 45: 17 as 'world without end' adroitly straddles the ambiguity.

[106] Maimonides' reading of this verse is no less idiosyncratic than his reading of Gen. 21: 33. Most of the classical medieval commentators take 'His work' to refer to God's actions as the world's judge rather than as its creator—see Rashi, Rashbam, and Nahmanides ad loc. That interpretation is also more sensitive to the convention of parallelism in biblical poetry (the verse is from the Song of Moses). The second half of the verse, 'a God of faithfulness and without iniquity, just and right is He', which is really the second line of a couplet, makes it clear that the first half, 'The Rock, His work is perfect; for all His ways are judgement', is entirely about God's justice, not creation.   [107] *Guide* i. 61 (p. 147).

books places the Torah of Moses in an Abrahamic frame. Circumcision, though, is that verse inscribed in the flesh.

Abraham's Discovery

Abraham was not a lawgiver. His mission was one of persuasion and example. He realized the existence and unity of God from his observation of natural phenomena, and he understood how moral obligation arose from that realization. He was capable of deriving the 'ought' from the 'is'. This is the state reached at the end of the *Guide*:[108] moral virtue—'loving-kindness, righteousness, and judgement'—flows from intellectual virtue, 'apprehension of Him' and knowledge of 'His providence extending over His creatures as manifested in the act of bringing them into being and in their governance as it is'. This is a state of knowledge and love that law can only communicate 'in a summary way'; the love that is demanded 'becomes valid only through the apprehension of the whole of being as it is and through the consideration of His wisdom as it is manifested in it'.[109] The commandments of the Torah, on the other hand, are, in the main, preparatory to intellectual virtue.[110] In this initial phase, moral virtue is not an intuitive flow from knowledge but a matter of careful calibration of one's temperament and control of one's actions. The function of the commandments is to educate and habituate in these ways.

As we have repeatedly stressed, circumcision encapsulates the entire law, so that the Torah may be regarded as an amplification of circumcision. But 'to be circumcised as Abraham, peace be upon him, was circumcised' ultimately means to reach the second phase, and to realize as Abraham did that morality follows upon knowledge.[111]

Circumcision did not perfect Abraham. Abraham was *called* perfect when

---

[108] *Guide* iii. 54 (p. 638). [109] See *Guide* iii. 28 (pp. 512–13).
[110] See *Guide* iii. 54 (p. 636): 'all the actions prescribed by the Law—I refer to the various species of worship and also the moral habits that are useful to all people in their mutual dealings—that all this is not to be compared with this ultimate end and does not equal it, being but preparations made for the sake of this end.' The 'ultimate end' is 'the apprehension of Him, may He be exalted', i.e. intellectual virtue. This passage is discussed further in Ch. 5 below. See also Maimonides, *Eight Chapters*, ch. 4, where the commandments are described as designed to keep a person just slightly on the more ascetic side of the middle path that constitutes moral virtue.
[111] Note too *Guide* iii. 11 (pp. 440–1), discussed in Ch. 14 below, where Maimonides states both the proposition that, in the days of the messiah, evildoing will be abolished thanks to 'the knowledge that men will then have concerning the true reality of the deity', and the reverse, that vices 'derive from ignorance, I mean from a privation of knowledge'.

he became circumcised because circumcision signified his hard-won understanding purely from contemplation of 'the whole of being as it is' that creation is good, that its perfection entails God's justice, and that the required human response is to imitate that perfection and that justice. Rather than representing a correction of an imperfection in nature, circumcision actually represents the human attempt to become assimilated to nature's perfection.

Abraham and the Torah thus each stand in their own perfection. Each independently reflects the meaning of 'The Rock, His work is perfect'.[112] The Torah cannot be partly of Abraham and partly of Moses, for that would breach the definition of perfection, which is a state in which nothing can be added and nothing can be taken away. The Torah of Moses is whole and perfect and the sole source of law. It can, however, refer to the perfection of Abraham as a universal ideal from which it derives and towards which it guides.

Moses apprehended the idea of God as the first principle, more clearly than anyone before or since, but Abraham personified it. The Torah of Moses is perfect, but it is secondary, a redaction of nature, as it were, not the raw text. The commandments of the Torah, moreover, foster fear, 'the awe before His command'.[113] Abraham represents the ideal of love tempered by fear, learned from nature itself,[114] and the Torah is preparation for each Jew to become his or her own Abraham and to enter the covenant of love.

The reflection of the perfection of creation in the mind of Moses and in the person of Abraham is the mutuality that is the real substance of the covenant. The covenant of love is the preoccupation with God that renders all other occupations secondary and mechanical, and from which moral virtue flows. This is made clear in the *Guide*:

And there may be a human individual who, through his apprehension of the true realities and his joy in what he has apprehended, achieves a state in which he talks with people and is occupied with his bodily necessities while his intellect is wholly turned toward Him, may He be exalted, so that in his heart he is always in His presence, may He be exalted, while outwardly he is with people, in the sort of way described by the poetical parables that have been invented for these notions: 'I sleep but my heart waketh; it is the voice of my beloved that knocketh', and

---

[112] In discussing the perfection of the Torah, Maimonides also cites Ps. 19: 8, 'The Torah of the Lord is perfect', where perfect translates *temimah*, the feminine form of *tamim*—see *Guide* ii. 39 (p. 380).

[113] *Guide* iii. 52 (p. 630). See also *Guide* iii. 24 (p. 501).

[114] See 'Laws of the Foundations of the Torah', 2: 1–2. At the peak of his career, in the binding of Isaac, Abraham demonstrated 'the limit of love for God, may He be exalted, and fear of Him—that is, up to what limit they must reach' (*Guide* iii. 24 (p. 500)).

so on.[115] I do not say that this rank is that of all the prophets; but I do say that this is the rank of Moses our Master . . . This was also the rank of the Patriarchs, the result of whose nearness to Him, may He be exalted, was that His name became known to the world through them: 'The God of Abraham, the God of Isaac, and the God of Jacob . . . this is My name for ever.'[116] Because of the union of their intellects through apprehension of Him, it came about that He made a lasting covenant with each of them.[117]

At this level of constant intellectual love of God, perfection and covenant are the same thing.

Abraham's Alacrity, Moses' Reluctance

Abraham may not have had Moses' intellectual stature, but he carried out everything he was required to do by God unquestioningly and with alacrity, even the near-sacrifice of his beloved son and circumcision. This is perhaps hinted at in 'Laws of Circumcision', 3: 9. Moses was reluctant to take up his mission, and was slow to circumcise his son. A Maimonidean explanation of this might be that Moses was the type of philosopher who fears political engagement as a risk to his intellectual pre-eminence and a disturbance to his communion with God, and who regards ritual as necessary for the masses but not for him. In Plato's image, Moses did not wish to return to the cave.[118] At the burning bush, Moses protests that he cannot translate divine matters into terms comprehensible by ordinary people; he is given the tools to do so. He still fails to see the need to conform to religious practice. It was suggested above that Abraham similarly was not in need of circumcision himself, but he did not hesitate to carry it out on himself, his sons, and all the males of his household.

Moses not only had an intellectual advantage over Abraham; he was also better educated. Abraham grew up in an idolatrous culture that extended even to his own family. In divine matters, he was a complete autodidact. Moses came from the tribe of Levi which stayed faithful to the Abrahamic

---

[115] S. of S. 5: 2.

[116] Exod. 3: 15. Pines notes 'The Hebrew expression translated: *for ever*, may also mean: *for the world.*' [117] *Guide* iii. 51 (pp. 623–4).

[118] In the Allegory of the Cave, Plato imagines Socrates likening the general run of humanity to prisoners chained in a cave, who only ever see shadows projected on a wall and take them for reality. Anyone taken out of the cave will come to understand that the sunlit world is real and the shadows in the cave are illusions. Such is the philosopher, who, Socrates demands, must return to the cave—that is, must engage in governing society with its false notions and values, even though he or she longs to remain in the sun—that is, to be left alone to pursue truth and enlightenment. See Plato, *Republic*, 514a–521b.

tradition and never succumbed to idolatry.[119] Both men displayed courage, and both had to flee the wrath of a ruler on account of courageous behaviour, but the courage of Abraham as recounted by Maimonides (on the basis of midrashic anecdotes, of course), defying the beliefs and mores of an entire society as well as the authority of the state, was arguably greater. Moreover, denied the certainty vouchsafed to Moses, Abraham was nevertheless committed to the ideas of God's will as creator and his wisdom as manifest in visible forms, and to the moral imperative that they imply. He thus exemplified 'the virtue of faith', a virtue with which he is explicitly associated.[120] So while Moses earned the status of lawgiver, it is Abraham who earned the title of lover, and whose spirit pervades the *Book of Love*, at the end of which his covenant of love is given priority over Moses' covenant of law.

Conversion

A further aspect of circumcision is its role in conversion. Maimonides describes the conversion process as a replica of the initiation of the Jewish nation into the covenant during the Exodus from Egypt. One component of that initiation was circumcision, which had fallen into abeyance (except among the tribe of Levi) and which Moses reinstated.[121] This is a particular example of Moses reviving through legislation the lost Abrahamic tradition.[122]

As we have noted, the common factor uniting the commandments discussed in the *Book of Love* is their constancy, and Maimonides stresses the constant fact of circumcision more than the original act. It is supposed to have a continual effect as a prompt 'to love God and remember him always'.[123] The love of God is not a fixed quantity. It is dependent on knowledge, and the acquisition of knowledge is a lifelong task. Circumcision, in other words, is not a one-time act of initiation but a sign of a continual process of conversion, a constant referral from the Mosaic covenant of law to the original Abrahamic covenant of love.[124] This idea of the precedence of the covenant of love over the covenant of law, both historically and in value, sets a pattern for several of the endings of the books of the *Mishneh torah*. In particular, it foreshadows Maimonides' treatment of conflict between the

---

[119] See 'Laws of Idolatry', 1: 3.
[120] *Guide* iii. 53 (pp. 630–2). See Kellner, 'The Virtue of Faith'.
[121] See 'Laws of Forbidden Intercourse', 13: 1–4.
[122] On this see J. Stern, *Problems and Parallels*, 95.   [123] *Mishneh torah*, introd.
[124] For a view of the convert as the embodiment of the Maimonidean ideal see Diamond, *Converts, Heretics, and Lepers*, 11–31.

legacy of Abraham and the legalities of Moses, to be found at the ends of certain books. It should be stressed, however, that this is not meant to imply any devaluation of the covenant of law. The law that Moses promulgated flowed from an even greater understanding of God's unity and the perfection of nature than did the love that Abraham preached. Maimonides' naturalism underwrites both. In short, love does not dispense with law, and of course it is Maimonides' deep commitment to both that makes his resolution of apparent conflict between them interesting.

Tension between love and law may be subjective, as well as an objective question of deciding behavioural norms. While it is possible to see 'Laws of Circumcision', 3: 8–9 as addressed to two different readerships on two different levels—Maimonides would certainly have taken into consideration the reader who would not venture beyond the homiletical level—a more interesting view, perhaps, is that the sophistication of Maimonides' writing as manifested in these *halakhot* is designed to draw the reader into participation in the process that he advocates. Through exploration of the text, and subjective amplification of its 'chapter headings', its hints and allusions, he or she graduates from a legal understanding of circumcision to a philosophical one. In other words, Maimonides projects an ideal reader not dissimilar from the one he projects in the introduction to the *Guide*, and engages with the oscillation between law and love within this reader.[125] At the start of this chapter we wrote of Maimonides dramatizing his source material. Such engagement is the dramatic effect.

Postscript: Circumcision and the Sabbath

We began this chapter by looking at the continuity between the *Book of Knowledge* and the *Book of Love*. It can now be appreciated that this is more than a matter of the second book picking up where the first left off. In the previous chapter, it was shown how Abraham is portrayed in the *Book of Knowledge* as the personification of the book's theme of knowledge, acquired through philosophical enquiry, and leading to the love of God. The Torah of Moses emerges as a specifically Jewish path to this universal ideal, its ultimate fulfilment being observance of the commandments informed by an Abrahamic spirit. The *Book of Love* is similarly permeated by the spirit of Abraham, and it concludes with a similar depiction of the relationship between his mission

---

[125] On such oblique, esoteric writing as a means of communicating the otherwise incommunicable as well as a political tactic, see Halbertal, *Concealment and Revelation* and Y. Lorberbaum, '"The men of knowledge"' (Heb.).

Abraham, Moses, and the Meaning of Circumcision

and that of Moses, expressed via the medium of the very concrete commandment of circumcision. The same outlines that were sketched on the level of theory in the *Book of Knowledge* are reproduced on the level of practical commandments in the *Book of Love*. A feature of the *Mishneh torah*'s microcosmic form is that its first ten books are arranged in a hierarchy that reflects the hierarchy of the angels and the process of emanation, each level from the one above it, that brings them into existence (see Appendix). The thematic echo of the *Book of Knowledge* in the *Book of Love*, amplified by the their endings, lends substance to this formal pattern: the second book can certainly be said to emanate from the first. Moreover, the final sentence of the *Book of Knowledge* explicitly returns us to its beginning, to the wonder at and investigation of the natural world that, according to the narrative in 'Laws of Idolatry', formed Abraham's knowledge and thereby prompted his love. In a more indirect way, the ending of the *Book of Love* similarly recalls us to the Abrahamic spirit of discovery.

If the concept of emanation makes it appropriate to look back, it also makes it appropriate to look forward, to the next volume, the *Book of Seasons*. The first section of that book is 'Laws of the Sabbath'. Like circumcision, the sabbath is a covenant[126] and a sign;[127] it too has both a physical and a pedagogic purpose: it procures rest, and 'At the same time it perpetuates throughout the periods of time an opinion whose value is very great, namely, the assertion that the world has been produced in time.'[128] Both circumcision and the sabbath feature in pre-Sinaitic legislation.[129]

The placing of 'Laws of Circumcision' last in the *Book of Love* may have been to some degree with an eye to 'Laws of the Sabbath'. This is not just because of the common characteristics listed above. It is possible to see circumcision and the sabbath as representing different degrees of understanding of the same thing. 'The assertion that the world has been produced in time' is 'an opinion whose value is very great', but it is not demonstrably true.[130] Abraham derived a theology and an ethic, and an unswerving commitment to both, from observation of nature and unaided speculation, that is, from knowledge. The transition from circumcision to the sabbath is a move slightly down the scale, from knowledge to traditional doctrine, and, since

---

[126] Exod. 31: 16. According to Kafih, this verse is not cited anywhere in Maimonides' works.

[127] Exod. 31: 17. This verse is cited in *Guide* i. 67 (p. 162), but only because the word *vayinafash* ('and he rested') which appears in it is an anthropomorphic description of God that requires explanation. [128] *Guide* iii. 43 (p. 570). See also *Guide* ii. 31 (pp. 359–60).

[129] See *Guide* iii. 32 (p. 531). [130] See *Guide* i. 71 (p. 180) and ii. 25 (pp. 327–30).

love is commensurate with knowledge, slightly down the scale of love. One could say that circumcision 'overrides the sabbath' not only halakhically, but philosophically as well. The juxtaposition of circumcision and the sabbath may be coincidence, but it may also be a way of highlighting the special status of circumcision as a Mosaic command with an Abrahamic pedigree.

Summary

On the surface, the ending of the *Book of Love* carries a particularistic, ethnocentric message. On that level, it seems intended to encourage obedience to the very difficult commandment to circumcise male babies. Maimonides' careful phrasing, however, makes it open to a universalistic reading. The commandment of circumcision derives its authority from the Torah of Moses, but in the final *halakhah* of 'Laws of Circumcision' Maimonides takes us back to Abraham, the rediscoverer of monotheism, whose mission was to humankind in general, and to circumcision as a means of promoting moral and social perfection and a sign of intellectual perfection. Circumcision symbolizes Abraham's understanding that recognition of the one incorporeal God entails a commitment to morality and justice.

This reading is supported by Maimonides' remarks about circumcision in the *Guide*, by his pointed reference to Abraham the lover of God at the end of the *Book of Knowledge*, and by other allusions to Abraham in the *Book of Love* itself. He presents circumcision as the commandment that directly connects the Mosaic covenant of law with the Abrahamic covenant of love. The implication is that the ultimate aim of the Torah of Moses is the emulation of Abraham, so that the path of obedience becomes the path of discovery.

THREE

SEASONS
Hanukah and Purim Reconfigured

The Hanukah Lamp and the Sabbath Lamp

The third book of the *Mishneh torah*, *Sefer zemanim* (the *Book of Seasons* or the *Book of Appointed Times*), contains ten sections (more than any other book in the *Mishneh torah*) and is the longest book in the work, with only the *Book of Ritual Purity* (Book 10) coming close. In his introduction to the *Mishneh torah* Maimonides explains that this book deals with commandments that are to be fulfilled at specific times. It thus follows logically from the *Book of Love*, which deals with commandments which are to be observed at all times. This book is the subject of *Guide* iii. 45,[1] in which its contents are described in detail. It contains: 'Laws of the Sabbath', 'Laws of *Eruvin*' (further sabbath restrictions), 'Laws of Repose on the Tenth of Tishrei' (restrictions concerning Yom Kippur), 'Laws of Repose on a Festival', 'Laws of Leavened and Unleavened Bread', 'Laws of the Ram's Horn', 'Laws of Sukkah', 'Laws of Lulav', 'Laws of Shekel Dues', 'Laws of Sanctification of the New Moon', 'Laws of Fasts', and, finally, 'Laws of Megillah' (the Scroll of Esther) and 'Laws of Hanukah'. In his introduction to the Yale Judaica series translation of the *Book of Seasons*,[2] Solomon Gandz points out that the first four treatises in this book 'represent a scale of descending degrees of holiness and strictness as far as the prohibition of work is concerned'. The rest of the book's sections deal with the other 'appointed times' in the Jewish calendar.

The *Book of Seasons* ends with the following paragraphs:

The commandment to light the Hanukah lamp is an exceedingly precious one, and one should be particularly careful to fulfil it, in order to make known the miracle, and to offer additional praise and thanksgiving to God for the miracles [*Al hanisim*] which He had wrought [for us].[3] Even if one has no food to eat except what he

---
[1] pp. 570–4.   [2] p. xxv.
[3] Hebrew: *lanu*—this word is not in Makbili's version of the text, nor in those of Kafih or Rabinovitch.

receives from charity, he should beg—or sell his garment to buy—oil and lamps, and light them.

If one has no more than a single *perutah*[4] and needs wine for the Sanctification benediction of the Sabbath and oil to light the Hanukah lamp, he should give preference to the purchase of oil for the Hanukah lamp over the purchase of wine for the Sanctification benediction. Since both commandments are based on the authority of the Scribes, it is best to give preference to the Hanukah lamp, since it serves as a memorial of the miracle of Hanukah.

If such a poor man has to choose between oil for both a Sabbath lamp and a Hanukah lamp, or oil for a Sabbath lamp and wine for the Sanctification benediction, the Sabbath lamp should have priority, for the sake of peace in the household,[5] seeing that even the Divine Name might be erased to make peace between husband and wife. Great indeed is peace, forasmuch as the purpose for which the whole of the Torah was given is to bring peace upon the world, as it is said, 'Her ways are ways of pleasantness, and all her paths are peace' [Prov. 3: 17].[6]

In order to understand the significance of Maimonides' decision to end his discussion of Purim and Hanukah with this passage, we must glance back at the beginning of his discussion of the festival. In that discussion Maimonides is uncharacteristically unclear about a central point. According to his account the festival of Hanukah appears to commemorate either the miracle of the oil or the victory of the Hasmoneans over the Hellenists:

In the time of the second Temple, when the Greeks ruled over Israel, they issued

---

[4] The smallest denomination of coin in mishnaic times.

[5] Maimonides' source is BT *Shab.* 23*b*:

Raba said: It is obvious to me [that if one must choose between] the house lamp [Rashi: i.e. the sabbath lamp] and the Hanukah lamp, the former is preferable, on account [of the importance] of the peace of the home; [between] the house lamp and [wine for] the Sanctification of the Day, the house lamp is preferable, on account of the peace of the home. Raba propounded: What [if the choice lies between] the Hanukah lamp and the Sanctification of the Day: is the latter more important, because it is permanent; or perhaps the Hanukah lamp is preferable, on account of advertising the miracle? After propounding, he himself solved it: The Hanukah lamp is preferable, on account of advertising the miracle.

Note that there is no explanation here as to which miracle is advertised—oil or victory? See also the next note.

[6] 'Laws of Megillah and Hanukah', 4: 12–13. See BT *Git.* 59*b*. We cite Maimonides here, with emendations, from the translation of Solomon Gandz and Hyman Klein. Here, too, as in the opening of his discussion of Hanukah, cited below, Maimonides is (purposely) unclear about the nature of the miracle that the Hanukah lamp advertises: the oil that lasted for eight days, or the victory over the enemies of Israel? For further discussion on this, and on the contemporary (often political) uses to which the rabbinic texts about Hanukah are put, see the fascinating discussion in Blidstein, 'Hanukah in Hazal'.

decrees against them, proscribing their religion and forbidding them to study the Torah and to fulfil the commandments. They laid hands on their property and on their daughters, and they entered the Temple and made breaches in it, and defiled that which was ritually pure. And Israel was in sore straits in consequence thereof, and suffered great persecution, until the God of our fathers took pity on them, and saved them from the hands of the Greeks. For the Hasmonean family of High Priests won a victory in which they slew the Greeks, and saved Israel from their hands. They set up a king from among the priests, and restored Israel's kingdom for a period of more than two hundred years—until the destruction of the second Temple.

The day on which the Israelites were victorious over their enemies and destroyed them was the twenty-fifth day of Kislev. When they re-entered the Temple, they found within its precincts only one cruse of ritually pure oil, enough to burn for but a single day. Yet they kept alight with it the required number of lamps for eight days, until they could press some olives and produce new ritually pure oil.

Consequently, the Sages of that generation ruled that the eight days beginning with the twenty-fifth of Kislev should be days of rejoicing on which the Hallel is to be recited, and that on each one of the eight nights lamps should be lit at eventide at the doors of the houses.[7] These days are known as Hanukah. Funeral eulogies and fasting are forbidden on them, just as they are on Purim, and the lighting of lamps on them is a commandment based on the authority of the Scribes, analogous to the commandment to read the Megillah.[8]

---

[7] Following many printed editions, the Yale translation adds here: 'to serve as manifestation and revelation of the miracle'. This addition is not found in the editions of Makbili, Kafih, or Rabinovitch. Frankel follows the traditional text, while noting in his textual notes that these words are lacking in all the manuscripts that he examined. The text as presented here may thus be safely taken to be correct. However, the question remains: why is the Hanukah lamp lit—because the oil lasted for eight days, or because of the victory over the Greek Syrians? There is reason to suppose that the latter is the case. The talmudic text (BT *Shab.* 21a) on the basis of which Maimonides codified the law here reads:

> What is [the reason of] Hanukah? For our Rabbis taught: On the twenty-fifth of Kislev [commence] the days of Hanukah, which are eight, on which a lamentation for the dead and fasting are forbidden. For when the Greeks entered the Temple, they defiled all the oils therein, and when the Hasmonean dynasty prevailed against and defeated them, they made search and found only one cruse of oil which lay with the seal of the High Priest, but which contained sufficient for one day's lighting only; *yet a miracle was wrought therein* and they lit [the lamp] therewith for eight days. The following year these [days] were appointed a festival with [the recital of] Hallel and thanksgiving.

Maimonides' decision to leave out the words 'yet a miracle was wrought therein' (*na'asah bo nes*) cannot be without significance, especially as this accords with his well-known and barely concealed antipathy to interruptions in the regular order of nature. The victory of the few over the many is easily explained in naturalistic terms. On Maimonides on miracles, see Langermann, 'Maimonides and Miracles' and Nehorai, 'Maimonides on Miracles' (Heb.).

[8] 'Laws of Megillah and Hanukah', 3: 1–3. It is worth noting that this long historical

Hanukah is treated together with Purim, it would seem, because of what Maimonides writes in the next *halakhah* (4) of chapter 3: 'Everyone obligated to read the Megillah is equally obligated to light a Hanukah menorah.' The connection drawn between the two festivals is technical–halakhic as opposed to substantive, even though, as we shall see, Maimonides manages to draw them together through the surprising motif of peace.

The Message of Hanukah and Purim

As noted above, Maimonides ends his discussion of Hanukah by emphasizing how exceedingly precious the commandment to light the Hanukah lamp is: if one can afford only to purchase oil for the Hanukah lamp or wine for the sanctification of the sabbath (kiddush), lighting the Hanukah lamp takes precedence. But if one has to choose between purchasing oil for a sabbath lamp and purchasing oil for the Hanukah lamp, or if one must choose between lighting the sabbath lamp and reciting the kiddush over wine, the sabbath lamp takes precedence, 'for the sake of peace in the household, seeing that even the Divine Name might be erased to make peace between husband and wife. Great indeed is peace, forasmuch as the purpose for which the whole of the Torah was given is to bring peace upon the world, as it is said, "Her ways are ways of pleasantness, and all her paths are peace" [Prov. 3: 17].'

Maimonides takes the opportunity provided by the laws of Purim and Hanukah (two festivals that hark back to wars between Jews and the non-Jewish world) to teach a lesson about the value of peace. It is the point of the whole Torah to bring about peace in the world.

This focus may help to explain an otherwise odd fact. Maimonides chooses to end his two chapters on Purim with the following:

In messianic times all the Prophetic Books and the Writings[9] will be abolished [*libatel*]—except the book of Esther. For this will continue to endure, just as the five books of the Torah and the laws of the Oral Torah will never be abolished. And so, although all memory of ancient troubles will disappear, in accordance with the verse, 'Because the former troubles are forgotten, and because they are hidden from mine eyes' [Isa. 65: 16],[10] the days of Purim will not cease to be observed, as it

---

account is a rare excursus in the *Mishneh torah*. Compare Gillis, *Reading Maimonides' Mishneh Torah*, 324 n. 156.

[9] i.e. the second and third sections of the Tanakh (Hebrew Bible).

[10] Maimonides also cites this verse in *Guide* ii. 29 (p. 342), but in another context altogether.

is said, 'And that these days of Purim should not fail from among the Jews, nor the memorial of them perish from their seed' [Esther 9: 28].[11]

As a prediction of the future, this passage has no halakhic significance and seems to contribute nothing to the discussion at hand. Indeed, it appears to be surprising, given Maimonides' general insistence on the permanence of halakhah and his concerns lest his views be used to support antinomian tendencies.[12] Coupling this passage at the end of the chapters on Purim, however, with the last *halakhot* of chapter 4, we are reminded by both Purim and Hanukah—two festivals that mark violent confrontations—that the messianic era is to be a period of peace, not of domination. This takes on added significance in light of Maimonides' intellectualist and universalist account of the messianic era (to which we will return in Chapter 14 below), with its emphasis on peace.

Peace between Husband and Wife

Let us return now to Maimonides' comments at the end of 'Laws of Megillah and Hanukah'.[13] Basing himself on the Talmud, he explains why the sabbath lamp takes precedence over the Hanukah lamp, assuming that his reader knows that the lighting of the sabbath lamp was ordained in order to maintain family peace (*shalom bayit*).[14]

He then adds a flourish of his own, proving that domestic harmony is a great value, since 'even a Divine Name might be erased to make peace between husband and wife'. He refers here to two separate laws in the *Mishneh torah*. The first states:

Any person who destroys any of the sacred and pure names by which the Holy One, blessed be He, is called, is whipped according to Torah law, for it says of idol

---

[11] 'Laws of Megillah and Hanukah', 2: 18. According to Kafih, *The Hebrew Bible in Maimonides* (Heb.), Maimonides cites the verse from Esther in his commentary on Mishnah *Meg.* 2: 1 and 2: 4; we found it in the second place, but not the first. The context there is not the permanence of the festival of Purim, but when the Megillah is meant to be read.

[12] See *Book of Commandments*, negative commandment 365 and 'Laws of Kings and their Wars', 11: 1 and 3. This is also a main motif in the *Epistle to Yemen* (on which see Friedman, *Maimonides, the Yemenite Messiah, and Forced Conversion* (Heb.), 113). The many studies on Maimonides on *ta'amei hamitsvot* (reasons for the commandments) are relevant here. See in particular, J. Stern, *Problems and Parables*, 51–2, 69–71, and 120–1. [13] 4: 12–13.

[14] BT *Shab.* 23b. In 'Laws of the Sabbath', 5: 1, Maimonides connects the obligation to light the sabbath lamp to sabbath joy (*oneg*) and in 30: 5, he connects the obligation to light the sabbath lamp to respect for the sabbath; a well-lit home is more peaceful because people can see well and will not collide with and annoy one another.

worship: 'You shall obliterate their name from that site. You shall not do likewise to the Lord, your God' [Deut. 12: 3–4].[15]

Despite that very clear prohibition, the Talmud states that one erases (blots from the parchment) God's name in order to prepare the 'bitter waters' of the *sotah* ordeal, which tests a woman suspected of adultery by her husband. Maimonides himself codifies this:

> Thereupon the priest brought a scroll made out of the hide of a clean animal, the same as used for a scroll of the Torah, and inscribed upon it—in the sacred tongue, with ink free of vitriol, and specifically in the name of that woman; exactly as in the case of a *get*—all the words wherewith he had just adjured her, letter for letter and word for word, spelling the Name as it is written, but without the concluding 'Amen, Amen'.
>
> He then brought an earthenware vessel that had never been used before, and that had not been made so long ago that it looked worn out. If, however, the aged vessel was first returned to the kiln to make it look like new, it might be used. Thereupon he poured into it one half-*log* of water from the laver, measuring it out with the half-*log* measure which was in the Temple, and entered into the Temple Hall with it. To the right, as one entered the Temple Hall, there was a space one cubit square, paved with a marble slab with a ring affixed to it. The priest lifted up the slab and scooped some earth out of the floor of the Tabernacle, poured it over the water so that it would remain visible upon the surface of it, and added to it some bitter ingredient, like wormwood, or the like, as it is said, 'the water of bitterness' [Num. 5: 18]. In this mixture he blotted out the writing on the scroll inscribed in the name of that woman, doing it with such thoroughness that no recognizable trace of the writing remained upon the scroll.[16]

Despite the explicit prohibition against erasing God's name, one is commanded to do so in the case of the *sotah*, the woman accused by her husband of unfaithfulness. Why? Not in order to emphasize the drama and significance of the ordeal, but 'to make peace between husband and wife'.[17] In our next chapter we will expand on the *sotah* ordeal, explaining that Maimonides sees it as a means of clearing the innocent rather than punishing the guilty.

After all this, Maimonides chooses to close his discussion of Purim and Hanukah in particular, and the *Book of Seasons* as a whole, with the following statement: 'Great indeed is peace, forasmuch as the purpose for which the whole of the Torah was given is to bring peace upon the world, as it is said, 'Her ways are ways of pleasantness, and all her paths are peace' [Prov. 3: 17].' This appears to be his own interpretation of the verse, rather than one bor-

---

[15] 'Laws of the Foundations of the Torah', 6: 1.
[16] 'Laws of the Sotah', 3: 8–10.
[17] This idea appears in *Sifrei Num.*, 42.

rowed from earlier sources. Maimonides' universalist reading of the verse is emphasized in the only other place where he cites it, in the context of a discussion of Jewish–Gentile relations:

Even with respect to heathens,[18] the Rabbis bid us visit their sick, bury their dead along with the dead of Israel, and maintain their poor with the poor of Israel in the interests of peace, as it is written: 'The Lord is good to all; and His tender mercies are over all His works' [Ps. 145: 9]. And it is also written, 'Her ways are ways of pleasantness, and all her paths are peace' [Prov. 3: 17].[19]

The Torah was given not only to bring peace between husband and wife, but among all human beings.

Al hanisim

It is of added interest that while Maimonides codifies the obligation to recite the paragraph *Al hanisim* on Purim and Hanukah in the Amidah and the Grace after Meals as a law of prayer,[20] and includes it in the schematic prayer book that he appended to his *Book of Love*,[21] he does not directly mention it in his discussion of the laws pertaining to Purim and Hanukah. The first two words of the prayer, 'for the miracles', are worked into 'Laws of Megillah and Hanukah',[22] as mentioned above. He does not cite the full text to be added, merely mentioning the *incipit*. The various versions of the prayer as known to us, and those found in the prayer book of Rabbi Sa'adyah Gaon, which in all likelihood was known to Maimonides, stress the motif of vengeance. One wonders if Maimonides' emphasis on (messianic?) peace reflects a response to that?

Here is the text of Sa'adyah's version, as translated by Stefan Reif:

[We thank you] for the miracles, the mighty deeds, the acts of salvation, the battles, the redemption and the rescue that you performed for us and for our forefathers in those days and at this time. In the days of Mattathias son of Johanan the High Priest, the Hasmonean, and his sons, when the kingdom of Greece arose against your people with the aim of making them forget your Torah and transgress your

---

[18] The Hebrew has *goyim*; Ya'akov Blidstein has shown that by this term Maimonides generally means idolaters. See Blidstein, 'On the Status of the Resident Alien' (Heb.), 44–5.

[19] 'Laws of Kings and their Wars', 10: 12. The source is BT *Git.* 61a, but the citation of Ps. 145: 9 in combination with Prov. 3: 17 in this context is original to Maimonides, and tends to confirm that he understood the rabbinic notion of 'in the interests of peace' (*mipenei darkhei shalom*) here as an ethical and universalistic one stemming from the Torah, rather than as a matter of policy in the face of possible Gentile antagonism.

[20] 'Laws of Prayer', 2: 13 and 10: 14; 'Laws of Blessings', 2: 6.

[21] See the *Book of Love*, trans. Kellner, 173–7.

[22] 4: 12.

express instructions, you stood up for them in your manifold mercies in their time of trouble, pleaded their cause, represented their case, took revenge for them, handing the mighty into the power of the weak, the many into the power of the few, the impure into the power of the pure, the wicked into the power of the righteous, and the insolent into the power of those who engage in Torah. You enhanced your great and holy reputation and brought about great salvation and rescue for your people Israel. Afterwards your people entered the shrine of your temple, cleansed your palace, purified your sanctuary and kindled lights in your holy courtyards. For all these things may you be blessed and exalted. Some then add here: They instituted eight days of praise and gratitude to your name. Just as you performed miracles for earlier generations, so do likewise for the later ones and save us these days as in those days, for all these things.[23]

Maimonides takes two festivals which are clearly associated with Jewish–Gentile warfare and makes their ultimate message one of peace among all human beings.[24] This is similar to the way in which he takes the figure of Elijah, a prophet presented in the Bible as unrelentingly vengeful (recall in particular his encounter with the prophets of Ba'al in 1 Kings 18), and makes him a messianic harbinger of universal peace:

Said the Rabbis: The sole difference between the present world and the messianic days is delivery from subjugation to powers [BT San. 91b].[25] Taking the words of the Prophets in their literal sense, it appears that the inauguration of the messianic era will be marked by the war of Gog and Magog; that prior to that war, a prophet will arise to guide Israel and set their hearts aright, as it is written: 'Behold, I will send you Elijah the prophet' [Mal. 3: 23]. He [Elijah] will come neither to declare the clean unclean, nor the unclean clean; neither to disqualify those who are presumed to be of legitimate descent, nor to pronounce qualified those who are presumed to be of illegitimate descent, but to bring peace in the world, as it is said: 'And he shall turn the hearts of the fathers to the children' [Mal. 3: 24].[26]

Maimonides leaves out the continuation of the verse from Malachi: 'and children with their fathers, so that, when I come, I do not strike the whole land with utter destruction'. Just as he does in 'Laws of Kings' so too here Maimonides turns Elijah into a harbinger of peace. Note that Maimonides has Elijah bringing peace in the *world*. This is all the more striking if we consider a *midrash* which Maimonides might or might not have known,

---

[23] Reif, *Problems with Prayers*, 295.

[24] This is all the more obvious if the miracle of Hanukah is the victory over the Greek Syrians, and not the miracle of the oil.

[25] This is usually taken to mean subjugation to *foreign* powers, but that is not what the text says (*shi'ebud malkhuyot*). It literally means that there will be no subjugation between nations at all.   [26] 'Laws of Kings and their Wars', 12: 2.

according to which Elijah is meant to bring peace between God and Israel. The midrash cites the same verse from Malachi cited here by Maimonides.[27] As we pointed out above, the Torah was given not only to bring peace between husband and wife, but among all human beings. This is hardly the message we would expect to find in a discussion of Purim and Hanukah. As we have seen in the previous chapters, and will see in those to follow, Maimonides uses the closing *halakhot* of the various books of the *Mishneh torah* to teach us perhaps unexpected and, for that reason, all the more important lessons.

Summary

Maimonides takes the festival of Hanukah as marking a military victory. He then turns around and indicates that the meaning of both Hanukah and Purim is to be found in a messianic future of peace among all nations. He ignores the bellicose nature of the special prayer added to the liturgy on these holidays, and focuses on the message of peace.

[27] *Yalkut shimoni*, 'Pinḥas', section 771.

FOUR

WOMEN
Marital and Universal Peace

Peace between Husband and Wife (Again)

The *Book of Women* (*Sefer nashim*), the fourth of the fourteen books of the *Mishneh torah*, deals with marital relations and is divided into five sections: 'Laws of Marriage', 'Laws of Divorce', 'Laws of Levirate Marriage and Ḥalitsah', 'Laws of the Virgin Maiden', and 'Laws of the Wayward Wife' (*sotah*). In this division Maimonides diverges from the order of subjects taken up in the Mishnah itself, in Seder *Nashim* ('Women'): *Yevamot* (levirate marriage and ḥalitsah), *Ketubot* (marriage contracts, contained in Maimonides' 'Laws of Marriage'), *Nedarim* (vows), *Nazir* (dealing with the Nazirite), *Sotah* (wayward wife), *Gitin* (divorce), and *Kidushin* (marriage).[1] In the introduction to his English translation of this book,[2] Isaac Klein offers the following explanation of the contents and order of the book. Unlike the Mishnah, he writes,

Maimonides adopted instead a logical sequence reflecting the usual situation in life. Accordingly, marriage comes first, followed by divorce. . . . Thereafter Mai-

---

[1] In *Reading Maimonides' Mishneh Torah*, David Gillis shows that the first ten books of the *Mishneh torah* become progressively more materially based (see also Appendix below). 'Laws of the Foundations of the Torah' in the *Book of Knowledge* is about eternal ideas, and the *Book of Love* is about constant reminders of those concepts throughout time. The *Book of Seasons* (*Zemanim*) is based on cycles within time. The *Book of Women* (*Nashim*) is based on the body, and ends this group of the first four books, in which holiness is presented in positive terms. In Book 5, the *Book of Holiness* (*Kedushah*), holiness is presented in negative terms, as a matter of separation from desires. 'Laws of the Wayward Wife' (*sotah*) at the end of the *Book of Women* fits with the pattern of loss and restoration in the *Mishneh torah* demonstrated by Gillis (e.g. idolatry followed by repentance at the end of the *Book of Knowledge*), in that it is about marriages breaking down; the final statement, as we shall see immediately below, is about how to avoid the breakdown of a marriage. The Gemara at the beginning of BT *Sot.* (2a) asks why tractate *Sotah* follows immediately upon tractate *Nedarim* (dealing with vows). Among the answers proposed is the following: 'To tell you that whoever witnesses a suspected wife in her disgrace should withhold himself [= vow abstinence] from wine' since, as Rashi explains there, wine leads to *kalut rosh*, i.e. inappropriate behaviour.

[2] (Yale Judaica Series), pp. xix–xx.

monides sets forth the laws that apply if the husband dies first. Seduction, rape, and waywardness (infidelity) are deviations that are not normal, but they do happen and the law must deal with them; they are discussed next. The Laws Concerning the Wayward Woman were left for the last, presumably because they are no longer in force.

We will suggest here that perhaps Maimonides had another end in view in ending this book with laws concerning the wayward wife.[3]

Maimonides chooses to end the fourth and final chapter of 'Laws of the Wayward Wife' with the following peroration:

The Sages have made it a religious duty[4] upon the sons of Israel to warn[5] their wives, for it is said, 'and he be jealous of his wife' [Num. 5: 14], and whosoever thus warns his wife should be moved by the spirit of purity.[6] He should not, however, warn his wife in a mood of playfulness, or in the course of conversation, or out of levity, or in consequence of a quarrel, or with the purpose of intimidating her. But if he transgresses and in the presence of witnesses does warn his wife while in one of the aforementioned moods, it is a valid warning.

It is improper for a man to act in haste and warn his wife in the first instance in the presence of witnesses. He should rather do so privately, gently, and in the spirit of purity and admonition, in order to guide her to the straight path and remove the stumbling block. Whosoever is not particular [*makpid*] about his wife, his children, and the members of his household, failing to warn them and watch constantly over

---

[3] In the *Guide* (iii. 35, p. 538), Maimonides offers an explanation for the laws governing forbidden sexual relations: 'to bring about a decrease of sexual intercourse and to diminish the desire for mating as far as possible, so that it should not be taken as an end, as is done by the ignorant'. Further on this, see above, Ch. 2, section on 'Circumcision in the *Guide*'.

[4] *Mitsvat ḥakhamim*; this expression occurs a total of eight times in the *Mishneh torah*. In his commentary *Kesef mishneh* on this passage, Joseph Karo wonders about Maimonides' use of the expression. For a recent discussion of Maimonides' various uses of the expression *mitsvah*, see Friedberg, *Crafting the 613 Commandments*, 272–8. In his commentary *Yad peshutah* on 'Laws of Marriage' (*ishut*) 15: 17, Nachum Rabinovitch argues that the expression there (and in our passage) means good advice, not something obligatory. On the related expression *tsivu ḥakhamim* ('the Sages commanded'), see Hacohen, 'On Maimonides' Terminology in the *Mishneh Torah*' (Heb.). Hacohen argues that Maimonides uses the expression to strengthen normative claims not based in technical halakhah.

[5] *Lekanot*: an unusual form from the same root as the word translated as 'jealous' in the verse about to be cited.

[6] Literally: 'and whosoever thus warns his wife—the spirit of purity enters him'. It does not appear that Maimonides could mean that literally, and we take him to be writing persuasively here, not descriptively, and translate accordingly. For a discussion of other statements by Maimonides phrased descriptively even when they are clearly meant persuasively, see Kellner, *They, Too, Are Called Human* (Heb.), ch. 8. We will take up below the question of what Maimonides is trying to persuade his readers.

their ways, so as to assure himself that they are free from all sin and iniquity [*ḥet ve'avon*], is himself a sinner, for it is said, 'And thou shalt know that thy tent is in peace; and thou shalt visit thy habitation, and shalt not sin' [Job 5: 24].[7]

The 'warning' spoken of here relates to a case where a husband suspects that his wife is having sexual relations with another man. The laws of *sotah* (based on Num. 5) detail the nature of the husband's jealousy, his technical 'warning' of his wife in the presence of two valid witnesses, and the ordeal to which she is subjected in order to prove her innocence. Maimonides devotes the four chapters of 'Laws of the Wayward Wife' to the detailed ways in which these matters are conducted. David Gillis has noted that our passage here 'rhymes', as it were, with the conclusion of the preceding volume, the *Book of Seasons*, as they both deal with peace between husband and wife.[8]

A number of technical points in our passage demand attention. What sort of 'religious duty' is it to warn one's wife? In his *Book of Commandments* Maimonides does not count warning one's wife as 'a religious duty'; the focus there is on the technicalities of the *sotah*, but there is no claim in that text that one is obligated to 'warn' one's wayward wife or that it is even praiseworthy to do so.[9] In a text parallel to ours,[10] Maimonides speaks of a 'duty' (*ḥovah*) to warn one's wife against infidelity. In neither place does he speak of a *mitsvat aseh* ('positive commandment'). The text, in 'Laws of Marriage', reads:

It is the duty [*ḥovah*] of every man to warn his wife against infidelity, and the Sages have said, 'A man should warn his wife only because the spirit of purity has entered into him.' Nevertheless, he should not carry his jealousy of her beyond reason, nor should he compel her to have intercourse with him against her will. Rather, he

---

[7] 'Laws of the Wayward Wife', 4: 18–19. On the use of the verse from Job here, see the following comment of Gillis in *Reading Maimonides' Mishneh Torah*, 241:

There is something of a play on words here, as the Hebrew for peace, *shalom*, is related to the word for perfect or whole, *shalem*, plural *shelemim*. The original behind "free of all sin" is *shelemim mikol ḥet*, literally "whole from all sin". "And thou shalt know that thy tabernacle shall be in peace" carries the overtone "thou shalt know that thy wife is whole", i.e. faithful. Similarly, the Hebrew verb behind "thou shalt visit" is *pakod*, which can also mean to oversee (reflected in the now almost obsolete use in English of the word "visitor" to mean auditor ["hearer"] or inspector, cf. the Modern Hebrew *mevaker*). Heard in this way, the verse therefore backs Maimonides' strictures on the master of the house to correct the morals of his wife and family. The idea of domestic peace nevertheless remains—it will be the result of the balance in this *halakhah* between gentleness and vigilance. For talmudic expositions of the verse from Job, see BT *Shab.* 34*a*; BT *Yev.* 62*b*; BT *San.* 76*b*. Maimonides' deployment of the verse does not quite correspond to any of the talmudic or midrashic treatments we have seen.

[8] Gillis, *Reading Maimonides' Mishneh Torah*, 241.
[9] Positive commandment 223.
[10] 'Laws of Marriage', 15: 17.

should do it only with her consent, accompanied by pleasant discourse and enjoyment.

In his *Commentary on the Mishnah*,[11] Maimonides says that one is *obligated* to warn his wife. Is he contradicting himself? It would seem that Maimonides there does not mean 'warn' in the technical sense (i.e. in front of two witnesses, and in the appropriate language), but, rather, informally, by way of maintaining family discipline, as will be seen below.[12]

Maimonides ends our passage by citing Job 5: 24. The only other place where this verse is cited in the *Mishneh torah* is irrelevant to our case here.[13] But it is very likely that the Talmud's use of the verse echoed in Maimonides' mind when he wrote this.[14] There we find: 'Our Rabbis taught: Concerning a man who loves his wife as himself, who honours her more than himself, who guides his sons and daughters in the right path, and arranges for them to be married near the period of their puberty, Scripture says, "And thou shalt know that thy tent is in peace".' Here we have an indication of what Maimonides may very well have had in mind when he wrote that a householder must be 'particular' about his wife and children.

To Warn with Wisdom

Turning to the broader issues which arise in our text, let us ignore the many ways that our passage does not sit well with contemporary values and try to understand the upshot of what Maimonides teaches here within the context of the *Mishneh torah* and the world in which Maimonides lived, and which he sought to influence.[15] Maimonides does not question the laws of the 'wayward wife', any more than he questions the laws of slavery included in the *Mishneh torah*.[16] But in both cases, as we shall see, he reads these laws in ways designed to lead to the moral improvement of all concerned.

The objective of the laws concerning the 'wayward wife' is to establish peace within a person's 'tent'. Maimonides thus connects the end of the *Book of Women* with the end of the *Book of Seasons* (Book 3, addressed in the previous chapter), reminding us that a major aim of the Torah is the establish-

[11] *Sot.* 1: 1.
[12] Rabinovitch, *Yad peshutah* on 'Laws of Marriage', 15: 17, understands the text in a similar fashion.   [13] 'Laws of Forbidden Sexual Relations', 21: 25.   [14] BT *Yev.* 62b.
[15] It should be noted, however, that Maimonides knew that the laws of the 'wayward wife' could only be applied when the Temple was standing. He includes them in the *Mishneh torah* in line with his aim to be comprehensive and also in line with his desire to milk the technical details of halakhah, as it were, for moral and metaphysical lessons.
[16] On the laws of slavery in the *Mishneh torah*, see below, Ch. 12.

ment of peace (among nations, as at the end of the *Book of Seasons*, and at the end of the *Mishneh torah* altogether) and within the family (our text here).[17] Peace is achieved through the avoidance of sin and iniquity.[18] Sin and iniquity, it will be recalled, are themselves a function of ignorance. This is the point of *Guide* iii. 11, the most messianic chapter of that work. Maimonides writes there:

> These great evils that come about because the human individuals who inflict them upon one another because of purposes, desires, opinions, and beliefs, are all of them likewise consequent upon privation. For all of them derive from ignorance, I mean from a privation of knowledge. Just as a blind man, because of absence of sight, does not cease stumbling, being wounded and also wounding others, because he has nobody to guide him on the way, the various sects of men—every individual according to the extent of his ignorance—does to himself and to others great evils from which individuals of the species suffer. If there were knowledge, whose relation to the human form is like that of the faculty of sight to the eye, they would refrain from doing any harm to themselves and to others. For through cognition of the truth, enmity and hatred are removed and the inflicting of harm by people on one another is abolished. It holds out this promise, saying: 'And the wolf shall dwell with the lamb, and the leopard shall lie down with the kid, and so on. And the cow and the bear shall feed', and so on [Isa. 11: 6–8]. Then it gives the reason for this, saying that the cause of the abolition of these enmities, these discords, and these tyrannies, will be the knowledge that men [*al-nas*] will have then concerning the true reality of the deity. For it says: 'They shall not hurt nor destroy in all My holy mountain; for the earth shall be full of the knowledge of the Lord, as the waters cover the sea' [Isa. 11: 9]. Know this.[19]

The same attitude, connecting knowledge to peace and ignorance to strife, undergirds our text. Establishing peace within the family setting is the responsibility of the head of the household, and failure to take the proper steps to guarantee that peace is itself sinful. The householder is furthermore enjoined to ensure that the family members remain free of sin and iniquity in ways that are likely to bring about *shalom bayit*, family peace. If one accuses his wife of adultery, it must be done out of a spirit of purity, not out of anger, never casually, never to intimidate her. On the one hand, Maimonides rejects such behaviour as inappropriate on the part of the *paterfamilias*, but on the other hand, if a person behaved in this manner, the accusation still stands

---

[17] Maimonides strengthens this connection by citing the ordeal of the *sotah* at the end of the *Book of Seasons* (see above, in Ch. 2). Cross-references in the *Mishneh torah* such as this ought not to be treated lightly.

[18] This will be addressed below, in Ch. 14. See also Kellner, 'And the Crooked Shall be Made Straight'.

[19] This passage is discussed below in Ch. 14.

and must be treated with all the formalities of the laws governing the wayward wife. Furthermore, even though Jewish law treats adultery with extreme severity, a husband who suspects his wife of adultery should 'do so privately, gently, and in the spirit of purity and admonition, in order to guide her to the straight path and remove the stumbling block'. He must behave in this fashion before levelling a formal 'warning' in the presence of witnesses.

A Spirit of Purity

Let us go back to Maimonides' text. He says that someone who warns his wife should be moved by a spirit of purity. In making this observation, he follows the Talmud:

It has been taught: Rabbi Meir used to say: If a person commits a transgression in secret, the Holy One, blessed be He, proclaims it against him in public; as it is said: 'And the spirit of jealousy came upon him' [Num. 5: 14], and the verb *avar* [came upon] means nothing but 'proclaiming', as it is said: 'And Moses gave commandment, and they caused it to be proclaimed [*vaya'aviru*] throughout the camp' [Exod. 36: 6]. Resh Lakish said: A person does not commit a transgression unless a spirit of folly [*shetut*] enters into him; as it is said: 'If any man's wife go aside' [Num. 5: 12] [The word is] written [so that it can be read] *sishteh*.[20]

Later on the same page we find:

The School of Rabbi Ishmael taught: A man does not warn his wife unless a spirit enters into him;[21] as it is said: 'And the spirit of jealousy came upon him and he be jealous of his wife' [Num. 5: 14]. What is the meaning [of the word] 'spirit'? The Rabbis declare, it is a spirit of impurity;[22] but Rabbi Ashi declares, It is a spirit of purity.[23] Reasonable is the view of him who declares that it is a spirit of purity, because it was taught: 'and he be jealous of his wife'—this is voluntary in the opinion of Rabbi Ishmael; but Rabbi Akiba says: It is obligatory. It is well if you say that it means a spirit of purity, then everything is right; but if you say that it means a spirit of impurity, is it voluntary or obligatory for a man to introduce a spirit of impurity into himself!

In following the view of Rabbi Ashi, Maimonides assimilates halakhah to the ideal, not to the real. In the real world, husbands may accuse their wives of adultery for all sorts of impure reasons; in the ideal world set before us as a standard by halakhah, they are meant to accuse their wives only for the purest of reasons. But Maimonides is no Pollyanna and knows that the real only very

---

[20] BT *Sot.* 3a. The word *sishteh* comes from the same root as *shetut*.
[21] Rashi: 'from God'.   [22] Rashi: 'from Satan, to cause him to sin'.
[23] Rashi: 'a spirit which hates lewdness'.

occasionally approximates the ideal; he accommodates himself to the real world, acknowledging that if a husband accuses his wife of adultery out of impure motives, the accusation stands and must be dealt with.

Maimonides wrote that one of the points of the laws concerning the 'wayward wife' is to teach husbands to see to it that their households are 'free from all sin and iniquity'. This may have led Yohai Makbili in his commentary on our text to suggest that one should read it in light of 'Laws of Impurity of Foodstuffs', 16: 12:[24]

Although it is permissible to eat ritually impure footstuffs and to drink ritually impure liquids, the pious of former times [*heḥasidim harishonim*] used to eat their common food in conditions of purity, and all their days they were wary of every impurity, and it is they who were called Pharisees, 'separated ones', and this is a greater holiness. It is the way of piety [*ḥasidut*] that a man keep himself separate and go apart from the rest of the people and neither touch them nor eat and drink with them. For separation [*perishut*] leads to the purification of the body from evil deeds, and the purification of the body [from evil deeds] leads to the sanctification of the soul from evil [moral] qualities [*de'ot*], and the sanctification of the soul [from evil moral qualities] leads to imitating [*lehidamot*] the *shekhinah*;[25] for it is said, 'Sanctify yourselves and be ye holy' [Lev. 11: 44], 'for I the Lord Who sanctify you am holy' [Lev. 21: 8].[26]

The spirit of purity which is meant to motivate the husband who warns his wife must thus be similar to what is described here: piety (*ḥasidut*), purification of the body from evil deeds, sanctification of the soul from evil (moral) qualities, all leading to an attempt to imitate God's *shekhinah*, or indwelling upon the earth.[27]

---

[24] This *halakhah* is the final paragraph in 'Laws of Impurity of Foodstuffs', which in turn is the sixth of the eight sections in the *Book of Ritual Purity*, the tenth book of the MT.

[25] Danby translates: 'leads to striving for likeness with the *Shekhinah*'. This is the only place where this expression occurs in the MT. The expression *lehidabek bashekhinah* occurs once, in 'Laws of Moral Qualities', 6: 2.

[26] In translating *de'ot* as moral qualities, we follow Maimonides himself in *Guide* iii. 35 (p. 335), where he writes: 'The third class [of commandments] comprises the commandments concerned with improvement of the moral qualities [Arabic: *al-ahlaq*]. They are those which we have enumerated in *Hilkhot de'ot*.' Septimus prefers to translate the expression as 'ethical dispositions'. See Septimus, 'What Did Maimonides Mean by *Madda*?', 96–102.

[27] It should be noted that this paragraph bears linguistic and structural comparison with the end of 'Laws of Immersion Pools', which closes the *Book of Ritual Purity*; with the end of 'Laws of Trespass' [*me'ilah*], which closes the *Book of Temple Service*; and with the end of 'Laws of Substituted Offerings' [*temurah*], which closes the *Book of Offerings*. See below, respectively Chs. 10, 8, and 9. In each case, Maimonides balances the objective and the subjective— the objective inscrutability of the law and subjective reasons for the law in 'Trespass' and

In applying the laws concerning the wayward wife, then, the ideals towards which we should strive are those which underlie the laws of ritual purity: purification of the body from evil deeds and purification of the soul from evil moral qualities, ultimately leading to the imitation of God. Relying upon our discussion of the imitation of God in our Introduction, we may state here confidently that Maimonides expects the person who seeks to fulfil the commandment to walk in God's ways, and thus imitate God, to achieve some combination of ethical perfection (for Maimonides a prerequisite of intellectual perfection) and intellectual perfection.

At first glance, we seem to have wandered far from the laws of the wayward wife. But have we? Here, as in so many other passages in the *Mishneh torah*, Maimonides takes a body of technical law, in this case concerned with a tragic breakdown in family relationships, and uses it to teach a number of lessons: about the responsibilities of a householder towards his family, about moral relationships within marriage, about striving for peace and, finally, and certainly not least, about the imitation of God, such imitation being open to all human beings.

Summary

Using the laws of the so-called 'wayward wife', Maimonides writes about the ways in which marital relations should be conducted, and about the ways in which a householder should relate to his (today we would add: her) household. The ultimate aim of familial and national relations should be to achieve peace. Peace can only be achieved through avoidance of sin. Sin, in turn, is a consequence of ignorance to which, sadly, all human beings are prone.

'Substituted Offerings'; the objective lack of physical change though *mikveh* and subjective moral change; and here, the objective, unavoidable obligation of a man to confront his wife (the 'spirit of purity' of *halakhah* 18) and the subjective tact and consideration he should apply in doing so (the 'way of purity' of *halakhah* 19). Perhaps Maimonides is also reminding the reader about the middle path, between being lax and indulgent on the one hand, and being a jealous martinet on the other. Maimonides strikes a delicate balance, and calls upon the reader to do the same.

FIVE

HOLINESS
Commandments as Instruments

Holiness as *Perishut* (Separation)

The fifth of the fourteen volumes of the *Mishneh torah* is *Sefer kedushah*, the *Book of Holiness*. This volume contains only three sections: 'Laws of Forbidden Intercourse', 'Laws of Forbidden Foods', and 'Laws of [Kosher] Slaughtering'. Before examining the closing paragraph in 'Laws of Slaughtering', the final paragraph in the book as a whole, it behoves us to ask what the three topics covered in the *Book of Holiness* have in common.[1] Maimonides offers an explanation of what they share in *Guide of the Perplexed*.[2] The purpose of the laws concerning forbidden foods, he tells us there, 'as we have explained in the Commentary on the *Mishnah* in the Introduction to *Aboth*,[3] is to put an end to the lusts and licentiousness manifested in seeking what is most pleasurable and to taking the desire for food and drink as an end'. The laws concerning forbidden intercourse, he adds, are designed:

> to bring about a decrease of sexual intercourse and to diminish the desire for mating as far as possible, so that it should not be taken as an end, as is done by the ignorant, according to what we have explained in the Commentary on *Tractate Aboth*.

Maimonides does not explicitly explain the purpose of the laws concerning ritual slaughter here (indeed, he does not mention them at all in this passage in the *Guide*), but it is not hard to see how they would fit into the rubric of forbidden foods, limiting what may be eaten, and how it may be prepared.

---

[1] See Gillis, *Reading Maimonides' Mishneh Torah*, 235: 'Next come two books on the core idea of holiness. The *Book of Holiness* and the *Book of Asseverations* are concerned with restraint of the appetites for food and sex. There is of course continuity between the *Book of Women* and the *Book of Holiness*, the first section of which is "Laws Concerning Forbidden Intercourse", but there is also a fundamental switch between the two books, from the idea of holiness as sanctification of the material and temporal, to holiness as detachment from the material and temporal.'   [2] *Guide* iii. 35 (p. 537).   [3] See Maimonides, *Eight Chapters*, ch. 4.

Indeed, Maimonides makes all this tolerably clear in his introduction to the *Mishneh torah*, where he describes the *Book of Holiness* as follows:

Fifth Book. It includes in it precepts having reference to illicit sexual unions, and those that relate to forbidden foods; because in these two regards, the Omnipresent sanctified us and separated us from the nations, and of both classes of precepts it is said, 'And I have set you apart from the peoples' [Lev. 20: 26], 'Who have set you apart from the peoples' [Lev. 20: 24]. I have called this book: *The Book of Holiness.*[4]

One achieves holiness by refraining from forbidden food and from forbidden sex.[5] That is why the laws concerning forbidden foods and the laws concerning ritual slaughtering (which transform certain classes of edibles from forbidden to permitted) are classed together in the *Book of Holiness*.

Maimonides derives this connection between holiness and refraining from forbidden activities from a midrashic passage cited in the fourth introductory principle to his *Book of Commandments*:

We are not to include charges which cover the whole body of the commandments of the Torah. There are injunctions and prohibitions in the Torah which do not pertain to any specific duty, but include all commandments . . . With respect to this principle other scholars have erred, counting 'You shall be holy' [Lev. 19: 2] as one of the positive commandments—not knowing that the verses, 'You shall be holy' [Lev. 19: 2] [and] 'Sanctify yourselves, and be you holy' [Lev. 11: 44] are charges to fulfil the whole Torah, as if He were saying: 'Be holy by doing all that I have commanded you to do, and guard against all things I have enjoined you from doing.' The *Sifra* says: '"You shall be holy", keep apart'; that is to say, hold aloof from all the abominations against which I have admonished you. In the *Mekhilta* the Sages say: '"And you shall be holy men unto Me" [Exod. 22: 30]—Issi the son of Yehudah says: With every new commandment the Holy One, blessed be He, issues to Israel He adds holiness to them.' That is to say, this charge is not an independent one, but is connected with the commandments wherein they have been enjoined there, since whoever fulfils that charge is called holy. Now this being so, there is then no difference between His saying, 'You shall be holy', and, 'Obey My commandments.' . . . The *Sifrei* [*Num.*] says: '"And you be holy" [Num. 15: 40], this refers to the holiness of the commandments.'[6]

Maimonides explains here that the biblical statement, 'You shall be holy', is

---

[4] We cite the translation of Moses Hyamson, *Maimonides, The Book of Knowledge*, 18b. It should be noted that the explanation given here is particularist ('separate us from the nations') and that of the *Guide* universalist. By the end of this chapter, it will be clear that the *Mishneh torah* also reaches a universalist conclusion.

[5] On this connection, see 'Laws of Moral Qualities', 5: 4, and *Guide* iii. 33 (p. 533). Also relevant is 'Laws of Forbidden Intercourse', 22: 20.

[6] See the Chavel translation, ii. 380–1 (emended).

not to be counted as one of the 613 commandments, since it encompasses the whole Torah. While doing so, Maimonides lets slip, as it were, a point crucial to our purposes: the Jews were not given the commandments because they are holy, nor were they made holy by having been given the commandments. Rather, they *become* holy when they fulfil the commandments. This does not mean that as one fulfils commandments one's ontological status changes from profane to holy; rather, it means that 'holiness' is the way in which the Torah characterizes obedience to the commandments. As Maimonides says at the end of the passage, holiness refers to the holiness of [fulfilling] the commandments.[7]

Returning to the exposition of this passage, Maimonides cites the explanation of Midrash *Sifra* on 'You shall be holy': keep yourself apart or separate yourself from illicit enjoyments (*perishut*). From what in particular must one refrain in order to achieve holiness? In the *Mishneh torah* Maimonides explains: from forbidden foods and from forbidden sex.[8]

Maimonides connects the *perishut* spoken of here with the *perushim*, or Pharisees, in the last *halakhah* of 'Laws of Ritual Impurity of Foods':

Although it is permissible to eat ritually impure foodstuffs and to drink ritually impure liquids, the pious of former times used to eat their common food in conditions of ritual purity, and all their days they were wary of every ritual impurity. And it is they who were called Pharisees, 'separated ones', and this is a higher holiness. It is the way of piety that a man keep himself separate and go apart from the rest of the people and neither touch them nor eat and drink with them. For separation leads to the purification of the body from evil deeds, and the purification of the body leads to the hallowing of the soul from evil thoughts, and the hallowing of the soul leads to striving for imitation of the Shekhinah; for it is said, 'Sanctify yourselves therefore and be ye holy' [Lev. 11: 44], 'for I the Lord Who sanctify you am holy' [Lev. 21: 8].[9]

Acting like the Pharisees is a form of 'higher holiness'. It involves separating

---

[7] These matters are the central theme of Kellner, *Maimonides' Confrontation*, ch. 3. Compare also Maimonides' discussion of ritual purity and impurity in *Guide* iii. 47 (pp. 595–6) and the discussion in *Maimonides' Confrontation*, ch. 4.

[8] It should be noted that in the fourth introductory principle to the *Book of Commandments*, Maimonides also says that holiness is an aspect of every commandment, so that the imperative 'be holy' amounts to no more than saying 'perform My commandments'. Gillis discusses this apparent contradiction in *Reading Maimonides' Mishneh Torah*, 224–36.

[9] 'Laws of Ritual Impurity of Foods', 16: 12. Compare *Guide* iii. 33 (p. 533) and, on the connection between holiness and *perishut*, 'Laws of the Foundations of the Torah', 7: 1 and 7: 7. See further Maimonides, *Commentary on the Mishnah*, Sotah 3: 3. This paragraph will be discussed at greater length below in Ch. 10.

oneself from all forms of ritual impurity and from all people who are in a state of ritual impurity. This is not because there is anything intrinsically wrong with being ritually impure.[10] It is because such separation 'leads to the purification of the body from evil deeds', which, in turn, 'leads to the hallowing of the soul from evil thoughts', which itself 'leads to striving for imitation of the Shekhinah'.

We understand Maimonides to be saying here that the aim of holiness, of *perishut*, is moral behaviour (separation from evil deeds), which in turn makes possible intellectual perfection (separation from evil thoughts); that, in turn, brings one to strive for *imitatio Dei*.[11] This is to translate Maimonides' rabbinic vocabulary into the language of medieval Aristotelianism.[12] But one need not agree with this translation to see that on the evidence of the text presented here, holiness for Maimonides means the outcome of a kind of behaviour. It is nothing which can be said to exist in and of itself, it is not some sort of superadded essence, it is nothing ontological. It is rather a name given to certain extremely important and highly valued types of behaviour, and, by extension, to persons, places, times, and objects. It is, and this is a point which must be emphasized, something which is not given, but must be earned. Holiness is not an inheritable status.[13]

---

[10] Maimonides writes in *halakhah* 9:

Just as it is permissible to eat and drink common food that is ritually impure, so it is permissible to allow ritual impurity to befall common food in the Land of Israel; and ritual impurity may be imparted to common food that is at the outset in fit and proper condition. Similarly, it is permissible to touch any things that are ritually impure, and to incur ritual impurity from them, for Scripture warns none but the sons of Aaron and the Nazirite against incurring ritual impurity from a corpse, thereby implying that for all other people it is permissible, and that it is permissible even for priests and Nazirites to incur ritual impurity from other ritually impure things, except only the ritual impurity of corpses.

[11] The point made here is well stated by Kreisel (*Maimonides' Political Thought*, 156): 'The dominant motif characterizing Maimonides' discussions of God is the negation of corporeality. His view of holiness as lying in the ethical virtues in general, and restraint of corporeal desires in particular, connects this notion with the negation of one's own corporeality. One must particularly negate that which is associated with the most corporeal of our senses.' The literature on Maimonides' conception of human perfection is vast. Much of it is summarized and analysed in Kellner, *Maimonides on Human Perfection*. See, more recently, Gillis, *Reading Maimonides' Mishneh Torah*, 150–4.

[12] For a defence of this approach, see Kellner, *Must a Jew Believe Anything?*, 127–41.

[13] On Maimonides on holiness, see Kellner, *Maimonides' Confrontation*, ch. 3. It is important to note, before carrying on with the line of interpretation being developed here, that for Maimonides holiness in this sense is not restricted to Jews. Non-Jews can also be as sanctified as the Holy of Holies. See below, Ch. 7.

Instrumental Commandments

With this background we may now to turn to our text itself, 'Laws Concerning Kosher Slaughtering [shehitah]', 14: 14–16:

> Whosoever performs shehitah must first spread dust underneath, then slaughter over it, and thereupon cover up the blood with more dust; he should not slaughter into a vessel and then cover up the blood with dust.
>
> It is he who performs shehitah who should also perform the covering up of the blood, as it is said, 'he shall . . . cover it with dust' [Lev. 17: 13]. If he does not cover it up and another man sees it, the latter must cover it up, since this is a separate commandment whose fulfilment does not depend solely upon the person who performs shehitah.[14]
>
> When one performs the commandment of covering up the blood, he should do it not with his foot, but with his hand, or with a knife or utensil, so as not to conduct the performance of the commandment in a contemptuous manner, thus treating God's commandments with scorn. For reverence is not due to the commandments themselves, but to Him who issued them, blessed be He, and has delivered us from groping in the darkness by making the commandments[15] a lamp to straighten out the crooked places and a light to teach us the paths of uprightness.[16] And so indeed Scripture says, 'Thy word is a lamp unto my feet, and a light unto my path' [Ps. 119: 105].[17]

We will focus here on the final sentences in this passage. What is Maimonides trying to teach us by insisting that the commandments are due no reverence in themselves, and serve as 'a lamp to straighten out the crooked places and a light to teach us the paths of uprightness', and thus deliver us 'from groping in the darkness'? He is, we suggest, hinting at his conception of the commandments as instrumental, having no inherent value in themselves.

In order to understand the significance of this, we must pay some atten-

---

[14] Compare *Book of Commandments*, positive commandment 147.

[15] Remarkably, many printed editions here have 'us' (*otanu*) instead of 'the commandments' (*otam*). This reading goes against the thrust of Maimonides' understanding of the commandments (to be discussed immediately below) and of the nature of the Jewish people (on which, see Kellner, *Maimonides on Judaism and the Jewish People*, and id., *They, Too, Are Called Human* (Heb.)). Kellner has further argued that this sort of 'correction' found its way into Maimonides' text by accident, as it were, and not due to any conscious attempt to subvert his meaning, or make it more 'kosher'. See Kellner, '"Farteitsht un Farbessert"'.

[16] Based on Isa. 42: 16: 'I will lead the blind by a road they did not know, and I will make them walk by paths they never knew. I will turn darkness before them into light, rough places into level ground. These are the promises—I will keep them without fail.'

[17] The commandments are 'a lamp unto my feet', and must never be treated contemptuously, as would be the case should one cover the blood with his or her 'foot'.

tion to Maimonides' understanding of the nature of the commandments.[18] He is notorious for having treated the commandments of the Torah as instruments to accomplish ends external to them. While certainly of great value, their value is not intrinsic (after all, they could have been different), but is a function of the social, religious, political, and especially philosophical ends that they help us accomplish.

One of the first places in which Maimonides makes this point about the instrumental character of the commandments is in a notorious passage near the beginning of the *Mishneh torah*:

> The topics connected with these five precepts, treated in the above four chapters, are what our wise men called *pardes*, as in the passage, 'Four went into the Pardes' [BT Ḥag. 14b]. And although those four were great men of Israel and great Sages, they did not all possess the capacity to know and grasp these subjects clearly. Therefore I say that it is not proper to dally in the *pardes* till one has first filled oneself with bread and meat; by which I mean knowledge of what is permitted and what is forbidden, and similar distinctions in other classes of precepts. Although these last subjects were called by the Sages 'a small thing' (when they say, 'a great thing, *ma'aseh merkavah*; a small thing, the discussion of Abaye and Raba'), still they should have the precedence. For the knowledge of these things gives primarily composure to the mind. They are the precious boon bestowed by God, to promote social well-being on earth, in order to inherit life in the world to come. Moreover, the knowledge of them is within the reach of all, old and young, men and women, those gifted with great intellectual capacity as well as those whose intelligence is limited.[19]

Another text which expresses the point well appears in the *Guide*:

> The Torah[20] as a whole aims at two things: the welfare of the soul and welfare of the body. As for the welfare of the soul, it consists in the multitude's acquiring correct opinions corresponding to their respective capacity . . . As for the welfare of the body, it comes about by the improvement of their ways of living one with another. This is achieved through two things. One of them is the abolition of their wronging

---

[18] For a fuller discussion, see Kellner, *Maimonides' Confrontation*, ch. 2.

[19] 'Laws of the Foundations of the Torah', 4: 13. We cite the translation of Isadore Twersky (with minor emendations), *Introduction to the Code*, 493. On this passage Joseph Karo famously glossed (in his *Kesef mishneh*, ad loc.): 'Maimonides wrote what he wished to write, and would that he had not done so.' On what Twersky calls the 'instrumental or teleological role' of the commandments, see his discussion, 418–30, and below in this chapter.

[20] Pines here has 'The Law', translating *al-sharia*. He is, so far as we know, consistent in translating in this fashion. This reflects his policy of seeking to translate terms in the same way throughout. To our mind, translating *al-shariah* literally as 'Law' instead of as 'Torah' often makes Maimonides sound overly 'Protestant'. 'Torah' can refer to the Pentateuch or to the entire body of sacred Jewish teaching.

each other. This is tantamount to every individual among the people not being permitted to act according to his will and up to the limits of his power, but being forced to do that which is useful to the whole. The second thing consists in the acquisition by every human individual of moral qualities that are useful for life in society so that the affairs of the city may be ordered.[21]

The Torah thus has two aims: the welfare of the soul, and the welfare of human society. The second aim is achieved by laws which abolish mutual wrongdoing and which inculcate elevated moral dispositions in the members of the society. Of these two aims, one is more sublime than the other. The passage continues:

Know that as between these two aims, one is indubitably greater in nobility, namely, the welfare of the soul—I mean the procuring of correct opinions—while the second aim—I mean the welfare of the body—is prior in nature and time . . . His ultimate perfection is to become rational *in actu*, I mean to have an intellect *in actu*; this would consist in his knowing everything concerning all beings that it is within the capacity of man to know in accordance with his ultimate perfection.

The Torah emphasizes the second aim more than the first because it applies to all Jews, while the first aim applies only to a relatively small subset of Jews. This is Maimonides' explanation for the fact that, while the first aim is more sublime than the second, and served by the second, the Torah spends much more time and energy on the second aim. Maimonides summarizes all this as follows:

The true Law[22] then . . . namely the Law of Moses our Master, has come to bring us both perfections, I mean the welfare of the states of people in their relations with one another through the abolition of reciprocal wrongdoing and through the acquisition of a noble and excellent character. In this way the preservation of the population of the country and their permanent existence in the same order become possible, so that every one of them achieves his first perfection; I mean also the soundness of the beliefs and the giving of correct opinions through which the ultimate perfection is achieved.

The commandments of the Torah are thus a tool, not an end in themselves.[23]

---

[21] *Guide* iii. 27 (pp. 510–11).

[22] Here Pines' translation helps us see how Maimonides distinguishes the (true) *sharia* of Moses from other putative divine laws, although (no doubt surprisingly to many readers), he sees them as belonging to the same genus. For more on this, see Diamond and Kellner, *Reinventing Maimonides*, ch. 5, n. 68.

[23] This view of Maimonides was well understood by Shem Tov ben Shem Tov Ibn Shem Tov (15th cent.) in his *Sefer ha'emunot*; there he criticizes Maimonides for denying that any

They were ordained in the Torah to educate Jews away from violence and oppression, and towards a morally elevated life. The commandments are tools, not forms of magical or mystical praxis. Their effects can be profound on those who fulfil them and on the societies in which they live, but they have no effects on 'supernal' realms, and have no effects on the 'inner workings' of the 'godhead'.[24]

The point of all the commandments is summarized in the following passage:

> Rather things are indubitably as we have mentioned: every commandment from among these six hundred and thirteen commandments exists either with a view to communicating a correct opinion, or to putting an end to an unhealthy opinion, or to communicating a rule of justice, or to warding off an injustice, or to endowing men with a noble moral quality, or to warning them against an evil moral quality. Thus all [the commandments] are bound up with three things: opinions, moral qualities, and political civic actions.[25]

All the commandments are tools, designed by God to teach truth, institute justice, or inculcate morality. There is no room here for a view of the commandments as effecting change in the world around us, still less in the world above.

The instrumental, educational character of the commandments is also made clear in the following passage:

> Know that all the practices of the worship, such as reading the Torah, prayer, and the performance of the other commandments, have only the end of training you to occupy yourself with His commandments, may He be exalted, rather than with matters pertaining to this world; you should act as if you were occupied with Him, may He be exalted, and not with that which is other than He.[26]

---

commandment is intrinsically valuable (*mekhuvenet le'atsmah*); see *Sefer ha'emunot*, Gate 1, ch. 1, p. 7a. For a recent exhaustive discussion of Ibn Shem Tov's critique of Maimonides, see Peleg, 'Between Philosophy and Kabbalah' (Heb.). For other criticisms by Ibn Shem Tov of Maimonides, see Davidson, *Moses Maimonides*, 415. Maimonides' position on this was succinctly captured (and treated very critically) by Joseph Soloveitchik: 'The net result of Maimonides' rationalization is that religion no longer operates with unique autonomous norms, but with technical rules, the employment of which would culminate in the attainment of some extraneous maximum bonum. In rationalizing the commandments genetically, Maimonides developed a religious "instrumentalism".' See Soloveitchik, *The Halakhic Mind*, 93 and our discussion of this issue below in this chapter and in Ch. 10.

[24] Thus those who seek to read Maimonides kabbalistically do violence to his words and his meaning. For an example of such a reading of Maimonides, see Toledano, *The Book of Speech and Thought* (Heb.).   [25] *Guide* iii. 31 (p. 524).

[26] *Guide* iii. 51 (p. 622). Compare 'Laws of Substituted Offerings', 4: 13. See the translation

This passage, both when read by itself and all the more when read in light of those cited just above, clearly teaches that fulfilling the commandments of the Torah does not accomplish anything 'pertaining to this world'; the commandments are part of a divinely ordained educational institution, not parts of a recipe for effecting ontological change in the universe.[27]

Our point is made even clearer in the context of Maimonides' discussion of various human perfections:

> The third species is a perfection that to a greater extent than the second species subsists in the individual's self. This is the perfection of the moral virtues. It consists in the individual's moral habits having attained their ultimate excellence. Most of the commandments serve no other end than the attainment of this species of perfection.[28] But this species of perfection is likewise a preparation for something else and is not an end in itself. For all moral habits are concerned with what occurs between a human individual and someone else. This perfection regarding moral habits is, as it were, only the disposition to be useful to people; consequently it is an instrument for someone else. For if you suppose a human individual is alone, acting on no one, you will find that all his moral virtues are in vain and without employment and unneeded, and that they do not perfect the individual in anything; for he only needs them and they again become useful to him in regard to someone else.[29]

In case the point wasn't made clearly enough, Maimonides reiterates it a few paragraphs later in the same chapter:

---

of that text and the discussion in Twersky, *Introduction to the Code*, 416–17, and below, Ch. 8. See also the following sentence in *Guide* iii. 52 (p. 630): 'the end of the actions prescribed by the whole Law is to bring about the passion of which it is correct that it be brought about . . . I refer to the fear of Him . . . and the awe before His command.' The commandments, Maimonides goes on to explain, bring one to awe of God, while the doctrines taught in the Torah bring one to love of God. The commandments are all means to an end external to them. On how the passage adduced here fits into Maimonides' doctrine of the reasons for the commandments (*ta'amei hamitsvot*), see J. Stern, *Problems and Parables*, chs. 4 and 6.

[27] Compare also *Guide* ii. 39 (p. 89) and the texts to which Maimonides apparently refers there (*Eight Chapters*, ch. 5 and 'Laws of the Foundations of the Torah', 2: 2).

[28] 'Most' but not all; as we saw above in the text cited from *Guide* iii. 27 (pp. 510–11), the commandments that do not inculcate virtuous behaviour teach metaphysical truths. There is thus no comfort here for those who might seek to read Maimonides as a halakhic ontologist.

[29] *Guide* iii. 54 (p. 635). This passage is truly remarkable. One could, mistakenly in our view, read it as implying that a Jew living alone on a desert island has no need to fulfil most of the commandments (although she would still have to build the proverbial two synagogues). For a bibliography of sources relating to a figure who apparently read Maimonides in that fashion, see Dienstag, 'Nachman Krochmal's Defence'.

The Sages, may their memory be blessed, apprehended from this verse[30] the very notions that we have mentioned and have explicitly stated that which I have explained to you in this chapter: namely that the term wisdom [ḥokhmah], used in an unrestricted sense and regarded as the end, means the apprehension of Him, may He be exalted; that the possession of the treasures acquired, and competed for, by man and thought to be perfection are not a perfection; and that similarly all the actions prescribed by the Law—I refer to the various species of worship and also the moral habits that are useful to all people in their mutual dealings—that all this is not to be compared with this ultimate end and does not equal it, being but preparations made for the sake of this end.[31]

All of the actions commanded by the Torah, Maimonides informs us in this final chapter of his *magnum opus*, are not to be compared to the ultimate end of the Torah (the teaching of true beliefs concerning metaphysical matters), nor are they its equal; rather, they serve as instruments which prepare people to seek their truly human end, the cognition of intelligibles about God.[32] One must feel sympathy for many of Maimonides' rabbinic contemporaries who, when faced with a passage such as this, responded, in effect, 'That's Greek to me!'[33] Indeed, he himself anticipated such a response, writing (in the context of his historical explanation of the sacrifices):

'I know that in thinking about this at first your soul will necessarily have a feeling of repugnance toward this notion and will feel aggrieved because of it; and you will ask me in your heart and say to me: How is it possible that *none* of the commandments, prohibitions, and great actions—which are very precisely set forth and prescribed for fixed seasons—should be intended for its own sake, but for the sake of something else'.[34]

---

[30] Jer. 9: 22–3: 'Thus says the Lord: Let not the wise man glory in his wisdom, neither let the mighty man glory in his might, let not the rich man glory in his riches; but let him that glories glory in this, that he understands and knows Me.' For discussions of this verse by Maimonides and other medieval Jewish thinkers, see Melamed, 'Al yithalel' (Heb.).

[31] *Guide* iii. 54 (p. 636).

[32] For Maimonides moral perfection is a necessary, but not sufficient, prerequisite for intellectual perfection. For sources, see *Guide* i. 34 (pp. 76–7), where Maimonides writes: 'the moral virtues are a preparation for the rational virtues, it being impossible to achieve true, rational acts—I mean perfect rationality—unless it be by a man thoroughly trained in his morals and endowed with the qualities of tranquillity and quiet'; and also *Guide* i. 62 (p. 152), iii. 27 (p. 510), and iii. 54 (p. 635) and *Commentary on Mishnah, Ḥag.* 2: 1. For discussion, see Kellner, *Maimonides on Human Perfection*, 26–8; id., 'Is Maimonides' Ideal Person Austerely Rationalist?', and Kreisel, *Maimonides' Political Thought*, 160, 238, and 317.

[33] Just to put the matter in sharp focus, compare Maimonides' devaluation of prayer here with Judah Halevi's elevation of it. See Schweid, 'Prayer in the Thought of Yehudah Halevi'.

[34] *Guide* iii. 32 (p. 527); emphasis added.

The position taken at the end of the *Guide* is also found, at least indirectly, at the very beginning of the work. Discussing biblical parables in the Introduction, Maimonides writes:

> Know that the key to the understanding of all that the prophets, peace be on them, have said, and to the knowledge of its truth, is an understanding of the parables, of their import, and of the meaning of the words occurring in them.... And it is said in the Midrash: 'To what were the words of the Torah to be compared before the advent of Solomon? To a well the waters of which are at a great depth and cool, yet no man could drink of them. Now what did one clever man do? He joined cord with cord and rope with rope and drank. Thus did Solomon say one parable after another and speak one word after another, until he understood the meaning of the words of the Torah.'[35] This is literally what they say.[36] I do not think that anyone possessing an unimpaired capacity imagines that 'the words of the Torah' referred to here that one contrives to understand through understanding the meaning of the parables are ordinances concerning the building of tabernacles, the *lulab*, and the law of the four trustees. Rather, what this text has in view here is, without any doubt, the understanding of obscure matters.[37]

Maimonides makes a clear distinction here between halakhah and the inner meaning of the Torah (which for him means physics and metaphysics, i.e. *ma'aseh bereshit* and *ma'aseh merkavah*). Halakhah has no mystical meaning which must be discovered with great difficulty and patience; it is what it is, namely, a social construct ordained by God. This is not to deny, of course, that the Torah uses many different stratagems to point us in the direction of philosophical enlightenment.

Lest it be thought that only in his *Guide* does Maimonides make the point we have been describing here, we would like to cite a passage from one of his halakhic works, the *Commentary on the Mishnah*, a text which every student of Maimonides would admit is addressed to all Jews and not just to the philosophers among them. In the sixth of the *Eight Chapters* with which he prefaces his commentary on Mishnah *Avot*, Maimonides distinguishes between a virtuous person and a self-disciplined person. The philosophers, he says, appear to prefer the former, the Sages of the Talmud, the latter. Against this background he writes:

---

[35] *S. of S. Rabbah*, 1: 1.   [36] This is not literally what they say in the texts before us today.
[37] (p. 10). For a profound discussion of this passage in the *Guide*, see Diamond, *Maimonides and the Hermeneutics of Concealment*, 13–20. Note also the implied equivalence here: tabernacles (sukkot) and *lulav* (palm branches used during the festival of Sukkot) are no more mysterious than the law of four trustees.

If the external meaning of the two accounts [i.e. by the philosophers and the Jewish sages] is understood superficially, the two views contradict each other. However, that is not the case; rather, both of them are true, and there is no conflict between them at all. For the bad things to which the philosophers referred when they said that someone who does not desire them is more virtuous than someone who does desire them and restrains himself—these are the things generally accepted by all the people as bad, such as murder, theft, robbery, fraud, harming an innocent man, repaying a benefactor with evil, degrading parents, and things like these. They are the laws about which the sages, peace be upon them, said [BT *Yoma* 67*b*]: 'If they were not written down, they would deserve to be written down'. . . . There is no doubt that the soul which craves and strongly desires any of them is defective and that the virtuous soul neither longs for any of these bad things at all nor suffers pain from the prohibition against them. When the sages said that the continent man is more virtuous and his reward is greater, they had in mind the traditional laws. This is correct because if it were not for the Law, they would not be bad at all. Therefore they said that a man needs to let his soul remain attracted to them and not place any obstacle before them other than the Law.[38]

What are the 'traditional laws' to which Maimonides refers here? He cites the following as examples: 'meat with milk, mixed fabric [*sha'atnez*], and illicit sexual unions'. A virtuous person will not want to kill, steal, or lie (Maimonides' examples), while such an individual may indeed want to eat non-kosher food, wear *sha'atnez*, or engage in illicit sex. Were it not for Torah prohibitions, such things 'would not be bad at all'.[39] Indeed, Maimonides believes that a normal person will be attracted to such activities, and there is clearly nothing wrong with that. It is the institution of Torah which makes such behaviour wrong (for a Jew); there is nothing about the ontological nature of the world which would make engaging in such behaviour damaging to the soul of a Jew. Maimonides clearly teaches here that halakhah is not linked to some mystical reality, but rather creates a social reality, without making any explicit or implicit claims whatsoever about the extra-social world.

Maimonides' text here coheres perfectly with a passage already cited from the *Guide*:

Know that all the practices of the worship, such as reading the Torah, prayer, and the performance of the other commandments, have only the end of training you to

[38] We cite the text as translated in Maimonides, *Ethical Writings*, 79–80.

[39] For many Jewish thinkers of a non-Maimonidean bent, practices outlawed by the ceremonial law of the Torah are bad (at least for Jews) in and of themselves; here Maimonides tells us that in and of themselves, they are not bad at all. For more on this, see Kellner, *Maimonides' Confrontation*, ch. 2.

occupy yourself with His commandments, may He be exalted, rather than with matters pertaining to this world.[40]

The practices of Judaism, we take Maimonides to be teaching here, were ordained *only* for purposes of training. To play on Maimonides' words, the commandments do not relate to matters pertaining to any objectively existent entities and distinctions in this world. Halakhah is therefore an instrument, not an end in itself; as such, it could have been different; it does not reflect any mystical reality beyond nature—rather, it is a divinely ordained response to historical realities and a divinely bestowed gift to be used as a tool for the religious, moral, and intellectual improvement of those bound to obey it.[41] Thus Maimonides writes that we are not to reverence the commandments themselves, since they are 'only' tools serving as 'a lamp to straighten out the crooked places and a light to teach us the paths of uprightness', and thus deliver us 'from groping in the darkness'.

The Opposite View

All this contrasts with a view according to which fulfilling the commandments actually accomplishes something concrete, as it were, in the metaphysical realm. That view finds one of its classic expressions in Halevi's parable of the physician's dispensary:

The sage said: Certainly the things that are fit to receive that divine influence are not within the capacity of human beings [to grasp], nor is it possible for them to determine their [specific] quantities and qualities. Moreover, even if people were to know their essential natures, they would not know their [proper] times, places, circumstances, and the means of preparing for them. For that, one would need consummate divine knowledge, explained thoroughly by God. Someone to whom this instruction has come and who conforms to it in accordance with its [specified] limits and conditions with pure intent is the faithful person. But someone who has tried to modify things in order to receive that [influence] by means of [his own] ingenuity, reasoning, and opinions [drawn] from what is found in the books of the astrologers (with respect to) summoning the influence of spiritual beings and making talismans, is the rebel because he offers sacrifices and burns incense on the basis of reasoning and conjecture. Thus, he does not understand the true character of what is necessary, [nor] how much, in what way, in which place, at what time,

---

[40] *Guide* iii. 51 (p. 622).

[41] Another text in which these ideas find indirect expression is the concluding chapter of the *Book of Knowledge*, namely, 'Laws of Repentance', 10. 'Laws of Trespass [*Me'ilah*]', 8: 8 (following the textual discussion and analysis of Henshke, 'On the Question of Unity' (Heb.)), also supports our interpretation. This text will be analysed in our next chapter.

through which person, how it should be handled, and many [other] circumstances, which it would take far too long to describe.[42]

Torah commandments serve as a means for calling down divine influence.[43] This can only be accomplished by one who carefully follows the 'recipes' found in the Torah. One who attempts to call down this influence without following the Torah instructions is like a fool who dispenses medicines without knowing what he is doing:

> He is [actually] like the fool who entered the pharmacy of a physician [who was] well-known for his effective medicines. The physician wasn't there, but people would come to that pharmacy seeking help [anyway]. The fool [in turn] would dispense [the contents] of the vials to them without knowing the medicines [they contained] nor even how much [of each] medicine should be dispensed to each individual. Therefore, he killed people by means of the very medicines that might have helped them. Now, if it happened by coincidence that one of them derived some benefit from [the contents of] one of those vials, the people took a liking to it and said that that one was the most beneficial [medicine] until it failed them or [until] they accidentally came to regard something else as beneficial, [so that] they also took a liking to it. They didn't know that what is beneficial in itself is only the advice of that learned physician who had prepared those medicines [in the first place], dispensed them properly, and would instruct the patient to prepare himself with the most appropriate regimen for [taking] each medicine, such as [the right] food, drink, exercise, rest, sleep, [time] awake, air, sedation, and other such things. So, too, people before Moses, except for a few, used to be deceived into [following] astrological and [other] natural *nomoi*, going from *nomos* to *nomos* and from deity to deity. Sometimes they would cling to several of them [at once] and forget the One who prepares them and dispenses them. They used to believe [those *nomoi* and deities] to be the cause of [all kinds of] benefits, when in themselves they are the cause of [all kinds of] harm, depending on their disposition and preparation. However, what is beneficial in itself is the divine order [*al-amr al-ilahi*], and what is harmful in itself is its absence.[44]

Halevi explicitly rejects what would become the Maimonidean approach as outlined in this chapter, attributing that view to Elisha ben Abuyah, the notorious apostate sage.[45] According to Halevi, Elisha mistakenly thought that the Torah's commandments are only instruments to bring one to a higher level of spirituality. Once that level is achieved, the commandments no longer need be obeyed.[46]

---

[42] *Kuzari* i. 79.
[43] On this matter, see Pines, 'On the Term *Ruḥaniyut*' (Heb.).
[44] *Kuzari* i. 79.
[45] *Kuzari* iii. 65.
[46] It may be that Halevi is not as far from Maimonides as he is here presented as being (on

Holiness for All

In contrast to Halevi, Maimonides sees the commandments as tools designed by God to deliver those who obey them 'from groping in the darkness'. The commandments (not the Jews!) thus become 'a lamp to straighten out the crooked places and a light to teach us the paths of uprightness'. This view is not just 'religious instrumentalism', as Joseph Soloveitchik dismissingly called it; it does not diminish the value of the commandments. On the contrary, it makes the person who fulfils them God's 'partner', not in repairing some imagined catastrophic breakdown within God, but in repairing the world in which we actually live, shedding light upon it, and straightening what Kant was later famously to call the crooked timber of humanity. Kant thought that timber could not be made straight; Maimonides, we submit, thought it could.[47]

There is another important consequence of Maimonides' view of the commandments as tools: it reflects his underlying universalism. Thinkers of the Halevian strain (i.e. almost all Jewish thinkers since the Middle Ages but for Maimonides and other rationalists) were convinced that only Jews could actually fulfil the commandments properly. Non-Jews lacked the requisite 'hardware' necessary to run Jewish 'software'.[48] For Maimonides, to fulfil the commandments, one needs proper behaviour and proper intent, not proper descent.

Following this long detour, we can return to the subject of our discussion, the closing words of the *Book of Holiness*:

For reverence is not due to the commandments themselves, but to Him who issued them, blessed be He, and has delivered us from groping in the darkness by making the commandments a lamp to straighten out the crooked places and a light to teach us the paths of uprightness. And so indeed Scripture says, 'Thy word is a lamp unto my feet, and a light unto my path' [Ps. 119: 105].

The commandments, as tools, are not objects of reverence themselves. They are, rather, lamps 'to straighten out the crooked places' and lights 'to teach us the paths of uprightness'. By this lamp and light God has 'delivered us from groping in the darkness'. As such, they can, in principle, be used by all human

that, the two authors of this book are not in total agreement), but the view attributed to Halevi here is certainly the widely held view of post-Zohar Judaism. For Maimonides, of course, the obligation to fulfil the commandments remains undiminished even after achieving the highest possible level of perfection.

[47] On this, see our discussion below in Ch. 14.
[48] For the source of this analogy, see Lasker, 'Proselyte Judaism'.

beings, whether born as Jews or converted to Judaism. But tools, when prized without reference to the ends they are meant to attain, can become fetishes. It will be seen in Chapter 7 that holiness, the goal towards which Book 5 of the *Mishneh torah* aims, can in principle be achieved by non-Jews who, using other tools, deliver themselves from groping in darkness and thus can become as sanctified as the Holy of Holies.[49]

Summary

The main theme of this chapter has been to demonstrate that for Maimonides the commandments of the Torah are tools designed to lead those who practise them properly to elevated morality, which, in turn, makes possible the true end of humanity: philosophical understanding. As tools, the commandments are valuable only when they accomplish the ends for which they were designed. When misused, obeyed improperly, they lose their value. The commandments of the Torah are the best, but not the only possible, way of achieving elevated morality and then human perfection.

---

[49] See below, Ch. 8. We will note there that the sentiment of our passage—that performance of the commandments should express respect for God who gave them—and its very language are echoed in the endings of both the *Book of Temple Service* and the *Book of Offerings*.

SIX

ASSEVERATIONS
Social Responsibility and Sanctifying God's Name

Introduction

The *Book of Asseverations* (*Sefer hafla'ah*) deals with the halakhic consequences of making various kinds of statements. It has four sections. The first is 'Laws of Oaths', which deals with oaths both as testimony to past events and as undertakings for the future. The following section is 'Laws of Vows'. There are two types of vows: vows of abstinence, which are dealt with in this section, and vows of consecration (such as to bring a sacrifice of one kind or another), for details of which we are referred to 'Laws of Sacrificial Procedures' in the *Book of Temple Service*. The main difference between oaths (with which this book begins) and vows (with constitute its bulk) is that God is not invoked in the former but only in the latter.

The last two sections of the book deal with unique vows that follow special rules. The third section is 'Laws of Naziriteship', which deals with the special case of a vow of abstinence in which a person undertakes to be a *nazir* for a period or even for life. A *nazir* is defined in Numbers 6: 1–21: a person who takes such a vow may not cut his or her hair, consume grapes or any grape product, or allow him or herself to become ritually impure. The fourth and final section is 'Laws of Valuation and Consecration', covering a special case of vows of consecration in which a person vows to give their own value or that of someone else, or some possession, to the priests or for the upkeep of the Temple. The final *halakhah* of that section reads:

A person should never consecrate or devote all of his possessions. He who does the reverse acts contrary to the intention of Scripture, for it says, '*of all* that he hath' [Lev. 27: 28], not '*all* that he hath', as was made clear by the Sages. Such an act is not piety but folly, since he forfeits all his valuables and makes himself dependent upon other people, and no pity should be shown toward him.[1] Of such, and those like

---

[1] The Yale Judaica translation, by B. D. Klein, has 'who may show no pity toward him'.

him, the Sages said, 'The pious fool is one of those who cause the world to perish.'

Rather, whosoever wishes to expend his money in good deeds, should disburse no more than one fifth, in order that he might be, as the Prophets have advised it, 'one that ordereth his affairs rightfully' [Ps. 112: 5], be it in matters of Torah or in the business of the world. Even in respect to the sacrifices which a person is obligated to offer, Scripture is sparing of his money, for it says he may bring an offering in accordance with his means. How much more so in respect to those things for which he is not liable except in consequence of his own vow, should he vow only what is within his means, for Scripture says, 'Every man shall give as he is able, according to the blessing of the Lord thy God, which He hath given thee' [Deut. 16: 17].

This conclusion to the *Book of Asseverations* amplifies previous *halakhot* that state that one should not consecrate all of one's possessions, but that if one does so, the oath is binding and they are considered consecrated.[2] Read cursorily, it may possibly come across as a bland piece of bourgeois morality. One must fulfil one's religious duties, but one should not thereby imperil one's financial soundness, or—horror!—one might become a burden on society. Perhaps such a view is to be expected of a physician to the Egyptian nobility from a family of the merchant class, such as Maimonides.

There is a vehemence in this *halakhah*, though, that cuts through any impression of blandness. If someone is foolish enough to consecrate all his worldly goods 'no pity should be shown toward him', writes the author for whom exhibiting mercy is the imitation of God,[3] and who at the end of the *Book of Acquisition* extols the quality of mercy with the words 'Whoever has compassion, will receive compassion.'[4] While the other expressions of condemnation in our *halakhah* can be traced to statements of the Sages, this denial of mercy is, as far as we have been able to ascertain, Maimonides' own contribution.[5] What leads him to refuse the succour that one would think extends even to fools, perhaps especially to them? What puts someone who gives up their possessions out of religious enthusiasm beyond the scope of mercy? Maimonides' thinking could be that a person who divests himself of all his wealth shows mercy neither to himself, nor to any dependants, nor to society at large, and therefore is not deserving of mercy. Nevertheless, since his general approach is that the exercise of moral virtues such as mercy is at

---

[2] See 'Laws of Valuation and Consecrations', 6: 2–3. Maimonides adopts the ruling in Mishnah *Arakh.* 6: 4 and Tosefta *Arakh.* 4: 23 (Zuckermandel), against the contrary opinion recorded in the latter and in Mishnah *Arakh.* 8: 4.   [3] See 'Laws of Moral Qualities', 1: 6.

[4] 'Laws of Slaves', 9: 8 (discussed below in Ch. 12), based on BT *Shab.* 151b.

[5] The view of R. Akiva (Mishnah *Ket.* 9: 2) that a poor person is not shown any special mercy in legal matters, which would presumably apply all the more to someone who makes themselves poor, may possibly be reflected here.

least as important for the reflexive effect on the subject as for the benefit conferred on the object, and since he defines ḥesed (loving-kindness) as including 'the exercise of beneficence toward one who has no right at all to claim this from you',[6] the reprobation here appears exceptionally severe.

Another original touch is the *a fortiori* argument at the very end of the final *halakhah*: if the Torah discourages overspending on obligatory sacrifices, then certainly when it comes to voluntary sacrifices, no-one should pledge more than they can really afford.[7] Such arguments are generally vulnerable to refutation, and here it is possible to make the counter-argument that it would be unreasonable for the Torah to demand that people should impoverish themselves, but what an individual decides to do with their own property is his or her affair. Moreover, it is not clear that, in the verse that Maimonides cites as a proof-text, the Torah means to curb spending. The verse 'every man shall give as he is able, according to the blessing of the Lord thy God which He hath given thee' sounds as though it is directed against parsimony rather than prodigality: one should be generous with sacrifices on festivals in appreciation of God's generosity.[8]

Perhaps our *halakhah* is only rhetoric. Perhaps Maimonides would not really spurn someone who had given away their last penny, and only writes this way for emphasis, while the *a fortiori* argument is designed to forestall any suggestion that such recklessness is what the Torah really demands. That could be one way of accounting for his tone here.

A Contemporary Issue?

Another possibility is that Maimonides was responding to contemporary ideas and practice. Whether or not poverty was an ideal was a matter of controversy among Islamic thinkers. While on the one hand al-Ghazali (c.1058–1111) held that 'Properly implemented, poverty leads to total concentration on acquiring knowledge of God',[9] the opinion of Abu Hafs al-Suhrawadi (1145–1234) was that 'The pauper is too concerned with the compensation God will award him for poverty to be properly devoted.'[10] On the Christian front, it is worth mentioning that Francis of Assisi (1181/2–1226), who for many people most strikingly represents deliberate poverty as a virtue, was a younger contemporary of Maimonides. As it happens, he did visit Egypt, and was report-

---

[6] *Guide* iii. 53 (pp. 631–2).

[7] Maimonides' argument is close in spirit to that of R. Elazar ben Azariah in Mishnah *Arakh*. 8: 4 and Tosefta (Zuckermandel edn.), *Arakh*. 4: 25, but not quite the same.

[8] This is the sense that Maimonides seems to give this verse in 'Laws of the Festal Offering', 1: 2, where the discussion is about the minimum that should be offered, not the maximum. [9] Sabra, *Poverty and Charity*, 22. [10] Ibid. 26.

edly received by the sultan, although, if that happened at all, it was after Maimonides' death.[11]

The doctrine of the mean propounded in the *Book of Knowledge*, 'Laws of Moral Qualities', entails steering a middle course between pauperism and avarice, and giving material existence its due. In the third chapter of 'Laws Concerning Moral Qualities', Maimonides decries asceticism in terms that strongly imply agreement with the view of Abu Hafs al-Suhrawadi mentioned above, namely that renunciation of the world is psychologically self-defeating for the person who seeks God.[12] Yet at the end of the *Book of Agriculture*, 'Laws of Sabbatical and Jubilee Years', the Levites, who have no land of their own and depend on tithes, are presented as a model for every earnest seeker after God, Jew or non-Jew.[13] Had Maimonides lived to see St Francis at the sultan's court, setting aside for the moment his negative view of Christianity,[14] what would he have made of him? Would he have classed him as someone who 'is as consecrated as the Holy of Holies, and his inheritance shall be in the Lord forever and ever', as in 'Laws of Sabbatical and Jubilee Years',[15] or with the crazy devotee who wastes the world of 'Laws of Valuation and Consecrations'?[16] Note, incidentally, that these two *halakhot* conclude adjacent books; Maimonides seemingly invites us to compare them.

What Is the *Book of Asseverations* About?

In order to gauge the tone of the final *halakhah* of 'Laws of Valuation and Consecrations' and understand what lies behind it, we need to be able to place it in context. We should expect it to be in some way a summation of the book that it concludes, illuminating the book's themes and guiding us to an understanding of the spirit of the laws it contains. That at least has been our approach to the book endings discussed so far.

The problem is that it is not obvious how this *halakhah* fulfils this function, and, in any case, to sum up the *Book of Asseverations* is a challenge. This volume of the *Mishneh torah* covers such disparate laws that it is not easy to

---

[11] See Lenihan, 'St. Francis of Assisi'; Moses, *The Saint and the Sultan*.

[12] The subject of asceticism in Maimonides' writings is a controversial one. See e.g. Schwarzschild, 'Moral Radicalism', and D. Shatz, 'Maimonides' Moral Theory'. We shall not enter this controversy for two reasons: it focuses on attitudes to emotions and desires, whereas the main concern here is the attitude to worldly goods; and it is largely over the extent to which Maimonides' ethical stance changed over his career, and particularly in the *Guide*, whereas our concern is mainly with the *Mishneh torah*.

[13] See below, Ch. 7, on the *Book of Agriculture*.

[14] See 'Laws of Idolatry', 9: 4.   [15] 13: 13.   [16] 8: 13.

say what it is about. As the title, *Book of Asseverations*, indicates, all of the laws it contains concern the consequences of making statements, but statements of very diverse kinds: giving evidence on oath in a court of law and vowing to donate the value of a field to the upkeep of the Temple, to take two examples, are both solemn utterances, but, on the face of it, in a consideration of where to classify them in a practical code of law, that commonality ought not to outweigh their very different circumstances and functions. If, as a contrary example, we look at laws concerning what goes into the mouth rather than what comes out of it, we find that these are placed in different books according to their different types: those occasioned by time, such as fasts and the prohibition on leaven during Passover, are in the *Book of Seasons*; prohibitions to do with the food itself are in the *Book of Holiness*; general dietary advice is in 'Laws of Moral Qualities' in the *Book of Knowledge*; and so on. Yet the diverse kinds of laws concerning asseverations are collected under one title. Noting the difficulty, Twersky remarks, 'The stresses and strains of conceptual arrangement are here illustrated.'[17] But what exactly is the concept?

To be sure, keeping one's solemn word and telling the truth are cardinal values, but so is restraint of appetite, certainly in Maimonides' scheme of things. Indeed, in the *Book of the Commandments*, all the various restrictions on eating, other than those concerning sanctified things such as sacrifices, are grouped together,[18] suggesting that Maimonides did consider them to be conceptually linked. The *Guide* retains the *Book of the Commandments*' grouping of the laws of the *nazir* (who, as mentioned, must refrain from the fruit of the vine) with the laws of forbidden foods, under the rubric of restraint of desire, which makes the link clear. This is of course a very pertinent case, and highlights the deliberate and distinct nature of the principle of classification adopted in the *Book of Asseverations*. Maimonides' departure in the *Mishneh torah* from his consistent line in the *Book of the Commandments* and the *Guide* by classifying the *nazir* according to the aspect of the *making* of vows, rather than that of the *substance* of the vow (i.e. the actual restrictions that the *nazir* undertakes) requires explanation.

That particular question might possibly be answered by referring to Maimonides' mishnaic sources, for 'Laws of Vows' and 'Laws of Naziriteship' are based on Mishnah *Nedarim* and Mishnah *Nazir*, consecutive tractates in Order *Nashim*, but that kind of solution certainly does not apply to our general difficulty for, as Twersky further notes, the other subjects treated in the

---

[17] Twersky, *Introduction to the Code*, 265.
[18] Negative commandments 172–206. The restrictions on eating sacrifices etc. are contained in negative commandments 125–53.

Book of Asseverations are dispersed about the Mishnah. 'Laws of Oaths' is mostly based on Mishnah *Shevuot*, from Order *Nezikin*; and 'Laws of Valuation and Consecrations' is based on Mishnah *Arakhin*, from Order *Kodashim*. What is more, these locations in the Mishnah are not arbitrary but quite understandable, as Maimonides himself explains in the introduction to his *Commentary on the Mishnah*.[19]

By bringing such heterogeneous subjects together in a single book of the *Mishneh torah*, Maimonides put himself in a position in which he was pretty well forced to divide some of them between that book and other books more suitable for the real substance of the laws in question, locations that in some cases correspond more to the mishnaic arrangement. To expand on the kind of heterogeneity already noted, oaths are of several different kinds: some are private, simply statements about the world, or having to do with the assumption of personal obligations and restrictions, while others are public, having to do with proceedings in torts and contract. The *Book of Acquisition*, the *Book of Civil Laws*, and the *Book of Judges* could have provided suitable homes for the laws concerning the latter kinds of oaths, and in fact 'Laws of Oaths' does contain cross-references to these places.

Vows are of two kinds: again, there is a private category, consisting of the assumption of restrictions beyond those imposed by the Torah, while the second category consists of pledges of voluntary sacrifices in the Temple. In this case, Maimonides makes a clean break and announces that the second category will be dealt with elsewhere, in 'Laws of Sacrificial Procedures', in Book 9 of the *Mishneh torah*.[20]

It is not that Maimonides' arrangement has no logic to it; far from it. The *Book of Asseverations* is a fine example of Maimonides' programme in the *Mishneh torah* of bringing together far-flung rabbinic material, 'one of a city and two of a family',[21] and unifying it under legal principles, stresses and strains notwithstanding. The answer to the problem of the deviation from the classification system in the *Guide* might then be that asseveration is a legal category appropriate to a code of law, while restraint of desire is a moral category appropriate to a discussion of the purposes of the law in a work of

---

[19] The explanations in the *Commentary on the Mishnah* are that *Shevuot* is the last of a group of three tractates in Order *Nezikin* that deal with court procedure; *Nedarim* comes into Order *Nashim* ('Women') because a husband has the power to annul his wife's vows, and is followed by *Nazir* because that is a particular instance of such a vow (this pairing is maintained in the *Book of Asseverations*); and *Arakhin* is positioned where it is because after tractates dealing with offerings in kind, it deals with monetary offerings.

[20] 'Laws of Vows', I: 3.

[21] 'Letter to Pinhas of Alexandria', in Maimonides, *Igerot harambam* (trans. Shailat), ii. 440.

philosophy. But that is not all that Maimonides does in the *Mishneh torah*. Take the immediately preceding volume, the *Book of Holiness*, for example. Can 'holiness' in this sense be called a legal category? The volume's sections 'Laws of Forbidden Intercourse' and 'Laws of Forbidden Foods' have in common not legal principles but moral purpose; restraint of desire again. Even the declared theme of that book in the Introduction to the *Mishneh torah*, namely laws that distinguish Israel from the other nations, is hardly a legal one.

That neighbouring example, together with the fact that the grouping in the *Book of Asseverations* is not smooth, indicates that it is probably worth looking for a stronger motivation for it than the fact that it collects laws to do with statements. Moreover, if the book is about the sanctity of asseverations, then the concluding *halakhah* goes off at a tangent, instead of being a peroration summarizing and reinforcing that theme. No rule says that it must conform to such a pattern; perhaps it has no further significance than the admonition it contains. If so, however, it is very much out of context. A more appropriate position for it would appear to be in 'Laws of Valuation and Consecrations', chapter 6, where the rule that a vow to consecrate all one's possessions is valid is found.[22] Were it removed to there, the last *halakhah* of the *Book of Asseverations* would be 'Laws of Valuation and Consecrations', 8: 12, which is about the making of vows in general rather than the moral and social consequences of a particular vow, making it perhaps a more suitable way of rounding off the volume. The apparent tangentiality of the actual concluding *halakhah* here could, however, serve as a prompt to seek a larger dimension—one that might encompass it—of the book as a whole.

Clash of Values

We have thus chalked up two questions about the *Book of Asseverations*: why does Maimonides conclude it with such downright condemnation of the person who consecrates too much of their wealth; and what is its unifying concept?

To this may be added a third question: if consecrating all one's wealth is so damaging, why does the Torah not prevent the damage by outlawing such a vow, or pronouncing it invalid?[23] The aversion that Maimonides expresses is certainly backed by rabbinic sentiment, which finds support in Torah verses, but all this fails to crystallize into a negative commandment.

[22] See n. 2 above.
[23] There is an opinion in the sources that such a vow is not binding, but Maimonides rules against it; see n. 2 above.

This question is particularly pointed for Maimonides, who asserts in the *Guide* that the law aims at the welfare of the body as well as the welfare of the soul. Allowing people to make themselves penniless is conducive neither to the welfare of the individual body nor to that of the body politic, as in fact Maimonides eloquently states in our *halakhah*. To put it another way, in this *halakhah* Maimonides confronts a potential clash within the Torah between the sacred obligation to keep one's word, and the promotion of the physical and moral welfare of the individual and the state. The clash is of course avoidable by refraining from making the vow that gives rise to it, but, besides deploying sheer rhetorical force, how does Maimonides establish a scale of values in the *Mishneh torah* that enables him to contain the contraries within a single system?

We shall attempt to link these questions, and to demonstrate that the final *halakhah* is not just a parting caution, but does express and connect fundamental themes of the *Book of Asseverations*, and reaches back to an even more basic underlying value than truthfulness—hence its urgency.

The Meaning of *Hafla'ah*

One cause of our difficulty with the conceptual basis of the *Book of Asseverations* is that this title does not capture all the nuances of the original Hebrew title, *Sefer hafla'ah*.[24] Although *hafla'ah* can be interpreted to mean 'specification', in the sense of making a clear, definite statement, especially in the context of vows,[25] it has a more general connotation of 'setting apart', and this covers other sub-meanings, such as 'separation',[26] and even 'wonder' (that is, something set apart from one's normal understanding), which 'asseveration' fails to convey. Maimonides' own description of the book in his Introduction to the *Mishneh torah* is as follows: 'I include in it precepts binding on one who has incurred an obligation by utterances, e.g. by taking oaths or making vows.' The Hebrew for 'incurred an obligation' is *asar atsmo*, which more literally means 'bound himself'. The verb *asar* means 'to bind' both literally and figuratively, but in rabbinic discourse it generally means 'to forbid'.[27]

---

[24] The *Oxford English Dictionary* defines asseveration as '1. The action of asseverating; solemn affirmation, emphatic assertion, positive declaration, avouchment. 2. That which is asseverated; a solemn or emphatic declaration or assertion. 3. Emphatic confirmation of a statement; a word or phrase used to express confirmation; an oath.'

[25] See e.g. BT *Naz.* 34a.

[26] See e.g. Exod. 9: 4 and Tobias ben Eliezer, *Pesikta zutarta*, which gives a reference to Exod. 8: 18.

[27] Not always, of course. *Asur* can mean bound in the sense of incarcerated. Modern

With both of these words, *hafla'ah* and *asar*, Maimonides displays great cunning. He conveys the idea of uttering specific, binding statements, but also the idea of things set apart or forbidden.[28]

Continuation of the *Book of Holiness*

The latter idea connects Book 6 to Book 5, the *Book of Holiness*, or *Sefer kedushah*, to give it its original title. The essential meaning of the Hebrew for holy, *kadosh*, is separate, set apart, something to which Maimonides draws attention in his introduction to the *Mishneh torah*, where he describes the content of the *Book of Holiness* as being the means whereby 'the Omnipresent sanctified us and separated us from the nations'. The two first sections of that book are *Hilkhot isurei biah*, 'Laws of Forbidden Intercourse', and *Hilkhot ma'akhalot asurot*, 'Laws of Forbidden Foods', the root of the word for 'forbidden' in both cases being *asar*. *Hafla'ah*, then, is almost synonymous with *kedushah*,[29] the implication being that Book 6 is a continuation of Book 5, and is about holiness, in the specific sense of restraint of physical appetite.

That being so, there is more harmony than at first appears between the classification scheme in the *Mishneh torah* and that of the *Guide*. As mentioned above, in the latter, Maimonides classes 'Laws of Forbidden Foods', from the *Book of Holiness*, together with vows and the *nazir*. He explains this as follows:

The thirteenth class comprises the *commandments* concerned with the prohibition of certain foods and what is connected therewith. These are the commandments that we have enumerated in the "Laws of Forbidden Foods". The [command-

---

Hebrew uses *asur* for 'forbidden' and *asir* for a prisoner in gaol (as opposed to a prisoner of war), both from the same root.

[28] Klein, *Comprehensive Etymological Dictionary* gives two meanings for *hafla'ah*: 'surprise, astonishment', and 'distinction'. He references the verb *pilei* for which he gives 'to distinguish, make special (said of a vow)', and lists the phrase *lefalei neder* which he translates as 'to make a special vow', citing Lev. 22: 21, Num. 15: 3, and Num. 15: 8, as well as Lev. 27: 2 (*yafli neder*), and Num. 6: 2 (*yafli lindor neder*). Jastrow, *Dictionary*, also gives two meanings: 'distinction, peculiarity' and 'distinct and solemn specification of a vow'. The dual meaning here is well captured by two of the classical commentators' paraphrases of *lefalei neder* in Lev. 22: 21. Rashi gives *lehafrish bediburo*, 'to set apart by his word'; Ibn Ezra gives *lefaresh*, 'to be explicit' (also, in other contexts, 'to explain', 'to interpret'), which is from the same root (*p-r-sh*) as Rashi's *lehafrish*.

[29] In his *New Concordance to the Bible*, Even-Shoshan states that the verb *pilei*, from which the verbal noun *hafla'ah* derives, is equivalent to *hikdish* (from the same root as *kadosh*), meaning 'to set apart' or 'to consecrate'. Under this sense he lists Lev. 22: 21 and 27: 2, and Num. 6: 2, 15: 3, and 15: 8 (corresponding to Klein's references—see previous note), all of them verses concerning the making of vows.

ments concerning] vows and the state of the Nazirites belong to this class. The purpose of all this is . . . to put an end to the lusts and licentiousness manifested in seeking what is most pleasurable and to taking the desire for food and drink as an end.[30]

This passage highlights the moral aspect of vows and the *nazir*, rather than the aspect of asseveration, but in fact both aspects are covered by the title *hafla'ah*, and we suggest that the dual meaning is intended. Vows and naziriteship are collected together in the *Book of Asseverations* not only because they both arise from making statements, but also because they have a common purpose.

As for 'Laws of Oaths', the commandments it contains are classed in the *Guide* in the first class, which 'comprises the commandments that are fundamental opinions':[31] 'To this class also belongs the commandment addressed to us to swear in His name and the prohibition addressed to us against breaking one's oath and swearing in vain. All this has a manifest reason; for it is intended to glorify Him, may he be exalted. Accordingly these are actions necessitating a belief in His greatness.'[32]

So far, we have only exacerbated our difficulty, for if the *Book of Asseverations* has the theme of self-imposed restrictions and is in that respect a continuation of the *Book of Holiness*, why mix that up with other kinds of declarations, such as evidence under oath in court? Why indeed make up a separate book at all? Why not have a fourth section of the *Book of Holiness* ('Laws of Self-Imposed Restrictions' might be its title) and consign the other matters to more appropriate places? For example, if, as explained in the *Guide*, the commandments in 'Laws of Oaths' belong to the class of fundamental opinions, would it not have made sense to include them (at least their theoretical aspects if not all their applications) in 'Laws of the Foundations of the Torah', where such fundamentals are discussed? It is not an answer to say that Maimonides may have conceived this notion of oaths only after he composed the *Mishneh torah* (the *Guide* being a later work). In the *Book of the Commandments* the commandment to swear in God's name (positive commandment 7) is grouped with commandments to do with basic principles of the relationship of human beings to God. This is another example of the *Mishneh torah* departing from a classification that is consistent between the *Book of the Commandments* and the *Guide*. Grouping oaths with fundamental doctrines in the *Guide* was not an innovation but a reversion to the method of a work written in preparation for the *Mishneh torah*.[33] Why the change in

---

[30] *Guide* iii. 35 (p. 537).   [31] Ibid. (p. 535).   [32] *Guide* iii. 36 (p. 538).
[33] For more on the *Guide*'s similarity to the *Book of the Commandments* in its treatment of

between? In this instance, the juxtaposition with the *Book of Holiness* does not help us.

It seems that the relationship between the *Book of Holiness* and the *Book of Asseverations* is less straightforward than we have so far supposed, or at least that the apparent continuity between them is not sufficient to solve the problem of the latter's apparent disunity.

Finding a solution will require us to put the *Book of Asseverations* and its final *halakhah* into a wider context, and to see how they fit into the *Mishneh torah* as a whole, and particularly how they relate to the first book of the *Mishneh torah* and its conceptual fountainhead, the *Book of Knowledge*. This will be done on two levels. We shall first trace explicit connections, and then look at more subtle references revealed by an understanding of underlying structures.

Oaths, Vows, and the Middle Path

The final *halakhah* of the *Book of Asseverations* clearly echoes 'Laws of Moral Qualities', 5: 12, which states: 'A person is forbidden to declare all his property derelict or devote it to the sanctuary and thus become a public charge . . . he should make it his aim to employ his capital successfully.' This tells us that giving up all one's worldly goods is unethical because it is socially irresponsible, more or less the idea with which we started. Other links between the *Book of Asseverations* and 'Laws of Moral Qualities' suggest a more inward dimension. 'Laws of Moral Qualities', chapter 3, which is about the undesirability of asceticism, states in its first *halakhah*:

Whoever persists in such a course is termed a sinner. Of the Nazirite, it is said 'He [the priest] shall make atonement for him, for the sin that he committed against the soul' [Num. 6: 11]. On this text, the Sages comment, 'The Nazirite who only abstained from wine stands in need of an atonement, how much more so one who deprives himself of all legitimate enjoyments'. The Sages accordingly enjoined us that we should only refrain from that which the Torah has expressly withdrawn from our use. And no one should, by vows and oaths, inhibit to himself the use of things permitted. 'Do not the prohibitions of the Torah', say our sages, 'suffice thee, that thou addest others for thyself?'

Compare the conclusions of 'Laws of Vows' and 'Laws of Naziriteship'. First, 'Laws of Vows':

the commandments, and the contrast with the *Mishneh torah*, see Gillis, *Reading Maimonides' Mishneh Torah*, 309–13.

Whoever makes a vow in order to discipline his moral disposition and to improve his conduct displays commendable zeal and is worthy of praise. For instance, one who is a glutton and forbids to himself meat for a year or two; or one who is addicted to wine and forbids it to himself for a long time, or at least binds himself never to become inebriated; or one who runs after bribes in his eagerness to amass wealth and binds himself to accept no presents or to derive no benefit from the people of his country; or one who is proud of his good looks and vows to become a Nazirite; or anyone else who makes vows of this kind. All such vows are ways of serving God, and of them and their like the Sages have said, 'Vows are a fence around self-restraint'.[34] Yet in spite of the fact that vows are ways of serving God, one should not multiply prohibitory vows nor employ them regularly, but should rather abstain from such things as should properly be abstained from, without making vows to do so.

Indeed, the Sages have said, 'Whosoever makes a vow is as though he had built a high place'.[35] If he nevertheless transgresses and vows, it his duty to seek absolution from the vow so that it might not become a snare before him. This, however, applies only to vows of prohibition. In the case of vows of consecration, it is one's duty to fulfil them and to seek absolution from them only under constraint, for Scripture says, 'I will pay my vows unto the Lord' [Ps. 116: 18].[36]

Now here is the conclusion to 'Laws of Naziriteship':

Whosoever says, 'I intend to become a Nazirite if I do', or 'do not do, a certain thing', or something similar, is a wicked person, and this kind of Naziriteship is accounted the Naziriteship of the wicked. On the other hand, whosoever vows to God in the way of holiness, does well and is praiseworthy. Of such a one Scripture says, 'His consecration unto God is upon his head . . . he is holy unto the Lord' [Num. 6: 7–8]. Indeed Scripture considers him the equal of a prophet, for it says, 'And I raised up of your sons for prophets, and of your young men for Nazirites' [Amos 2: 11].

We see in these three passages that whether vows and naziriteship are good or bad is entirely a question of motivation. In 'Laws of Moral Qualities', Maimonides asserts that religious devotion is not to be confused with a morbid tendency to abnegation, of which vows of abstinence may be a symptom. At the end of 'Laws of Vows', he nevertheless recognizes the merit of someone with an essentially healthy personality using such vows to counter some particular fault, with the reservation that such reformation is preferably to be achieved without making vows (a reservation that will be of importance later on in our discussion). Similarly, someone who takes the wrong cue from the

---

[34] Mishnah *Avot* 3: 17.
[35] i.e. a forbidden place of sacrifice outside the Temple. See BT *Ned.* 60b.
[36] 'Laws of Vows', 13: 25.

Torah's prohibitions and assumes a vow of naziriteship as a form of asceticism earns the Sages' reprimand, and treating naziriteship lightly is considered wicked, but someone who becomes a *nazir* in a spirit of holiness is close to the very highest status to which a human being can aspire, that of a prophet.[37]

The same spirit pervades the *Book of Asseverations'* concluding *halakhot*. Having got our bearings by looking at vows and the *nazir*, we can appreciate that the book's final *halakhah* is a continuation of its penultimate one:

> Although vows of consecration, devotion, and valuation are matters of religious duty, and it is fitting for a person to conduct himself in these things in such a manner as to subdue his inclination and avoid avarice, thus fulfilling the command of the Prophets, 'Honour the Lord with thy substance' [Prov. 3: 9], nevertheless if he never makes any such vows, it does not matter at all, and Scripture itself bears witness to this when it says, 'But if thou shalt forbear to vow, it shall be no sin in thee' [Deut. 23: 23].[38]

The Torah does not demand vows—they are in fact preferably avoided, as we learned from the end of 'Laws of Vows'. In the case of a commandment of the Torah, it is possible to apply the principle 'from doing something out of ulterior motives, one will eventually come to do it out of the right motives': performance of the commandment will ultimately yield a beneficial effect on the character and itself cure the faulty motivation.[39] In the case of vows, this is apparently not so. Motivation is crucial.

Vows and Piety

This background enables us to read the final *halakhah* of the *Book of Asseverations* as being about an inward state of mind as much as about social irresponsibility. What we have seen in 'Laws of Moral Qualities' puts the spotlight on a key phrase: 'Such an act is not piety but folly.' 'Piety' (*ḥasidut*) has a specific meaning in Maimonides' moral system. The basic commandment in 'Laws

---

[37] Although *nazir* is used in Hebrew to mean a Christian monk, being a *nazir* in Judaism does not involve poverty (nor chastity or obedience, for that matter). A wealthy *nazir* is entirely conceivable.   [38] 'Laws of Valuation and Consecration', 8: 13.

[39] Maimonides applies this principle particularly to Torah study (see 'Laws of Torah Study', 3: 5, 'Laws of Repentance', 10: 5). In *Lam. Rabbah* proem 2, it is cited in the name of Rav Huna concerning Torah study only, but in the Babylonian Talmud (*Pes.* 50b, *Sot.* 22b and 47a, *San.* 105b, *Hor.* 10b, *Arakh.* 17b) it is cited in the name of Rav Yehudah in the name of Rav, in a formulation closer to that of Maimonides but concerning both Torah study and performance of the commandments. It seems likely that at least in 'Laws of Repentance' Maimonides intended 'Torah' to include performance of the commandments of the Torah, and not only study.

of Moral Qualities' is to imitate God. This means imitating the attributes of God's actions in nature; that is to say (since God has no attributes) the characteristics we should ascribe to what we observe in nature were such actions to proceed from a human being.[40] 'Even as God is called gracious, so be thou gracious; even as He is called merciful, so be thou merciful; even as He is called holy, so be thou holy.'[41] The characteristic that these attributes share is that they exemplify the middle path, the mean between excess and deficiency. Holiness in its core meaning for Maimonides is restraint of appetite. But restraint is not to be taken to excess. Genuine holiness must be a middle path between self-indulgence and self-denial.

The line that perfectly bisects these extremes is the way of the wise, the philosopher (ḥakham), but it is very difficult to maintain. It is therefore advisable to err slightly on one side of the mean, the less selfish side, to counter the normal human tendency to self-centredness.

This is the way of the pious (ḥasid).[42] It is also the way of the Torah. As already mentioned in Chapter 2, Maimonides explains in *Eight Chapters*, chapter 4, that the commandments of the Torah are designed to inculcate a modicum of extra self-restraint in order to reinforce adherence to the mean. The compulsory restrictions of the *Book of Holiness* embody this approach. But there will be those for whom this is not enough, who diagnose their own characters as being too inclined to one extreme for the commandments by themselves to be a sufficient corrective. Such people will want to take the remedy that Maimonides prescribes in 'Laws of Moral Qualities' for distorted personalities: they should temporarily distort themselves in the other direction by going to the opposite extreme and thereby make themselves straight.[43] This form of *extra* piety is the subject of the *Book of Asseverations*. A person who realizes that he or she is prone to gluttony will make a vow of abstinence; someone who wishes to correct a miserly disposition will vow extra contributions to the Temple; someone who wishes to detach themselves from worldliness altogether and assume greater seriousness in their service of God will become a *nazir*. The ultimate aim, though, should be to regain the middle path, for that is 'the way of God'.[44]

Extra restrictions or obligations undertaken in this spirit are praiseworthy.[45] To pursue the medical image Maimonides uses in 'Laws of Moral

---

[40] See *Guide* i. 54 (pp. 125–6).   [41] *Sifrei* on Deut. 11: 22.

[42] On the varying use that Maimonides makes of the terms ḥakham and ḥasid, see Kasher, '"Hakham", "Hasid", and "Tov"'.

[43] See 'Laws of Moral Qualities', 2: 2.   [44] See ibid. 1: 7.

[45] See 'Laws of Vows', 13: 23; 'Laws of Nazirites', 10: 12; 'Laws of Valuation and Consecrations', 8: 12.

Qualities', they are like drugs that are necessary for the sick but a risk to the healthy. In any event, they are not good in themselves.

Understanding of this background also helps to bolster the *a fortiori* argument in 'Laws of Valuation and Consecrations', 8: 13, and helps to explain why that argument forms the conclusion to the *Book of Asseverations*. The commandments of the Torah are meant to keep people close to the middle path. This presumably applies to sacrifices as much as to other commandments. The prescribed sacrifices train individuals in generosity, keeping those who bring them slightly to one side of the desirable middle path between prodigality and meanness. Some people will feel that they need to give a little more in order to achieve this object, but someone who consecrates all they have defeats the object entirely; rather than improving his or her character this person spoils it. Sacrifices are not a tax paid to God, who does not need them, but a means of developing a correct attitude towards the material world, an attitude that should apply in all circumstances. So one is actually not at liberty to dispose of one's property as one sees fit; one must always have regard to the effect on one's moral character. The attempt made above at refuting Maimonides' argument thus fails. At least within his system, it is logical to argue on the basis of the Torah's stipulation of moderate spending on compulsory sacrifices that voluntary sacrifices should not be overdone.[46] Moreover, the closing proof-text, 'Every man shall give as he is able, according to the blessing of the Lord thy God which He hath given thee',[47] puts the whole subject of oaths, vows, and consecrations into perspective, serving as a reminder that giving to God, as it were, is only worthwhile insofar as it brings us truly closer to the God who gives to us.

'Honour the Lord'

This gives us the beginnings of an answer to the question of what unifying idea underlies the different subjects in the *Book of Asseverations*. In chapter 3 of 'Laws of Moral Qualities', the *halakhah* cited above about the sinfulness of self-denial immediately precedes the exhortation: 'A man should direct all his thoughts and activities to the knowledge of God, alone.'[48] The implication is that not only should the satisfaction of material needs not be pursued for its

---

[46] It is still difficult to understand why the case of voluntary consecrations should be considered stricter in this respect than sacrifices imposed by the Torah. Possibly the argument hinges on the statement at the end of 'Laws of Vows' (13: 25) to the effect that from the point of view of the Torah it is preferable not to make vows at all. That being so, if one does make a vow of consecration, one should certainly not exceed the Torah's guideline for sacrifices.

[47] Deut. 16: 17.   [48] 'Laws of Moral Qualities', 3: 2.

own sake, as Maimonides goes on to discuss, but that the denial of such needs is equally distracting from the overriding aim of acquiring knowledge of God. In 'Laws of Moral Qualities',[49] the prohibition on divesting oneself of all one's wealth and the directive to exercise good judgement in managing one's financial affairs are part of a series of instructions to the *talmid ḥakham*, the scholar, which culminates in the very next *halakhah* in his becoming the person 'of whom the verse says "Thou art my servant in Israel in whom I will be glorified" [Isa. 49: 3]'. Self-denial and pauperism result in inward distancing from God and outward dishonouring of him, achieving the opposite of the purpose of swearing in God's name. The *Guide*, as already mentioned, states that purpose as 'to glorify Him, may he be exalted', while 'Laws of Oaths' similarly states: 'for the oath in his great and holy name is a form of worship, and it is a great adornment and sanctification to swear in his name'.[50]

The different subjects of the *Book of Asseverations* can now be seen to hang together better, and the underlying themes we have detected find expression in the closing *halakhah*. Consecrating all one's possessions is not just socially damaging; it betokens inward moral and intellectual perversion. Nor does it redound to the glory of God. Both these concerns—moral self-correction and the glorification of God—also characterize Maimonides' treatment of vows and oaths in the *Book of Asseverations* generally. The penultimate *halakhah* of 'Laws of Valuation and Consecrations' cited above expresses these two dimensions in saying 'it is fitting for a person to conduct himself in these things in such a manner as to subdue his inclination and avoid avarice, thus fulfilling the command of the Prophets, "Honour the Lord with thy substance".' Someone who gives away all their wealth, we may take it, neither improves their character nor honours the Lord. No motivation can justify it.

Structural Hints

So much for the explicit connections branching out from the ending of the *Book of Asseverations*. Consideration of underlying structures in the *Mishneh torah* reveals other connections that supplement what we have discovered so far. A feature of the *Mishneh torah*'s structure is that the ten chapters of its very first section, 'Laws of the Foundations of the Torah', form a template for its first ten books (see Appendix). On that basis, Books 5 and 6 are keyed to chapters 5 and 6 of that opening section.

The fifth chapter of 'Laws of the Foundations of the Torah' is about holiness in the sense of sanctification of the name of God (*kidush hashem*)

[49] Ch. 5. [50] II: 1.

by bearing witness to God's existence and unity, through martyrdom when circumstances unavoidably demand it, but more usually through exemplary manners and conduct. The chapter also covers the negative commandment prohibiting profanation of the name of God, but this is discussed as a corollary of sanctification: someone who fails to undergo martyrdom when it is demanded profanes the name of God, as does a person of religion whose conduct is disreputable.

The sixth chapter is about avoiding the desecration of the name of God. It forbids causing damage to anything associated with God, specifically erasure of God's written name, and vandalism of scriptural books and of the Temple and its fixtures.

The association of the fifth chapter of 'Laws of the Foundations of the Torah', with the *Book of Holiness* begins with the word 'holy'. It is an association that deepens the connection between the inner and outer dimensions of holiness.[51] It was mentioned above that Maimonides views the commandments in the *Book of Holiness* as distinguishing the Jewish people from the nations. The sanctification of God's name has in common with this the fact that it is the first commandment in the *Mishneh torah* that is specifically addressed to 'the House of Israel'. Non-Jews are enjoined to recognize God and avoid idolatry, but not to undergo martyrdom or otherwise sanctify the name of God.[52] Moreover, the ideal scholar described at the end of the chapter is characterized by being set apart: he is gracious to people, but not overly familiar with them, rather withdrawing, 'occupied with the Torah, wrapped in *tsitsit* and crowned with tefillin'. Self-restraint is his hallmark—the kind of self-restraint in which the *Book of Holiness* provides training.

On the negative side, the profanation of God's name comes about not just in the extreme case of failure to submit to martyrdom, but also through the everyday conduct of someone who treats the commandments with contempt, deriding them and transgressing them provocatively, while sanctification of the name arises from performance of the commandments without ulterior motives, for the sake of God.[53] Similarly, as we saw in the previous chapter, the *Book of Holiness* ends with the idea of not performing the commandments perfunctorily and with disdain, but respectfully, mindful of the God who commanded them. In these various ways, the *Book of Holiness* is linked to the fifth chapter of 'Laws of the Foundations of the Torah'.

---

[51] On the concept of holiness in Maimonides, see Seeskin, 'Holiness as an Ethical Ideal'.

[52] The exclusion of non-Jews from the scope of this commandment is given greater emphasis in the *Book of the Commandments*, positive commandment 9.

[53] See 'Laws of the Foundations of the Torah', 5: 10.

The affinity of the *Book of Asseverations* with the sixth chapter of 'Laws of the Foundations of the Torah' (about the desecration of God's name) is expressed in the commandments that form the subjects of the book's first section, 'Laws of Oaths'. Three out of the five commandments discussed here directly concern God's name: not to swear in his name falsely; not to bear his name in vain; to swear in his name truthfully. The other two (not to deny having someone else's property in your possession, and not to deny a financial debt), although they do not include mention of 'the name' in the listing at the beginning of the book, do in fact also relate to oaths sworn invoking it. The underlying theme of 'Laws of Oaths' can therefore be said to be the same as the theme of chapter 6 of 'Laws of the Foundations of the Torah', namely avoidance of desecration of the name of God. This theme is very much stressed in the final chapter of 'Laws of Oaths', where Maimonides goes so far as to state that swearing falsely is something one should be wary of 'more than any other transgression'[54] and that it involves 'profanation of the sacrosanct name, which is the greatest of sins'.[55] So while the subject of oaths is not actually located in 'Laws of the Foundations of the Torah', as the *Guide*'s characterization of oaths as 'intended to glorify Him, may He be exalted' implies that it perhaps should be, 'Laws of Oaths' is related to that opening section structurally, as though deriving from it.

The *Book of Holiness* and the *Book of Asseverations* are thus paired in the same way as the fifth and sixth chapters of 'Laws of the Foundations of the Torah', representing the positive and negative sides of holiness: sanctification and avoidance of desecration.

'The Name'

Thus far, we have emphasized the moral aspects of asseverations, but these structural features add an intellectual layer. To follow this, it is necessary to examine more closely what Maimonides means by 'the name' and 'desecration of the name'.

The first time we encounter 'the name' in the *Mishneh torah* is in the context of the pursuit of scientific knowledge. In 'Laws of the Foundations of the Torah', we are told that there is a commandment to love God, and that the way to fulfil this commandment is through contemplation of nature, in which God's infinite wisdom is reflected, leading to a desire 'to know the great name'.[56] 'The name' here is, in effect, the laws of nature. Since God is

---

[54] 'Laws of Oaths', 12: 1. [55] Ibid. 12: 2.
[56] 'Laws of the Foundations of the Torah', 2: 1–2.

unknowable in himself, that is all the knowledge of God to be had. Even to state the fundamental doctrine of God's unity conveys no positive knowledge, since the unity of God has nothing in common with our normal conception of unity.[57] We can, however, approach the idea of that unity by understanding the regular unifying principles behind nature's diverse and changing appearances.

In 'Laws of Moral Qualities', we come across the phrase 'the names', which refers to the manifestation of God in the very plurality of natural phenomena, to be understood not through objectification as scientific knowledge but through subjective absorption as rules of conduct:

> And we are commanded to walk in these middle ways, and they are the good and straight ways, as it says 'And thou shalt walk in His ways.' This is explicitly how they understood this commandment: 'As he is called gracious, so you be gracious; as he is called merciful; so you be merciful; as he is called holy, so you be holy', and in this way the prophets called God by all those epithets: patient, very kind, righteous, straight, perfect, mighty, strong, and so forth, to inform us that these are the good and straight ways, and a person must train himself in them and assimilate in accordance with his ability . . .
>
> And because these names by which the creator is called are the middle path that we must follow, this way is called 'the way of God'.[58]

What does it mean to call God by these names? The *Guide* glosses this for us:

> Accordingly, whenever one of His actions is apprehended, the attribute from which this action proceeds is predicated of Him, may He be exalted, and the name deriving from that action is applied to Him. For instance, one apprehends the kindness of His governance in the production of the embryos of living beings, the bringing of various faculties in existence in them and in those who rear things after birth . . . Now actions of this kind proceed from us only after we feel a certain affection and compassion, and this is the meaning of mercy.[59]

According to this, the names of God are our subjective interpretations of natural phenomena, which we are supposed to adopt as guides to the middle path.

'The name' and 'desecration of the name' are thus not just of ritual significance: they carry overtones of intellectual and moral health and degeneracy, and of the spread or contraction of the awareness of God in the world. What is more, most people do not follow Maimonides' prescription: they do not study physics, and they do not consider the moral significance of natural

---

[57] See 'Laws of the Foundations of the Torah', 1: 7 and 2: 10.
[58] 'Laws of Moral Qualities', 1: 5.   [59] *Guide* i. 54 (p. 125).

phenomena. They are mostly influenced by the society around them, and by those to whom they look as models. After his exposition of the doctrine of the mean in chapters 1–5 of 'Laws of Moral Qualities', in chapter 6 Maimonides stresses the need to keep the company of the righteous and to live in a virtuous community. Chapters 5 of both 'Laws of the Foundations of the Torah' and 'Laws of Moral Qualities' end on the theme of the religious scholar as an example to others; virtuous conduct on his part sanctifies the name and leads to the glorification of God.

Given these significances of 'the name', the sixth chapter of 'Laws of the Foundations of the Torah' can be taken to refer not just to erasure of the written name of God, its ostensible subject, but to the eclipse of the knowledge of God.[60] In this light, 'Laws of Valuation and Consecrations', 8: 13 is seen to concern not just appropriate management of one's financial affairs, or even adherence to the middle path, but also 'the name'. Maimonides is not specific about the motivation of the person who consecrates all their wealth. He gives certain hints and leaves the rest to the reader's imagination. The main hint is the word *ḥasidut*, piety.

Poverty Will Not Buy Divine Favour

In the comparison with the passage from 'Laws of Moral Qualities' above, this word was understood to refer to precautions and corrective measures taken to ensure adherence to the mean, so that 'not piety but foolishness' would mean a dangerous overdose of such moral medicine. But it is possible to understand Maimonides as meaning here that to consecrate all one's worldly wealth is not a matter of excess piety, of over-motivation, but of wrong motivation. It perhaps indicates a fundamentally diseased mentality that sees charity, consecrations, and self-denial as ways of warding off forces of evil or bribing forces of good.

In Maimonides there are simply no such shortcuts to grace. Just as idol worship begins in seeing created beings as worthy of worship in themselves,[61] here there is a mistaken estimation of the place of worldly wealth in the scheme of things. Just as wealth is not an end in itself, neither is poverty. Nobody wins points merely for self-deprivation. Nor is repudiation of the world as evil, another possible motivation for divesting oneself of material possessions, compatible with Maimonides' assertion that creation is 'indubitably a good'.[62] What counts is having a balanced temperament that

---

[60] Quite amazingly, this name refers to the God of Aristotle as well as the God of Abraham, Isaac, and Jacob! See above, Chs. 1–2.
[61] See 'Laws of Idolatry', 1: 1 and 2: 1.
[62] *Guide* iii. 25 (p. 506).

facilitates fulfilment of a human being's sole purpose, which is to acquire knowledge of God, going from 'the names' to 'the name'. (Even that is not quite an end in itself, for from knowledge will flow a disposition to kindness, righteousness, and justice, as we are told at the end of the *Guide*.) The moral deviation is a product of intellectual error, and is liable to be a multiplier of it, and that is an erasure of God's name. Even if the motives of the person in question are deep and sincere, and they feel that their spiritual welfare requires being stripped of worldly goods, they may not pursue such ends at the expense of others. This would be an example of the kind of conflict between the individual and society discussed in the Introduction, but again we stress that the conflict is not just on the material plane: the act of social vandalism is also an act of intellectual vandalism.

Maimonides' harsh language in 'Laws of Valuation and Consecrations', 8: 13 can now be better understood. Someone who deliberately impoverishes themselves deserves condemnation on social and economic grounds alone. When they do so for supposedly religious reasons, they inwardly harbour an erroneous concept of God and outwardly profane God's name. They are morally deviant in that they are not merciful as God is merciful, either to themselves or to others. They misrepresent to themselves and to others one of God's 'names', and so do not deserve mercy. Moreover, the obligation to imitate God is another factor that bolsters the *a fortiori* argument that the requirement of moderation in obligatory sacrifices implies an even greater requirement of moderation in voluntary sacrifices.

Comparision with Torah Study

Both the tone and the content of the *halakhot* that conclude the *Book of Asseverations* bear comparison with the no less vehement terms in which Maimonides condemns anyone who abandons a livelihood and becomes dependent on charity in order to study Torah in 'Laws of Torah Study'.[63] There, he explicitly charges such a person with profanation of the name, and there, as here, the condemnation is both on the intellectual plane, such conduct being an abuse of the Torah, and on the moral and social plane, since it is liable to lead to a life of crime. Moreover, there too we find an allusion to what constitutes true piety: Maimonides cites the 'way of the pious of old' (*midat ḥasidim harishonim*) who would earn their living by labour.

There is probably much to be learned from this comparison, but suffice it

[63] 3: 10–11. See Rappoport, '"The Virtue of He Who Earns His Living from His Labour"' (Heb.). See also 'Laws of Gifts to the Poor', 10: 18; *Commentary on the Mishnah*, Avot 4: 7.

to say for the present that if Maimonides expresses such a view in the realm of intellectual development, it is not surprising that he should express a similar view in what he regarded as the less important (though, it must be stressed, not unimportant) realm of ritual.

Conclusion: Inner Virtue and the Glory of God

What we see in this analysis of the end of the *Book of Asseverations* is how extraordinarily closely woven are the moral, political, and metaphysical strands of Maimonides' thought, and how deftly the *Mishneh torah* moves between the law's interiority and its exteriority. To coerce desire and to honour the Lord are part and parcel of the same thing, and if we perceive this, we can perceive how the diverse subjects of the *Book of Asseverations* are conceptually united. The verse on which the book ends, 'Every man shall give as he is able, according to the blessing of the Lord thy God which He hath given thee', gains overtones of the way in which, in general, a human being turns towards the God from which he derives his existence, striving morally and intellectually to 'know the great name', 'according to his ability' (*kefi koho*) as Maimonides ubiquitously qualifies that endeavour. The separateness reflected in the very titles of *Sefer kedushah* and *Sefer hafla'ah* (*Holiness* and *Asseverations*), as well as that delineated by the Torah and by the commandment to sanctify the name of God, is not an ontological separateness, but an acquired one.

What, then, would Maimonides have made of St Francis? We shall have to remain disappointingly non-committal about this question. It is all too easy to delude oneself into believing one has the key to what a great and influential thinker would say about anyone and anything at all. What can be said is that it is possible to trace a nuanced discussion in the *Mishneh torah* of the quest for truth versus the demands of worldly, social existence, of piety versus what masquerades as piety, of what sanctifies the name and what profanes it, of the particular and the universal, a discussion in which the next book, the *Book of Agriculture*, represents something of a countercurrent to the trend of thought at the end of the *Book of Asseverations*.

Summary

'Laws of Valuation and Consecration', 8: 13, appears to be a straightforward piece of practical wisdom: do not consecrate all your wealth and become a burden to others. Both this concluding *halakhah* and the *Book of Asseverations* as a whole, however, are problematic. The *halakhah* seems excessively sharp in expression, and also out of place, removed from the legal ruling that gives rise to it. As for the *Book of Asseverations*, the difficulty lies in finding the concept that might unite its diverse topics.

The connotation of 'separateness' of the word *hafla'ah* provides a clue to the answers to these difficulties. The *Book of Asseverations* is a continuation of the *Book of Holiness*, the essential meaning of 'holiness' (*kedushah*) being 'separateness'. The *Book of Holiness* contains laws that educate in detachment from physical appetites, thereby safeguarding the middle path between extremes that represents moral virtue. The *Book of Asseverations* provides for those who wish to undertake extra restrictions in order to curb some extreme tendency with the aim of returning to the middle path. Consecrating all one's wealth, as the embracing of an extreme, is not only a social wrong but morally self-destructive. It is also evidence of intellectual error. The person in question seems to imagine that consecrations in themselves bring a person closer to God, when the only means of closeness is the acquisition of knowledge, for which moral virtue is a precondition. Rather than fulfilment of the command 'Honour the Lord with thy substance', the result of deliberate self-impoverishment is dishonour and the desecration of God's name—hence Maimonides' vehement tone.

The *Book of Asseverations* is largely about undertakings made invoking the name of God. In the *Guide* (and also within the *Book of Asseverations* itself) the purpose of swearing in God's name is stated to be the glorification of God. The structural scheme whereby the ten chapters of 'Laws of the Foundations of the Torah' form a template for the first ten books of the *Mishneh torah* supports the view that this represents the unifying idea of the *Book of Asseverations*. The *Book of Holiness* corresponds to chapter 5 of the 'Laws', about sanctification of God's name, while the *Book of Asseverations* corresponds to chapter 6, about avoiding desecration of the name. In the conclusion of 'Laws of Moral Qualities', which itself warns of the general undesirability of vows of abstinence, the glorification of God's name is seen to be the final purpose of moral perfection as well.

Through these connections, Maimonides unites the *Book of Asseverations*' technical concerns and moral themes under a single governing idea. Desecration of God's name means moral and intellectual degradation as well as disregard for God's honour. The final *halakhah* is not just about financial misjudgement but carries overtones of both outward and inward desecration.

SEVEN

AGRICULTURE
Sanctifying All Human Beings

The Text at the Middle of the *Mishneh Torah*: 'All Those Who Come into the World'

The seventh volume of the *Mishneh torah* is the *Book of Agriculture* (literally, the *Book of Seeds* (*Zera'im*)), which deals with laws concerning agricultural issues. It comprises seven sections: 'Laws of Diverse Kinds', 'Laws of Gifts to the Poor', 'Laws of Heave Offerings', 'Laws of Tithes', 'Laws of the Second Tithe and the Fourth Year's Fruit', 'Laws of First Fruits', and 'Laws of the Sabbatical Year and the Jubilee'. The final chapter of this last section deals largely with the special restrictions of the Levites concerning land-owning, and other issues connected with the cities given over to them, in lieu of inheriting portions of the Land itself.[1] In the *Guide* Maimonides comments:

> With regard to the commandments that we have enumerated in 'Laws Concerning the Sabbatical Year and the Jubilee', some of them are meant to lead to pity and help for all men[2]—as the text has it: 'That the poor of thy people may eat; and what they leave the beasts of the field shall eat', and so on [Exod. 23: 11]—and are meant to make the earth more fertile and stronger through letting it lie fallow. Others are meant to lead towards benevolence toward slaves and poor people.[3]

This explanation helps provide context for the argument we will develop in this chapter, about the text at the end of the *Book of Agriculture*. It also explains why laws concerning charity ('gifts to the poor') are included in this volume.[4]

The precise position within the *Mishneh torah* of the text we will study in this chapter is highly suggestive. While we are not devotees of the sort of Maimonidean numerology indulged in by Leo Strauss, sometimes it is simply too striking to be ignored. As noted many times in this study, the *Mishneh*

---

[1] Translations from this book are taken, with emendations, from Isaac Klein's translation of the *Book of Agriculture* (Yale Judaica Series).
[2] Arab.: *al-nas*; Schwarz translates: *benei adam*.
[3] *Guide* iii. 39 (p. 553).   [4] See below, Ch. 12, on 'Laws of Slaves'.

torah comprises fourteen books. The precise mid-point of the work, then, is the end of Book 7 (the volume under consideration here). This (and only this) book is itself divided into precisely seven sections. Devoted to laws relating to agricultural matters, Book 7 is brought to a close by a section with messianic overtones, since it deals with matters which will only obtain after the coming of the messiah: 'Laws of the Sabbatical Year and Jubilee'. This seventh section of the seventh book is itself divided into thirteen chapters. The thirteenth chapter is, as it happens, divided into thirteen paragraphs.[5]

As long as we are talking about numbers, the number seven is not only a standard typological number in Judaism, it is also half of fourteen, a number of which Maimonides was particularly fond. As Aryeh Tepper notes, 'Fourteen is, of course, seven plus seven. It should also be noted that Maimonides divided his *Treatise on the Art of Logic* into fourteen chapters, laid down fourteen legal principles in his introduction to *Sefer HaMitzvot*, divided the *Mishneh Torah* into fourteen books, and parallel to those books included fourteen chapters on reasons for the commandments in the *Guide*.'[6] Fourteen is furthermore ten plus four. This last is an observation to which Maimonides himself drew attention in a dramatic fashion,[7] and to which he seemed partial in many contexts. There is no need to talk about the significance of the number ten in human societies composed of individuals having ten fingers (and toes), nor is it necessary to talk about the significance of ten multiplied by four in biblical and later Judaism, forty and its multiples being numbers which crop up over and over again.[8] Ten and four represent the thematic division of the *Mishneh torah* into books on commandments between humans and God (*bein adam lamakom*) and commandments concerning human relations (*bein adam leḥavero*), but the arithmetical division (7 + 7) also turns out to be significant.[9]

[5] In all the carefully edited versions of the *Mishneh torah* (Frankel, Kafih, Makbili, Rabinovitch, Shailat) the last paragraph is numbered as 13. But this is simply the widely accepted standard numeration, adopted by these editors as a matter of convenience (following early printed editions). Maimonides himself did not number the paragraphs (*halakhot*) in the *Mishneh torah* and the surviving manuscripts are inconsistent, some numbering our *halakhah* as 12, others as 13. For an interesting study on Maimonides' methods in composing the *Mishneh torah* see Langermann, '*Fusul Musa*, on Maimonides' Method of Composition'.

[6] Tepper, *Progressive Minds, Conservative Politics*, 27. See also Strauss, 'How to Begin to Study the *Guide of the Perplexed*', p. xiii, Kraemer, 'Moses Maimonides: An Intellectual Portrait', 20 and 24, and Berman, 'The Structure of the Commandments of the Torah'.

[7] *Guide*, ii. 9–10 (pp. 268–73).

[8] On Maimonides' fascination with the number 14, see Gillis, *Reading Maimonides' Mishneh Torah*, 192–4. On the number 4, see ibid. 273–7, and Freudenthal, 'Four Observations'.

[9] Rabinovitch, 'Sanctuary, Society, and History', argues that the first seven books of the *MT* deal with the private sphere and the last seven with the public sphere.

Sanctifying All Human Beings 131

Thirteen, of course, is also a number of considerable significance for Judaism: thirteen attributes of divine mercy,[10] thirteen as the age of majority for males, thirteen rules for the derivation of halakhah from the text of the Torah,[11] and also for Maimonides, who listed thirteen principles of faith, neither more nor less.[12]

What, then, do we find at the precise midpoint of the *Mishneh torah*, in this apparently significant place (7/7/13/13)? We find the following passage:

12. Why was the Tribe of Levi granted no right to a share in the Land of Israel and in its spoils, together with his brothers?[13] Because they were set apart to worship the Lord, 'to serve Him' [Deut. 10: 8], and to teach His upright ways and His righteous judgments to the many, as it is said, 'They shall teach Jacob Thine ordinances, and Israel Thy law' [Deut. 33: 10]. They were consequently set apart from the ways of the world: they do not wage war as do the rest of Israel, they have no share in the Land, and they may acquire nothing for themselves by physical force. They are rather the host of God, as it is said, 'Bless, Lord, his host' [Deut. 33: 11]. It is He, blessed be He, who acquires for them, as it is said, 'I am thy portion and thine inheritance' [Num. 18: 20].

13. Not only the Tribe of Levi, but also each and every individual of those who come into the world, whose spirit moves him and whose mind [*mada'o*][14] gives him understanding to withdraw from the world in order to stand before the Lord, 'to serve Him, to worship Him',[15] and to know Him, who walks upright [*yashar*] as God had made him,[16] and frees his neck from the yoke of the manifold contrivances

---

[10] Exod. 34: 6–7.   [11] *Sifra*, introd.

[12] Isaac Abravanel wonders why Maimonides listed precisely thirteen principles, which forced him to leave out some beliefs the importance of which he emphasizes in other contexts (such as free will, which he himself calls a 'great principle' (*ikar gadol*) in 'Laws of Repentance', 6: 3). See Abravanel, *Principles of Faith (Rosh Amanah)*, ch. 10 and Kellner, *Dogma in Medieval Jewish Thought*, 53–61.

[13] As established in *halakhah* 10, preceding our text.

[14] We follow Septimus in this translation of *mada'o* as 'his mind'. See Septimus, 'What Did Maimonides Mean by *Madda*?', 90.

[15] Based on Deut. 11: 13, Josh. 22: 5, and Zeph. 3: 9. There are good reasons to think that this last, and messianic, verse is the most significant. As we will see when we reach the end of Book 14 of the *Mishneh torah*, Maimonides emphasizes the re-establishment of the laws of the sabbatical year and jubilee in connection with his account of the messianic era. Note should also be taken of Isa. 56: 6–7: 'As to the foreigners who attach themselves [*nilvim*] to the Lord, to serve Him [*leshoreto*], and to love the name of the Lord, to be His servants—all who keep the Sabbath and do not profane it, and hold fast to my covenant—I will bring them to My sacred mount and let them rejoice in My house of prayer. Their burnt offerings and sacrifices shall be welcome on My altar, for My house shall be called a house of prayer for all peoples.' On this verse, and on the expression *nilvim*, see below, Chs. 9 and 11.

[16] Compare Eccles. 7: 29: 'Behold, this only have I found, that God made man upright

[*ḥeshbonot*] that human beings are wont to pursue—such an individual is as consecrated as the Holy of Holies,[17] and his portion 'and his inheritance' [Deut. 18: 1] shall be in the Lord forever and ever. The Lord will acquire for him in this world whatsoever is sufficient for him, the same as He did 'for the priests and for the Levites' [Isa. 66: 21].[18] Thus indeed did David, upon whom be peace, say, 'O Lord, the portion of mine inheritance and of my cup. Thou maintainest my lot' [Ps. 16: 5].[19]

For our purposes, the key phrase here is: 'each and every individual of those who come into the world' (*kol ish va'ish mekol ba'ei olam*).[20] To whom does this refer? This phrase has become a matter of considerable controversy in the contemporary Jewish world. Traditionalists, seeking to find in Maimonides (of all people!)[21] support for their insistence that the broader Jewish community (and Israeli taxpayers) owe support to Talmud scholars, often point to this text and take it to refer to Torah scholars, who are due support as were the ancient Levites.[22] In their eyes, it certainly does not refer to all human beings. Many of these traditionalists, no doubt, are misled into thinking that our

[*yashar*]; but they have sought out many inventions [*ḥeshbonot*].' Perhaps Maimonides is quietly rejecting the Christian notion of original sin? It should be noted that this doctrine infiltrated medieval Judaism as well. See Nahmanides on Lev. 26: 6 and Bahya ben Asher on Lev. 12: 7. See further Lasker, 'Original Sin and Its Atonement' (Heb.) and Schechterman, 'The Doctrine of Original Sin' (Heb.).

[17] This word-pair (*kodesh kedoshim*) occurs twenty-six times in Scripture. For Maimonides' specific source here, see 1 Chron. 23: 13.

[18] For a fascinating discussion of the possible universalist implications of this verse (and a response to some attempts to avoid those implications) see Roth, 'Moralization and Demoralization in Jewish Ethics'.

[19] This translation is based on both Isaac Klein's version and that of Twersky, *Introduction to the Code*, 441–2. Hartman, *Maimonides: Torah and Philosophic Quest*, 222, makes the interesting point that Spinoza, Hermann Cohen, and Leo Strauss 'never refer to this important statement'. As to Spinoza, it might reflect his desire to present Maimonides in a particularist light, something which caused Moses Mendelssohn great distress. For details, see Schwarzschild, 'Do Noachites Have to Believe in Revelation?' In his translation of the *Mishneh torah* Eliyahu Touger translates our phrase: 'Not only the tribe of Levi, but any one of the inhabitants of the world.' In a note he adds, 'This wording could also imply gentiles.'

[20] This expression may also be literally translated as 'all who enter the world'. This is the translation favoured by Kimelman, '*U-N'taneh Tokef* as a Midrashic Poem'.

[21] On Maimonides' notorious opposition to paying people to study Torah, see the recent studies of Buchman, 'Rambam and Zevulun: *Boz Yavuzu Lo*', and Leibowitz, 'The Pursuit of Scholarship'.

[22] Even some academic scholars mistakenly see this text as a retreat from Maimonides' settled opposition to paying people to study Torah. See e.g. Brown, *The Hazon Ish* (Heb.), 239, and the sources cited there.

expression refers only to Jews because of their familiarity with the term from the synagogue hymn (*piyut*), *Unetaneh tokef*.[23]

Maimonides himself may or may not have known this liturgical poem,[24] but he certainly knew its sources. Tracing these will be instructive for our purposes. Here is the relevant passage in the hymn:

We acclaim this day's pure sanctity, its awesome power. This day, Lord, Your dominion is deeply felt. Compassion and truth, its foundations, are perceived. In truth do You judge and prosecute, discern motives and bear witness, record and seal, count and measure, remembering all that we have forgotten. You open the Book of Remembrance and it speaks for itself, for every man has signed it with his deeds. The great shofar is sounded. A still, small voice is heard. This day even angels are alarmed, seized with fear and trembling as they declare: 'The day of judgement is here!' For even the hosts of heaven are judged. This day all *who walk the world* [*kol ba'ei olam*] pass before You as a flock of sheep. And like a shepherd who gathers his flock, bringing them under his staff, You bring everything that lives before You for review. You determine the life and decree the destiny of every creature.[25]

The author of our poem clearly had in mind the following mishnaic text:[26]

At four seasons [divine] judgement is passed on the world: at Passover in respect of produce; at Pentecost in respect of fruit; at Rosh Hashanah *all creatures* [*kol ba'ei olam*][27] pass before God like children of *maron*,[28] as it says, 'he fashions their hearts alike; he considers all their deeds' [Ps. 38: 15]; and on Tabernacles judgement is passed in respect of rain.

Let us look at the verse from Psalm 38, cited here in its original context (verses 10–15):

---

[23] When one of us (MK) taught 'Laws of the Sabbatical Year and the Jubilee' 13: 13 in his synagogue, a learned member of the congregation insisted that *kol ba'ei olam* must refer only to Jews because of its use in *Unetaneh tokef*!

[24] On the hymn and its history, see Kimelman, '*U-N'taneh Tokef* as a Midrashic Poem'.

[25] We cite the translation of Jules Harlow from the *High Holidays Prayer Book* (*mahzor*) that he published in 1972. It ought to be noted that the author of this poem takes it as a given that God judges *kol ba'ei olam* on Rosh Hashanah. He thus presumably held that God judges each and every individual human being (and perhaps all living creatures); a trivial point, perhaps, but one that surprises many contemporary Jews, even learned ones. For a survey of many authorities who would probably be surprised by this, see Balk, 'The Soul of a Jew'.

[26] Mishnah *RH* 1: 2.

[27] The Soncino translator here understood our expression with crushing literalism; *kol ba'ei olam* is taken to mean all of God's creatures, and not just all human beings, and certainly not just Jews. This translation probably reflects the Talmud's explanation of the phrase 'children of *maron*', as deriving from the way a shepherd counts his flock. See the article cited in the following note. Compare further David Kimhi (Radak) on Ps. 145: 10.

[28] On this expression, see Wieder, 'A Controversial Mishnaic and Liturgical Expression'.

The Lord brings the counsel of the nations to naught; he frustrates the schemes of the people. The counsel of the Lord stands forever, the thoughts of his heart to all generations. Happy is the nation whose God is the Lord; and the people whom he has chosen for his own inheritance. The Lord looks down from heaven; he beholds all the sons of men. From the place of his habitation he looks upon all the inhabitants of the world. He fashions their hearts alike; he considers all their deeds.

These verses teach us that God looks down from heaven and beholds all human beings (*benei ha'adam*) and all the inhabitants of the world (*yoshvei ha'arets*); he fashioned all their hearts alike, and considers all their deeds. It is obvious that the Psalmist was convinced that God created all humans alike, and that hence God also judges all human beings. It is this verse that the authors of the Mishnah chose as their prooftext for the idea of divine judgement on Rosh Hashanah, and it is this verse to which the author of our poem alludes. The Psalmist, the *tana'im* in Mishnah *Rosh hashanah*, and, it would seem, the author of *Unetaneh tokef* all agree that on the New Year God judges *kol ba'ei olam*, and mean by that each and every individual human being, not just Jews. Despite that, it is safe to say that for very many Jews today the idea that God judges each and every human being on the High Holidays is ludicrous.

'All Who Come into the World' in Maimonides' Writings

How does Maimonides himself use the expression in the *Mishneh torah*? There are variants of it in five other places in the work. In each place Maimonides means 'all human beings'. This fact alone conclusively refutes the possibility that in our text alone Maimonides uses the expression *kol ba'ei olam* to mean 'each and every individual *Jewish* human being'. We do not expect the reader to take our word for this, so we will examine each of these sources in turn.

The first is from 'Laws of Repentance':

Whoever regrets the commandments [*mitsvot*] that he had fulfilled and wonders at his meritorious deeds, saying to himself, 'What profit have I of them? Would that I had not done them', forfeits the credit for all of them, and none of his meritorious deeds is ever remembered in his favour, as it is said, 'The righteousness of the righteous shall not deliver him on the day of his wickedness'[29] [Ezek. 33: 12]; that is, if he regrets his former good deeds. And even as a man's meritorious deeds and

---

[29] The standard text of Ezekiel has *pisho* (transgression), while Makbili's Maimonides has *risho* (wickedness).

iniquities are balanced at the hour of death, so are the iniquities of *every single inhabitant of the world* [*kol eḥad ve'eḥad meba'ei ha'olam*] weighed against his merits annually on the Rosh Hashanah holiday. He who is found righteous is sealed unto life; he who is found wicked is sealed unto death. If one belongs to the intermediate class, sentence on him is suspended till the Day of Atonement. If he repents, he is sealed unto life; if he does not do so, he is sealed unto death.[30]

Maimonides here follows Mishnah *Rosh hashanah* 1: 1–2 (cited above), almost quoting it verbatim. Just as the Mishnah there refers to all humanity, so does Maimonides.[31]

Our second instance is also from 'Laws of Repentance':

A man may commit so great a sin or such numerous sins that justice requires of the true judge, as the penalty to be exacted from this particular sinner for the sins, committed by him voluntarily and of his own mind, that repentance shall be withheld from him and liberty to turn from his wickedness shall not be accorded him, so that he may die and perish in the sins which he committed. So God saith through Isaiah, 'Make the heart of this people fat, and make their ears heavy, and close their eyes, lest they see with their eyes, and hear with their ears, and understand with their heart, and turn and be healed' [Isa. 6: 10]; and thus it is said, 'But they mocked the messengers of God, and despised His words, and scoffed at His prophets, until the wrath of the Lord arose against His people, till there was no remedy' [2 Chron. 36: 16]. This means that they sinned, of their own will, and multiplied transgressions to such an extent that they incurred the penalty of having repentance, which is the remedy for sin, withheld from them. Hence also, it is written in the Pentateuch, 'And I will harden Pharaoh's heart' [Exod. 4: 21]. Because Pharaoh sinned on his own impulse and ill-treated the Israelites who sojourned in his land, as is said 'Come let us deal wisely with them . . .' [Exod. 1: 10], justice required that repentance should be withheld from him till retribution had been visited upon him. The Holy One, blessed be He, accordingly hardened his heart. But why did He send him a message through Moses, bidding him release the Israelites and repent, when He had already told him, thou wilt not release them, as it is said, 'But as for thee and thy servants, I know that ye will not fear the Lord God'

---

[30] 'Laws of Repentance', 3: 3. The translation by Moses Hyamson is cited here, with our emphasis.

[31] Admittedly, in the continuation of our passage Maimonides refers to the Day of Atonement, which is definitely only for Jews ('Laws of Repentance', 2: 7), but that should not be construed as undercutting our claim here. Maimonides' law, as we have seen, is based upon a mishnaic text that begins 'At four seasons [divine] judgement is passed on the world'. That text in turn cites a psalm referencing all creatures. It should be noted that Isaac Abravanel was puzzled by the apparent universalism of our mishnaic text; see his commentary on Lev. 23: 26 (*Perush vayikra*, 253). Abravanel's worries aside, Maimonides appears to hold that Rosh Hashanah is for all humanity, while the Day of Atonement is a special gift for Jews alone. Be that as it may, he certainly holds that all human beings are judged on Rosh Hashanah.

[Exod. 9: 30], 'But in very deed for this cause have I made thee to stand [to show thee power that my name be declared throughout all the earth]' [Exod. 9: 16]? The purpose was to instruct *the inhabitants of the world [leba'ei olam]*, that when the Holy One Blessed be He withholds repentance from the sinner, he cannot return, but will die in his wickedness which he had originally committed of his own will.[32]

The context here is crystal clear: Pharaoh was made an example of obstinate wickedness before all humanity.

Humanity is called upon again in the next instance, in 'Laws of Tefillin, Mezuzah, and the Torah Scroll':

If one has gone from place to place with a Torah scroll, he may not place it in a sack on the back of an ass and ride on the ass. But if he has done so for fear of robbers, it is permitted. But if there is no cause for fear, he holds it near his breast opposite his heart and rides on the beast. Anyone who sits in the presence of a Torah scroll must comport himself gravely, in awe and fear, since the Torah is the trustworthy witness before *all the inhabitants of the world [al kol ba'ei olam]*, as it says, '[Take this book of Teaching and place it beside the Ark of the Covenant of the Lord your God], and let it remain there as a witness against you' [Deut. 31: 26].[33] One must respect the Torah to the utmost of one's capacity. The early Sages said [*Avot* 4: 1]: 'Anyone who profanes the Torah will be profaned by others, while one who respects the Torah will be respected by others.'[34]

Before whom is the Torah meant to be a witness? Maimonides makes himself entirely clear: before *kol ba'ei olam*. But what does that expression mean here? The commentator Abraham Ibn Ezra (1089–1167), for example, takes the Deuteronomy verse to be referring to the people of Israel—the Torah bears witness to *them*. Maimonides himself cites the verse in two other places,[35] but in both his object is to elucidate questions concerning the writing of Torah scrolls and their placement in the Ark of Covenant, so his citations there do not bear upon our question.

There is another place where Maimonides explains before whom the Torah is meant to be a witness. In the context of a withering critique of preachers (*darshanim*) who take rabbinic *agadot* literally, Maimonides writes:

The members of this group are poor in knowledge. One can only regret their folly. Their very effort to honour and exalt the sages in accordance with their own meager understanding actually humiliates them. As God lives, this group destroys the glory

---

[32] 'Laws of Repentance', 6: 3 (Hyamson trans.), with our emphasis.
[33] *Vehayah sham bekha la'ed*: a witness against you should you abandon it.
[34] 'Laws of Tefillin, Mezuzah, and the Torah Scroll', 10: 11.
[35] Near the beginning of the introduction to his *Commentary on the Mishnah*, and in *Teshuvot harambam*, i, no. 136.

of the Torah and extinguishes its light, since they make the Torah of God say the opposite of what it intended. For He said in his perfect Torah, 'The nations who hear of these statutes shall say: Surely this great nation is a wise and understanding people' [Deut. 4: 6]. But this group expounds the laws and teachings of our sages in such a way that when the other peoples hear them they say that this little people is foolish and ignoble.[36]

The glory of Torah and its light, then, are matters which the nations of the world are meant to understand and appreciate. We understand Maimonides to mean that it is *against them* also that the Torah stands as a witness. We take this as further support for the claim that the *ba'ei olam* before whom the Torah witnesses are precisely that, *ba'ei olam*.

Our fourth passage is from 'Laws of the Sanhedrin':

For this reason, but a single man was created, to teach us that if any man destroys a single life in the world, Scripture imputes it to him as though he had destroyed the whole world; and if any man preserves one life, Scripture ascribes it to him as though he had preserved the whole world. Furthermore, *all human beings [kol ba'ei olam]* are fashioned after the pattern of the first man, yet no two faces are exactly alike. Therefore, every man may well say, 'For my sake the world was created.'[37]

The many fascinating questions about this text and its relation to parallel texts in the *Mishneh torah* and in Maimonides' *Commentary on the Mishnah* need not detain us here.[38] Our interest is in the phrase *kol ba'ei olam*, which in this context (dealing as it does with the creation of Adam) can only mean all human beings.

So, also, we find in 'Laws of Kings', the last place in the *Mishneh torah* where our phrase occurs:

Moses, our teacher, bequeathed the Law and commandments to Israel, as it is said 'an inheritance of the congregation of Jacob' [Deut. 33: 4], and to those of other nations who are willing to be converted [to Judaism], as it is said: 'One law and one ordinance shall be both for you, and for the resident alien' [Num. 15: 15]. But no coercion to accept the Law and commandments is practised on those who are unwilling to do so. Moreover, Moses, our teacher, was commanded by God to compel *all human beings [kol ba'ei olam]* to accept the commandments enjoined upon the descendants of Noah. Anyone who does not accept them is put to death. He who does accept them is invariably styled a resident alien. He must declare his acceptance in the presence of three associates. Anyone who has declared his intention to

---

[36] *Perek ḥelek*; We cite the translation as cited and discussed in Twersky, *Introduction to the Code*, 380–7. [37] 'Laws of the Sanhedrin', 13: 3.
[38] See the discussion in Kellner, *They, Too, Are Called Human* (Heb.), 40–4.

be circumcised and fails to do so within twelve months is treated like a heathen infidel.[39]

There can be no doubt that here, as well, our expression means 'all human beings', nothing less.

Thus, in addition to our passage from the end of the *Book of Agriculture*, we find that Maimonides uses the expression *kol ba'ei olam* in five other places in the *Mishneh torah*. In three of these instances we have shown that the term cannot mean anything other than all human beings, and we have given good reasons to read the remaining instances in that way as well. Generally, it should be remembered that Maimonides, like the written Torah before him, denies that there is any inherent distinction between Jews and non-Jews,[40] so that even if anyone finds our readings of some of these texts unconvincing, there is no reason to suspect that by *kol ba'ei olam* Maimonides means anything other than all human beings. In any case, since there are instances in which the phrase means this beyond any doubt, had he wished to refer specifically to Jews in our original passage in 'Laws of the Sabbatical Year' he should have used an expression like *kol yisra'el* ('all Israel'). The burden of proof is on those who wish to give a narrow interpretation to a phrase whose basic meaning is clearly inclusive, and the evidence is against them. There is no reason in the world other than prejudice, therefore, to think that in our passage he restricts the meaning of *kol ba'ei olam* to Jews, let alone to yeshiva students.

We have seen, therefore, that Maimonides chooses the very midpoint of the *Mishneh torah*, a place whose numerological significance can hardly have been a coincidence, to state unambiguously[41] that *all* human beings can become as sanctified as the Holy of Holies in the Temple (and thereby earn shares in the world to come).[42]

Human Sanctification

How does one go about becoming sanctified in this fashion? Maimonides tells us: a person whose spirit moves her[43] and whose mind gives her under-

---

[39] 'Laws of Kings', 8: 9.

[40] This is proved in detail in Kellner, *They, Too, Are Called Human* (Heb.).

[41] This is obviously an exaggeration, since many readers do misinterpret or misrepresent Maimonides here, thus proving the truth of Herzl's dictum: 'If you wish it, it is no dream.'

[42] For other scholars who read the text as we do, see Kellner, *They, Too, Are Called Human* (Heb.), 166. To this list we may now add Friedman, 'Ten *Betelin* in the Synagogue' (Heb.).

[43] In Maimonides' case, this inclusive language is justified. See Kellner, 'Misogyny: Gersonides vs. Maimonides'.

standing to set herself apart from the rest of humanity to serve, worship, and know God, and who walks upright as God created her, and who frees herself from the many calculations that preoccupy human beings, becomes as sanctified as the Holy of Holies in the Jerusalem Temple, and God becomes her portion, as it were, in this world (and, by very clear implication, in the next).[44] It must be noted that none of these steps is easy to accomplish—Maimonides did not expect many individuals, Jew or non-Jew, to achieve this exalted state.

Let us look in detail how Maimonides does this. He takes the verse Exodus 35: 21—'And they came, every one whose heart stirred him up, and every one whom his spirit made willing, and brought the Lord's offering, for the work of the tent of meeting, and for all the service thereof, and for the holy garments'—which relates to the gifts made by Israelites for the Tabernacle, and introduces into it the expression *kol ba'ei olam*, as if the Torah had written: 'And they came, *each and every individual of those who come into the world*, whose heart stirred him up, and every one whom his spirit made willing, and brought the Lord's offering, for the work of the tent of meeting, and for all the service thereof, and for the holy garments.'

Let us now see how Maimonides understands the expression 'whom his spirit made willing' (*asher nadvah ruḥo*). The expression *ruaḥ nedivah* is found in Psalm 51: 14 and is quoted by Maimonides in 'Laws of Repentance':[45]

And thus the prophets and the righteous beseech the Almighty, in their prayers, to help them to the way of truth [*derekh ha'emet*], as David said, 'Teach me, O Lord, thy way [that I may walk in Thy truth; make one my heart to fear Thy name]' [Ps. 86: 11]; that is, 'May my sins not keep the way of truth [*derekh ha'emet*] from me, that I may learn from it Thy ways [*derakhekha*] and the Unity of Thy Name [*yiḥud shemekha*].' So also his prayer, 'let a willing spirit [*ruaḥ nedivah*][46] uphold me' [Ps. 51: 14] means, 'Suffer my spirit to accomplish its desire, and may not my sins cause repentance to be withheld from me, but let me have free will [*reshut*], till I return and understand and know the way of truth [*derekh ha'emet*]'. Every text similar to the above can be explained in the same way.

For Maimonides 'the true way' (*derekh ha'emet*) mentioned here is the way of Abraham, who turned to all humanity with a call to acknowledge the one true God.[47] God's way is the way of truth, discovered by Abraham, who did

---

[44] Immortality, to the extent that Maimonides thought it could be achieved, is certainly not restricted to Jews. See Kellner, *Maimonides on Judaism and the Jewish People*, 23–32.

[45] 'Laws of Repentance', 6: 4.   [46] NJPS has 'vigorous spirit'.

[47] See Maimonides' letters to Obadiah the Proselyte. On this text, see Diamond, *Converts, Heretics, and Lepers*, ch. 1; for some of the vicissitudes to which the text has been subjected (and specifically on the term *derekh ha'emet*), see Kellner, '"Farteitsht un Farbessert"'. See also our discussion in the Conclusion on the way of Abraham.

not know the commandments of the Torah, and who obviously preached God's way to the humans (Noahides in every sense of the term) whom he encountered. Maimonides further makes it clear that repentance is open to all human beings—even to an Amalekite.[48] (It was Pharaoh's unique punishment that he was not allowed to repent.) This reading of the text supports our claim that by *kol ba'ei olam* in 'Laws of the Sabbatical Year', 13: 13 Maimonides means exactly that—namely 'each and every individual of those who come into the world'.

This last point is clarified and supported by examining the expression 'whose mind gives him or her understanding to withdraw from the world' (*vehevino mada'o lehibadel*). We have seen above that the term *mada* can mean a property of mind, or simply knowledge.[49] In the present context it seems to mean mind, knowledge, or understanding. Either way, it is certainly not something unique to Jews.

In this context, it behooves us to re-examine 'Laws of Idolatry':[50]

Thus was the world declining by degrees, till the World's Pillar, our Father Abraham, was born. No sooner was this hero weaned than he began to ponder, though but a child, and to meditate day and night, wondering: 'How can the Sphere forever follow its course with none to conduct it? Who causes it to rotate? For it cannot possibly cause *itself* to rotate?' He had no one to teach or instruct him in anything, but was immersed in [the culture of] Ur of the Chaldees among the foolish adherents of alien worship. His father, mother, and the entire populace worshipped alien deities, and he worshipped along with them, while his mind was searching and seeking to understand—till he grasped the true way [*derekh ha'emet*] and understood the right course of his own sound reason. He realized that: there is a single God, He conducts the Sphere, He created the universe, and, in all that exists, there is no god but He. And he realized that all the people were in error, and [that] what had caused them to err was worshipping the stars and images for so long that the truth [of God's existence] was lost to their minds. It was at the age of forty that Abraham recognized his Creator.[51]

The patriarch Abraham is a perfect example of an individual 'whose mind gives him or her understanding to set himself or herself apart from the rest of

---

[48] For details, see Kellner, 'And Yet, the TextsRemain'. In his *Epistle to Yemen* (in Lerner, *Maimonides' Empire of Light*, 116; Maimonides, *Igerot harambam* (trans. Shailat), i. 138–9) Maimonides opines that even an Amalekite can aspire to prophecy. This also appears to be the upshot of 'Laws of Kings and their Wars', 6: 4, especially in light of the harsh gloss by Abraham ben David on that text. For the creativity which Maimonides brought to bear on his sources in order to arrive at this (innovative) conclusion, see Korn, 'Moralization in Jewish Law'.   [49] See above, n. 14.

[50] See above, Ch. 1, and below, Conclusion.   [51] 'Laws of Idolatry', 1: 3.

humanity'. Abraham achieved this knowledge through reasoned conviction (*hekhra hada'at*) alone (we will explain this term below). This is an important point for our understanding of Maimonides in general, and of our text from the end of the *Book of Agriculture* in particular. The upshot of all this is that Abraham discovered God on his own, so to speak.[52] God did not choose Abraham, God did not seek him out, God did not make himself known to Abraham. God waited till someone discovered the truth about him; that someone happened to be Abraham, progenitor of the Jews. It did not have to be Abraham. Had the first human being to discover the truth about God been, say, a Navajo Indian, and had that Navajo philosopher possessed the courage and effectiveness of Abraham, then the Navajo would be the chosen people, the Torah would have been composed in the Navajo language, its narratives would reflect their history, and many of its commandments would reflect that history and the nature of Navajo society at the time of the giving of the Torah to them. The inner meaning of the Torah, its philosophical content, and its spiritual message would all be equivalent to the inner meaning, philosophical content, and spiritual message of the Torah as it was indeed revealed to Moses at Sinai, but its outer garment would be dramatically different.[53]

The importance of this point is brought out in a famous passage in 'Laws of Kings and their Wars':

> Anyone who accepts the seven [Noahide] commandments and observes them scrupulously is one of the righteous of the nations of the earth and has a share in the world to come, on condition that he accept them and perform them because the Holy One, blessed be He, commanded them in the Torah and made known to us through Moses our Teacher that Noahides had been commanded to obey them before [the giving of the Torah]. But if he observed them because his reason compels him [*hekhra hada'at*], he is not a resident alien [*ger toshav*], nor one of the righteous gentiles [*meḥasidei umot ha'olam*], but[54] one of their wise men.[55]

---

[52] In addition to discovering God on his own, through reasoned conviction Abraham also brought his contemporaries (Noahides in the most literal sense of the term) to acceptance of monotheism through *hekhra hada'at*. It is a safe assumption that on Maimonides' view Abraham himself and those whom he brought near to God achieved shares in the world to come; that being the case, the standard reading of 'Laws of Kings and their Wars', 8: 11 (according to which even wise non-Jews have no share in the world to come) cannot be correct. This is taken up in the coming paragraphs.

[53] On Maimonides' view of the Torah as an account of what actually happened to happen, as it were, as opposed to being an account of what *had* to happen, see Kellner, 'Did the Torah Precede the Cosmos?' (Heb.).

[54] The famous question concerning the correct reading here (*ela* [but] or *velo* [and not]) need not detain us. For discussion, see Kellner, *Maimonides' Confrontation*, 241–50, and the sources cited there. [55] 'Laws of Kings and their Wars', 8: 11.

Abraham reached his knowledge of God through *hekhra hada'at* exclusively.⁵⁶ Returning to our original text from 'Laws of the Sabbatical Year and Jubilee', he is the prototype of 'every individual of those who come into the world, whose spirit moves him and whose mind gives him understanding to withdraw from the world in order to stand before the Lord, *to serve Him, to worship Him*, and to know Him, who walks upright as God had made him, and frees his neck from the yoke of the manifold contrivances that human beings are wont to pursue'.⁵⁷ Abraham, it must be remembered, was born, lived, and died as a non-Jew; he reached the truth through his own efforts.⁵⁸ Abraham's students followed him in adopting the 'true way' (*derekh ha'emet*), without being Jews. A student such as this, 'who walks upright as God had made him, and frees his neck from the yoke of the many manifold contrivances that human beings are wont to pursue', is 'as consecrated as the Holy of Holies'. In consequence of that his portion 'and his inheritance' (see Deut. 18: 1) shall be in the Lord forever and ever more. The Lord will grant him in this world whatsoever is sufficient for him, as was promised by David, who said, concerning such an individual, 'O Lord, the portion of mine inheritance and of my cup, Thou maintainest my lot' (Ps. 16: 5).

Who has a chance to become 'as consecrated as the Holy of Holies'? One 'who walks upright as God had made him'. God created all human beings in the divine image. This is a further indication that in our passage Maimonides speaks of human beings generally, *kol ba'ei olam*, and not just Jews, let alone only that subset of Jews who subsist on public charity to 'work themselves to death in the tents of Torah'. God created all human beings upright,⁵⁹ and instilled in each and every one of them the ability to free 'his neck from the yoke of the manifold contrivances that human beings are wont to pursue'.⁶⁰

⁵⁶ For discussion, see Kellner, *Maimonides' Confrontation*, 77–83.

⁵⁷ 'Laws of the Sabbatical Year and Jubilee', 13: 13.

⁵⁸ And not because of his lineage, or because God chose him as a three-year-old child. See the passage cited above, n. 51.

⁵⁹ BT *AZ* 22*b* has been used by some to prove that while all human beings were created equal in the beginning, after the sin of Adam and Eve, all human beings were polluted, and only Jews, who stood at Sinai, were eventually freed of that pollution. For Maimonides' rejection of this use of the passage see the discussion in Kellner, *They, Too, Are Called Human* (Heb.), 44–51. It should be noted that, following the then regnant theory of climates, Maimonides may have been more restrictive than we are in whom he called human. In *Guide* iii. 51 (p. 618) he dismisses pale Northerners and dark Southerners as subhuman. On this, see Melamed, *The Image of the Black in Jewish Culture*, 127–35 (on the theory of climates) and 139–48 (on Maimonides). For our purposes, the important point is that Maimonides made no racial or ethnic distinctions among those considered human in his day.

⁶⁰ On human freedom Maimonides writes in 'Laws of Repentance', 6: 1:

Reshut is given to all human beings: if one chose to direct himself to a good way and

Any human being who fulfils the criteria outlined in 'Laws of the Sabbatical Year', 13: 13 will become as consecrated as the Holy of Holies. In his usual way, Maimonides ends the precise midpoint of the *Mishneh torah* with a challenge and a promise. He challenges his reader to fulfil the listed criteria and promises that one who does will indeed become 'as consecrated as the Holy of Holies'. Furthermore, by challenging the reader (Jew or non-Jew) to seek to be as consecrated as the Holy of Holies, Maimonides implies that such consecration is possible.

Summary

At the precise midpoint of the *Mishneh torah*, at a spot with messianic overtones, Maimonides teaches that each and every single human being can be as sanctified as the Holy of Holies. The next book of the *Mishneh torah*, the *Book of Temple Service*, gives details of the laws concerning the physical Holy of Holies, part of the Temple that is a national institution of the Jewish people, and entered only once a year, by the High Priest on Yom Kippur. This encounter with holiness can of course take place only when the Temple is rebuilt, in the days of the messiah. By ending the *Book of Agriculture* in the way he does, Maimonides prefaces this with the concept of a moral and intellectual Holy of Holies, available at all times, to anybody.

This is an outstanding example of the way in which the endings of the books of the *Mishneh torah* not only summarize and colour the current book, but also provide a perspective on the next. Moreover, the transition from moral and intellectual sanctity to a sanctum of stone and wood can be seen as part of the general movement over the first ten books of the *Mishneh torah* from the less to the more physical, which for Maimonides means a decline in intellectual clarity that parallels the cosmic process of emanation. All the same, we shall see over the next three chapters that, through the Maimonidean concept of a commandment as a 'hint', the physical Temple rituals can express philosophical notions.

> become a righteous person, *reshut* [to do so] is in his hands; [but] if one chose to direct himself to an evil way and become a wicked person, *reshut* [to do so] is in his hands. This as is written in the Torah: '[And the Lord God said:] Behold, the man is unique, knowing good and evil from himself' [Gen. 3: 22]. That is to say: this species of man is unique in the world, no other species being similar to it in this regard, that he himself, with his *da'at* and thought knows good and evil, and does whatever he desires, there being no one to restrain him from doing either good or evil. This being the case—'lest he put forth his hand [and take also of the tree of life, and eat, and live forever]' [Gen. 3: 22].
>
> The word *reshut* in this context clearly means 'freedom'.

EIGHT

TEMPLE SERVICE
The Divinity of the Commandments

Introduction

Books 8, 9, and 10 of the *Mishnah torah* are closely linked. In the case of Book 8, the *Book of Temple Service*, and Book 9, the *Book of Offerings*, this is very obviously so: both books are about the Temple and its rituals. Book 10, the *Book of Purity*, belongs with them because the main consequence of impurity is exclusion from the Temple precincts.[1] The *Guide* explains that the point is to make visits to the Temple rare,[2] and so maintain the sense of awe that the Temple is meant to inspire.[3] All three books thus concern the Temple.

A second common thread is that the endings of these books constitute a three-part discussion of *ta'amei hamitsvot*, the reasons for the commandments.[4]

We shall establish that these two unifying factors are connected. The way that Maimonides structures the laws of the Temple, sacrifices, and purity turns these three books into a parable about the reasons for the commandments that gives access to a profoundly philosophical, and universalist, conception of the Temple ritual.

This is the ultimate goal of our argument. We shall, however, first look at the endings of Books 8, 9, and 10 individually, before considering their interrelationships and their wider context.

The *Book of Temple Service* (*Sefer avodah*) has nine sections. The first, 'Laws of the Temple', opens with the commandment 'to make a house for

---

[1] See 'Laws of Entrance into the Sanctuary', 3–4; 'Laws of Impurity of Foodstuffs', 16: 8.
[2] See *Guide* iii. 47 (pp. 593–4).
[3] See 'Laws of the Temple', 7: 1, and *Guide* iii. 45 (pp. 577–81).
[4] See Twersky, *Introduction to the Code*, 371–447; this constitutes essential reading on reasons for the commandments in the *Mishneh torah*, and in Maimonides in general. Note especially the analyses of 'Laws of Trespass', 8: 8 (the end of the *Book of Temple Service*), and 'Laws of Substituted Offerings', 4: 13 (the end of the *Book of Offerings*) (pp. 407–18). See also Twersky's articles, 'A Clarification of Maimonides' Remarks'; 'On Law and Ethics in the *Mishneh Torah*'; and Heinemann, *Reasons for the Commandments* (Heb.), i. 79–97.

God established for the offering of sacrifices'. It affirms the Temple on Mount Moriah in Jerusalem as the sole venue for sacrifices, and describes the design and proportions of the Temple structure itself and its main appurtenances: two altars, one for sacrifices with a ramp leading up to it and a smaller one for burning incense; the basin in which the priests wash their hands and feet; the seven-branched candelabrum; and the table on which the shewbread is placed.[5] Most importantly, the Ark of the Covenant containing the stone tablets of the Ten Commandments is mentioned as having been hidden under the spot where, in the First Temple, it stood in the inner sanctum, the Holy of Holies.[6] This section also presents the keynote commandment to be in awe of the Temple.[7]

'Laws of Temple Utensils and Servers' covers the anointing of high priests and kings, the organization and functions of priests, Levites, and lay representatives in the Temple, and the priestly garments. 'Laws of Entrance into the Sanctuary' is about preparations for and disqualifications from service in the Temple, the main exclusions being of priests with physical deformities and, as already mentioned, all people in a state of ritual impurity. 'Laws of Things Forbidden for the Altar' discusses deformed animals and other things that may not be brought as offerings. 'Laws of Sacrificial Procedures' lists the different types of communal and individual sacrifices and other offerings, and the procedures for each. 'Laws of Daily and Additional Offerings' details the regular communal offerings, mostly of the *olah* (burnt offering) type. It also prescribes the daily counting of the seven week period between the Passover and Shavuot festivals. 'Laws of Offerings Rendered Unfit' is about procedural flaws that can disqualify an offering, whether physical, or in the state of mind of the priest who carries out the procedures, or that of the worshipper on whose behalf he acts. 'Laws of the Day of Atonement' is about the high priest's preparations for the Day of Atonement and the special order of service on that day, with its fifteen sacrifices, including the scapegoat.

The concluding section is 'Laws of Trespass', which is about deriving illicit personal benefit from anything to do with the Temple. The penalty for doing so deliberately is lashes plus payment of whatever loss of value may have been caused, while inadvertent transgressors must reimburse the loss of value plus one fifth, and also make a guilt offering.[8]

---

[5] See 'Laws of the Temple', 1: 6.   [6] See ibid. 4: 1.   [7] See ibid. 7: 1.

[8] Trespass can mean, for example, eating the meat of a sacrifice that is meant to be entirely burnt on the altar (see 'Laws of Trespass', 1: 3), but it can also mean something as slight as a building worker benefitting from the shade given by a wall of the Temple under construction (see 'Laws of Trespass', 7: 4, which provides a solution to the practical problems that inevitably arise from this).

'Laws of Trespass' ends as follows:

It is fitting for man to meditate upon the laws of the Holy Torah and to comprehend their full meaning to the extent of his ability. Nevertheless, a law for which he finds no reason and understands no cause should not be trivial in his eyes. Let him not 'break through to rise up against the Lord lest the Lord break forth upon him' [Exod. 19: 24]; nor should his thought concerning these things be like his thought concerning profane matters. Come and consider how strict the Torah was in the law of trespass! Now if sticks and stones and earth and ashes became hallowed by words alone as soon as the name of the Master of the Universe was invoked upon them, and anyone who comported with them as with a profane thing committed trespass and required atonement even if he acted unwittingly, how much more should man be on guard not to rebel against a commandment decreed for us by the Holy One, Blessed be He, only because he does not understand its reason; or to heap words that are not right against the Lord; or to regard the commandments in the manner he regards ordinary affairs.

Behold it is said in Scripture: 'Ye shall therefore keep all My statutes [*ḥukim*] and all Mine ordinances [*mishpatim*], and do them' [Lev. 20: 22]; whereupon our Sages have commented that 'keeping' and 'doing' refer to the statutes as well as to the 'ordinances'. 'Doing' is well known; namely to perform the statutes. And 'keeping' means that one should be careful concerning them and not imagine that they are less important than the ordinances. Now the 'ordinances' are commandments whose reason is obvious, and the benefit derived in this world from doing them is well known; for example the prohibition against robbery and murder, or the commandment of honouring one's father and mother. The 'statutes', on the other hand, are commandments whose reason is not obvious.[9] Our Sages have said: I have legislated statutes for thee, and thou art not permitted to question them. A man's impulse pricks him concerning them and the gentiles reprove us about them, such as the statutes concerning the prohibition against the flesh of the pig and that against meat seethed with milk, the law of the heifer whose neck is broken, the Red Heifer, or the he-goat that is sent away.

How much was King David distressed by heretics and pagans who disputed the statutes! Yet the more they pursued him with false questions, which they plied according to the narrowness of man's mind, the more he increased his cleaving to the Torah; as it is said: 'The proud have forged a lie against me; But I with my whole

---

[9] The Yale translation has 'not known'. In the Vilna edition of the *Mishneh torah* the expression is *lo yadua*, which does translate into English as 'not known'. The Makbili edition, however, gives *lo galui*—'not obvious'. Whatever the manuscript evidence, this reading in any case seems more likely, as it balances the definition of statutes against the definition of ordinances as 'commandments whose reason is obvious' (*galui* in the original, in all editions we have inspected). Hence we emend to 'not obvious'. This is preferable to a flat 'not known' for substantive reasons too, as should become clear in the course of this and subsequent chapters.

heart will keep thy precepts' [Ps. 119: 69]. It is also said there concerning this: 'All Thy commandments are faithful; they persecute me falsely, help Thou me' [Ps. 119: 86].

All the [laws concerning the] offerings are in the category of statutes. Therefore the Sages have said that the world stands even because of the service of the offerings;[10] for through the performance of the statutes and the ordinances the righteous merit life in the world to come. Indeed, the Torah puts the commandment concerning the statutes first, as it is said: 'Ye shall therefore keep My statutes, and Mine ordinances, which if a man do, he shall live by them' [Lev. 18: 5].[11]

It may be useful to present a skeleton summary of this complex *halakhah*, as follows:

- A person should try to understand the commandments of the Torah to the extent that he or she is able.
- A commandment whose reason is not obvious should nevertheless be observed respectfully.
- Commandments the reasons for which are obvious are called *mishpatim*.
- Commandments the reasons for which are not obvious are called *ḥukim*.
- Sacrifices are *ḥukim*.
- Performing both *mishpatim* and *ḥukim* leads to the world to come.

This *halakhah* is, as mentioned, the first part of a three-part essay on the subject of reasons for the commandments. It concerns the appropriate attitude to *ḥukim* (sing. *ḥok*), which are those commandments for which the reason is not apparent, as opposed to *mishpatim*, which are those commandments that are readily understandable. It provides many points for discussion, but the focus here will be in accordance with our theme of universalism.

The *Mishneh Torah* versus the *Guide* 1: Non-Jews and the Commandments

Our *halakhah* is about observance of the commandments, which is not universally mandatory, at least not in pre-messianic times.[12] There is a two-tier system: 613 Torah commandments and countless rabbinic regulations specifically for Jews, and seven Noahide commandments incumbent on all

---

[10] The addition of 'even' is a further emendation of the Yale translation, in accordance with the Makbili edition. [11] 'Laws of Trespass', 8: 8.
[12] The question of Maimonides' position on the status of non-Jews in the messianic era is debated in scholarship. For an entrée into the discussion, see Kellner, 'Maimonides' "True Religion"' and the response by Chaim Rappoport that follows the article (pp. 25–8).

mankind.¹³ Nevertheless, according to the *Guide*, all 613 Torah commandments are universal in the sense that they are universally comprehensible, even by those not committed to observing them. Maimonides condemns the school of thought that holds that the value of the statutes lies precisely in their inscrutability, so that performing them denotes pure obedience to the divine will. This idea, he says, is repugnant, for it would make human beings, who always act with some useful end in view, superior to their maker, who would be acting in a manner that is futile.¹⁴

Instead, Maimonides asserts that every commandment promotes some recognizable human good. He does so on the basis of the verse 'Which shall hear all these statutes and say: Surely this great community is a wise and understanding people' (Deut. 4: 6). Maimonides comments on this verse:

> Thus it states explicitly that even all the 'statutes' [*ḥukim*] will show to all the nations that they have been given with 'wisdom and understanding'. Now if there is a thing for which no reason is known and that does not either procure something useful or ward off something harmful, why should one say of one who believes in it or practises it that he is 'wise and understanding' and of great worth? And why should the religious communities think it a wonder? Rather things are indubitably as we have mentioned: every commandment exists either with a view to communicating a correct opinion, or to putting an end to an unhealthy opinion, or to communicating a rule of justice, or to warding off an injustice, or to endowing men with a noble moral quality, or to warning them against an evil moral quality. Thus all [the commandments] are bound up with three things: opinions, moral qualities, and political civic actions.¹⁵

According to this passage, all of the commandments, without distinction between ordinances and statutes, are intelligible by Jew and non-Jew alike as means to intellectual, moral, and political ends about which there is universal consent. This makes the commandments universally admired.

The closing *halakhah* of the *Book of Temple Service* depicts the opposite situation. The commandments are beset from without and within. Maimonides has to defend commandments that might seem pointless against reason's attack.¹⁶ Besides being denigrated because of incomprehension at the begin-

---

¹³ The seven commandments that apply to all mankind since Noah are prohibitions against idolatry, blasphemy, murder, theft, sexual immorality (incest and adultery), and eating flesh from a living animal, and one positive commandment, which is to set up a system of justice; see 'Laws of Kings and their Wars', ch. 9.   ¹⁴ See *Guide* iii. 31 (pp. 523–4).
¹⁵ *Guide* iii. 31 (p. 524). Twersky discusses this passage in *Introduction to the Code*, 385–6.
¹⁶ Twersky identifies in this *halakhah* three possible reprehensible attitudes to com-

ning of the *halakhah*, the commandments are liable to be flouted because they would thwart desire, and 'a man's impulse pricks him concerning them'. For their part, the non-Jews, far from admiring the wisdom of the commandments, are assigned an antagonistic role: they 'reprove us about them'. The first example of a *ḥok* is 'the prohibition against the flesh of the pig'. This prohibition is part of the dietary laws dealt with in the *Book of Holiness*. In the introduction to the *Mishneh torah*, the *Book of Holiness* is described as containing laws designed to separate the Jewish people from the other nations.[17] So here we have an incomprehensible, particularist law that is meant to promote exclusiveness—not exactly the spirit of universalism. Furthermore, the response in our *halakhah* to criticism by heretics and pagans is not an attempt to engage them and explain, but only redoubled, inward-looking devotion, as expressed in the verses quoted from Psalms.

The final particularist gesture is the statement that 'through the performance of the statutes and the ordinances the righteous merit life in the world to come'. If it takes performance of the statutes to qualify for the life hereafter, then, whatever it may say elsewhere in the *Mishneh torah*, non-Jews are ruled out from the start.[18]

mandments that are not understood, which can be summarized as: contemptuous neglect; irresponsible invention of unfounded reasons; routine, unreflective performance. See ibid. 411–12.

[17] This makes the commandments in the *Book of Holiness* transparent in general, but the particular prohibition on the flesh of the pig remains opaque.

[18] See 'Laws of Kings and their Wars', 8: 11. Maimonides' essential position is that what survives death is the developed intellect, and that there is no difference between a Jewish intellect and a non-Jewish intellect. There are, however, many places in the *Mishneh torah* in which immortality is said to depend upon deeds, specifically obedience to the commandments, as well as on knowledge. In general, this is explicable by the fact that Maimonides regards morality and knowledge as a continuum, because the barrier to knowledge is the human material condition (see *Guide* iii. 9 (p. 436)), and morality is the regulation of, even detachment from, material desires, appetites, and concerns, which is what the commandments are in large part intended to achieve. An important text in this respect is Maimonides' commentary on Mishnah *Mak.* 3: 17, in which he appears to state that performance of even a single commandment (appropriately, honestly, and without ulterior motives) can earn immortality, but prefaces this (in his commentary on the preceding *mishnah*) with a characterization of the commandments in general as designed to purge the appetites; here he stresses the idea and intention of the commandment, thereby intellectualizing it. The commentary mentions performance of the commandment 'for its own sake, out of love, as I explained to you', which Kafih takes to be a reference to the commentary on Mishnah *San.* 10: 1 (*Perek ḥelek*), where the idea of the world to come and the opposition of intellect and matter are explained. See also the commentary on Mishnah *Kid.* 1: 10, which discusses the significance of a single commandment for attaining the world to come, and makes a similar reference. For a summary of Maimonides' view of the issue of non-Jews and the world to

In short, in contrast to the *Guide*, in which Judaism encounters the outside world and justifies itself in universal, philosophical terms, our *halakhah* encapsulates the intimate relationship between God and a people that obeys his commandments out of pure, unquestioning, self-justifying love, something outsiders will never understand. The *halakhah* builds up to an intensity of faith in King David's cleaving to the commandments in the face of a doubting world, and to a consummation of that faith in immortality. One might be led to conclude that, with all due respect to universalism, here it is simply *de trop*, and that this perhaps captures the true spirit of the *Mishneh torah* as a whole, which is of Judaism in a quite different mood from that of the *Guide*.

The *Mishneh Torah* versus the *Guide* 2: Sacrifices

This conclusion seems to be reinforced by what 'Laws of Trespass', 8: 8 has to say about sacrifices. The *halakhah* concerns the concept of *ḥok* in general, but appropriately for the end of the *Book of Temple Service*, it builds up to the statement: 'All the [laws concerning the] offerings are in the category of statutes.' In the *Guide*, however, Maimonides famously, or notoriously, explains sacrifices as a concession to historical conventions of worship. People find it hard to adjust to radical change, and it was not possible for the Jewish people, fresh out of Egypt, to abandon overnight the kind of rituals with which they were familiar. So while sacrifices do not directly contribute towards achieving the primary goals of the law, the welfare of the soul (which means expunging idolatry) and the welfare of the body, they do fulfil its 'second intention', which is to take existing kinds of religious practices based on false pagan notions and use them to educate people gradually in true monotheistic doctrines, accommodating the familiar while changing its significance.[19] Actually, explanations are provided in the *Guide* not just for sacrifices but for every single one of the commandments listed as statutes in 'Laws of Trespass', 8: 8,[20] but it is

come, see Kellner, *Maimonides on Judaism and the Jewish People*, 29–32. The subject of observance of the commandments and immortality is taken up again at the end of this chapter.

[19] See *Guide* iii. 32 (pp. 525–8).

[20] For the prohibition against eating the flesh of the pig, see *Guide* iii. 48 (p. 598); for meat seethed with milk, see ibid. (p. 599); for the heifer whose neck is broken, see *Guide* iii. 40 (p. 557); for the red heifer, see *Guide* iii. 47 (p. 594); and for the he-goat that is sent away (the scapegoat), see *Guide* iii. 46 (p. 591). The explanation of the purification ritual using the ashes of a red heifer is in general terms only. Towards the end of *Guide* iii. 47 (p. 597), Maimonides confesses that he does not know the reason for the use of hyssop, scarlet thread, and cedar wood in this ritual and in the procedure for purification from leprosy. The red heifer was the one commandment that even Solomon failed to understand; see *Guide* iii. 26 (pp. 507–8).

the apparent tension with the *Guide* over sacrifices that tends to disturb those who comment on this *halakhah*. Twersky, for example, makes clear that its main point is not to explain sacrifices. 'We have a general affirmation concerning the implicit worth of a legal genre, *hukkim*, but we are not given a specific rationalization for sacrifices',[21] he writes, but still concludes, apropos sacrifices, 'It is clear, nevertheless, that the *Moreh*'s [*Guide*'s] socio-historical explanation... is not easily integrated here.'[22]

Maimonides brings matters to a head with the statement 'Therefore the Sages have said that the world stands even because of the service of the offerings.' The source of this is Mishnah *Avot* 1: 2: 'Simon the Just was one of the last of the men of the Great Assembly. He used to say, "The world stands upon three things, on the Torah, on the Temple service, and on kind deeds."' According to the *Guide*, though, the world can get along very well without the Temple service, and indeed ought preferably to do so, the highest form of worship of God being pure cogitation, with prayer ranked second, and sacrifices a poor third.[23] How can a practice that accommodates pagan custom be regarded as essential to the world's very existence? We understand from the way our *halakhah* continues—'for through the performance of the statutes and the ordinances the righteous merit life in the world to come'—that Maimonides takes Simon the Just to refer to behaviour in this world that earns immortality, but that scarcely alleviates the difficulty.

Glaring as the problem might appear, Maimonides shows no self-consciousness about it. In any case, explanations of commandments against a background of pagan practices are not a new phenomenon in the *Guide*. They are found in the *Book of the Commandments*[24] and in the *Mishneh torah* itself.[25] The idea of accommodation to pagan custom, as opposed to countering it, does make its debut in the *Guide* (as far as we are aware), but the chapters in that work on reasons for the commandments are strewn with cross-references to the *Mishneh torah*, with no hint that Maimonides saw any inconsistency on this subject between the two works.

We shall argue that this is because there is no inconsistency. The *Mishneh torah* and the *Guide* clearly do have different ambiences, but the difference

---

[21] Twersky, *Introduction to the Code*, 414.
[22] Ibid. 415.   [23] See *Guide* i. 59 (pp. 139–43); iii. 32 (pp. 526 and 530).
[24] See e.g. negative commandments 40–5.
[25] See 'Laws of Idolatry', 12: 7. Given that Maimonides forbids reading idolatrous works (ibid. 2: 2–3), his admission that he read every one he could find (*Guide* iii. 29 (pp. 518, 521)) has aroused debate. See e.g. Berger and Kaplan, 'On Freedom of Inquiry in the Rambam and Today', 37–50. See also Kellner, *Maimonides' Confrontation*, 18 n. 47 and 25.

does not arise from one having a more universal orientation than the other. As far as our *halakhah* is concerned, we shall find on close inspection that, while it does not preach universalism on the face of it, nothing in it contradicts a universalist position. At a deeper level, its general approach will be shown to be the same as that of the *Guide*, namely that the commandments can be explained on the basis of universally acknowledged rational principles. The difference between the *Guide* and the *Mishneh torah* on this subject is that each fulfils a different requirement of Maimonides' model of what constitutes an explanation. What we are looking at is two aspects of the same, universal, philosophical system. The two works are complementary, not contradictory.

What Is a Ḥok? Maimonides versus Midrash

Before we look at Maimonides' explanatory model, we need to understand what it is that requires explanation. What exactly does Maimonides mean by a *ḥok*? In this respect, the differences between our *halakhah* and the rabbinic sources are just as interesting as the apparent differences with the *Guide*, and they shed light on Maimonides' concept of a *ḥok*—what it is, and what it is not.

As often, Maimonides concocts an artful blend of several sources. Besides the direct citations, he alludes in almost every phrase to the Bible, Talmud, or Midrash. There are, however, two deceptively simple-looking general statements in the *halakhah*, that, as far as we are aware, do not have parallels in the classical rabbinic literature.

The first is the definition of statutes as 'commandments whose reason is not obvious', as opposed to ordinances, which are 'commandments whose reason is obvious'. The implication of this contrast is that the difficulty with statutes is epistemological rather than inherent. The reasons for them are not obvious, but research might discover something. This is also implied in the opening of the *halakhah*: 'It is fitting for man to meditate upon the laws of the Holy Torah and to comprehend their full meaning to the extent of his ability.' The limit on understanding is the extent of one's ability, which we take to mean perspicacity, together with the patience and determination required to master the disciplines necessary to comprehend these matters.[26]

---

[26] On the idea that natural ability and perseverance in an orderly course of studies are prerequisites for the understanding of 'divine science', see *Guide* i. 34 (pp. 72–9). Maimonides' conclusion there is that 'these matters are only for a very few solitary individuals, of a very special sort, not for the multitude'.

Comprehension is attained through meditation, not access to occult lore.[27] 'It is fitting for man [*le'adam*]', taken at face value, means fitting for any human being. Maimonides probably does mean at this point a practising Jew (commonly but not always the referent of *adam* in the *Mishneh torah*) trying to make sense of the commandments, but it is a Jew as a citizen of the world, not a breed apart, using the normal tools of human intelligence. This interpretation receives support from the description that follows of the heretics and pagans who distress King David by deriding the statutes. They do so 'according to the narrowness of man's [*ha'adam*] mind'. Jews and non-Jews face the same epistemological difficulty in contemplating the commandments; the difference is one of attitude.

The definitions of ordinances as 'commandments whose reason is obvious' and statutes as 'commandments whose reason is not obvious' are paralleled by the definitions in the *Guide* of ordinances as 'commandments whose utility is clear to the multitude' and of statutes as commandments 'whose utility is not clear to the multitude'.[28] The epistemological nature of the problem of the *ḥukim* is expressed fairly clearly in the *Guide*, which states that the end of the *ḥukim* is 'hidden from us either because of the incapacity of our intellects or the deficiency of our knowledge'.[29] This is as opposed to an end that is in principle unknowable, other than that it is God's will, or one that is not knowable using normal heuristic methods, but only through a hermetic body of knowledge subject neither to the scrutiny of logic nor to factual verification, such as kabbalah. Maimonides explicitly rules out both these possibilities. He states apropos statutes that 'some say that there is no utility in them at all except the fact of mere commandment, whereas others say that there is a utility in them that is hidden from us', and summarily dismisses such obscurantism.[30]

Besides their not being inherently incomprehensible, a further characteristic of the *ḥukim* that emerges from our *halakhah* is that they are not inherently potent in any way. This is brought out by the *a fortiori* argument in the first part of it. The commandments are compared to the fabric and contents of the Temple, 'sticks and stones and earth and ashes', which 'became hallowed by words alone as soon as the name of the Master of the Universe was

---

[27] Compare Maimonides' remark in his preface to his interpretation of the visions in Ezek. 1 and 10 in the *Guide*, that he received no divine revelation and no tradition from a teacher (see *Guide* iii. Introd. (p. 416)).

[28] *Guide* iii. 26 (p. 507). Pines uses the term 'judgements' rather than 'ordinances', but he is translating the same Hebrew word as in 'Laws of Trespass', 8: 8, i.e. *mishpatim*.

[29] *Guide* iii. 26 (p. 507). See J. Stern, 'The Idea of a Hoq'.   [30] *Guide* iii. 28 (p. 513).

invoked upon them', that is, they are considered holy only because they are nominated as such, not because of anything essential in them. The comparison is intended to impress upon the reader the high respect due to the commandments: if sticks and stones are treated as sacrosanct even though there is nothing perceptibly sacred about them, then all the more so should the commandments be treated that way, even if they have no perceptible reason, since God has nominated these specific acts as his commandments. At the same time, the idea is conveyed that the commandments are sticks and stones, in the sense that their significance is not intrinsic to the act.[31]

Are Ḥukim Contradictory, or Simply Unexplained?

These are not necessarily the conclusions one would draw from Maimonides' sources,[32] which seem to imply that certain commandments are ordinances while others are, inherently, statutes. According to what we have seen so far,

---

[31] This implication of Maimonides' argument is well brought out in Henshke, 'On the Question of Unity' (Heb.), 122–3. On holiness in Maimonides, see Kellner, *Maimonides' Confrontation*, 85–126, who cautions that 'in Maimonides, holiness is, indeed, only institutional, but still extremely important' (ibid. 87 n. 6).

[32] The relationship between 'Laws of Trespass', 8: 8, and its sources is complicated, and made the more so by variant readings in the latter. The main source is recognized as being BT *Yoma* 67b (*Sifra* on Lev. 18: 4 is very similar), where ordinances are characterized as commandments that 'had they not been written, ought to have been written', in other words, human intelligence would have dictated them even without divine decree, while statutes are characterized as commandments that 'Satan [*Sifra* has 'a man's impulse'] pricks him concerning them and the gentiles reprove us about them', as in 'Laws of Trespass', 8: 8, but without the general description 'commandments whose reason is not obvious'. The lists of commandments in each category are not entirely the same as in 'Laws of Trespass', 8: 8, but variant readings may be at play here; see the Steinsaltz edition of the Talmud and the paraphrastic commentary of Hananel ben Hushiel (Rabbenu Hananel) on *Yoma* 67b.

In *Eight Chapters*, ch. 6, Maimonides himself uses the phrase 'had they not been written, they ought to have been written' to describe commandments that ought to become second nature, as opposed to those the transgression of which should remain a temptation, which he calls there *ḥukim*. This would seem to put a limit on rationalization of the *ḥukim*, since a true philosopher would never wish to transgress a rational law, but see Kaplan, 'Philosophy and the Divine Law'. At any rate, Maimonides does not revisit this definition of *ḥok* in his later works. Notably, forbidden sexual relations are listed both among the commandments that 'had they not been written, they ought to have been written' in BT *Yoma* 67b, and among the transgressions that should remain a temptation in *Sifra* on Lev. 20: 26, the presumed source for the discussion in *Eight Chapters*, ch. 6. This means either that the Sages were not in agreement about whether forbidden sexual relations should be classed as a statute or as an ordinance, or, alternatively, that the category of things that ought to remain a temptation is not in their eyes coextensive with the category of statute as Maimonides would have it in *Eight Chapters*, ch. 6. Forbidden sexual relations are conspicuously absent from 'Laws of Trespass', 8: 8. See also Kafih's note 5 to his translation of *Guide* iii. 26 (p. 334 in his edition).

in Maimonides' approach 'statute' is not a fixed category; what that category contains depends on one's state of knowledge, so that commandment *x* might be a statute to *A* but not to *B*, or a statute today but not tomorrow, or even vice versa if knowledge is lost—as indeed happened in the case of sacrifices, according to the *Guide*, when knowledge of their pagan background faded.[33]

Moreover, in one *midrash*, commandments are characterized as statutes not so much because the reasons for them are unknown as because they are contradictory; either conflicting with other commandments, such as the prohibition on marrying a brother's wife, which conflicts with the law of levirate marriage, or self-contradictory, such as the ritual of sprinkling the ashes of the red heifer, which makes the impure pure and the pure impure.[34] Characterizing statutes in this way implies an essentialist view of them. If the ashes of the red heifer have the inherent property of purifying, then it is highly mysterious that they should also make impure.[35] On a nominalist view, there is less of a mystery, since the consequence of contact with the ashes of the red heifer is a matter of definition only, and there is no real effect.[36] Consistently with this view, Maimonides eschews the reason that the *midrash* gives for this ritual being considered a statute—its paradoxical character—and instead includes it under the simple rubric of 'commandments whose reason is not obvious'.

Apropos the red heifer as a commandment about which 'the gentiles reprove us', an anecdote about the mishnaic sage Raban Yohanan ben Zakai offers support for the nominalist position. In this story, Raban Yohanan is challenged by a pagan with the charge that the purification procedure for someone who has had contact with a corpse using water mixed with the ashes of a red heifer looks like witchcraft. He responds that it is similar to the kind of exorcism of an unquiet spirit with which the challenger is familiar. When the pagan departs, Raban Yohanan's students protest that this response may have been a sufficient rebuttal for him, but will not satisfy them, upon which the sage says, 'By your lives! The corpse does not defile, and the water does not purify. Rather it is a decree of the Holy One, blessed be He. The Holy One,

---

[33] Josef Stern stresses that Maimonides transformed the *ḥukim* from arbitrary and mysterious commandments to problematic commandments, and notes that everyone except Maimonides considers the list of statutes in BT *Yoma* 67b (see previous note) to be exhaustive; see id., *Problems and Parables of Law*, 117.

[34] See *Num. Rabbah* 19: 5; *Midrash tanḥuma* (Warsaw), 'Ḥukat', 7.

[35] Cf. Sa'adiah Gaon, *Book of Beliefs and Opinions*, iii. 10 (p. 177).

[36] Cf. *Guide* iii. 47 (p. 597), where uncleanness and purification are associated with sin and expiation.

blessed be He said, I have legislated a statute, I have decreed a decree, and you are not permitted to transgress my decree.'[37]

Although similar expressions are found elsewhere,[38] the precise phrase 'I have legislated a statute' is found only in this source, and is echoed in our *halakhah*. Here we are dealing with a non-Jew who is evidently knowledgeable about the Torah, and who charges it with inconsistency, so that again a statute is seen as a law that involves contradiction. In this case, however, the contradiction is ideological rather than technical: the Torah outlaws witchcraft, but prescribes a law that looks just like it. The pagan's accusation is that the Torah purports to be, or is held up as, a rational creed, but its commandments reveal it to be otherwise—at least that might be Maimonides' interpretation of his remark. The allusion to Raban Yohanan's ultimate response to his students on this question, that impurity and the means of purification have no substance, reinforces the inference drawn from the beginning of 'Laws of Trespass', 8: 8, that the Temple ritual and ancillary practices have no actual effect. This prepares the ground for the ending of the *Book of Purity*, where the non-real character of purity and impurity is given full and highly charged expression.

Sacrifices as Ḥukim: an Original Generalization

The other generalization that Maimonides makes without support in the sources is that 'All the [laws concerning the] offerings are in the category of statutes.' We have found no such wholesale categorization in the discussions of statutes in the Talmud and Midrash. These discussions do mention some Temple rituals, but the singling out of particular rituals as problematic implies that sacrifices in general make sense.[39] Categorizing all the sacrifices as statutes may seem to make them mysterious, but given the characterizations of statutes we have just discussed, it actually demystifies them. It entails that sacrifices have the characteristics of statutes expressed or implied in our *halakhah*: the reasons for them are 'not obvious', but possibly discoverable, and they have no essential efficacy.

If, moreover, we accept Josef Stern's thesis that Maimonides applies to commandments the same method of interpretation that he applies to para-

---

[37] *Num. Rabbah* 19: 8; *Pesikta derav kahana* (Mandelbaum), 'Parah adumah', §4: 7. See Kellner, *Maimonides' Confrontation*, 130–1.

[38] In BT *Yoma* 67b and *Sifra* on Lev. 18: 4; see above, nn. 32–3.

[39] It is true that in the *Guide* Maimonides distinguishes between the general idea of sacrifices, which he rationalizes as an accommodation to the familiar, and the details of the sacrificial rites, which he says may sometimes be arbitrary.

bles, namely that they have an external significance to do with 'the welfare of human societies' and an internal significance to do with 'the truth as it is',[40] that is, individual apprehension of physics and metaphysics,[41] then by calling sacrifices *ḥukim* Maimonides proposes that rather than being non-rational, they are super-rational. Unlike the kind of *mishpatim* mentioned in 'Laws of Trespass', 8: 8, which are readily understandable because they concern what is conventionally perceived as good and bad, that is, they concern the welfare of society only and at most inculcate some ethical virtue, *ḥukim* contain an inner core of truth, some educative message about physics and metaphysics. It is this message that we ultimately seek to decipher.

At any rate, the point we have reached is that Maimonides' definition of 'statute' as a commandment whose reason is not obvious, and his inclusion of sacrifices in general within that definition, are both original to him, and indicate the possibility that there is more to our *halakhah* than an appeal for obedience.

Opposing Views on Reasons for the Commandments

It is certainly possible to put a different construction on the concept of a *ḥok* and on the examples that Maimonides mentions. Sa'adyah Gaon divides the commandment into two divisions: 'rational' commandments that God imposes because reason demands it, such as prohibitions on theft and murder; and 'revealed' commandments—roughly coterminous with *ḥukim*—which are not compelled by reason but which God imposes 'in order thereby to increase our reward and happiness' from obedience to his word (although Sa'adyah does mention incidental benefits arising from them).[42] Maimonides rejects this view, insisting that all commandments have both poles: that of reason, and that of acceptance of God's authority.[43]

On sacrifices, the view of Judah Halevi, for example, was that they cause the divine presence to dwell with the Jewish people,[44] while Nahmanides believed that they mend a rupture in the divine realm.[45] According to this kind of approach, the Temple ritual is a uniquely Jewish franchise, a formula for procuring a special divine favour of which Jews are the unique object, and the details of this formula are necessary and must be followed precisely in

---

[40] *Guide* i, Introduction (p. 12).   [41] See J. Stern, *Problems and Parables of Law*, 74.

[42] See Sa'adiah Gaon, *Book of Beliefs and Opinions*, iii. 1 (pp. 138–41).

[43] As far as *ḥukim* are concerned, this is the point of 'Laws of Trespass', 8: 8. For its application to the commandments in general, see Funkenstein, *Maimonides: Nature, History, and Messianic Beliefs* (Heb.), 21–9.

[44] See *Kuzari* ii. 26.   [45] See Schwartz, 'From Theurgy to Magic'.

order for it to work. Indeed Halevi makes a comparison to pharmaceuticals,[46] which places special emphasis on the mechanics of the act.

Maimonides did not believe in the existence of a populated divine realm: as far as he is concerned, there is only God on the one hand, beyond our intellectual horizon, and nature on the other, with nothing in between. Moreover, God's non-contingency entails that he is eternally unchanging, which in turn entails that he is not affected by anything outside himself, including performance of the commandments.[47] In this approach, any ritual act is more or less contingent, and its effect is solely on the state of mind of the person who performs it, and through that to his or her society. It can have no effect beyond this.

An interesting outcome of these two approaches is two opposing views on seeking reasons for sacrifices and other commandments. After a lengthy explanation of the Temple furnishings and utensils, Halevi disavows any real knowledge of the divine intention behind them, and states that it is preferable simply to accept the Temple ritual as divine wisdom without attempting to penetrate the reasons for it. Only for someone who is incapable of such acceptance is it advisable to find reasons to motivate performance of the commandments rather than abandon them.[48] Reason is only a fall-back.

In 'Laws of Trespass', 8: 8, Maimonides puts the matter the other way round. He starts with the proposition that one should strive to find reasons for the commandments. When ratiocination falls short it is necessary to resort to the idea of submission to divine fiat, but nowhere in the halakhah is it suggested that this attitude is superior. Reasoned observance of the commandments is always preferable. The intensity of the appeal to divine decree tends to divert the reader's attention from the fact that our *halakhah* does not idealize blind acceptance. Unlike Halevi, Maimonides believes that, as with the comprehension of nature, comprehending the commandments to the best of our limited ability brings us closer to the true love and knowledge of God.[49]

To sum up, while 'Laws of Trespass', 8: 8 may sound particularist in tone, it actually maintains a universalist stance, insofar as it presents the *ḥukim* not as occult mysteries or theurgies that give Jews unique access to the divine, but as institutional laws susceptible of understanding in accordance with universal reason.

---

[46] See *Kuzari* i. 79, discussed in Ch. 5 above.
[47] See 'Laws of the Foundations of the Torah', 1: 11–12; *Guide* i. 55 (pp. 128–9).
[48] See *Kuzari* ii. 26.
[49] See discussion of *Book of the Commandments*, positive commandment 3, in Ch. 1 above.

The Multitude versus the Elite?

It might be thought that in the course of the foregoing analysis we have unearthed explanations for the apparent divergence between the *Mishneh torah* and the *Guide* on ḥukim in general and on sacrifices in particular. If a ḥok is a commandment 'whose utility is not clear to the multitude', then the explanation for the stress on obedience in the *Mishneh torah* versus the sociohistorical explanations of the *Guide* must be that the former work is intended for the multitude and the latter for the elite. The multitude does not know, nor is it desirable that it should know, the kinds of reasons for sacrifices and so on that are put forward in the *Guide*. It is preferable that it should regard such commandments as divine decrees with no reasons known or even knowable, and be warned severely against treating them lightly on that account.

Moreover, the *Mishneh torah* is a book written for the present and the future, not the past. It looks forward to the restoration of sacrifices and accompanying purification rituals, such as the red heifer, when the messiah comes and rebuilds the Temple. Since such things have long since been dropped from the repertoires of non-Jewish religions, and Jews themselves have become accustomed to their absence, the principle of accommodation cannot support their reintroduction. The pole of reason for these kinds of commandments therefore fails, and we are left with the pole of divine authority alone.

But neither of these explanations holds water. If 'Laws of Trespass', 8: 8 is addressed only to the multitude, why did Maimonides write it at all? It gives no practical information, but only awakens questions that might have been better left dormant. When Maimonides eventually wrote the *Guide*, he took no steps to shield the multitude, and presented the relativist approach to sacrifices overtly. Even if most readers of the *Mishneh torah* could be expected never to open the *Guide*, they would very likely be exposed to this idea. The scathing attack on it by Nahmanides in his commentary on the Torah seems to indicate that it was widely known. Presumably people can say to themselves that the *Mishneh torah* represents Maimonides' true position for true believers, while the *Guide* is for those who have become corrupted by philosophy, but that is hardly adequate. 'Laws of Trespass', 8: 8 needs to be reconciled with the *Guide* on a more respectable basis.

Moreover, it is not at all clear that the reason for categorizing sacrifices as statutes in 'Laws of Trespass', 8: 8 is because of the explanation based on accommodation to idolatrous practice offered in the *Guide*. That is not consistent with the way statutes are characterized in that *halakhah*. If sacrifices were a concession to convention no man's impulse would have pricked him concerning them, since they were meant precisely to accommodate the impulse to give tangible expression to the relationship with God; nor would the non-Jews have reproved Jews about them—they ought positively to have approved such conformity with their own custom. Maimonides does describe many of the detailed practices in the Temple as demonstrative rejections of pagan notions, but any non-Jewish criticism that such practices might have drawn would only have clarified to the Jews the logic of what they were doing. It could not have caused the kind of consternation on the part of King David that we find in our *halakhah*.

That brings us to the idea of sacrifices in the future being purely a matter of obedience, since the rationale of accommodation to familiar religious practices will no longer apply. Such theocentricity is certainly part of Maimonides' ideology of the commandments, but by itself it comes rather close to the idea he lampoons in the *Guide*,[50] that obedience to a commandment is actually preferable if its performer is ignorant of any reason for it. In Maimonides' view, positing that a commandment has no intelligible reason makes it futile and frivolous: all commandments, *ḥukim* and *mishpatim* alike, express both God's will and God's wisdom,[51] which means that all, including sacrifices, are conducive to human moral and/or intellectual welfare.[52] In fact, unless sacrifices have an enduring, comprehensible purpose that transcends their historical origins, their reinstatement will be worse than frivolous, it will be positively harmful, since it will represent a reversion to an inferior, second-intention mode of worship, which will amount to intellectual regression. 'Laws of Trespass', 8: 8 tells us that ignorance of the purpose will be no excuse for not fulfilling the commandments about sacrifices when they once again become applicable, since they are God's will, but some purpose must exist, embodying God's wisdom. In Chapter 10, once we have acquired a perspective on all three books of the *Mishneh torah* that deal with the Temple, we shall be in a position to consider how, according to Maimonides, this is so. For the present we should simply note that, as far as he is concerned, the nexus between human beings and God is the intellect actualized through the study of creation. Therefore, whatever its national role, if the Temple is to represent the service of God at the highest level, its rituals should carry some intellectual significance. Otherwise, the time, effort, and funds might be better spent on building a particle accelerator.

---

[50] *Guide* iii. 31 (pp. 523–4).   [51] See *Guide* iii. 26 (pp. 506–7).
[52] See *Guide* iii. 27 (p. 510).

It is true that a little later in the *Guide* the commandments are commended as spiritual exercises,[53] as means of detaching the mind from worldly affairs and focusing on God, but this is not achieved through regarding them as otherwise pointless. On the contrary, understanding the content of the commandment is part of the exercise:

> If, however, you pray merely by moving your lips while facing a wall; or if you read the Torah with your tongue while your heart is set upon the building of your habitation and does not consider what you read; and similarly in all cases in which you perform a commandment merely with your limbs . . . without reflecting either upon the meaning of that action or upon Him from whom the commandment proceeds or upon the end of the action, you should not think that you have achieved the end.[54]

It would appear from this that reflecting upon 'Him from whom the commandment proceeds' is only part of the required mental approach: one should understand what one reads or the meaning and purpose of what one does, 'the end of the action'. In other words, all commandments have both poles: the pole of God and the pole of discernible utility.

In any case, it is not characteristic of the *Mishneh torah* to distinguish between periods of history when it comes to the applicability of commandments. 'Laws of Trespass', 8: 8 itself ranges over a long period of Jewish history, starting from before the First Temple, without showing any consciousness of different conditions applying at different times. The defender of the *ḥukim* in this *halakhah* is King David, who certainly lived in the age of sacrifices as a universal convention. This is not necessarily fatal, since the intention could be that we should keep what are considered *ḥukim* in our day just as David kept what were considered *ḥukim* in his day, but, as already noted, the *halakhah* also refers to the statement of the Sages that 'the world stands even because of the service of the offerings'. If the idea is to affirm the validity of sacrifices in a post-sacrificial age, that statement is clearly anachronistic, since Simon the Just, the sage in question, lived at the time of the Second Temple, and as it happens was himself a high priest. If on the other hand we want to say that, both in the past and for the future, 'the world stands

---

[53] *Guide* iii. 51 (pp. 618–28).

[54] *Guide* iii. 51 (p. 622). Note Twersky's comment, 'It should be emphasized—and Maimonides' philosophic posture sharply illustrates this—that medieval religious rationalism did not mean "religion within the limits of reason alone". . . . It meant pressing the intellect into the service of religion, using reason for purposes of spirituality and self-fulfilment, to avoid religious routinization and unreflective existence' (*Introduction to the Code*, 88).

because of the service of the offerings' refers to mere obedience to God's word, we are back to the first difficulty: the service of the offerings becomes frivolous.

On this statement of Simon the Just, Maimonides comments that 'He said that in science [Arabic: *'ilm*], which is the Torah, and in moral virtue, which is kind deeds, and in observance of the commandments, which is the sacrifices, lies the continued soundness of the world and its orderly existence in the most perfect fashion.'[55] We shall have reason to discuss this *mishnah* and Maimonides' commentary upon it in more detail later on, but for the time being the point to note is that he makes sacrifices representative of 'observance of the commandments', and he does the same in our *halakhah*: the discussion is of *ḥukim* in general, of which sacrifices are an example. In other words, Maimonides is not concerned with justifying sacrifices particularly or with the obsolescence of that institution implied by the explanation that he later offered in the *Guide* (which we assume he had already thought of), but with a difficulty that applies to all, or most, of the commandments, including sacrifices, *and always has, and always will*.

Integrating the *Mishneh torah*'s approach to sacrifices and to the laws of purity with the socio-historical explanation of the *Guide* will be the object of the formal analysis to come later, but a great deal of ground-clearing can be done at this stage. The essential point is that the *Mishneh torah* and the *Guide* deal in different dimensions of the commandments and different kinds of explanation for them.

To sum up, when Maimonides describes *ḥukim* as 'commandments whose reason is not obvious', he is giving a definition of his own. He does not mean that *ḥukim* have some mystical significance, or that their function is purely to test obedience to God. The problem of the *ḥukim*, according to Maimonides, is an epistemological problem. The difficulty standing in the way of explaining some commandments is the same in the *Mishneh torah* as in the *Guide*, namely a lack of intellectual capacity and/or a lack of information that make it impossible to meet the criteria for a causal explanation, whether of the commandments or of any other phenomenon. The difference between the two works lies in the kind of cause for the commandments each seeks to demonstrate, the kind of information each requires in order to do so, and the particular obstacles that lie in the way of obtaining that information.

---

[55] *Commentary on the Mishnah, Avot* 1: 2, translated into English from Kafih's Hebrew version. Note that this comment makes the statement refer to this world, not the world to come.

Aristotle's Four Causes and the Reasons for the Commandments

How do we explain things? As far Maimonides is concerned, an explanation requires knowledge of Aristotle's four causes: the final cause, or end-purpose of the act or thing; the formal cause; the efficient cause; and the material cause. To take Aristotle's own example, in the casting of a bronze statue, the final cause is the existence of the finished statue itself (which is the artist's goal); the formal cause is the pre-existing shape in the artist's mind; the efficient cause is the art of bronze-casting; and the material cause is the bronze out of which the statue is made.[56]

In the case of natural phenomena, the final and formal causes often coincide. In human procreation, for example, the formal cause and the final cause are both a human being: 'For Aristotle, the ultimate moving principle responsible for the generation of a man is a fully developed living creature of the same kind; that is, a man who is formally the same as the end of generation. Thus the student of nature is often left with three types of causes: the formal/final cause, the efficient cause, and the material cause.'[57] We should note that, in Maimonides' own account of these causes, God is the ultimate formal, final, and efficient cause of any phenomenon.[58]

How does this apply to the commandments? Our fundamental observation about the structure of the *Mishneh torah* in the Introduction to this book is that it has the form of a microcosm. The idea of a human being as a microcosm is also embedded in it. This is interpreted to mean that the formal cause of the commandments is the form of the cosmos, and that their final cause is a human being who has realized his or her microcosmic potential.[59] That is to say, the ideal human being and the ideal human society govern themselves by laws that formally replicate the laws by which God governs his perfect creation. The world is moved by the love of God. This is ultimately what causes the rotations of the spheres and, through them, natural process on earth. A human being who aspires to the knowledge and love of God reproduces in himself or herself an analogous form of self-regulation, which is promoted by the commandments of the Torah. Looked at in this way, the formal cause of the commandments and their final cause are the same, namely the form of the cosmos, which is reflected in the microcosmic form of the perfect human being. God is the ultimate formal and efficient cause

---

[56] See *Phys.* II.3, 194b16–195b30; *Met.* V.2, 1013a24–1013b27.
[57] Falcon, 'Aristotle on Causality'. [58] See *Guide* i. 69 (pp. 166–71).
[59] See Appendix below and Gillis, *Reading Maimonides' Mishneh Torah*, 93–6.

of the commandments as he is of the entire world, and their final cause in that the knowledge, love, and imitation of God is their ultimate goal.

In the *Guide*, the final cause of the commandments is expressed differently, as the perfection of the soul and the perfection of the body, without direct reference to a formal cause. The *Guide* focuses more on material causes. These are the things that are used to fulfil commandments, such as a palm branch, a citron, and myrtle and willow twigs in the case of the commandment of the four species, or pigeons, sheep, goats, and bulls in the case of sacrifices. More broadly, the material causes of the commandments are the environmental and cultural conditions that prevailed when they were given. For example, Maimonides explains that the four species commemorate the joy of the Children of Israel at leaving the desert and entering the Land of Israel, and that they are specified because they are plentiful in the land, beautiful to look at, and stay fresh.[60] Sacrifices, as mentioned, are explained as an adaptation of existing modes of worship, by way of concession to familiar practices, so that the Jewish people will gradually be led away from idolatry and towards true doctrines. In this way, the material causes of the commandments can be correlated with their final cause, which is human perfection.

In very general terms, then, the *Guide* looks at contingent causes of the commandments, whereas the *Mishneh torah* looks at absolute causes.[61] In the former, the information required in order to explain a commandment is historical and anthropological, and sometimes geographical; in the latter it is in the natural sciences.

In both works, the information that is available falls short. In the *Guide*, Maimonides relies on books about the Sabian cult to furnish clues to the cultural causes of the commandments, but the information they supply is incomplete, so that for some commandments explanations elude him, at least for their details.[62] In the case of the *Mishneh torah* and formal causes, the difficulty is that we do not have reliable knowledge of all the laws of nature. Specifically, those that apply above the earth are beyond us:

All that Aristotle states about that which is beneath the sphere of the moon is in accordance with reasoning; these are things that have a known cause, that follow one upon the other, and concerning which it is clear and manifest at what points wisdom and natural providence are effective. However, regarding all that is in the heavens, man grasps nothing but a small measure of what is mathematical; and

---

[60] See *Guide* iii. 43 (pp. 573–4).

[61] Ultimately, nature too is contingent, as we learn in the very first *halakhah* of the *Mishneh torah*, but it is absolute in that, post-Creation, it is unchanging.

[62] See *Guide* iii. 49 (p. 612).

The Divinity of the Commandments

you know what is in it. I shall accordingly say in the manner of poetical preciousness: 'The heavens are the heavens of the Lord, but the earth hath He given to the sons of man'.[63] I mean thereby that the deity alone knows the true reality, the nature, the substance, the form, the motions, and the causes of the heavens. But He has enabled man to have knowledge of what is beneath the heavens, for that is his world and his dwelling-place in which he has been placed and of which he himself is a part. This is the truth. For it is impossible for us to accede to the points starting from which conclusions may be drawn about the heavens; for the latter are too far away from us and too high in place and in rank.[64]

This being so, the commandments cannot be fully explained. Maimonides himself makes the connection between understanding the commandments and understanding nature, or rather the limitations of our understanding of both:

Marvel exceedingly at the wisdom of His commandments, may He be exalted, just as you should marvel at the wisdom manifested in the things He has made. It says: 'The Rock, His work is perfect; for all His ways are judgement.'[65] It says that just as the things made by Him are consummately perfect, so are His commandments consummately just. However, our intellects are incapable of apprehending the perfection of everything that He has made and the justice of everything He has commanded. We only apprehend the justice of some of His commandments just as we only apprehend some of the marvels in the things He has made, in the parts of the body of animals and in the motions of the spheres. What is hidden from us in both these classes of things is much more considerable than what is manifest.[66]

The message of the *Mishneh torah*'s structure is that our inability to understand the commandments completely is not just parallel to our inability to understand nature completely but is actually a consequence of it.

The difficulty in the *Mishneh torah* is actually worse than in the *Guide*. In the latter, commandments can be explained individually, and if the historical background is lacking for commandment *x* this does not affect the ability to explain commandment *y* for which the background is known. In the former, the commandments as a system are supposed to reflect nature as a system; there is no direct link between any particular commandment and any particular natural phenomenon. A fully integrated system is either understood in its entirety or not at all, because the significance of the parts derives from the whole, and the parts are all interlinked. Our inadequate grasp of what is in the heavens therefore seems to dash any hope of being able to understand the formal cause of the commandments.

[63] Ps. 115: 16. [64] *Guide* ii. 24 (pp. 326–7).
[65] Deut. 32: 14. [66] *Guide* iii. 49 (p. 605).

Moses' Special Knowledge

There is one exception. Ordinary mortals acquire knowledge through syllogistic reasoning, but Moses, the lawgiver and greatest of the prophets, gained an access of knowledge that bypassed such reasoning and exceeded the knowledge of any human being before or since.[67] Hence Maimonides' discussion of our epistemological limitations concludes:

> Let us then stop at a point that is within our capacity, and let us give over the things that cannot be grasped by reasoning to him who was reached by the mighty divine overflow so that it could be fittingly said of him: 'With him do I speak mouth to mouth' [Num. 12: 8].[68]

With this we have found the proximate efficient cause of the commandments, the equivalent in their case of the art of bronze-casting, namely prophecy. Prophecy in general is an elevated insight into physics and metaphysics that can be translated through the prophet's imagination into concrete terms transmittable to the masses and into knowledge of the future—and hence into recommendations for action in the present. But the supreme prophecy of Moses gave him comprehensive understanding of physics and metaphysics paralleled by a comprehensive, eternal law.

We therefore propose that *ḥok* in our *halakhah* means a commandment the formal cause of which in nature is not obvious to us—but was obvious to Moses.[69] In that case, classifying commandments as *ḥukim* is not anti-universalist; quite the contrary, their formal causes lie in nature's universal laws. The problem is simply that these causes are inaccessible to human beings below the level of Moses.

We may, however, have been unduly pessimistic about the possibility of understanding nature and hence being able to explain the commandments. In the first place, as the above-quoted passage shows, Maimonides had confidence in the Aristotelian/Neoplatonic account of nature below the moon.

---

[67] *Guide* ii. 45 (p. 403). [68] *Guide* ii. 24 (p. 327).

[69] Note *Num. Rabbah* 19: 6: 'The Holy One, blessed be He, said to Moses, "To you I reveal the reason for the [red] heifer, but for anyone else it is a statute"' (our translation). What Maimonides' view was of the degree of Moses' agency in writing the Torah is not settled in scholarship; see Manekin, 'Maimonides on the Divine Authorship of the Law'. The question is whether Moses derived the Torah from his knowledge of physics and metaphysics, or whether the Torah was transmitted to him directly word for word by God. Since, however, we find a formal parallel between the structure of the cosmos and the structure of the *Mishneh torah*, we find it reasonable to assume that, at the very least, Maimonides held that Moses was able to understand the Torah in terms of physics and metaphysics, certainly much better than we can, so that commandments that for us are opaque statutes were transparent to him.

This gives scope for understanding the many commandments whose province is chiefly earthly things.[70]

Secondly, it is not really true that one cannot have partial knowledge of a system. Physicists nowadays acknowledge that their models are incomplete or are not unified, but that does not mean that they cannot tell us anything at all. Moreover, different scientific disciplines concern different parts of the system that is the universe. Although Maimonides was well aware of the shortcomings of Aristotelian theory when it came to the heavens, and of its failure to match observation (which he called 'the true perplexity'),[71] he did not consider it worthless. After all, he spent four sections of the *Mishneh torah* and the entire middle part of the *Guide* expounding it, and he considered it to be the subject of the vision in the first chapter of Ezekiel. We shall never reach Moses' complete understanding, but at least a schematic, if provisional, account of the heavens is possible, from which can be derived a schematic and provisional account of the commandments between human beings and God as a system. That is the significance of the way in which the structure and dynamics of the first ten books of the *Mishneh torah* reflect the hierarchies of the angels and spheres and the forces that move them, as Maimonides understood them.

Thirdly, the idea of human beings as microcosms means that human self-understanding sheds light on the formal causes of the commandments: natural causes can be deduced from human effects.

It follows from the foregoing that the *Mishneh torah* is, if anything, more esoteric than the *Guide* in respect of reasons for the commandments, since its ultimate reasons depend on knowledge of the esoteric disciplines of physics and metaphysics. It is not that the *Mishneh torah* presents reasons for the commandments for the multitude and the *Guide* presents reasons for the elite; the *Mishneh torah* is for both, and gradations of intellectual capacity are reflected within it.[72]

---

[70] In the Appendix we propose, on the basis of Gillis, *Reading Maimonides' Mishneh Torah*, that the last four books of the *Mishneh torah* (which are about the social commandments, and which in their sequence depict a society progressing from disorder towards order and harmony) reflect Alfarabi's notion of sublunary nature evolving towards perfection.

[71] *Guide* ii. 24 (p. 326). For a recent salvo in the scholarly wrangling over this passage, see Davidson, 'The Problematic Passage'.

[72] This bears out a comment by Strauss that might at first sight seem paradoxical, if not perverse: 'Now, an exoteric book, if it is the work of an unexoteric or initiated mind, is, by its very nature, more difficult to decipher than is an esoteric book. . . . One may venture to say that an exoteric work such as *Sefer ha-Madda* (or the *Mishneh Torah* as a whole) is much more esoteric than are most esoteric works', quoted in Green, *Leo Strauss on Maimonides*, 338. Absolutely right!

The full justification of that assertion must await our discussion of Books 8, 9, and 10 as a unit. In this chapter we present the negative side of the argument, and aim to demonstrate that, even taken by itself, 'Laws of Trespass', 8: 8 is not inconsistent with the view that explaining the commandments means explaining them according to universally acknowledged criteria of intelligibility, by means of knowledge that is accessible universally, insofar as it is accessible at all.

We have posited that Moses did understand all the commandments, as he understood all of creation. Maimonides distinguishes the prophecy of Moses from that of other prophets on several counts, but the object of his knowledge was still the same as in the case of lesser prophets, and even non-prophets—namely physics and metaphysics. His knowledge was the most comprehensive possible, but it did not exceed the boundaries of creation.[73] It was not of some arcane mystery. After all, if such a mystery existed, one would expect King David to have been party to it. It is possible to imagine that in our *halakhah* King David knows the reasons for the statutes but refuses to divulge them to his provoking challengers because they will be lost on them, but the plainer understanding, the one that does not require any extra entity in the form of special knowledge on David's part, is that he is as ignorant of the reasons as they are; the difference is that, unlike those who challenge him, he heeds the exhortation at the beginning of the *halakhah* not to hold the commandments in less esteem on that account. In short, while it certainly could be read differently, our *halakhah* is by no means incompatible with the idea that understanding the *ḥukim* is a matter of degree, not kind, of knowledge. If they were willing to apply themselves, even the heretics and pagans might get somewhere.

The World to Come

The point that the ceremonial commandments operate purely through the minds of those who fulfil them and that their significance lies in the thought of God rather than in the act itself is made earlier in the *Mishneh torah*, in 'Laws of Ritual Slaughtering', in a *halakhah* about the commandment to cover the blood of a bird or a non-domestic animal after slaughtering it:

When one performs the commandment of covering up the blood, he should do it, not with his foot, but with his hand, or with a knife or utensil, so as not to conduct the performance of the commandment in a contemptuous manner, thus treating

[73] See *Eight Chapters*, ch. 7 and *Guide* i. 54 (pp. 124–5).

God's commandments with scorn. For reverence is due not to the commandments themselves, but to Him who issued them, blessed be He.[74]

The idea is repeated in the *Book of Temple Service* itself:

It is a positive commandment to reverence the Sanctuary, for it is said: 'Ye shall . . . reverence My Sanctuary' [Lev. 19: 30]. This does not bid you fear the Sanctuary itself, but Him Who commanded that we reverence it.[75]

Our *halakhah* thus participates in a general theme that commandments are particular means to a universal end, and are valuable only insofar as they assist correct thinking. Again, the comparison with nature is pertinent. Nature is not entirely comprehensible, but we are not free to desist from attempting to understand it, for that is the route to the love of God; in considering nature, too, what should inspire reverence is not natural phenomena themselves but the thought of the God who created them. In 'Laws of the Foundations of the Torah',[76] Maimonides prescribes contemplation of nature as a means of arousing the love and fear of God, but he is careful to specify that what inspires love is the thought of God's wisdom, and that what inspires awe is awareness of the gap between God's knowledge and ours. Revering natural objects and phenomena themselves, even if it is ostensibly out of respect for their creator, is the error that leads to idolatry and ultimately to forgetfulness of God.[77]

Undue emphasis on the act or object of the commandment, whether out of disrespect (such as by performing the act of covering blood but doing so casually) or out of misapplied respect (such as by revering the Sanctuary itself), therefore smacks of idolatry. Religious ritual in Maimonides is thus a risky activity, as likely to dim the intellect as to enlighten it. Calibrating one's attitude towards ritual is not simple, for meticulous observance must be combined with thought that penetrates beyond observance. Hence the complexity of the discussion in the *halakhot* we are considering. At any rate, the statutes in general, and sacrifices in particular, are not exclusive formulae with substantive properties, but contingent means of inculcating universal truths. Performance of the ceremonial commandments does not help in reserving a place in the world to come, except insofar as the truths that those commandments are meant to impart are actually absorbed.

This may seem to be contradicted by the statement in 'Laws of Trespass', 8: 8 that 'through the performance of the statutes and the ordinances the righteous merit life in the world to come'. As noted at the beginning of this

---

[74] 'Laws of Ritual Slaughtering', 14: 16. See Ch. 5 above for full discussion of this passage.
[75] 'Laws of the Temple', 7: 1.   [76] 2: 1.   [77] See 'Laws of Idolatry', 1: 1–2.

discussion, this might imply that performance of the commandments is in itself a direct ticket to immortality, a particularist interpretation apparently backed by what is said about the Noahide laws in 'Laws of Kings and their Wars'.

This interpretation, however, is not warranted. We should note that it is through the performance of the statutes and the ordinances alike that the righteous gain immortality. It is not that performance of the ordinances is rewarded in this world and performance of the statutes in the world to come. Statutes and ordinances both confer benefits in this world, the ultimate one being that a person becomes worthy of life in the world to come.

As far as Maimonides is concerned, the world to come is a disembodied existence of pure contemplation of the divine.[78] It is attained through development of the intellect until it is on a par with the separate intellects and can exist without a body, so that it survives physical death.[79] There is no heavenly scorer recording how many statutes you observe. All the commandments ultimately have value only insofar as they contribute to fulfilment of your intellectual potential. For Maimonides, this encompasses all human activity, since he sees social harmony and individual moral uprightness as necessary conditions for intellectual development. The social and moral commandments, besides their obvious, direct benefits in this world, thus also fall into line with the ultimate aim. For their part, the ceremonial commandments act directly on the intellect by countering idolatrous ideas and inculcating correct, monotheistic doctrine. The statutes are therefore not a passport to eternal life. They are an aid to fulfilling the universal condition for immortality for Jew and non-Jew alike, namely a fully developed intellect, and our *halakhah* implies nothing different from this. The question why acknowledgment of the Torah's mandate is required even though the conditions are universal remains, but at least some of the difficulty has been removed: performance of the commandments is not in itself a route to heaven.

This provides an opportunity for bringing the *Mishneh torah* and the *Guide* together, after we have set them facing in different directions on reasons for the commandments. *Guide* iii. 51–2 is a secondary discourse on reasons for the commandments, for the philosopher who seeks purpose in them after their basic didactic functions have been fulfilled. Maimonides says he will explain 'the worship as practised by one who has apprehended the true realities peculiar only to Him after he has obtained an apprehension of what He is; and it also guides him toward achieving this worship, which is the end of

---

[78] See 'Laws of Repentance', 8: 2–3.
[79] See 'Laws of the Foundations of the Torah', 4: 8–9.

man, and makes known to him how providence watches over him in this habitation until he is brought over to the *bundle of life*,[80] which, as Pines points out, means eternal life. In other words, he will explain what was puzzling in 'Laws of Trespass', 8: 8, namely, how practising the commandments leads to immortality.

The explanation is that immortality is not attained through the commandments themselves—the physical actions that they entail—but through the way they are performed. In this phase, they are a means of training the mind to be occupied with God alone. Those who achieve this level of meditation on God, whose thoughts constantly transcend their material condition, will, at the moment of death, experience an ecstasy of love that is pure thought, and will remain permanently in that state. At the same time, because the commandments train people to be mindful of God at all times—which means submitting to the constant scrutiny of their intellects—they will always act correctly, even in secret, for they constantly experience awe.

The *Book of Temple Service*, and especially its ending, can be interpreted in this light. The Temple is a place of awe. Those who visit it will conduct themselves circumspectly out of a feeling that they are in God's presence, and 'Man does not sit, move, and occupy himself when he is alone in his house, as he sits, moves, and occupies himself when he is in the presence of a great king.'[81] But a person should always feel that way, because he or she is always accompanied by the king: 'This king who cleaves to him and accompanies him is the intellect that overflows towards us and is the bond between us and Him, may He be exalted.'[82] As mentioned, in discussing the commandment to be in awe of the Temple, Maimonides stresses that the awe is not of the place but of the one who issued the commandment. The sense of awe inspired by being in God's house should carry over into one's behaviour alone in one's own house, for God's presence is equally close, through the intellect, in both places.

This is the kind of awe underlying 'Laws of Trespass', 8: 8. Relative to the God who commanded them, the commandments themselves are only sticks and stones. Their function is to keep the thought of God constantly in mind, a thought that will ultimately ensure immortality.

Summary

In 'Laws of Trespass', 8: 8, Maimonides does not retreat from universalism. He seeks to bolster respectful observance of the commandments in

[80] *Guide* iii. 51 (p. 618).   [81] *Guide* iii. 52 (p. 629).   [82] Ibid.

awareness of their source even when no reason can be supplied for them, but he goes about this without undermining the principles on which a universalistic reading of the *Mishneh torah* is based. Reason is not denigrated. The problem of the statutes is an epistemological problem arising from the difficulty in attaining certain kinds of knowledge: historical in the case of the *Guide*, scientific in the case of the *Mishneh torah*. In neither case is it a question of an arcane mystery, and the difficulty is common to all human beings. The commandments are presented as helping a human being fulfil the criterion for admission to the world to come, namely a developed intellect, but immortality is not promised as a direct reward for keeping them.

Much work still needs to be done to uncover the positive universalistic message of which the ending of the *Book of Temple Service* forms part, and to demonstrate how the natural order is manifest in Maimonides' presentation of the laws of sacrifices and purity. Meanwhile, however, we turn to the *Book of Offerings* and the next instalment of the discussion of reasons for the commandments.

NINE

OFFERINGS
The Morality of the Commandments

Introduction

The *Book of Offerings* (*Sefer korbanot*) is described in the *Mishneh torah*'s introduction as being about individual offerings, as opposed to the *Book of Temple Service*, which is described as being about 'the Temple building and the regular communal offerings'. This distinction will be highly important later on.

The *Book of Offerings* has six sections. The first, 'Laws of the Passover Offering', is about the paschal lamb (or kid) which is slaughtered in the Temple in the afternoon of the day before Passover and consumed, roasted, in family groups that night, commemorating the Exodus from Egypt. The brief second section, 'Laws of the Festal Offering', is about the three kinds of offerings that each householder brings on the three pilgrim festivals: one is a burnt offering, while the other two are consumed by him and his family. Maimonides characteristically stresses the obligation to give portions to the poor and the Levites so that they too will rejoice on the festival.[1] The third chapter of this section covers the commandment of *hakhel*, the ceremony held every seven years on the festival of Tabernacles following the sabbatical year, in which the people assemble in the Temple to hear the king read certain portions of Deuteronomy. The next section, 'Laws of Firstlings', is about the requirement to offer firstborn kosher animals and animal tithes. The fourth section is 'Laws of Offerings for Transgressions Committed through Error', the title of which is description enough. The next section, 'Laws of Those whose Atonement Is Not Complete', is about the sacrifices required to complete the purification process in certain cases of impurity.

The sixth and final section, 'Laws of Substituted Offerings', is about the prohibition against substituting an animal designated for sacrifice with another one—even a superior one. The penalty for this is lashes, and both animals become consecrated.[2]

[1] See 'Laws of the Festal Offering', 2: 14.
[2] Lashes are an unusual penalty for an offence not involving an action but only a statement such as 'this instead of that'. See 'Laws of Substituted Offerings', 1: 1.

The final *halakhah* of 'Laws of Substituted Offerings' reads:

Although the statutes in the Law are all of them divine edicts, as we have explained at the close of Laws of Trespass, yet it is proper to ponder over them and to give a reason for them, so far as we are able to give them a reason. The Sages of former times said that King Solomon understood most of the reasons for all the statutes of the Law. It seems to me that in so far as Scripture has said: 'Both it and that for which it is changed shall be holy' [Lev. 27: 10]—as also in that matter whereof it has said: 'And if he that sanctified it will redeem his house then he shall add the fifth part of the money of thy valuation' [Lev. 27: 15]—the Law has plumbed the depths of man's mind and the extremity of his evil impulse. For it is man's nature to increase his possessions and to be sparing of his wealth. Even though a man had made a vow and declared something, it may be that later he drew back and repented and would now redeem it with something less than its value. But the Law has said, 'If he redeems it for himself he shall add the fifth.' So, too, if a man dedicated a beast to a sanctity of its body, perchance he would draw back, and since he cannot redeem it, would change it for something of less worth. And if the right was given to him to change the bad for the good he would change the good for the bad and say, 'It is good.' Therefore Scripture has stopped the way against him so that he should not change it, and has penalized him if he should change it and has said: 'Both it and that for which it was changed shall be holy.' And both these laws serve to suppress man's natural tendency and correct his moral qualities. And the greater part of the rules in the Law are but 'counsels from of old' [Isa. 25: 1], from Him 'who is great in counsel' [Jer. 32: 19], to correct moral qualities [*de'ot*] and to make straight all doings.[3] And so He saith: 'Have not I written unto thee excellent things of counsels and knowledge, that I might make thee know the certainty of the words of truth, that thou mightest bring back words of truth to them that sent thee' [Prov. 22: 20–1].[4]

This *halakhah* complements the ending of the *Book of Temple Service*, which is explicitly referenced. Whereas in the *Book of Temple Service* the emphasis is on the need to obey the commandments even when reason fails to find a cause, here the matter is presented the other way around: although the commandments are divine edicts, it is proper to attempt to discover reasons for them. Maimonides does not divide the commandments into two kinds; all of them are divine edicts and at the same time susceptible of reasoned explanation.

In the particular case of 'Laws of Substituted Offerings', the reason that Maimonides proposes is a psychological one: the Torah understands human frailty. A person may designate a fine animal as an offering in a sudden access

---

[3] Danby's translation (Yale Judaica Series) gives 'our moral qualities' and 'all our doings', but 'our' is not warranted by the original.

[4] 'Laws of Substituted Offerings', 4: 13, trans. Herbert Danby, slightly modified.

of feelings of gratitude for good fortune, but when the enthusiasm begins to wear off and the person starts to reflect, he or she may decide that what befell them was not so remarkable after all, and that in any case it is the thought that counts. Another animal will do just as well, and there's one that could be just right; in fact, who's to say it might not be better than the first one?

The law penalizing the substitution of offerings, like the law imposing a penalty payment of one-fifth extra for someone who wishes to redeem property donated to the Temple, is intended to discipline cupidity. These ceremonial laws thus act as correctives in the manner that Maimonides recommends in 'Laws of Moral Qualities' for curing deviation from the ethically desirable middle path—to go to the opposite extreme, only in this case the cure is imposed rather than being undertaken voluntarily. This is not a new Maimonidean theory of the function of the commandments. As mentioned in the previous chapter, Maimonides describes all the commandments of the Torah as designed to safeguard virtue by keeping human behaviour just to one side of the ideal, philosophically approved mean, in order to counter the propensity to veer to the other side.[5] If appropriate generosity is the virtuous middle way, the more common vice, 'man's natural tendency', is miserliness rather than profligacy. Hence the Torah institutes commandments designed to steer people away from it towards virtue.

Just as interesting as the explanation Maimonides does provide is the one he does not. It would have been possible to justify the rule that 'Both it and that for which it is changed shall be holy' on quite different grounds, namely that once an animal is designated for sacrifice, it acquires a quality called 'holiness' which is irremovable. We saw in the previous chapter, however, that as far as Maimonides is concerned, holiness is not something that inheres in places or objects. Thus while 'Laws of Substituted Offerings', 4: 13, presents the opposite perspective on rationalization of the commandments from that of 'Laws of Trespass', 8: 8, there is an underlying consistency between these two endings, and we shall see it extend to the ending of the *Book of Purity* as well.

An objection that might be raised is that, on this basis, the substitution of a better animal for a worse one ought to incur no penalty, since the person concerned is only going further in bending his or her character towards generosity; yet in this case, too, both animals have to be sacrificed. On the basis of the concept of inherent holiness, this presents no difficulty: a holy animal remains holy regardless of the worshipper's motives. But Maimonides anticipates this objection by presenting this aspect of the rule as evidence of the

[5] See *Eight Chapters*, ch. 4.

Torah's insight into 'the depths of man's mind and the extremity of his evil impulse', as he explains: 'And if the right was given to him to change the bad for the good he would change the good for the bad and say, "It is good".' The *halakhah* plumbs the human capacity for dissimulation, even self-deception, where material interests are at stake.[6]

Very clearly, this way of rationalizing the commandments concerning sacrificial animals and consecrated property has a universal character. There is no indication here that Maimonides considers the moral constitution of Jews to be different from that of non-Jews, either better or worse. As in the ending of the *Book of Temple Service*, he speaks of the nature of *adam*, a generic human being. Moreover, he generalizes from these particular instances to the commandments as a whole: 'And the greater part of the rules in the Law are "but counsels from of old", from Him who is great in counsel, to correct moral qualities and to keep straight all doings.'[7] The purpose of 'the greater part of the rules in the Law', then, is to guide people towards attainment of the Aristotelian ideal of moral virtue. The only particularity is that the Jewish people is privileged with God-given means, '"counsels from of old", from Him "who is great in counsel"', to achieve this universal end.

'The Seed of Our Father Abraham'

But are things really so straightforward? Maimonides' drift in our *halakhah* is that the point of these laws about sacrifices is not to protect God's property but to uproot a moral failing from human beings, namely meanness, and to instil the moral quality of generosity. In relation to these qualities we read in 'Laws of Gifts to the Poor':

It is our duty to be more careful in the performance of the commandment of almsgiving [*tsedakah*] than in that of any other positive commandment, for almsgiving is the mark of the righteous man who is of the seed of our father Abraham, as it is said, 'For I have known him, to the end that he may command his children . . . to do righteousness [*tsedakah*]' [Gen. 18: 19]. The throne of Israel cannot be established, nor true faith made to stand up, except through charity [*tsedakah*], as it is said, 'In

---

[6] *Guide* iii. 46 (p. 584) provides the same psychological (as opposed to ontological) explanation of the basis of these commandments in the tendency to be careful about one's property, but in explaining their purpose it emphasizes reinforcement of respect for the Temple: 'All this is prescribed in order that what has been named as consecrated to God and whereby one may come near to Him should not be held in little esteem'—rather than moral improvement. A similar idea is expressed in 'Laws of Things Forbidden for the Altar', 7: 11.

[7] The Hebrew *rov* is here translated 'the greater part of', but it could also be translated 'the many'.

righteousness shalt thou be established' [Isa. 54: 14]; nor will Israel be redeemed, except through the practice of charity, as it is said, 'Zion shall be redeemed with justice, and they that return of her with righteousness' [Isa. 1: 27] . . .

Whosoever is cruel and merciless lays himself open to suspicion as to his descent, for cruelty is found only among the heathens, as it is said, 'They are cruel, and have no compassion' [Jer. 50: 42]. All Israelites and those that have attached themselves to them are to each other like brothers, as it is said, 'Ye are the children of the Lord your God' [Deut. 14: 1]. If brother will show no compassion to brother, who will? And unto whom shall the poor of Israel raise their eyes? Unto the heathens, who hate them and persecute them? Their eyes are therefore hanging solely upon their brethren.

He who turns his eyes away from charity is called a base fellow, just as is he who worships idols.[8]

On the face of it, these *halakhot* indicate that Maimonides considered liberality to be a peculiarly Jewish trait, and one inborn at that, not culturally transmitted. In that case, the kind of moral traits in which the commandments train those who observe them[9] may not in his view be universal values after all, but essentially Jewish characteristics. Such characteristics perhaps need encouragement in the form of divine precepts in order to develop and be expressed, as every talent requires training in order to flourish, but they remain a specifically and innately Jewish potential, so much so that the origins of anyone who fails to manifest them are suspect.

This reading has been effectively rebutted, and there is no need to rehearse the arguments at length.[10] In outline, the main one is that Maimonides did not really consider 'the seed of our father Abraham' to be a biological category; it is, in his eyes, a cultural one, referring to those who share Abraham's beliefs. He adopts the language of genetics here as a rhetorical ploy, to impress upon those who think in those terms the importance of a charitable disposition, but his true position is revealed not only by what he says elsewhere, but also by the inclusion here in the category of 'the children of the Lord your God' not only of Israelites but also of 'those who have attached themselves to them'.[11] This clearly rules out the idea that charity is an inherited trait that is unique to those born Jewish. The verse about Abraham, 'For I have known him, to the end that he may command his children . . . to do righteousness', is also cited at the end of the first chapter of 'Laws of Moral

---

[8] 'Laws of Gifts to the Poor', 10: 1–3. See also below, Ch. 11.
[9] Such as the commandment about substituted offerings.
[10] See Kellner, *Maimonides' Confrontation*, 254–5, and Kellner, *They, Too, Are Called Human* (Heb.), ch. 7.   [11] This phrase is discussed in Ch. 11 below.

Qualities', where moral virtue is introduced as pertaining to 'all human beings'; Abraham and his legacy are only an instance of virtue in action.

Morality and Truth

Maimonides does not stop, however, at impugning the ancestry of a person who fails to perform charity. He associates that trait with idol worship. In other words, a mean person repudiates not only Abraham's moral legacy, but his intellectual legacy as well. It is a constant in Maimonides' writings that moral virtue is both a preparation for intellectual virtue and an outcome of it.[12] Truth and goodness go together.

We find this very idea expressed at the end of the *Book of Offerings*:

And both these laws serve to suppress man's natural tendency and correct his moral qualities. And the greater part of the rules in the Law are but 'counsels from of old' [Isa. 25: 1], from Him 'who is great in counsel' [Jer. 32: 19], to correct moral qualities and to keep straight all doings. And so He saith: 'Have not I written unto thee excellent things of counsels and knowledge, that I might make thee know the certainty of the words of truth, that thou mightest bring back words of truth to them that sent thee' [Prov. 22: 20–1].

This passage leads from correct moral qualities and actions to knowledge and truth. Twersky remarks of it that 'The use of Prov. 22: 20–21 is novel.'[13] In that case, it is probably worth dwelling on what exactly Maimonides means by citing these verses here.[14] A first point to note is that the Hebrew translated by 'moral qualities' is *de'ot*, which can mean opinions, but which in the *Mishneh torah* almost always refers to traits of character.[15] This clearly echoes the Hebrew title of 'Laws of Moral Qualities', *Hilkhot de'ot*, and constitutes the keyword of that entire section. Moreover, the psychological deviancy described in 'Laws of Substituted Offerings', 4: 13—'for if you allow him to exchange the bad for the good, he will exchange the good for the bad and say "It is good"'—can be seen as an example of the general pathology discussed in 'Laws of Moral Qualities', 2: 1 of moral judgement perverted by desire,[16] concerning which Maimonides cites the verse 'O, they that say of evil that it is good, and of good that it is evil'.[17] The person who substitutes a bad animal for

---

[12] See Gillis, *Reading Maimonides' Mishneh Torah*, 100–9.

[13] Twersky, *Introduction to the Code*, 417 n. 148.

[14] According to Kafih, *The Hebrew Bible in Maimonides* (Heb.), 124, this is the only place where Maimonides refers to these verses.

[15] It is also used to refer to the separate intellects or angels, on which see Gillis, *Reading Maimonides' Mishneh Torah*, 96.   [16] 'Laws of Moral Qualities', 2: 1.   [17] Isa. 5: 20.

a good one not only succumbs to avarice, but is in danger of letting such motives corrupt his or her judgement entirely, and is well on the way to general moral confusion.

To return to the close of 'Laws of Substituted Offerings', 4: 13, the context of commandments that 'suppress man's natural tendency' and the pairing with 'all our doings', which is also on the moral plane, tend to confirm that *de'ot* refers to character traits. In Proverbs 22: 20, however, rather than *de'ot* we find the related word *da'at*, here translated as 'knowledge', but which in the *Mishneh torah* is more generally used in the sense of 'intellect', the form or defining characteristic of the human species.[18] In the end, though, there is really no difference, since the developed intellect, which is what makes a human being truly human, is theoretical knowledge, and ultimately knowledge of God. The word 'counsels' (*etsot*), on the other hand, appears to retain its moral connotation from 'counsels of old . . . to correct our moral qualities'. In short, the 'excellent things' are the commandments, and 'of counsels and knowledge' can be paraphrased as 'concerning moral virtue and intellectual virtue',[19] which are the main headings of the purposes of the commandments in the *Guide*: 'the welfare of the soul and the welfare of the body'.[20] The use of the words *de'ot* and *da'at*, here and elsewhere in the *Mishneh torah*,[21] conveys the way in which one shades into the other.

Who Sent Whom?

Somewhat puzzling is the closing phrase 'that thou mightest bring back words of truth to them that sent thee'. Who is bringing back which words of truth, and to whom? The classic medieval commentators offer various interpretations. Rashi suggests that the phrase means that you should be capable of giving appropriate responses to those who seek instruction from you. This is a plausible reading in our context. The *halakhah* is about giving reasons for the commandments, and the closing words could mean that a person should be able to demonstrate to his and others' satisfaction how the command-

---

[18] See 'Laws of the Foundations of the Torah', 4: 8.

[19] Supporting evidence can be adduced from a similar interpretative move that Maimonides makes in *Eight Chapters*, ch. 4, where he comments on the phrase in Zech. 8: 19, 'therefore love ye truth and peace': 'And know that "truth" refers to the intellectual virtues, because they are unchanging truths . . . and "peace" refers to the moral virtues, through which there will be peace in the world.'

[20] *Guide* iii. 27 (p. 510). Kafih, ad loc., makes a similar reference.

[21] Commenting on the nuances of *de'ot*, Twersky (*Introduction to the Code*, 417 n. 148) recommends a list of passages in the *Mishneh torah* 'to be studied and correlated'.

ments act 'to correct our moral qualities and to keep straight all our doings'. The 'words of truth' would be a true understanding of the commandments that can be reached if their moral aim is fulfilled.

More interesting in the light of what we have already said is the approach of Abraham Ibn Ezra (1089–1167), who comments:

> And the sense of 'to bring back'[22] is as in 'And Moses returned the words of the people unto the Lord',[23] meaning, when I make you know the certainty of the words of truth I also return words to him, as in 'we will do and be obedient'.[24] 'To them that sent thee' [means] to God who sent me to you to try you, because the intellect is the messenger of God. 'To them that sent thee' is in the plural like 'God my maker'.[25]

In other words, the sender is God, what is sent is the intellect, and what is brought back is an expression of compliance with the intellect's directive. That is at least approximately what Ibn Ezra seems to be saying. It puts one in mind of a passage from the *Guide*: 'the intellect that flows towards us and is the bond between us and Him'.[26]

At any rate, what Maimonides seeks to express through the verses from Proverbs is probably something not far from Ibn Ezra's interpretation of them. There is, though, a slightly different emphasis. As in the *Guide*,[27] while most of the commandments, the 'counsels from afar', instil fear and obedience and bring about correct behaviour, the 'words of truth' are 'the opinions taught by the Law, which includes the apprehension of His being as He, may He be exalted, is in truth', and inspire love.

Being Straight and Becoming Straight

By a different route, then, we arrive at a similar position to that at the end of the *Book of Temple Service*. There, 'through the performance of the statutes and the ordinances the righteous merit life in the world to come'. 'The righteous' translates the Hebrew *hayesharim*, literally 'the straight'. At the end of the *Book of Offerings*, the function of the commandments is 'to correct our moral qualities', where 'to correct' translates the verb *leyasher*, literally 'to straighten'. This is as a platform for acquiring the truth, which is the qualification for the world to come.

---

[22] The original simply has *lehashiv*, 'to bring back' or 'to reply', that is, the infinitive with no person mentioned. The translation 'That thou mightest bring back' is already a gloss.
[23] Exod. 19: 8.   [24] Exod. 24: 7.
[25] Job 35: 10. The Hebrew for 'my maker' is *osai*, which literally means 'my makers'.
[26] *Guide* iii. 52 (p. 629).   [27] Ibid. (p. 630).

The contrast between being and becoming in these two endings, between 'straight' and 'to straighten', is foreshadowed earlier in the *Mishneh torah*, in the transition between the first section of the *Book of Knowledge*, 'Laws of the Foundations of the Torah', and the second, 'Laws of Moral Qualities'. The former section is directed towards God. It concerns what we can know about God himself, God's creation, and prophecy. It aims at intellectual virtue. In it, human beings are described as created in God's image, in respect of their intellects.[28] In the latter section, attention shifts to human beings. The subject is moral virtue, acquired through human beings *becoming* like God by applying their intellects to the imitation of God's ways.

This parallel between the respective orientations of the first two sections of the *Book of Knowledge* and of books 8 and 9 of the *Mishneh torah* will be important in chapter 10, where books 8, 9, and 10 will be considered together. For the time being, we should remember that, although book 10, the *Book of Purity*, is connected to the Temple, 'Laws of Substituted Offerings', 4: 13 is Maimonides' last word on the Temple ritual per se. Its radical nature should be appreciated. Through his explanation of the penalty for attempted substitution of offerings, Maimonides apparently takes these laws out of the sphere of sacred ritual altogether and relocates them, along with 'the greater part of the rules in the Law', in the sphere of ethics. At stake is not the value of gifts that God does not need, but the welfare of the human soul. Through the closing quotation from Proverbs, Maimonides traces the link between ethics and intellectual clarity, and implies that the offering that God really demands is knowledge of the truth.[29]

This is the anchor of Maimonides' universalism in the *Mishneh torah*.

---

[28] See 'Laws of the Foundations of the Torah', 4: 8. In fact, the intellect also goes through a process of becoming: through study of the sciences it develops from a hylic intellect into an acquired intellect. Nevertheless, 'Laws of the Foundations of the Torah' treats it as a fixed quality through which human beings are 'in God's image'.

[29] See M. Y. Shatz (Bransky; 1817–91), *Har hamoriyah*, a commentary that links this ending to the distinction in the *Guide* between knowledge of true and false as absolutes and knowledge of good and bad as conventional. The Torah, Shatz avers, is true because it corresponds to the order of nature, which Moses understood in its entirety but which Solomon did not; hence the latter was able to understand some commandments only in terms of good and bad. Admittedly Shatz bases his notion of the correspondence between the Torah and nature on the *midrashim* in *Gen. Rabbah* (1: 1, 4 and 8: 2) to the effect that the Torah was the pre-existent blueprint of creation, which does not accord with our understanding of Maimonides' version of the concept (see Kellner, *Maimonides' Confrontation*, 68–76). Nevertheless, his comment here is close to the interpretation we have advanced that the ending of the *Book of Offerings* traces the transition from moral virtue to intellectual virtue. We are not aware of any other rabbinic commentary that deals with this ending so extensively.

The commandments may wear Jewish national costume (although, according to the *Guide*, sacrifices themselves are borrowed robes), but they ultimately derive from the bare truth and are meant to lead back to it. As far as Maimonides is concerned, there is but one truth upon which all other things, whatever the differences between them, are equally contingent, namely the existence and unity of God.[30]

Summary

The ending of the *Book of Offerings* complements the ending of the *Book of Temple Service*. In both cases, the commandments are presented as divine edicts and at the same time comprehensible within human limitations, but whereas before the emphasis was on observance of commandments despite our failure to find reasons for them (it was suggested this is because of shortcomings in knowledge of physics and metaphysics), here the emphasis is on finding reasons in the moral sphere (where full knowledge is available). The attempt to substitute one sacrificial animal for another results in both being consecrated, not because the animals acquire an inherent quality of holiness, but as a moral corrective. Maimonides' explanation relates to universal moral theory.

The endings of Books 8 and 9 are also complementary in a broader way. The former ultimately touches on immortality, a state of permanent intellectual being reached by a human mind that has attained universal truth. The latter is about a state of moral becoming, and truth as an aspiration. In the next chapter we examine how Book 10, the *Book of Purity*, represents the bridging of these two states through devotion to knowledge.

[30] See 'Laws of the Foundations of the Torah', 1: 1–4.

TEN

RITUAL PURITY
Intellectual and Moral Purity

Introduction

The *Book of Ritual Purity* (*Sefer tohorah*)[1] covers a large and complicated area of Jewish law that was once as important to observant Jews as, say, the dietary laws still are today, but that since the destruction of the Second Temple has been mostly without practical application. This is because a bar on admission to the Temple is the main consequence of most types of impurity—a point that, as we shall see, Maimonides stresses. Nevertheless, the laws of purity and impurity occupy a complete volume of his code. Part of the aim of this chapter is to demonstrate that this is not merely for the sake of completeness, or only in anticipation of the messiah and the Temple's reconstruction. The *Book of Purity*, together with the previous two volumes on the Temple and its rites, is part of a meaningful structure whereby Maimonides conveys what he sees as the timeless value of comprehending the Torah in its entirety as a system of divine law, irrespective of temporary hiatuses in its applicability. He derives this value, we argue, by relating the law to universal philosophical concepts.

The book has eight sections. 'Laws of Corpse Impurity' is about impurity from touching, carrying, or even being under the same roof as a human corpse. 'Laws of the Red Heifer' is about purification from such impurity, involving a waiting period of seven days and being sprinkled with the ashes of a perfectly red heifer mingled with water on day three and day seven—recognized as the most obscure commandment of the Torah. 'Laws of Impurity of

---

[1] In *Guide* iii. 47 (pp. 592–7), and in the passage studied in this chapter, Maimonides emphasizes that the purity/impurity spoken of here is a matter of law only, and has nothing to do with cleanliness or morality. As he points out there, most people spend most of their lives in a state of ritual impurity. For details, see Kellner, *Maimonides' Confrontation*, ch. 4. For the sake of simplicity, however, we will henceforth use the expressions purity/impurity, without adding the modifier 'ritual'. Pines, whose translation of the *Guide* we cite, prefers 'clean/unclean'.

Leprosy' is about *tsora'at* (generally translated 'leprosy'), a condition that can afflict people, garments, and houses, rendering them impure. 'Laws of Those who Render Couch and Seat Impure' is about impurity transmitted by people who have had issues from their bodies. 'Laws of Other Fathers of Impurity' is about other sources of impurity, such as animal corpses. Idols and things associated with idolatry also come under this heading. 'Laws of Impurity of Foodstuffs' describes how foods wetted by certain liquids become impure on contact with things from which impurity derives. 'Laws of Utensils' describes how garments and containers made of certain materials may become impure.

The final section is 'Laws of Immersion Pools', about the complete immersion in a pool of water known as a *mikveh* that is a component of all purification rituals. A *mikveh* is a body of natural ('undrawn') water, of about 575 litres minimum volume. Besides being required for purification, immersion in a *mikveh* is also undergone by a woman before she resumes sexual relations with her husband after menstruation or childbirth, by a convert to Judaism, and by anyone wishing to enter the Temple, even if they are in a state of purity. The section ends as follows:

It is plain and manifest that the laws about impurity and purity are decrees laid down by Scripture and not matters about which human understanding is capable of forming a judgement; for behold, they are included among the divine statutes. So, too, immersion as a means of freeing oneself from impurity is included among the divine statutes. Now 'impurity' is not mud or filth which water can remove, but is a matter of scriptural decree and dependent on the intention of the heart. Therefore the Sages have said, If a man immerses himself, but without special intention, it is as though he has not immersed himself at all.

Nevertheless, we may find some indication [*remez*] of this: just as one who sets his heart on becoming pure becomes pure as soon as he has immersed himself, although nothing new has befallen his body, so, too, one who sets his heart on purifying himself from the impurity that besets men's souls—namely wrongful thoughts and bad dispositions[2]—becomes pure as soon as he consents to shun those counsels and brings his soul into the waters of intellect.[3] Behold, Scripture says, 'And I will sprinkle pure water upon you and ye shall be pure; from all your

---

[2] Danby renders *vede'ot hara'ot* here as 'and false convictions'. We emend to 'bad dispositions' on the grounds that *ra* means bad rather than false, and so cannot qualify 'convictions', which, especially in Maimonides, are true or false, not good or bad (see *Guide* i. 2 (pp. 24–5)). Throughout the *Mishneh torah*, the word *de'ot*, when applied to human beings, has a meaning in the field of moral dispositions, ethical traits, and the like, as in 'Laws of Moral Qualities', which translates *hilkhot de'ot*. In 'Laws of Moral Qualities', 2: 3, anger is described as *de'ah ra'ah*, which must mean a bad disposition, not a false conviction, and there are similar examples elsewhere in the *Mishneh torah*; see Gillis, *Reading Maimonides' Mishneh Torah*, 126 n. 53.   [3] Danby gives 'waters of pure reason'.

impurity and from all your idols will I cleanse you' [Ezek. 36: 25]. May God, in his great mercy, purify us from every sin, iniquity, and guilt.[4]

The *Book of Purity* is the last of the ten books of the *Mishneh torah* that almost entirely concern *mitsvot bein adam lamakom*, commandments between human beings and God, mostly ceremonial commandments. The remaining four books concern *mitsvot bein adam leḥavero*, the social commandments. Since the *Book of Purity* is situated at such an important position, at the end of the first of the *Mishneh torah*'s two major divisions, we might expect its own ending, the point of inflection between the divine and human orientations of the commandments, to be special. It is. Uniquely in Maimonides' oeuvre, the final *halakhah* in the book presents a figurative interpretation of a commandment, making *mikveh* a metaphor for 'the waters of intellect'.[5]

This striking image does have some basis in the rabbinic sources. In the Talmud, Resh Lakish takes the verse 'And the stability of thy times shall be a hoard of salvation, wisdom, and knowledge, and the fear of the Lord which is His treasure' (Isa. 33: 6) and breaks it down into six separate expressions, which he interprets as referring to the six orders of the Mishnah.[6] 'Knowledge' is said to stand for Order *Tohorot*, on which Maimonides' *Book of Purity* is based. The Hebrew translated as 'knowledge' in the verse is *da'at*, the word used in 'Laws of Immersion Pools', 11: 12 to mean 'intellect'. In other words, the third-century sage Resh Lakish established a link between the laws of purity and intellect. It is unlikely that he had in mind quite the reverberations that are set off in our *halakhah*,[7] but it is not at all unlikely that Maimonides saw that link as something on which he could build, at least a hint to his hint.

Mikveh as Unifying Image

Mikveh as an image of the purifying intellect is remarkable in itself, but the position of this image at the end of the *Book of Purity* amplifies its significance. This positioning is deliberate. Tractate *Mikva'ot*, to which 'Laws of

---

[4] 'Laws of Immersion Pools', 11: 12, trans. Danby.
[5] In *Guide* iii. 43 (pp. 572–4) Maimonides criticizes literal-minded approaches to midrashic, symbolic interpretations of the commandments, which he says have 'the status of poetical conceits'. It is after all a short step from a poetical conceit to talismanic or theurgic beliefs—if *a* stands for *x*, perhaps it can affect *x* or partake in its powers—and to an intellectually and morally depleted notion of religion. [6] See BT *Shab.* 31a.
[7] He probably means that the material of Order *Tohorot* is mentally taxing, but it is worth noting that in a continuation of the same passage Rava makes the word 'knowledge' in the verse refer to the power of deduction in general.

Immersion Pools' corresponds, is in the middle of Order *Tohorot*, the sixth out of twelve tractates in that order altogether, so that Maimonides had to rearrange the mishnaic material in order to place his own treatment of *mikveh*, and his potent metaphor, at this crucial juncture.

The image of the *mikveh* as 'the waters of intellect' looks both back and forwards. It sums up all that has gone before, in that all the commandments between human beings and God can be thought of as an immersion in the waters of intellect. They are designed to bring all appetites, desires, and faculties within reason's scope, and to subordinate them to reason's quest, the knowledge of God, which is the *Mishneh torah*'s very first commandment. Seen thus as not just an ending but a summary, the final *halakhah* of the *Book of Purity* places even the largely particularist commandments between human beings and God in a universal context, for, certainly as far as Maimonides is concerned, there is no such thing as specifically Jewish intellect. *Mikveh* itself may, along with all the laws of purity and impurity, be peculiarly Jewish,[8] but all mankind is invited to immerse itself in 'the waters of intellect'. The notion that the commandments are particular means to universal ends, which may sound trite when stated so barely, is thus given subtle and powerful expression.

This universal ideal is realized at the very end of the *Mishneh torah* when, in the time of the messiah, 'the earth will be full of the knowledge of God as the waters cover the sea' (Hab. 2: 14). Again, water is a metaphor for knowledge or intellect. For Jewish ritual purposes the sea is a valid *mikveh*.[9] At the end of the *Mishneh torah* it is a *mikveh* in which the whole world is metaphorically immersed. Through the association that Maimonides creates between water and intellect, we can understand that what he means by citing this verse from Isaiah at the end of his code of Jewish law is not the triumph of Judaism but the perfection of human nature, for in his philosophy the knowledge of God is not a matter of tradition but of correct thinking, discoverable by all who sincerely seek it (whether or not it will lead to universal observance of the commandments is another question),[10] and the Jews in the age of the messiah will not be overlords but peaceful pursuers of enlightenment.[11]

---

[8] The corpse of a non-Jew can be a source of impurity like that of a Jew, but, at least on the level of Torah legislation (as opposed to regulations of the rabbis), purity and impurity have no application to living non-Jews. See 'Laws of Corpse Impurity', 1: 17.

[9] The sea is actually the original *mikveh*: in the verse from the story of the Creation 'and the gathering together of the waters called He seas' (Gen. 1: 10), the Hebrew for 'the gathering together of the waters' is *mikveh hamayim*.   [10] See Ch. 14 below on these issues.

[11] See 'Laws of Kings and their Wars', 12: 4, the subject of Ch. 14 below.

This foreshadowing of the *Mishneh torah*'s climax demonstrates that Maimonides conceived of the endings of the different volumes as more than simply appropriate places at which to step back from halakhah and reflect. The structure of the work is co-ordinated with its purpose. Through its repetition at two crucial places—the end of the volumes on commandments between human beings and God, and the end of the work as a whole—the idea of 'the waters of intellect' becomes a meaningful structural feature. With the aid of *mikveh* turned metaphor, the beginning, middle, and end of the *Mishneh torah* are linked by the universal values of reason and knowledge.[12]

Water as Metaphor for Emanation

Furthermore, through the symbolic form of the *Mishneh torah*, Maimonides' 'hint' is backed by the full force of his metaphysics. In the work's microcosmic structure, its first ten books correspond to the ten orders of angels described in 'Laws of the Foundations of the Torah', as existing in a hierarchy in accordance with the Neoplatonic idea of emanation: each angel, or separate intellect, emanates from the one above it (see Appendix).[13] The process begins with an emanation from God, a superfluity of goodness. This is compared in the *Guide* to a flow of water from a source: 'it has been said that the world derives from the overflow from God and that He has caused to overflow to it everything in it that is produced in time'.[14] The flow is also a flow of knowledge: 'In the same way it is said that He caused his Knowledge to overflow to the prophets.'[15]

In the *Mishneh torah*, the first volume, the *Book of Knowledge*, represents the fountainhead of knowledge and form, which flow down through the following books until they pool in the *mikveh* at the end of the *Book of Purity*. The *mikveh* receives into it the flow of all these commandments which, whatever the individual, immediate significance of each one, all ultimately aim at the knowledge of God. It is because of this philosophical background that *mikveh* becomes such an appropriate emblem of their collective meaning, of the way they are intended to bring moral and intellectual purity, goodness, and truth into the world. At the end of the *Book of Purity*, this is an ideal for the individual; at the end of the *Mishneh torah* as a whole, it is fulfilled for the world as a whole.

---

[12] Middle here refers to the thematic middle, the dividing point at the end of the *Book of Purity* between ceremonial commandments and social commandments, but the arithmetic middle, that is, the end of Book 7, certainly participates in the same idea, as discussed in Ch. 7 above.
[13] 'Laws of the Foundations of the Torah', 2: 4.   [14] *Guide* ii. 12 (p. 279).   [15] Ibid.

'The waters of intellect' are therefore not an *ad hoc* image, but one that represents the quintessence of the entire work. This all-embracing scope of an image that at first sight is only a solution to a local difficulty—the need to provide a rational justification for the *mikveh* rite—is another demonstration that the universalism of the *Mishneh torah* is not a matter of occasional sorties into philosophy, but is systematic and deep, and informs the entire theory and practice of the commandments.

Purity and the Temple

Let us now narrow our focus and look at the *Book of Purity* in its more immediate context as the last of the three books that deal with the Temple.

As mentioned, in the absence of a Temple, the laws in the *Book of Temple Service* and the *Book of Offerings* are almost all in abeyance, and the same applies to most of the laws in the *Book of Purity*.[16] The main consequences of being impure are that one may not enter the Temple precincts,[17] or consume sacrifices.[18] Apart from certain special restrictions for priests, impurity has no further practical effect, nor is being impure itself reprehensible.[19]

This is just as well, because impurity is very easily contracted, for example through direct or indirect contact with a human corpse—merely entering a cemetery, or even a hospital, or touching someone else who has touched a corpse is liable to suffice. It is thus almost unavoidable. Furthermore, the elaborate procedure for removing the impurity that arises from contact with a corpse will be revived only by the messiah,[20] who will also rebuild the Temple.[21] All Jews are therefore presumed for the time being to be in a state of impurity of a kind that cannot currently be removed. This does not prevent them from leading lives fully conformable with the commandments in their pre-messianic, sans-Temple scope.

Maimonides strongly emphasizes the connection between purity and the Temple. 'Laws of Impurity of Foodstuffs' states: 'Whatever is written in Scripture and in traditional teaching about the laws relating to things impure and

---

[16] Surviving exceptions are the laws concerning a married menstruating woman, who may not resume sexual relations with her husband until seven days after her period ends and after she has immersed in a *mikveh*; ritual hand washing before partaking of bread; and avoidance of cemeteries by those of priestly descent.

[17] See 'Laws of Entrance into the Sanctuary', 3. Precisely which parts of the Temple and its surrounds are out of bounds depends on the type of impurity.

[18] See 'Laws of Offerings for Transgressions Committed Through Error', 10: 5; 11.

[19] See 'Laws of Impurity of Foodstuffs', 16: 9, but note ibid., *halakhah* 12.

[20] See 'Laws of the Red Heifer', 3: 4.   [21] See 'Laws of Kings and their Wars', 11: 1.

pure is relevant only to the Temple and to its Hallowed Things and to heave offerings and second tithe, for it warns those who are impure against entering the Temple or eating in impurity anything that is hallowed or heave offering or tithe. But no such prohibition applies to common food, and it is permissible to eat common food that is impure and to drink liquids that are impure.'[22] Echoing this, the *Guide* states: 'this matter of uncleanness and cleanness concerns only the Holy Place and holy things, nothing else'.[23]

The Jewish idea of impurity is thus restricted in scope, and Maimonides contrasts it with pagan practices in this respect.[24] It is also purely notional. Niels Bohr is said to have been asked how a great scientist like him could hang a lucky horseshoe over his door, and to have responded, 'They say it works even if you don't believe in it.'[25] *Mikveh*, according to Maimonides, does not 'work' even if you do believe in it.[26] There is nothing in which to believe. Immersion in a *mikveh* is a prescribed act that, if completed with the intention of fulfilling the commandment, makes it possible to enter the Temple. Other than that, it does nothing at all. Maimonides draws a contrast with someone who bathes in a pool of water with mud on their body; they will emerge clean whether they meant to or not. But with purification in a *mikveh*, the thought makes the act.[27]

The *Guide*: Laws of Purity Serve the Individual

Thus far, the *Mishneh torah* and the *Guide* march in step. Elsewhere in the *Guide*,[28] Maimonides distinguishes three senses of impurity—or perhaps 'pollution' would be a better rendering of the Hebrew *tumah* here. There is

---

[22] 'Laws of Impurity of Foodstuffs', 16: 8. To have the force of Torah commandments, contributions to priests and tithes are not dependent on the existence of a Temple, but rather on the entire Jewish people living in the Land of Israel (see 'Laws of Heave Offerings', 1: 1 and 26). Since, however, the coming of the messiah, the rebuilding of the Temple, and the ingathering of the exiles are envisaged as stages of a single process (see 'Laws of Kings and their Wars', 11: 1), the difference may be regarded as technical.

[23] *Guide* iii. 47 (p. 595). There were those who would take upon themselves extra strictness and observe the laws of purity and impurity in their daily lives as well. See 'Laws of Impurity of Foodstuffs', 16: 12, also discussed below.   [24] See *Guide* iii. 47 (p. 595).

[25] Sad to say, this oft-repeated anecdote is reckoned to be apocryphal. A similar tale has been told of Albert Einstein.

[26] Worthy of note here is the debate between Maimonides and Nahmanides on this point. According to the latter, magic is forbidden because it *does* work. See Nahmanides' commentary on Deut. 18: 9–12.

[27] This does not necessarily apply to a woman who immerses in a *mikveh* after menstruation. If her immersion was involuntary or simply to refresh herself, it still makes her 'permitted to her husband', although it does not count for sacred purposes—see 'Laws of Immersion Pools', 1: 8.   [28] *Guide* iii. 47 (p. 595).

physical pollution, i.e. dirt; there is moral and intellectual pollution, in which sense the word *tumah* is used in relation to disobeying the commandments; and there is notional pollution, which is the subject of the *Book of Purity*. In other words, the impurity discussed in that book is a halakhic construct only, not a physical or spiritual illness to be cured; it is not an ontological condition at all.[29] From here, the *Mishneh torah* and the *Guide* diverge. The *Guide* is very clear about reasons for the laws of purity and impurity, both their origin and their purpose. *Guide* iii. 35 states that the general purpose of all the laws of purity and impurity is 'to make people avoid entering the Sanctuary, so that it should be considered as great by the soul and feared and venerated'. A little later in the *Guide*, where this class of commandments is discussed in detail,[30] Maimonides reiterates the idea of awe of the Temple:

We have already explained that the whole intention with regard to the Sanctuary was to affect those that come to it with a feeling of awe and fear; as it says: 'Ye shall fear My Sanctuary'. Now if one is continually in contact with a venerable object, the impression received from it in the soul diminishes and the feeling it provokes becomes slight. . . . This being the intention, He, may He be exalted, forbade the unclean to enter the Sanctuary.

According to the *Guide*, then, the bar on entering the Temple is not just a technical halakhic consequence of being impure, but represents the entire point of the laws of purity and impurity: to make Temple visits difficult and rare, and hence always awe-inspiring, which in turn is the entire point of the Temple itself.

The *Mishneh Torah:* Laws of Purity Serve the Temple

In the *Mishneh torah*, despite ample opportunity to do so, Maimonides refrains from making the very short leap from exclusion from the Temple as a *consequence* of being impure to declaring it as the *purpose* of the laws of purity and impurity. We have already observed that *Guide* iii. 47 echoes 'Laws of Impurity of Foodstuffs', 16: 8 in confining the relevance of the laws of purity and impurity to 'the Holy Place and holy things, nothing else', but whereas the passage in the *Guide* goes on to describe the connection to the Temple as the laws' rationale, the passage in 'Laws of Impurity of Foodstuffs' stops at the halakhic fact. In the seventh chapter of 'Laws of the Temple', which opens with the commandment to be in awe of the Temple, the restrictions on access for those who are impure are listed together with restrictions that apply to other categories of people, and are not specifically linked to the theme of awe.

[29] See Kellner, *Maimonides' Confrontation*, 127–54. [30] *Guide* iii. 47 (p. 595).

In general, awe is treated in this chapter as a matter of preserving the dignity of the institution and, as it were, of God himself, rather than as of inward, psychological significance, as though the entry of the impure, and others, into the Temple would be *lèse-majesté*. The third and fourth chapters of 'Laws of Entrance into the Sanctuary', which deal with the specific commandments that exclude people in a state of impurity from the Temple, do not mention the idea of awe at all.

The very fact that the prohibition on people in a state of impurity entering the Temple is dealt with in the *Book of Temple Service* rather than in the *Book of Purity*, that is, from the point of view of the Temple rather from the point of view of the impure person as a function of their impurity, is telling. 'Laws of Entrance into the Sanctuary' sets the tone by presenting a positive commandment to eject those who are impure from the Temple—again, the point of view is that of the objective requirement of the institution.[31] It is incumbent on the impure themselves to refrain from entering the Temple,[32] but the impression given by 'Laws of Entrance into the Sanctuary' is that such measures are designed to prevent the Temple itself from becoming tainted and the Temple service from becoming invalid, rather than to ensure a correct state of mind on the part of the Temple visitor.[33] All the pieces are found in the *Mishneh torah*, but never assembled into an argument that the purpose of the laws of purity and impurity is to maintain awe of the Temple. Instead of ascribing direct psychological usefulness to these laws, 'Laws of Immersion Pools' presents them as *ḥukim*, the reason for which is obscure.[34]

The contrast between the *Mishneh torah* and the *Guide* in their treatments of the laws of purity and impurity should be seen in the context of their different general approaches to reasons for the commandments. As we have several times had occasion to observe, the *Guide* defines two main purposes of a divine law, namely the welfare of the soul and the welfare of the body, and then sets out to demonstrate that the commandments of the Torah fulfil these purposes and that they are therefore reasonable and can be considered to be the product of a wise legislator. The awe of God is part of the welfare of the soul, and the laws of purity and impurity contribute indirectly to the soul's welfare by ensuring that the Temple, which is meant to inspire the awe of God, will fulfil its function. In the *Mishneh torah* the commandments are not measured against antecedent, external criteria; the extraneous utilitarian

---

[31] 'Laws of Entrance into the Sanctuary', 3: 1.   [32] See ibid. 3: 10.
[33] This emphasis is actually more in keeping with that of the presentation of the laws of purity and impurity in the Torah than is the idea of preserving awe—see e.g. Lev. 19: 13 and 20.   [34] 'Laws of Immersion Pools', 11: 12.

purpose of the laws of purity is therefore not considered. This opens the way to something much more inspiring. In the *Mishneh torah*, reasons for the commandments emerge from the commandments themselves: 'Laws of Immersion Pools', 11: 12 is the most dramatic example of this. Maimonides drains the *mikveh* of ontological significance, and fills it with metaphorical significance.

Contrast with Shofar

We prefer the expression 'metaphorical' to 'symbolic' here because symbolic acts are like speech acts: they can have effects, and this is exactly the connotation that Maimonides seeks to avoid. Immersion in a *mikveh* does not make a person morally purer; it is not even an outward sign of that inner process. It changes a person's status from 'unable to enter the Temple' to 'able to enter the Temple', but the Temple is not technically out of bounds to the morally degenerate, however much the prophets may have railed against their hypocritical presence there, and in both the *Mishneh torah* and the *Guide* Maimonides insists upon the *mikveh*'s wholly technical function. What he does allow is an 'indication' or 'hint' (the Hebrew word is *remez*). Immersion in a pool of water suggests the idea of the immersion of one's entire being in intellect, and of the instantaneous transformation in one's outlook that such immersion can work.

The notion of a hint is used differently here from the way in which it is used in the other instance in which Maimonides applies it to a commandment in the *Mishneh torah*, namely that of the shofar, the ram's horn blown on Rosh Hashanah.[35] The shofar is described as a wake-up call to repentance, but this is only an extension of the fact that the startling and penetrating sound of the shofar actually is an alarm. Rather than being a warning of physical danger or a call to arms, on Rosh Hashanah it rouses the conscience. It requires a little imagination to think of the shofar this way, but that does not make it a metaphor, for most of the ordinary, one could say literal, meaning of the sounding of a shofar remains. By contrast, writing about the human mind as though it were a pool of water—'the waters of intellect'—does qualify as a metaphor, for there is no literal sense in which that description holds

---

[35] See 'Laws of Repentance', 3: 4.

[36] In Maimonides' figurative treatments of commandments, the explanation of the scapegoat ritual in *Guide* iii. 46 (p. 591) as a parable 'serving to bring forth a form in the soul' (discussed at length below) is perhaps somewhere between the shofar and the *mikveh* as far as the level of conversion of physical action into mental process is concerned, but in the case of *mikveh* the conversion rate reaches 100 per cent, and the difference in degree becomes a difference in kind.

true. The difference is subtle, but it justifies describing Maimonides' treatment of *mikveh* as unique in his oeuvre.[36]

Three Endings: Thesis, Antithesis, Synthesis

The conceptual link that makes the metaphor work is intention. To be valid, immersion in a *mikveh* requires a mental operation, the intention to fulfil the commandment. Self-regeneration is similarly a mental operation, the application of thought to appetite, desire, and action. The final *halakhah* of 'Laws of Immersion Pools' thus encapsulates 'Laws of Moral Qualities', which is about applying the singular intellect, or *da'at* in Maimonides' Hebrew, to the rectification of one's multifarious dispositions and desires, which he terms *de'ot*. The important verb in this process is *lekhaven*, 'to direct', from the same root as *kavanah*, meaning 'intention'. In our halakhah, the phrase 'waters of intellect' is *mei hada'at* in the original, and 'bad dispositions' is *de'ot ra'ot*, while 'one who sets his heart' translates *hamekhaven libo*. In short, the end of 'Laws of Immersion Pools' employs key words—*de'ot*, *kaven*—that invoke 'Laws of Moral Qualities'.

In this way, Maimonides provides a conceptual link between the *Book of Temple Service*, the *Book of Offerings*, and the *Book of Purity*, beyond the mere fact that they each concern the Temple, and he does this through their endings. The ending of the *Book of Purity* synthesizes the endings of the previous two books. The ending of the *Book of Temple Service* stresses observance of *ḥukim*, commandments that are not understood, out of sheer obedience.[37] In the closing *halakhah* of the *Book of Offerings*, Maimonides urges the reader to endow the commandments with meaning, and himself provides an example of how the commandments reach into the shadowy and crooked alleys of the human mind 'to make straight all doings' and train moral character.

At the end of the *Book of Purity*, Maimonides synthesizes the ideas of the previous two endings. The commandment of *mikveh* is described as an inscrutable *ḥok*: 'the laws about impurity and purity are decrees laid down

---

[37] The idea of *ḥok* is introduced at the end of the *Book of Temple Service* in relation to sacrifices, but one of the main rabbinic sources alluded to there actually concerns purification, namely the response of R. Yohanan ben Zakai to his students who enquired after the real reason for the red heifer purification ritual, cited in Ch. 8 above: 'The corpse does not defile, and the water does not purify. Rather it is a decree of the Holy One, blessed be He. The Holy One, blessed be He, said, I have legislated a statute, I have decreed a decree, and you are not permitted to transgress my decree' (*Num. Rabbah* 19: 8; *Pesikta derav kahana*, 'Parah adumah', §4: 7). Similarly, Maimonides states that immersion in a *mikveh* has no tangible effect, and no apparent meaning. In that respect, it is a *ḥok*. See above, Ch. 9.

by Scripture and not matters about which human understanding is capable of forming a judgement; for behold, they are included among the divine statutes'.[38] This, however, is combined with the idea that *mikveh* suggests (but cannot itself effect) a process of moral regeneration. Objective divine law practically merges with subjective experience, and extremes meet as this non-rational *ḥok* is made to stand compellingly for rationality itself.

The Endings and Their Contexts: Creating a Parable

We now turn to examination of Books 8, 9, and 10 as a group. Why did Maimonides deliver his discussion of the reasons for the commandments in three instalments spread over three volumes? We must presume that each instalment is somehow appropriate to the particular book that it concludes, that its significance lies not just in what it says, but also in where it appears. This structural feature adds another dimension to the dialectic we have found in our three endings. It turns Maimonides' whole presentation of the laws of sacrifices and purity into a parable.

The subject of the parable is the proper orientation of the human mind towards itself, the world, and God. The key to it lies in Maimonides' very original arrangement of the laws relating to the Temple ritual. The arrangement, moreover, is according to a plan first found in the *Book of Knowledge*. Maimonides thus relates the Temple ritual to the basic concepts treated in that book, and in this way gives it a permanent value that transcends the historical explanation for it presented in the *Guide*.

Actions as Parables: The Case of the Scapegoat

Law as parable may seem a strange idea; a parable is usually thought of as a brief story that conveys an abstract notion, usually a moral. For Maimonides, however, a parable is 'any text, narrative or not, with multiple levels of external and internal meaning'.[39] In fact, he does not stop at texts. Actions too can be parables, an idea that he applies to at least one Temple ritual, but with an implication that it can be extended to sacrifices in general. This is how Maimonides explains the scapegoat, the goat sent into the desert (actually thrown off a cliff, according to the account in the Mishnah[40]) as part of the Yom Kippur service. In the *Guide*, on the verse 'And the goat shall bear upon him all their iniquities unto a land not inhabited',[41] he comments:

---

[38] 'Laws of Immersion Pools', 11: 12.
[39] J. Stern, *Problems and Parables of Law*, 10.
[40] Mishnah *Yoma* 6: 6.   [41] Lev. 16: 22.

No one has any doubt that sins are not bodies that may be transported from the back of one individual to that of another. But all these actions are parables serving to bring forth a form in the soul so that a passion toward repentance should result: we have freed ourselves from all our previous actions, cast them behind our backs, and removed them to an extreme distance.[42]

The verse, and the action it commands, cannot be taken literally: a goat cannot carry sins on its back. Rather, the form of the action must be abstracted from the concrete details and internalized as 'a form in the soul' to induce 'a passion for repentance'. Maimonides characterizes the function of sacrifices generally in a similar way:

If, however, he believes in repentance, he can correct himself and return to a better and more perfect state than the one he was in before he sinned. For this reason there are many actions that are meant to establish this correct and very useful opinion, I mean the confessions, the sacrifices in expiation of negligence and also of certain sins committed intentionally, and the fasts.[43]

Sacrifices do not directly accomplish atonement; they rather encourage the belief that repentance and atonement are possible, that sin is not binding but can be objectified and discarded, opening the way to a process of self-examination and self-repair.[44]

It is sometimes overlooked that, despite his general explanation of sacrifices as a concession to pagan convention, as discussed in Chapter 8, Maimonides does assign didactic or moral value to components of the Temple ritual. In many cases this is a matter of demonstrative rejection of pagan ideas, such as the stipulation that the Temple itself should face west, thus symbolically negating pagan deification of the rising sun.[45] The passages just cited go further than this and allow ritual inherent value, independently of pagan association. The scapegoat ritual is described as having a direct effect on the human mind, on the mind's permanent, native disposition, with no need for any external, cultural key to its meaning. Although the scapegoat would presumably not exist were it not for the general pagan custom of

---

[42] *Guide* iii. 46 (p. 591).   [43] *Guide* iii. 36 (p. 540).

[44] It is perhaps necessary at this point to distinguish between parable and symbol. For present purposes, we characterize a parable as a text or action that invites interpretation, whereas a symbol is an agreed token of meaning. Moreover, in symbolic ritual there are the elements of efficacy and vicariousness in the act itself which seem to be precisely what Maimonides seeks to avoid in his discussion of the scapegoat. But see 'Laws of Repentance', 1: 2, which states that the scapegoat does atone for minor transgressions even without repentance.   [45] See *Guide* iii. 45 (p. 575).

achieving expiation through animal sacrifice, once it does exist, it can be interpreted in its own terms.

Soloveitchik's Subjective Correlative

Maimonides' critics down the centuries have perceived his treatment of sacrifices in the *Guide* as a travesty,[46] even as heresy.[47] In our time, J. B. Soloveitchik has castigated him for his whole approach to rationalization of the commandments in the *Guide*, finding it alien and dispiriting. 'The reluctance on the part of the Jewish *homo religiosus* to accept Maimonidean rationalistic ideas is not ascribable to any agnostic tendencies, but to the incontrovertible fact that such explanations neither edify nor inspire the religious consciousness', he writes.[48] But Maimonides' idea about the scapegoat does not seem to lack edification and inspiration. It is very close to the method of investing the commandments with meaning that Soloveitchik sees as characteristic of the *Mishneh torah*, where, according to him, Maimonides is not interested in extraneous philosophical goals for halakhah or in its causes, but rather in its experiential effect, its 'subjective correlative'.[49] The enquiring religious mind discovers this by reconstructing from the objective halakhic data an autonomous realm of ideas, one that is independent of philosophical and scientific concepts and categories.

Soloveitchik's main example is the 'hint' that Maimonides suggests is conveyed by the sound of the shofar, discussed above. The objective commandment of blowing the shofar is internalized as a subjective prompt to repentance. The 'form in the soul' that the scapegoat ritual brings forth surely furnishes another example. The question is whether it is really independent of philosophy.

In what follows, we propose a resolution of this great crux in the study of Maimonides, the apparent incompatibility of the *Mishneh torah* and the *Guide* on sacrifices, through the idea of the Temple ritual as parable. Rather than the *Mishneh torah* being a bastion of halakhic autonomy in which *homo*

[46] For a prominent example, see Nahmanides on Lev. 1: 9. On Nahmanides' approach to sacrifices, see Schwartz, 'From Theurgy to Magic'; Pinchot, 'The Deeper Conflict between Maimonides and Ramban over the Sacrifices'.

[47] See Emden, *Mitpaḥat sefarim*, 61 (pt. 2, ch. 8). R. Emden concludes that the *Guide* could not have been written by the Maimonides of the *Mishneh torah* and is a forgery.

[48] Soloveitchik, *The Halakhic Mind*, 92.

[49] Ibid. 94. In less impassioned terms than Soloveitchik, Twersky similarly contrasts the 'historical and abstract' kind of rationalization of the commandments in the *Guide* with the 'experiential and immediate' kind in the *Mishneh torah*, and, as noted above in Ch. 8, observes that, in the case of sacrifices, the two approaches appear incompatible. See his *Introduction to the Code*, 437, and our Introduction above.

religiosus clings to the commandments, and specifically sacrifices, like King David at the end of the *Book of Temple Service*, in defiance of the world's incomprehension and hostility, while the *Guide* offers a universalist, philosophical (and, for Soloveitchik, unsatisfactory) gloss upon them, we offer an alternative view that sees philosophy as underlying the approaches of both works. The Temple ritual is a parable of the metaphysics of the philosophers. The basis for this is simple. Since a human being is a microcosm, his or her subjective world is, or ought to be, a reflection of the world that physics and metaphysics describe. The subjective correlative or 'form in the soul' that ritual subtends thus does not relate to something uniquely Jewish but to universal philosophy (at least up to the critical point of belief in Creation)—only Judaism understands it better than the philosophers.

Does this make matters better or worse for the Jewish *homo religiosus* whom Soloveitchik projects? On the one hand, the primacy of halakhah in the *Mishneh torah* is upheld, in that a rationale immanent in the commandments themselves is reconstructed through study and practice as a subjective correlative. On the other hand, the content of the subjective correlative turns out to be precisely the scientific philosophy that Soloveitchik was trying to get away from. The frame of reference is the same as in the *Guide*. On the basis of our reading, then, the *Mishneh torah* does not appear to support Soloveitchik's conception of halakhah as intellectually self-sufficient. There is, however, no loss of spiritual intensity. For Maimonides, philosophy is not just cognitive but experiential. The virtuous life is the absorption of scientific truths into one's very being, self-formation according to the forms of God's creation, and the commandments are the conduits of those forms and the agents of the self-forming process.[50] For our purposes, at any rate, the chief point is that the perceived dichotomy between the *Mishneh torah* and the *Guide* is not real

First Rungs of the Ladder

On the specific question of sacrifices, a partial reconciliation of the *Mishneh torah* and the *Guide* along these lines is suggested by Gillis in *Reading*

---

[50] The assessment of Soloveitchik's position presented here is based on what he writes in *The Halakhic Mind*, but he is also on record as having expressed greater appreciation for the role that Maimonides assigns to scientific knowledge in the fulfilment of the commandments and the study of the Torah, and even for the idea of the Torah as a means of assimilating oneself to the scientifically understood cosmos. See Kaplan (ed.), *Maimonides: Between Philosophy and Halakhah*, 181–218. Perhaps the real problem for *homo religiosus* is that Maimonides' science has been shot away. An attempt to solve this problem is made in Gillis, *Reading Maimonides' Mishneh Torah*, 375–85. See also above, Introduction, n. 24.

Maimonides' *Mishneh Torah*.⁵¹ It is based on the parallel between the first ten books of the *Mishneh torah* and the Neoplatonic hierarchy of the separate intellects (angels), referred to earlier in this chapter. The separate intellects are ranked according to the degree of their knowledge of God. Correspondingly, the first ten volumes of the *Mishneh torah* are arranged according to how closely the laws they contain concern the knowledge of God. Hence sacrifices and the laws of purity, which are remotest from knowledge, are in Books 8, 9, and 10, at the bottom of the hierarchy, and represent the first rungs of a ladder leading to enlightenment, at the top of which is Book 1, the *Book of Knowledge*. Thus where the *Guide* evaluates sacrifices as a stage in a historical process, the *Mishneh torah* evaluates them as a stage in individual intellectual development. In Maimonides' vision of the messianic age, human nature remains unchanged, and the need to start from concrete expressions of faith and progress to more abstract ones and ultimately to pure contemplation still applies. All that will happen is that better political circumstances, of which of course the Temple itself is part, will facilitate that process.

This account narrows the gap between the *Mishneh torah* and the *Guide* on sacrifices, but it is still lacking. It explains the value of sacrifices relative to the other commandments, but fails to assign them any intrinsic value that would transcend their original historical context and justify restoring them in the future. 'Expression of faith' is a vague phrase. What exactly do sacrifices express? What is it possible to see in them that will make them an engine of intellectual growth?

'Consider Them Closely'

Aside from the care and effort required to present all the laws of sacrifices systematically in the *Mishneh torah*, and the condemnation in 'Laws of Kings and their Wars' of any denial of the messianic hope as apostasy,⁵² Maimonides' remarks at the end of his commentary on tractate *Menaḥot* make it clear that he did consider sacrifices to have lasting value:

And they further said 'This is the law of the burnt offering' [Lev. 7: 37]. Anyone who engages in the study of Torah is considered as though he has offered a burnt offering and a meal offering and a sin offering and a guilt offering. And the sages said that those who engage in the study of the laws of the Temple worship are considered by the verse as though the Temple had been built in their days [BT *Men.* 110a]. And therefore it is appropriate for a person to engage in the study of matters

---

⁵¹ pp. 260–2.   ⁵² See 'Laws of Kings and their Wars', 11: 1.

concerning the sacrifices and to consider them closely, and not to say that they are things that are not needful nowadays, as many people say.[53]

This statement that the laws of the Temple worship are of current and not just historical importance makes the contradiction between the *Mishneh torah*, where the treatment of sacrifices is faithful to this rallying cry, and the *Guide*, which seems to side with what 'many people say', appear all the more stark. What Maimonides stresses, however, is the need 'to engage in the study of matters concerning the sacrifices and to consider them closely'. Consistent with what we have seen of Maimonides' view of sacrifices as stimulants to reflection and repentance, the implication is that the lasting value of sacrifices lies not so much in the acts as in the meaning that can be extracted from them and from the laws pertaining to them. Our close consideration of the way these matters are presented in the *Mishneh torah* aims at completing the comparison between that and Maimonides' physics and metaphysics. We shall discuss each side of the comparison separately before bringing them together.

Originality of Classification

As far as the presentation in the *Mishneh torah* is concerned, the trail starts in another passage from the *Commentary on the Mishnah*. In the introduction to that work, Maimonides goes to considerable lengths to explain and justify the order of the Mishnah. He generally explains the sequence of the tractates in Order *Kodashim*, which deals with the Temple, sacrifices, and allied topics, as being in accordance with the sequence of the subjects as they occur in the Torah. This is his default explanation for the structures of the other orders as well.[54] The attention that Maimonides pays to the structure of the Mishnah indicates that we should be alert to the changes he makes to that structure in his own schematization of halakhah.

Sacrifices as a Prompt to Thought

The introduction to Maimonides' commentary on Mishnah *Zevaḥim*, the first

---

[53] *Commentary on the Mishnah*, Men. 13: 11.

[54] The scholarly consensus is that the sequence of tractates in each order as we have it is actually governed simply by the number of chapters that each tractate contains, and Order *Kodashim* is no exception in this respect. To take them in order, *Zevaḥim* has 14 chapters, *Menaḥot* 13, *Ḥulin* 12, *Bekhorot* 9, *Arakhin* 9, *Temurah* 7, *Keritot* 6, *Me'ilah* 6, *Tamid* 6, *Midot* 4, and *Kinim* 3. An external explanation of the sequence may possibly be required as a tie-breaker where several tractates have the same number of chapters, as here, but otherwise the numerical principle seems to need no elaboration.

tractate in Order *Kodashim*, presents a systematic outline of the various kinds of sacrifices, opening with an explanation of his motive for this:

> I saw fit to provide a preface on the divisions of the sacrifices and a survey of their types before I start the commentary on this Order. What prompted me to do so, even though their division is a simple matter and they are all verses in the Torah and it is not possible to introduce anything wonderful or any deep analysis, is that this thing, namely the sacrifices, is lost because of our many sins, and no-one takes an interest in it except for a few people, and its topics are not frequently brought to people's attention such that they will remember them even if they have at some time studied them, since there is no active performance that will make them revise what they have learned, and nobody enquires about anything to do with them, to the point that all have become equal in respect of them, the greatest sage and the most foolish of the multitude, and most students are ignorant about the sacrifices and do not even know what is said about them in many verses.[55]

It is perhaps not entirely clear what is intended by 'it is not possible to introduce anything wonderful or any deep analysis', but we take the passage as a whole to mean that because for the time being the subject is entirely theoretical, people are not aware of the taxonomy of the sacrifices and do not take the trouble to study it, even though it is readily understood from plain verses in the Torah and does not require any difficult deduction. What grieves Maimonides here, as in the extract from the commentary on Mishnah *Menaḥot* cited above, is not so much the absence of sacrifices as that, in their absence, there is nothing to prompt the study of their laws and ensure that people will have the system of sacrifices clear in their minds.[56] This is nascent parable. What counts is not the thing itself, but what can be abstracted from it—its form.

In the introduction to the commentary on Mishnah *Kelim*, the first tractate in Order *Tohorot*, we find a similar lament that lack of practical application has led to neglect of this area of study, and a similar essay that systematizes the laws of purity and impurity. This time, however, Maimonides stresses the complexity of the subject and urges the student to read his exposition again and again until it is thoroughly understood and absorbed.

---

[55] Our English translation is based on Maimonides, *Commentary on the Mishnah*, Order *Kodashim* (Heb.), trans. Kafih, vol. iii, p. 9.

[56] This is an interesting reversal of Maimonides' refrain in 'Laws of Torah Study' that study leads to action, but action does not lead to study. Cf. the exposition in the introduction to the *Commentary on the Mishnah* of the rabbinic statement 'God has nothing in his world besides the four cubits of halakhah' (BT *Ber.* 8a). This statement is analysed in detail in Diamond and Kellner, *Reinventing Maimonides*, ch. 6.

Communal versus Individual

To return to the introduction to Mishnah *Zevaḥim*: following the preface Maimonides proceeds to map all the animal sacrifices. He first sets out a classification according to the nature of the sacrifice itself and its procedures, there being four categories: burnt offering, sin offering, guilt offering, and peace offering. But then he introduces a second classification according to what could be called the domain of the sacrifice, which again turns out to be fourfold:

- Communal
- Individual
- Communal with characteristics of individual
- Individual with characteristics of communal

It is this second classification that forms the basis of the division of the laws of the Temple ritual between the *Book of Temple Service* and the *Book of Offerings* in the *Mishneh torah*.

This distinction between communal and individual sacrifices has some importance in rabbinic literature, but it is by no means a primary principle of organization there. In the Mishnah, the main division is between animal sacrifices, in Mishnah *Zevaḥim*, and meal offerings, in Mishnah *Menaḥot*. Furthermore, Mishnah *Zevaḥim* begins by discussing individual sacrifices, and they are also the type mentioned first in the Torah,[57] but, as we have already noted, in the introduction to Mishnah *Zevaḥim* Maimonides discusses communal sacrifices first, and he follows suit in the *Mishneh torah*.

Maimonides makes the continuity between the *Commentary on the Mishnah* and the *Mishneh torah* very clear in the introduction to the latter, where, in listing the general contents of each of the fourteen books, he states that the *Book of Temple Service* deals with commandments concerning communal sacrifices and that the *Book of Offerings* deals with commandments concerning individual sacrifices.[58]

---

[57] The regular service of the Tabernacle/Temple is first described in Lev. 1, which is about sacrifices offered by an individual, with an emphasis on atonement. Communal sacrifices offered on festivals are described in Lev. 23, but even there they are preceded by instructions about individual sacrifices in Lev. 22. The regular daily communal sacrifices are not commanded until Num. 28. In Exod. 19 too, where the procedure for the induction of Aaron and his sons as priests is described, the first sacrifices mentioned are their personal ones, with reference also being made in verse 28 to individual peace offerings by the children of Israel, and only towards the end of the chapter, starting in verse 38, are the regular daily communal offerings mentioned.

[58] The stress on commandments is important. They are the building blocks of the *Mish-*

To sum up, Maimonides placed great emphasis on understanding sacrifices as an ordered system. The primary feature of his system in the *Mishneh torah* is a distinction between communal sacrifices and individual sacrifices, with communal sacrifices placed first. This has no traditional basis and little practical importance. What idea does it serve?

Mishnaic Material Significantly Rearranged

Maimonides' originality is evident not just at the level of the general division of the laws of the Temple and sacrifices between the *Book of Temple Service* and the *Book of Offerings*, but also in the ordering of the laws within those volumes. It would be tedious to trace every move in his reshuffle of the mishnaic tractates. Suffice it to say that in relation to the locations within the Mishnah of the tractates on which they are based, 'Laws of Trespass', 'Laws of Substituted Offerings', and 'Laws of Immersion Pools' are all out of place,[59] and the first two are also out of sequence. Moreover, this is despite the justification of the mishnaic structure that Maimonides offers in his introduction to the *Commentary on the Mishnah*, leaving no doubt that, for reasons of his own, he deliberately lined up 'Laws of Trespass', 'Laws of Substituted Offerings', and 'Laws of Immersion Pools' at the ends of three successive books of the *Mishneh torah*. This confirms that it is not enough to note that the endings of these sections offer a continuous discussion about reasons for the commandments. We are looking at a carefully planned arrangement of the topics that constitute the infrastructure of that discussion. The whole scheme must be presumed to be significant.

The Dialectic Writ Large

The endings of Books 8, 9, and 10 were described above as forming a kind of Hegelian dialectic of thesis, antithesis, and synthesis: first, commandments as *ḥukim*, God's unquestionable decrees; next, commandments as applied

---

neh torah. Among other procedures, the *Book of Temple Service* deals with those for voluntary offerings and sin offerings, which are individual sacrifices. This might seem to vitiate the communal versus individual distinction between that book and the *Book of Offerings*. By definition, however, there can be no commandment to bring a voluntary offering, while the commandment that initiates sin offerings is found in the *Book of Offerings*, in 'Laws of Offerings for Transgressions Committed through Error'. In terms of commandments, therefore, the distinction between Books 8 and 9 as announced in the introduction to the *Mishneh torah* is maintained.

[59] It was noted above that Tractate *Mikva'ot* is in the middle of Order *Tohorot* of the Mishnah.

psychology, plumbing human material desires and fostering moral reformation; finally, commandments as unfathomable decrees that nevertheless stand for moral and intellectual regeneration. We can generalize from these three approaches to the commandments to three orientations of a human being: (1) towards God; (2) towards him or herself; (3) a movement away from the material self towards intellect.

The conclusions of the books reflect the themes of the books as a whole. The *Book of Temple Service*, on communal sacrifices, concerns the institutional, public, objective aspect of the Temple ritual and the awesomeness of the place. It is orientated towards God.

The change as we move to the *Book of Offerings* is clear: individual, personal sacrifices instead of communal sacrifices; the self rather than the unknowable God.

As for the *Book of Purity*, if the first ten books of the *Mishneh torah* correspond to the ten orders of angels, then it corresponds to angel number ten, the *ishim*, or agent intellect. The significance of this correspondence is that human moral and intellectual virtue involve turning away from material desires and material existence towards the knowledge that the agent intellect emanates. It is no coincidence that Maimonides describes the angels as *hatsurot hatehorot hanifradot mehagolmim*, 'pure forms separate from materiality'.[60] To turn towards the agent intellect is to turn towards purity. In 'Laws of Impurity of Foodstuffs', commenting on the pious who voluntarily adhere to the laws of purity not only when they wish to enter the Temple but also in their daily lives, which means isolating themselves from those less strict who might make them or their food impure, Maimonides writes:

> It is the way of piety that a man keep himself separate and go apart from the rest of the people and neither touch them nor eat and drink with them. For separation leads to the cleansing of the body from evil deeds, and the cleansing of the body leads to the hallowing of the soul from evil traits, and the hallowing of the soul leads to striving for likeness with the Shekhinah.[61]

In philosophical terms, 'likeness with the Shekhinah' (usually translated 'divine presence') would mean here communion with the agent intellect.[62] This passage prefigures the ending of the *Book of Purity*. It also indicates that that ending is not an abrupt addendum but flows from what Maimonides saw

---

[60] 'Laws of the Foundations of the Torah', 4: 12. See also ibid. 7: 1.
[61] 'Laws of Impurity of Foodstuffs', 16: 12.
[62] See Kellner, *Maimonides' Confrontation*, 213; Eisenmann, 'The Term "Created Light" in Maimonides' Philosophy'.

Table 10.1 Co-ordination of the *Mishneh torah*, Books 8–10, with the orientations of the human psyche

Book	Theme	Ending	Orientation
Temple Service	Communal sacrifices	Commandments are inscrutable decrees	God
Offerings	Individual sacrifices	Commandments are comprehensible as moral therapy	Self
Purity	Attaining purity	Commandments are decrees but also hint at moral and intellectual regeneration	Agent intellect

as the idea of the whole volume: the *ḥok* of purity and impurity reorientates a human being towards intellect.

It may be helpful to summarize what we have seen so far in a table (see Table 10.1).

How Stars, Spheres, and Humans Think

Our aim is to demonstrate that the structure described in the table reflects Maimonides' metaphysics. In the classical and medieval worldview, it is not only human beings that have intellects. The universe is alive, and spheres, and the stars and planets that they contain, possess consciousness and are moved by love (see Appendix). We learn of this early on in the *Mishneh torah*:

> Every star and sphere has a soul and is endowed with knowledge and intelligence. They are living beings who apprehend 'Him who spake and the world was'. They praise and glorify their Creator, just as the angels do, each according to its greatness and degree. And as they apprehend God, so are they conscious of themselves and the angels above them. The knowledge possessed by the stars and spheres is less than that of angels, more than that of human beings.[63]

God and Self

This passage expresses in religious terms the Neoplatonic theory (filtered through Alfarabi and Avicenna) of the structure of thought in all beings possessed of intellect. A star or sphere has three thoughts: a thought of God ('They praise and glorify their Creator'); a thought of itself ('so are they conscious of themselves'); and a thought of the angel from which it emanated ('and the angels above them').

---

[63] 'Laws of the Foundations of the Torah', 3: 9.

We are told in this *halakhah* that human beings possess less knowledge than stars and spheres. Nevertheless, their intellectual activity has the same structure. This emerges from the description of the way to fulfil the commandments to love and fear God.

And what is the way that will lead to the love of Him and the fear of Him? When a person contemplates His great and wondrous works and creatures and from them obtains a glimpse of His wisdom which is incomparable and infinite, he will straightway love Him, praise Him, glorify Him, and long with an exceeding longing to know His great Name. . . . And when he ponders these matters, he will recoil affrighted, and realize that he is a small creature, lowly and obscure, endowed with slight and slender intelligence, standing in the presence of Him who is perfect in knowledge.[64]

Here we have the archetypal human being confronting the universe. He has two thoughts: a thought of God ('he will straightway love Him, praise Him, glorify Him') and a thought of himself in relation to God ('he will . . . realize that he is a small creature'). Thus far, a human being is similar to a star or sphere.[65] The difference is that the heavenly bodies are made of an ethereal, imperishable substance that, although it is a barrier to perfect knowledge, like all matter, is nevertheless not corrupting, so that they maintain unwavering knowledge and love of God, each at a level in accordance with its rank. A human being, in contrast, is made of gross, perishable earthly matter that constantly tempts him or her with low appetites and desires that deflect the individual from intellectual activity.[66] The thought of God induces a desire for knowledge, but immediately the thought of the self with its physical proclivities causes a retreat in awe.

Acquisition of Knowledge

How can a human being reconcile these antitheses and overcome this distressing bipolar condition? Through the impulse of love being tempered by awe, that is, through the gradual, patient acquisition of knowledge, mastering the various disciplines in the right order, and thereby establishing a firm basis on which love can flourish.[67] Thus our *halakhah* ends:

And accordingly, I explicate general laws of what the master of the world has made, so that they will be an opening for the one who understands to love the name, as the

---

[64] 'Laws of the Foundations of the Torah', 2: 2.
[65] For comparison of the relationship between intellect and body in the heavens to their relationship in human beings, see *Guide* i. 72 (p. 193).
[66] See *Guide* iii. 8–9 (pp. 430–7).
[67] On the importance of pursuing an orderly course of studies gradually leading up to

sages said concerning love, 'Through that you recognize the one who spoke and the world came into being.'[68]

This process of understanding the laws of nature is one of communion with the agent intellect, which emanates human form (along with every form on earth), and radiates knowledge. In order to become intellectually developed and avoid floundering in materiality, that is, in order to become fully human, a human being needs to turn back towards the origin of his or her form in a way that is analogous to the third thought of the stars and spheres, the thought of 'the angels above them'. In this way, the thought of the self and the sense of awe that it engenders, rather than being simply dismaying, becomes a reality check, a measure of the effort required to climb the ladder to knowledge and love.

Adam as Archetype

In the Jewish tradition, the archetypal human being has a name: Adam. It may seem curious that in the *Mishneh torah*, human history appears to start 'in the days of Enosh', with the account in 'Laws of Idolatry' of how idolatry came about. If Maimonides sees fit to recount that lapse, why does he not also recount the original lapse, that of Adam and Eve?

The answer is that actually he does. The first four chapters of 'Laws of the Foundations of the Torah' are a philosophized retelling of the Creation story in Genesis. In this account of 'all that the Holy One, blessed be He, created in his world',[69] Adam as an individual is absent, but this is consistent with Maimonides' statement in the *Guide* that he based his theological discussion in the *Mishneh torah* on the idea of the eternity of the world.[70] If the world has always existed, there was no first human being, or at least the story of Adam and Eve loses its literal meaning. It is true that he uses the word 'created', as we have just seen, but nothing else in the account implies creation as a succession of events in time.

The description of the human archetype in 'Laws of the Foundations of the Torah', 2: 2, can be seen as representing the parabolic interpretation offered in the *Guide* of the biblical story of Adam and Eve and the snake in the

---

metaphysics, and of adequate moral training as a prerequisite for studying that discipline, see *Commentary on the Mishnah*, Ḥag. 2: 1; *Guide* i. 34 (pp. 72–9).

[68] 'Laws of the Foundations of the Torah', 2: 3.   [69] Ibid. 2: 2.

[70] 'You will always find that whenever, in what I have written in books of jurisprudence, I happen to mention the foundations and start upon establishing the existence of the deity, I establish it by discourses that adopt the way of the doctrine of the eternity of the world' (*Guide* i. 71 (p. 182)).

Garden of Eden.[71] In the *Guide*'s interpretation, Adam represents the form of a human being, or the intellect, Eve represents the body, and the snake, imagination and desire. In his or her intellectual striving, a human being is always prey to the danger of being overwhelmed by material impulses, and of declining from the perception of absolute truth to the merely conventional perception of good and bad, which is how Maimonides describes the change that came over Adam following his sin.[72]

In 'Laws of the Foundations of the Torah', 2: 2, the human situation is expressed in different terms and with different emphases. Here it is actually a positive commandment to be aware of one's material condition and of the impediment to knowledge that it constitutes. The underlying idea, however, is the same as in the *Guide*. The story of Adam in Genesis conveys the essential, eternal tension in human beings between form and matter, intellect and body, the thought of God and the thought of the self.[73] This tension is resolved by harnessing both material and intellectual drives in the service of the acquisition of knowledge.[74]

Ritual Enacts the Intellectual Process

We thus have a match between the Temple ritual and Maimonides' metaphysics. The laws of sacrifices and purity in the *Mishneh torah* are configured according to the structure of intellect in stars and spheres and in human beings. The themes and orientations of Books 8, 9, and 10 correspond to the three thoughts of any being possessed of intellect of whatever rank: the thought of God; the thought of itself; and the thought of the entity from which it emanated.

In treating Books 8, 9, and 10 as a parable, we thus have one stage in Maimonides' parabolic model of interpretation of the scapegoat in the *Guide*: the 'form in the soul', or more precisely, the form of the soul. What we have not seen so far is the 'passion for repentance'. This will emerge in the next stage of our inquiry into the morphology of the *Mishneh torah*.

---

[71] In *Guide* i. 14 (p. 40), Maimonides notes that the Hebrew word *adam* can refer to Adam the first human being or to the human species in general. See Klein-Braslavy, *Maimonides' Interpretation of the Adam Stories in Genesis* (Heb.). [72] See *Guide* i. 2 (pp. 24–5).

[73] Adam is mentioned by name in 'Laws of the Temple', 2: 2 in connection with the location of the altar. David Gillis hopes to discuss elsewhere the significance of this in relation to the argument of this chapter.

[74] See the reference in *Guide* iii. 22 (p. 489) to the rabbinical saying in Mishnah Ber. 9: 5 about serving God with both good and evil inclinations.

God, Self, Study, Repentance: The Pattern of the *Book of Knowledge*

A basic structural feature of the *Mishneh torah* is that the *Book of Knowledge* not only contains the essential concepts that underlie the rest of the work, but is also a formal template for it.[75] The relationships between 'Laws of the Foundations of the Torah' and the ending of the *Book of Temple Service*, and between 'Laws of Moral Qualities' and the ending of the *Book of Offerings* were outlined in the previous chapter. What follows is a development of the pattern identified there, restating it in relation to the tripartite structure of intellect, and bringing the *Book of Purity* into the picture.

The first section of the *Book of Knowledge*, 'Laws of the Foundations of the Torah', is orientated towards God. Its opening injunction to know God's existence illustrates this, but the whole section is theocentric, covering God's immateriality and unity, God the Creator, sanctification of God, and God as bestower of prophecy.

The second section, 'Laws of Moral Qualities', has a human orientation. It is about a human being's self-understanding and self-direction in following the middle path between extremes of temperament.

The third section, 'Laws of Torah Study', is about the acquisition of knowledge, which ultimately means physics and metaphysics, the theoretical knowledge emanated by the agent intellect.[76]

This sequence reflects the three thoughts of the stars and spheres, and forms a pattern that underlies Books 8, 9, and 10 and their endings: the divine orientation of Book 8 corresponds to 'Laws of the Foundations of the Torah'; the ethical aspect of the commandments stressed in Book 9, concerning not just right action but reform of character, corresponds to 'Laws of Moral Qualities'; and the soul turning towards intellect in Book 10 corresponds to 'Laws of Torah Study'.

Repentance as State of Mind

What though of the remaining sections of the *Book of Knowledge*, 'Laws of Idolatry' and 'Laws of Repentance'? To take the latter section first, its ending recapitulates the pivot away from the material world towards intellect and love, and stresses that this is accomplished through the acquisition of knowledge:

---

[75] See Gillis, *Reading Maimonides' Mishneh Torah*, 239–60.

[76] Torah study ultimately means study of *pardes* (see 'Laws of Torah Study', 1: 12), which for Maimonides means physics and metaphysics (see 'Laws of the Foundations of the Torah', 4: 13).

It is plainly known that love of the Holy One, blessed be He, becomes bound up in one's heart (so that he is always enthralled by it as he should be, forsaking all else, as He charged, '[Love the Lord your God] with all your heart and all your soul' [Deut. 6: 5]), only through the knowledge he attains of Him. As is one's knowledge [*de'ah*] so is his love: if [the one be] little, [the other will be] little, if [the one be] great, [the other will be] great. One must, therefore, be single-minded in studying and reflecting on the disciplines and sciences that give him such knowledge of his Master as humans can understand and apprehend, as we have explained in 'Laws of the Foundations of the Torah'.[77]

If this is the climax of 'Laws of Repentance', we must understand repentance not only as remorse for wrongdoing, or even as reform of one's character, but as a consistent posture of the human mind, the directing of one's being towards knowledge and love.

The acquisition of knowledge, the subject of 'Laws of Torah Study', and repentance as it is presented in 'Laws of Repentance', are two aspects of the same thing. Both are rooted in the Neoplatonic idea of return: 'The theory of emanation accorded reason an exalted position in the hierarchy of being and set up the soul as the link between the intelligible and material world. So long as it is incarcerated in the body, this soul will yearn for return to its original abode in the higher world and will eventually be liberated through the therapeutic study of philosophy.'[78]

It is through this turning back in yearning to contemplate the superior hypostasis from which it emanated that the lower hypostasis comes into full existence. In the case of human beings, this means turning back towards the agent intellect, from which their form, the human intellect, emanates. In this sense, through repentance, a human being is self-creating.[79] Thus at the end of 'Laws of Repentance' Maimonides provides the metaphysical underpinning of the 'passion for repentance', the source of the hope that we are not bound by our materiality, but can cast our sins—always the fault of our material side—behind our backs.

As for 'Laws of Idolatry', the origin of idolatry is depicted in this section as intellectual error, the thought that created beings should be venerated like their creator.[80] Undoing that error means a search for knowledge and truth. It is, therefore, no coincidence that 'Laws of Repentance', which follows 'Laws of Idolatry', indicating that is intended to be the antidote to it, ends on the theme of acquisition of knowledge.

---

[77] 'Laws of Repentance', 10: 6.
[78] Fakhry, *Al-Farabi, Founder of Islamic Neoplatonism*, 78.
[79] See *Guide* i. 7 (pp. 32–3) and iii. 54 (p. 635).   [80] 'Laws of Idolatry', 1: 1.

Torah and Water

All these aspects of return—repentance, 'the therapeutic study of philosophy', and redemption from idolatry—are present at the close of the *Book of Purity*. The phrase 'one who sets his heart on cleansing himself from the impurity that besets men's souls—namely wrongful thoughts and bad dispositions' describes an attitude of repentance. 'One who sets his heart' (*hamekhaven et libo*) suggests that what counts is not so much where one stands as which way one is looking, which is consistent with the Neoplatonic idea of Soul turning away from matter back towards Intellect whence it came, as is the instantaneous quality of the transformation in the continuation: '[he] becomes pure as soon as he consents to shun those counsels and brings his soul into the waters of intellect'. This is the application of reason to a person's moral disposition, but also implies a turn towards intellectual pursuits. In 'Laws of Torah Study',[81] Maimonides compares the Torah to water in making precisely this point: just as water finds the lowest level, so humility and diminution of appetites are preconditions for intellectual progress.

This comparison of the Torah to water is one of a series on that theme found in *Song of Songs Rabbah*.[82] Another in the series runs: 'Just as water cleanses a person from impurity, as it says: "And I will sprinkle clean water upon you and ye shall be clean" [Ezek. 36: 25], so Torah cleanses the impure person from impurity, as it says: "The words of the Lord are pure words" [Ps. 12: 7]'.[83] The verse from Ezekiel is of course the very one cited in 'Laws of Immersion Pools', 11: 12, only there its reference is transferred from the literal water of the *mikveh* to the metaphorical 'waters of intellect'. All this, together with the arguments from structure, makes it not unlikely that an allusion to Torah study is intended in that *halakhah*, at least as one brand of 'the waters of intellect'. In fact, given the midrashic associations, we might well have expected 'waters of Torah', rather than 'waters of intellect'. That is to say, there is a subtle universalization of Torah here, elevating it to its highest level, at which it means the study of philosophy, physics, and metaphysics, disciplines in which human beings are aided to knowledge by emanation from the agent intellect

Finally, in the verse from Ezekiel, we have elimination of idolatry: 'And I will sprinkle clean water upon you and ye shall be pure; from all your impurity and from all your idols will I cleanse you'. The direction of flow ('And I will sprinkle') makes Maimonides' use of this verse a harbinger of his use in

---

[81] 3: 9. [82] 1: 19.
[83] Our translation. Torah as water is a trope that goes back to Isa. 55: 19, which is cited in 'Laws of Torah Study', 3: 9.

Table 10.2 The universal structure of intellect as a template for the human archetype and for *Mishneh torah*, Book 1 and Books 8–10

1	2	3	4	5
Spheres and stars	Adam	*Mishneh torah*		
'Foundations of the Torah', 3: 9	'Foundations of the Torah', 2: 2	Book 1 (*Book of Knowledge*)	Books 8–10	Books 8–10: endings
Thought of God	Love	'Foundations of the Torah'	*Book of Temple Service* (communal sacrifices)	Commandments as decrees
Thought of self	Awe	'Moral Qualities'	*Book of Offerings* (individual sacrifices)	'Give reasons for the commandments'; commandments as ethical 'counsels from afar'
Thought of separate intellect	Acquisition of knowledge	'Torah Study' 'Idolatry' 'Repentance'	*Book of Purity*	Commandments as decrees, but also 'hint' at 'waters of intellect'

the *Guide* of a flow of water as a metaphor for emanation. In philosophical terms, it signifies purification of the notion of God by purging it of physical attributes, which is the intellect's lifelong endeavour,[84] and the reciprocal flow of knowledge from the agent intellect precipitated by the mind's turn towards it.

The argument is summed up in Table 10.2, which is an expansion of Table 10.1. It shows how the configuration of the laws of sacrifices and purity, and of the discussion of the reasons for the commandments, can be traced from the fundamental structures that the *Mishneh torah* both expounds and displays. Read from left to right, the table traces the way in which three directions of thought found in spheres and stars (column 1) are replicated in the intellectual processes of the archetypal human being described in 'Laws of the Foundations of the Torah', 2: 2 (column 2); in the structure of the *Book of Knowledge* (column 3); in the structure of the laws of sacrifices in Books 8, 9, and 10 of the *Mishneh torah* (column 4); and in the structure of the discussion of reasons for the commandments at the ends of those books (column 5).

---

[84] See *Guide* i. 59 (p. 139) and i. 60 (p. 144), and also *Guide* i. 36 (pp. 82–5), where Maimonides describes those who ascribe corporeal attributes to God as worse than those who worship forms in stone and wood.

The Temple ritual and the laws of purity, taken together, thus stand for a whole and healthy psyche in proper, balanced relationship with God, itself, and the world. This form in the soul is certainly a subjective correlative of the laws in question, but, because of the fundamental idea of human beings as microcosms, it co-ordinates with the objective forms of nature, with the distinct Neoplatonic colouring that characterizes Maimonides' understanding of them.

'Commune with Your Own Heart upon Your Bed, and Be Still'

In *Guide* ii. 5,[85] Maimonides turns his attention to the verse 'The heavens tell of the glory of God' [Ps. 19: 2]. The psalm quoted continues: 'the sky proclaims His handiwork. Day to day makes utterance, night to night speaks out. There is no utterance, there are no words, whose sound goes unheard.'

This might seem to mean that the heavenly bodies are endowed with the faculty of speech and utter hymns of praise to God. Maimonides explains that this is not so. The spheres that make up the heavens, he explains, do not actually speak. There is no heavenly choir.[86] The sphere has an idea of God, and its praise of God is the idea itself. It tells of the glory of God through its very being.

Human beings do speak, but speech is only the way in which they communicate the ideas that exist in their minds. The idea is primary; speech is secondary. When it comes to divine worship, prayer and songs of praise are only inadequate ways of uttering what the mind has comprehended of God. The ultimate praise is silent contemplation: 'For he who praises in speech only makes known what he has represented to himself. Now this very representation is the true praise, whereas the words concerning it are meant to instruct someone else or to make it clear concerning oneself that one has had the apprehension in question. Thus it says, "Commune with your own heart upon your bed, and be still",[87] as we have explained.' In that state, a human being resembles the spheres in their silent glorification of God.[88]

'As we have explained' in this passage refers to two earlier chapters of the *Guide*. In *Guide* i. 50, Maimonides states that those who 'represent to themselves the unity of the Name' are preferable to 'those who merely proclaim it with their mouth', and concludes 'But men ought rather to belong to the cate-

---

[85] pp. 259–61.
[86] Cf. *Guide* ii. 8 (p. 267), where Maimonides asserts, with Aristotle and contra the talmudic Sages, that the spheres make no sound.   [87] Ps. 4: 5.
[88] See also *Guide* i. 64, on God's glory, and Kellner, *Maimonides' Confrontation*, 189–215.

gory of those who represent the truth[89] to themselves and apprehend it, even if they do not utter it, as the virtuous are commanded to do—for they are told "Commune with your own heart upon your bed, and be still".' Similarly, in *Guide* i. 59, he criticizes the attempt to describe God's perfection in prayer as resulting in denigration, since it inevitably involves material attributes. He invokes Psalm 65: 2, 'Silence is praise to thee', and continues, 'silence and limiting oneself to the apprehensions of the intellects are more appropriate—just as the perfect ones have enjoined when they said: "Commune with your own heart upon your bed, and be still".'

This is as much as to say that those who read and understand the *Book of Knowledge*, 'Laws of Foundations of the Torah', 1–2 on God's unity are preferable to those who merely fulfil the commandment in the *Book of Love*, 'Laws of Recitation of the Shema', to proclaim 'the Lord is one'.[90] Hence in the hierarchy of the division of the *Mishneh torah* that concerns relations 'between human beings and God', the *Book of Knowledge*, which is motivated by 'the apprehensions of the intellects', precedes the *Book of Love*, which is about the articulation of those apprehensions in the Shema, prayer, blessings, and circumcision.

If apprehension has priority over speech, which must involve some mental engagement, then *a fortiori* it has priority over sacrifices, which are yet further removed from the 'apprehensions of the intellect', and over ritual purity, which, beyond the intention of fulfilling a commandment, has no mental component at all. This order finds expression in *Guide* iii. 32,[91] which presents sacrifices as a concession to ancient convention, prayer and fasts as concessions to current convention, and worship consisting 'solely in meditation' as the ideal. In the *Mishneh torah*, as already explained, it is expressed in the relegation of sacrifices and ritual purity to the bottom of the 'between human beings and God' division.

Yet just as Maimonides explicitly makes the non-rational commandment of *mikveh* represent rationality itself, implicit in his treatment of the laws pertaining to the Temple, sacrifices, and purity taken as a whole is that the lowest form of worship is representative of the very highest, in which, like the spheres, human beings glorify God through the very operation of their intellects, the realization of their form. The perfected human intellect is like the intellect of the spheres with its three thoughts—of God, of self, and of the

---

[89] Pines notes that 'The word may also mean "God".'

[90] Of course the best thing is to recite the Shema, but in awareness of the significance of what one is saying, and not just with the intention of fulfilling the commandment—see *Guide* iii. 51 (p. 622).   [91] p. 526.

immediately superior angel—but all three thoughts are ultimately thoughts of God. As we have already pointed out, a human being's self-consciousness arises from awareness of the gulf between his or her intellect and that of God. Perfection of the self is through the imitation of God, with the aim of becoming capable of acquiring knowledge of God. As for the thought of the agent intellect, that consists in the study of physics and metaphysics, which is the only positive knowledge of God to be had. A human being's real worship of God is thus the proper functioning of the intellect itself in all its orientations. As we saw in Chapter 7 above, Maimonides already gives notice in the ending to Book 7 that the Holy of Holies is a virtuous mind as much as a physical structure. Over the following three books, he develops that idea with full philosophical rigour.

In this way, Books 8, 9, and 10 of the Mishneh torah fulfil all the criteria of a Maimonidean parable, as set out in the introduction to the Guide[92] in the exposition of Proverbs 25: 11: 'A word fitly spoken is like apples of gold in settings of silver.' The parable's literal meaning is the laws of sacrifices and purity themselves. The silver level of meaning, which 'contains wisdom that is useful in many respects, among which is the welfare of human societies',[93] concerns the Temple as a symbol of national sovereignty and unity, and a place of awe before God, whose Torah is unquestionable law (in Book 8); the idea of moral virtue, on which social cohesion depends (in Book 9); and the morally and intellectually regenerated individual's pursuit of knowledge, the purpose of a state governed by divine law (in Book 10).

At this level there is also 'something that indicates to someone considering it what is to be found in its internal meaning',[94] such as the hint we found at the end of Book 9 that the offering God truly seeks is knowledge of the truth, and the Neoplatonic overtones of the metaphorical treatment of *mikveh* at the end of Book 10. Moreover, the sealing of the three books on the Temple ritual with the parable of the *mikveh* 'indicates to someone considering it' not just the matter but also the method. It hints at the possibility that the exposition of the Temple ritual as a whole (which, like the *mikveh*, is characterized as a *ḥok*), might be a great parable that the parable of the *mikveh* synecdochically summarizes.

The golden layer confirms that indication. At this level we understand that the glory of God is ultimately not in the sacrifices offered in the Temple, nor even in the songs of the Levites and the recitations and prayers, but, as with the spheres, in the intellect's own self-realization. Moreover, the realized intellect is that which survives death, and the parable suggests that this is

---

[92] *Guide* i. Introduction (p. 12).   [93] Ibid.   [94] Ibid.

how the *ḥukim* lead to immortality as promised at the end of Book 8: at the silver level, through their effects on the mind and character; at the golden level, through the abstraction and internalization of their form. The very perception of the laws of sacrifices and purity as a parable is this idea in performance. Thus out of the most active, material-bound, and contingent commandments, Maimonides creates a still communion with the heart.[95]

'The World Stands upon Three Things'

In Chapter 8 we noted that the statement in 'Laws of Trespass', 8: 8, that 'The sages said that even on the service of sacrifices the world stands' is a reference to Mishnah *Avot* 1: 2: 'Simon the Just was one of the last of the men of the Great Assembly. He used to say, "The world stands upon three things, on the Torah, on the Temple service, and on kind deeds"';[96] we also referred

---

[95] Maimonides' order of priorities in worship, placing 'apprehensions of the intellect' above prayer and both above sacrifices, not only reflects the Neoplatonic hierarchy of being, but also has affinities with views on worship expressed by Neoplatonic writers. The late pagan Neoplatonists Porphyry (c.234–c.305 CE) and Iamblichus (c.245–c.325 CE) posit matching hierarchies of gods and human beings. The lowest gods, which are associated with matter, and the lowest rank of human beings, need food offerings. Next comes a middling kind of god, and a middle rank of human beings, for which the appropriate mode of worship is hymns and prayers. The highest god is free of any material association, and is worshipped by human beings of the highest rank, i.e. philosophers, through contemplation only, 'in profound silence with a pure soul, and with pure conceptions about him' (Porphyry, *On Abstinence from Animal Food*, ii. 34, pp. 69–70). The idea that a perfected human being in himself represents the most meaningful offering is echoed in Porphyry's statement that 'the most excellent offering is a pure intellect and an impassive soul' (ibid. ii. 61, p. 91). See further *Iamblichus on the Mysteries of the Egyptians, Chaldeans, and Assyrians*, v. 14–26 (pp. 249–74); Zeper, 'Blood Sacrifice and Bloodless Sacrifice', 97–107; Lobel, 'Silence Is Praise to You'; ead., 'Being and the Good'.

Maimonides' rationalization of sacrifices is more akin to that of the pagan philosophers than to that of, for example, *Sifrei* on Num. 28: 8. *Sifrei* replaces the undesirable implication of the verse that the daily offerings satisfy God's appetite with the idea that they fulfil God's will. As we have argued, that idea by itself runs contrary to Maimonides' conception of commandments as products of both God's will and God's wisdom.

We are grateful to Professor Azzan Yadin-Israel for directing our attention to the Neoplatonic and rabbinic sources cited here, in his lecture at the 17th World Congress of Jewish Studies: 'A Theological Critique of Sacrifice: The Rabbis and Porphyry', and in subsequent private correspondence. It is highly unlikely that Maimonides was directly acquainted with the works of Porphyry and Iamblichus; they are not among the Greek books currently known to have circulated in Arabic versions by Maimonides' time. See D'Ancona, 'Greek Sources'. A Porphyry is mentioned in Maimonides' letter to Ibn Tibbon (see Maimonides, *Igerot harambam* (trans. Shailat), ii. 563), but it is not clear what writings might be meant, especially as this Porphyry is listed as belonging to 'early philosophy', i.e. before Plato and Aristotle. See Davidson, *Moses Maimonides*, 112 n. 176.   [96] See also JT *Meg.* 3: 6.

to Maimonides' comment on this *mishnah*, 'He said that in science, which is the Torah, and in moral virtue, which is kind deeds, and in observance of the commandments, which is the sacrifices, lies the continued soundness of the world and its orderly existence in the most perfect fashion.'[97]

This is a prime example of Maimonides putting a philosophical construction on statements of the talmudic Sages. He does not treat the three things listed by Simon the Just as specific areas of religious observance, but generalizes from them to philosophical categories: from kind deeds to moral virtue, and from Torah to science. As far as sacrifices are concerned, he makes them representative of 'observance of the commandments', and we have seen what Maimonides ultimately means by this: not the actions, but the constant thought of the God who commanded them. We thus have in Maimonides' reading of this *mishnah* the three orientations of the psyche: the thought of God, in observance of the commandments; the thought of the self, in moral virtue; and the thought of the agent intellect, in the study of science.[98]

This philosophical reading, we submit, is invoked by the allusion to Mishnah *Avot* 1: 2 in 'Laws of Trespass', 8: 8. It tends to justify the assertion in Chapter 8 that by classifying the sacrifices as *ḥukim* Maimonides intends them as representative of all the commandments in their '*ḥok* dimension', that is, from the point of view of their formal cause, which is God, or all that we can perceive of God, namely the laws of nature.

It is plausible, then, to conjecture that the significance of the pattern we have identified in Books 8, 9, and 10 of the *Mishneh torah* was in Maimonides' mind in his earliest cogitations on the commandments, and particularly in the schematization of sacrifices presented in the commentary on Mishnah *Zevaḥim*.

Reversing Halevi

At the outset of this discussion, in Chapter 8, it was mentioned that Maimonides' preference for reasoned observance of the commandments is the opposite of Judah Halevi's preference for pure obedience, with observance

---

[97] Our translation from *Commentary on the Mishnah* (Heb.), trans. Kafih, vol. 4, p. 267.
[98] It is also worth noting Maimonides' comment on the closing *mishnah* of the first chapter of *Avot*. That *mishnah* reads: 'Raban Shimon ben Gamliel says, "The world exists by virtue of three things: justice, truth, and peace."' Maimonides comments: 'Justice is the just direction of the state. And we have already explained in the fourth chapter [of *Eight Chapters*] that truth is the intellectual virtues and peace is the moral virtues.' This re-emerges in *Guide* iii. 51 (p. 524): 'Thus all [the commandments] are bound up with three things: opinions, moral qualities, and political civic actions.'

supported by reason as second best. This difference emerges in their approaches to explanation of the Temple ritual. It turns out that Maimonides' position is the reverse of Halevi's in the substance of his explanation as well as in his general approach. Halevi draws an analogy from the well-ordered human personality required for the flourishing of the intellect to the order of the Temple service, the orderly and precise performance of which is required, he argues, so that the 'divine matter' will become attached to the nation of Israel, which is uniquely capable of receiving it.[99] The functioning of the individual human intellect is the *mashal*, the model or parable, and the Temple ritual is the *nimshal*, the reference or lesson. What we have found in the esoteric layer of Books 8, 9, and 10 of the *Mishneh torah* is precisely the opposite: the Temple ritual is the *mashal*, and the functioning of the individual intellect is the *nimshal*.

This reversal is so neat that it raises the suspicion that Maimonides' treatment represents a direct reaction to Halevi. It also clarifies Maimonides' universalism. Halevi uses universal human psychology as a basis for conveying the divine mystery of a peculiarly Jewish set of rituals—and then retreats even from that merely analogical contact with philosophy. Maimonides takes those rituals, which amount to the most prominent Jewish national symbol, and makes them emblematic of the universal human condition.

Halevi's idea of the Temple is of course predicated on the existence of a metaphysical entity called the nation of Israel to which the divine can attach. Maimonides' philosophical position precludes that. He writes in the *Guide*: 'I say that it is known that no species exists outside the mind, but that the species and the other universals are, as you know, mental notions and that every existent outside the mind is an individual or a group of individuals'.[100] The Jewish nation is simply a collection of Jews, and Maimonides refuses to reify it. The Temple has its political importance, for the individual needs order and cohesion in the state in order to pursue enlightenment, and the Temple is the institution around which the nation coalesces, but knowledge of the divine can subsist only in an individual mind.

The Love within Awe

Taking our cue from the *Guide*'s treatment of the scapegoat, we have arrived at an interpretation of the Temple ritual in the *Mishneh torah* as a parable that

---

[99] See *Kuzari* ii. 26. Kreisel, 'Reasons for the Commandments', surveys several medieval interpretations of the Temple and its rites as a microcosm or macro-anthropos.

[100] *Guide* iii. 18 (p. 474).

underwrites its continued validity. It is a parable of the human intellect and soul assuming their proper roles and relationship, and thereby becoming like the intellect and soul of a sphere (see Appendix). The heavenly spheres are moved by love. The Temple rites, on the other hand, are designed to inspire awe, but if their inner meaning is a parable of the soul and intellect, and love is proportionate to the product of intellect, that is, knowledge, then within a setting of awe, the Temple ritual has a core of love.[101]

It emerges that the approach of the *Mishneh torah* to sacrifices and purity requires greater philosophical knowledge to be fully understood than does the approach of the *Guide*. This is enough to upset the view that the approach to rationalization of the commandments in the *Mishneh torah* is designed to encourage practical observance, while the *Guide* is speculative.[102] It is also more universal. From a once universal but now obsolete religious practice, the *Guide* converges on an explanation, in the light of that practice, of the particular rituals of Judaism.[103] The *Mishneh torah*, by contrast, expands from Jewish ritual to universal, eternal truths. The universalist horizons of the *Mishneh torah* could not be wider.

The question arises, what is the status of this parable? Is it meant to be a final truth, delivered covertly in order to conceal it from the masses, or is the covert treatment a way of conveying a poetic truth that cannot be stated apodictically without spoiling it? After all, to the extent that Maimonides' physics and metaphysics are schematic and provisional, as discussed in Chapter 8, rationalizations of the commandments based on his physics and metaphysics must be schematic and provisional too. Perhaps what counts is not the thought so much as the stimulus to thought, and Maimonides' intention is not to serve the fruit but to plant a seed? The question is really beyond our scope.[104] At the very least, we can observe that the *Mishneh torah* practises what it preaches: 'Give reasons for the commandments' it says, and through its reflective endings and symbolic structure, it does so.

---

[101] Perhaps this is hinted at by the motto of the *Book of Temple Service*, 'Pray for the peace of Jerusalem; may they prosper that love thee' (Ps. 122: 6).

[102] See Heinemann, *Reasons for the Commandments* (Heb.), 79.

[103] Note, however, that part iii of the *Guide*, the latter half of which contains the discussion of reasons for the commandments, opens with Maimonides' exposition of *ma'aseh merkavah*; that is to say, there may be a structural hint to the formal cause of the commandments in the *Guide* as well as in the *Mishneh torah*. Don Seeman, in his article 'Reasons for the Commandments', sees a similar significance in the sequence of topics in the third part of the *Guide*.

[104] See Gillis, *Reading Maimonides' Mishneh Torah*, 375–85; Twersky, *Introduction to the Code*, 401–3.

Summary

Maimonides deliberately placed 'Laws of Immersion Pools' at the end of the *Book of Purity*, rearranging the mishnaic source material in order to do so. This enabled him to conclude this volume with the idea of the *mikveh* as a metaphor for the human intellect. The positioning of this metaphor is highly significant. If the first ten books of the *Mishneh torah*, on commandments between human beings and God, are seen as representing a process of emanation from the primary commandment to know God, and given that Maimonides likens emanation to a flow of water, then the *mikveh* at the end is where this process culminates. This sums up all the ceremonial commandments as contributing towards bringing the soul into 'the waters of intellect'. The metaphorical treatment of *mikveh* also prefigures the ending of the *Mishneh torah* as a whole, where knowledge, now the property of all mankind, is again associated with water, this time as the sea, a universal *mikveh*.

In the *Guide*, Maimonides states that the reason for the laws of purity is to create a barrier to entry to the Temple, so that visits there will be rare and therefore always awe-inspiring. In the *Mishneh torah*, he avoids assigning these laws such a utilitarian purpose. His insistence in that work that they are *ḥukim* allows him to offer his metaphorical 'hint'.

The endings of Books 8, 9, and 10 present a three-part discussion of reasons for the commandments that forms a dialectic of thesis, antithesis, and synthesis: commandments as incomprehensible divine edicts (Book 8); commandments comprehensible as moral correctives (Book 9); commandments as edicts but hinting at moral and intellectual regeneration—which means acquiring knowledge (Book 10).

This last idea opens the way to seeing Maimonides' entire treatment of the Temple and its rituals in the *Mishneh torah* as a parable of soul and intellect, along lines suggested by his description in the *Guide* of the scapegoat as 'parables serving to bring forth a form in the soul so that a passion for repentance should result'. Books 8, 9, and 10 of the *Mishneh torah* are configured according to the triple orientation of thought in all created things endowed with intellect: a thought of God; a thought of self; and a thought of the entity from which the self emanated. In the case of human beings, this last entity is the agent intellect, from which emanate both form and knowledge. At the end of the *Book of Purity*, the human soul turns away from material concerns and towards knowledge in a movement of repentance.

The ending of the *Book of Purity* is also an appropriate interface with the following book, the *Book of Damages*. At the very end of 'Laws of Moral

Qualities', inward moral virtue is presented as the basis of constructive social and commercial transactions. The idea of individual moral regeneration at the end of the *Book of Purity* thus leads in to the laws dealing with wrongdoing between people in the *Book of Damages*, which begin the process of social regeneration that spans Books 11 to 14 of the *Mishneh torah*.

Throughout his writings, Maimonides stresses that the point of the commandments is not just their performance but also the systematic study of them in order to extract their form. Maimonides imprints on the laws of the Temple, sacrifices, and ritual purity a form that originates in the *Book of Knowledge*. He thereby turns them into a parable of the properly functioning human psyche, which is the true worship of God. The *Guide* explains sacrifices in general by their historical context. The parable in the *Mishneh torah* invests them with an enduring significance that transcends that context, and it is perhaps this that, in Maimonides' eyes, justifies their future reinstatement.

ELEVEN

DAMAGES
Who Is a Jew?

Introduction

The eleventh book of the *Mishneh torah* is *Sefer nezakim*, the *Book of Damages* (or *Torts*). As noted in the previous chapter, the *Book of Ritual Purity* is the last of the ten books of the *Mishneh torah* that mostly concern commandments between human beings and God, that is to say, ceremonial commandments. The remaining four books mostly concern social commandments (*bein adam leḥavero*).[1] Our volume is thus the first of that four-book series. It contains five sections: 'Laws of Monetary Damage', 'Laws of Theft', 'Laws of Robbery and Lost Property', 'Laws of Wounding and Damaging', and 'Laws of Murder and the Preservation of Life'. This last section deals with the following topics: homicide, manslaughter, exile to cities of refuge, cities of refuge, the rite of breaking the neck of a heifer, building a parapet around a roof, and other actions meant to avoid accidental death and to safeguard from danger. The last chapter includes discussions of the duty to help load or unload the burden of a pack animal and the right to pass or overtake on a narrow road or river, and ends with the following statement concerning the commandment to assist someone in trouble on the road, even if they are an enemy:

The enemy [*hasone*] mentioned in the Torah[2] does not mean a foreign enemy but an

---

[1] See the book synopses in Maimonides' Introduction to the *Mishneh torah*, and the Appendix below. The title *Sefer nezakim* follows Makbili's text. The book is more usually called *Sefer nezikin*, after the order in the Mishnah (and Talmud) upon which it is largely based.

[2] Exod. 23: 5: 'If thou see the ass of him that hateth thee lying under its burden, thou shalt forbear to pass by him; thou shalt surely release it with him.' Maimonides' reference here is to his previous paragraph: 'If one encounters two animals, one crouching under its burden and the other unburdened because the owner cannot find anyone to help him load, he is obligated to unload first to relieve the animal's suffering, and then to load the other. This rule applies only if the owners of the animals are both friends or are both enemies [of the person who comes upon them]. But if one is an enemy and the other a friend, he is obligated to load

Israelite[3] one. How can an Israelite have an Israelite enemy when Scripture says, 'Thou shalt not hate thy brother in thy heart' [Lev. 19: 17]? The Sages explained that this could occur if one all alone sees another committing a crime and warns him against it and he does not desist, one is obligated to hate him until he repents and leaves his evil ways. Yet even if he has not yet repented and one finds him in difficulties with his burden, one is obligated to help him load or unload, and not leave him possibly to die, lest he tarry because of his property and meet with danger. The Torah is very solicitous for the lives of Israelites, whether of the wicked or of the righteous, since all Israelites are joined with [*nilvim el*] God and believe [*ma'aminin*] in the principles of religion [*ikarei hadat*]. For it is said, 'Say unto them; As I live, saith the Lord God, I have no pleasure in the death of the wicked but that the wicked turn from his way and live' [Ezek. 33: 11].[4]

'Those who Join Themselves'

Two terms at the end of this passage call out for attention: *nilvim* and *ikarei hadat*. We shall examine them both, beginning with the first, which occurs twice in the Bible, in Isaiah 56: 3 and 6 and in Esther 9: 27. The New Jewish Publication Society translation renders these verses as follows (we cite the verses in their immediate contexts):

Isaiah 56: 1–8: Thus said the Lord: Observe what is right and do what is just; for soon My salvation shall come, and my deliverance be revealed. Happy is the man who does this, the man who holds fast to it: who keeps the sabbath and does not profane it, and stays his hand from doing any evil. Let not the foreigner say, *who has attached himself to the Lord*, 'The Lord will keep me apart from His people'; and let not the eunuch say, 'I am a withered tree.' For thus said the Lord: 'As for the eunuchs who keep My sabbaths, who have chosen what I desire and hold fast to My covenant—I will give them, in My House and within My walls, a monument and a name better than sons or daughters. I will give them an everlasting name which shall not perish. As for *the foreigners who attach themselves to the Lord*, to

---

the [animal of the] enemy first, in order to subdue his evil impulse.' It is of interest to note that the term translated here as 'is obligated' is *mitsvah*, which often connotes a supererogatory good deed, not a technical halakhic obligation. On this last, see Friedberg, *Crafting the 613 Commandments*.

[3] Hebrew: *yisra'el*. It will become clear below why we do not translate this more colloquially as 'Jews'.

[4] 'Laws of Murder and the Preservation of Life', 13: 14. We quote here and below from the translation of Klein, *The Book of Torts* (Yale Judaica Series), with emendations. According to Kafih, *The Hebrew Bible in Maimonides* (Heb.), the verse from Ezekiel is cited nowhere else in Maimonides' writings. On this passage, see also Gillis, *Reading Maimonides' Mishneh Torah*, 278–85, and Buchman, 'The Order of the Books of the *Mishneh Torah*' (Heb.), 21.

minister to Him, and to love the name of the Lord, to be His servants—all who keep the sabbath and do not profane it, and who hold fast to My covenant—I will bring them to My sacred mount and let them rejoice in My house of prayer. Their burnt offerings and sacrifices shall be welcome on My altar; for My House shall be called a house of prayer for all peoples.' Thus declares the Lord God, who gathers the dispersed of Israel: 'I will gather still more to those already gathered.'

Esther 9: 26–8: For that reason these days were named Purim, after *pur*.[5] In view, then, of all the instructions in the said letter and of what they had experienced in that matter and what had befallen them, the Jews undertook and irrevocably obligated themselves and their descendants, *and all who might join them*, to observe these two days in the manner prescribed and at the proper time each year. Consequently, these days are recalled and observed in every generation: by every family, every province, and every city. And these days of Purim shall never cease among the Jews, and the memory of them shall never perish among their descendants.

Despite what might be taken as a more universalist referent in these verses, the commentators Rashi and David Kimhi (Radak, 1160–1235) take the expression in Isaiah 56: 3 to refer to proselytes (and one assumes they would read 56: 6 similarly). On the Esther passage, Rashi and Ibn Ezra (and later commentators in their wake) also take our term to refer to proselytes. In this, they follow those rabbinic texts which relate to the term.

Maimonides himself uses the term in four places in the *Mishneh torah*, aside from our text. These are 'Laws of Idolatry', 1: 3, 'Laws of Repose on Festivals', 6: 17, 'Laws of Fasts', 4: 4, and 'Laws of Gifts to the Poor', 10: 2. We cited the first text in its entirety above, in Chapter 1. Here we cite the directly relevant passage, once again in the exemplary translation of Bernard Septimus:

When the people gathered about him [Abraham], questioning him about his message, he would instruct each individual according to his intelligence, so as to turn him to the true path. [He continued] till thousands and tens of thousands had joined him, these being 'the people of Abraham's house' [Gen. 17: 23]. He planted this great root in their hearts, composed books on it, and imparted it to his son Isaac. Isaac continued to teach and turn [his students to the truth]. Isaac imparted it to Jacob and assigned him to teach. [Jacob] continued to teach and to turn *all who joined him* [*kol hanilvim elav*] [to the true path].

Our Father Jacob taught all his children; but he singled out Levi, appointing him 'head' and installing him in an academy to teach 'the way of the Lord' [Gen. 18:

---

[5] *Pur* means 'lot', referring to the lots cast by the chief vizier Haman to determine the date for massacring the Jews of the Persian empire, a plan thwarted by Esther's courage and sagacity.

19] and keep Abraham's charge. He directed his children that there be an uninterrupted succession of Levite appointees, so that the teaching not be forgotten.

This enterprise was gathering strength among Jacob's children *and those who joined them [uvanilvim aleihem]*, a God-knowing nation was coming into being—till Israel's stay in Egypt became prolonged and they retrogressed, learning [the Egyptians'] deeds and worshipping alien deities like them (the sole exception being the tribe of Levi, which remained steadfast to the Patriarchal charge: never did the tribe of Levi worship alien deities).

The root planted by Abraham was on the verge of being uprooted and Jacob's descendants, of reverting to the error and aberrance of the nations. But because God loved us and stood by [his] oath to Our Father, Abraham, he elected Moses—Our Master and the Master of all the Prophets—and charged him with his [prophetic] mission.

When Moses our Master attained to prophecy and God chose Israel as His own, He crowned them with commandments, and taught them: how to worship Him and what rules should govern alien worship and all who stray after it.[6]

For Maimonides there is no possibility of conversion before Sinai (there being nothing to convert to, since the Jewish religion as such does not precede Sinai).[7] That being the case, whatever the status of those described as *nilvim el* Jacob and his children, it is not that of proselytes and certainly not that of the actual descendants of Jacob (or of his father or grandfather).

The second passage is in 'Laws of Repose on Festivals':

The seven days of Passover, the eight days of the Feast of Tabernacles, and the other festival days are all days on which funeral eulogies and fasting are forbidden. It is one's duty to rejoice and be of cheerful heart on these days, together with his children, his wife, his household [*uvnei beito*], *and all the other members of his household* [*vekol hanilvim alav*], for Scripture says, 'And thou shalt rejoice in thy feast, thou and thy son and thy daughter, your male and female slave [the Levite, the stranger the

---

[6] 'Laws of Idolatry', 1: 3. For discussions of this text, see Kellner, *Maimonides' Confrontation*, 77–83, and the studies cited there.

[7] Note the way Maimonides introduces the laws of conversion in 'Laws of Forbidden Intercourse', ch. 13, comparing the conversion of proselytes to Judaism to the conversion of the Israelites who left Egypt at Sinai: 'With three things did Israel enter the covenant: circumcision, immersion, and sacrifice . . . and so it is for all generations, when a Gentile wishes to enter the covenant and shelter under [lit. 'stand at the threshold of'] the wings of the Shekhinah, and accept upon himself the yoke of the Torah, he needs circumcision, immersion, and the bringing of a sacrifice . . . and when the Temple will be [re]built, he will bring his sacrifice.' For discussion, see Kellner, *Maimonides on Judaism and the Jewish People*, 52. Maimonides certainly did not accept the rabbinic legend that the Patriarchs (and their pre-Sinaitic descendants) observed the 613 commandments before Sinai. See Kellner, *Maimonides' Confrontation*, 76–7, and above, Ch. 2.

fatherless and the widow in your communities]' [Deut. 16: 14]. Although rejoicing in this context refers to the peace offering to be brought on festivals, as we shall explain in 'Laws of the Festal Offering' [1: 1], it includes also the duty incumbent upon each man, his children, and his household [*uvnei beito*], to rejoice in the appropriate manner.[8]

In this text Maimonides distinguishes the householder, his children, his wife, his household (*benei beito*) from those who are *nilvim* to him. Are the *nilvim* here only those specified in the verse, or anyone dependent upon the householder? We will come back to this question below.

The third passage is in 'Laws of Fasts':

Who was regarded as eligible to recite the prayers on such fast days? A person who was accustomed to reciting prayers and reading from the Torah, the Prophets, and the Writings; one who had small children; a poor man responsible for a wife and children and dependent upon his labour in the field; one whose household was free from transgression—i.e. none of whose sons, family members [*uvnei beito*],[9] relatives, or *other dependents* [*vehanilvim alav*] was a transgressor—and who had a blameless reputation in his youth; a person of humble disposition, and held in favour by the people, and one who understood melody and had a sweet voice. If an elder could be found with all these qualifications, he was given preference;[10] otherwise one who was not an elder was appointed to lead the congregation in prayer, so long as he answered all these requirements.[11]

In this case the *nilvim* are neither children of the householder in question, members of the family, nor other relatives. It appears that they are dependent upon the householder, but in what capacity it is not clear.

Our fourth passage is from 'Laws of Gifts to the Poor':

No one is ever impoverished by almsgiving, nor does evil or harm befall anyone by reason of it, as it is said, 'And the work of righteousness shall be peace' [Isa. 32: 17]. He who has compassion upon others, others will have compassion on him, as it said, 'That the Lord may . . . show thee mercy and have compassion upon thee' [Deut. 13: 18]. Whoever is cruel and merciless lays himself open to suspicion as to his descent, for cruelty is found only among the heathens [*goyim*], as it is said, 'They are cruel, and have no compassion' [Jer. 50: 42]. All Israelites and *those who have attached themselves to them* [*vehanilvim aleihem*] are to each other like brothers, as it

---

[8] 'Laws of Repose on Festivals', 6: 17. We cite the passage, slightly emended, from the Yale Judaica translation by Solomon Gandz and Hyman Klein, p. 303.

[9] Gandz and Klein translate this as 'household members', but that seems clearly wrong in this context. [10] Lit.: 'that is splendid'.

[11] 'Laws of Fasts', 4: 4. We cite the passage, slightly emended, from the Gandz and Klein translation, p. 444.

is said, 'Ye are the children of the Lord your God' [Deut. 14: 1]. If brother will show no compassion to brother, who will? And unto whom shall the poor of Israel raise their eyes? Unto the heathens [*goyim*], who hate them and persecute them? Their eyes are therefore hanging solely upon their brethren.[12]

Who are those who have attached themselves to Israelites? The term could not mean proselytes in this context, since they are as obligated to give alms as any other Jew and have a stronger claim to receive alms than other Jews.[13]

Whether we translate *nilvim* in these passages as 'members of his household' or as 'dependents', we are left with a question: does the term include non-Jewish slaves or other hangers-on? Since the joy of the festivals is not incumbent upon non-Jews, slaves or otherwise,[14] it seems apparent that the term in the first passage is restricted to Jews.[15] The other passages are not so clear.

Be that as it may, these passages do not seem to shed much light on the expression 'joined (*nilvim*) with God' in our text at the end of the *Book of Damages*. The first passage that we examined, from 'Laws of Idolatry', on the other hand, clearly indicates that those who are joined (*nilvim*) with God are people who attach themselves to God without being descendants of the Patriarchs, and without being formal converts. This reading is supported by one version of Maimonides' famous responsum to Obadiah the Proselyte, which contains the following passage:[16]

> The reason for this is, that Abraham our father taught the people, opened their minds, and revealed to them the true religion [*dat*][17] and the unity of God; he rejected the idols and abolished their adoration; he brought many . . . under the wings of the Divine Presence; he gave them counsel and advice and ordered his sons and the members of his household after him to keep the ways of the Lord . . . as it is written, 'For I have known him to the end that he may command his children and his household after him, that they may keep the way of the Lord, to do righteousness and justice' [Gen. 18: 19]. Ever since then whoever adopts Judaism

---

[12] 'Laws of Gifts to the Poor', 10: 2. That Maimonides writes persuasively here, not descriptively, should be clear. For proof, see Kellner, *They, Too, Are Called Human* (Heb.), ch. 8. This text is also discussed above in Ch. 9, p. 176.

[13] See Kellner, *Maimonides on Judaism*, ch. 7.

[14] One could make a case that BT *Pes.* 109a and Maimonides, *Book of Commandments*, positive commandment 109 imply that one has an obligation to include non-Jewish dependents in the joy of the holiday, but proving it would take us too far afield. On joy in Maimonides' thought generally, see Blidstein, 'Joy in Maimonides' Ethical Teaching' (Heb.).

[15] Actually, this may not be so clear in light of 'Laws of Slaves', 9: 8, in which one is urged to share food and drink with non-Jewish slaves, as discussed in Ch. 13 below.

[16] As cited in *Teshuvot harambam* (no. 293, p. 549). The discussion here is drawn from Kellner, '"Farteitsht un Farbessert"'. [17] On this term, see above, Ch. 1, n. 2.

and confesses the unity of the divine name, as it is written in the Torah—they are all disciples of Abraham our Father, peace be with him, and members of his household, and he turned them to righteousness. In the same way as he turned his contemporaries through his words and teaching, so does he turn all who will convert in the future through the testament he left to his children and household after him. Thus Abraham our Father . . . is the father of his pious posterity who walk in his ways, and the father of his disciples and of every proselyte who converts.

Admittedly, there is another version of this letter, found in Shailat's edition of the responsa, which makes it easier (but by no means necessary) to limit Abraham's future disciples to proselytes.[18] But even if Shailat's reading is preferred, the text from 'Laws of Idolatry' presents us with an example of how Maimonides clearly uses *nilvim* to mean non-Jews.[19]

'The Principles of Religion'

Let us now return to the text which is the focus of our discussion in this chapter, the last paragraph in the *Book of Damages*:

The enemy [*hasone*] mentioned in the Torah does not mean a foreign enemy but an Israelite one. How can an Israelite have an Israelite enemy when Scripture says, 'Thou shalt not hate thy brother in thy heart' [Lev. 19: 17]? The Sages decreed that if one all alone sees another committing a crime and warns him against it and he does not desist, one is obligated to hate him until he repents and leaves his evil ways. Yet even if he has not yet repented and one finds him in difficulties with his burden, one is obligated to help him load or unload, and not leave him possibly to die, lest he tarry because of his property and meet with danger. The Torah is very solicitous for the lives of Israelites, whether of the wicked or of the righteous, since all Israelites are joined with [*nilvim el*] God and believe in the principles of religion. For it is said, 'Say unto them; As I live, saith the Lord God, I have no pleasure in the death of the wicked but that the wicked turn from his way and live' [Ezek. 33: 11].

It is immediately obvious that Maimonides does not mean to be taken literally here, since he knew very well that not all Israelites are joined (*nilveh*) to God and believe in the principles of the Jewish religion (*ikarei hadat*). We know this latter fact from an interesting responsum.

Maimonides was asked a pointed question on his position concerning the place of heretics in the Jewish community and in the world to come. His questioner had pointed out an apparent inconsistency in the master's *Mishneh torah*.[20] In 'Laws of Idolatry',[21] Maimonides had stated in no uncertain

---

[18] For details, see Kellner's article cited in n. 16 above.
[19] For further discussion of the term *nilvim*, see above, Ch. 7, n. 15.
[20] See Maimonides, *Teshuvot harambam*, ii, no. 264.   [21] 2: 5.

terms that 'Israelite sectarians [*minim*] are not considered as Israelites in any fashion, and they are never accepted as penitents.'[22] In 'Laws of Repentance',[23] on the other hand, Maimonides maintained that sectarians and heretics 'are excluded from the world to come only if they die unrepentant. But if he repents his evil, and is a penitent [*ba'al teshuvah*], he has a share in the world to come, since nothing stands in the way of repentance.' The apparent contradiction is obvious. In his responsum, Maimonides replied to his questioner as follows (emphasis added):

What you consider to be a contradiction concerning sectarians—there is no contradiction whatsoever. One of the texts states 'they are never accepted as penitents', i.e. *we* do not accept their repentance and do not see them as falling under the category of penitents, but, rather, continue to see them as the sectarians they were, and assume that the righteousness of their behaviour is motivated by fear or a desire to fool people. But the second text states that if they truthfully repented in all that concerns their relationship with their Creator, they have a share in the world to come. This [second] law concerns their relationship with their Creator, while the first concerns their relationship with other human beings.

It is thus clear that Maimonides in the *Mishneh torah* was well aware of the fact that there were Jews who did not accept the principles of the Jewish religion, who persisted in their denial until their deaths, and who, therefore, certainly were not joined to God.

Maimonides often writes persuasively even when he presents himself as writing descriptively. This is a very good example of such writing. He does not for a moment delude himself into thinking that all Jews are joined to God and believe in the principles of the Jewish religion. But he certainly wants to *persuade* Jews to do those things.[24]

But it is likely that there are more things going on here behind the scenes, as it were. It would take us too far afield to follow in detail some of the novellae implied by Maimonides here. Maimonides is very likely the first Jewish thinker self-consciously to posit the existence of an entity which we today call Judaism (not knowing Modern Hebrew, German, or English, he had no clear-cut term for it) which was one of several competing *datot*, 'religions'.[25] Adherence to this *dat* consists first and foremost in accepting dogmas,

---

[22] On Maimonides' use of the term *min*, see Kasher, *Sectarians, Epicureans, and Heretics* (Heb.). [23] 3: 14.

[24] For further discussion of persuasive vis-à-vis descriptive writing in Maimonides, see Kellner, *They, Too, Are Called Human* (Heb.), ch. 8.

[25] Melamed, 'Religion': *From Law to Religion* (Heb.). See also Batnitzky, *How Judaism Became a Religion*. See our discussion of this matter above, Introduction.

defined in the strict sense of the term. Leaving these contentious matters aside, let us ask, what are the *ikarei hadat* which all Israelites believe, and what is the significance of that claim?

Many medieval and post-medieval Jewish thinkers were convinced that Jews have some quality or property whereby they are distinguished from non-Jews 'up front', as it were; Jews are said to be ontologically distinct from (and superior to) non-Jews. Maimonides, however, consistently denies that Jews as such have any advantage over non-Jews as such in matters such as immortality, providence, prophecy, and so on.[26]

Let us focus here on the question of immortality, and state Maimonides' position succinctly: Jews who actualize their intellects achieve shares in the world to come; the same is true of non-Jews. Similarly, Jews who fail to actualize their intellects cease to exist with their deaths; the same is true of non-Jews. While it is certainly true that in all likelihood Maimonides expected the world to come to be much more heavily 'populated' by the actualized intellects of Jews than of non-Jews (to the extent that it is populated at all), this is a consequence of obedience to the Torah in the fullest sense of the term, not of any inborn characteristic which Jews have and non-Jews lack. The Jews have an advantage over non-Jews because the Torah guides them more effectively than any other system of laws, first to moral perfection (a prerequisite for intellectual perfection[27]) and then to intellectual perfection. This advantage is relative, not absolute.

Our point may be expressed in the following, admittedly extreme terms: Maimonides distinguishes (or should have distinguished) between what may be called Israel of the commandments and Israel of the mind.[28] Israel of the commandments includes all Jews by birth or conversion. Israel of the mind includes all human beings who apprehend the truth and who thereby achieve a share in the world to come, whatever their ethnic background or confessional status. Maimonides is driven (or should be driven) to distinguish three groups:

---

[26] This claim is defended in several books and articles by Kellner. For recent studies, see *Maimonides' Confrontation*, ch. 7 and *They, Too, Are Called Human* (Heb.).

[27] See Gillis, *Reading Maimonides' Mishneh Torah*, 105–9; Kellner, *They, Too, Are Called Human* (Heb.), 135–43; and id., *Maimonides' Confrontation*, index, s.v. 'perfection, intellectual and moral'. This matter is taken up in various ways throughout this book; see especially above, Chs. 2, 5 (n. 32), 8, and 9, and below in Chs. 12 and 14.

[28] We write 'or should have distinguished' since it is sufficient here to show that this distinction is implicit in Maimonides' writings, even if he was possibly unaware of this implication of his views.

- descendants of Abraham, Isaac, and Jacob, all of whom are obligated to fulfil the commandments of the Torah and to accept its doctrinal teachings, but many of whom do neither.
- descendants of Abraham, Isaac, and Jacob who fulfil the commandments and correctly accept its doctrinal teachings.
- unconverted individuals who are not descendants of Abraham, Isaac, and Jacob, who do not (and need not) observe the commandments of the Torah, but who do accept the philosophical teachings of the Torah.[29] These latter are those whom Steven Schwarzschild has called 'Jewish Non-Jews'.[30]

Members of the first group, to the extent that they do not correctly accept the doctrinal teachings of Torah, are Israel of the commandments alone; members of the second group are Israel of the commandments and of the mind; members of the third group are Israel of the mind alone.

We write 'Israel of the mind' and not 'of the spirit' both in order to distinguish Maimonides from Christianity (the parallelism suggested by our language is only linguistic, not substantial) and in order to emphasize that the issue at hand is essentially philosophical; it is the correct understanding and acceptance of philosophically necessary statements which bring one into 'Israel of the mind'.

Maimonides never explicitly draws the tripartite distinction outlined here. It is even remotely possible that he was not consciously aware of it. It is, however, a distinction which grows out of his writings.

In general terms, it may be said that Sa'adyah Gaon and Rabenu Bahya Ibn Pakuda (eleventh century) began the process of turning Judaism into a religion defined by a systematic theology. Sa'adyah offered his *Book of Beliefs*

---

[29] This in fact is the way that Maimonides' 'parable of the palace' in *Guide* iii. 51 is often interpreted (an interpretation which led the 15th-cent. Iberian commentator on the *Guide*, Shem Tov ben Joseph ibn Shem Tov, to comment ad loc.: 'Many rabbinic scholars said that Maimonides did not write this chapter and if he did write it, it ought to be hidden away or, most appropriately, burned. For how could he say that those who know physics are on a higher level than those who engage in religion, and even more that they are with the ruler in the inner chamber, for on this basis the scholars who are engaged with physics and metaphysics have achieved a higher level than those engaged with Torah!'). For what it is worth, Kellner has argued that this interpretation of the parable is incorrect. See Kellner, *Maimonides on Human Perfection*, ch. 3.

[30] Schwarzschild, 'An Agenda for Jewish Philosophy in the 1980s'. See also Kellner, *Maimonides' Confrontation*, 240–9, and Kellner, 'Steven Schwarzschild, Moses Maimonides, and "Jewish Non-Jews"'.

and Opinions to those Jews who felt the need for the kind of certainty which only rational proof provides. Jews who did not feel that need had no need of his book.[31] Rabenu Bahya took the process one step further, maintaining that Jews were religiously obligated to prove the truth of the tenets of their religion. He excused from this obligation only those Jews who were incapable of understanding such proofs.[32] In this he follows standard halakhic practice: no-one is obligated to do what cannot be done.[33] Maimonides, in effect, took these matters two steps forward. First, he insisted that the obligation to understand (i.e. be able to prove rationally) the tenets of Torah falls upon all Jews. Those who do not or cannot do that fail to earn a share in the world to come and, in effect, exclude themselves from the community of Israel (or, more precisely, fail to achieve membership in that community).[34] Second, he maintained that some tenets of Torah are more fundamental than others; in other words, he maintained that what we today call Judaism had dogmas.

The following text is crucial. It follows Maimonides' exposition of what came to be known as his 'Thirteen Principles of Faith':

When all these foundations are perfectly understood and believed in by a person he is within the community of Israel and one is obligated to love and pity him and to act towards him in all the ways in which the Creator has commanded that one should act towards his brother, with love and fraternity. Even were he to commit every possible transgression, because of lust and because of being overpowered by the evil inclination, he will be punished according to his rebelliousness, but he has a portion [of the world to come]; he is one of the sinners of Israel. But if a man doubts any of these foundations, he leaves the community [of Israel], denies the fundamental, and is called a sectarian, *epikoros*, and one who 'cuts among the plantings'. One is required to hate him and destroy him. About such a person it was said, 'Do I not hate them, O Lord, who hate thee?' [Ps. 139: 21].[35]

Maimonides makes no exceptions: all Jews must accept all the principles.[36] One who does not thereby excludes himself or herself from the community of Israel and from the world to come. Even more surprisingly, Maimonides

---

[31] See *Beliefs and Opinions*, introd., ch. 6 (pp. 26–33).
[32] See *Duties of the Heart*, Treatise 1, ch. 3 (pp. 114–18).
[33] A man without a head, for example, is freed of the obligation of donning tefillin of the head; similarly, as Zev Harvey pointed out to us, a man without a head metaphorically does not have to prove the tenets of Judaism.
[34] 'Fail to earn'; not 'are not given'. Existence in the world to come is not a *reward* in the sense that God judges and grants it; rather, it is something we *create* through our intellectual activity. For details, see Kasher, 'Torah for its Own Sake'.
[35] *Perek ḥelek*, in Maimonides, *Commentary on the Mishnah*, Order Nezikin, 145.
[36] For detailed analysis, see Kellner, *Dogma in Medieval Jewish Thought*, 10–65.

here makes acceptance of the principles the only criterion for being included in the community of Israel.[37] This does not mean that Maimonides is redefining accepted halakhic norms, which establish that one joins the community of Israel through birth or conversion. Rather, Maimonides is here redefining the notion of 'the community of Israel'. The community of Israel is no longer constituted by the descendants of Abraham, Isaac, and Jacob, but by all human beings who properly understand and accept the tenets of the Torah.

This point is hinted at by the eschatological context and nature of Maimonides' discussion.[38] He presents his 'Thirteen Principles' as part of a commentary on a mishnaic text which opens with the words, 'All Israelites have a share in the world to come'.[39] In the text cited above, Maimonides makes it clear that acceptance of the principles guarantees one a share in the world to come and that rejection of them costs one his or her share in the world to come. He even goes so far as to drive an unprecedented wedge between theological orthodoxy and halakhic observance: 'Even were he to commit every possible transgression, because of lust and because of being overpowered by the evil inclination, he will be punished according to his rebelliousness, but he has a portion [of the world to come]; he is one of the sinners of Israel.'[40]

If we shift gears for a moment, and ask again whom Maimonides expected to meet in the world to come, we can only answer: individuals who have achieved a sufficient level of intellectual perfection to have acquired actual intellects (which is another way of saying: have understood (i.e. can rationally prove the truth of) the first five of the 'Thirteen Principles').[41] We have no doubt that Maimonides fully expected that most of these disembodied intellects would have been earned by individuals who in this world were descendants of Abraham, Isaac, and Jacob (and of converts to Judaism), but that is a technical point. Intellectual perfection is impossible without ante-

---

[37] By 'accept' Maimonides means 'understand' (i.e. be able to prove rationally). On this, see the discussion in Kellner, *Must a Jew Believe Anything?*, 61–5.

[38] For a recent discussion, see Hyman, *Eschatological Themes in Medieval Jewish Philosophy*, 74–89.

[39] Mishnah *San.* 10: 1. R. Isaac Abravanel was the first to point out that Maimonides presented his principles by way of defining the term 'Israel'. See Abravanel, *Principles of Faith*, chs. 6 and 24.

[40] Norman Lamm is amazed by this: 'If we take [Maimonides] literally, we reach the astonishing conclusion that he who observes *mitzvot* but has not reflected upon their theological basis would also be excluded from the Children of Israel.' See Lamm, 'Loving and Hating Jews', 115. Rabbi Lamm should actually have written: 'but has not *correctly* reflected upon their theological basis'.

[41] On the distinction between the first five of the Thirteen Principles and the last seven, see Kellner, *Maimonides' Confrontation*, 233–8.

cedent moral perfection and the Torah is the best (but not only!) guide to moral perfection. In the pre-messianic world, at least, descendants of Abraham, Isaac, and Jacob (and of converts to Judaism) who wholeheartedly observe the commandments of the Torah thus have a tremendous advantage over non-Jews and over descendants of Abraham, Isaac, and Jacob (and of converts to Judaism) who do not observe the commandments of the Torah.

Let us now return to our text at the end of the *Book of Damages*. Those who are joined to God are those who accept the principles of the Jewish religion. This includes 'non-Jewish Jews' but excludes born Jews who do not affirm the principles and thus are not joined to God. Maimonides' strict notions of doctrinal orthodoxy[42] lead him to exclude from the community of Israel heterodox Jews, but to include within it moral non-Jews who are philosophical monotheists.

We might add that we are not passing judgement here, moral or Jewish, on Maimonides' strict intellectual elitism. Rather, we are pointing out that, however the notion of election is construed, it is not descent which is crucial, but what one does with what one is given.

Summary

The *Book of Damages* ends by declaring that a person must come to the aid of all Israelites, even wicked ones, because all of them are 'joined with God' and 'believe in the principles of religion'.

Maimonides uses the first phrase in some other places to refer to proselytes or perhaps, more ambiguously, to non-Jews who are socially attached to the Israelites. But there are also Maimonidean passages that clearly speak of those who have joined themselves to the God of Israel without being formal converts.

Such people who have joined with the God of Israel are those who accept the principles of religion. It is possible to do so, intellectually, even for someone who is not born Jewish and does not formally become a Jew. Such non-Jews join 'Israel of the mind' through their discovery and acceptance of the truth taught by Abraham, Isaac, and Jacob.

When born Jews, however, reject 'the principles of religion', they remove themselves from the true Israel, the 'Israel of the mind', even though they remain formally Jewish.

This chapter focuses directly on Maimonides' redefinition of 'Jew' on the axis of particularism versus universalism, and at the beginning of the books

---

[42] Criticized by Kellner in *Must a Jew Believe Anything?*

of the *Mishneh torah* that focus on social laws, *bein adam laḥavero*. It thus provides a transition from the first ten books of the *Mishneh torah* to the last four.

Looking ahead, the subject of aid to an enemy on the road represents a first step away from the disorder and violence of the *Book of Damages* towards an orderly society in which knowledge of God and immortality can be universally pursued, a start on which the next volume, the *Book of Acquisition*, builds.[43]

[43] See Gillis, *Reading Maimonides' Mishneh Torah*, 278–85.

TWELVE

ACQUISITION
Slavery versus Universal Humanity

Introduction

The *Book of Acquisition* (*Sefer kinyan*) mainly covers the law of contract and of property. Its first section is 'Laws of Sales', on the various mechanisms for acquiring real estate, chattels, slaves, and animals, and on fairness in sale transactions. The second section, 'Laws of Acquisition and Gifts', covers acquisitions in which there is no consideration,[1] as in the case of seizure of ownerless property and of gifts, and the special rules governing gifts by the dying (the laws of inheritance form a section in the next book). This is followed by 'Laws of Neighbours', which deals with rights and obligations between owners and/or occupiers of neighbouring homes and fields, town planning law and obligations to the municipality, and also partnerships in real estate. 'Laws of Agents and Partners' deals with agency, and partnerships in trade. 'Laws of Slaves', the final section, covers transactions in and treatment of slaves, the rules of which differ for Jewish and non-Jewish slaves. It ends as follows:

It is permitted to work a Canaanite[2] slave with rigour. Though such is the rule, it is the quality of piety and the way of wisdom that a man be merciful and pursue justice and not make his yoke heavy on the slave or distress him, but give him to eat and drink of all foods and drinks. The Sages of old were wont to let the slave partake of every dish that they themselves ate of and to give the meal of the cattle and of the slaves precedence over their own. Is it not said: 'As the eyes of slaves unto the hand of their master, as the eyes of a female servant unto the hand of her mistress' [Ps. 123: 2].

Thus also the master should not disgrace them by hand or by word, because scriptural law has delivered them only unto slavery and not unto disgrace. Nor should he heap upon the slave oral abuse and anger, but should rather speak to him

---

[1] In the law of contract, the term 'consideration' refers to a benefit that must be bargained for between the parties.   [2] i.e. non-Jewish.

softly and listen to his claims. So it is also explained in the good paths of Job, in which he prided himself:

> 'If I did despise the cause of my manservant,
> Or of my maidservant, when they contended with me...
> Did not He that made me in the womb make him?
> And did not One fashion us in the womb?' [Job 31: 13, 15]

Cruelty and effrontery are not frequent except with uncircumcised non-Jews. The children of our father Abraham, however, i.e. the Israelites, upon whom the Holy One, blessed be He, bestowed the favour of the Torah and laid upon them righteous statutes and judgements,[3] are merciful people who have mercy upon all. Thus also it is declared by the attributes of the Holy One, blessed be He, which we are enjoined to imitate: 'And His mercies are over all His works' [Ps. 145: 9].

Furthermore, whoever has compassion will receive compassion, as it is said: 'And He will show thee mercy, and have compassion upon thee, and multiply thee' [Deut. 13: 18].[4]

Slavery as a Jewish institution is perhaps not a comfortable subject for a modern reader, who may wonder at the Torah condoning it at all. For his part, in his closing words on the subject, Maimonides stands the institution on its head, and turns it into a platform for eloquent advocacy of human equality. He outlaws the indignity and cruelty associated with slavery, undercuts any supremacist argument that might be used to justify the enslavement of one race by another, and insists that Jewish doctrine demands the fair treatment of all people, regardless of origin.

Slavery was a reality in Maimonides' world. In the medieval period, Bernard Lewis writes, 'Non-Muslim subjects of the Muslim state, that is, *dhimmis*, were in practice allowed to own slaves; and Christian and Jewish families who could afford it owned and employed slaves in the same way as their Muslim counterparts.'[5] The close of 'Laws Concerning Slaves' should therefore not be regarded as purely theoretical; we may imagine that Maimonides was speaking out against phenomena that he knew and that dismayed him. In doing so, he goes beyond generalized condemnation of injustice. He places the thrust of his entire religious philosophy behind a vision of the equality of all people before God, and co-opts the reader to this vision, in a piece of cleverly crafted rhetoric that is well worth analysing.

Maimonides begins by making things difficult for himself, for the final

---

[3] Klein's translation (Yale Judaica Series) omits 'righteous'.
[4] 'Laws of Slaves', 9: 8, trans. Klein, emended.
[5] Lewis, *Race and Slavery in the Middle East*, 8–9. See also Abrahams, *Jewish Life in the Middle Ages*, 96–101.

halakhah of 'Laws of Slaves' actually begins with a discriminatory provision: 'It is permitted to work a Canaanite slave with rigour.'[6] As we shall immediately see, such behaviour is impermissible in the case of a Jewish slave. This could be taken as an argument for a particularistic view of Judaism and a doctrine of Jewish supremacy. Instead, Maimonides uses it as the starting point for the opposite case.

'To work with rigour' has a special meaning here; it does not mean simply to make the slave work hard. Following *Sifra*,[7] Maimonides defines it as the assignment of work that is either indeterminate (the example given is 'hoe under the grapevines until I return') or pointless, even if it is very light, with the sole purpose that the slave should not be idle.[8] It is, then, a matter of humiliating and dehumanizing treatment, or of gratifying the owner's need for a sense of lordship,[9] rather than what we normally understand by 'slave-

---

[6] 'Laws of Slaves', 9: 8. The Hebrew term *eved kena'ani* ('Canaanite slave') that Maimonides uses here is translated 'heathen slave' by Klein, but in fact the slave in question is not a heathen. There are three kinds of non-Jewish slave: (1) a slave who undergoes the conversion rites of circumcision (if male) and immersion in a *mikveh*, and thereby becomes bound by all the negative commandments and all positive commandments not occasioned by a particular time, requiring only manumission in order to be considered fully Jewish; (2) a slave who undertakes to observe the seven Noahide laws, one of which is a prohibition on idolatry (see 'Laws of Kings and their Wars', 9: 1); and (3) a slave who will make neither of these commitments, who remains a heathen and may therefore not be kept (see 'Laws of Forbidden Intercourse', 14: 9; 'Laws of Slaves', 8: 12; 'Laws of Circumcision', 1: 6). In other words, a Jew may only maintain a slave who subscribes to at least the basic tenets of monotheistic religion. From the slave's point of view, an advantage of the procedures in (1) and (2) is that, following them, he or she cannot be made to do work on the sabbath (see 'Laws of the Sabbath', 20: 14). The fact that the slave in our *halakhah* is not a heathen distinguishes this case, in which Maimonides goes out of his way to nullify a law that seems inhumane towards a non-Jew, from other cases in which he does not, but simply records a discriminatory law (e.g. 'Laws of Murder and Preservation of Life', 4: 11). Those cases concern non-Jews who actually are idolatrous heathens. Maimonides considered idolatry to be intellectual and moral degeneracy, and the intellect to be the form or essence of a human being (see 'Laws of the Foundations of the Torah', 4: 8; *Guide* iii. 54 (p. 635)). It follows that a heathen is less than fully human and liable to be a corrupting, dehumanizing influence, and therefore deserves to be discriminated against—and in fact the same applies to Jews who are idol worshippers or openly contemptuous of the Torah (as in 'Laws of Murder and Preservation of Life', 4: 10, 12). In other words, while such discrimination may still be unpalatable to a liberal conscience (although it may sometimes be theoretical rather than practical), its basis is moral and intellectual, not ethnic or racial. As we argue throughout, and as demonstrated below concerning our *halakhah* in particular, Maimonides attributes no inherent moral or intellectual superiority to Jews over non-Jews.   [7] On Lev. 25: 43.   [8] See 'Laws of Slaves', 1: 6.

[9] *Sifra* stresses that God knows the slave-owner's motive, implying that the slave himself may not even be aware that he is being exploited for something other than genuine economic need.

driving'. The Torah expressly prohibits 'rigour' in this sense in the case of a Jewish slave.[10] It is silent on the subject in relation to a non-Jewish slave, but *Sifra* turns this default into a positive licence. When it comes to a Jewish slave, a master is supposed to be careful of the dignity of labour; he need not show such care towards a non-Jewish slave.

Maimonides does not revoke this licence in as many words. He cannot. In the *Mishneh torah*, he is faithful to halakhah, its sources, and its methods, to the letter. Instead, he goes on to urge the utmost consideration by a Jew towards a non-Jewish slave. He should not overburden or distress him and should feed him as he feeds himself, and even give him priority over food; he should not disgrace him in any way; and he should not raise his voice at him or be angry with him, but should rather be attentive to his requests. These adjurations all have sources in statements of the Sages of the Talmud or in accounts of their conduct.[11] The upshot is that the treatment of a non-Jewish slave is on a par with the treatment of a Jewish slave.

Ostensibly, the position is that a non-Jewish slave may be worked with rigour, but at the same time, under a separate provision, he should not be overburdened and should be given of all foods and drinks, and so on. The message is that we should not extrapolate from one discriminatory provision to the idea that the Torah seeks mistreatment of a non-Jewish slave in general. But if piety, wisdom, mercy, and justice demand that we should not make the yoke heavy on the slave or distress him, then surely distress should be avoided in the way he is employed just as much as in the way he is fed?

The argument of the *halakhah* climaxes in the citation of the basic commandment of 'Laws of Moral Qualities', that of *imitatio Dei*. It emerges that while it may be technically permissible to work a non-Jewish slave with rigour, to do so would be counter to a basic tenet of Judaism, as well as to the living tradition in which the rabbis treated non-Jewish slaves with respect. In that case, the rule, though not expressly revoked, has been neutralized: one may not in fact work a non-Jewish slave with rigour. It follows that the discriminatory law cannot be taken as indicative of the attitude that should be adopted towards a non-Jew.

Many people will feel sympathetic towards Maimonides' position here and therefore be willing to accept his argument without close scrutiny. Nevertheless, the question must be asked: on what exact grounds does he give priority to a universalistic principle over a particular, and particularistic, provision of the law, negating a property right in the process?[12] In the course of

---

[10] Lev. 25: 43.   [11] Maimonides' sources here are considered in detail below.
[12] Concerning opposition to moves in the 19th century to abolish slavery in Islamic

analysing the *halakhah*, we shall attempt to answer this question, and to demonstrate that what it presents is not a vague appeal to liberal feelings; rather Maimonides makes his universalistic case with force and precision.

Conflict within the Torah

The question just raised leads to a larger one. If Maimonides uses the commandment of *imitatio Dei* to override a law concerning slaves, or at least the implications of that law, this means that he recognizes the possibility of a clash of values within the law. How can that happen in a God-given, and therefore presumably monolithic, system? Maimonides continually refers to the Torah's perfection. Self-contradiction must surely render it imperfect.

There are of course instances in which the demands of different laws or principles are incompatible, and one is set aside. For example, the laws of the sabbath must be broken where human life is at stake. The values of the sabbath and of preserving life are not at root opposed; it is only that they can sometimes come into conflict, and it is then necessary to determine the scope of the laws in question.[13] Conversely, the building of the Temple is suspended on the sabbath,[14] but again there is no essential inconsistency; from Sunday to Friday there is no problem at all.

In other cases, there is a head-on clash, as in the law of levirate marriage, which calls for a man to marry the widow of a brother who dies childless,[15] despite the general prohibition on sexual intercourse with a brother's wife even after the brother's death.[16] In this and other instances the Torah makes a rule and makes an exception to the rule. The rabbis developed general

countries, Bernard Lewis writes that 'From a traditional Muslim point of view . . . To forbid what God permits is almost as great an offense as to permit what God forbids', although he also notes that 'the position of the slave in Muslim society was incomparably better than in either classical antiquity or nineteenth-century North and South America' (*What Went Wrong?*, 95). The rabbis have of course forbidden many things that the Torah permits, but one can still imagine a Jewish slave-owner protesting here.

[13] There is a debate over whether breaching the laws of the sabbath in order to save life is a provision within those laws or an exemption from them (see Steinberg, *Encyclopedia of Jewish Medical Ethics*, 866), but on neither side of that nice distinction is there a basic conflict between observing the sabbath and saving life.

[14] See 'Laws of the Temple', 1: 12, which states that construction of the Temple may not take place on a festival, implying *a fortiori* that it may not take place on the sabbath.

[15] See Deut. 25: 5.

[16] See Lev. 18: 16 and 'Laws of Forbidden Intercourse', 2: 1. It is worth noting that even though conflicts of laws such as in the case of the commandment of levirate marriage are resolvable at the jurisprudential level, the rabbis still found something incomprehensible about them, leading them to classify the commandments in question as *ḥukim*, that is,

principles for understanding or resolving such contradictions, the main one being that a positive commandment overrides a conflicting negative commandment.[17]

'Laws of Slaves', 9: 8 does not fit these models. There, one law is permanently, radically at odds with another: either non-Jewish slaves deserve to be discriminated against, or they deserve to be treated like their Jewish counterparts; it cannot be both. The sabbath model therefore does not apply.

The levirate marriage model also does not apply. It might have been possible to argue that non-Jewish slaves are equal to Jewish slaves in some ways but not in others, were it not for the fact that Maimonides bases the argument for equality on the obligation to imitate the mercy of God that extends to all creatures, without differentiation. Such imitation of God, it must be stressed, is not a recommendation or suggestion, but, according to Maimonides, is a positive commandment of the Torah, enjoined by the verse 'and you shall walk in His ways'.[18] Mercy is one of the ways of God that Maimonides specifically mentions that we should imitate: 'The sages taught, "Even as God is called gracious, so be thou gracious; Even as He is called merciful, so be thou merciful".'[19] The idea of being commanded to be merciful as God is called merciful except where God's law states otherwise is altogether strange—the non-Jewish slave has, after all, committed no offence.[20] Even stranger is that, rather than the exception overriding the rule, as in the levirate marriage case, Maimonides proposes that the rule should override the exception, that mercy should prevail over the permission to work a slave with rigour. What, then, is the point of the exception in the first place?

We are left in a position in which Maimonides brings two laws of the Torah into direct conflict, and makes one override the other without a recognized mechanism for doing so.

Lifnim mishurat hadin?

The phrase 'though such is the rule' might appear to indicate that the kind of treatment of the non-Jewish slave called for in the *halakhah* is supererogatory,

---

commandments that cannot be rationalized—see *Num. Rabbah* 19: 5; *Midrash tanhuma* (Warsaw), 'Ḥukat', 7, cited in the discussion of *ḥukim* in Ch. 8 above.

[17] See BT *Men.* 40a and 'Laws of Levirate Marriage', 6: 10.   [18] Deut. 28: 9.

[19] 'Laws of Moral Qualities', 1: 6, following *Sifrei* on Deut. 11: 22. See also *Book of the Commandments*, positive commandment 8, which cites *Sifrei*, and BT *Shab.* 133b.

[20] Cf. 'Laws of Valuation and Consecration', 8: 13, where Maimonides states that mercy should not be shown to a person who deliberately impoverishes himself by giving away all his possessions to charity. This *halakhah* is the subject of Ch. 6 above.

and that the principle at work here is *lifnim mishurat hadin*, literally 'within the line of the law', that is, decently stopping short of prosecuting one's full legal rights. 'Laws of the Foundations of the Torah', 5: 11, which describes the way in which the everyday conduct of a scholar is supposed to fulfil the commandment to sanctify the name of God, states that all of the scholar's actions will be *lifnim mishurat hadin*. If it is in that spirit that our *halakhah* calls for the fair treatment of a non-Jewish slave, then there is actually no clash of values within the law. The law provides for a certain standard of behaviour, but 'though such is the rule' (the word for 'rule' is *din*, the opposite of *lifnim mishurat hadin*) we are encouraged to aim for a higher standard.[21]

This would also leave a particularist interpretation of the law intact. After all, even animals must be treated humanely.[22] In Judah Halevi's *Kuzari*, the *ḥaver* (the representative of Judaism) certainly takes the view that Jews are innately superior to non-Jews, in that only the former are capable of true prophecy,[23] but he does not on that account advocate cruelty towards the latter, or even their exclusion. On the contrary, non-Jews are welcome to convert to Judaism, only they can never quite attain equal status with those born Jewish.[24]

On this view, it is very reasonable that the Torah should allow discrimination against non-Jewish slaves, but that at the same time Jews should be exhorted not to take undue advantage of the discriminatory rule. The citation of the verse 'His mercy is over all His works' can be construed as encourage-

---

[21] Num. 6: 18, 'And thou shalt do that which is right and good', is seen as a basis in the Torah for *lifnim mishurat hadin*—see Rashi and Nahmanides ad loc. It is not, however, found in Maimonides' listing of the commandments. It would in any case presumably be excluded by the fourth of the fourteen criteria enumerated in the introduction to the *Book of the Commandments* for determining which imperative statements in the Torah qualify for inclusion among the 613 commandments (the traditional number according to BT *Mak.* 23*b*), which is that general exhortations that cover all the commandments do not count as commandments in themselves. Nor is this verse among Nahmanides' amendments to Maimonides' list. According to Kafih, *The Hebrew Bible in Maimonides* (Heb.), Maimonides cites it only once in all his writings, in 'Laws of Creditor and Debtor', 22: 16, which is based upon BT *BM* 35*a*. The scholarly debate on *lifnim mishurat hadin* and how it relates to *din* is extensive and many-sided—see e.g. Eisen, '*Lifnim mi-Shurat ha-Din* in Maimonides' *Mishneh Torah*'; Lichtenstein, 'Does Jewish Tradition Recognize an Ethic Independent of Halakha?'; Newman, 'Law, Virtue, and Supererogation in the Halakha'.

[22] See *Commentary on the Mishnah, Beits.*, 3: 4; 'Laws of the Sabbath', 21: 9–10 and 25: 26; 'Laws of Resting on Festivals', 2: 4; 'Laws of Murder and the Preservation of Life', 13: 13.

[23] See *Kuzari* i. 31–43.

[24] See *Kuzari* i. 27, 115. This of course distinguishes Halevi from ideologies that call for the extermination of inferior races. A Jew could not convert to become even a second-class Aryan. There is at least a place for everyone in Halevi's ecology.

ment to act *lifnim mishurat hadin* in this case, rather than as a basis for a specific legal provision. *Lifnim mishurat hadin* therefore seems to fit the bill well as a rationale for our *halakhah*. It allows for an approach that is perhaps patronizing, but not downright brutal. Twersky states unequivocally that 'the mercy shown in this case is supererogatory rather than mandatory'.[25]

Another element in constructing a particularist reading of our *halakhah* is expressed by Kafih, who, summing up the classical commentators' remarks on it, writes that it concerns 'the trait of piety and mercy innate in the descendants of Abraham'.[26]

Such readings keep Maimonides' discussion comfortably within what is conventionally perceived as a rabbinic framework. We shall, however, challenge Twersky's assessment as well as Kafih's. There are good grounds for wondering whether our *halakhah* is really about, or only about, *lifnim mishurat hadin*, and for arguing that mercy here is mandatory, not supererogatory, and that it is an acquired characteristic rather than an inherited one. This means that there is a clash of values—the law allows ill treatment, yet mandates mercy—and a framework needs to be found that will contain it. We assert that a framework exists within which 'Laws of Slaves', 9: 8 expresses not a kind of condescending particularism (which would be the upshot of applying *lifnim mishurat hadin*) but a thoroughgoing universalism.

Lifnim mishurat hadin initially seems a plausible basis for the concluding *halakhah* of 'Laws of Slaves', and as we shall see later on, at a certain level that concept does come into play. Right from the beginning of the *halakhah*, however, Maimonides signals that he is taking us on a more challenging journey.

Wisdom and Piety

First, let us note that the principle of *lifnim mishurat hadin* is not explicitly mentioned here. In other instances in the *Mishneh torah* where it is recommended to refrain from enforcing one's full legal rights, *lifnim mishurat hadin* is explicitly invoked. We might have expected Maimonides to do the same in our *halakhah* if that was what he had in mind. Deliberately or otherwise, the phrase 'though such is the rule' seems to allude to it, but if it was really the applicable principle, the *halakhah* should have been formulated approximately as follows: 'It is permitted to work a heathen slave with rigour. Though such is the rule, *one should refrain from doing so, for* it is the quality of piety and the way of wisdom that a man be merciful' and so forth. However,

---

[25] Twersky, *Introduction to the Code*, 427.
[26] *Mishneh torah*, ed. Joseph Kafih, ad loc. (our translation).

the italicized words do not appear in the text. Instead, the *halakhah* goes on to mention the general ways in which a non-Jewish slave should be treated well, and quickly switches to the subject of food. The narrow rule about pointless or undefined work is left untouched. It is outflanked rather than confronted. If Maimonides had directly countered it with *lifnim mishurat hadin*, that would have closed off the discussion. He might have tacked on further ideas, but his more open approach enabled him develop an argument smoothly and powerfully.

The cases in which *lifnim mishurat hadin* is explicitly mentioned are: the return of a lost article to its owner even though the circumstances in which it was found make the finder legally entitled to keep it;[27] the return of a lost article to its owner even though the finder is exempt from doing so because their social standing is such that it is beneath their dignity to handle it;[28] and assisting someone in loading or unloading his beast of burden even though one is exempt, again because of one's status.[29] Acting *lifnim mishurat hadin* in such circumstances involves foregoing an economic benefit or waiving one's own dignity, and, although expected of the scholar, it remains discretionary. In none of these instances do we find the impassioned tone of our passage from 'Laws of Slaves'. By contrast, what is at stake in this *halakhah* is the dignity of the other, and the force of Maimonides' rhetoric blows away any notion that respecting human dignity might be at our discretion, or a concern for the scholar, who is supposed to set a higher example, but not for the average Jew. The concept of *lifnim mishurat hadin*, noble though it is, does not have the leverage to exert such force. Instead, the concept deployed is *imitatio Dei*, which is the fundamental commandment upon which Maimonides builds the theory and practice of moral virtue.

The early signal that *lifnim mishurat hadin* is not the sole underlying concept in 'Laws of Slaves', 9: 8 is the statement that to treat a slave mercifully and justly is 'the quality of piety and the way of wisdom'. The terms 'piety' (*ḥasidut*) and 'wisdom' (*ḥokhmah*) in Maimonides do not refer to general dispositions to do good; they have specific meanings. In 'Laws of Moral Qualities', he introduces the idea of the middle path between extremes of temperament as the basis of moral virtue, and terms it 'the way of God'.[30] According to Maimonides, this is what is referred to in the commandment 'and you shall walk in His ways'. In relation to this, Maimonides describes two types. The first is the *ḥakham* (the wise person or philosopher), who keeps precisely

---

[27] See 'Laws of Robbery and Lost Property', 11: 7.
[28] Ibid. 11: 17.   [29] See 'Laws of Murder and the Preservation of Life', 13: 4.
[30] 'Laws of Moral Qualities', 1: 7.

to the middle path. The second is the *ḥasid* (the pious person), who deviates slightly from the middle towards the more self-denying extreme. The way of the *ḥasid* is described as *lifnim mishurat hadin*.[31] In the context of 'Laws of Moral Qualities', *lifnim mishurat hadin* is the cultivation of a trait of character rather than a waiver of legal rights, but we can take it that Maimonides sees practical instances of supererogatory behaviour as expressions of this inward quality—in fact he explicitly uses the term *ḥasid* to describe the person who assists in loading and unloading an animal despite not being obliged to do so. He is very consistent in applying this terminology. In instances in the *Mishneh torah* where he commends conduct that is more liberal to others or more self-restrictive than halakhah demands, but without explicitly mentioning *lifnim mishurat hadin* (even though that is clearly the principle involved), he characterizes such conduct as *ḥasidut*, not *ḥokhmah*.[32] As far as we are aware, the combination of *ḥokhmah* and *ḥasidut* that we find in 'Laws of Slaves', 9: 8 is unique in the work.[33] Maimonides apparently seeks to convey a more complex and far-reaching message at this point than the desirability of 'the quality of piety' by itself.

The addition of 'the way of wisdom' indicates that both *ḥasid* and *ḥakham* will treat a non-Jewish slave respectfully, and that this is not just an option under the heading of *lifnim mishurat hadin* but a requirement of *din* (law) as well.

If mercy is the middle path between cruelty and indulgence, then the *ḥakham* will follow 'the way of wisdom' and treat a non-Jewish slave in a manner precisely gauged to coincide with that path. Piety, with the idea of *lifnim mishurat hadin*, comes into play as the principle that guides us in deciding on which side to err; the *ḥasid* will exercise 'the quality of piety' by veering slightly towards indulgence in order to counter the widespread tendency to inconsiderate treatment of social inferiors. For *ḥakham* and *ḥasid* alike, however, exercising mercy in the first place, not making the slave's yoke heavy or distressing him, is a requirement of the law, not a concession or a waiver of rights.

---

[31] 'Laws of Moral Qualities', 1: 5.

[32] See 'Laws of Forbidden Intercourse', 21: 9; 'Laws of Valuation and Consecrations', 8: 13; 'Laws of Gifts to the Poor', 4: 8; 'Laws of Second Tithe and Fourth Year's Fruit', 2: 2; 'Laws of Impurity of Foodstuffs', 16: 12; 'Laws of Sales', 12: 12; 'Laws of Neighbours', 14: 5; 'Laws of Hiring', 7: 7; 'Laws of Inheritance', 6: 11; 'Laws of Kings and their Wars', 5: 9.

[33] *Ḥasidut* and *ḥokhmah* do come together in descriptions of the ideal person who combines wisdom with gracious behaviour that is *lifnim mishurat hadin*—see, for example, 'Laws of the Foundations of the Torah', 5: 11—but the terms are not used interchangeably to describe the same sort of act.

Nor is the next phrase in our *halakhah*, 'and pursue justice', part of the language of *lifnim mishurat hadin* in Maimonides. He defines justice as 'the granting to everyone who has a right to something, that which he has a right to'.[34] *Lifnim mishurat hadin* is the granting of something to someone who does not have a right to it. Justice is not only about relations with others. It includes moral virtue, 'For when you walk in the way of the moral virtues, you do justice unto your rational soul, giving her the due that is her right.'[35] With this in mind we can begin to see the kind of framework within which a permit to work a non-Jewish slave with rigour can be reconciled with a requirement to be merciful that would countermand it. Mercy is a moral virtue that one owes it to oneself to cultivate, independently of the rights of other people. In itself, this idea might not seem remarkable; what is important is its status in Maimonides' philosophical system, and hence, as the substance of the specific positive commandment 'to walk in His ways', in his legal system.

Slave and Sage

The path to the final position in our *halakhah* runs, as mentioned, via allusions to several talmudic anecdotes illustrating a humane attitude towards slaves on the part of the Sages. We should note that the *halakhah* refers here to 'the sages of old' (*ḥakhamim harishonim*), rather than to 'the pious men of old' (*ḥasidim harishonim*), the latter being the designation Maimonides uses in contexts of supererogatory behaviour, notably in 'Laws of Moral Qualities', 1: 5. We thus have a further hint that we are in the realm of *din* rather than *lifnim mishurat hadin*.

The statement that 'the sages of old would give a slave to eat from every dish that they themselves would eat' appears to be based upon JT *Bava kama* 8: 4, where we find: 'Rabbi Yohanan would eat meat and give some to his slave, would drink wine and give some to his slave, and concerning himself would cite the verse: "Did not he that made me in the womb make him?" [Job 31: 15].' In the Talmud, this is presented as a difficulty, for it follows the recording of a ruling by the same Rabbi Yohanan that if someone injures and incapacitates someone else's slave, they are liable to pay the owner under the various heads of damages, while the slave himself receives nothing and is left to beg for charity. His reasoning is that in any case the owner of a non-Jewish slave has no obligation to feed him.[36] One would then not expect to find Rabbi

---

[34] *Guide* iii. 53 (p. 631).
[35] Ibid. We are assuming that the *Guide* can be used as a gloss here, but this is the best evidence we have of what Maimonides' terms mean.   [36] See 'Laws of Slaves', 9: 7.

Yohanan sharing meals with his slave. The conclusion in the Talmud is that the ruling is in accordance with *midat hadin*, the measure of strict law, while Rabbi Yohanan's actual conduct is in accordance with *midat harahamim*, the measure of mercy.

The rule that the master receives the damages if his slave is injured by a third party is recorded, unadorned, in 'Laws of Wounding and Damaging', 4: 10, quite a long way from 'Laws of Slaves', 9: 8. Maimonides saves the account of Rabbi Yohanan's conduct towards his own slave for his general appeal for humane treatment of slaves. He takes a source that is about *lifnim mishurat hadin*, for that in essence is the explanation in the Jerusalem Talmud for Rabbi Yohanan's conduct being inconsistent with his legal ruling, and uses it to further the case that merciful treatment of slaves is a matter of *din*.[37]

Animals and Slaves First

In 'Laws of Slaves', 9: 8, the verse from Job 'Did not he that made me in the womb make him?', used by Rabbi Yohanan to justify his actions, is detached from the context of giving food to slaves, and deployed later in the argument, something that we shall expand on shortly. Instead of the reference to Job, what comes next in the *halakhah*, after the sharing of food with non-Jewish slaves, is a requirement that animals and slaves should actually receive priority when it comes to food. Maimonides here extends to slaves a rule that originally applied to animals only.[38] In support of this, he cites Psalm 123: 2: 'As the eyes of slaves look to the hand of their master, as the eyes of a female slave look to the hand of her mistress'. This psalm is actually about mercy:

> I lift up my eyes to you, to you who sit enthroned in heaven. As the eyes of slaves look to the hand of their master, as the eyes of a female slave look to the hand of her mistress, so our eyes look to the Lord our God, till he shows us his mercy. Have mercy on us, Lord, have mercy on us, for we have endured no end of contempt. We have endured no end of ridicule from the arrogant, of contempt from the proud. [Ps. 123: 1–4]

The psalmist humbles himself by putting himself in relation to God as a slave is to his master or her mistress, in an appeal for relief from persecution. It is possible that in citing his prooftext Maimonides is not just making a reference to the dependent status of slaves, but is playing with his source by

---

[37] Maimonides' source opposes mercy to strict law—*midat hadin* versus *midat harahamim* is of course a classic opposition—whereas we have just been at pains to explain that as far as Maimonides is concerned, mercy is itself demanded by law, and he makes mercy and justice practically equivalent. This may be a further reason that he separated the idea of mercy from his allusion to the story of R. Yohanan and his slave.   [38] See BT *Ber.* 40a.

reversing its sense, so that instead of the appeal of the slave it comes to be about the duty of the master or mistress to show mercy just as God shows mercy. He thereby turns the psalm into a scenario of *imitatio Dei*.[39]

Certainly, awareness of the source, which expresses at least possible identification with the status of a slave, gives a sense of continuity with the next stage of the *halakhah*, which is about not putting a slave to shame. The psalmist looks for relief in God's mercy from the 'ridicule of the arrogant' and the 'contempt of the proud'. 'Similarly he should not show contempt towards him with his hand or with words', the *halakhah* states.

From Physical to Psychological

The adjuration not to put a slave to shame by word or deed is a step up. From seeing to the slave's physical wants, we progress to his psychological and spiritual welfare. This means recognizing his underlying equal human worth. The talmudic source from which this derives appears to be an incident involving the *amora* Samuel, who, after carrying out an examination of his female slave's breasts in an investigation of the signs of sexual maturity, recompensed her for the humiliation she had undergone, with the words 'scripture gave them over to slavery, not to degradation'.[40] Again, Maimonides stretches his source. Samuel's act was one of physical interference; Maimonides extends his stricture to verbal abuse. Once again, he supports the extension with a prooftext: 'If I did despise the cause of my manservant or of my maidservant, when they contended with me . . . Did not he that made me in the womb make him? And did not one fashion us in the womb?' (Job 31: 13, 15).

The second verse here is the one Rabbi Yohanan cited to explain why he allowed his slave to partake of the same food as he ate himself. We observed above that Maimonides omits it from his allusion to that story. He now cites it at this point together with a previous verse that suits his adjuration to be attentive to a slave's petitions and not talk to him angrily. This is a more pointed deployment of a powerfully suggestive source. It takes us from consideration towards inferiors (animals and slaves) to recognition of essential equality.[41]

---

[39] The Hebrew phrase translated as 'until he shows us his mercy' here is *ad sheyeḥoneinu*, the latter word being from the same root as *ḥanun*, which is generally translated as 'gracious'. The word usually translated as 'merciful' is *raḥum*. Since, however, both *raḥum* and *ḥanun* appear in the list of attributes of God's actions that should be imitated (see 'Laws of Moral Qualities', 1: 6), and since *imitatio Dei* itself is the key point here, the precise English equivalent of the attribute in question should not be a concern.   [40] BT *Nid*. 47a.

[41] The identity of Job, or even whether he existed at all, was a matter of controversy among the talmudic Sages, but as it happens there is an opinion attributed to R. Yohanan that Job

The invocation of the figure of Job is in itself suggestive. In the *Guide*, the book of Job is interpreted as one man's progress from a self-centred to a God-centred perspective on the world. That is also the track followed in our *halakhah*. Since Maimonides does not copy the Talmud's use of this reference exactly but gives it his own twist, it is possible that the general trend of the book of Job, as he understands it, is meant to reverberate here.[42]

The series of allusions to the Talmud thus begins with the basic need for food and progresses towards universal respect for human dignity, with the sources being slightly modified along the way.

Rabbi Judah the Prince and the Calf

The extrapolation from a duty to animals to a duty to slaves concerning their food prefigures the use of the legend alluded to next. The citation of the verse 'And His mercy is over all His works' leading to the statement 'anyone who is compassionate receives compassion' is a reference to a story told in the Talmud of Rabbi Judah the Prince.[43] The context is a discussion of the sufferings of the righteous. A calf being led to slaughter sought shelter under Rabbi Judah's cloak and sobbed. Rabbi Judah pushed it away with the words 'Go, this is what you were created for.' Because he failed to show compassion, he underwent years of suffering, apparently from kidney stones: his screams of agony when he went to the toilet were so loud that not even the lowing of his cattle, which were so numerous that they could be heard for miles around, could drown them out. His sufferings ceased one day when he prevented the maidservant who was sweeping his house from disturbing a litter of weasels, with the words 'And His mercy is over all His works', upon which they said in heaven, 'Since he is compassionate, let us be compassionate towards him.'

There are at least two ways of understanding what was wrong with Rabbi Judah's original act of pushing away the calf. One way is that he was correct, that indeed the calf was created to provide food for human beings, that this is

---

was Jewish, in fact one of those who returned from the Babylonian exile—see JT *Sot*. 5: 6. Maimonides, in his exposition on the book of Job in the *Guide*, states that the multitude of opinions about when and where Job lived strengthens the view that he never really existed, but he is not categorical about this—see *Guide* iii. 22 (p. 486).

[42] See Raffel, 'Providence as Consequent Upon the Intellect'. The fact that the *Guide* was written after the *Mishneh torah* is not a bar to seeing interpretations of Scripture and Midrash presented in the former as implied in the latter, since we know that, quite early on, Maimonides started writing books on these matters that he eventually abandoned (see 'Introduction to *Perek ḥelek*', in *Commentary on the Mishnah*, Order Nezikin, 140). It is a reasonable assumption, therefore, that he had settled on his interpretation of Job before he started on the *Mishneh torah*.   [43] BT *BM* 85a.

as it were *din*, but he should have acted *lifnim mishurat hadin* and at least shown some sympathy for the frightened animal.

Another, possibly more Maimonidean, way is that what he said was just as wrong as what he did. Rabbi Judah was not just emotionally cold; he was also intellectually mistaken, for the calf was not created to provide food. As Maimonides puts it in the *Guide*, 'It should not be believed that all the beings exist for the sake of the existence of man. On the contrary, all the other beings too have been intended for their own sakes and not for the sake of something else.'[44] The arrangement whereby people eat animals, and assume the right to do so out of a sense of superiority, implies nothing about the animals' essential being.

This interpretation is perhaps hinted at by the detail in the story about the lowing of Rabbi Judah's cattle failing to drown out his screams. Rabbi Judah, in performing his lowest bodily function, is as it were the animal who cries, while the cattle with their voices try, vainly, at least to cover his shame, if not comfort him for his pain. The situation at the beginning of the story is reversed, and what we take as the normal order of things is upturned, showing that it is not essential. It is true that human beings possess an intellectual potential that animals lack, but that does not devalue an animal's intrinsic worth as God's creation, or justify an entirely instrumentalist attitude towards it.[45]

The same applies to slavery, only more so. That one person is a master and another a slave implies nothing about the human essence of either, and moreover the intellectual potential of both is the same. The difficult thing demanded here is that an economic arrangement should not be internalized as an instrumentalist attitude towards one's fellow creatures.

Raban Gamliel and Heaven's Mercy

The final statement and prooftext in 'Laws of Slaves', 9: 8, come from the Talmud:[46]

---

[44] *Guide* iii. 13 (p. 452). This appears to represent a shift from the position expressed in the introduction to the *Commentary on the Mishnah*, that all sublunary entities were created for the sake of human beings. The validity of our interpretation here depends of course on the *Mishneh torah* being identified with the position of the *Guide* on this question rather than with that of the *Commentary*.

[45] R. Judah also said that an ignorant person who has not studied Torah should not eat meat (see BT *Pes.* 49*b*). In other words, someone who has not actualized their intellectual potential is not superior to an animal.

[46] BT *Shab.* 151*b*. Other sources are Tosefta *BK* 9: 11 (where the attribution is 'R. Judah in the name of Raban Gamliel'—this would be R. Judah II, son of Gamliel III); JT *BK* 8: 7

Raban Gamliel son of the Rabbi says: '[God] will show you mercy, and will have compassion on you. He will increase your numbers' [Deut. 13: 18]—whoever shows mercy towards people is shown mercy from heaven, and whoever does not show mercy towards people is not shown mercy from heaven.

The first thing to note is that this statement is cited in the name of Gamliel III, and that his father 'the Rabbi' is Rabbi Judah the Prince, providing dynastic as well as thematic continuity from the preceding talmudic citation. The context is a discussion about poverty and how to avoid it. Raban Gamliel is perhaps extending the lesson his father learned from experience with animals to the human arena.

What is translated here as '[God] will show you mercy' more literally means '[God] will give you mercy', which Raban Gamliel appears to interpret as 'God will make you merciful'—that at least is how Rashi seems to read him.[47] A Maimonidean understanding of how God makes someone merciful would be that, having acquired knowledge of God to the extent of his capacity, a person is then attuned to God's governance and, like him, is compassionate to all creatures. This also makes such a person a recipient of God's providence,[48] in the sense that Job comes to understand it. This final talmudic allusion is a more emphatic statement of the lesson of the preceding one, and a culmination of the tendency of the *halakhah* as a whole.[49]

It will have been noticed that the sayings and actions of Rabbi Judah the Prince and Raban Gamliel alluded to do not actually concern slaves, much less non-Jewish slaves. It is Maimonides who generalizes to humanity as such,[50] and in fact makes the non-Jewish slave the test of mercy. Animals and poor people can easily arouse compassion, and being kind and charitable towards them can be a matter of indulging feelings of pity, which may even reinforce a sense of superiority and privilege. There are worse indulgences, of course, but Maimonides demands something more stringent than pity, namely a sense of basic equality.

(attribution as in Tosefta); *Sifrei* on Deut. 13: 18 (attribution as in BT *Shab.*); *Pesikta rabati* 38 (different attribution altogether). The same part of Deut. 13: 18 is cited in 'Laws of Gifts to the Poor', 10: 2, in support of exactly the same statement. On further similarity between 'Laws of Slaves', 9: 8 and 'Laws of Gifts to the Poor', 10: 2, see below, n. 51.

[47] See Rashi on BT *Shab.* 151b, s.v. *venatan lekha raḥamim*.
[48] 'I believe that providence is consequent upon the intellect and attached to it' (*Guide* iii. 17 (p. 474)).
[49] This reading also makes the *halakhah* echo the ending of the *Guide*.
[50] In 'Laws of Kings and their Wars', 10: 12, where he rules that poor non-Jews should be supported alongside Jews, Maimonides again cites the verse 'And His mercy is over all His works', although it is not cited in his source (BT *Git.* 61a).

'The Children of Our Father Abraham'

The statement that the distinguishing trait of the descendants of Abraham is mercy, while cruelty is only found among the uncircumcised non-Jews, can be understood in several ways.[51] It can be read as an argument that Jews should treat their non-Jewish slaves well out of a sense of *noblesse oblige*. It can also be read as a piece of rhetorical judo in which Maimonides uses his readers' prejudices to defeat them. Anyone with particularist views will readily approve the extolling of 'the children of our father Abraham', only to find themselves thereby committed to treating non-Jews as equals.

But does Maimonides really embrace a racial definition of Jewishness here? Who are 'the children of our father Abraham', and what actually makes them different? On this question we have already referred to the 'Letter to Obadiah the Proselyte' and its statement that 'Abraham our Father, peace be with him, is the father of his pious posterity who keep his ways, and the father of his disciples and of all proselytes who adopt Judaism' as evidence that Maimonides regarded the children of Abraham as a cultural identity, not a biological one.

In our *halakhah*, this interpretation of 'the children of our father Abraham' is bolstered by other phrases. Non-Jews are designated 'uncircumcised'. Why introduce circumcision here? The answer would appear to be that it marks a cultural rather than a biological difference between Jews and non-Jews, and of course it was Abraham who was first commanded to undergo circumcision, as a sign of adherence to the belief in the one God, according to Maimonides.[52]

It is also possible, given the context, that Maimonides seeks to evoke the idea in the Bible of circumcision of the heart.[53] In discussing the purposes of the law in the *Guide*, he states, 'Similarly to the totality of intentions of the Law there belong gentleness and docility; man should not be hard and rough, but responsive, obedient, acquiescent, and docile. You know already His commandment, may He be exalted: "Circumcise therefore the foreskin of your heart, and be no more stiffnecked".'[54] The word 'commandment' is used

---

[51] The apparently particularist nature of our text is analysed by Kellner in *Maimonides' Confrontation* (pp. 252–63) and in id., *They, Too, Are Called Human* (Heb.) (pp. 203–11). Similar rhetoric is deployed earlier in *Mishneh torah*, in 'Laws of Forbidden Intercourse', 19: 17, and in 'Laws of Gifts to the Poor', 10: 2. The reading here is according to the Makbili edition. Other editions have 'idolatrous' instead of 'uncircumcised', and this is followed by Klein's translation, which gives 'heathen who worship idols'. The source is BT *Bets.* 32b. See also above, Ch. 2.   [52] See *Guide* iii. 49 (p. 610).   [53] See above, Ch. 2.
[54] *Guide* iii. 33 (p. 532). The verse cited is Deut. 10: 16. See also Lev. 26: 41; Deut. 30: 6; Jer. 4: 4; and Ezek. 44: 7.

loosely here; there is no separate commandment to circumcise the heart. Since, however, this statement follows a discussion of the restraint of desire as one of the purposes of the law, and such restraint is explicitly stated later on to be the reason for actual physical circumcision,[55] we can take it that the mildness of temperament described is associated with circumcision causally as well as metaphorically. Either way, it is not innate, but is a trait that needs to be cultivated.

Moreover, in the introduction to the *Book of the Commandments*, in setting out the fourteen principles underlying his enumeration of the commandments, Maimonides states, under the fourth principle, that the injunction to circumcise the heart is one of those imperative statements in the Torah that are too general to be included in the canonical list of 613 commandments, and that its import, like that of other such statements, is that one should keep all the commandments, in this particular case with an emphasis on the spirit of submission in which they should be accepted. With this in mind, 'uncircumcised non-Jews' in our *halakhah* can be taken to mean both 'non-Jews who have not been physically circumcised' and 'non-Jews who are without the commandments', and therefore uncircumcised of heart. This fits the text well, since it provides a basis for the contrast with 'the Israelites, upon whom the Holy One, blessed be He, bestowed the favour of the Law'. Circumcision in the metaphorical sense means both submission to God's commandments, and the gentleness that obedience to the commandments is supposed to produce. The implication is that 'the children of our father Abraham' are 'compassionate to all' not innately, but thanks to the commandments, and only to the degree to which they observe them.

'The Israelites, upon whom the Holy One, blessed be He, bestowed the favour of the Law' could be seen simply as an identifier; alternatively, it can be construed as meaning that, as the descendants of Abraham, characterized by mercy, Israel were worthy to receive the Torah. It makes more sense, though, to interpret it as meaning that Israelites are merciful by virtue of having, and observing, the Torah, and are not necessarily inherently so. After all, if Jews were so innately compassionate, Maimonides would not need to urge merciful behaviour in the way he does here. Nor would 'Laws of Moral Qualities' be at all coherent.

Twersky, who, as mentioned above, sees *lifnim mishurat hadin* as the basis of the behaviour urged in our *halakhah*, finds the reference to the Torah incongruous:

---

[55] *Guide* iii. 49 (p. 609). For further discussion of the word 'commandment' here, see above, Ch. 4 n. 4.

Inasmuch as the mercy shown in this case is supererogatory rather than mandatory—it is avowedly not legislated—why refer to the laws of the Torah? The mention of 'statutes and judgments' would seem to be gratuitous, inasmuch as they do not prescribe the 'way of wisdom' and piety being recommended. The clear inference, however, is that all the laws are a springboard for the highest morality and perfection which emanate slowly and steadily from them.[56]

In asserting that 'the mercy shown in this case' is 'avowedly *not* legislated', Twersky presumably alludes to the phrase 'though such is the rule', taking it to mean that what follows it is not a legal rule. Our approach is that there are two rules, and they conflict. If we assume 'wisdom' and 'piety' to have the specific meanings that they have in 'Laws of Moral Qualities', then they actually are prescribed by the 'statutes and judgements', the mention of which is not at all gratuitous. 'The quality of piety' may perhaps only be recommended, but 'the way of wisdom' is absolutely mandated. It was Abraham who discovered this ideal of the mean and *imitatio Dei* and passed it on to his 'children'.[57] Moses later embodied this ideal in a commandment that specifies mercy as one of the chief attributes of God's actions that should be imitated.[58] Through the allusion to these two stages in the development of Jewish ideology and law, Maimonides builds towards his explicit mention of the commandment of *imitatio Dei*, and provides further indication that he regards mercy towards a non-Jewish slave as *din* and not as *lifnim mishurat hadin*. Or to put it another way, the laws are not 'a springboard for the highest morality and perfection'; the highest morality and perfection are legislated. A reading of the *halakhah* as based upon conflict within the laws of the Torah, and a resolution of the conflict through a universal principle overriding a particular law, thus avoids Twersky's difficulty, and is smoother than a reading based upon *lifnim mishurat hadin*.

Imitating God's Wisdom and Imitating God's Will

That said, it is only fair that we should reverse our observation and ask why, if the background to our *halakhah* is *din* and not *lifnim mishurat hadin*, 'the quality of piety', associated with the latter, is mentioned at all? All that is required to ensure humane treatment of slaves is 'the way of wisdom' and the pursuit of justice.

We should first observe that our *halakhah* may be divided into three parts,

---

[56] Twersky, *Introduction to the Code*, 427–8. [57] See 'Laws of Moral Qualities', 1: 7.
[58] See 'Laws of Idolatry', 1: 5–6.

each ending with a prooftext or prooftexts,[59] and remind ourselves that Maimonides remoulded his sources in order to arrive at this arrangement, so that it is reasonable to suppose that it conveys some message.

The first part, urging consideration for the slave's physical needs, ends with the prooftext 'As the eyes of slaves look unto the hand of their master'. In our survey of Maimonides' sources we discerned two strands in his argument for considerate treatment of a non-Jewish slave: the strand of mercy and the strand of equality, and noted that the continuation of this verse from Psalms, which compares a slave's dependence on his master to our dependence on God, suggests the idea of mercy as *imitatio Dei*. This verse keeps the discussion within the framework of the master/slave relationship, and the ethical demand arises out of that very relationship. The exercise of mercy, after all, is always in a situation of inequality; one can only be called upon to act mercifully if one is in a position of power over another person. In treating the slave mercifully, the slave-owner imitates God's mercy in governing the world.

The second part, about the slave's psychological well-being, ends with the prooftext from Job, 'Did not He that made me in the womb make him?', which, as we noted, expresses the idea of equality. This verse dissolves the master/slave relationship. Here God is evoked not as governor of the world, but as its maker. The slave-owner and slave were not made as such; they are equal before their creator. The ethical demand arises out of that fact.

This implies that there are two possible forms of *imitatio Dei*: the imitation of God's governance—that is, the wisdom of God as manifest in nature—and the imitation of God as creator—that is, the will of God in bringing the world into being in the first place. We suggest that the first form of *imitatio* is *ḥokhmah*, while the second form is *ḥasidut*. The first form, in which moral and social law is modelled upon laws of nature, is *din*, while the second, which is the imitation of God's mindset, as it were, is *lifnim mishurat hadin*.[60] The ethical demands of our *halakhah* involve both.

---

[59] In the traditional editions of the *Mishneh torah*, the *halakhah* appears as a single continuous paragraph, but in the Makbili edition, which we consider more reliable, the three parts form three separate paragraphs.

[60] *Sifrei* on Deut. 11: 22 (Maimonides' main source for his presentation of *imitatio Dei*—see n. 19 above) states, *inter alia*, 'Just as the Holy One, blessed be He, is called righteous [*tsadik*], as it says ... so you also should be righteous. The Holy One, blessed be He, is called kind [*ḥasid*], as it says ... so you also should be kind.' The prooftext we have omitted from this citation is Ps. 145: 17, which the NJPS translation gives as 'The Lord is beneficent [*tsadik*] in all His ways and faithful [*ḥasid*] in all His works.' The 1917 JPS translation gives 'The Lord is righteous in all His ways, and gracious in all His works', which is nearer to Maimonides' understanding of *tsadik* and *ḥasid* as applied to God—at any rate, *ḥasid* cannot mean pious

This may seem to apply too much system to what could be read as simply an appeal for a little decency and humanity, but our suggestion is well supported by the *Guide*. We saw that, in the *Guide*, justice is defined as giving someone their due. In that chapter of the *Guide*, God is described as '*tsadik* [righteous] because of His mercy toward the weak—I refer to the governance of the living being by means of its forces'. As Pines notes, *tsadik* is 'A word deriving from the same verbal root as *tsedakah*', which in turn Maimonides states 'is derived from *tsedek*, which means justice'. The exercise of mercy by human beings is thus the imitation of an attribute of God's justice in governing the world.

In that same chapter, *ḥesed* ('loving-kindness'), which is from the same root as *ḥasid* and as *ḥasidut*, is defined as beneficence towards someone who has no right to claim it, or in excess of their claims. Applied to God, it refers to creation: 'Hence this reality as a whole—I mean that He, may He be exalted, has brought it into being—is *ḥesed* . . . Accordingly He is called *ḥasid* ['one possessing loving-kindness'] because He has brought the all into being.' In other words, the world's very existence is *lifnim mishurat hadin*. Once created, the world is governed by natural laws (which God could alter but will not),[61] but the idea of law does not apply to the act of creation itself. The *ḥasid* may thus be said to think and act out of appreciation of 'this reality as a whole', which no law says has to exist, unlike the *ḥakham*, who analyses and imitates the laws governing the world as a system of interrelated parts. The *Guide* thus corroborates the association we detected in our *halakhah* of mercy with *ḥokhmah* and the imitation of God's wisdom as observed in nature, and of equality with *ḥesed* and the imitation of God's will in creating the world, which levels master and slave.[62] The perfected human being, that is the human being who comes as near as possible to imitating God's perfection, will incorporate both these traits.

What then of the third part of our *halakhah*?

---

here. This part of the *midrash* from *Sifrei* is not cited in the exposition of 'walk in His ways' in 'Laws of Moral Qualities', 1: 6, but it is in the *Book of the Commandments*, positive commandment 8. 'And His mercies are over all His works', as cited in 'Laws of Slaves', 9: 8, is from verse 9 of the same psalm. Eisen, '*Lifnim mi-Shurat ha-Din* in Maimonides' *Mishneh Torah*', also sees *lifnim mishurat hadin* in the *Mishneh torah* as an aspect of *imitatio Dei*, but not in the same way as proposed here.

[61] See *Guide* ii. 29 (p. 346).

[62] It is worth noting that J. B. Soloveitchik also sees Maimonides' conception of *ḥesed* as dissolving social differences, and indeed differences between Jews and non-Jews. See Kaplan (ed.), *Maimonides: Between Philosophy and Halakhah*, 205–8.

Cruelty and effrontery are not frequent except with uncircumcised non-Jews. The children of our father Abraham, however, i.e. the Israelites, upon whom the Holy One, blessed be He, bestowed the favour of the Torah and laid upon them righteous statutes and judgements, are merciful people who have mercy upon all. Thus also it is declared by the attributes of the Holy One, blessed be He, which we are enjoined to imitate: 'And His mercies are over all His works' [Ps. 145: 9].

Furthermore, whoever has compassion will receive compassion, as it is said: 'And He will show thee mercy, and have compassion upon thee, and multiply thee' [Deut. 13: 18].

The first prooftext cited here is the second half of a verse from Psalms that reads in full: 'The Lord is good to all; and His mercies are over all His works.' In *Guide* iii. 12, which is about the problem of apparent evil in the world, this verse is used to summarize an argument that synthesizes the two aspects of God that we have been discussing: the goodness of creation and equality, and the mercy manifest in the laws of nature. On the discernment of God's wisdom in nature Maimonides writes here:

On the other hand, men of excellence and knowledge have grasped and understood the wisdom manifested in that which exists, as David has set forth, saying: 'All the paths of the Lord are mercy and truth unto such as keep His covenant and His testimonies.'[63] By this he says that those who keep to the nature of that which exists, keep the commandments of the Law, and know the ends of both, apprehend clearly the excellency and the true reality of the whole. For this reason they take as their end that for which they were intended as men, namely apprehension.

In other words, understanding both the universal and universally accessible laws of 'that which exists' and the particularist laws of the Torah leads to the same end, 'apprehension', the ultimate purpose of all human beings, who all share the same means of apprehension, even if some enjoy a superior moral and cognitive education in the shape of 'His covenant and His testimonies'.

The chapter continues with the statement, already noted in Chapter 2, that God's beneficence is manifest 'in that He brings into existence what is necessary according to its order of importance and in that He makes individuals of the same species equal at their creation'. This is where Maimonides deploys the prooftext he cites in our *halakhah*: 'David also says explicitly: "The Lord is good to all; and His tender mercies are over all His works."' The chapter concludes:

For his bringing us into existence is absolutely the great good, as we have made clear, and the creation of the governing faculty in the living beings is an indication of His mercifulness with regard to them, as we have made clear.

[63] Ps. 25: 10.

The verse thus combines creation as 'the great good', and governance as mercy.

Bestowal of the Torah

The third part of our *halakhah* also achieves a synthesis, but in a somewhat different way. The first subject of this part is a distinction between non-Jews and the Israelites, which we have already discussed, and the bestowal of the Torah. The word translated as 'bestow' here is *hishpia*, which, in this context, can be translated more literally as 'cause to flow' or 'pour out'.[64] In his introduction to the *Book of the Commandments*, written in preparation for compiling the *Mishneh torah*, Maimonides announces that the language of his projected code of law will be mishnaic Hebrew, and the way he uses the word *hishpia* in our *halakhah* has good antecedents in the Mishnah and other tannaitic literature, where, by extension, it can mean 'to supply in abundance/in excess'. Nevertheless, there is a slight adaptation here, for although the Sages of the Mishnah use this word to describe God showering blessings on human beings, these are generally of a material, or at least this-worldly kind. As far as we have been able to ascertain, they never apply it to the giving of the Torah.

This latter use of the word *hishpia* has a philosophical connotation. In medieval literature, the root *shafa*, from which *hishpia* derives, is used to refer to the Neoplatonic doctrine of emanation, which in Modern Hebrew is *torat hashefa*. Ibn Tibbon uses the word *shefa* in this way throughout his Hebrew translation of the *Guide*, and in *Guide* ii. 12, in the course of a discussion of the concept of emanation, Maimonides himself remarks, 'This term, I mean "overflow" [*shefa*], is sometimes also applied in Hebrew to God, may He be exalted, with a view to likening Him to an overflowing spring of water.' Just before this, he states that, just as water spreads from a wellspring in all directions and does not flow from one particular point to another, so 'it has been said that the world derives from the overflow of God and that He has caused to overflow to it everything in it that is produced in time. In the same way it is said that He caused His knowledge to overflow to the prophets.'

So while it looks as though what Maimonides is saying in our *halakhah* is that God selected the Jewish people to bestow upon them the gift of the Torah, the undertone of the word *hishpia* is that the Torah is a flow from God received by a uniquely talented prophet, Moses.[65] While the experience of the

[64] It can also mean 'cause to slope' but that is not relevant here. Presumably the connection is that liquids flow down slopes. In Modern Hebrew it means 'to affect' or 'to influence'.

[65] Scholars disagree on what Maimonides held to be the precise way in which the Torah was transmitted from God to Moses, and on how far he regarded Moses as the Torah's author. See above, Ch. 8 n. 69.

miracles of the Exodus was supposed to make the Jewish people receptive to the Torah,[66] no special aptitude on their part is implied, and a Jew has no inborn advantage or divinely bestowed privilege over his or her non-Jewish slave.

The conclusion of 'Laws of Slaves', 9: 8: 'Furthermore, whoever has compassion will receive compassion, as it is said: "And He will show thee mercy, and have compassion upon thee, and multiply thee"', can be thought of as a continuation of the idea of *shefa*, emanation. The fulfilment of the Torah, that is, the acquisition of moral and (though not separately stated here) intellectual virtue makes a person receptive to the divine flow.

As explained in Chapter 2, moral virtue, that is, *imitatio Dei*, has two phases: the first phase, which is preparatory to the acquisition of intellectual virtue, requires deliberate adjustment of one's temperament to the middle path. *Lifnim mishurat hadin* at that stage is a separate precautionary, or sometimes remedial, mode. Intellectual virtue itself, the 'final perfection', is described in the *Guide* as the apprehension of God and his providence 'as manifested in the act of bringing them into being'[67] (which is *ḥesed*, God's will, and *lifnim mishurat hadin*), and also 'in their governance'[68] (which is *tsedek*, God's wisdom, and *din*). The consequence of this apprehension is the cancellation of what was always a false, if necessary, distinction, since God is a unity and does not have will or wisdom separately from his essence. In the final phase, 'The way of life of such an individual, after he has achieved this apprehension, will always have in view loving-kindness, righteousness, and judgement, through assimilation to his actions', that is, apparently, assimilation to both sorts of actions: the act of creation, and the actions in the world. In this phase of moral virtue, there is no differentiation between wisdom and piety, and moreover the assimilation to divine actions means that showing compassion and receiving compassion are the same divine flow.

Mercy Indivisible

As already indicated above, at least in 'Laws of Moral Qualities', the imitation of God is not only a matter of outwardly replicating God's actions, but also a matter of cultivating an inward God-like state. The essence of the commandment is not acting mercifully, but becoming merciful. Actions are divisible: one can envisage being commanded to act mercifully towards some people but not towards others, for reasons that one might not fully understand. Virtuous character is indivisible, and independent of the object of one's actions. There are undoubtedly people of unstable temperament capable of

[66] See Exod. 19: 4. [67] *Guide* iii. 54 (p. 638). [68] Ibid.

displaying what looks like mercy on some occasions and vicious cruelty on others, but the point of 'Laws of Moral Qualities' is the cultivation of a steadily virtuous temperament, in which mercy is an ingrained personality trait, and exercised with judgement, not on a whim or to make an impression. This is a wholly rational undertaking, and largely autonomous. It depends on one's understanding of oneself and the world. It will not admit of unintelligible distinctions.

We have already mentioned that mercy is one of 'God's ways' listed in the discussion of *imitatio Dei* in 'Laws of Moral Qualities', 1: 6: 'Even as He is called merciful, so be thou merciful.' In our *halakhah*, Maimonides assumes this background. Mercy is one of the attributes of God's actions that we should imitate, and now we are informed of the scope of God's mercy: it is indivisible and universal. Our mercy should have the same integrity and scope.

The Intellect's Tripartite Orientation Again

As we have interpreted them, the three parts of the *halakhah* that ends the *Book of Acquisition* exhibit a tripartite pattern similar to that identified in Books 8, 9, and 10. This dialectical pattern seems ingrained in Maimonides' mind, and emerges at points of greatest tension between the particular and the universal: between the service of sacrifices and the service of intellect, and here, between discrimination against a non-Jewish slave and the imitation of God.

The first part of our *halakhah* represents the thought of the self, in the subjective idea of *imitatio Dei* as the replication within oneself of God's wisdom in governing the world, and of fair treatment of the slave as a question of consistent moral virtue. This orientation is appropriate in relation to the slave's physical needs, which are the subject of this part of the *halakhah*. Just as God provides for all creatures, the slave-owner should provide for the slave.

The second part represents the thought of God. Rather than the internalization of the attributes of God's actions in the world, it concerns the objective recognition of creation as the product of God's will, and hence recognition of the slave as essentially equal. This suits the subject of this part of the *halakhah*, which is the slave's psychological well-being. 'Scriptural law has delivered them only unto slavery and not unto disgrace': just as God as he is in himself is indefinable, so the slave is not completely defined by his status and function. In this respect, the guide to right conduct is not internal moral consistency, but acceptance of the slave's objective, separate existence, and listening to what he has to say.

The third part of the ending of the *Book of Acquisition* exhibits a movement very similar to what we saw at the end of the *Book of Purity*, where immersion in 'the waters of intellect' precipitates a cleansing divine flow. It represents the interface with the agent intellect in the reciprocity of mercy shown and mercy received, apprehension of the agent intellect being the closest that a human being can come to the divine. This kind of reciprocity can be seen as anticipating the ending of endings, the climax of Maimonides' oeuvre, namely the end of the *Guide*, where the ascent to 'apprehension of Him, may He be exalted' precipitates assimilation with the divine flow of 'loving-kindness, righteousness, and judgement'.

Our *halakhah* can thus be seen as the application to social ethics of the correct intellectual and moral disposition represented by the endings of Books 8, 9, and 10. The order of phases one and two is, however, reversed. In the ten-book *bein adam lamakom* division of the *Mishneh torah*, governed by emanation, the movement is from God downwards, and from recognition of God's objective existence and authority to internalization of God's laws observed in nature, a pattern set at the start in the sequence of 'Laws of the Foundations of the Torah' followed by 'Laws of Moral Qualities', and replicated in the sequence of Books 8 and 9. Here, in the *bein adam laḥavero* division of the work, the movement is upwards, from God in nature, material conditions, and subjective morality, to God separate from nature, the non-physical realm, and objectivity.

Towards the Messianic Society

This leads to consideration of the wider context of our halakhah. The last four books of the *Mishneh torah*, which deal with the social commandments, proceed from dystopia to utopia.[69] The first book in this division, the *Book of Damages*, is about dysfunction in society—robbery, injury, even murder. It ends, however, with laws about aiding an enemy in distress on the road, a move towards the rehabilitation of society. The *Book of Acquisition*, which follows, is about a society in co-operative mode, in which normal commercial transactions are possible. Underlying this transition is a reformation in the attitude of human beings towards one another. The enemy in distress at the end of the *Book of Damages* is a Jew. There are hostile feelings towards him, but at the same time there exists an obvious basis for fellowship. At the end of the *Book of Acquisition*, Maimonides goes a step further and takes an outsider,

[69] This is discussed at length in Gillis, *Reading Maimonides' Mishneh Torah*, 178–85.

a non-Jewish slave, someone vulnerable to discrimination and exploitation, and makes him as it were the agent of discovery of the basis of a universal human bond.[70]

One factor in the transformation from dystopia to utopia is the infusion, one could say emanation, into human relations of the values of 'Laws of Moral Qualities'.

The conclusion of 'Laws of Slaves', 9: 8 echoes very closely the end of the first chapter of 'Laws of Moral Qualities':

> And as the Creator is called by these attributes, which constitute the middle path in which we are to walk, this path is called the Way of God and this is what the patriarch Abraham taught his children, as it is said 'For I love him, because he will charge his children and his household after him, that they may keep the way of the Lord' [Gen. 18: 19]. Whoever walks in this way secures for himself happiness and blessing, as the text continues, 'In order that the Lord might bring upon Abraham that which He spoke concerning him' [Gen. 18: 19].[71]

All the elements of our *halakhah* are here, only arranged slightly differently. There is the invocation of Abraham and his legacy; the conversion of that legacy into a set of commandments, or obligations, of which *imitatio Dei* is one of the most fundamental; the reference to justice and righteousness; and the idea of reciprocity—whoever walks in 'the way of God' receives goodness and blessing, and, in our *halakhah*, whoever displays compassion receives compassion. The reform of human society is 'Laws of Moral Qualities' at work in the realities of material existence.

The final character traits treated in 'Laws of Moral Qualities' are vengefulness and resentment, the most destructive of human dispositions. The latter leads to the former, and so should be removed from the heart. 'This is the right principle. It alone makes civilized life and social intercourse possible.'[72] Really, the whole weight of 'Laws of Moral Qualities' is behind this final statement. The removal of resentment from the heart makes the civilized transactions of the *Book of Acquisition* emerge from the violence and disorder, which we may imagine to stem from vengefulness, of the *Book of Damages*. Thus the first two books of the social commandments division of the *Mishneh torah* work their way back to the virtues that 'Laws of Moral Qualities' propounds.

---

[70] On the outsider as a catalyst of virtue in Maimonides, see Diamond, *Converts, Heretics, and Lepers*. On p. 89, Diamond cites *Guide* iii. 13 in the context of an argument similar to the one made here. For more on the 'human bond' mentioned here, see Maimonides on Mishnah *Avot* 3: 15 (in Kafih's edition; 3: 12 in standard editions), to the effect that one ought to receive all human beings, the lowly and the great, free and slave, with joy and gladness.

[71] 'Laws of Moral Qualities', 1: 7.   [72] Ibid. 7: 8.

The climax of this process is in our *halakhah*, at the end of 'Laws of Slaves', which returns us to *imitatio Dei*, the governing commandment of 'Laws of Moral Qualities'. It is permissible to work a non-Jewish slave with rigour. Maimonides does not try to cancel this law, evade it, extenuate it, or mitigate it with *lifnim mishurat hadin*. Nevertheless, through his rhetorical skill in our *halakhah*, as well as through the *Mishneh torah*'s general structure, the superior value of 'Laws of Moral Qualities' trumps it.

Accommodation

Universal social values are nowadays generally thought of in terms of rights,[73] whereas, as is well known, Judaism speaks of obligations. Generally, this makes little practical difference, since one person's right implies another's obligation and vice versa. In our case, it does make a difference, and this enables us to see a possible resolution of the apparent clash of values in the *halakhah* under discussion.

Some provisions of the laws concerning slaves can be thought of as symmetrical as far as rights and obligations are concerned. For example, the owner of a non-Jewish slave who causes him permanent visible bodily injury must free him.[74] This implies a right of the slave to go free, and it probably does not matter which way it is expressed. In the case of the obligation to show mercy, however, there is no symmetry, because, as we saw above, it is not in the first instance a duty that the master owes the slave as a social obligation, but rather one that he owes himself; it is part of the duty to imitate God, in the pursuit of moral and intellectual perfection. It can therefore coexist with the law permitting a non-Jewish slave to be worked with rigour, for the latter is on a different plane.

All this points back to our analysis in Chapter 2 of the ending of the *Book of Love*, and the idea adumbrated there that the two-tier system presented in 'Laws of Circumcision', 3: 8–9, the Abrahamic covenant of love and the Mosaic covenant of law, can be used to arbitrate conflicts within the Torah. In that light, the references in 'Laws of Slaves', 9: 8 to Abraham and circumcision are not at all surprising. The Torah commands male Jews to be circumcised 'as Abraham circumcised'. Circumcision represents the idea that the ethnically particular covenant of law, the Torah, flows from the universal covenant of love, the covenant with Abraham, and directs towards a return

---

[73] Article 4 of the Universal Declaration of Human Rights adopted by the United Nations in 1948 states: 'No one shall be held in slavery or servitude; slavery and the slave trade shall be prohibited in all their forms.'   [74] See 'Laws of Slaves', 5: 4.

to it. The Torah works on the principle of accommodation. It is adapted to the realities of social and economic needs and of human understanding, and seeks to transform and elevate them. Moreover, the Abrahamic covenant was characterized in Chapter 2 as a covenant of discovery. The Torah, it was suggested, is ultimately intended to turn each person into his or her own Abraham, discoverer of moral and intellectual truth. The complications and nuances of 'Laws of Slaves', 9: 8, particularly the blending of *din* and *lifnim mishurat hadin*, are perhaps intended to provoke that spirit of discovery. Maimonides' moral theory is a heuristic rather than an algorithm.

Maimonides expresses the idea of accommodation most clearly in relation to sacrifices, which he sees as a concession to convention, but it can be applied to our *halakhah* on the treatment of non-Jewish slaves.[75] The ideal is equal treatment of all human beings, and probably the elimination of slavery altogether. The legitimation of slavery in general accommodates prevailing economic realities, while the law that a non-Jewish slave may be worked with rigour can be regarded as a concession to a human need to lord it over someone—an interpretation that is actually quite consistent with the language of *Sifra*. Although 'rigour' in the technical sense that we have assumed is possibly more insidiously cruel and degrading than hard labour (and perhaps for this very reason Maimonides chose to take his universalist stance on this matter), there do at least exist in the law provisions that protect against outright brutality, such as that a non-Jewish slave goes free if his master injures him. It is therefore reasonable to argue that the law does not condone ill treatment, but recognizes that certain tendencies take time to eradicate. Our *halakhah* can then be read as a progression from a kind of regulated xenophobia to enlightened universalism.

We thus have two complementary ways of resolving the conflict that Maimonides sets up between the licence to work a non-Jewish slave with rigour and the requirement to treat him as mercifully as a Jewish slave must be treated. The first is the principle of indivisibility. It may be permissible to act in inconsistent ways on the basis of ethnic distinction, but the inward traits that we are commanded to cultivate are an imitation of God's ways in nature, and indeed should reflect God's unity as far as is humanly possible, which allows no such discrimination. The second is the principle of accommodation. The law takes into account the real human situation, but, in its hierarchy of values, Abrahamic laws (in this case 'and you shall walk in His ways') take precedence over purely Mosaic laws.

---

[75] For an extended discussion of this idea, see Rabinovitch, *The Way of the Torah* (Heb.), 11–19. For a history of the idea of divine accommodation, see Benin, *The Footprints of God*.

One point should be made clear: Maimonides does not countenance two covenants post-Torah. The covenant of love is incorporated into the covenant of law. The Torah does not aim at an external perfection. It is itself perfect, but it has gradations, and 'Laws of Slaves', 9: 8 presents a ladder for ascending through them.

Slavery Social, not Racial

Maimonides saw slavery as a purely social and economic institution. There is no trace in his treatment of it of any notion of natural slavery, or of any kind of inborn inferiority of one race to another. To be sure, there are biologically determined differences between human beings, but these are differences of degree, a matter of varying characteristics and aptitudes.[76] The essential human form, an intellect capable of abstract thought, is identical in all human beings, and the essential knowledge that God has no physical attributes is within everyone's grasp. This is in spite of the fact that some people are capable of developing their understanding of this idea and its implications further than others. Even if someone insists that there is a family resemblance among Jews in that they are especially given to kindness and mercy, this mandates equal treatment of the others rather than their subjugation.

An indication of Maimonides' view of slavery is the very fact that it is dealt with in the *Book of Acquisition*. This volume is in the division of the *Mishneh torah* that deals with the social commandments, comprising the last four books. Some of the material of 'Laws of Slaves' derives from Order *Nezikin* of the Mishnah, which is the basis for those four books, and from the Tosefta and halakhic Midrash, but the source for much of it is Order *Nashim* ('Women'), which is mainly about marriage and divorce. Both marriage and slavery involve rights in the person and property of another, and the formalities whereby these relationships are created and dissolved are similar. But Maimonides treats these two institutions under quite different rubrics. In the *Mishneh torah*, the *Book of Women*, containing 'Laws of Marriage', 'Laws of Divorce', and 'Laws of Levirate Marriage', is in the division comprising the first ten books that deal with man–God commandments. The thread that connects these books is holiness, in its various guises. 'Laws of Marriage' has a preamble which is precisely about the way in which the Torah transformed a purely contractual relationship between a man and woman into a relationship with a dimension of holiness.

---

[76] See Freudenthal, 'Biological Limitations'.

Slavery, by contrast, remains purely in the contractual sphere. It fulfils no godly purpose, and has no touch of holiness. It therefore finds its place in the *Book of Acquisition*. Holiness in fact only comes in with the idea of *imitatio Dei*,[77] which demands that a master should rise above the contractual relationship to treat his slave humanely. It forms no part of the relationship itself.

Torah in the Eyes of the Slave

A final word on the passage in our *halakhah*: 'the Israelites, upon whom the Holy One, blessed be He, bestowed the favour of the Law and laid upon them righteous statutes and judgements, are merciful people who have mercy upon all'. 'Righteous statutes and judgements' [*ḥukim umishpatim tsadikim*] recalls Deuteronomy 4: 5–8:

Behold, I have taught you statutes and ordinances [*ḥukim umishpatim*], even as the Lord my God commanded me, that ye should do so in the midst of the land whither ye go in to possess it. Observe therefore and do them; for this is your wisdom and your understanding in the sight of the peoples, that, when they hear all these statutes, shall say: 'Surely this great nation is a wise and understanding people.' For what great nation is there, that hath God so nigh unto them, as the Lord our God is whensoever we call upon Him? And what great nation is there, that hath statutes and ordinances so righteous [*ḥukim umishpatim tsadikim*] as all this law, which I set before you this day?

It is this passage (specifically, verse 7) that Maimonides uses as proof that all the commandments have rational purposes, in a way comprehensible even to outsiders: 'Thus it states explicitly that even all statutes [*ḥukim*] will show to all the nations that they have been given with wisdom and understanding.'[78] He continues, 'every commandment from among these six hundred and thirteen commandments exists either with a view to communicating a correct opinion, or to putting an end to an unhealthy opinion, or to communicating a rule of justice, or to warding off an injustice, or to endowing men with a noble moral quality, or to warning them against an evil moral quality.' The phrase 'righteous statutes and judgements' is thus at the interface between the practising Jew and the discerning non-Jew, and no-one is in a better position to judge the righteousness of the commandments, and whether they are truly efficacious in the manner Maimonides describes, than the Israelite's non-Jewish slave.

The conclusion to the *Book of Acquisition* encapsulates Maimonides' ethics. It brings together the doctrine of the mean, Abraham as the discoverer

---

[77] See W. Z. Harvey, 'Holiness'.   [78] *Guide* iii. 31 (p. 524), discussed in Ch. 8 above.

of ethical and theological truths through speculation, the commandments as Moses' embodiment of these truths in law, and *imitatio Dei*. The encapsulation occurs at this point in the *Mishneh torah* because the *Book of Acquisition* represents a critical stage in the repair of society and its progress towards the messianic ideal in which social structures and mores are entirely conducive to the pursuit of perfection.

Summary

In the final *halakhah* of 'Laws of Slaves', Maimonides records the law that a non-Jewish slave, unlike a Jewish slave, may be worked 'with rigour'. In effect, however, he overrides that law and in impassioned rhetoric calls for sensitive and considerate treatment of a non-Jewish slave, concluding with the verse 'And His mercy is over all His works'. The question is, what is the basis for this manoeuvre?

The consensus answer is *lifnim mishurat hadin*, a supererogatory waiver of legal rights. This leaves intact the non-Jewish slave's inferior status, and a particularist view of the Torah. It does not, however, fit the text well. Although the *halakhah* might appear to be about condescension from a position of inborn moral superiority inherited from Abraham, Maimonides' wording, his allusions to 'Laws of Moral Qualities' (particularly through the terms 'wisdom' and 'piety'), and his refashioning of his rabbinic sources, suggest that he actually sees a conflict within the law, which he decides on the basis of a hierarchy of values in which the commandment of *imitatio Dei*, which entails the indivisibility of moral virtue and the recognition of the equality of all human beings as created by God, prevails over the discriminatory provision concerning a non-Jewish slave. The persistence of that provision in the Torah can perhaps be explained by the principle of accommodation.

Out of halakhah and aggadah, Maimonides constructs a *halakhah* that moves smoothly but pointedly from seeing the non-Jewish slave as an alien who can be treated as an inferior to seeing him as an equal fellow human being. The upshot is a statement of thoroughgoing universalism, as Maimonides builds towards the establishment of a truly Abrahamic society at the very end of the *Mishneh torah*.

THIRTEEN

CIVIL LAWS
God of Aristotle in the God of Abraham

Introduction

The thirteenth book of the *Mishneh torah*, the *Book of Civil Laws* (*Sefer mishpatim*), is the third of the four-book division dealing explicitly with laws regulating social behaviour (*bein adam leḥavero*).[1] It is a natural continuation of Book 12, the *Book of Acquisition*, a point emphasized by the last section of the book, which deals with inheritances. Like all the books in the *Mishneh torah*, this book opens with a quotation from Genesis 21: 33: 'In the name of the Lord, God of the world', and then adds a citation or motto unique to it, this time from Psalms: 'I will praise you with a sincere heart as I learn Your just rules [*mishpetei tsidkekha*]',[2] indicating in advance that the book is about justice. We shall return to this opening motto at the end of the chapter.

Like its biblical namesake, the weekly pericope (*parashah*) of 'Mishpatim',[3] this book contains a wide variety of civil laws, divided into five sections: 'Laws of Hiring', 'Laws of Borrowing and Depositing', 'Laws of Creditor and Debtor', 'Laws of Pleading [*to'en venitan*]', and 'Laws of Inheritance'.

The last chapter of 'Laws of Inheritance', and of the book as a whole, deals with the court-appointed guardian for individuals orphaned as minors. Maimonides chooses to phrase the last *halakhah* of that chapter as follows:

Although the guardian is not required to render an account, as we have stated,[4] he must make reckoning to himself privately with great care and beware of the father of these orphans[5] who rides upon the skies, as it written, 'Extol Him that

---

[1] On the division of the *Mishneh torah* into sections of ten and four books, see the discussion in the Appendix, which is based on the in-depth study by Gillis in *Reading Maimonides' Mishneh Torah*, 158–62.   [2] Ps. 119: 7.   [3] Exod. 21–4.   [4] 'Laws of Inheritance', 11: 5.
[5] Given that Maimonides uses three infinitives in a row here, a less polished but more accurate translation of this clause might be: 'to reckon with himself, and to be exacting, and to *greatly* beware of the father of these orphans'.

rideth upon the *aravot*⁶. . . . a father of the fatherless' [Ps. 68: 5–6].⁷

This paragraph bears out an observation made by Isaac Klein in the introduction to his translation of Book 12: 'Book 12 fully confirms the often made observation to the effect that Maimonides tends to detect a moral–ethical point of view even in laws that at first sight seem to be of purely civic and ritual nature.'⁸ Our text is certainly an attempt to detect a moral–ethical point in what otherwise might be taken as a series of technical laws about inheritance, and serves as a coda to Books 11, 12, and 13. The last *halakhah* may be meant to reflect on the book(s) as a whole, in that all the formal laws of contract and property cannot guarantee an upright society unless there is also inner integrity. This would also reflect the end of 'Laws of Moral Qualities',⁹ which deals with the danger posed to society by the bearing of grudges: 'The Torah, accordingly, emphatically warns us not to bear a grudge, so that the impression of the wrong shall be quite obliterated and be no longer remembered. This is the right principle. It alone makes civilized life and social intercourse possible.'¹⁰ The three books that deal with the laws of 'social intercourse' end with the ethical dealing and upright character that support those laws.

Jacob Rabinowitz, the translator of Book 13, makes a similar point:

In three of the five treatises of our book (1, 4, 5) the last section represents a sort of peroration, with an appropriate passage from Scripture skillfully woven into the text. These perorations, which are also found in many of the other treatises of the Code, reveal a depth of feeling and beauty of style rarely matched in Halakhaic [sic] literature.¹¹

Both Klein and Rabinowitz reflect a point made by Maimonides himself, in his discussion of the specific commandments dealt with in these two books (and elsewhere). In the *Guide*, apropos of some of the commandments in the two books under discussion here, Maimonides comments:

If you consider all these commandments one by one, you will find that they are manifestly useful through instilling pity for the weak and wretched, giving strength in various ways to the poor, and inciting us not to press hard upon those in straits and not inflict the hearts of individuals who are in a weak position.¹²

---

⁶ This word is variously translated as 'skies', 'heavens', or 'clouds'. In *Guide* i. 70 (p. 171, cited below) Maimonides informs us that *aravot* is the name of the outermost sphere of the cosmos, furthest from earth. In 'Laws of the Foundations of the Torah', 3: 1 Maimonides uses it as one of the names for the heavenly spheres generally. We choose to leave it untranslated for the purposes of this chapter.

⁷ 'Laws of Inheritance', 11: 12   ⁸ *The Book of Acquisition*, trans. Klein, p. xiv.   ⁹ 7: 8.
¹⁰ *The Book of Knowledge*, trans. Hyamson, 57a.
¹¹ *The Book of Civil Laws*, trans. Rabinowitz, p. xx.   ¹² *Guide* iii: 39 (p. 551).

Orphaned children are certainly examples of individuals in a weak position.

With specific reference to section 3 of Book 13 ('Laws of Creditor and Debtor'), Maimonides writes that all of the commandments enumerated there 'are imbued with benevolence, pity, and kindness for the weak; they forbid depriving anyone of a utility necessary for his nourishment; I mean: "No man shall take the nether or upper millstone to pledge" [Deut. 24: 6].'[13]

Maimonides himself links Books 11, 12, and 13 together in his Introduction to the *Mishneh torah*:

Eleventh book: I include in it commandments referring to civil relations [*bein adam leḥavero*] which from the outset cause damage to property or injury to persons . . . Twelfth book: I include in it commandments referring to sales and other modes of acquisition . . . Thirteenth book: I include in it commandments referring to civil relations that do not, from the outset, cause damage.[14]

All three books, in other words, relate to what we might call financial relations among people.[15]

A Father of the Fatherless

With this background, let us look again at the final paragraph of this three-book division of the *Mishneh torah*:

Although the guardian is not required to render an account, as we have stated, he must make reckoning to himself privately with great care and beware of the father of these orphans who rides upon the skies, as it written, 'Extol Him that rideth upon the *aravot* . . . a father of the fatherless' [Ps. 68: 5–6].

Here are the complete verses that Maimonides cites: 'Sing to God, chant hymns to His name, extol Him that rideth [*harokhev*] upon the *aravot*; the Lord [*Yah*] is His name. Exult in His presence—the father of the fatherless, the champion of widows, God in His holy habitation [*beme'on kodesho*].' The

---

[13] Ibid., p. 553.
[14] *The Book of Knowledge*, trans. Hyamson, 19b (heavily emended). Of Book 14 he writes there: 'Fourteenth Book: I include therein precepts, the fulfilment of which is assigned to the Sanhedrin, as for example, infliction of capital punishment, reception of evidence, administration of the laws affecting the sovereign, and wars.' See the discussion in Gillis, *Reading Maimonides' Mishneh Torah*, 281.
[15] This was already noted by Hyman Klein, the translator of the *Book of Torts (Damages)*: 'Book eleven of the Code of Maimonides and the three following books . . . form a unit concerned mainly with civil and criminal law, that is, with affairs "between man and his fellow-man"—in contrast to the preceding ten books that are given over for the most part, to the symbolic and ritual observances of the Law, and thus deal with provisions between "man and God"' (p. xi). See also the Appendix.

legal guardian of orphans must always remember that such work is supervised, as it were, by 'the father of orphans' on high. The temptation to take advantage of those 'who are in a weak position' is always great, and so Maimonides uses this discussion to remind legal guardians of orphans that their work is never 'unsupervised'.[16]

Maimonides glosses these very verses in the *Guide*:

> In this sense it is said of God, may He be exalted: 'The rider [*rokhev*] of the heavens [*shamayim*] is helping you' [Deut. 33: 26]; the interpretation of which is: He who dominates the heavens. Similarly: 'The rider [*rokhev*] in the *aravot*' [Ps. 68: 5], meaning: He who dominates the highest heaven encompassing the universe ...
>
> Similarly the deity, may His name be held sublime, is the mover of the highest heaven, by whose motion everything that is in motion within this heaven is moved; at the same time, He, may He be exalted, is separate from this heaven and not a force subsisting within it. Accordingly the Sages interpreting His speech, may He be exalted, 'The eternal God [*elohei kedem*] is a dwelling place [*me'onah*]' [Deut. 33: 27], say in *Genesis Rabbah*: 'He is the dwelling place of the world, [whereas] the world is not his dwelling place.'[17] ...
>
> Consider it, and it shall become clear to you how they explained His relation, may He be exalted, to heaven: that it is His instrument by means of which He governs that which is existent. For whenever you find that according to the Sages, may their memory be blessed, there exists one thing in one particular heaven and another thing in another, the meaning of the passage is not that in that particular heaven there are to be found bodies other than that heaven, but that the forces generating the particular thing in question and safeguarding its order come from that heaven. A proof of what I have said to you is their saying:[18] '*Aravot*—that in which [exist] righteousness, right-dealing, justice, the treasures of life, the treasures of peace, the treasures of blessing, the soul of the righteous ones, the souls and the spirits that shall be created in the future, and the dew by means of which the Holy One, blessed be He, will revive the dead'.[19]

Maimonides' main point in this chapter of the *Guide* is a metaphysical one about the relation between God and the universe. This finds expression in the first two passages from the chapter cited here. But along the way he allows us to elaborate (perhaps a trifle midrashically) on our passage from the end of the *Book of Civil Laws*. In the third paragraph cited just above we learn that the same 'rider of the *aravot*', metaphysically distant from the cosmos, which he governs through many intermediaries, is also concerned, among other

---

[16] Note should be taken of other verses that Maimonides might have chosen to emphasize his point: Deut 10: 18 (but there, too, see the previous verse); Ps. 146: 9; Prov. 23: 10–11. That he chose the verses he did allows us, nay, encourages us, to make the points that follow.

[17] *Gen. Rabbah*, 68.   [18] BT Ḥag. 12b.   [19] *Guide* i. 70 (pp. 171–3).

things, with 'righteousness, right-dealing, justice, the treasures of life, the treasures of peace, the treasures of blessing'.

This reminds us of the great care that a legal guardian must take in protecting the assets of his orphaned charges, whose father is, on the one hand, the metaphysically distant rider of the skies, and yet, on the other hand, a 'father of the fatherless'. It may not be too much of a stretch to say that here Maimonides is hinting that the relationship of the guardian to the orphan should be parallel to that of God and the cosmos.

This connection, as it were, between the transcendent God and the needs of widows and orphans brings another passage from the *Guide* to mind,[20] in which Maimonides explains two verses from Jeremiah—'Thus saith the Lord: Let not the wise man glory in his wisdom, neither let the mighty man glory in his might, let not the rich man glory in his riches; but let him that glorieth glory in this, that he understandeth and knoweth Me, that I am the Lord who exercises loving-kindness, judgement, and righteousness in the earth'[21]—as teaching that it is God's purpose that 'there should come from you loving-kindness, judgement, and righteousness in the earth in the way I have explained'. We take Maimonides' point here to be that God expects all human beings to emulate His actions of 'loving-kindness, judgement, and righteousness in the earth' after each has reached the highest level of intellectual perfection available to her or to him.[22]

So, too, our passage from the end of the 'Laws of Inheritance' reminds us that one is expected to imitate God, known through the movement of the outermost sphere (*aravah*), who is also father to widows and orphans.[23]

A further point: as noted above, Maimonides could have chosen any number of verses to indicate God's concern for the weak in general and orphans in particular. Deuteronomy 10: 18, for example, comes to mind: 'But He upholds the cause of the fatherless and the widow, and befriends the stranger, providing him with food and clothing.'[24] But in our text he chose a

---

[20] *Guide* iii. 54 (p. 637).   [21] Jer. 9: 22–3.
[22] For a detailed analysis of this passage, see Kellner, *Maimonides on Human Perfection*, ch. 4. See further Gillis, *Reading Maimonides' Mishneh Torah*, who points out that the intellectual self-sufficiency of the fourth perfection is an *imitatio Dei* from which follows moral *imitatio* (p. 103). See also Melamed, '*Al Yithalel*' (Heb.).
[23] Buchman, 'The Order of the Books of the *Mishneh Torah*' (Heb.), makes a similar claim, arguing that succouring a widow is not only a matter of loving-kindness (*ḥesed*), but a reflection of the fact that God is a 'champion of widows' (p. 24). Even though God rides the heavens, he still does justice for widows and orphans and is father to the weak, making sure they get what is due to them.
[24] Maimonides cites this verse in 'Laws of Moral Qualities', 6: 4 and in his commentary on Mishnah *Avot* 4: 4. See above, n. 16.

specific verse in which God is called *rokhev aravot*. It is hard to read that verse and not think of *ma'aseh merkavah*, the 'Account of the Chariot'. The same root, *r-kh-v*, has pride of place in both contexts. The God of *ma'aseh merkavah* is the God whose existence is proven through metaphysics, not the personal God of the biblical narratives, the God of history.

The Names of God

Maimonides thus takes advantage of a text concerning the proper treatment of the weak and powerless (in this case, orphans and widows) to teach a lesson about which kind of God, as it were, protects those unfortunates and remind us we should emulate him. Maimonides was no less aware than Judah Halevi of the strain between the remote God of Aristotle and the personal God of the Patriarchs. In a famous passage in his *Kuzari*, Halevi writes in the name of the Khazar king:

The difference between *Elohim* and *YHVH* has now become clear to me, and I have also understood the difference between the God of Abraham and the God of Aristotle. One longs for *YHVH*, exalted be He, by way of savoring and witnessing for oneself, whereas one inclines towards *Elohim* by way of reasoning. Moreover, that [same] savoring calls upon the one who has experienced it to do the utmost for the sake of His love, and even [to prefer] death [to living] without Him, whereas the reasoning [which I just mentioned] makes one see that exalting Him is obligatory as long as one is not harmed and one does not undergo hardship because of it. Therefore, Aristotle should be excused for attaching no importance to the actions [associated with] the *nomos*, since he doubts whether God knows anything about that.[25]

In our chapter on the *Book of Knowledge*,[26] we showed how the first four chapters of 'Laws of the Foundations of the Torah'—the first four chapters of the *Mishneh torah* overall—can easily be construed as referring to the essentially minimalistic God of Aristotle, whose existence can be proven philosophically. In previous works Kellner has had occasion to show that this God is the deity discovered by Abraham, *Elohim* in Halevi's view, as opposed to *YHVH*, the more personal God whose Torah Moses brought to the Jewish people.[27]

Maimonides takes advantage of our text to annoy Leo Strauss, Shlomo Pines, and their followers by teaching that the metaphysical God of Aristotle (and of Abraham)[28]—the 'rider of the *aravot*'— is also 'the father of orphans,

---

[25] *Kuzari* iv. 16.   [26] See above, Ch. 1.   [27] *Maimonides' Confrontation*, 81–3.

[28] Judah Halevi contrasted the metaphysical God of Aristotle with the historical God of Abraham, Isaac, and Jacob. Maimonides, in opposition to this, presents the God of Abraham

the champion of widows'. Here is one of the many places in which Maimonides the philosopher and Rambam the rabbi show themselves to be the same person. Maimonides does this in two ways. First, he chooses as a prooftext verses in which 'the father of orphans, the champion of widows' is also called the 'rider of the *aravot*'. Then, instead of just citing the relevant portion of the passage, as he so often does, Maimonides cites most of the text, including apparently irrelevant portions: 'extol Him who rides the clouds; the Lord [*Yah*] is His name . . . the father of orphans, the champion of widows, God in His holy habitation.' There are three parts of this verse which could have been left out without weakening the argument:

- extol Him who rides the clouds
- the Lord [*Yah*] is His name
- God [*Elohim*] in His holy habitation [*beme'on kodesho*]

As we have seen in the texts cited above,[29] God as rider of the *aravot* is the God who dominates the heavens, especially the highest heaven encompassing the universe (*Elohim* in Halevi's terminology). This highest heaven is the sphere which revolves eternally, as Maimonides writes in 'Laws of the Foundations of the Torah' i: 5 and explains in *Guide* i. 71.[30] In that chapter, Maimonides goes on to explain that this domination of the heavens involves being the mover of the outermost sphere of the cosmos, while remaining at the same time entirely transcendent.[31] In this connection, as we have seen, Maimonides cites Deuteronomy 33: 27, glossing that verse to teach that God (*Elohim*) is distinct (transcendent) from the cosmos.[32] In that verse we also find the root *m-'-n*, which also appears in the prooftext used in our passage in 'Laws of Inheritance'.

What do we know about God's names, especially *Yah*? Maimonides

---

as being, in effect, the God of Aristotle. The existence of this God is proved through *hekhra hada'at* (see above, Ch. 7 n. 52)—'reasoning' in Halevi's terms from the paragraph quoted just above—in opposition to the God of history, known through 'savouring and witnessing'.

[29] *Guide* i. 70 (p. 171).

[30] (p. 182). Maimonides' description of the cosmos (in the first paragraphs of the *Mishneh torah*) as existing eternally without beginning or end in what we might call a 'steady state' would seem to stand in stark contrast with the rest of the book, which is all about divinely revealed commandments. We will return to this apparent contradiction at the end of this chapter.   [31] *Guide* i. 70 (pp. 172–3).

[32] He cites it in one other place, the fourth of his so-called 'Thirteen Principles', to prove that God, in the first 'edition' of that text, is logically antecedent to the universe, if not necessarily temporally antecedent to it. For discussion, see Kellner, *Dogma*, 53–61.

devotes several chapters in the first part of the *Guide* to a discussion of this matter.[33] He states,

All the names of God, may He be exalted, that are to be found in any of the books derive from actions. There is nothing secret in this matter. The only exception is the Name: namely, *yod, heh, vav, heh*. This is the name of God, may He be exalted, that has been originated without any derivation and for this reason it is called the articulated name [*shem hameforash*]. This means that this name gives a clear unequivocal indication of His essence, may He be exalted.[34]

Maimonides continues:

There can be no doubt about the fact that this great name . . . is indicative of a notion with reference to which there is no association between God, may He be exalted, and what is other than He. Perhaps it indicates the notion of a necessary existence. . . . As for the other names, all of them, because of their being derived, indicate attributes; that is, not an essence alone, but an essence possessing attributes.[35]

The Tetragrammaton names a wholly transcendent necessary existent; put simply, the philosophic God of Aristotle discovered through reason alone by Abraham.

But how can such a God be the author, not only of the cosmos, but also of the Torah and its commandments? Maimonides addresses that issue:

Accordingly, when God, may He be held sublime and magnified, revealed Himself to Moses our Master and ordered him to address a call to people and convey to them his prophetic mission, [Moses] said: the first thing they will ask of me is that I should make them acquire true knowledge that there exists a god with reference to the world; after that I shall make the claim that He has sent me. For at that time all the people except a few were not aware of the existence of the deity.[36]

Moses clearly thought that the Children of Israel were philosophers like himself, who would want proof of God's existence. It is at this stage that God tells Moses that His name is 'I am that I am' (Exod. 3: 14), a name derived from the verb 'to be', and which indicates 'a true notion of the existence of God'. This knowledge 'is what demonstration necessarily leads to: namely to the view that there is a necessarily existent thing that has never been, or ever will be, nonexistent'.

Skipping to the end of the chapter, we find Maimonides summarizing this point:

---

[33] *Guide* i. 61–4 (pp. 147–57). [34] *Guide* i. 61 (p. 147).
[35] Ibid. (p. 148). [36] *Guide* i. 63 (p. 154).

> Accordingly it has become clear to you that all names are derived or are used equivocally, as 'Rock' and others similar to it. He, may He be exalted, has no name that is not derivative except the name having four letters, which is the articulated name. This name is not indicative of an attribute but of simple existence and nothing else. Now absolute existence implies that He shall always be, I mean He who is necessarily existent. Understand the point at which this discourse has finally arrived.[37]

On the same page, Maimonides also informs us that 'The name *Yah* refers similarly to the notion of the eternity of existence.'

Once provided with proof that a transcendent necessarily existent deity exists, the Children of Israel will quite properly be perplexed (as were many of Maimonides' readers through the generations) as to how such a deity might be connected to concrete events taking place, to history, and to commandments. Thus Maimonides continues:

> Accordingly, when He, may He be exalted, made known to [Moses] the proofs that would establish His existence among their men of knowledge ... [Moses], peace be upon him, posed another question, saying: once they have accepted by means of these intellectual demonstrations the view that there is an existent deity, what shall be my proof that that this existent deity has sent me? Thereupon he was granted the miracle. Thus it has been made clear that the meaning of his saying, 'What is His name?' means only: who is He who you think has sent you?[38]

It is no surprise to learn that the rider of the *aravot*, knowledge concerning whom is the subject matter of metaphysics (*ma'aseh merkavah*), is named *Yah*, the necessary existent.

So far as we could discover, Maimonides makes no relevant use of the term *beme'on kodsho* in any of his writings.[39]

Transcendent and Manifest at Once

In previous chapters we have shown that while writing the *Mishneh torah* as, at the very least, a halakhic compendium (and perhaps more: as the halakhah itself, as Moshe Halbertal argues[40]) addressed to Jews, Maimonides also had a broader audience in mind, namely the whole human race, which would one day acknowledge the truth of the Torah. Here, in the penultimate section of his majestic book, Maimonides starts tying everything together before

---

[37] *Guide* i. 63, (p. 155).   [38] Ibid. (p. 156).
[39] We examined his use of verses in which the root *m-'-n* appears (using both Kafih, *The Hebrew Bible in Maimonides* (Heb.) and the Bar Ilan database).
[40] Halbertal, *Maimonides*, 181–96.

the grand finale, his strikingly universalist account of the messianic era. Maimonides here combines the universalist God of Aristotle with the more particularist God of history and Torah. But more than that, Maimonides may be teaching that the commandments of the Torah flow from the God of the philosophers (which, of course, brings us back to the very opening of the *Mishneh torah*).

As noted at the beginning of this chapter, this thirteenth book opens with a quotation of part of Genesis 21: 33: '[Abraham planted a tamarisk at Beersheba,] in the name of the Lord, God of the World'. Like the other fourteen books of the *Mishneh torah* this one also has a motto unique to it, Psalm 119: 7. This verse contains a reference to the title of the book (*Mishpatim*) and a hint to the effect that the book is about justice: 'I will praise you with a sincere heart as I learn Your just rules [*mishpetei tsidkekha*].' Here, too, we see Maimonides combining the unknowable, transcendent God of the cosmos with the God of the commandments of the Torah—God as manifest in the world.[41]

Summary

The *Book of Civil Laws* closes with an exhortation to legal guardians of orphans, urging them to take care to act with inner integrity, and to 'beware of the father of these orphans who rides upon the skies'. In this passage Maimonides writes as a rabbi and as a philosopher at once, indicating that the transcendent God of the philosophers ('who rides upon the skies') is also the immanent God of the Torah ('the father of these orphans'). Immediately before the next and final book of the *Mishneh torah*, which closes with a universalist vision for the messianic age, Maimonides presents the God of Abraham and the God of Aristotle as one and the same.

[41] See also Kaplan (ed.), *Maimonides: Between Philosophy and Halakhah*, 75–87.

FOURTEEN

JUDGES
Messianic Universalism

What Are the Two Final Chapters Doing in the *Mishneh Torah*?

The fourteenth and final book of the *Mishneh torah* is *Sefer shoftim*, the *Book of Judges*. It ends the entire *Mishneh torah* as well as the last four-book division of laws governing behaviour among human beings. The *Book of Judges* consists of five sections: 'Laws of the Sanhedrin', 'Laws of Testimony', 'Laws of the Rebellious Elders',[1] 'Laws of Mourning', and, closing this book and the work as a whole, 'Laws of Kings and their Wars'. Chapters 11 and 12 of this final section deal with the messianic king and the messianic era. With the startling exception of 'Laws of Mourning', all the sections deal with questions of how to order civil society and administer justice (one of the central tasks of the king).[2]

The closing two chapters—of the *Book of Judges* and of the *Mishneh torah*—are surprising in much the same way as the opening four chapters ('Laws of the Foundations of the Torah', 1–4). All six of these initial and final chapters deal with matters that had not been considered part of halakhah before Maimonides (and were rarely considered in this way after him). The first four chapters, however, contain references to specific commandments (to acknowledge God's existence and unity, to love God, to hold God in awe,

---

[1] i.e. members of the Sanhedrin who do not abide by its decisions.
[2] Maimonides' own explanation for why he included 'mourning' in this volume is hardly convincing: 'but no mourning is to be observed for those who have been condemned to death by the court; I have nevertheless included this treatise in this Book because it embodies the duty of burying the deceased on the day of death, which (as in the case of one who is executed by order of the court) is a positive commandment.' We cite here and below from the translation of Abraham Hershman (Yale Judaica Series), with many emendations. The passage just quoted is on p. 173. For further discussion of why Maimonides placed 'Laws of Mourning' here, see Gillis, *Reading Maimonides' Mishneh Torah*, 319–24. See also Aviram Ravitzky, 'Why Were the Laws of Mourning Introduced in the *Book of Judges*?' (Heb.), and Halbertal, *Maimonides*, 236–43.

and to deny idolatry, for example)—at least according to Maimonides' own list of commandments. The last two chapters do not. Moreover, Maimonides explicitly tells us that these two chapters deal with matters about which no one, not even the rabbinic Sages, can be certain, and that they do not deal with matters on which one should focus one's attention, implying that they are not matters of halakhah at all.[3] We propose that Maimonides added these two chapters for two main reasons.

The first reason has to do with symmetry between the beginning of the *Mishneh torah* and its end. Let us recall that, in our Introduction to this book, we pointed out that the codas that Maimonides added to each book of the *Mishneh torah* (and to many of its parts) have parallels in the codas with which Rabbi Judah the Prince, editor of the Mishnah, ended at least some mishnaic tractates; we also suggested that Rabbi Judah may have added tractate *Avot* to the Mishnah in order to demonstrate that the specific *halakhot* out of which the body of the Mishnah is composed are not the ultimate aim of the work. The ultimate aim of the Mishnah according to this reading is to create an individual who embodies the values described in *Avot*. There is no way of knowing if this was indeed Rabbi Judah's aim. Concerning Maimonides, however, there can be no question: for him the commandments are a tool.[4] The question must then be asked: a tool to accomplish what? The chapters of this book have been an attempt to answer that question.

Since the codas give us hints as to the moral, spiritual, and religious themes of individual books of the *Mishneh torah*, what do we learn from the coda of the book as a whole? Maimonides may or may not have intended the *Mishneh torah* to be a constitution for a messianic state or as a way of ushering in that state,[5] but there is little doubt that he believed that a world organized along the lines of the commandments of the Torah as presented in

---

[3] 'Laws of Kings and their Wars', 12: 2. This is hotly denied by followers of the late Lubavitcher Rebbe, who maintain that Maimonides' account of the messianic era at the end of the *Mishneh torah* (but not his account in *Perek ḥelek*) is to be taken as strictly halakhic and obligatory. See e.g. *A Booklet on Maimonides' Thought on the Messianic Era* (Heb.), published anonymously in Kefar Habad in 2007. See further Gottlieb, *Intellectualism in Hasidic Garb* (Heb.), 173–203.   [4] See above, especially Ch. 5 on the *Book of Holiness*.

[5] See Zeitlin, 'Maimonides', 80 and Yuval, 'Moses Redivivus' (Heb.), 172–5. See further Kraemer, 'On Maimonides' Messianic Posture', 110 and 114–16, and the sources cited there. Twersky himself points to other scholars who interpreted the *Mishneh torah* in this fashion in 'The *Mishneh Torah* of Maimonides', 271. Friedman, *Maimonides, the Yemenite Messiah, and Forced Conversion* (Heb.), 64–79, provides convincing evidence to the effect that when Maimonides wrote his *Epistle to Yemen* he took the imminent renewal of prophecy (the first stage of the messianic process) very seriously. This supports those who see the *Mishneh torah* as the intended constitution of a messianic government.

the *Mishneh torah* (emphatically including the first four chapters) would be a messianic world. The messianic world described at the end of the book is the world towards which the entire work aims. As we shall see in the present chapter, however, that messianic world itself is not an end, but a means towards another end, namely, achieving the world to come. For Maimonides, the key to the world to come is intellectual perfection (made possible but not necessary by antecedent moral perfection). The point of the *Mishneh torah* as a whole, then, is the creation of a society which gives its members the greatest chance of achieving their perfection as human beings. In this way, the end of the *Mishneh torah* comes round to its beginning: just as the beginning of the *Mishneh torah* deals with matters that relate to all human beings, so do the last chapters. Similarly, the *Guide* opens with an emphasis on intellectual perfection[6]—again, open in principle to all human beings—and closes with a focus on the imitation of God through doing 'loving-kindness, righteousness, and judgement in the earth'.[7] So also, the *Mishneh torah*'s establishment of a perfected society makes possible the achievement of philosophical perfection, which, in turn, enables highly perfected individuals to imitate God in the best way possible (and become as sanctified as the holy of holies).

As we will see in what follows, Maimonidean messianism is a process, not an event. It should thus surprise no one that there will be differences between the opening and closing stages of that process. Writing in the twelfth century, Maimonides envisioned the opening of that process in terms of warfare. The messianic king is no pacifist (at least not at the beginning of his career). Second, as will be argued below, the aim of the messianic process is to bring about a world that, as Isaiah prophesied, will be 'full of the knowledge of the Lord, as the waters cover the sea'.[8] Such an aim can only be achieved through teaching and persuasion, not through warfare. This is all the more the case when we recall that the ultimate aim of 'the knowledge of the Lord' is intellectual perfection, and consequent upon that, a share in the world to come.

We saw above in Chapter 1 how Maimonides sought to connect the end of the *Book of Knowledge* with its beginning. We see now how that this is also true of the beginning and the end of the *Mishneh torah* as a whole. The first four chapters of the *Mishneh torah* deal with matters (philosophical truth) that con-

---

[6] *Guide*, i. 1–2 (pp. 21–6).

[7] *Guide* iii. 54 (p. 638); the biblical verses cited here are Jer. 9: 22–3. See the argument for this interpretation in Kellner, *Maimonides on Human Perfection*. The closing verses and (Hebrew) poem of the *Guide* can also be read in a messianic light. On the poems in the *Guide*, see Zory, 'Notes on the Prefatory and Concluding Verses' (Heb.) and Kozodoy, 'Prefatory Verse'. See also n. 9.   [8] Isa. 11: 9.

cern all human beings and in that sense may be said to be addressed to all human beings. The final two chapters of the *Mishneh torah* deal with the world to be shared by all humans once they accept the truths taught in the first chapters of the work. Another way of putting this is to note that God's original intent was Abrahamic religion, the religion described in the first four chapters of the *Mishneh torah*.[9] God's aim was frustrated by the inability of Abraham's descendants and followers to remain steadfast to that religion.[10] The messianic world is the closest that the world as it actually is (and not as God would have liked it to be, as it were) can come to the Abrahamic faith.[11] Yet another way of putting this point (as pointed out to us by Avram Montag) is to see that the *Mishneh torah* prepares the groundwork for the *Guide of the Perplexed*. The *Mishneh torah* enables us to pursue the knowledge of God, the subject of the *Guide*.

We find a further symmetry between the beginning and end of the *Mishneh torah*. In the opening two sections of the first book, the *Book of Knowledge*, knowledge of God precedes *imitatio Dei*; in the closing two sections of the final book, the *Book of Judges*, *imitatio Dei*, as embodied in the acts of kindness prescribed by 'Laws of Mourning', precedes the universal knowledge of God with which the work concludes. This symmetry is expressive of the theme of restoration, especially as it reflects a similar symmetry within the *Book of Knowledge* itself, where love serves as a stimulus to knowledge in 'Laws of the Foundations of the Torah', matched by knowledge as a ladder back to love in 'Laws of Repentance'.[12]

Furthermore, a tension winds through all of Maimonides' writings—the tension between the individual and the community—and this leads us to

[9] One should recall Maimonides' penchant for using Gen. 21: 23 ('In the name of the Lord, God of the world') as a motto for his works. The *Mishneh torah* is meant to complete the work of Abraham in ridding the world of idolatry and bringing all humans to call 'in the name of the Lord', as Abraham sought to do.

[10] 'Laws of Idolatry', ch. 1 (quoted at length above in our Ch. 1), as adumbrated in Kellner, *Maimonides' Confrontation*, 77–84.

[11] Aviezer Ravitzky made a similar point; he connects the end of *Mishneh torah* with Maimonides' allegorical interpretation of Eden as opposed to connecting it to Abraham, as do we. For Ravitzky, the key to Maimonides' messianic vision 'is to be found precisely in Maimonides' allegorical interpretation of the story of the Garden of Eden in the opening chapters of the *Guide* . . . the opening of human history is united with its final perfection . . . the universal redemption of the human race . . . refers in fact to man's return to his original stature represented by the human archetype.' See Ravitzky, 'To the Utmost of Human Capacity', 230–3.

[12] For more on this, see Gillis, *Reading Maimonides' Mishneh Torah*, 323. Kraemer (above, n. 5) also notes that both the *Mishneh torah* and the *Guide* begin and end 'on the theme of knowledge, specifically the knowledge of God' (p. 115).

the second reason for Maimonides to add these two chapters. A good way of illustrating the tension between individual and society is to recall Maimonides' brief comments on the Song of Songs, elaborated after him in great detail by Gersonides.[13] Rabbinic tradition sees the Song of Songs as a paean of love between God and the people of Israel. Maimonides sees the Song of Songs as an expression of the individual's yearning for personal intellectual (hence, human) perfection. The first four chapters of the *Mishneh torah* are all about that individual search for perfection. The last two chapters shift the focus from individuals seeking their own perfection to a society of such individuals. One is tempted to say that just as Maimonides the Jew overwhelms Maimonides the philosopher at the end of the *Guide of the Perplexed*, so Maimonides the Jew overwhelms Maimonides the philosopher at the end of the *Mishneh torah*, focusing, not on individual perfection, but on perfected society.

The Messiah in the *Commentary on the Mishnah* and Elsewhere in the *Mishneh Torah*

In this chapter we will expand our vision, focusing not only on the last paragraph of the book under discussion (as we have done in earlier chapters), but upon the entire rousing finale of the *Mishneh torah*, 'Laws of Kings and their Wars', chapters 11 and 12. This is made necessary by the fact that in the case of each of the previous books, the added coda was generally the last *halakhah*. In the present case, it is the last two chapters as a whole. These chapters, in turn, lead to the final, culminating *halakhah*, 'Laws of Kings and their Wars', 12: 5.[14]

First, however, we will briefly examine what Maimonides says about the nature of the messianic era in his other writings.[15] Our focus here will be on the messianic era itself, not the processes leading up to it.[16] Messianism is a

---

[13] For Maimonides, see Diamond, *Maimonides and the Shaping of the Jewish Canon*, 52–61; on Gersonides, see id., *Commentary on Song of Songs*.

[14] The end of the *Mishneh torah* has drawn the attention of many scholars. Among them, Don Seeman sees the conclusion of the work, like the *Guide* according to his reading of it, as marking 'a transition from political to intellectual perfection'. He then asks, 'Is it too much to suggest that Maimonides here frames the *Guide* itself as an act of virtue friendship *par excellence*?' See Seeman, 'Maimonides and Friendship', 23.

[15] To our surprise, and despite all that has been written on Maimonides' messianism, we have found no systematic survey of his statements on the subject. Many of the texts summarized here are presented and analysed in Kellner, 'And the Crooked Shall Be Made Straight'.

[16] On that issue, see Kellner, 'Messianic Postures in Israel Today'.

process which takes place in the world as we know it.[17] There are steps leading to the messianic advent, and after the messiah's coming the process must continue to its eventual fruition. After presenting and analysing Maimonides' statements on the nature of the messianic era, we will point out, following what we have learned from Steven Schwarzschild (who always insisted that he was only following Hermann Cohen), if not necessarily from Maimonides himself, that ends should determine means. That being the case, if we can show that Maimonides anticipated a messianic era characterized by enlightenment[18] and (therefore) peace, we can then point out to him (whatever he himself may have thought in the midst of the Crusades) that war will never achieve that end.

Maimonides' earliest messianic statement is in his introduction to the tenth chapter of the mishnaic tractate *Sanhedrin*, known as *Perek ḥelek*.[19] The

---

[17] This is an important point, not only because it makes Orthodox Zionism possible. While Maimonides rarely specifies the precise stages of the messianic process, to read him as if everything happens at once, *behese'aḥ hada'at* (BT *San.* 97a), as it were, is radically to misunderstand him. He expects the messianic process to *unfold* within nature as we know it. For the connection between Maimonides' messianism and Orthodox Zionism, see Kellner, 'Messianic Postures in Israel Today'.

[18] There is an interesting debate between Hermann Cohen and his followers, on the one hand, and Leo Strauss and his followers, on the other hand, over how extensive Maimonides thought messianic enlightenment could be. Cohen's position is much more optimistic than that of Strauss. For Cohen, see Schwarzschild, 'Moral Radicalism and "Middlingness"'; for Strauss, see Kochin, 'Morality, Nature, and Esotericism'.

[19] A Hebrew translation of Maimonides' text may be found in Maimonides, *Hakdamot*. For English translations, see *Maimonides' Commentary on the Mishnah, Tractate Sanhedrin*, trans. Rosner, 147–8; and Twersky, *A Maimonides Reader*, 414–16. Here are the main points in the text (quoted from the translation in Twersky, with emphases added):

> The days of the messiah refers to the time when sovereignty will *return* to Israel, and the people of Israel will *return* to the Land of Israel. The king will reign at that time from his royal capital Zion [= Jerusalem]. His name will be renowned to the very ends of the earth, and his kingdom will be greater even than Solomon's. All the nations will make peace with him, and the states will all obey him *because* of his great righteousness; he will be seen to work wonders and all who rise against him—God will cut them off and deliver them to his hand.... Nothing that now exists will be changed, other than the fact that Israel will be sovereign ... The great advantage of that era will be that we will be relieved of *subjugation* to evil kingdom[s] which prevents us from achieving all the virtues; *wisdom* will increase ... Strife and war will end ... One who lives at that time will achieve great perfection and *through it* merit life in the world to come.... The messiah will die, and he will be succeeded by his son and grandson.... His kingdom will last for a very great time, and the life spans of human beings will be increased as well, for when sorrows and tribulations disappear, life is lengthened. It is entirely possible that his kingdom might last for even thousands of years, since, as the wise have pointed out that

following issues in that text need to be emphasized: Maimonides' vision is restorative, not utopian. From this it follows that the messianic era will in principle be not unlike the present world. Hollywood will not be called upon for special effects. Since the messianic era is constituted by the reconstitution of a past golden age, it is possible to find our way forward to what once was in the past (not 'Back to the Future' but 'Forward to the Past') without miracles, and nature will therefore continue in its accustomed patterns (as Maimonides makes clear in a text to be cited below), and hence the messianic era must be brought about through human effort.[20] Note well: in this text Maimonides says, 'The days of the messiah refers to the time when sovereignty will return to Israel, and the people of Israel will return to the Land of Israel.' Nowhere does he say that God will send the messiah; rather, he implies, it is up to humans to bring the messiah. From this it follows (and Maimonides will make this clear as well) that the coming of the messiah is a process, not an event. This passage repeatedly focuses on political freedom and sovereignty. But peace and freedom from subjugation are not ends in themselves; they are means towards the constitution of a world in which virtue is cultivated. Even morality is not the end. Rather, morality is a means towards the achievement of wisdom, and wisdom is the only key to earning a share in the world to come. For Maimonides, even in the messianic era one lives one's life in deferment, as it were,[21] looking forward to the ultimate end of human existence, the bodiless contemplation of eternal verities.[22] This point is important to emphasize, since many of our contemporaries (mis)read Maimon-

---

a highly perfected polity, once organized, will not easily fall apart . . . The days of the messiah were not desired so that grain and money be increased, nor so that we ride on horses, nor drink at musical parties as those with confused minds think. Rather, the prophets desired the days of the messiah and the righteous yearned for them, in that they would be characterized by perfected society, excellent governance, wisdom, the righteousness of the king, his great wisdom, and his nearness to his Creator . . . [The prophets and righteous further desired the days of the messiah because they would be characterized by] the fulfillment of the entire Torah of Moses without weakness, worry, or *compulsion*.

[20] For examples of this effort, see David Berger's discussion of Maimonides on the renewal of rabbinic ordination (*semikhah*) and the re-establishment of the Sanhedrin in 'Some Ironic Consequences'.

[21] Borrowing Gershom Scholem's famous expression in his essay, 'Toward an Understanding of the Messianic Idea in Judaism', 35.

[22] This is not the place to go into the question of whether or not Maimonides actually thought that such eternal life was truly possible. For a recent summary of the scholarly wrangle over this, see J. Stern, 'Maimonides' Epistemology'.

ides as teaching that the point of the messianic era is Jewish sovereignty over the (whole) Land of Israel (not to mention dominion over it).[23]

By way of emphasizing messianic naturalism, and by way of countering Christian messianism, Maimonides stresses that the messiah will die and will be succeeded by his son and further descendants. He then makes the unusual claim that the messianic kingdom will last for a very long time, *but not forever*.[24] This last point is of capital importance, since it explains why the Torah, including the sacrificial cult, must remain undisturbed in the messianic era. As Kenneth Seeskin has argued, for Maimonides idolatry is an ever-present threat.[25] Idolatry consists in worship of anything other than God; the objects of idolatry may or may not be idols of wood, clay, or metal—they might be 'American idols'. Since the messianic era will not last forever (another expression of Maimonides' naturalism, and his desire to keep his messianism on a low flame), the Torah, as antidote to idolatry, must be preserved in all its specificity even during the messianic era—when, presumably, no one will be tempted to worship idols—against the day when that temptation will once again rear its head.[26]

In the continuation of this passage, Maimonides counters other mistaken views of the nature of the messianic era and explains its true significance. The point of the this-worldly messianic era is to make it more likely that one achieves a share in the immaterial and eternal world to come. How so? In a well-governed society, ruled by a wise, righteous, and devout king, the Torah can be obeyed 'without weakness, worry, or compulsion'. In a way typical of Maimonides, such obedience is not presented as an end in itself but, rather, as a means for achieving a share in the world to come.

At the end of his introduction to *Perek ḥelek*, Maimonides presents his Thirteen Principles of faith, of which the twelfth reads:

---

[23] For an influential example, see Aviner, *Maimonides' Laws Concerning the Messiah* (Heb.), 26. [24] But Maimonides seems to withdraw from this position in *Guide*, ii. 29 (p. 341).

[25] Seeskin, *No Other Gods*.

[26] It is also possible that here Maimonides is countering views later articulated by Nahmanides (1194–1270), according to which there is an 'era of Torah' that ends with the transition from this world (*olam hazeh*) to the coming world (*olam haba*). See Nahmanides, *Disputation at Barcelona*, para. 40 (in *Ramban: Writings and Discourses*, ii. 669), and his commentary on Gen. 2: 9. Nahmanides' views were articulated in response to Maimonides, but they can also be seen as reflecting traditional views that came before Maimonides. In 'The Gate of Reward' (*Sha'ar hagemul*) Nahmanides defends the plain meaning of *olam hazeh* and *olam haba* as successive eras by gathering textual evidence that the Sages used them in this way, and not as Maimonides understood them (for Maimonides 'this world' exists parallel in time to 'the coming world', but the latter is fully experienced by humans only after death); see *Ramban: Writings and Discourses*, ii. 419–551.

The twelfth foundation is the days of the messiah; to wit, the belief in, and the assertion of, the truth of his coming. He shall not be a long time, 'and if he tarries, wait for him' [Hab. 2: 3]. No time for his coming may be set nor may the verses of Scripture be interpreted to reveal the time of his coming, as our Sages have said, 'Blasted be the bones of those who reckon out the end.'[27] One must believe in him by praising him, loving him, and praying for his coming according to that which has been revealed by all the prophets from Moses to Malachi. He who doubts, or treats this command lightly, says that the Torah, which promised his coming specifically in the weekly readings of 'Bilam' and 'Atem nitsavim',[28] is lying. One of the general ideas of this foundation is that Israel will have no king except from David, and that he will be descended especially from the seed of Solomon.[29] Whoever disobeys the command of this dynasty denies God and the verses of the prophets.[30]

Maimonides does not add much to his earlier discussion; here his aim is to strengthen belief in the eventual messianic advent, not to describe the world that the messiah will usher in. However, he does repeat his anti-Christian emphasis on a messianic *dynasty*.

Maimonides' most extensive discussion of the messianic era is found in his *Mishneh torah*, towards the beginning (in 'Laws of Repentance') and in our passage at the very end of the book. The issue comes up in 'Laws of Repentance' in a discussion of the rewards promised for the fulfilment of the commandments. In 'Laws of Repentance', 9: 1, Maimonides explains that the blessings promised for obedience to the commandments are not ends in themselves; rather, they are means so that individuals 'grow wise in Torah and engage in it[s study], *in order* that [they] attain to the life of the world to come.'[31] Life in the world to come is the ultimate aim; obedience to the Torah makes it more likely that one will earn a share in the world to come. This is so since, for Maimonides, intellectual perfection cannot be attained by someone who is undisciplined, dissolute, and immoral. The Torah, being God-given, is the *best* route to moral perfection.[32] It is in this context that Maimonides

---

[27] BT *San.* 97b. Maimonides is notorious for having himself violated this proscription. See his *Epistle to Yemen*, 125 and Friedman, *Maimonides, the Yemenite Messiah, and Forced Conversion* (Heb.), 50–63. There are some textual issues with the citation from *Sanhedrin*, but they do not affect the meaning and will be ignored here.

[28] i.e. Num. 22: 5–25: 9 and Deut. 29: 9–30: 2.

[29] *Contra* the account of Jesus's ancestry at Luke 3: 31.

[30] I cite David Blumenthal's translation as found in Kellner, *Must a Jew Believe Anything?*, 173.

[31] Emphasis added in order to stress the instrumental character of the commandments.

[32] But not necessarily the only route, Maimonides would be forced to admit. For discussion of the relationship between moral and intellectual perfection in his thought, see Kellner,

turns to a discussion of the messianic era. In effect, he has to answer the following question: if the ultimate aim is the world to come, why are all the Torah's promised rewards this-worldly?[33] Maimonides explains that the point of the messianic era is to enable Israel (which by the time the process reaches fruition should mean all humanity, as hinted by the citation from Isaiah 11: 9[34]) to 'engage with the Torah and commandments *properly*,[35] and to acquire composure and grow in wisdom, [in order] to attain to the life of the world to come'. The defining characteristic of the messianic era is that 'knowledge, wisdom and truth will abound'. It is the job of the messianic king, wiser than Solomon and a prophet almost as great as Moses, to bring this about. Maimonides takes the opportunity to reaffirm the naturalistic character of the messianic era (and advent): the world will follow its normal course. In the messianic era pain-free low-cholesterol steaks will not grow on trees, and we will still need to have rubbish collected and plumbing repaired.

'Laws of Kings and their Wars', 11-12

This emphasis on the natural course of events in the messianic era is the point with which Maimonides chooses to open the twelfth and last chapter of the last book of the *Mishneh torah*. But before looking at that text, we must examine what he says in the eleventh, penultimate chapter of the work:

King messiah will arise and *restore* the kingdom of David to its *former* state and *original* sovereignty. He will *rebuild* the sanctuary and gather the dispersed of Israel. All the ancient laws will be *reinstituted* in his days; sacrifices will *again* be offered;

Maimonides on Human Perfection and Kellner, *Maimonides' Confrontation*, index, s.v. 'perfection, intellectual and moral'. This relationship has come up throughout our book, as we examined the commandments in terms of their contribution to moral perfection and their universal goal of intellectual perfection.

[33] This is a question which exercised many Jewish thinkers. See, for example, the discussion of Isaac Abravanel, *Commentary on Leviticus* (Heb., pp. 306–11), and Rosenbloom, 'Rationale for the Omission of Eschatology from the Bible'.

[34] This verse, quoted below, closes 'Laws of Kings and their Wars' and the *Mishneh torah* as a whole. For an argument supporting the interpretation proposed here, see Kellner, 'Maimonides' True Religion'. See also the surprisingly universalist sources cited by Kimelman, '*Lekha Dodi*' and *Kabalat Shabat* (Heb.), ch. 4.

[35] We emphasize this word since we see here a hint towards Maimonides' doctrine (on which, see Kellner, *Maimonides' Confrontation*, 59–66) that formal fulfilment of the commandments by itself carries no reward. The *proper* fulfilment of the commandments must both lead to and follow from intellectual perfection, which latter is the key to achieving a share in the world to come.

the sabbatical and jubilee years will *again* be observed in accordance with the commandments set forth in the Law.[36]

Maimonides thus opens his account of the messianic era by emphasizing its restorative character. The messiah will re-establish what once was and thus miracles will not be necessary. The non-miraculous restoration of what once was must be a process, not an event. As such, it is a challenge to those alive at that time to help the process forward. The messiah is thus a *king* (a purely human figure) who will *restore* the kingdom of David to its former glory. He will *rebuild* the Temple in Jerusalem (i.e. it will not drop down from heaven fully formed, flattening in one second the Dome of the Rock)[37] and after that gather the dispersed of Israel, reinstituting all the laws connected with the Temple, especially sacrifices and the sabbatical and jubilee years.[38]

Apparently aware of claims that eschatology is a late import into Judaism, Maimonides insists that the coming of the messiah is taught in the Torah itself, and not just in the later prophetic writings:

> He who does not believe in him or does not look forward to the coming of the messiah denies not only the Prophets but also the Torah and Moses, our teacher, for Scripture testifies to him, as it is said: 'Then the Lord thy God will turn thy captivity, and have compassion upon thee, and will return and gather thee . . . if any of thine that are dispersed be in the uttermost parts of heaven . . . and the Lord thy God will bring thee into the land which thy fathers possessed' [Deut. 30: 3, 4, 5]. These words explicitly stated in Scripture include that which all the Prophets said. This is correct also with respect to the section treating of Balaam. The prophecy in that section bears upon the two messiahs: the first, namely, David, who saved Israel from the hand of their enemies; and the later messiah, a descendant of David, who will achieve the final salvation of Israel.[39]

---

[36] Emphases here are, of course, ours, not Maimonides', who had to work without the assistance of Bill Gates or Steve Jobs, who have both eased and frustrated our lives.

[37] On this motif, see Aptowitzer, 'The Celestial Temple as Viewed in the Aggadah', and Berger, 'Some Ironic Consequences', 85–7.

[38] Given the way that thinkers like Hermann Cohen wanted to see these laws as anticipations of democratic socialism, it would be nice to think that Maimonides included them here to make such thinkers happy. See Schwarzschild, 'The Democratic Socialism of Hermann Cohen'.

[39] For the sake of completeness and some further points, here is the full passage:

There it is said: 'I see him, but not now' [Num. 24: 17], this refers to David; 'I behold him, but not nigh' [ibid.], this refers to King messiah. 'There shall step forth a star out of Jacob' [ibid.], this refers to David; 'And a sceptre shall rise out of Israel' [ibid.], this refers to King messiah. 'And shall smite through the corners of Moab' [ibid.], this refers to David, for we are told: 'And he smote Moab, and measured them with the line' [2 Sam. 8: 2]; 'and break down all the sons of Seth' [Num. 24: 17], this refers to King messiah, as it is

Maimonides casually introduces a very important point here. By his day, the notion of two messiahs had become a staple of messianic apocalypticism: messiah ben Ephraim, who would die in a titanic battle against the forces of evil, at which point all would appear to be lost, leaving only a small 'saving remnant' to welcome the true messiah ben David.[40] Quietly and nonchalantly, Maimonides undermines that entire view in a few sentences, reaffirming the naturalistic, non-apocalyptic nature of his messianism.

Having laid out the broad outlines of his naturalistic messianic doctrine, and having proved to his satisfaction that the messiah is promised in the Pentateuch, and not only in the prophetic works, Maimonides hastens to insist further on the naturalistic, this-worldly nature of the messianic advent:

> Do not think that King messiah will have to perform signs and wonders, bring anything new into being, revive the dead, or do similar things which the fools talk about. It is not so. Rabbi Akiba was a great sage, one of the sages of the Mishnah, yet he was also the armour-bearer of Koziba the King [= Bar Kokhba]. He affirmed that the latter was King messiah; he and all the wise men of his generation thought that was so until he [Koziba] was slain because of iniquity. Since he was killed, it became known that he was not the messiah. Yet the Rabbis had not asked him for a sign or token. The general principle [*ikar hadevarim*] is: this Torah [of ours] with its statutes and ordinances [is not subject to change]. They stand forever and to all eternity; they are not to be added to or to be taken away from. Whoever adds aught to it, or takes away aught from it, or misinterprets it, and strips the commandments of their literal sense, is certainly a wicked man, and an *epikoros*.

> written concerning him: 'And his dominion shall be from sea to sea' [Zech. 9: 10]. 'And Edom shall be a possession' [Num. 24: 18], this refers to David, as it is written: 'And all the Edomites became servants to David' [2 Sam. 8: 14]; 'And Seir shall be a possession' [Num. 24: 18], this refers to (the days of) King messiah, as it is written: 'And saviours shall come up on Mount Zion to judge the mount of Esau' [Obad. 1: 21]. So too, with reference to the cities of refuge, the Bible says: 'And if the Lord thy God enlarge thy borders . . . then thou shalt add three cities more for thee' [Deut. 19: 8, 9]—a precept which has never been carried out. Yet not in vain did the Holy One, blessed be He, give us this commandment. As for the prophetic utterances on the subject [of the messiah], no citations are necessary, as all their books are full of this theme.

We thus see that Maimonides foresees the need for cities of refuge in the messianic world—that means he anticipated that accidental killings would take place, and the relatives of those accidentally killed would seek to exact blood vengeance from those responsible for the death of their relations. The human world as we know it will certainly be improved, but not changed beyond recognition.

[40] For an entry into this world, see Sa'adiah Gaon's account of the messianic advent in his *Book of Beliefs and Opinions*, treatise 8 and 'The Scroll of Zerubavel' (one of Sa'adiah's sources) in Stern and Mirsky, *Rabbinic Fantasies*.

Proof that the messiah is not expected to perform miracles is provided by Rabbi Akiva's support of Bar Kokhba. This, and the way in which it is phrased, is truly surprising. The more standard reading of rabbinic texts has Bar Kokhba rejected by the overwhelming majority of the rabbis who ultimately executed him,[41] as noted in the gloss of Rabbi Abraham ben David on this passage.

Particularly noteworthy is Maimonides' separation between the messiah and resurrection, a point repeated in his *Treatise on Resurrection*: the two simply have nothing to do with each other. The important point to remember in all this, Maimonides insists, is that the Torah and all its laws 'stand forever and to all eternity'. Not only does Maimonides here stake out a stance against the antinomian nature of Christian messianism; he may also have been aware of positions, later adumbrated by Nahmanides and other kabbalists, that the era of Torah will be brought to an end by the coming of the messiah.[42] For Maimonides, the messianic era is this-worldly (belonging to *olam hazeh*)— and this world will never end[43]—while for Nahmanides it is other-worldly (belonging to *olam haba*).[44]

Maimonides emphasizes the naturalistic, this-worldly, and fundamentally normal, political nature of his messianism at the beginning of *halakhah* 4. Here we are told that the proof of the messianic pudding is in the eating thereof. A saintly Davidic king might arise who tries, but fails, to be the messiah. This is no defect in such a king:

If there arise a king from the House of David who meditates on the Torah, occupies himself with the commandments, as did his ancestor David, observes the precepts prescribed in the Written and the Oral Torah, forces [*vayekhof*] Israel to walk in the way of the Torah and to repair its breaches, and fights the battles of the Lord, it may be assumed that he is the messiah. If he does these things and succeeds, defeats the nations around him, rebuilds the sanctuary on its site, and gathers the dispersed of Israel, he is beyond all doubt the messiah. But if he does not meet with full success,

---

[41] BT *San.* 93b.   [42] See above, n. 26.

[43] Scholars are divided on the question whether for Maimonides the universe will ever come to an end. For the debate, see Feldman, 'The End of the Universe' and Weiss, 'Maimonides on the End of the World'.

[44] Maimonides was not a prophet (*contra* Abraham Joshua Heschel) and thus could have been unaware, while writing these passages, that he would later, in *Guide* iii. 32 (pp. 525–31), give some readers reason to think that he did not anticipate the renewal of the sacrificial cult in the messianic era. Compare our discussion above concerning the limited time-frame of the messianic era. For Heschel on Maimonides' prophetic aspirations, see his 'Prophetic Inspiration in the Middle Ages'. On *Guide* iii. 32 and how it relates to the structure and message of the *Mishneh torah*, see our extensive discussion above in Ch. 10.

or is slain, it will be known that he is not the messiah promised in the Torah. He is [to be regarded] like all the other wholehearted and worthy kings of the House of David who died and whom the Holy One, blessed be He, raised up to test the multitude, as it is written, 'Some of the knowledgeable will fail, that they may be refined and purged and whitened until the time of the end, for an interval still remains until the appointed time' [Dan. 11: 35].

The normal and political context of the messianic era is stressed here. Maimonides anticipates the restoration of the monarchy independently of the coming of the messiah.

Maimonides now takes the opportunity, in a passage censored in most printed editions of the *Mishneh torah*, to explain the careers of Jesus and Mohammed in ways which confirm the truth of Jewish messianic claims.[45] This text is germane to our discussion, even though it does not further illuminate Maimonides' ideas on the *nature* of the messianic era, and it is also of great intrinsic interest.

Even of Jesus of Nazareth, who imagined that he was the messiah, and was put to death by the court, Daniel had prophesied, as it is written, 'And the children of the violent among thy people shall lift themselves up to establish the vision; but they shall stumble' [Dan. 11: 14]. For has there ever been a greater stumbling-block than this? All the prophets affirmed that the messiah would redeem Israel, save them, gather their dispersed, and strengthen [observance of] the commandments. But he [Jesus] caused Israel to be destroyed by the sword, their remnant to be dispersed and humiliated. He was instrumental in changing the Torah and causing the world to err and serve another beside God. But it is beyond the human mind to fathom the designs of the Creator; for our ways are not His ways, neither are our thoughts His thoughts. All these matters relating to Jesus of Nazareth, and the Ishmaelite [Mohammed] who came after him, only serve to clear the way for King messiah, to prepare [*letaken*] the whole world to worship God with one accord,[46] as it is written, 'For then will I turn to the peoples a pure language, that they all call upon the name of the Lord to serve Him with one consent' [Zeph. 3: 9]. How so? The messianic hope, the Torah, and the commandments have become familiar topics—topics of conversation [among the inhabitants] of the far isles and many people, uncircumcised of heart and flesh. They are discussing these matters and the commandments of the Torah. Some say, 'Those commandments were true, but have lost their validity and are no longer binding'; others declare that they had an esoteric meaning and were not to be taken literally; that the messiah has already come and revealed their

---

[45] On this passage, and for proof of its authenticity, see the analysis by Goldfeld, 'The Laws of Kings' (Heb.). See also Hershman, 'Textual Problems'.

[46] Compare the *Aleinu* prayer: *letaken olam bemalkhut shadai* 'to establish the world under the sovereignty of God'. On Maimonides' use of the now trite expression *tikun olam*, see M. Lorberbaum, 'Maimonides on *Tikun olam*' (Heb.).

occult significance. But when the true King messiah will appear and succeed, be exalted and lifted up, they will forthwith recant and realize that they have inherited nothing but lies from their fathers, that their prophets and forebears led them astray.

In a passage which anticipates Franz Rosenzweig, Maimonides affirms that Christianity and Islam have crucial roles in the messianic advent.[47] Since the task of the messiah is 'to prepare the *whole* world to worship God with *one accord*', and since, as he often stresses, no miracles are to be involved, for the messiah to come the world must be monotheized, as it were. That is the role assigned by God(!) to Christianity and to Islam.[48] Here again we see that messianism is a historical process, not an event, and that its culmination must involve universal enlightenment.[49] Note also how the verse from Zephaniah contrasts with the story of the Tower of Babel, anticipating a time when peace reigns because all people speak one language (presumably Hebrew, not Esperanto).

Having dealt with Christianity and Islam, Maimonides turns, in the final, climactic chapter of the *Mishneh torah*, to the main contours of the messianic era. In the first paragraph of the last chapter of the *Mishneh torah*,[50] he writes:

Let it not enter your mind that in the days of the messiah any aspect of the regular order of nature will be abolished or some innovation will be introduced into the world of nature; rather, the world follows its accustomed course. The verse in Isaiah [11: 6], 'The wolf shall dwell with the lamb, the leopard lie down with the kid' is an allegory and metaphor. Its meaning is that Israel will dwell in security with [those who were] the wicked nations of the earth, which are allegorically represented as wolves and leopards, as it says [Jer. 5: 6]: 'the wolf of the desert ravages them. A leopard lies in wait by their towns.' Those nations will all adopt the true religion [*dat ha'emet*]. [In consequence,] they will neither rob not destroy; rather, they will eat permitted foods in peace and quiet as[51] Israelites, as it says, 'the lion, like the ox, shall eat straw'.[52] All similar things written about the messiah are allegories, and

---

[47] It may be significant that Nahmanides cites this passage without comment. See *Ramban: Writings and Discourses*, i. 39–40.

[48] Maimonides condemned Christianity as idolatry, but acknowledged Christian acceptance of the idea of Torah and commandments. See Lasker, 'Tradition and Innovation in Maimonides' Attitude towards Other Religions' (Heb.) and the studies cited there.

[49] One can well imagine that this passage was offensive to Christians and Muslims ('what, our role is only to facilitate the Jewish messiah's coming?!') and to many medieval Jews ('what, our oppressors have a role in the messiah's coming!?'); many had reason to censor Maimonides here.   [50] 'Laws of Kings and their Wars', 12: 1.

[51] Following the text in Makbili's edition of the *Mishneh torah*; printed editions and some manuscripts read: 'with'.

[52] Note that according to this prooftext, the lion and the ox eat the *same* food. For an alter-

in the days of the messianic king everyone will understand which matters were allegories, and also the meaning hinted at by them.

What does the expression *dat ha'emet* mean in this context? In a number of places Menachem Kellner has argued that Maimonides means that in the messianic era (or, more accurately, by the time it reaches fruition since it is, after all, a process and not an event) all human beings will worship God from a position of absolute spiritual equality.[53] Whether that means that all non-Jews will convert formally to Judaism,[54] that they will be absorbed into Israel in some other fashion, or that the distinction will become in some way significantly less important than it is now,[55] is open to question. What is clear is that the distinction between Jew and non-Jew will disappear by the time that the messianic process has reached completion.[56] In making this claim, we stand opposed to those who interpret Maimonides in a more particularist

native reading of this paragraph, according to which messianic non-Jews fulfil the seven Noahide commandments but remain non-Jews, see Rappoport, 'Critique of M. Kellner'.

[53] See Kellner, 'Maimonides' True Religion'.

[54] As Kellner argues in *Maimonides on Judaism and the Jewish People*, 39–58. Maimonides was not alone in this view. See the surprising number of kabbalists who also looked forward to a redemption characterized by wholesale conversion to Judaism, cited by Kimelman, *'Lekha Dodi' and Kabalat Shabat* (Heb.), ch. 4. Maimonides' son Abraham probably understood his father in much the way we present him here:

> And the meaning of 'a kingdom of priests' [Exod. 19: 6] is that the priest of a congregation is its leader, for he is its most honoured member and serves as its model, inasmuch as the members of the congregation will walk in his footsteps and through him will find the straight path. Thus, God said, 'You, by observing My commandments, will become the leaders of the world. Your relationship to them [the nations of the world] will be like the relationship of the priest to his congregation. All the world will follow in your wake, they will imitate your actions, and walk in your path.' This is the understanding that I received as the explanation of this verse from my father and master, of blessed memory.

See Abraham ben Maimonides, *Commentary on Genesis and Exodus*, 303 (Arabic original) and 302 (Hebrew trans.) (this book is available for download on hebrewbooks.org).

The term 'Judaism' sounds anachronistic—it is clearly a 19th-century coinage. But it is also clear from his writings that Maimonides had a conception of something that we now call Judaism as distinguished from what we now call Christianity and Islam, even if he did not use those precise terms. If nothing else, his use of the term *dat emet* instead of *torat emet* is an indication of this. Maimonides may or may not have been the first Jewish thinker to use the term *dat* in the sense of 'religion' (as opposed to 'law', its biblical meaning), but he certainly did so extensively. His claim that Judaism has a firm dogmatic basis is a reflection of his understanding of Judaism as a religion. On this, see Melamed, *'Religion': From Law to Religion* (Heb.). We previously broached this topic in Ch. 11.

[55] Blidstein, *Political Concepts* (Heb.), 245–8.

[56] It is not clear to us that Maimonides himself addressed this question self-consciously; it may have been among the things he expected would be clarified after the coming of the messiah, issues about which he will counsel us below not to spend time wondering.

fashion, according to which even at the end of days for Maimonides the Jews will remain God's chosen people, especially beloved, and distinct from the mass of humanity. We also stand opposed to those who might want to read Maimonides in a pluralist fashion, as if he holds that in the messianic era many different paths will lead equally to God.[57] Rather, we read him as a messianic universalist.

We thus see that Maimonides chooses to open his only extended discussion of the messianic era in a strictly halakhic context[58] with an emphasis on messianic universalism and messianic naturalism. This can hardly be an accident.

The next topic Maimonides takes up in this chapter is the nature of the messianic advent:

Said the Rabbis: The sole difference between the present world and the messianic days is delivery from servitude to foreign powers [BT *San.* 91b].[59] Taking the words of the Prophets in their literal sense, it appears that the inauguration of the messianic era will be marked by the war of Gog and Magog; that prior to that war, a prophet will arise to guide Israel and set their hearts aright, as it is written: 'Behold, I will send you Elijah the prophet' [Mal. 3: 23]. He [Elijah] will come neither to declare the clean unclean, nor the unclean clean; neither to disqualify those who are presumed to be of legitimate descent, nor to pronounce qualified those who are presumed to be of illegitimate descent, but to bring peace in the world, as it is said: 'And he shall turn the hearts of the fathers to the children' [Mal. 3: 24]. Some of our Sages say that the coming of Elijah will precede the advent of the King messiah. But no one is in a position to know the details of this and similar things until they have come to pass. They are not explicitly stated by the Prophets. Nor have the Sages any tradition with regard to these matters. They are guided solely by what the scriptural texts seem to imply. Hence there is a divergence of opinion on the subject. But be

---

[57] Raphael Jospe points to Netanel ibn al-Fayyumi (Yemen, c.1165) as a medieval Jew who held a pluralist view of religious revelation. This is surely a case of an exception proving a rule. For sources and discussion, see the debate between Jospe on the one hand and Jolene and Menachem Kellner on the other; Jospe, 'Pluralism out of the Sources of Judaism' and J. and M. Kellner, 'Respectful Disagreement'. The philosopher cited by Halevi at the beginning of the *Kuzari* might be cited as an example of a medieval religious pluralist, but that is surely a mistake: his pluralism consists in saying that all religions are equally false, not equally true.

[58] Followers of Habad make much of this, arguing (tendentiously and disingenuously, in our view) that Maimonides' discussion in *Perek ḥelek* (according to which the late Lubavitcher Rebbe could not be the messiah, since he died) is not normative, in that it is not found in a strictly halakhic context.

[59] Literally: 'subjugation to powers'. It may even be that Maimonides understood this to mean that no nation will be subjugated to any other nation, as opposed to the more common interpretation, according to which Israel will be freed of subjugation to other powers.

that as it may, neither the exact sequence of those events nor the details thereof constitute religious dogmas [*ikar badat*]. No one should ever occupy himself with the aggadic texts or spend much time on midrashic statements bearing on this and like subjects. He should not deem them of prime importance [*ikar*], since they lead neither to the love of God nor to the awe of Him. Nor should one calculate the end. Said the Rabbis: 'Blasted be the bones of those who reckon out the end' [BT *San.* 97b]. Rather, one should wait [for his coming] and believe in this generally, as we have stated before.

Maimonides makes great efforts here to take the wind out of the sails of messianic enthusiasm: no one, not even the Sages of the Talmud, really knows what will happen, and one ought not to be overly involved in these matters. He continues:

In the days of King messiah, when his kingdom will be established and all Israel will gather around him, their pedigrees will be determined by him through the Holy Spirit which will rest upon him, as it is written: 'And he shall sit as a refiner and purifier' [Mal. 3: 3]. First he will purify the descendants of Levi, declaring: 'This one is a priest; this one is a Levite.' Those who are not of levitical descent will be placed in the rank of Israelites, for it is written: 'And the Tirshatha said unto them that they should not eat of the most holy things, till there stood up a priest with Urim and Tummim' [Ezra 2: 63]. It is inferred therefrom that lineage will be traced by means of the Holy Spirit. The descent of the Israelites will be recorded according to their tribes. He will announce: 'This one is of such-and-such a tribe, and this one of such-and-such a tribe.' But he will not say concerning those who are presumed to be of pure descent: 'This is a bastard; this is a slave.' For the rule is: once a family has been intermingled with others, it remains intermingled.

That is not to say that there is not something to look forward to, but what Jews ought to look forward to is not what people ordinarily think will be the case. Maimonides makes the point in the resounding last paragraph of the *Mishneh torah*:

The Sages and Prophets did not long for[60] the days of the messiah that they might

---

[60] Compare 'Laws of Repentance', 9: 2. Maimonides uses the same verb in both places: *nitavu*, 'desired', 'longed for', 'yearned for'. The same point is made in *Perek ḥelek*:

The prophets and the virtuous only longed for the days of the messiah for the sake of the virtuous community [*al-jam al-fadil*] that will then exist, the fine conduct and knowledge that will then be, the justice of the king [the messiah], his great knowledge and proximity to his Creator, as He said to him; 'You are my son' [Ps. 20: 7], and adherence to the entire Law of Moses, without care, anxiety, or constraint, as He has promised, 'No longer will they need to teach one another and say to one another, "Heed the Lord"; for all of them, from the least of them to the greatest, shall heed Me—declares the Lord' [Jer. 31: 34]; 'I will put My Teaching into their inmost being' [Jer. 31: 33]; '[And I will give you a new

exercise dominion over the world, or rule over the nations, or be exalted by the peoples, and not in order to eat and drink and rejoice,[61] but so that they be free to devote themselves to the Torah and *its wisdom*,[62] with no one to oppress or disturb them, and thus be worthy of life in the world to come, as we explained in 'Laws of Repentance'.[63] Then there will be[64] neither famine nor war, neither jealousy nor strife. Good things will be abundant, and delicacies as common as dust. The one preoccupation of the whole world will be only to know [*lada'at*] the Lord. Hence [they][65] will be very wise, knowing [*yodim*] things now unknown and will apprehend knowledge [*da'at*] of their Creator to the utmost capacity of the human mind,[66] as it is written: 'For the land[67] shall be full [*ki malah*

---

heart and put a new spirit into you:] I will remove the heart of stone from your body [and give you a heart of flesh]' [Ezek. 36: 26].

We cite the passage as translated by Kraemer, 'On Maimonides' Messianic Posture', 111.

[61] Probably a critique of quranic descriptions of the afterlife.

[62] Emphasis added. See Maimonides' distinction on the very first page of the *Guide* between the legalistic study of the Law and the science of the Law in its true sense (introd., p. 5). For Maimonides' use of 'wisdom' (*ḥokhmah*) see Kellner, *They, Too, Are Called Human* (Heb.), ch. 3. [63] 'Laws of Repentance', 9: 2.

[64] Hebrew: *lo yiheyeh sham*. This Arabism calls to mind the very first paragraph of the *Mishneh torah*, a text addressed to all human beings.

[65] Presumably the inhabitants 'of the whole world', the *ba'ei olam* who, Maimonides says, can achieve the highest possible level of sanctity even in this dispensation (see above, Ch. 7). On the textual issues here, see Schwarzfuchs, 'Les Lois royales de Maimonide'. On pp. 81–2 Schwarzfuchs shows that many printed editions and manuscripts add the word 'Israel' here. Makbili includes the word in the first printing of his edition, with a note that Shailat excludes the word from his text. Makbili excluded the word in subsequent editions. On literary grounds alone it appears clear that the word is an emendation since the prooftext from Isaiah speaks of the entire earth. See Kellner, '"Farteitsht un Farbessert"' and also below, n. 67.

[66] On this expression, and many of the issues raised here, see Aviezer Ravitzky, '"To the Utmost of Human Capacity"'. It must be recalled that in this context the intellectual perfection to which Maimonides refers here is relative, not absolute. Human beings, even in the messianic era, achieve intellectual perfection to different degrees. When Maimonides says here that humans will come to know God *kefi ko'aḥ ha'adam*, he means, to translate him literally, 'according to each person's abilities' and not 'according to human ability'. The latter reading would involve a miraculous change in human nature. See further Gillis, *Reading Maimonides' Mishneh Torah*, 188 n. 122. Our passage here harks back to the final paragraph in 'Laws of Repentance' (see above, Ch. 1) which can hardly be an accident. Both passages deal with human beings as such.

[67] On the question of what this land is (and for more on the textual issues) see Blidstein, *Political Concepts* (Heb.), 246 n. 56. In his commentary, Makbili points out that the root *d-'-h* occurs four times in these closing sentences. This can hardly be a coincidence. Knowledge is a *human* (not uniquely Jewish) trait, indeed the trait which distinguishes us from animals, and the trait by virtue of which we can be said to be made in the image of God. This emphasis on *d-'-h* also brings us back to the very first sentence in the *Mishneh torah* with its universalistic emphasis on human perfection.

ha'arets[68]] of the knowledge [*de'ah*] of the Lord, as the waters cover the sea[69] [Isa. 11: 9].

Recall that, according to the twelfth of Maimonides' Thirteen Principles, Jews are bidden to anticipate the coming of the messiah, even though he tarries, and to pray for his coming. Why? Here we are told: not in order to enjoy power and dominion, or this-worldly pleasures, but in order to be free to devote themselves to the Torah *and its wisdom*. Such devotion will make those wise enough to engage in it 'worthy of life in the world to come'. In such a well-organized and enlightened world, in which its natural riches are shared among human beings rationally as opposed to selfishly, not only will war disappear, but delicacies will be as common as dust. This is not a function of miracles, but of proper organization and the self-restraint of a population focused on important matters. Is it any wonder that in such a world human beings (not just Jews) will achieve great wisdom? Thus, the point of the messiah's coming is to help human beings bring about a peaceful society enjoying the just allocation of resources and devoted to the cultivation of the intellect.

Lest it be thought that we personally want to live in such a world, let us make clear that we understand that Maimonides might be one of the open society's enemies criticized by Karl Popper, and that his vision of liberty is not the one that Isaiah Berlin and we ourselves prefer. Maimonides, after all, was a universalist, not a pluralist, and he was convinced that truth is one, objective, and unchanging—no relativist he. If virtue is knowledge, then ignorance of the truth is immoral and also a form of mental illness. But, on the other hand, because of his universalism, Maimonides adopted a kind of pluralism: there can be salvation outside the synagogue, so long as one accepts the

[68] The verse from Isaiah recalls Gen. 6: 13 ('God said to Noah: I have decided to put an end to all flesh, for the earth is filled [*ki malah ha'arets*] with lawlessness because of them: I am about to destroy them with the earth'). We are tempted to say that just as that verse surely relates to humans in the general sense, and not to Jews only, Maimonides uses the parallel verse from Isaiah in the same way. The prophet is surely alluding to the difference between the messianic and antediluvian eras through the use of the expression *ki malah ha'arets*; it is a safe bet that if we noticed it, Maimonides certainly did.

[69] Rabbi Jeffrey Bienenfeld pointed out to us that the meaning of the word 'sea' here is 'seabed' and that just as water spreads to cover every part of any enclosure in which it is placed, seeping into every nook and cranny (as anyone who has had plumbing problems knows), so too will the knowledge of God extend to and seep into every nook and cranny of the world, and, hence, into the hearts of all human beings. For extensive discussion of this text, see Kellner, 'Maimonides' True Religion'. See above, Ch. 10 for a comparison of the use of water as a metaphor for knowledge or intellect here and at the end of the *Book of Purity*, and for discussion of the structural significance and Neoplatonic overtones of this metaphor.

philosophical truth ultimately taught by the synagogue. Thus, *contra* Isaac Deutscher's 'non-Jewish Jews', Maimonides, through Steven Schwarzschild channelling, as it were, Hermann Cohen, could (but, of course, did not) speak of Jewish non-Jews.[70]

Messiah in the *Guide*

The last passage in which Maimonides describes the messianic world is *Guide of the Perplexed* iii. 11.[71] Warren Harvey has pointed out that this chapter of the *Guide* is a kind of poetic and philosophical rendition of the last paragraph of the *Mishneh torah*, glossing it in the way Maimonides meant it to be read.[72] Since we agree with Harvey, we will discuss the chapter here by way of expanding our discussion of the end of the *Mishneh torah*. Here is the chapter in its entirety:

These great evils that come about because the human individuals who inflict them upon one another because of purposes, desires, opinions, and beliefs, are all of them likewise consequent upon privation. For all of them derive from ignorance, I mean from a privation of knowledge. Just as a blind man, because of absence of sight, does not cease stumbling, being wounded and also wounding others, because he has nobody to guide him on the way, the various sects of men—every individual according to the extent of his ignorance—does to himself and to others great evils from which individuals of the species suffer. If there were knowledge, whose relation to the human form is like that of the faculty of sight to the eye, they would refrain from doing any harm to themselves and to others. For through cognition of the truth, enmity and hatred are removed and the inflicting of harm by people on one another is abolished. It holds out this promise, saying: 'And the wolf shall dwell with the lamb, and the leopard shall lie down with the kid', and so on. 'And the cow and the bear shall feed', and so on [Isa. 11: 6–8]. Then it gives the reason for this, saying that the cause of the abolition of these enmities, these

---

[70] See Kellner, *Maimonides' Confrontation*, 240–9. On Cohen on this topic, see Batnitzky, *How Judaism Became a Religion*.

[71] Maimonides has comments on the messianic advent, but little on the nature of the messianic era itself, in his *Epistle to Yemen* and *Letter on Resurrection*. We do not address these texts here for a number of reasons. Maimonides himself tells us that one should read every text in its context, and he clearly indicates the polemical nature of these two texts. For the contextual reading of texts, see his *Epistle to Yemen* in Lerner, *Maimonides' Empire of Light*, 114. For his comments on the messianic era, see there, pp. 124–7, and (in the *Letter on Resurrection*), 166–7. In these two passages Maimonides reiterates the points surveyed here, but also accepts the idea that the messianic advent will involve miraculous events and more or less predicts when the messiah will come. This latter is a very clear indication that Maimonides addressed these texts to the masses, and did not mean them to be taken as seriously as one takes the texts analysed in this chapter.

[72] See W. Z. Harvey, 'Averroes, Maimonides, and the Virtuous State', 23–4.

discords, and these tyrannies, will be the knowledge that men [*al-nas*] will have then concerning the true reality of the deity. For it says: 'They shall not hurt nor destroy in all My holy mountain; for the earth shall be full of the knowledge of the Lord, as the waters cover the sea' [Isa. 11: 9]. Know this.

This chapter comes near the end of Maimonides' discussion of the problem of evil. His overall position is that evil in and of itself does not exist: all that God created is good, even very good. Just as darkness is nothing in and of itself, but the absence of light, and just as a shadow cannot actually be said to exist since it is just the consequence of the blocking of light, so evil is the absence ('privation') of good. It is thus no surprise that another privation, that of knowledge, i.e. ignorance, is the cause of much evil. People properly guided by knowledge do not harm themselves or each other; they treat themselves and each other like lambs, not like wolves. This will be brought about when human beings (and not just Jews) focus their energies on knowing 'the true reality of the deity'. When 'the earth shall be full of the knowledge of the Lord', then people 'shall not hurt or destroy in all God's holy mountain'.

It is noteworthy how this chapter appears to envisage a process opposite to the one at the end of the *Mishneh torah*—rather than moral and political reform and regeneration leading to conditions for the pursuit of knowledge, knowledge leads to peace and goodwill, foreshadowing *Guide* iii. 54. But in reality there is no conflict here: moral progress and intellectual progress actually advance each other, in a dialectical relationship. Thus, the *Guide*, a book of philosophy aimed at the individual, ends on a political ideal, while the *Mishneh torah*, the law and constitution of the ideal state, ends on the ideal of philosophy.[73]

The Logic of Messianism

Wisdom, apprehension, and knowledge cannot be achieved by war, only by study. The whole world can become preoccupied with the knowledge of the Lord only if war is replaced by education. To the extent that it is rational for ends to determine means, then the only way to bring about the fulfilment of the messianic redemption, at least as it is understood by Maimonides, is to make the study of true Torah (which includes *ma'aseh bereshit*, physics, and *ma'aseh merkavah*, metaphysics) our aim, and not domination of one group by another.

[73] Aviezer Ravitzky sees this as a paradox; see his 'Philosophy and Leadership in Maimonides'. Compare Gillis, *Reading Maimonides' Mishneh Torah*, 105–9: the *Book of Knowledge* presents moral virtue in both phases, as a precondition for knowledge and as flowing from knowledge.

The peak of messianism for Maimonides is to bring all human beings to the point where they abandon idolatry (and all that idolatry stands for, namely, brutality and stupidity) and embrace monotheism.[74] Remember, the messiah will 'prepare the whole world to worship God with one accord, as it is written, "For then will I turn to the peoples a pure language, that they all call upon the name of the Lord to serve Him with one consent" [Zeph. 3: 9]'. This will come about without miraculous intervention. If the messiah is meant to 'to prepare the whole world to worship God with one accord', then the world must be made ready to accept belief in one God in order to make the messiah's mission possible. Converting the entire world from paganism to refined monotheism in one fell swoop would be a miracle of gargantuan proportions. Such a change can only come about miraculously since, as Maimonides teaches in the *Guide*, 'a sudden transition from one opposite to another is impossible. And therefore man, according to his nature, is not capable of abandoning suddenly all to which he was accustomed.'[75] Thus, in order for Judaic messianism to reach fruition, the world needs Christianity and Islam to pave the way for the messiah's advent.

Relevant here is another aspect of Maimonides' overall approach. God makes demands of human beings; God does not hand out presents. Nothing is given one on a silver platter, not one's humanity (to be human is to be a rational animal, and not all children of human parents achieve that), and not one's membership in the community of Israel.[76] It is certainly the case that for Maimonides humanity must earn the coming of the messiah by making the world a place in which the messiah can function.

Similarly, since a reign of universal peace and enlightenment is a prerequisite for the messiah to succeed completely in the task of ushering in a situation in which 'the earth shall be full of the knowledge of the Lord, as the waters cover the sea', and since peace is the opposite of war, it is logically incoherent to think that war is the way in which this goal can ultimately be reached. If one wishes to raise humane children, brutalizing them is not the way to go. In order to achieve any end, one must adopt means consistent with that end. Bolsheviks did not understand this, but Maimonides did, and so should other Jews.

---

[74] Relevant here, we believe, is the way in which Maimonides construes the wars against the seven Canaanite nations and even against Amalek, as wars against idolatry and brutality, and not as wars against people. One wages war against people, not because of who they are, but because of their dangerous ideas and behaviour. See 'Laws of Kings and their Wars', 5 and Korn, 'Moralization in Jewish Law'. See also Kellner, 'And Yet, the Texts Remain'.

[75] *Guide* iii: 32 (p. 526).

[76] For a defence of these claims, see Kellner, *Maimonides' Confrontation*, ch. 7.

The messianic universalism sketched out here is an outgrowth of Maimonides' understanding of world history. It was not God's original intention to choose the Jews, Halevi and most other Jewish thinkers through the generations to the contrary, or any national group for that matter. Abraham chose God, not the other way round. Had the first individual to discover God through rational means after humanity had degenerated into paganism been a Navajo philosopher, then the Torah would have been written in the Navajo language, its narratives would have reflected the history of the Navajo people, and its commandments would have sought to purify, sanctify, and exalt the Navajo way of life. But the Torah in its innermost essence would not be different; it would teach the same truths it teaches today, only clothed differently. Indeed, Abraham sought to create a universal religion, not one connected to a particular lineage, but this experiment failed. Moses sought to create a religion of reason, not one of cultic ritual, but this experiment also failed. By envisioning a universal religion at the end of days, Maimonides is consistent with his understanding of how history should have worked itself out, had humanity been up to the task.

Maimonides' messianic universalism is also an outgrowth of his understanding of the nature of humanity. Human beings are rational animals. By that Maimonides meant that people are born with the capacity to exercise their intellects through the rational apprehension of truths about important topics, pre-eminently about God. In this Jews and non-Jews are precisely alike, created in the image of God. Only those who actualize their intellectual potential can be said to have realized the image of God potentially in them. But, as noted above, such actualization is very hard work and can only be achieved by highly disciplined individuals living lives of self-restraint. It is in this sense that Maimonides (and other medieval philosophers, Jews, Muslims, and Christians, working in the Aristotelian tradition) was convinced that a morally dissolute person (such as Martin Heidegger) could not possibly be a philosopher. For Maimonides, who was not only a philosopher but also a rabbi, the Torah is the best tool for achieving a life of moral perfection. Moral perfection is a prerequisite for intellectual (i.e. truly human) perfection. This is God's aim, as it were, for all of humanity, an aim which will be realized in the messianic era.

Hermann Cohen and, following him, Yeshayahu Leibowitz would say that Maimonides did not really expect this to happen, that we may come ever closer to the messianic era, but will never actually reach it.[77] That may or may not have been Maimonides' actual position; we do not really have a settled

---

[77] See Schwarzschild, 'The Democratic Socialism of Hermann Cohen'.

opinion on the subject. What is crucial to understand is that—whether actually achievable, or an ever-receding while paradoxically ever-closer dream—Maimonides' messianic vision is one of ultimate universal peace and enlightenment. This is a vision which will be realized only if human beings do not wait for God, but bring it about themselves.

Midrash *Sifra* teaches *kol yisra'el arevim zeh lazeh*: all Jews are responsible for (or better, to) one another.[78] Maimonides teaches that the messiah will have come when all human beings are responsible for (or better, to) one another.

Summary

As we have seen, the book-endings in the *Mishneh torah* touch upon the reasons and goals of the commandments found within the individual books. The *Book of Judges* and the *Mishneh torah* as a whole conclude with two climactic chapters about the messianic era. These two messianic chapters form a symmetry with the beginning of the book, as the messianic process establishes a perfected society which fosters the kind of intellectual perfection that Maimonides wrote about at the outset. In the perfected messianic world, all peoples will be able to realize the faith of Abraham. This universalism is, it would seem, the goal of the Torah's commandments and of the *Mishneh torah* as a whole.

Similarly, in the *Commentary on the Mishnah* and elsewhere in the *Mishneh Torah*, Maimonides described messianism as a natural, non-miraculous process whose goal is to foster intellectual perfection, and emphasized the central role of the Torah as the means to achieve this.

Our in-depth analysis of the final two chapters deepens these themes, especially that of universal enlightenment as the meaning and the goal of the Torah and the messianic age, the final thought with which the text of the *Mishneh torah* concludes. When Maimonides returned to the messianic idea for the last time in the *Guide*, he returned to precisely this point. A comparison of the two passages shows that moral progress and intellectual progress each help to advance the other in coming ever closer to realization of the ideal. In this blessed reality, no group will subjugate another, and all peoples will need to contribute towards its coming. The process was set in motion by Abraham, and continued by Moses, but its full realization will be by all peoples and for all peoples.

[78] *Sifra*, 'Beḥukotai', 7: 5.

CONCLUSION

The Messages of the *Mishneh Torah*'s 'Endings'

Let us begin by reviewing the main points of our individual chapters.

Maimonides ends the first book of the *Mishneh torah*, the *Book of Knowledge*, with 'Laws of Repentance'. The final *halakhah* of that section (10: 6), and hence of the book as a whole, tells us that love of God (positive commandment 3 in Maimonides' *Book of Commandments*) depends upon knowledge of God. The last sentence reads: 'One must, therefore, be single-minded in studying and reflecting on the disciplines and sciences that give him such knowledge of his Master as humans can understand and apprehend, as we have explained in "Laws of the Foundations of the Torah".' In this section, it will be recalled, Maimonides spent two chapters on metaphysical matters and two chapters on physical matters, all four aimed at making it possible for his readers to approach love of God. The metaphysics and physics taught in those four chapters (which according to Maimonides represent what the rabbis called *pardes*) are the standard sciences of the medieval world, derived ultimately from Greek texts and aimed at all human beings. The opening of the *Book of Knowledge*, which of course is the opening of the *Mishneh torah*, is moreover matched by the closing passage of the work as a whole, which has a similarly clear universal thrust.

The *Book of Love* (Book 2) ends by elevating the Abrahamic covenant of love above the Mosaic covenant of law in relation to the commandment of circumcision, which links the two. Circumcision symbolizes Abraham's discovery of the one incorporeal God, and his understanding of that discovery's moral and social consequences. The implication, found elsewhere in the *Mishneh torah* and in the *Guide* but conveyed most forcefully here, is that the ultimate aim of the Torah of Moses is the emulation of Abraham by graduating from obedience to discovery.

The *Book of Seasons* (Book 3) ends by taking the stories of Purim and Hanukah away from their bellicose historical character and using them to teach that the Torah was given, not only to bring peace between husband and wife, but among all people.

The *Book of Women* (Book 4) ends with 'Laws of the Wayward Wife'. Maimonides takes a discussion of the consequences of the tragic breakdown of marital relations and uses it to teach a number of lessons: about the responsibilities of a householder towards his family, about moral relationships within marriage, about striving for peace, and last, but certainly not least, about the imitation of God, such imitation being open to all human beings.

The *Book of Holiness* (Book 5) ends by emphasizing the instrumental character of the commandments: they accomplish nothing metaphysical and certainly have no theurgic value. As instruments, the commandments can, in principle, be used by anyone—no special soul is required. Instruments must be judged in terms of the aims that they are designed to accomplish (and their effectiveness in accomplishing those aims); one of the aims of the commandments is to direct those capable of it to approach a philosophical understanding of the nature of God.

The *Book of Asseverations* (Book 6) brings together two underlying themes of the book in its conclusion. One is the glorification of God through making solemn statements in his name. The other is voluntary restrictions undertaken in addition to those prescribed in the *Book of Holiness* in order to preserve moral virtue. We suggested that the grounds of the concluding condemnation of excessive self-deprivation are that it neither redounds to God's glory nor promotes moral health, and is thus altogether unholy.

The *Book of Agriculture* (Book 7) brings the first half of the *Mishneh torah* to an end. One of the aims of the book is to bring those who obey its prescriptions to a state of (non-ontological) holiness. In the closing *halakhah* of this volume, 'Laws of the Sabbatical Year', 13: 13, Maimonides marks the precise midpoint of the *Mishneh torah* by challenging the reader to aspire to holiness, and by promising that any human being, whether Jew or non-Jew, who fulfils the criteria that the *halakhah* lists will indeed become 'as consecrated as the holy of holies'.

The second half of the *Mishneh torah* opens with Book 8, the *Book of Temple Service*. In its final *halakhah*, 'Laws of Trespass', 8: 8, Maimonides asserts that rational appreciation of the commandments is desirable, but warns that if this is not attainable, the commandments must still be observed. Maimonides' writings in general indicate that, in his view, the cause of failure to rationalize any commandment is lack of scientific or historical knowledge rather than exclusion from some peculiarly Jewish mystery, or that the commandment is simply God's inscrutable will. This *halakhah* is consistent with that view and maintains a universalistic approach to understanding the commandments.

Focus on the Temple continues in Book 9, the *Book of Offerings*. The ending of the *Book of Offerings* is the obverse of the ending of the *Book of Temple Service*. Although the commandments must in any case be obeyed, they are comprehensible as correctives to moral failings common to all human beings.

Since, as Maimonides teaches in the *Guide of the Perplexed*, the reason for the laws of ritual purity and impurity is to create a barrier to entry to the Temple so that visits there will be rare and therefore always awe-inspiring, it is no surprise that Book 10 is the *Book of Purity*. Its conclusion presents a metaphor of intellect as water that binds the *Mishneh torah* together: the flow of intellect emanating from the *Book of Knowledge* gathers in this transfigured *mikveh*, which also foreshadows the image of universal knowledge of God as the waters of the sea in the final *halakhah* of the whole work. In tandem with the endings of the previous two books, it presents the order that underlies the entire sentient universe: the tripartite division of intellect between the thought of God, the thought of the self, and the thought of the immediately superior entity in the process of emanation. Maimonides' configuration of the laws of the Temple ritual thus lends that ritual enduring significance by relating it to the enduring, universally cognizable laws of nature. The ultimate offering to God is the intellectual and moral perfection attained by assimilating oneself to those laws.

The *Book of Damages* (Book 11) is the first of four books dealing largely with social relations, in the form of commandments relating to obligations among human beings. The conclusion of this book discusses those who are 'joined' to God, and says that they are those who accept the 'principles of the Jewish religion'. This includes non-Jewish 'Jews of the mind', but excludes born Jews who deny the principles and thus are not 'joined' to God. Maimonides' strict notions of doctrinal orthodoxy lead him to exclude heterodox Jews from the community of Israel, but to include within it moral non-Jews who are philosophical monotheists.

The *Book of Acquisition* (Book 12) ends with the transformation of what could be seen as a harsh and discriminatory law concerning a non-Jewish slave into an embrace of universalism, concluding with the verse 'And His mercy is on all His works'. Commentators have explained this as an example of supererogation. Our conclusion is that Maimonides intends something more radical: he applies a hierarchy of values to resolve a conflict within the Torah between universal ethical principles and a particularist provision.

The motto of Book 13, the *Book of Civil Laws*, is Psalm 119: 7, which contains a reference to the title of the book (*Mishpatim*) and a hint to the effect that the book is about justice: 'I will praise you with a sincere heart as I learn Your just rules [*mishpetei tsidkekha*].' At the end of this book, we see Maimonides combining the unknowable, transcendent God of the cosmos with the God of the commandments of the Torah, which constitute God's justice as manifest in the world.

The last two chapters of Book 14, the *Book of Judges*, are the end of the *Mishneh torah* as a whole, and in them Maimonides sets forth his messianic universalism, which is an outgrowth of his understanding of world history. It was not God's original intention to choose the Jews. Abraham chose God, not the other way round. He sought to create a universal religion, not one connected to a particular lineage, but his experiment failed. Moses sought to create a religion of reason, not one of cultic ritual, but his experiment also failed. By envisioning a universal religion at the end of days, Maimonides is consistent with his understanding of how history should have worked itself out, had humanity been up to the task.

The *Mishneh torah*'s messianic universalism is also an outgrowth of Maimonides' understanding of the nature of humanity. Human beings are rational animals. By that Maimonides meant that people are born with the capacity to exercise their intellect through the rational apprehension of truths about important topics, first and foremost about God. This is God's aim, as it were, for all of humanity, an aim that will be realized in the messianic era.

Pulling all this together, among the central themes found in the statements concluding each of the fourteen books of the *Mishneh torah* we find knowledge/love of God, the tension between Abrahamic and Mosaic Torahs (a tension which will be overcome in the messianic era), and, connected to messianism, an emphasis on peace as an overarching goal. This goal is a universal utopia, not a national triumph, and throughout, 'Israel' is defined culturally rather than ethnically. We find in these endings expressions of reciprocity and intense closeness between human beings and God, but the basis of this is the virtues that the commandments are meant to promote rather than performance of the commandments as such, since they have no theurgic function. The ends to which the commandments are meant to bring one are moral perfection, which is the imitation of God (who does justice, loving-kindness, and righteousness in the earth), and which includes social harmony and political stability; and the attainment of philosophical enlightenment, which is ultimately the knowledge of God. The former is a prerequisite for the latter, since knowledge cannot flourish in a corrupt person or a violent society, and also an outcome of it, since enlightenment makes people intuitively good. The rationality and utility of the commandments is repeatedly emphasized, as is the integration of philosophy and halakhah.

Abraham and Moses

The *Mishneh torah*'s motto, like that of all Maimonides' works, is the verse 'in the name of the Lord, God of the world', Abraham's invocation of God in Genesis 21: 33.[1] Abraham preached monotheism and decent behaviour to the whole world. In this respect, and hence with respect to the ultimate aim of the commandments, Jews have no inborn, essential advantage over non-Jews. In our introduction, we suggested that Maimonides may have taken Rabbi Judah the Prince as his model in adding moral and spiritual codas to the halakhic content of the *Mishneh torah*. We have reached the point where we can see that, no less than Rabbi Judah, his models were Abraham and Moses.

We have indicated in several places the different significances that these models held for Maimonides. The Abrahamic model involves the creation of a monotheism with almost no ritual aspects (with the obvious exception of circumcision). The Mosaic model involves 613 highly detailed commandments. Maimonides expresses the distinction between the Abrahamic and Mosaic models most clearly in two texts: 'Laws of Idolatry', chapter 1 (quoted at length and analysed above in Chapter 1) and *Guide of the Perplexed* iii. 32. In 'Laws of Idolatry' we are taught that the community called together by Abraham, 'in the name of the Lord, God of the world', consisted of his family, household, and 'the persons they had gotten in Haran',[2] referring to the individuals whom Abraham and Sarah had brought close to God. This community, held together only by shared (minimalistic) theology, did not survive the descent into Egypt. The community would have disappeared altogether had not God, fulfilling his promise to Abraham, sent Moses to be their teacher. Having 'learned' that philosophical theology was not enough to hold the community together, God's next step was to constitute them as a people, and not only as a religious community. The nature of that move is the subject matter of *Guide* iii. 32. There we learn that God, as it were, made two efforts in this direction, with only the second being successful.

The *Guide of the Perplexed* contains many 'outrageous' chapters; this may be the most provocative of them all. Here Maimonides teaches that God

---

[1] See the discussion in Ch. 2 on the interpretation of this verse.
[2] Gen. 12: 5 and *Guide* i. 63 (p. 154).

behaves with 'wily graciousness'[3] (close to what Plato would have called 'noble lies'), in effect misleading the people of Israel for their benefit.[4] The point of his extended discussion is to explain why the God of all creation would command the bringing of sacrifices. Maimonides' answer is one towards which the reader's 'soul will necessarily have a feeling of repugnance' and 'will feel aggrieved because of it'.[5] What is that answer which arouses such repugnance? It is that God's original intention after the Exodus was to command a Torah consisting only of the sabbath (which teaches the creation of the world by God) and of laws governing social relations.[6] But this Torah, God's primary intention as Maimonides explains in our chapter, turned out to be deficient. The Israelites apparently found this religion too abstract. At the first opportunity, when Moses disappeared on Mount Sinai, the Israelites slid back into idolatry, creating and worshipping the Golden Calf. Seeing this, God *realized* that the Torah revealed at Marah was insufficient, and was *forced* to reveal a Torah full of sacrifices and detailed ritual—all this according to what Maimonides calls God's second intention.[7] Since the people of Israel had proved themselves unable to worship God without a concrete focus for their worship (the Golden Calf), God exercised a 'gracious ruse' and made the people think that God desired them to offer sacrifices to him. Sacrifices demand a place in which to bring them (the Tabernacle in the Sinai wilderness and then the Temple in Jerusalem), a priesthood to officiate, laws of ritual purity and impurity to guarantee that the Temple be treated with awe, and festivals marked by huge numbers of sacrifices and focused on the Temple.[8] All of these are God's second intention, a clear accommodation to the primitive spirituality of the Israelites leaving Egypt.

Once revealed, however, the Torah became obligatory and remains so.

---

[3] Ar.: *talattuf*. On this term, see Pines, 'Translator's Introduction', *Guide*, p. lxxii, n. 32, and Schwarz's Hebrew translation, iii. 32 n. 2.

[4] The clearest examples of such misleading expressions are the many verses in the Torah that lead people to attribute corporeality and personality to God.   [5] *Guide* iii. 32 (p. 527).

[6] While Maimonides does not make the point explicitly in *Guide* iii. 32, it is obvious that these are the laws expressed in the Decalogue: God, sabbath, and social relations.

[7] The italicized words in this sentence are drawn from Isaac Abravanel's presentation of this idea in his commentary on Jeremiah 7. Maimonides ignores the status of the paschal lamb, which together with the prohibition on eating leaven on Passover is established in Exod. 12 as 'an ordinance for ever' before the legislation at Marah.

[8] In his commentary on Lev. 1: 9, Nahmanides gives every indication of having been personally offended by this account of the sacrifices. No wonder! The clear implication of Maimonides' account is that anyone who thinks that God really *wants* sacrifices, and that sacrifices actually accomplish anything ontological (views definitely held by Nahmanides), is marked by a primitive, pagan sensibility. See further Schwartz, "From Theurgy to Magic'.

This reflects Maimonides' well-known position that the (often historical) explanation of why a commandment was given in no way impacts upon its normative character.[9]

According to Maimonides, then, the Torah was meant to be Abrahamic—consisting in effect of what was later to be called ethical monotheism—while the actual Torah of Moses was divine accommodation to the spiritual weakness of the ancient Israelites. Thus, the *Mishneh torah* as we present it in this book is Mosaic in content (halakhah) but Abrahamic in the overarching, messianic goal towards which the passages studied in this book lead.[10]

The point of the *Mishneh torah* as a whole, then, is the creation of a society which gives its members the greatest chance of achieving their perfection as *human beings*. In this way, the end of the *Mishneh torah* comes round to its beginning: just as the beginning of the work deals with matters that relate to all human beings, so do the last chapters. Similarly, the *Guide* opens with an emphasis on intellectual perfection—again, open in principle to all human beings—and closes with a focus on the imitation of God through doing 'loving-kindness, righteousness, and judgement in the earth'.[11] So also, the *Mishneh torah*'s establishment of a perfected society makes possible the achievement of philosophical perfection, which, in turn, enables highly perfected individuals (Jewish or non-Jewish) to imitate God in the best way possible (and become as consecrated as the holy of holies).

The microcosmic form of the *Mishneh torah*, which we have found to bear significantly on the interpretation of the book endings, is also expressive of the work's Abrahamic and Mosaic layers.

On the Mosaic level, this form reflects the interpretation in *Guide* i: 54 of Moses' two requests of God: to be shown 'thy ways', and to be shown 'thy glory'. The latter request, which Maimonides interprets as referring to God's essence, is denied, since 'His essence cannot be grasped as it really is'; God as he is known to himself is beyond human (and even angelic) comprehension.[12] The request to be shown God's ways is granted, however, with the words 'I will make all My goodness pass before thee', which Maimonides says

---

[9] See above, Ch. 8.

[10] Twersky writes: 'Messianism may be described as the ultimate triumph of Abraham when true belief will be universally restored' (*Introduction to the Code*, 451). Each of the endings of the books has its local significance, but each is also part of a general trend directing all of halakhah towards these universal goals.

[11] Jer. 9: 22–3. See *Guide* iii. 54 (p. 638) and the argument for this interpretation in Kellner, *Maimonides on Human Perfection*. The closing verses and (Hebrew) poem of the *Guide of the Perplexed* can also be read in a messianic light.

[12] See also 'Laws of the Foundations of the Torah', 1: 10.

'alludes to the display to him of all existing things . . . I mean that he will apprehend their nature and the way they are mutually connected so that he will know how He governs them in general and in detail'.[13] Moses' motive for making this request is not just for his own edification, but 'that I may find grace in Thy sight and consider that this nation is Thy people', meaning, according to Maimonides, 'a people for the government of which I need to perform actions that I must seek to make similar to Thy actions in governing them'.[14] In other words, the governance of the people should reflect the way God governs the world, and the more perfectly Moses understood God's governance, that is, the laws of nature, the more perfect his governance would be.

Moses governed by means of the Torah. The Torah should therefore presumably reflect the laws of nature. The microcosmic structure of the *Mishneh torah* confirms this presumption and demonstrates its truth 'in general and in detail'. This provides a rationale for the doctrine cited above that a historical explanation for a commandment does not impinge on its normative character. However adventitious may have been the physical and cultural materials out of which the Torah was made, its form reflects the perfect and permanent form of nature. Just as an artist creates out of the materials at hand a form that any alteration is liable to mar, so the Torah of Moses is unalterable: nothing may be added to it and nothing may be taken away.[15]

Our approach to the analysis of the endings of the *Mishneh torah*'s books, in themselves and in relation to the general structure, is intended, if we may adapt Maimonides' language, to apprehend the nature of each book and the way the books are mutually connected, and thus bring out the universal ideas and values that they embody.

That is at the Mosaic level of understanding. There is also another, Abrahamic, level. Abraham discovered God through observation of the motions of the heavens, and he too understood God's governance of the world, if less comprehensively than did Moses.[16] From there he went on to found an ethical community guided by correct ideas.[17] In other words, Abraham knew the physics and metaphysics that Maimonides sets out at the beginning of the *Mishneh torah*. In the biography of Abraham in 'Laws of Idolatry', 1: 3, Maimonides describes how Abraham wondered, 'How can the Sphere forever follow its course with none to conduct it? Who causes it to rotate? For it can-

---

[13] *Guide* i. 54 (p. 124). [14] Ibid. (p. 125).
[15] See 'Laws of the Foundations of the Torah', 9: 1. Maimonides' notion of the perfection of the Torah and Aristotle's notion of aesthetic perfection are compared in Gillis, *Reading Maimonides' Mishneh Torah*, 35–44. [16] See 'Laws of Idolatry', 1: 3. [17] Ibid.

not possibly cause *itself* to rotate', which echoes the proof given for God's existence in 'Laws of the Foundations of the Torah', 1: 5: 'For the Sphere is always revolving; and it is impossible for it to revolve without someone making it revolve. God, blessed be He, it is, who, without hand or body, causes it to revolve.'

Abraham is portrayed as discovering the ideas that form the basis of morality and of a society dedicated to the pursuit of knowledge, unlike the kind of idolatrous state in which he grew up, where general ignorance is a mainstay of monarchical and priestly power, and advocates of truth like him are persecuted. In short, the foundations of the Torah and of the Abrahamic community are the same: appreciation of physics and metaphysics, of the laws of nature, and of God as separate from nature.

The Torah of Moses teaches that knowledge expressly only 'in a summary way'.[18] It commands the love of God, but 'We have already explained in the *Mishneh Torah* that this love becomes valid only through the apprehension of the whole of being as it is and through the consideration of His wisdom as it is manifested in it';[19] in other words the love of God arises from comprehensive knowledge of physics and metaphysics, which is beyond the scope of the Torah itself. What the Torah does do is to make its followers morally fit for cultivation of this knowledge, while also instituting a social and political order that facilitates that activity. The *Mishneh torah*'s microcosmic form thus signifies not only that physics and metaphysics are the Torah's foundation, but that knowledge of them is its Abrahamic, messianic goal. Its formal and final causes are equal.

A further implication of the parallel between the *Mishneh torah*'s form and the structure of the universe is that the two systems are equivalent, in the sense that contemplation of the commandments—the apprehension of their nature and the way they are mutually connected, and the consideration of God's wisdom as it is manifested in them—is itself a route to the knowledge and love of God as much as is the contemplation of creation.[20] The fulfilment of a human being's microcosmic potential is not only a way of promoting right conduct, but is also a form of knowledge, the internalization of the structures of the commandments, and hence of cosmic structures, as the law of one's being.[21] This, we believe, lies behind the importance that Maimonides attached throughout his career to systematic understanding of the

---

[18] *Guide* iii. 28 (p. 512). [19] Ibid.
[20] See Gillis, *Reading Maimonides' Mishneh Torah*, 317–19; Seeman, 'Reasons for the Commandments as Contemplative Practice'; and discussion in Ch. 1 above.
[21] See Gillis, *Reading Maimonides' Mishneh Torah*, 110–34.

commandments, culminating in his systematization of the entire halakhah in the *Mishneh torah*. He insists that the Torah is binding as God's will, but through his systematization he also makes it accessible as God's wisdom.

The Abrahamic phase of Torah, the knowledge of universal laws, is thus immanent in the commandments themselves, although only those who have gone on to study physics and metaphysics will consciously appreciate that. It is particularly at this level that the book endings and the general form of the *Mishneh torah* co-ordinate. This was the theme of the second half of Chapter 10, and we shall shortly examine to what extent the dialectical pattern discussed there is applicable to the *Mishneh torah* generally. For the moment, the point we emphasize is that the Abrahamic and Mosaic models do not just apply to stages of history, but are present synchronically in the *Mishneh torah* as levels of understanding of the commandments.

The Endings as Genre

We stated in the Introduction that we would treat the endings of the books of the *Mishneh torah* as a distinct genre. Is such treatment justified? Looking back, we would point to certain shared characteristics that put these closing statements into a special category.

Biblical Citation

A simple observation is that all the books of the *Mishneh torah* except the first end by citing the Bible. Of course, citation of biblical verses is by no means a rarity in the *Mishneh torah*. Nevertheless, the regularity of the phenomenon at the endings of the books suggests some collective significance as a stylistic motif. In fact, both the rule and the exception to the rule resonate with our theme of universalism.

The *Mishneh torah* is a codification of the Oral Torah organized around the 613 commandments of the Written Torah. Maimonides states in the introduction to the work that while his code renders the record of the Oral Torah (the Mishnah, the two Talmuds, and so on) dispensable, the Bible is still required reading: 'A person who reads first the Written Torah and then this compilation, will know from it the whole of the Oral Torah, without having occasion to consult any other book between them.'[22]

The *Mishneh torah* refers constantly to the Written Torah (in the broad sense of the Hebrew Bible as a whole rather than just the Pentateuch), to the

---

[22] *Book of Knowledge*, trans. Hyamson, 28.

extent that Twersky remarks that this phenomenon calls for 'a redefinition of the codificatory form' and that 'in many respects it [the *Mishneh torah*] turns out to be a suggestive and selective commentary cast as a code'.[23]

The biblical citations at the endings of the books seem to take the phenomenon beyond incidental commentary. Their consistent placing suggests that they are a systematic device. They direct the halakhic material of the books that they conclude towards the moral and intellectual virtues that halakhah is meant to serve and that find expression in the Bible. Each division of Maimonides' account of the Oral Law thus originates in the Written Law as a source of the commandments, and ends in the Written Law as a source of wisdom.

What, then, of the exception? Why is the *Book of Knowledge*, the book most directly concerned with moral and intellectual virtue, and with prophecy, the one book not capped by a biblical verse? The answer we propose is that this is an indication that the ultimate moral, intellectual, and prophetic goals are pre-biblical and pre-halakhic. They are, in short, Abrahamic, universal. There is no biblical signpost to direct us, because this is the final destination. Instead, the ending of the *Book of Knowledge* directs us back to its own beginning. That beginning too is not biblical. The book opens with a short series of philosophical propositions before it presents the first commandment, 'I am the Lord thy God' (although it does cite a couple of biblical prooftexts along the way).[24] This circularity, and the absence of biblical reference, suggests that the *Book of Knowledge* is, on the whole, concerned with self-sufficient, universally intelligible ideas that are indeed expressed in commandments of the Bible but do not necessarily originate in them. The collective message of the endings of the books of the *Mishneh torah* is, then, that there are universal goals, and that halakhah is valuable insofar as it leads towards those goals.

Argumentation

A further distinctive, though by no means exclusive, feature is argumentation. The endings do not merely state moral or philosophical ideas; rather, they argue a point, and thereby engage the reader. Maimonides confronts false assumptions and steers determinedly towards truth. The general model is 'You might have thought this, but the truth is that.' The phrase 'even though' (*af al pi*) is common, but even when it is not present it is implied. Thus at the end of the *Book of Offerings* we find: 'Although the statutes in the Law are all of them divine edicts, as we have explained at the close of "Laws of Trespass", yet it is proper to ponder over them and to give a reason for them.'

[23] Twersky, *Introduction to the Code*, 143.   [24] 'Laws of the Foundations of the Torah', 1: 6.

The idea that the commandments should all be regarded simply as divine edicts is raised and countered. Similarly, at the end of the final book, the idea that the messianic age will mean some sort of Jewish suzerainty is raised and countered with the idea of general freedom from oppression and pursuit of knowledge.

The argumentation is not necessarily involved or heavily rhetorical. Take, for example, the ending of the *Book of Holiness*: 'For reverence is not due to the commandments themselves, but to Him who issued them, blessed be He.' The wrong way and the right way of regarding the commandment to cover the blood after slaughter are stated briefly and plainly, but the moral is no less pointed for that.

One notable ploy is the use of the reader's false assumptions to lead to true conclusions. Thus at the end of the *Book of Acquisition* we saw a false notion of the superiority of the descendants of Abraham leading the reader to consent to the notion of equality. This *halakhah* is also an outstanding example of Maimonides using his endings to give what he sees as the correct bias to the *halakhot* he has been enumerating. The Bible and halakhah are, after all, open to all kinds of ideological construction through selective quotation and tendentious emphasis. In this case, the discriminatory permit to work a non-Jewish slave 'with rigour' could easily be taken as indicative of the general attitude Jews should adopt towards themselves and towards outsiders. Maimonides' peroration here disabuses his reader of that thought and asserts quite the opposite view.

The endings are, moreover, argued with halakhic stringency. They are not philosophical addenda. The tensions that they address are not those between the Torah and philosophy, but tensions *within* the Torah as Maimonides conceives of it. For if the basic commandments to know and imitate God mean knowledge and imitation of nature, then it is not possible to say where halakhah ends and philosophy begins. This gives the endings a tautness and a complexity that make them, individually and collectively, compelling objects of study.

Altogether the argumentation of the endings of the books of the *Mishneh torah* involves the reader in a process of balancing and calibration that guides him or her towards a true appreciation of halakhah in all its dimensions.

The Three-Beat Rhythm of Intellect

A similar process takes place between the book endings, which are distinguished and unified by interconnections that are sometimes subtle and sometimes quite explicit. The dialectic identified in Books 8, 9, and 10, which their endings play a prominent part in creating, is a clear example of the latter kind. This dialectic is not, however, confined to those books but is to some extent discernible in the earlier ones as well.

Again, the *Book of Knowledge* must be regarded as being in a class of its own. It is integrated into the pattern not as part of it but as its origin. As explained in Chapter 10, the sequence in that volume of 'Laws of the Foundations of the Torah', 'Laws of Moral Qualities', and 'Laws of Torah Study' reflects the three orientations of the human intellect: towards God, towards the self, and, in a motion of return, towards the agent intellect.

Looking at Books 2 to 4, we can see certain parallels with Books 8 to 10. Book 2, the *Book of Love*, is about commandments 'which we have been bidden to keep, in order that we may always love God and be ever mindful of Him'. It ends on the subject of covenants with God. It thus firmly directs the reader towards the thought of God, which we identified as the orientation of Book 8, the *Book of Temple Service*.

According to the *Guide*, the sabbath and festivals are dual-purpose commandments. They are reminders of correct doctrines—that is, they promote the welfare of the soul, which is the same as the thought of God—and they also procure rest and encourage social intercourse—that is, they promote the welfare of the body, which is the same as the thought of the self. The *Book of Seasons* reflects this duality: the sabbath, for example, is described as a sign between the Jewish people and God, and breach of its laws is compared to idolatry, but the book's final gesture is towards the social theme. It ends on the idea of harmony between husband and wife, and on the assertion that peace is the whole purpose of the Torah, ideas that themselves harmonize with 'Laws of Moral Qualities', which ends on the theme of order and harmony in the state. It can at least be said, then, that the book moves from the thought of God to the thought of the self, from the theological to the ethical and moral perspective.

As noted in Chapter 4, a clear connection exists between the ending of the *Book of Women* and that of the *Book of Purity*. The former ends with a man 'moved by the spirit of purity' in warning his wife not to stray, and on his household being 'free from all sin and iniquity', which is exactly the idea on which the latter book also closes ('May God, in his great mercy, purify us from every sin, iniquity and guilt'). Purification is an important element in the Neoplatonic idea of the soul turning away from the world back towards intellect. Moreover, the positioning of 'Laws of the Wayward Woman' at the end of the *Book of Women* (which is at variance with the position of the corresponding mishnaic tractate *Sotah* within Order *Nashim*) can be seen as an example of Maimonides creating a sequence that ends on the idea of breakdown and repair. The point of the ordeal of the woman accused of adultery is not so much to punish the guilty as to clear the innocent, and to save a marriage by restoring a jealous and suspicious husband's faith. This is expressed powerfully at the end of the *Book of Seasons*: 'even a Divine Name might be erased to make peace between husband and wife'. The ending of the *Book of Women* thus interacts with the ending of the previous volume, and more remotely with the ending of the *Book of Purity*, through verbal echo, and more generally through participation in its theme of restoration and return. Thus there are also undertones here of 'Laws of Repentance', where return is the underlying idea.

In retrospect, the *Book of Love* can also be seen to participate in the marital theme, ending as it does on 'Laws of Circumcision'. In the *Guide*, circumcision is explained as both a sign of belief in God's unity and a damper on desire, restraint of the sexual appetite being a prerequisite of both social order and the pursuit of knowledge, so that the second function of circumcision serves the first. In the *Mishneh torah*, the stated function is more like the first one,[25] but the second helps to tie these three volumes together in interesting ways. At any rate, although there is no rigid symmetry, Books 2, 3, and 4 do exhibit distinct traces of the God–self–agent-intellect pattern of Books 8–10.

Moving on to Books 5 to 7, Book 5, the *Book of Holiness*, expresses the thought of God, in that it concerns divinely imposed restrictions on appetite, and, as we have just seen, it certainly ends on that thought, with the commandments as signs of reverence to God, 'to Him who issued them, blessed be He'.[26]

Book 6, the *Book of Asseverations*, expresses the thought of the self, in that it concerns self-imposed restrictions as moral correctives. The message of its ending (at least the explicit message) concerns social responsibility, again echoing 'Laws of Moral Qualities', and orientating the book towards the welfare of the body, or the thought of the self. Book 7, the *Book of Agriculture*, has an ending very similar to that of Book 10, the *Book of Purity*, in that it describes a renunciation of worldly vanities and a turn towards intellect. Here too a balance is struck with the ending of the previous book, the *Book of Asseverations*, with its caution against excessive otherworldliness. Thus the pattern repeats itself.

There are, then, signs of a certain idea permeating Maimonides' conceptualization and arrangement of the commandments throughout the first ten

[25] See the comment on circumcision in the listing of the books in Maimonides' introduction.   [26] 'Laws of Slaughtering', 4: 16.

books of the *Mishneh torah*. It is not necessarily the main idea, but it is traceable beyond Books 8 to 10, where it is dominant, as a kind of underlying rhythm. It is the endings of the books as much as anything that establishes this rhythm, the three beats of which represent the universal triple orientation of all intellectual beings. The pattern is emblematic of the process on which Maimonides expatiates in the *Guide*,[27] after he has explained the origin and utility of the commandments, which is that performance of the commandments is an aid to the constant awareness of God, the conversion, as it were, of action into thought.

Social Regeneration and Messiah

All this is in contrast with the last four books, which proceed in linear fashion, like the motions of the elements, towards the perfected, messianic society. Again, the endings of the books help to establish the trend. A common feature of the endings of Books 11–13 is that they all express the idea of God's care for his creatures and the obligation of human beings to imitate it. Thus, at the end of Book 11, the *Book of Damages*, the duty to assist a sinful Jew in distress is backed by God's desire for the sinner's repentance rather than his or her perdition; at the end of Book 12, the *Book of Acquisition*, the commandment of *imitatio Dei* is mentioned explicitly in connection with God's mercy 'on all His works'; at the end of Book 13, the *Book of Civil Laws*, the duty of honest stewardship of the affairs of orphans is linked to the quasi-paternal care of orphans by 'Him that rideth upon the *aravot*'.

Here too, we see the *Book of Knowledge* functioning as a pattern. The most direct connection with that book is via *imitatio Dei*, which is the basic commandment in its second section, 'Laws of Moral Qualities'. As remarked in Chapter 13, Books 11 to 13 reflect the closing words of that section on the avoidance of vengefulness and resentment: 'This is the right principle. It alone makes civilized life and social intercourse possible.' These books infuse the principles of 'Laws of Moral Qualities' into society. If, however, we bring the very last book, the *Book of Judges*, into the picture, we can see a broader reflection of the *Book of Knowledge* as a whole. The *Book of Knowledge* begins with the subject of knowledge of God and ends on the subject of repentance (in the shape of 'Laws of Repentance'). The last four books of the *Mishneh torah* proceed in the opposite direction. As we have just seen, the subject of the ending of Book 11 is repentance, while Book 14 closes on the subject of universal knowledge of God.

---

[27] *Guide* iii. 50–2 (pp. 613–28).

There is nothing coincidental about this. It fits precisely the paradigm of the process of emanation in the universe above the earth, in which power and perfection diminish with progression from the source, and the converse process on earth of increasing perfection (see Appendix). The former process is associated with the first ten books of the *Mishneh torah*, on commandments between human beings and God, and the latter with the last four books, on the earth-bound social commandments. Accordingly, the endings of the last four books go from repentance, a turning away from vice, through the inculcation of moral virtue, towards a society in which there is maximum receptivity to knowledge. We have, moreover, often observed in the course of the preceding chapters that the ending of one book serves both as an epilogue to that book and as a prologue to the next. This concatenation contributes to artistic unity and hints at the underlying ideas of emanation in the *Mishneh torah*'s first ten books and of gradual regeneration in the last four.

Our observation that, in the ending of the *Book of Civil Laws*, the transcendent, ultimately unknowable God is nevertheless present in the world, in caring for orphans and widows, is applicable to the endings of all three of Books 11 to 13, and it reflects the motto of the *Mishneh torah* and of every single book within it (and of all three parts of the *Guide*): Abraham's call 'In the name of the Lord, God of the world', that is, the remote, indescribable 'Lord' (*YHWH*) who is at the same time an immanent God (*el*). The relationship between the remote *Book of Knowledge*, where the doctrine of God's complete separateness from the world is stated, and the last four books of the *Mishneh torah* is a literary enactment of that paradoxical motto. We stress again that the book endings are key to this effect. They are one of the most important devices whereby the parts of the *Mishneh torah* are networked into a meaningful whole.

The Straight Way

We shall not attempt to summarize all the verbal and thematic links between the *Mishneh torah*'s book endings discussed in the above chapters. Another repeated idea that we would highlight here, however, is that of a way or path and of walking straight, together with the associated idea of being, or being made, straight. The first ending in which it appears is that of Book 2: 'Walk in My ways and be blameless. I will establish my covenant between Me and you.' Here Maimonides cites God's words to Abraham introducing the command to be circumcised. The motif of the way and/or of straightness reappears in one form or another in more than half the subsequent endings.[28]

[28] See the ends of the *Book of Seasons* ('all her paths are peace'); the *Book of Women* ('to

These endings resonate with the essential idea of the middle path, 'the straight way' (*haderekh hayesharah*),²⁹ towards which it is the business of the Torah to guide us.³⁰ This way is associated with Abraham: 'this path is called the Way of God and this is what the patriarch Abraham taught his children, as it is said "For I love him, because he will charge his children and his household after him, that they may keep the way of the Lord to do righteousness and justice".'³¹ Consciously or not, through this motif Maimonides channels halakhah towards its Abrahamic purpose.

Style and Expression

A final common aspect of the endings is their expressive power. This is partly generated by their argumentation, but altogether they are fine examples of Maimonides' literary skill. All of them are eloquent and pointed, and some are also densely allusive, producing deep consent to their spiritualization of halakhah. In the *Mishneh torah* such lyricism is by no means limited to the endings of the books, but in those places it is especially resonant and purposive. The *Guide* opens and closes with short poems (in Hebrew). The endings of the *Mishneh torah*'s books are not poetry as such (although they occasionally slip into a verse metre, and possibly even intentional rhyme),³² but all the same they have a poetic intensity, a heightened form of expression that elevates them above the surrounding material, drawing attention to them and opening channels of communication between them.

This is an important feature to take into account in assessing the persuasiveness of Maimonides' universalist case. After all, the construction that we claim he places on the Bible and halakhah could be criticized as no less tendentious than any other. Our analysis of the endings testifies against this charge. Their individual content, their expressiveness, their own inter-

---

guide her to the straight path' [*baderekh hayesharah*]); the *Book of Holiness* ('and has delivered us from groping in the darkness by making the commandments a lamp to straighten out [*leyasher*] the crooked places and a light to teach us the paths of uprightness' [*netivot hayosher*, lit. 'paths of straightness']); the *Book of Agriculture* ('who walks upright [*yashar*—'straight'] as God had made him'), while earlier in that passage the tribe of Levi is described as 'set apart to worship the Lord, to serve Him, and to teach His upright ways [*derakhav hayesharim*—more literally 'straight paths'] and His righteous judgements'; the *Book of Temple Service* ('through the performance of the statutes and the ordinances the righteous [*hayesharim*—'the straight'] merit life in the world to come'); the *Book of Offerings* ('to make straight [*leyasher*] all doings'); and the *Book of Acquisition* ('the way of wisdom [*derekh haḥokhmah*]').

²⁹ 'Laws of Moral Qualities', 1: 4.   ³⁰ See Maimonides, *Eight Chapters*, ch. 4.
³¹ 'Laws of Moral Qualities', 1: 7, citing Gen. 18: 19.
³² As in 'Laws of Sabbatical and Jubilee Years', 13: 13.

connectedness, and the connections that they help to form create a fine balance between the parts of halakhah. They are, moreover, one of the formal devices that mobilize the force of Maimonides' philosophy behind the valuations and the scale of values that he applies. His judgements on the values that halakhah enshrines and on priorities within those values are felt to be based upon a sensible appreciation of the whole, and upon a system in which everything finds its place, rather than upon the seizure of convenient parts.

In short, the endings of the books of the *Mishneh torah* are carefully crafted and deployed. They adjust the tendency of each individual book, generally in a universalist direction, and compose a balanced and integrated picture of halakhah, oriented towards universal conceptions of individual and social perfection. They guide the reader towards an understanding of all the ceremonial commandments as intellectually and morally purposive, and of the social commandments as infused with the divine, creating a sense of reciprocity between intellectual virtue and moral virtue. This, combined with their shared stylistic and tonal attributes, makes them worthy of separate consideration, a study in which we hope to have made at least a fair beginning.

How much of Maimonides' construction still stands and how well it competes with rival ideologies of Judaism are questions beyond our scope. It is sometimes compared unfavourably with the approach of Judah Halevi, for being magnificent but inauthentic, ingenious but uninspiring. Our isolation and inspection of the endings of the books of the *Mishneh torah* are partly meant to help demonstrate that Maimonides' construct is so intricate and involving, and so sensitive in its handling of the biblical and rabbinic material, that such criticisms fall away. In his rendering of that material, the essential components of his universalism, namely that there is no innate difference between Jews and the rest of humanity, and that the Torah's ideal is general enlightenment and peace, grow organically out of halakhah, or are distilled from it—and the book endings are the distillation. At the same time, the *Mishneh torah* has extra-halakhic bearings: historical, in the figure of Abraham, and ontological, in the natural order after which its structure is modelled. The correlation of these two thrusts, from within halakhah outwards and from science and philosophy inwards, is just one of the things that make the *Mishneh torah* a literary marvel. The message of our book endings is that halakhah is a Mosaic means to an Abrahamic end, but in Maimonides' presentation it becomes a medium for apprehending that end, an invitation and guide to discovery, and this is perhaps the *Mishneh torah*'s most profoundly Abrahamic attribute. The standard notion of competition between universal reason and particularist revelation dissolves in an artistic creation that, like nature, is constantly revelatory. The result is not a wan compromise with, or a capitulation to, alien philosophy, but genuinely both Jewish and universal.

APPENDIX

MAIMONIDES' COSMIC PARADIGM

IN DAVID GILLIS'S *Reading Maimonides' Mishneh Torah*, the *Mishneh torah* is shown to have a structure based on the cosmology outlined in its first section, 'Laws of the Foundations of the Torah'. This is interpreted as a device whereby Maimonides incorporates his Aristotelian/Neoplatonic philosophy into his code of Jewish law. Since this theory underlies parts of the present book, we present a summary of it below.

The idea is intricate in detail, but in outline it is simple. The *Mishneh torah* has fourteen books. Following a classic rabbinic distinction, these are divided between ten books on *mitsvot bein adam lamakom* (commandments between man and God, or ceremonial commandments), and four books on *mitsvot bein adam leḥavero* (commandments between man and his fellow, or social commandments).[1] In 'Laws of the Foundations of the Torah', the main components of the universe are ten orders of angels, which govern the spheres containing the stars, planets, sun, and moon, and the four elements of matter—fire, air, water, and earth—of which everything in the world beneath the moon, including human beings, is composed. The ten books on the heavenward-aspiring *mitsvot bein adam lamakom* correspond to the ten angels, while the four books on *mitsvot bein adam leḥavero*, with their mundane orientation, correspond to the four elements.

The *Mishneh torah* is thus constructed as a microcosm.

What might this structure tell us about Maimonides' view of the status and function of the commandments?

Cosmology and Law

We must first understand why the *Mishneh torah* discusses cosmology at all. What has cosmology to do with halakhah, the *Mishneh torah*'s ostensible

[1] That this is Maimonides' plan is demonstrated in Gillis, *Reading Maimonides' Mishneh Torah*, 158–62, where apparent anomalies in this division are also discussed.

subject?² The answer is that Maimonides determines that there are commandments to know, love, and be in awe of God,³ but since God himself is absolutely unknowable,⁴ there is 'no way to apprehend Him except it be through the things He has made'.⁵ It is through the study of these things, that is, the laws of nature, that one comes to love God and to be in awe of him.⁶ Moreover, the principal commandment of 'Laws of Moral Qualities' is the imitation of God,⁷ but if God cannot be directly known, he cannot be directly imitated; the fulfilment of this commandment lies in the imitation of God's ways in nature.⁸ The fundamental commandments of the Torah in the realms of what Aristotle called intellectual and moral virtue are thus bound up with knowledge of science and philosophy, and so Maimonides provides a condensed account of the cosmos and of God's relationship to it at the beginning of his code of law, 'that they may serve the intelligent individual as a door to the love of God'.⁹

The relationship between human virtue and cosmology goes deeper than this, however, and in order to appreciate it more fully we need to look in more detail at the *Mishneh torah*'s account of the cosmos (with some supplementary material from the *Guide* and from Maimonides' philosophical sources), while suspending our belief in modern science and attempting to see the world through Maimonides' eyes.

The Model

In the Aristotelian model of the universe,¹⁰ the standard model in Maimonides' time, the earth is at the centre, surrounded by nine invisible nested spheres, 'like the layers of onions'.¹¹ The earth is still while the spheres rotate,

---

² Cosmological theory needs to be distinguished from astronomical observation and calculation, which are very pertinent to halakhah, as evidenced by 'Laws of Sanctification of the New Moon'. ³ See 'Laws of the Foundation of the Torah', 1: 6 and 2: 1. ⁴ Ibid. 2: 10.
⁵ *Guide* i. 34 (p. 74). ⁶ 'Laws of the Foundations of the Torah', 2: 2.
⁷ 'Laws of Moral Qualities', 1: 5. ⁸ Ibid. See also *Guide* i. 54 (p. 125).
⁹ 'Laws of the Foundations of the Torah', 2: 2.
¹⁰ The account that follows is very much simplified, and ignores, among other things, differences between the cosmologies presented in the *Mishneh torah* and the *Guide*, on which see Rudavsky, *Time Matters*, 24–30; Langermann, 'Astronomical Problems' (Heb.); Freudenthal, 'Four Observations' (Heb.).
¹¹ 'Laws of the Foundations of the Torah', 3: 1–2. At this point Maimonides reveals that the nine spheres are subdivided into many more spheres, which are required, together with epicycles (ibid. 3: 4), in order to account for the complicated movements of the planets as seen from earth, but nine is the basic number given at the start of the description of the spheres in 'Laws of the Foundations of the Torah', 3: 1. Aristotle thought that there could be

accounting for the observed movements of the moon, the sun, the five known planets, and the stars, which are embedded in spheres one to eight. The motions of these spheres are partly controlled by the ninth and highest sphere (which contains no stars or planets) as it rotates once every twenty-four hours from east to west.[12]

Copernicus and Kepler put the earth along with the other planets in elliptical motion around the sun, and astronomy now teaches that the stars exist in billions of galaxies, but that change from the medieval model does not represent the greatest gap between modern science and the worldview of Maimonides (who, incidentally, was well aware that the model was flawed).[13] More significant in this respect than the architecture of the universe is what makes it work.

A Moral Universe

It would be fair to say that nowadays even those who believe in a creator God consider the fabric of the universe as morally neutral. As far as we know, human beings are the only moral agents in existence, and the only creatures capable of abstract thought. We certainly do not attribute thoughts and feelings to the stars and all the other amalgamations of rock, dust, and gas that circulate in space under the effect of gravity. Beyond the fact that planet earth is home, we do not privilege one part of the universe over any other, and we assume the laws of physics and chemistry and the elements of matter to be the same everywhere, in an expanding universe that is constantly evolving, as stars explode and new ones are formed.

The medieval view was very different. Maimonides considered the cosmos as a living, thinking organism. He held the spheres and the stars and planets they contain to possess souls and intellects far superior to those of human beings.[14] In his system, it is the consciousness and yearnings of these living creatures that make them move in the ways they do.

Emanation and the Celestial Hierarchy

The celestial bodies are not equally intellectually endowed. The higher you go, the greater the intellectual capacity you encounter.[15] This universe is

---

as many as fifty-five spheres (*Met.* XII.8,1074a, 1–14), on which see *Guide* ii. 4 (p. 257). See also n. 20 below.

[12] 'Laws of the Foundations of the Torah', 3: 1. [13] See *Guide* ii. 24 (pp. 322–7).
[14] See 'Laws of the Foundations of the Torah', 3: 9. [15] Ibid. 2: 5–8.

thus not egalitarian like ours, but hierarchical. Nor is it uniform in its composition. Celestial bodies are composed of a refined, imperishable material, unlike terrestrial objects, which are subject to change and decay.[16] In the heavens there is movement, but no change.

The hierarchy of the heavens is a result of the phenomenon behind their existence, known as emanation. This concept was developed by the Neoplatonic philosophers of the third century CE onwards, first and foremost Plotinus, and adapted by the Islamic writers Alfarabi (d. 950) and Avicenna (980–1037) to fit the Aristotelian model of the visible universe.

In the system of emanation propounded by Plotinus there are three levels. At the top is the ineffable One or Good (the 'First Being' of 'Laws of the Foundations of the Torah', 1: 1). A flow of goodness from the One turns back in love towards it, and in doing so becomes Intellect.[17] Intellect contemplates the One, and also itself, but it is not able to comprehend the unity of the One as it truly is, and fragments it into the Forms, the ideal essences of things. In turn, a flow from Intellect turns back towards it and becomes Soul. Soul carries the process of fragmentation further, so that Intellect's timeless, holistic vision of the Forms becomes successive, bringing space and time into existence. Soul itself has two levels: the higher level remains in contemplation of Intellect, while the lower level imposes the Forms on Matter, which is a kind of darkness left after emanation peters out. This gives rise to the tangible world.

In Aristotle's cosmology, each sphere has an intelligence associated with it that makes it move, but the intelligence does not produce the sphere, and there is no causal relationship between the intelligences. In Alfarabi and Avicenna, the idea of emanation supplies these connections. The cosmology that Maimonides presents is this amalgam of Aristotle and Neoplatonism (see the diagram on p. 337 below).[18]

Maimonides compares emanation to a flow of water from a fountain.[19] From the First Being or God, a first non-corporeal intelligence or separate intellect (i.e. separate from any kind of matter) flows, or emanates. This first separate intellect has two directions of thought: back towards God, and

---

[16] Ibid. 2: 3 and 3: 3.

[17] 'Intellect', 'Soul', 'Form', and 'Matter' are given initial capitals to distinguish Plotinus's use of these concepts from their derivative and general use.

[18] For an account of Maimonides' adoption and adaptation of the emanation theories of Alfarabi and Avicenna, see Davidson, *Alfarabi, Avicenna, and Averroes on Intellect*, 198–201.

[19] See *Guide* ii. 12 (p. 279). Maimonides admits that 'the mental representation of the action of one that is separate from matter is very difficult'.

towards itself. From its thought of God, it emanates the second separate intellect. From its thought of itself, it emanates the highest, outermost sphere, the one that holds no stars or planets.

The Neoplatonic hierarchy is replicated within the sphere: it has an intellect, a soul, and a material body. Its intellect perceives the separate intellect, its soul loves and yearns to be united with it, and this yearning causes its body to move in constant rotation (because the separate intellect, as a non-corporeal being, has no location towards which there could be linear motion).[20]

Like a separate intellect, a sphere too has three directions of thought. Besides the separate intellect from which it emanates, it also contemplates God, and itself, but the intellectual power of the spheres is less than that of the angels, though greater than that of human beings.[21]

The second separate intellect contemplates the first separate intellect, to which it longs to return. It also has a thought of God, from which emanates the third separate intellect, and a thought of itself, from which emanates the intellect, soul, and body of the second-highest sphere, that of the fixed stars (so called because they appear fixed in relation to one another and rotate once every twenty-four hours in fixed synchronization with the outermost sphere).

The flow continues in similar fashion but with diminishing power and diminishing knowledge of God, along the way producing all the rest of the spheres containing the planets, the sun, and the moon, down to the tenth and last separate intellect, known as the agent intellect.

In the *Mishneh torah*, the ten separate intellects are presented as the ten orders of angels. The first separate intellect is the *ḥayot*, which possesses knowledge of God in the highest possible degree; the second is the *ofanim*; the third is the *erelim*; and so on down to the tenth, which is the angel known as *ishim*.[22] The whole system can be thought of as the devolution of form and knowledge from God, and what holds it together and makes it move is not gravity, but love.

---

[20] Ibid. ii. 4 (p. 256). Here, the sphere's rotary movement is attributed to its love of God, but in *Guide* ii. 6 (p. 265) it is made clear that this works through the separate intellect.

[21] See 'Laws of the Foundations of the Torah', 3: 9.

[22] The emanation and intellectual hierarchy of the angels is described in 'Laws of the Foundations of the Torah', 2: 5–8. Although the angels' Hebrew names are in the plural, Maimonides treats them as singular. As far as Maimonides is concerned angels are natural, not supernatural, beings. They are a part of creation, though a superior part. In *Guide* ii. 6 (pp. 261–5) they are identified with natural forces. In *Guide* ii. 4 (p. 257), the 'opinion of the later philosophers' is cited that there are ten separate intellects and nine 'globes', some of which are subdivided into several spheres.

The Four Elements of Matter

With the *ishim*, emanation is at an end. After that come the four elements of terrestrial matter.[23] These elements are insensate, possessing neither souls nor intellects.[24] Each has its natural place—fire is above air, which is above water, which is above earth—but they combine, separate, and recombine under the influence of the revolutions of the spheres.[25] The *ishim*, which is not sufficiently powerful to emanate another angel or a sphere, instead projects forms onto terrestrial matter.[26] Each combination of elements receives the form appropriate to it, turning it into a stone, a flower, an animal, or a human being: the entire variety of things we see.[27] Form is the essence of something, that which makes it what it is. The *ishim* also broadcasts knowledge, which is received by suitably trained and attuned human minds.[28] These two functions are essentially the same, knowledge being the apprehension of forms and their abstraction from matter.[29]

Since the material of which the heavens are made is permanent, the forms that inhere in it, of the spheres, stars, and planets, are permanent too, whereas terrestrial forms perish when the combinations of elements that receive them disintegrate.[30]

Emanation is not a process in time. It is a logical progression, not a temporal one.[31] The existence of each angel depends on that of the immediately prior one in the hierarchy.[32] Beneath the moon, the generation and decay of entities composed of the four elements is a process in time. In that region, there are no permanent individual forms; only permanent processes and permanent species.[33] A further contrast is that, whereas in emanation perfection diminishes with each level after the source, terrestrial processes tend towards greater perfection.[34]

[23] See 'Laws of the Foundations of the Torah', 3: 10.
[24] Ibid. 3: 11.   [25] Ibid. 4: 5–6; *Guide* ii. 10 (pp. 269–73).
[26] *Guide* ii. 12 (p. 278); 'Laws of the Foundations of the Torah', 4: 6.
[27] 'Laws of the Foundations of the Torah', 4: 1.
[28] See *Guide* ii. 36–7 (pp. 369–75); 'Laws of the Foundations of the Torah', 7: 1. This marks another feature that distinguishes medieval from modern thought. We regard science as a construct created by the human mind. For Maimonides, theoretical knowledge is something that the mind receives. This is in accordance with the Aristotelian principle that a potential cannot become actual unless the actual pre-exists. So the realization of the human intellect's potential is the reception of knowledge pre-existing in the agent intellect.
[29] 'Laws of the Foundations of the Torah', 4: 7.   [30] Ibid. 2: 3.
[31] See *Guide* ii. 21 (p. 316).   [32] See 'Laws of the Foundations of the Torah', 2: 5–6.
[33] See *Guide* i. 72 (pp. 186 and 189).
[34] This is according to Alfarabi; see Fakhry, *A History of Islamic Philosophy*, 123. See also *Guide* iii. 13 (p. 450).

To sum up, the basic components of Maimonides' universe are ten angels, existing in a hierarchy determined by degree of knowledge of God, and four elements of terrestrial matter. The first nine angels produce, and induce the motions of, nine spheres in which are embedded the stars and planets, while the tenth serves as the interface with the terrestrial region. The existence of everything ultimately depends on God, who is the only independent existent, and it is the love of God that moves and regulates the whole system.[35]

Human Beings: Straddling Matter and Intellect

Maimonides did not consider human beings to be the glory of creation. They represent the pinnacle of terrestrial life, but they are outclassed by the spheres and stars, and the fact that the spheres revolve around planet earth does not mean that everything exists for the sake of humankind.[36] On the contrary, earth is the least salubrious neighbourhood of the universe, and Maimonides considers it absurd to think that nobler entities could exist for the sake of less noble ones.[37]

Human beings are interesting, though, because they occupy the border between the universe's two divisions. The human form, that which distinguishes human beings and in respect of which they are said to be 'in the image of God', is the intellect.[38] Possession of an intellect, inferior though it is, puts human beings (all human beings)[39] on the side of the angels, spheres, and stars. At the same time, human beings have bodies made up of the four elements of terrestrial matter. Moreover, the intellect with which we are born is only a potential, and our material condition impedes its fulfilment, for in Maimonides' worldview, matter and intellect are opposites.[40]

In order to realize this potential, a human being must first educate the soul and discipline his or her bodily appetites and desires, that is, acquire moral virtue, which, as we have seen, Maimonides defines as the imitation of God, and then become devoted to acquiring knowledge, that is, intellectual virtue,[41] which ultimately means the knowledge of God. The acquisition of knowledge is equivalent to the phase of return in the emanation of the angels,

---

[35] See 'Laws of the Foundations of the Torah', 1: 1–3, 2: 9. The crucial difference between Maimonides and the philosophers is that he regards God as active in the process of emanation, which 'takes place not through eternal necessity but through a noneternal act of will' (Davidson, *Alfarabi, Avicenna, and Averroes on Intellect*, 200).   [36] See *Guide* iii. 13 (p. 452).
[37] *Guide* iii. 14 (p. 458).   [38] See 'Laws of the Foundations of the Torah', 4: 8.
[39] See *Guide* iii. 12 (p. 447).   [40] *Guide* iii. 9 (p. 436).
[41] *Guide* iii. 27 (pp. 510–11). See also 'Laws of the Foundations of the Torah', 4: 13; 'Laws of Torah Study', 3: 9 and 4: 1.

for in this process the human intellect turns back towards the agent intellect from which it derives and which radiates knowledge. This pivot away from matter and towards intellect constitutes a human being as fully human.[42] The developed human intellect (the 'acquired intellect') survives the death of the body.[43] An undeveloped intellect perishes when the body perishes.

The Human Microcosm

Human beings thus reflect the composition and dynamics of the cosmos. They are microcosms, or rather, potential microcosms. This echoes the Neoplatonic idea that the levels of emanation also exist within human beings, who at the temporal, particularized level of Soul need to turn away from the desires induced by Matter towards timeless and holistic Intellect, and aspire to transcendent unity with the One.

In the version of microcosm theory that Maimonides expounds in the *Guide*, human beings, like the universe, have ruling parts and ruled parts.[44] Just as God rules the terrestrial world via the hierarchy of angels, so in a human being the intellect ought to rule the emotions, desires, and appetites, and thereby rule the actions of the material body. All of a human being's faculties then serve the intellect in its pursuit of knowledge and immortality.

A stable and harmonious society, as in the messianic era reached at the end of the *Mishneh torah*, provides conditions conducive to this pursuit, which then occupies all humankind.

So when we look up at the heavens, what we see is not dead matter whirled about by blind forces but an ideal of love and harmony, a pattern of perfection that we should desire to replicate within ourselves and our society. In its totality, the cosmos is as it were the externalization of God, all of God that a human being (or even an angel) can know. The knowledge of God therefore consists in the apprehension of the divine laws that govern the cosmos, and the imitation of God consists in their internalization as the laws governing our own being. Then, our intellects, souls, and bodies will

---

[42] 'through it man is man' (*Guide* iii. 54 (p. 635)).

[43] For the distinction between intellect and soul and the way intellect becomes immortal, see 'Laws of the Foundations of the Torah', 4: 8–9.

[44] *Guide* i. 72. Scholarship has underplayed the significance of this chapter of the *Guide* (for a dismissive view, see Bland, *The Artless Jew*, 80–1). Within the *Mishneh torah*, the idea of the human being as microcosm is implied in structural correspondences between 'Laws of the Foundations of the Torah', which is about God and the universe, and 'Laws of Moral Qualities', which is about human beings and human societies; see Gillis, *Reading Maimonides' Mishneh Torah*, 93–6.

function like the intellects, souls, and bodies of the spheres, and we too will be moved and regulated by the love of God.

Unfortunately, our borderline condition represents an obstacle to the realization of this ideal. The universe's highest sentient components, the angels, stars, and spheres, are self-aware and have moral choice—but they will always choose the good.[45] They will always praise and love God, with the love that gives the universe its unswerving motions, contemplating him with unclouded intellects, each according to its rank. Human beings, composed of a corruptible and corrupting kind of matter that provokes in the soul desires subversive of intellect, do not always choose the good, and lack intellectual clarity. They need help.

The commandments of the Torah, transmitted by a prophet who transcended human limitations to the greatest extent possible, are designed to assist human beings in realizing their microcosmic potential. They are meant to perfect the human personality and human society by shaping them according to the perfect cosmic order, translating the laws of nature into laws of human conduct.[46] This renders human beings fit and able to attain the ultimate fulfilment of the knowledge of God, which the commandments also inculcate.

Hence the *Mishneh torah* is configured as a microcosm. Its overall form embodies this general rationalization of the commandments. This raises the expectation that closer analysis of the *Mishneh torah*'s form along these lines might reveal in greater detail and depth how the commandments function, by analogy with the processes, structures, and relationships found in nature, the macrocosm.

The Hierarchy of the Commandments

We began this summary by describing the first ten books of the *Mishneh torah*, on commandments between human beings and God, as corresponding to the ten orders of angels. These books concern a human being's relationship with God as formulated in certain essential doctrines and expressed in ritual.[47] The first ten books mediate between human beings and God as the angels mediate between God and earth, while the last four books, on

---

[45] See *Guide* ii. 7 (p. 266).

[46] That the Torah reflects the order of nature is a well-recognized Maimonidean motif. For full-length treatments of the subject see Hadad, *Torah and Nature* (Heb.), and Funkenstein, *Maimonides: Nature, History, and Messianic Beliefs* (Heb.).

[47] Laws designed to inculcate moral qualities are placed in this division, even though they clearly have social ramifications, because the basis for moral virtue in Maimonides is the imitation of God.

'commandments between man and his fellow', concern social, commercial, and political matters, corresponding to the inanimate four elements that form the material objects, and hence the material interests, that are the subject of these commandments.

The implication is that, like the angels, the first ten books of the *Mishneh torah* form a hierarchy. If we examine them by the criterion that determines the angelic hierarchy, which we said is the degree of knowledge of God, we can see that this is indeed the case. The order of the books can be explained by how closely the commandments that each contains concern the ultimate human goal of knowledge of God, or their degree of intellectuality, as opposed to materiality. Thus the highest book in the hierarchy is called, unsurprisingly, the *Book of Knowledge*, and it contains commandments that are absolutely logical, such as to apprehend the existence, unity, uniqueness, and incorporeality of God (all demonstrable propositions as far as Maimonides is concerned), or that are closely related to these essential doctrines, and that involve mental rather than physical operations. The *Book of Knowledge* contemplates God, perceiving him with the highest possible degree of clarity. It is followed by the *Book of Love*, which, as declared in the introduction to the *Mishneh torah*, has as its theme the constant love and remembrance of God, and contains commandments that continually reinforce the doctrines in the *Book of Knowledge* but that involve physical objects and acts (mostly speech acts).

At the other end of the scale are the books dealing with the Temple ritual and purity, which contain the most arbitrary and physical commandments, and the ones furthest removed from intellectual apprehension of God.[48]

In between we have the *Book of Seasons* (Book 3), which, although it contains commandments that are reminders of correct doctrines, is a step down from the *Book of Love* in that these commandments are more physical and contingent, since they involve the physical property of time and in many cases commemorate historical events, and they procure physical benefits, such as bodily rest, as well as intellectual ones. This is followed by three books that contain commandments regulating bodily desires and appetites (the *Book of Women*, the *Book of Holiness*, and the *Book of Asseverations*) and one that regulates attitudes to possessions (the *Book of Agriculture*), being concerned with

---

[48] It should be stressed that as far as Maimonides is concerned the laws of purity are entirely technical, having no spiritual or metaphysical significance whatsoever (see *Guide* iii. 47 (p. 595)). At the end of the *Book of Purity*, Maimonides turns the purification ritual of immersion in a *mikveh* into a metaphor for steeping oneself in intellect, while maintaining its non-metaphysical character. See the discussion in Ch. 10 above.

restrictions on land use and obligations to the poor and the landless. The trend is away from the intellectual towards the moral and social.

Besides intellectual and absolute versus physical and contingent, the hierarchy of books can be understood in terms of two other scales of value in Maimonides. One is love of God versus awe of God. Love, according to Maimonides, prompts desire for knowledge and is commensurate with it, whereas awe arises from consciousness of one's low, material condition and intellectual inadequacy.[49] Service of God out of love is preferable to service of God out of awe.[50] The *Book of Knowledge* thus represents love, while the title of the *Book of Love* speaks for itself. At the other end of the scale, the keynote commandment concerning the Temple is to be in awe of it, and hence in awe of God.[51] The other scale of value arises out of the distinction that Maimonides draws in the *Guide* between the 'first intention' of the Torah and its 'second intention'. The Torah's first intention is 'the apprehension of Him, may He be exalted, and the rejection of idolatry'.[52] The second intention is actually to use the forms of idolatry, such as sacrifices, to defeat the ideology of idolatry. The hierarchy of the first ten books of the *Mishneh torah* promotes first-intention commandments over second-intention commandments.

Permanence versus Process

The cosmic divide between a region of being, of distinct permanent forms, from the sphere of the moon upwards, and below the moon a region of becoming, of process, involving intermingling elements and changing forms, is also reflected in the *Mishneh torah*'s structure. The first ten books form a system, but each has its own governing concept. The last four books, on the other hand, are all part of a single process of the rehabilitation and perfection of society, from the dysfunctional world of Book 11, the *Book of Damages*, characterized by robbery, violence, and murder, via the co-operative and constructive relations between people in the *Book of Acquisition* and the *Book of Civil Law* (Books 12 and 13), to the harmonious society governed by stable institutions of the *Book of Judges* (Book 14), ending with the ideal state of the messianic age. This reflects the tendency towards perfection of natural terrestrial processes.

The distinction between being and becoming can be traced by means of specific commandments. The most prominent is the knowledge of God—a

---

[49] See 'Laws of the Foundations of the Torah', 2: 2, and 'Laws of Repentance', 10: 6.
[50] 'Laws of Repentance', 10: 5.   [51] See 'Laws of the Temple', 7: 1.
[52] *Guide* iii. 32 (p. 327).

timeless imperative at the opening of the *Mishneh torah*, but a historical outcome at its close. The building of the Temple provides a further example. At the opening of the *Book of Temple Service* (Book 8), this too is presented as a timeless commandment: 'It is a positive commandment to make a house for the Lord, suitable for bringing sacrifices.'[53] At the end of the *Book of Judges*, building the Temple is a task for the messiah, again as the culmination of a historical process.

The structure and dynamics of the *Mishneh torah* thus reproduce in literary form the structure and dynamics of the Maimonidean cosmos, and thereby render the commandments intelligible as a system. This form also enables us to understand what Maimonides means when he says that physics and metaphysics are 'a great thing' while halakhah is 'a small thing'.[54] It is not just that halakhah is easier to learn, or that it promotes the moral perfection required as a prelude to studying those loftier disciplines; halakhah is actually a projection of physics and metaphysics.

Emanation from the *Book of Knowledge*

In a further analogy of the cosmic process of emanation and return, the practical commandments in the subsequent books can be said to emanate from, or to be informed by, the essential concepts in the *Book of Knowledge*, and to educate our moral and intellectual faculties in those concepts, thus returning us to them. This too is represented structurally, in that the *Book of Knowledge*, and within it the first section, 'Laws of the Foundations of the Torah' (which has ten chapters), constitute templates for the ten books of the 'between man and God' division.[55] In Neoplatonic terms, the *Book of Knowledge* is Intellect, holding within it the Forms, or concepts, that acquire tangible expression in space and time through the practical commandments in the subsequent books, which in turn guide Soul away from Matter and back towards Intellect.

This is not the place to go into great detail on this feature.[56] A couple of

---

[53] 'Laws of the Temple', 1: 1.   [54] 'Laws of the Foundations of the Torah', 4: 13.

[55] In the introduction to the *Mishneh torah*, Maimonides describes the *Book of Knowledge* as containing the commandments that are 'the root of the faith taught by Moses, our teacher'. (Hyamson has 'the very essence and principle', but 'root' is a more faithful rendering of the Hebrew *ikar*.) The other books are thus the branches. The title 'Laws of the Foundations of the Torah' of course expresses something similar itself, using an architectural metaphor: if these are the foundations, then the rest of the commandments are the superstructure, following the plan of the foundations. The parallel with cosmic structures gives the jurisprudential idea of roots and branches of the law a philosophical dimension.

[56] For a fuller exposition, see Gillis, *Reading Maimonides' Mishneh Torah*, 239–60.

examples will illustrate what is meant. Chapter 2 of 'Laws of the Foundations of the Torah' discusses the commandment to love God. Correspondingly, Book 2 is the *Book of Love*, which particularizes that love as regular actions. Chapter 5 of 'Laws of the Foundations of the Torah' discusses the commandment to sanctify (in Hebrew, *lekadesh*) the name of God, which means to bear witness to God, if necessary through martyrdom This is the first commandment in the *Mishneh torah* addressed specifically to the Jewish people rather than being of universal application. Correspondingly, Book 5 is the *Book of Holiness* (in Hebrew, *Sefer kedushah*, from the same root as *lekadesh*). The commandments it contains regulate the desires for food and sex. Moreover, in the synopsis of Book 5 in the introduction to the *Mishneh torah*, these commandments are described as distinguishing the Jewish people from the other nations (the basic meaning of *lekadesh* being 'to set apart'). We can conclude that the self-sanctification through moral discipline demanded in Book 5 leads to the sanctification of the name of God demanded in 'Laws of the Foundations of the Torah', chapter 5. This very idea is indeed embodied at the end of that chapter by the portrayal of the sage who bears witness to God through his virtuous conduct, which encourages piety in others. This is a further example, in addition to those discussed in the body of this book, of the way in which structure makes connections that can enrich our understanding of the supra-halakhic perorations found at the end of chapters, sections, and books of the *Mishneh torah*. In this case, the formal patterns link the intellectual and moral significances of sanctification, and bring out the distinctive role that the commandments (and, according to Maimonides, *only* the commandments) give the Jewish people in this respect.[57]

To state that Maimonides arranged the commandments hierarchically does not imply that any commandment is dispensable or unimportant. All are part of the system, just as in the cosmos there are higher entities and lower entities, but each has a function to perform; or, as in the human microcosm, there are higher faculties and lower ones, but all are required in order to keep a human being alive.

A Relational Correspondence

It is stressed that the correspondence between microcosm and macrocosm is only relational, and not direct. It is a comparison of relations between the parts of one system with the relations between the parts of another; there is no actual correspondence between the parts of the two systems. Or to put it

---

[57] The application to Book 5 (and Book 6) is expanded upon in Ch. 6 above.

another way, it is a comparison between classes of entities, not between particular entities. Thus when Maimonides discusses the idea of human beings as microcosms in the *Guide*,[58] he compares the relationship between the celestial bodies and the earthly elements to 'ruling parts and ruled parts' in a human being, but he does not suggest that there is something in a human being directly corresponding to, say, the planet Jupiter. When a component is the only member of its class, it might look as though there is such a direct correspondence. In the same passage in the *Guide*, the heart (which Maimonides considered to be the seat of the intellect) is compared to the outer sphere. But in fact here too the comparison is relational: just as the outer sphere governs the motions of the universe as a whole, so the human intellect governs, or ought to govern, the human being as a whole.[59]

Similarly, there is no direct correspondence between parts of the *Mishneh torah*, considered as a microcosm, and particular parts of the macrocosm. The *Book of Knowledge* is to the rest of the *Mishneh torah* as the outer sphere is to the rest of the universe: just as the outer sphere drives the inner spheres, the *Book of Knowledge* is the conceptual driver of the subsequent books. The *Book of Love* also has a similar relationship to the *Book of Knowledge* as the sphere of the fixed stars has to the outer sphere: just as the motion of the fixed stars (unlike that of the planets) is geared directly and consistently to the motion of the outer sphere, so the commandments in the *Book of Love* are direct and constant reminders of the truths expounded in the *Book of Knowledge*. The rest of the angels and spheres, however, are similar in type and function, and represent a single class,[60] so no direct correspondence should be sought between, for example, the *Book of Seasons* (Book 3), and the third angel (the *erelim*) and its sphere (that of Saturn). Such a correspondence would be more like astrology, which Maimonides condemned, than science, which he exalted.[61] What is significant is the hierarchical relation-

[58] See above, n. 44.

[59] This account of Maimonides' argument in *Guide* i. 72 is compressed and simplified, but adequate for the point being made. Other medieval Jewish thinkers treat the idea of human beings as microcosms in a much more literal way; see Conger, *Theories of Macrocosms and Microcosms*, 37–45. Maimonides' version of emanation and his naturalistic microcosm theory also need to be distinguished from the *sefirot* of kabbalah, which similarly derive, partly at least, from Neoplatonism. See Gillis, *Reading Maimonides' Mishneh Torah*, 200–7.

[60] The tenth angel, the *ishim*, is admittedly different, and in fact unique, but discussion of that point would over-complicate this outline. It is touched upon in Ch. 10 above.

[61] See 'Letter to the Rabbis of Montpelier on Astrology', *Igerot harambam* (trans. Shailat), ii. 3, 474–90. This is not to pretend that what Maimonides called science is precisely the same as the mathematically and empirically based science of our time.

ships among angels and spheres, which for Maimonides constituted scientific theory, reflected in a hierarchical arrangement of the first ten books of the *Mishneh torah*.

So, too, the last four books of the *Mishneh torah* correspond to the four elements, but there is no direct correspondence between any one book and any one element. There is a correspondence between the idea of process in sublunary nature and process in human societies.

All this is not an imposition on the *Mishneh torah* of ideas external to it.[62] The *Mishneh torah* is an organic unity. The cosmology set out in its first four chapters is 'a door to the love of God', and at the same time a door to the appreciation of the *Mishneh torah* itself.

[62] In order to bring out this point, we have endeavoured above to provide references to the *Mishneh torah* itself to support statements about Maimonides' cosmology.

The Maimonidean Cosmos

The diagram shows the emanation of the ten separate intellects, or angels (named as in 'Laws of the Foundations of the Torah', 2: 7), and the spheres. The angels do not actually have physical locations.

Emanation is unidirectional from the First Being, or God, down to the *ishim*, or agent intellect. Lower entities have thoughts of higher ones, but do not affect them in any way.

As shown in the enlarged diagram of the activity of the separate intellect/angel, each angel has a thought of the First Being, or God, a thought of itself, and a thought of the prior angel from which it emanates. From its thought of God emanates the next angel, while from its thought of itself emanates the intellect, soul, and body of a sphere.

Each sphere has three directions of thought similar to those of the angels: of God, of itself, and of the angel from which it emanates. When the sphere's intellect represents the angel to its soul, the soul's love of the angel makes it desire to unite with it. Since the angel has no location and the sphere cannot move from its position, this desire causes it to rotate.

The power of emanation diminishes as we descend the hierarchy, so that the *ishim*/agent intellect is too weak to produce another separate intellect. Instead, by analogy with emanation, it projects forms onto the various combinations of the four terrestrial elements, and radiates knowledge.

The number and order of the spheres shown here accords with 'Laws of the Foundations of the Torah', 3: 1. *Guide* ii. 9 (pp. 268–9) puts Venus and Mercury above the sun.

The four elements are arranged in spherical layers, but, having no souls, they do not rotate. Under the influence of the rotating spheres, small amounts of them move up and down and mingle to form different combinations, though each element tends to return to its original, natural place—see 'Laws of the Foundations of the Torah', 3: 10–4: 6.

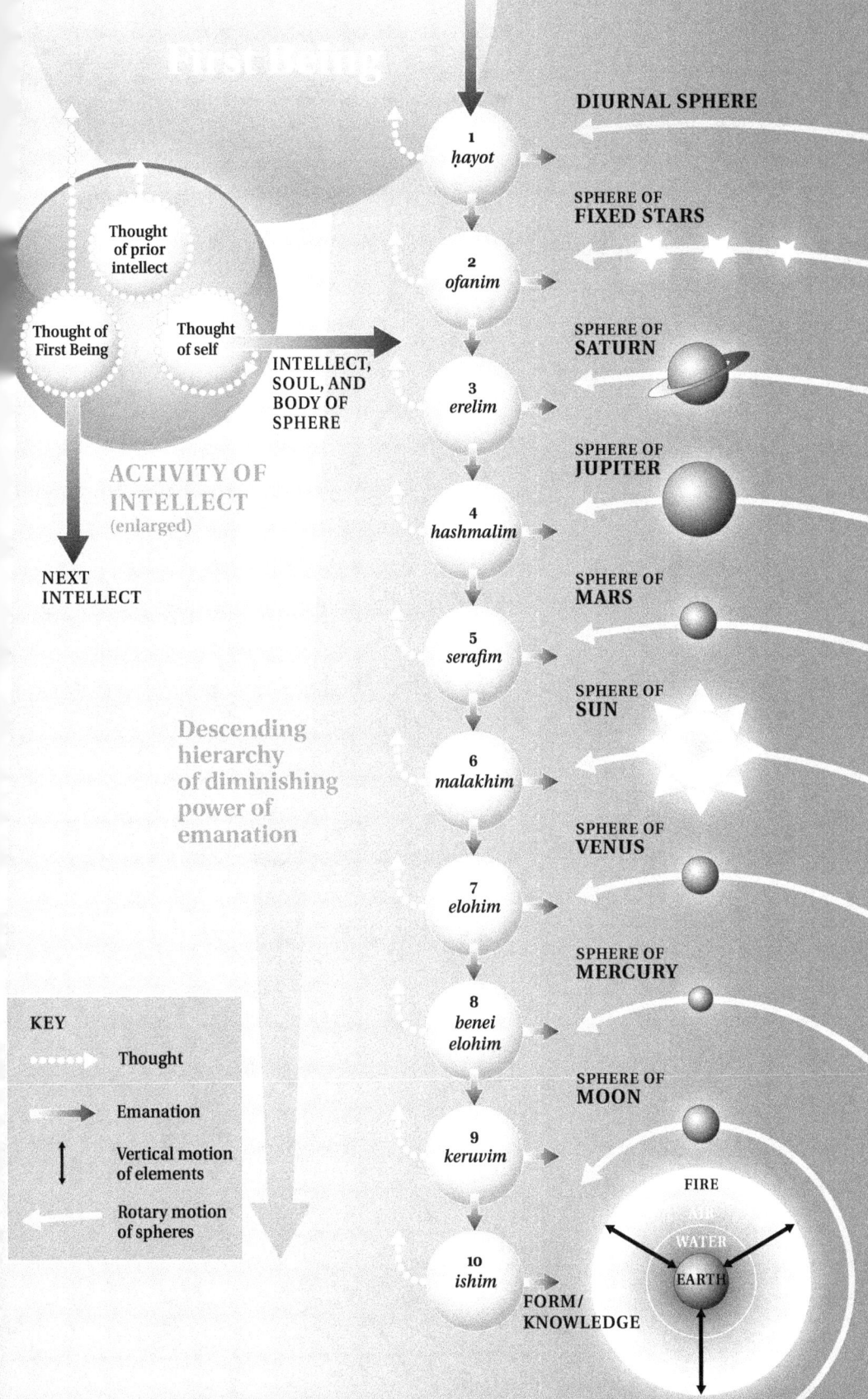

Bibliography

Works by Maimonides

The following editions and translations have been cited throughout, unless stated otherwise in the notes; other translations are by the authors of this book. Published translations have occasionally been emended without comment where a more literal rendering was required in order to make a point, and in cases of slight disagreement with the translator.

Mishneh torah

The Book of Knowledge, trans. Moses Hyamson (Jerusalem, 1974).

The Code of Maimonides, 14 vols., Yale Judaica (New Haven, 1949–2004): *The Book of Knowledge*, trans. Bernard Septimus (forthcoming); *The Book of Love*, trans. Menachem Kellner (2004); *The Book of Seasons*, trans. Solomon Gandz and Hyman Klein (1961); *The Book of Women*, trans. Isaac Klein (1972); *The Book of Holiness*, trans. Louis I. Rabinowitz and Phillip Grossman (1965); *The Book of Asseverations*, trans. B. D. Klein (1977); *The Book of Agriculture*, trans. Isaac Klein (1979); *The Book of Temple Service*, trans. Mendel Lewittes (1957); *The Book of Offerings*, trans. Herbert Danby (1963); *The Book of Cleanness*, trans. Herbert Danby (1954); *The Book of Torts*, trans. Hyman Klein (1954); *The Book of Acquisition*, trans. Isaac Klein (1951); *The Book of Civil Laws*, trans. Jacob J. Rabinowitz (1949); *The Book of Judges*, trans. Abraham M. Hershman (1949).

Mishneh torah, with commentary by Shmuel Tanhum Rubinstein, 20 vols. (*Rambam la'am*) (Jerusalem, 1981); ed. Shabse Frankel, 15 vols. (Jerusalem, 2000); with commentary *Yad peshutah* by Nachum Eliezer Rabinovitch, 20 vols. (Jerusalem, 1990–2011); ed. with commentary by J. Kafih, 25 vols. (Kiryat Ono, 1984–96); ed. Yitshak Shailat, 9 vols. (*Rambam meduyak*) (Ma'aleh Adumim, 2004–11); ed. Yohai Makbili (*Mifal mishneh torah*) (Haifa, 2008).

Other Works by Maimonides

The Book of Commandments [Sefer hamitsvot], ed. Chaim Heller (Jerusalem 1946). *The Book of Divine Commandments (Sefer ha-Mitzvoth of Moses Maimonides)*, trans. Charles B. Chavel, 2 vols. (London, 1967).

Commentary on Avot [Avot im perush harambam], ed. and trans. from the Arabic by Isaac Shailat (Ma'aleh Adumim, 1994).

Commentary on the Mishnah [Mishnah im perush rabenu mosheh ben maimon], ed. and trans. from Arabic Joseph Kafih, 6 vols. (Jerusalem, 1963–7).

Eight Chapters = 'Introduction to Tractate *Avot*', *Commentary on the Mishnah*, trans. in

Raymond L. Weiss and Charles E. Butterworth (eds.), *Ethical Writings of Maimonides* (New York, 1975), 59–104.

Epistle to Yemen, trans. in Abraham Halkin and David Hartman, *Epistles of Maimonides: Crisis and Leadership* (Philadelphia, 1985), 91–131; also trans. by Ralph Lerner in id., *Maimonides' Empire of Light: Popular Enlightenment in an Age of Belief* (Chicago, 2000), 99–132.

Essay on Resurrection, trans. in Abraham Halkin and David Hartman, *Epistles of Maimonides: Crisis and Leadership* (Philadelphia, 1985), 209–33.

Ethical Writings of Maimonides, trans. Raymond Weiss and Charles Butterworth (New York, 1983).

Guide of the Perplexed [Dalalat al-ḥa'irin, Moreh nevukhim], English trans. from Arabic, Shlomo Pines (Chicago, 1963); Hebrew trans., J. Kafih (Jerusalem, 1972); Hebrew trans., Michael Schwarz, 2 vols. (Ramat Aviv, 2002). Page references in the footnotes are to the Pines translation.

Hakdamot harambam lamishnah [Maimonides' Introductions to the Mishnah], ed. Isaac Shailat (Jerusalem, 1992).

Igerot harambam [Maimonides' Epistles], Hebrew trans., J. Kafih (Jerusalem, 1972); Hebrew trans., Isaac Shailat, 2 vols. (Jerusalem, 1987).

Maimonides' Commentary on the Mishnah, Tractate Sanhedrin, trans. Fred Rosner (New York, 1981).

Medical Aphorisms of Maimonides, trans. Fred Rosner and Suessman Muntner, 2 vols. (New York, 1970).

Perek ḥelek = 'Introduction to Chapter 10 of Tractate *Sanhedrin*', *Commentary on the Mishnah*

Teshuvot harambam [Maimonides' Responsa], ed. and trans. Joshua Blau, 4 vols. (Jerusalem, 1957–61) (available on the Bar Ilan Global Jewish Database).

Treatise on Logic [= Logical Terms], trans. I. Efros (New York, 1938).

Other Works

ABRAHAM MAIMONIDES, *Commentary on Genesis and Exodus*, ed. S. D. Sassoon and E. Weisenberg (London, 1958).

ABRAHAMS, ISRAEL, *Jewish Life in the Middle Ages* (New York, 1896; repr. Mineola, NY, 2004).

ABRAVANEL, ISAAC, *Commentary on Leviticus* [Perush vayikra] (Jerusalem, 2005).
—— *Principles of Faith*, trans. Menachem Kellner (Oxford, 1982).

American Heritage Dictionary of the English Language, internet edn. <https://ahdictionary.com/> (accessed 1 July 2019).

APTOWITZER, VICTOR, 'The Celestial Temple as Viewed in the Aggadah', in J. Dan (ed.), *Binah: Studies in Jewish History, Thought, and Culture*, ii (New York, 1989), 1–29.

AVERROES, *On the Harmony of Religion and Philosophy* (*Kitab faṣl al-maqal*), trans. George F. Hourani (London, 1976).

AVINER, SHLOMO, *Maimonides' Laws Concerning the Messiah and the Pamphlet 'Not to Ascend as a Wall'* [Hilkhot mashiaḥ larambam betosefet kunteres shelo ya'alu biḥomah] (Jerusalem, 2002).

BAHYA IBN PAKUDA, *Duties of the Heart*, trans. Menahem Mansour (London, 1973).

BALK, HANAN, 'The Soul of a Jew and the Soul of a Non-Jew: An Inconvenient Truth and the Search for an Alternative', *Hakirah: The Flatbush Journal of Jewish Law and Thought*, 16 (2013), 47–76.

BARIS, MICHAEL, 'Limited Knowledge, Unlimited Love: A Maimonidean Paradox', *University of Toronto Journal for Jewish Thought*, 3 (2013), 1–28. <http://tjjt.cjs.utoronto.ca/wp-content/uploads/2013/11/Michael-Baris-Limited-Knowledge-Unlimited-Love-A-Maimonidean-Paradox-Vol.-3.pdf> (accessed 9 July 2019).

BATNITZKY, LEORA, *How Judaism Became a Religion: An Introduction to Modern Jewish Thought* (Princeton, NJ, 2011).

BENIN, STEPHEN, *The Footprints of God: Divine Accommodation in Jewish and Christian Thought* (Albany, NY, 1993).

BERGER, DAVID, 'Some Ironic Consequences of Maimonides' Rationalistic Messianism', in Y. Levy and S. Carmy (eds.), *The Legacy of Maimonides: Religion, Reason, and Community* (New York, 2006), 79–88.

—— and LAWRENCE KAPLAN, 'On Freedom of Inquiry in the Rambam—and Today', *Torah u-Madda Journal*, 2 (1990), 37–50.

BERMAN, LAWRENCE, 'The Ethical Views of Maimonides within the Context of Islamicate Civilization', in J. Kraemer (ed.), *Perspectives on Maimonides* (Oxford, 1991), 13–32.

—— 'The Structure of the Commandments of the Torah in the Thought of Maimonides', in S. Stein and R. Loewe (eds.), *Studies in Jewish Religious and Intellectual History in Honor of Alexander Altmann* (Tuscaloosa, Ala., 1979), 51–66.

BLAND, KALMAN, *The Artless Jew* (Princeton, NJ, 2000).

BLIDSTEIN, GERALD (YA'AKOV), 'Hanukkah in Hazal: The Missing Players', *Tradition*, 35 (2001), 20–3.

—— 'Joy in Maimonides' Ethical Teaching' (Heb.), *Eshel be'ersheva*, 2 (1980), 145–63.

—— 'Menahem Ha-Me'iri: Aspects of an Intellectual Profile', *Journal of Jewish Thought and Philosophy*, 5 (1995), 63–79.

—— 'On the Status of the Resident Alien in Maimonides' Thought' (Heb.), *Sinai*, 101 (1988), 44–52.

—— *Political Concepts in Maimonidean Halakhah* [Ekronot mediniyim bemishnat harambam] (Ramat Gan, 2001).

—— *A Booklet on Maimonides' Thought on the Messianic Era* [Kunteres shitat harambam begeder yemot hamashiaḥ] (Kefar Habad, 2007).

BROWN, BENJAMIN, *The Hazon Ish: Halakhist, Believer, and Leader of the Haredi Revolution* [Haḥazon ish: haposek, hama'amin, umanhig hamahepekhah haḥaredit] (Jerusalem, 2011).

BRUCKSTEIN, ALMUT, *Hermann Cohen on 'Maimonides' Ethics'* (Madison, Wis., 2003).

BUCHMAN, ASHER BENZION, 'The Order of the Books of the *Mishneh Torah*' (Heb.), *Hakirah: The Flatbush Journal of Jewish Law and Thought*, 18 (2014), 5–26.

—— 'Rambam and Zevulun: *Boz Yavuzu Lo*', *Hakirah: The Flatbush Journal of Jewish Law and Thought*, 5 (2007), 47–78.

CONGER, GEORGE PERRIGO, *Theories of Macrocosms and Microcosms in the History of Philosophy* (New York, 1922; repr. 1967).

D'ANCONA, CRISTINA, 'Greek Sources in Arabic and Islamic Philosophy', in Edward N. Zalta (ed.), *The Stanford Encyclopedia of Philosophy* (Spring 2016 edn.), <https://plato.stanford.edu/archives/spr2016/entries/arabic-islamic-greek/> (accessed 22 Aug. 2017).

DAVIDSON, HERBERT A., *Alfarabi, Avicenna, and Averroes on Intellect* (Oxford, 1992).

—— *Moses Maimonides: The Man and his Works* (Oxford, 2005).

—— 'The Problematic Passage in *Guide for the Perplexed* 2: 24', *Aleph: Historical Studies in Science and Judaism*, 8 (2008), 163–93.

—— 'The Study of Philosophy as a Religious Obligation', in S. D. Goitein (ed.), *Religion in a Religious Age* (Cambridge, 1974), 53–68.

DIAMOND, JAMES, *Converts, Heretics, and Lepers: Maimonides and the Outsider* (Notre Dame, Ind., 2007).

—— 'The Failed Theodicy of a Rabbinic Pariah: A Maimonidean Recasting of Elisha Ben Abuyah', *Jewish Studies Quarterly*, 9 (2002), 353–80.

—— *Maimonides and the Hermeneutics of Concealment: Deciphering Scripture and Midrash in the Guide of the Perplexed* (Albany, NY, 2002).

—— *Maimonides and the Shaping of the Jewish Canon* (New York, 2014).

—— and MENACHEM KELLNER, *Reinventing Maimonides in Contemporary Jewish Thought* (London, 2019).

DIENSTAG, JACOB I., 'Nachman Krochmal's Defence of Maimonides in the Light of the Critique of S. D. Luzzatto' (Heb.), *Bitsaron*, 55 (1967), 34–7.

EISEN, ROBERT, '*Lifnim mi-Shurat ha-Din* in Maimonides' *Mishneh Torah*', *Jewish Quarterly Review*, 89 (1999), 291–317.

EISENMANN, ESTI, 'The Term "Created Light" in Maimonides' Philosophy' (Heb.), *Da'at*, 55 (2005), 41–57.

EMDEN, JACOB, *Mitpaḥat sefarim* (Lvov, 1870).

EPSTEIN, J. N., *Mavo lenusaḥ hamishnah* [Introduction to the Mishnaic Text], 2 vols. (Jerusalem, 1948; repr. 2000).

EVEN-SHOSHAN, ABRAHAM, *A New Concordance of the Bible* [Konkordantsiyah ḥadashah letorah nevi'im ukhetuvim] (Jerusalem, 1988).

FAKHRY, MAJID, *Al-Farabi, Founder of Islamic Neoplatonism: His Life, Works, and Influence* (Oxford, 2002).

—— *A History of Islamic Philosophy* (New York, 1970).

FALCON, ANDREA, 'Aristotle on Causality', in Edward N. Zalta (ed.), *The Stanford Encyclopedia of Philosophy* (2015), <https://plato.stanford.edu/archives/spr2019/entries/aristotle-causality/> (accessed 11 June 2019).

FEINTUCH, ABRAHAM, *Maimonides' Book of Commandments with the Commentary* Pikudei yesharim [Sefer hamitsvot larambam im perush pikudei yesharim], 2 vols. (Jerusalem, 2000).

FELDMAN, SEYMOUR, 'The End of the Universe in Medieval Jewish Philosophy', *Association for Jewish Studies Review*, 11 (1986), 53–77.

FRIEDBERG, ALBERT D., *Crafting the 613 Commandments: Maimonides on the Enumeration, Classification, and Formulation of the Scriptural Commandments* (Boston, Mass., 2013).

FRIEDMAN, MORDECAI AKIVA, *Maimonides, the Yemenite Messiah, and Forced Conversion* [Harambam, hamashiaḥ beteiman vehashemad] (Jerusalem, 2002).

—— 'Ten *Betelin* in the Synagogue in the Thought of Maimonides and Abraham Maimuni' (Heb.), in Zvi Haber and Carmiel Cohen (eds.), *Mibirkat mosheh: kovets likhvodo . . . naḥum eli'ezer rabinovits*, ii (Ma'aleh Adumim, 2012), 796–835.

FREUDENTHAL, GAD, 'The Biological Limitations of Man's Intellectual Perfection According to Maimonides', in Georges Tamer (ed.), *The Trias of Maimonides* (Berlin, 2005), 137–49.

—— 'Four Observations on Maimonides' Four Celestial Globes (*Guide* ii. 9–10)' (Heb.), in Aviezer Ravitzky (ed.), *Maimonides: Conservatism, Originality, Revolution* [Harambam: shamranut, mekoriyut, mahapkhanut], ii (Jerusalem, 2008), 499–527.

FUNKENSTEIN, AMOS, *Maimonides: Nature, History, and Messianic Beliefs* [Teva, historiyah umeshiḥiyut etsel harambam] (Tel Aviv, 1983; repr. 1986).

GERSONIDES (LEVI BEN GERSHON), *Commentary on Song of Songs*, trans. Menachem Kellner (New Haven, 1998).

GILLIS, DAVID, *Reading Maimonides' Mishneh Torah* (Oxford, 2015).

GOLDFELD, LEAH NAOMI, 'The Laws of Kings' (Heb.), *Sinai*, 96 (1984), 67–79.

GOTTLIEB, YA'AKOV, *Intellectualism in Hasidic Garb: The Image of Maimonides in Habad Hasidism* [Sakhaltanut belevush ḥasidi: demuto shel harambam beḥasidut ḥabad] (Ramat Gan, 2009).

GREEN, KENNETH HART, *Leo Strauss and the Rediscovery of Maimonides* (Chicago, 2013).

—— (ed.), *Leo Strauss on Maimonides: The Complete Writings* (Chicago, 2013).

GROSS, ABRAHAM, 'Reasons for Circumcision: Trends and Historical Influences' (Heb.), *Da'at*, 21 (1988), 25–46.

HACOHEN, AVIAD, 'On Maimonides' Terminology in *Mishneh torah*' (Heb.), *Shenaton hamishpat ha'ivri: Annual of the Institute for Research in Jewish Law*, 14–15 (1988), 113–20.

HADAD, ELIEZER, *The Torah and Nature in Maimonides' Writings* [Hatorah vehateva bekhitvei harambam] (Jerusalem, 2012).

HALBERTAL, MOSHE, *Concealment and Revelation: Esotericism in Jewish Thought and Its Philosophical Implications*, trans. Jackie Feldman (Princeton, NJ, 2007).

—— *Maimonides: Life and Thought* (Princeton, NJ, 2015).

HALEVI, JUDAH, *Kuzari*, trans. Barry Kogan (forthcoming).

HARLOW, JULES (ed.), *High Holidays Prayer Book* (New York, 1972).

HARTMAN, DAVID, *Maimonides: Torah and Philosophic Quest* (Philadelphia, 1976).

HARVEY, STEVEN, 'Alghazali and Maimonides and their Books of Knowledge', in Jay Harris (ed.), *Be'erot Yitzhak: Studies in Memory of Isadore Twersky* (Cambridge, Mass., 2005), 99–117.

—— 'The Meaning of Terms Designating Love in Judaeo-Arabic Thought and Some Remarks on the Judaeo-Arabic Interpretation of Maimonides', in N. Golb (ed.), *Judaeo-Arabic Studies* (Amsterdam, 1997), 175–96.

HARVEY, WARREN ZEV, 'Averroes, Maimonides, and the Virtuous State' (Heb.), in *Iyunim bisugyot filosofiyot likhevod shelomoh pines* (Jerusalem, 1992), 19–31.

—— 'Holiness: A Command to Imitatio Dei', *Tradition*, 16 (1977), 7–28.

HEINEMANN, ISAAC, *Reasons for the Commandments* [Ta'amei hamitsvot], 2 vols., 6th edn. (Jerusalem, 1993).

HENSHKE, DAVID, 'On the Question of Unity in Maimonides' Thought' (Heb.), *Da'at*, 37 (1996), 37–52.

HERFORD, R. TRAVERS, *The Ethics of the Talmud: Sayings of the Fathers* (New York, 1962).

HERSHMAN, A. M., 'Textual Problems of Book Fourteen of the *Mishne Torah*', *Jewish Quarterly Review*, 40 (1950), 401–12.

HESCHEL, ABRAHAM JOSHUA, 'Prophetic Inspiration in the Middle Ages', in Morris M. Faierstein (ed.), *Prophetic Inspiration after the Prophets: Maimonides and Other Medieval Authorities* (New York, 1996), 1–67.

HIRSHMAN, MENACHEM, 'Rabbinic Universalism in the Second and Third Centuries', *Harvard Theological Review*, 93 (2000), 101–15.

—— *Torah for All Human Beings: A Universalist Stream in Tannaitic Literature and Its Relation to Gentile Wisdom* [Torah lekhol ba'ei olam: zerem universali besifrut hatana'im veyaḥaso leḥokhmat he'amim] (Tel Aviv, 1999).

HYMAN, ARTHUR, *Eschatological Themes in Medieval Jewish Philosophy* (Milwaukee, Wis., 2002).

Iamblichus on the Mysteries of the Egyptians, Chaldeans, and Assyrians, trans. Thomas Taylor, 2nd edn. (London, 1895).

IBN ATTAR, HAYIM, *Or haḥayim*, 2 vols. (Venice, 1742).

IBN SHEM TOV, SHEM TOV BEN SHEM TOV, *Sefer emunot* (Ferrara, 1556).

JASSEN, ALEX, 'Reading Midrash with Maimonides: An Inquiry into the Sources of Maimonides' Account of the Origins of Idolatry', *Australian Journal of Jewish Studies*, 21 (2007), 170–200.

JASTROW, MARCUS, *A Dictionary of the Targumim, the Talmud Babli and Yerushalmi, and the Midrashic Literature*, 2 vols. (New York, 1903; repr. 1989).

JOSPE, RAPHAEL, 'Pluralism out of the Sources of Judaism: The Quest for Religious Pluralism without Relativism', in A. Goshen-Gottstein and E. Korn (eds.), *Jewish Theology and World Religions* (Oxford, 2012), 87–121.

KADARI, ADIEL, *Studies in Repentance: Law, Philosophy, and Educational Thought in Maimonides' 'Laws of Repentance'* [Iyunei teshuvah: halakhah, hagut umaḥshavah ḥinukhit behilkhot teshuvah leharambam] (Be'ersheva, 2009).

KAFIH, JOSEPH, *The Hebrew Bible in Maimonides* [Hamikra barambam] (Jerusalem, 1972).

KAPLAN, LAWRENCE (ed.), *Maimonides: Between Philosophy and Halakhah: Rabbi Joseph B. Soloveitchik's Lectures on the Guide of the Perplexed* (New York, 2016).

—— 'Maimonides on the Singularity of the Jewish People', *Da'at*, 15 (1985), pp. v–xxvii.

—— 'Philosophy and the Divine Law in Maimonides and Al-Farabi in Light of Maimonides' *Eight Chapters* and Al-Farabi's *Chapters of the Statesman*', in Charles Selengut (ed.), *Jewish–Muslim Encounters: History, Philosophy, and Culture* (St Paul, Minn., 2001), 1–34.

KASHER, HANNAH, 'Does "Ought" Imply "Can" in Maimonides?' (Heb.), *Iyun*, 36 (1987), 13–34.

—— '"Hakham", "Hasid", and "Tov" in Maimonides' Writings: A Study in Terms and their Reference', *Maimonidean Studies*, 4 (2000), 81–105.

—— 'Maimonides' Interpretations of the Story of the Divine Revelation in the Cleft of the Rock' (Heb.), *Da'at*, 35 (1995), 29–66.

—— 'Maimonides' View of Circumcision as a Factor Uniting the Jewish and Muslim Communities', in Ronald I. Nettler (ed.), *Medieval and Modern Perspectives on Muslim–Jewish Relations* (Luxembourg, 1995), 103–8.

—— *Sectarians, Epicureans, and Heretics in Maimonides' Thought* [Al haminim, epikorsim vekofrim bemishnat harambam] (Tel Aviv, 2011).

—— '"Torah for Its Own Sake", Torah Not for Its Own Sake, and the Third Way', *Jewish Quarterly Review*, 79 (1988–9), 153–63.

KATZ, JACOB, 'The Vicissitudes of Three Apologetic Statements' (Heb.), *Zion*, 23–4 (1958–9), 174–93.

KELLNER, JOLENE S., and MENACHEM KELLNER, 'Respectful Disagreement: A Response to Raphael Jospe', in A. Goshen-Gottstein and E. Korn (eds.), *Jewish Theology and World Religions* (Oxford, 2012), 123–33.

KELLNER, MENACHEM, 'And the Crooked Shall be Made Straight: Twisted Messianic Visions—A Maimonidean Corrective', in Michael Morgan and Steven Weitzman (eds.), *Rethinking the Messianic Idea: New Perspectives on Jewish Messianism* (Indianapolis, 2014), 108–40.

—— 'And Yet, the Texts Remain: The Problem of the Command to Destroy the Canaanites', in Katell Berthelot, Menachem Hirshman, and Josef David (eds.), *The Gift of the Land and the Fate of the Canaanites in Jewish Thought* (Oxford, 2014), 153–79.

KELLNER, MENACHEM, 'The Conception of the Torah as a Deductive Science in Medieval Jewish Thought', *Revue des Études Juives*, 146 (1987), 265–79.
—— 'Did the Torah Precede the Cosmos? A Maimonidean Study' (Heb.), *Da'at*, 61 (2007), 83–96.
—— *Dogma in Medieval Jewish Thought: From Maimonides to Abravanel* (Oxford, 1986).
—— '"Farteitsht un Farbessert": Comments on Tendentious "Corrections" to Maimonidean Texts' (Heb.), in B. Ish-Shalom (ed.), *Bedarkei shalom: iyunim behagut yehudit mugashim lishalom rosenberg* (Jerusalem, 2006), 255–63; English trans.: 'Farteitcht un Farbessert (On "Correcting" Maimonides)', *Me'orot [Edah Journal]* 6/2 (2007), <https://www.academia.edu/36128094/Menachem_Kellner_Farteitcht_un_Farbessert_On_Correcting_Maimonides_Meorot_Edah_Journal_6_2_2007_1-11> (accessed 14 June 2019).
—— 'Is Maimonides' Ideal Person Austerely Rationalist?', *American Catholic Philosophical Quarterly*, 76 (2002), 125–43.
—— 'The Literary Character of the *Mishneh Torah*: On the Art of Writing in Maimonides' Halakhic Works', in E. Fleisher, G. Blidstein, C. Horowitz, and B. Septimus (eds.), *Me'ah She'arim: Studies in Medieval Jewish Spiritual Life in Memory of Isadore Twersky* (Jerusalem, 2001), 29–45.
—— 'Maimonides' Commentary on *Mishnah Hagigah* ii.1', in Marc D. Angel (ed.), *From Strength to Strength: Lectures from Shearith Israel* (New York, 1998), 101–11.
—— *Maimonides' Confrontation with Mysticism* (Oxford, 2006).
—— *Maimonides on Human Perfection* (Atlanta, Ga., 1990).
—— *Maimonides on Judaism and the Jewish People* (Albany, NY, 1991).
—— 'Maimonides' "True Religion": For Jews or All Humanity?', in id., *Science in the Bet Midrash: Studies in Maimonides* (Boston, Mass., 2009), 291–319.
—— 'Messianic Postures in Israel Today', *Modern Judaism*, 6 (1986), 197–209. Repr. in Marc Saperstein (ed.), *Essential Papers on Messianic Movements in Jewish History* (New York, 1992), 504–19.
—— '*Mishneh Torah*: Why?' (Heb.), *Mesorah leyosef*, 4 (2005), 316–29.
—— 'Misogyny: Gersonides vs. Maimonides', in id., *Torah in the Observatory: Gersonides, Maimonides, Song of Songs* (Boston, Mass., 2012), 283–304.
—— *Must a Jew Believe Anything?*, 2nd edn. (Oxford, 2006).
—— 'Steven Schwarzschild, Moses Maimonides, and "Jewish Non-Jews"', in Görge K. Hasselhoff and Otfried Fraisse (eds.), *Moses Maimonides (1138–1204): His Religious, Scientific, and Philosophical Wirkungsgeschichte in Different Cultural Contexts* (Wuerzburg, 2004), 587–606.
—— 'The Virtue of Faith', in Lenn E. Goodman (ed.), *Neoplatonism and Jewish Thought* (Albany, NY, 1992), 195–205.
—— *They, Too, Are Called Human: Gentiles in the Eyes of Maimonides* [Gam hem keruim adam: hanokhri be'einei harambam] (Ramat Gan, 2016).
KIMELMAN, REUVEN, '*Lekha Dodi*' *and Kabalat Shabat: Their Mystical Meaning* [Lekha dodi vekabalat shabat: hamashma'ut hamistit] (Jerusalem, 2003).

—— 'U-N'taneh Tokef as a Midrashic Poem', in Debra Reed Blank (ed.), *The Experience of Jewish Liturgy: Studies Dedicated to Menahem Schmelzer* (Leiden, 2011), 115–46.

KLEIN, ERNEST, *A Comprehensive Etymological Dictionary of the Hebrew Language for Readers of English* (Jerusalem, 1987).

KLEIN-BRASLAVY, SARA, *Maimonides' Interpretation of the Adam Stories in Genesis* [Perush harambam lesipurim al adam beparashat bereshit] (Jerusalem, 1986).

KOCHIN, MICHAEL, 'Morality, Nature and Esotericism in Leo Strauss' *Persecution and the Art of Writing*', *Review of Politics*, 64 (2002), 261–83.

KORN, EUGENE, 'Gentiles, the World to Come and Judaism: The Odyssey of a Rabbinic Text', *Modern Judaism*, 14 (1994), 265–87.

—— 'Moralization in Jewish Law: Genocide, Divine Commands, and Rabbinic Reasoning', *Edah Journal*, 5/2 (2006) <http://www.edah.org/backend/Journal Article/KORN_5_2.pdf> (accessed 11 June 2019).

KOZODOY, MAUD, 'Prefatory Verse and the Reception of the Guide of the Perplexed', *Jewish Quarterly Review*, 106 (2016), 257–82.

KRAEMER, JOEL, 'Alfarabi's *Opinions of the Virtuous City* and Maimonides' *Foundations of the Law*', in J. Blau et al. (eds.), *Studia Orientalia: Memoriae D. H. Baneth Dedicata* (Jerusalem, 1979), 107–53.

—— 'Maimonides, the Great Healer', *Maimonidean Studies*, 5 (2008), 1–30.

—— 'Maimonides' Intellectual Milieu in Cairo', in Tony Levy and Roshdi Rashed (eds.), *Maimonide philosophe et savant* (Louvain, 2004), 1–37.

—— 'Moses Maimonides: An Intellectual Portrait', in Kenneth Seeskin (ed.), *The Cambridge Companion to Maimonides* (New York, 2005), 11–57.

—— 'On Maimonides' Messianic Posture', in I. Twersky (ed.), *Studies in Medieval Jewish History and Literature*, ii (Cambridge, Mass., 1984), 109–142.

KREISEL, HOWARD (HAIM), *Maimonides' Political Thought: Studies in Ethics, Law, and the Human Ideal* (Albany, NY, 1999).

—— 'Reasons for the Commandments in Maimonides' *Guide of the Perplexed* and in Provençal Jewish Philosophy', *Maimonidean Studies*, 5 (2008), 159–88.

LAMM, NORMAN, 'Loving and Hating Jews as Halakhic Categories', *Tradition*, 24 (1989), 98–122.

—— 'Maimonides on the Love of God', *Maimonidean Studies*, 3 (1992–3), 131–42.

LANGERMANN, Y. TZVI, 'Astronomical Problems in Maimonides' Thought' (Heb.), *Da'at*, 37 (1996), 107–18.

—— '*Fusul Musa*, on Maimonides' Method of Composition', *Maimonidean Studies*, 5 (2008), 325–44.

—— 'Maimonides and Miracles: The Growth of a (Dis)Belief', *Jewish History*, 18 (2004), 147–72.

LASKER, DANIEL J., 'Original Sin and Its Atonement According to Hasdai Crescas' (Heb.), *Da'at*, 20 (1988), 127–35.

LASKER, DANIEL J., 'Proselyte Judaism, Christianity, and Islam in the Thought of Judah Halevi', *Jewish Quarterly Review*, 81 (1990), 75–91.

—— 'Tradition and Innovation in Maimonides' Attitude towards Other Religions' (Heb.), in Aviezer Ravitzky (ed.), *Maimonides: Conservatism, Originality, Revolution* [Harambam: shamranut, mekoriyut, mahapkhanut], i (Jerusalem, 2008), 79–94.

LEIBOWITZ, ARYEH, 'The Pursuit of Scholarship and Economic Self-Sufficiency: Revisiting Maimonides' Commentary to *Pirkei Avot*', *Tradition*, 40 (2007), 31–41.

LENIHAN, THOMAS, 'St. Francis of Assisi and Sultan Malik Al-Kamil: The Legend in History & Art', National Endowment for the Humanities Seminar: The Thirteenth Century 'Lives' of St. Francis of Assisi, State University of New York College at Geneseo, 2009, <https://www.academia.edu/7384455/St._Francis_of_Assisi_and_Sultan_Malik_al-Kamil_The_Legend_in_History_and_Art>.

LERNER, RALPH, *Maimonides' Empire of Light: Popular Enlightenment in an Age of Belief* (Chicago, 2000).

LEVI BEN GERSHOM *see* GERSONIDES

LEWIS, BERNARD, *Race and Slavery in the Middle East: An Historical Enquiry* (Oxford, 1990).

—— *What Went Wrong? Western Impact and Middle Eastern Response* (London, 2002).

LICHTENSTEIN, AHARON, 'Does Jewish Tradition Recognize an Ethic Independent of Halakha?', in Marvin Fox (ed.), *Modern Jewish Ethics: Theory and Practice* (Columbus, Ohio, 1975), 62–88. Repr. in Menachem Kellner (ed.), *Contemporary Jewish Ethics* (New York, 1978), 102–24.

LOBEL, DIANA, 'Being and the Good: Maimonides on Ontological Beauty, *Journal of Jewish Thought and Philosophy*, 19/1 (2011), 1–45.

—— '"Silence Is Praise to You": Maimonides on Negative Theology, Looseness of Expression, and Religious Experience', *American Catholic Philosophical Quarterly*, 76/1 (2002), 25–51.

LORBERBAUM, MENACHEM, 'Maimonides on *tikun olam*' (Heb.), *Tarbiz*, 64 (1995), 65–82.

LORBERBAUM, YAIR, '"The men of knowledge and the sages are drawn, as it were, toward this purpose by the divine will" (*Guide*, introd): On Maimonides' Conception of Parables' (Heb.), *Tarbiz*, 71 (5762/2001), 87–132.

MANEKIN, CHARLES H., 'Maimonides on the Divine Authorship of the Law', in id. and Daniel Davies (eds.), *Interpreting Maimonides* (Cambridge, 2018), 133–51.

MELAMED, ABRAHAM, '*Al Yithalel*: Philosophical Commentaries on Jeremiah 9: 22–3 in Medieval and Renaissance Jewish Thought' (Heb.), *Jerusalem Studies in Jewish Thought*, 4 (1985), 31–82.

—— *The Image of the Black in Jewish Culture: A History of the Other* (London, 2003).

—— '*Religion*': From Law to Religion—The History of a Formative Term [Dat: meḥok le'emunah—korotav shel minuaḥ mekhonen] (Tel Aviv, 2014).

METZGER, DAVID, 'The "Commentator" on Maimonides' "Laws of the Foundations of the Torah"' (Heb.), *Tsefunot*, 1 (1988/9), 99–100.

Moses ben Nahman *see* Nahmanides
Moses, Paul, *The Saint and the Sultan: The Crusades, Islam, and Francis of Assisi's Mission of Peace* (New York, 2009).
Nadler, Steven (ed.), *Spinoza and Medieval Jewish Philosophy* (Cambridge, 2014).
Nahmanides (Moses ben Nahman), *Ramban: Writings and Discourses*, trans. Charles B. Chavel, 2 vols. (New York, 1978).
Nehorai, Michael Zvi, 'Maimonides on Miracles' (Heb.), *Jerusalem Studies in Jewish Thought*, 9 (1990), 1–18.
Newman, Louis E., 'Law, Virtue, and Supererogation in the Halakha: The Problem of *Lifnim Mishurat Hadin* Reconsidered', *Journal of Jewish Studies*, 40 (1989), 61–88.
Numbers Rabbah, Bar Ilan Global Jewish Database ('Responsa Project').
Nuriel, Avraham, 'The Concept "Faith" in Maimonides' (Heb.), in id., *Concealed and Revealed in Mediaeval Jewish Philosophy* [Galui vesamui bafilosofyah hayehudit biyemei habeinayim] (Jerusalem, 2000), 78–82.
Peleg, Erez, 'Between Philosophy and Kabbalah: Criticism of Jewish Philosophy in the Thought of Rabbi Shem-Tov ben Shem-Tov' [Bein filosofiyah lekabalah: bikoret hasekhaltanut hayehudit bihaguto shel r. shem tov ibn shem tov], Ph.D. diss., University of Haifa, 2003.
Pesikta derav kahana, ed. Bernard Mandelbaum (New York, 1962).
Pessin, Sarah, 'The Influence of Islamic Thought on Maimonides', in Edward N. Zalta (ed.), *The Stanford Encyclopedia of Philosophy*(Spring 2016), <https://plato.stanford.edu/archives/spr2016/entries/maimonides-islamic/> (accessed 11 June 2019).
Pinchot, Roy, 'The Deeper Conflict between Maimonides and Ramban over the Sacrifices', *Tradition*, 33 (1999), 24–33.
Pines, Shlomo, 'On the Term *Ruḥaniyut* and its Origin, and on Judah Halevi's Doctrine' (Heb.), *Tarbiz*, 57 (1988), 511–34.
Porphyry, *On Abstinence from Animal Food*, trans. Thomas Taylor, in *Selected Works of Porphyry* (London, 1823), 1–170.
Rabinovitch, Nachum E., 'Sanctuary, Society, and History: The Uniqueness of Maimonides' (Heb.), in Aviezer Ravitzky (ed.), *Maimonides: Conservatism, Originality, and Revolution* [Rambam: shamranut, mekoriyut, mahapkhanut] (Jerusalem, 2008), 63–77.
—— *The Way of the Torah* [Darkah shel torah] (Jerusalem, 5769).
Raffel, Charles M., 'Providence as Consequent upon the Intellect: Maimonides' Theory of Providence', *AJS Review*, 12 (1987), 25–71.
Rappoport, Chaim, 'Critique of M. Kellner', *Me'orot* 7/1 (Tishrei 5769), <https://library.yctorah.org/files/2016/07/Kellner-III-with-Rapoport-response-revision6.pdf> (accessed 14 June 2019).
—— '"The Virtue of He Who Earns His Living from His Labour": An Interpretation of Maimonides "Laws of Torah Study"' (Heb.), *Hama'ayan*, 49/4 (5769/2008), <http://shaalvim.co.il/torah/maayan-article.asp?id=295> (accessed 19 Feb. 2015).

RAVITZKY, AVIEZER, 'The Binding of Isaac and the Covenant: Abraham and His Sons in Jewish Thought' (Heb.), in Moshe Hallamish, Hannah Kasher, and Yohanan Silman (eds.), *The Faith of Abraham in the Light of Interpretation throughout the Ages* [Avraham avi hama'aminim: demuto bere'i hehagut ledoroteiha] (Ramat Gan, 2002), 11–38.

—— 'Philosophy and Leadership in Maimonides', in Jay Harris (ed.), *Maimonides after 800 Years: Essays on Maimonides and his Influence* (Cambridge, Mass., 2007), 257–90.

—— '"To the Utmost of Human Capacity": Maimonides on the Days of the Messiah', in J. Kraemer (ed.), *Perspectives on Maimonides: Philosophical and Historical Studies* (Oxford, 1991), 221–56.

RAVITZKY, AVIRAM, 'Why Were the Laws of Mourning Introduced in the *Book of Judges*? Moses' Authority in Maimonides' Thought and the Principles of Arrangement of the *Mishneh Torah*' (Heb.), in Howard Kreisel, Boaz Huss, and Uri Ehrlich (eds.), *Spiritual Authority: Struggles over Cultural Power in Jewish Thought* [Samkhut ruḥanit: ma'avakim al ko'aḥ tarbuti bahagut hayehudit] (Beersheva, 2009), 71–82.

REIF, STEFAN C., *Problems with Prayers: Studies in the Textual History of Early Rabbinic Liturgy* (Berlin, 2006).

ROSENBERG, SHALOM, 'The Concept of "Emunah" in Post-Maimonidean Jewish Philosophy', in I. Twersky (ed.), *Studies in Medieval Jewish History and Literature*, ii (Cambridge, 1984), 273–307.

—— 'You Shall Walk in His Ways', *Edah Journal*, 2 (2002), 1–17. <http://www.edah.org/backend/JournalArticle/rosenberg2_2.pdf> (accessed 9 July 2019).

ROSENBLOOM, NOAH H., 'Rationale for the Omission of Eschatology from the Bible', *Judaism*, 170 (1994), 149–58.

ROTH, LEON, 'Moralization and Demoralization in Jewish Ethics', in id., *Is There a Jewish Philosophy?* (London, 1999), 128–43.

RUDAVSKY, TAMAR, *Time Matters: Time, Creation, and Cosmology in Medieval Jewish Philosophy* (Albany, NY, 2000).

SA'ADYAH GAON, *The Book of Beliefs and Opinions*, trans. Samuel Rosenblatt (New Haven, 1948).

SABRA, ADAM, *Poverty and Charity in Medieval Islam: Mamluk Egypt 1250–1517* (Cambridge, 2000).

SCHECHTERMAN, DEBORAH, 'The Doctrine of Original Sin and Commentaries on Maimonides in Jewish Philosophy of the Thirteenth and Fourteenth Centuries' (Heb.), *Da'at*, 20 (1988), 65–90.

SCHNEERSOHN, MENACHEM MENDEL, *Maimonidean Rules* [Kelalei harambam] (New York, 1991).

SCHOLEM, GERSHOM, 'Toward an Understanding of the Messianic Idea in Judaism', in id., *The Messianic Idea in Judaism and Other Essays on Jewish Spirituality* (New York, 1971), 1–36.

SCHWARTZ, DOV, 'From Theurgy to Magic: The Evolution of the Magical-Talismanic Justification of Sacrifice in the Circle of Nahmanides and his Interpreters', *Aleph: Historical Studies in Science and Judaism*, 1 (2001), 165–213.

SCHWARZFUCHS, SIMON-RAYMOND, 'Les Lois royales de Maimonide', *Revue des Etudes Juives*, 111 (1951–2), 63–86.

SCHWARZSCHILD, STEVEN S., 'An Agenda for Jewish Philosophy in the 1980s', in Norbert Samuelson (ed.), *Studies in Jewish Philosophy: Collected Essays of the Academy for Jewish Philosophy, 1980–5* (Lanham, Md., 1987), 101–25.

—— 'The Democratic Socialism of Hermann Cohen', *Hebrew Union College Annual*, 27 (1956), 417–38.

—— 'Do Noachites Have to Believe in Revelation? (A Passage in Dispute between Maimonides, Spinoza, Mendelssohn, and Herman Cohen): A Contribution to a Jewish View of Natural Law', in Menachem Kellner (ed.), *The Pursuit of the Ideal: Jewish Writings of Steven Schwarzschild* (Albany, NY, 1990), 29–59.

—— 'Moral Radicalism and "Middlingness" in the Ethics of Maimonides', in Menachem Kellner (ed.), *The Pursuit of the Ideal: Jewish Writings of Steven Schwarzschild* (Albany, NY, 1990), 137–61 and 302–18.

SCHWEID, ELIEZER, 'Prayer in the Thought of Yehudah Halevi', in Gabriel H. Cohn and Harold Fisch (eds.), *Prayer in Judaism: Continuity and Change* (Northvale, NJ, 1996), 109–17.

SEEMAN, DON, 'Maimonides and Friendship', *Jewish Studies Internet Journal*, 13 (2015), 1–36.

—— 'Reasons for the Commandments as Contemplative Practice in Maimonides', *Jewish Quarterly Review*, 103 (2013), 298–327.

SEESKIN, KENNETH, 'Holiness as an Ethical Ideal', *Journal of Jewish Thought and Philosophy*, 5/2 (1996), 191–203.

—— *No Other Gods: The Modern Struggle against Idolatry* (New York, 1995).

SEPTIMUS, BERNARD, 'What Did Maimonides Mean by *Madda*?', in G. Blidstein, E. Fleischer, C. Horowitz, and B. Septimus (eds.), *Me'ah She'arim: Studies in Medieval Jewish Spiritual Life in Memory of Isadore Twersky* (Jerusalem, 2001), 83–110.

SHATZ, DAVID, 'Maimonides' Moral Theory', in Kenneth Seeskin (ed.), *The Cambridge Companion to Maimonides* (Cambridge, 2005), 167–92.

SHATZ, MEIR YONAH [MEIR YONAH BRANSKY], *Har hamoriyah* (Warsaw, 1890).

SOLOVEITCHIK, JOSEPH B., *The Halakhic Mind: An Essay on Jewish Tradition and Modern Thought* (New York, 1986).

—— *On Repentance: The Thought and Oral Discourses of Rabbi Joseph Dov Soloveitchik*, ed. and trans. Pinchas Peli (Northvale, NJ, 1984).

STEINBERG, AVRAHAM, *Encyclopedia of Jewish Medical Ethics*, trans. Fred Rosner, 3 vols. (Jerusalem, 2003).

STERN, DAVID, and MARK J. MIRSKY, *Rabbinic Fantasies: Imaginative Narratives from Classical Hebrew Literature* (New Haven, 1990).

STERN, JOSEF, 'The Idea of a Hoq in Maimonides' Explanation of the Law', in Shlomo Pines and Yirmiyahu Yovel (eds.), *Maimonides and Philosophy. Papers Presented at the Sixth Jerusalem Philosophical Encounter, May 1985*, International Archives of the History of Ideas (Dordrecht, 1986), 92–130; repr. in Josef Stern, *Problems and Parables of Law: Maimonides and Nahmanides on Reasons for the Commandments (Ta'amei Ha-Mitsvot)* (Albany, NY, 1998), 15–48.

—— 'Maimonides' Epistemology', in Kenneth Seeskin (ed.), *The Cambridge Companion to Maimonides* (Cambridge, 2005), 105–33.

—— *The Matter and Form of Maimonides' Guide* (Cambridge, Mass., 2013).

—— *Problems and Parables of Law: Maimonides and Nahmanides on Reasons for the Commandments (Ta'amei Ha-Mitsvot)* (Albany, NY, 1998).

STRAUSS, LEO, 'How to Begin to Study the *Guide of the Perplexed*: Introductory Essay', in Maimonides, *Guide of the Perplexed*, English trans. Shlomo Pines (Chicago, 1963), pp. xi–lvi.

Talmud bavli im shinuyei nushaot: Sotah (Jerusalem, 1977).

TEPPER, ARYEH, *Progressive Minds, Conservative Politics: Leo Strauss's Later Writings on Maimonides* (Albany, NY, 2013).

TOBIAS BEN ELIEZER, *Pesikta zutarta (Midrash lekah tov)* (Venice, 1546; Vilna, 1880).

TOLEDANO, SHLOMO, *The Book of Speech and Thought: A Summary of Maimonides' Holy Guide of the Perplexed, with the Commentary* Mevikh Maskilim [Sefer dibur umahashavah, sikum hasefer hakadosh moreh nevukhim leraban mosheh ben maimon, im haperush mevikh maskilim], 2 vols. (Jerusalem, 2006).

Tosefta, ed. Moses Samuel Zuckermandel (Pasewalk, 1880; repr. Jerusalem, 1937, 1970).

TURNER, MASHA, 'The Patriarch Abraham in Maimonidean Thought' (Heb.), in Moshe Hallamish, Hannah Kasher, and Yohanan Silman (eds.), *The Faith of Abraham in the Light of Interpretation throughout the Ages* [Avraham avi ha-ma'aminim: demuto bere'i hehagut ledoroteiha] (Ramat Gan, 2002), 143–54.

TWERSKY, ISADORE (YITSHAK), 'A Clarification of Maimonides' Remarks in "Laws of Trespass" Chapter 8 Halakhah 8: Towards Understanding Maimonides' Reasons for the Commandments' (Heb.), in Immanuel Etkes (ed.), *Studies in the History of Jewish Society in the Middle Ages and in the Modern Period Presented to Professor Jacob Katz* [Perakim betoledot hahevrah hayehudit biyemei habeinayim uva'et hehadashah: mukdashim leprofesor ya'akov kats] (Jerusalem, 1980), 24–33.

—— *Introduction to the Code of Maimonides* (New Haven, 1980).

—— *A Maimonides Reader* (New York, 1972).

—— 'The *Mishneh Torah* of Maimonides', *Proceedings of the Israel Academy of Sciences and Humanities*, 5 (1976), 265–96.

—— 'On Law and Ethics in the *Mishneh Torah*: A Case Study of *Hilkhot Megillah* ii: 17', *Tradition*, 24 (1989), 138–49.

—— 'Some Non-Halakic Aspects of the Mishneh Torah', in A. Altmann (ed.), *Jewish Medieval and Renaissance Studies* (Cambridge, Mass., 1967), 95–118.

WEISS, ROSLYN, 'Maimonides on the End of the World', *Maimonidean Studies*, 3 (1992–3), 195–218.

WIEDER, NAFTALI, 'A Controversial Mishnaic and Liturgical Expression', *Journal of Jewish Studies*, 18 (1967), 1–7.

YADIN-ISRAEL, AZZAN, 'A Theological Critique of Sacrifice: The Rabbis and Porphyry'. Paper presented at the 17th World Congress of Jewish Studies, Jerusalem (2017).

Yalkut shimoni, Bar Ilan Global Jewish Database ('Responsa Project').

YUVAL, ISRAEL J., 'Moses Redivivus: Maimonides as a "Helper to the King" Messiah' (Heb.), *Zion*, 72 (2007), 161–88.

ZEITLIN, SOLOMON, 'Maimonides', *American Jewish Yearbook*, 37 (1935–6), 60–97.

ZEPER, ELEONORA, 'Blood Sacrifice and Bloodless Sacrifice in Porphyry and Iamblichus', *Syzetesis—Semestrale di filosofia*, NS 2/2 (2015), 97–107.

ZORY, DAVID, 'Notes on the Prefatory and Concluding Verses' (Heb.), in Maimonides, *Guide of the Perplexed*, Hebrew trans. Michael Schwarz, ii (Ramat Aviv, 2002), 767–9.

Index of Citations

Mishneh torah
Page numbers in bold indicate the location of the main discussion of the *halakhah/halakhot* or chapter(s) in question as the ending of a book of the *Mishneh torah*.

Introduction 9, 14, 40, 41, 57, 59, 73, 91, 112, 113, 114, 149, 201, 202 n. 58, 221 n. 1, 269, 330, 332 n. 55, 333

Book of Knowledge
'Laws of the Foundations of the Torah'
    1   24
    1: 1   **22–8**, 324
    1: 1–3   327 n. 35
    1: 1–4   182 n. 30
    1: 1–6   22 n. 41
    1: 4   17 n. 16, 19 n. 24
    1: 5   273, 310
    1: 6   312 n. 24, 322 n. 3
    1: 7   48 n. 30, 124 n. 57
    1: 10   308 n. 12
    1: 11–12   158 n. 47
    1–2   17, 17–18 n. 20, 213
    1–4   17, 206, 272, 277
    1–10   121, 128, 332
    2   25, 27, 333
    2: 1   29 n. 58, 34 n. 76, 169, 322 n. 3
    2: 1–2   **22–8**, 30, 67 n. 114, 123 n. 56
    2: 2   10 n. 30, 26 n. 52, 28, 98 n. 27, 205 n. 64, 206, 206 n. 69, 207, 211, 322 n. 6, 322 n. 9, 331 n. 49
    2: 3   206 n. 68, 324 n. 16, 326 n. 30
    2: 4   187 n. 13
    2: 5–6   326 n. 32
    2: 5–8   323 n. 15, 325 n. 22
    2: 7   336
    2: 9   327 n. 35
    2: 10   124 n. 57, 322 n. 4
    2: 11   18 n. 20
    3: 1   268 n. 6, 322 n. 11, 323 n. 12, 336
    3: 1–2   322 n. 11
    3: 3   324 n. 16
    3: 4   322 n. 11
    3: 9   204 n. 63, 211, 323 n. 14, 325 n. 21
    3: 10   326 n. 23
    3: 10–4: 6   336
    3: 11   326 n. 24
    3–4   18 n. 20
    3–5   28
    4: 1   326 n. 27
    4: 5–6   326 n. 25
    4: 6   326 n. 26
    4: 7   326 n. 29
    4: 8   179 n. 18, 181 n. 28, 237 n. 6, 327 n. 38
    4: 8–9   170 n. 79, 328 n. 43
    4: 10   18 n. 20
    4: 12   203 n. 60
    4: 13   2 n. 3, 18 n. 20, 95 n. 19, 208 n. 76, 327 n. 41, 332 n. 54
    5   121, 122, 123, 125, 128, 333
    5: 10   122 n. 53
    5: 11   241, 244 n. 33
    5–6   121
    6   123, 125, 128
    6: 1   78 n. 15
    7: 1   92 n. 9, 203 n. 60, 326 n. 28
    7: 6–7   52 n. 45
    7: 7   92 n. 9
    8   7
    9   52 n. 45
    9: 1   309 n. 15

'Laws of Moral Qualities'
    1   177–8, 261

'Laws of Moral Qualities' (*cont.*):
- 1: 4   318 n. 29
- 1: 5   124 n. 58, 244 n. 31, 245, 322 n. 7, 322 n. 8
- 1: 6   56 n. 60, 107 n. 3, 240 n. 19, 247 n. 39, 255 n. 60, 259
- 1: 7   53 n. 51, 119 n. 44, 243 n. 30, 253 n. 57, 261 n. 71, 318 n. 31
- 1–5   125
- 2: 1   178, 178 n. 16
- 2: 2   119 n. 43
- 2: 3   184 n. 2
- 3   116, 120
- 3: 2   35 n. 79, 120 n. 48
- 5   121, 125
- 5: 4   91 n. 5
- 5: 12   116
- 6   125
- 6: 2   88 n. 25
- 6: 4   271 n. 24
- 6: 6   64 n. 95
- 7: 8   261 n. 72, 268 n. 9

'Laws of Torah Study'
- 1: 12   1 n. 2, 208 n. 76
- 3: 5   118 n. 39
- 3: 9   210 n. 83, 327 n. 41
- 3: 10–11   126 n. 63
- 4: 1   327 n. 41

'Laws of Idolatry'
- 1   63, 280 n. 10, 306
- 1: 1   30 n. 62, 125 n. 61, 209 n. 80
- 1: 1–2   169 n. 77
- 1: 2   64 n. 101
- 1: 2–3   31 n. 66, 60 n. 79
- 1: 3   30 n. 61, 32 n. 71, 54, 61, 61 n. 83, 69 n. 119, 140 n. 51, 223, 224 n. 6, 309, 309 n. 16, 309 n. 17
- 1: 5–6   253 n. 58
- 2: 1   125 n. 61
- 2: 2–3   151 n. 25
- 2: 5   46 n. 23, 227 n. 21
- 9: 4   109 n. 14
- 12: 7   151 n. 25

'Laws of Repentance'
- 1: 2   195 n. 44
- 1–10   15
- 2: 7   135 n. 31
- 3: 3   135 n. 30
- 3: 4   192 n. 35
- 3: 14   228 n. 23
- 5: 4   44 n. 15
- 6: 1   142 n. 60
- 6: 3   131 n. 12, 136 n. 32
- 6: 4   139 n. 45
- 8: 1   60 n. 77
- 8: 2   43 n. 7
- 8: 2–3   170 n. 78
- 8: 5   60 n. 77
- 9   16
- 9: 1   285
- 9: 2   52 n. 45, 294 n. 60, 295 n. 63
- 10   17, **18–21**, 25, 37, 55, 56, 102 n. 41
- 10: 2   56, 62 n. 84, 62 n. 85
- 10: 3   35 n. 82
- 10: 5   118 n. 39, 331 n. 50
- 10: 6   **14–39**, 34 n. 77, 209 n. 77, 302, 331 n. 49

Book of Love

'Laws of Recitation of the Shema'
- 1: 4   54

'Laws of Prayer and the Priestly Blessing'
- 1   55
- 2: 13   79 n. 20
- 10: 14   79 n. 20

'Laws of Tefillin, Mezuzah, and the Torah Scroll'
- 10: 11   136 n. 34

'Laws of Blessings'
- 2: 6   79 n. 20

'Laws of Circumcision'
- 1: 6   237 n. 6
- 1: 8   60 n. 76
- 3: 4–5   51 n. 41
- 3: 8   49 n. 32, 53, 62 n. 86, 63
- 3: 8–9   **40–72**, 262
- 3: 9   68

Index of Citations

Book of Seasons
'Laws of the Sabbath'
 5: 1 77 n. 14
 20: 14 237 n. 6
 21: 9–10 241 n. 22
 25: 26 241 n. 22
 30: 5 77 n. 14

'Laws of Resting (Repose) on a Festival'
 2: 4 241 n. 22
 6: 17 223, 225 n. 8

'Laws of Fasts'
 4: 4 223, 225 n. 11

'Laws of Megillah and Hanukah'
 2: 18 77 n. 11
 3: 1–3 75 n. 8
 4: 12 79 n. 22
 4: 12–13 **73–81**

Book of Women
'Laws of Marriage'
 15: 17 83 n. 4, 84, 85 n. 12

'Laws of Levirate Marriage'
 6: 10 240 n. 17

'Laws of the Wayward Wife (*Sotah*)'
 3: 8–10 78 n. 16
 4: 18–19 **82–9**

Book of Holiness
'Laws of Forbidden Intercourse (Sexual Relations)'
 2: 1 239 n. 16
 13 224 n. 7
 13: 1–4 69 n. 121
 14: 9 237 n. 6
 19: 17 251 n. 51
 21: 9 244 n. 32
 21: 25 85 n. 13
 22: 20 91 n. 5

'Laws of Ritual Slaughtering'
 4: 16 315 n. 26
 14: 14–16 **90–105**
 14: 16 169 n. 74

Book of Asseverations
'Laws of Oaths'
 11: 1 121 n. 50
 12: 1 123 n. 54
 12: 2 123 n. 55

'Laws of Vows'
 1: 3 111 n. 20
 13: 23 119 n. 45
 13: 25 117 n. 36, 120 n. 46

'Laws of Nazirites'
 10: 12 119 n. 45

'Laws of Valuation and Consecrations'
 6 112
 6: 2–3 107 n. 2
 8: 12 112, 119 n. 45
 8: 13 **106–28**, 240 n. 20, 244 n. 32

Book of Agriculture
'Laws of Gifts to the Poor'
 4: 8 244 n. 32
 10: 1 64 n. 96
 10: 1–3 177 n. 8
 10: 2 223, 226 n. 12, 250 n. 46, 251 n. 51
 10: 18 126 n. 63

'Laws of Heave Offerings'
 1: 1 189 n. 22
 1: 26 189 n. 22

'Laws of Second Tithe and Fourth Year's Fruit'
 2: 2 244 n. 32

'Laws of First Fruits and other Priestly Offerings'
 4: 3 47 n. 28

'Laws of Sabbatical and Jubilee Years'
 13: 12–13 **129–43**
 13: 13 8, 109 n. 15, 133 n. 23, 140, 142 n. 57, 143, 303, 318 n. 32

Book of Temple Service
'Laws of the Temple'
 1: 1 332 n. 53
 1: 6 145 n. 5

'Laws of the Temple' (cont.):
    1: 12   239 n. 14
    2: 2   207 n. 73
    4: 1   145 n. 6
    7   190
    7: 1   144 n. 3, 145 n. 7, 169 n. 75, 331 n. 51

'Laws of Entrance into the Sanctuary'
    3   188 n. 17
    3: 1   191 n. 31
    3: 10   191 n. 32
    3–4   144 n. 1, 191

'Laws of Things Forbidden for the Altar'
    7: 11   176 n. 6

'Laws of Trespass'
    1: 3   145 n. 8
    7: 4   145 n. 8
    8: 8   102 n. 41, **144–72**, 175, 215, 216, 303

Book of Offerings
'Laws of the Festal Offering'
    1: 1   225
    1: 2   108 n. 8
    2: 14   173 n. 1

'Laws of Offerings for Transgressions Committed through Error'
    10: 5   188 n. 18
    10: 11   188 n. 18

'Laws of Substituted Offerings'
    1: 1   173 n. 2
    4: 13   97 n. 26, 144 n. 4, **173–82**

Book of Purity
'Laws of Corpse Impurity'
    1: 17   186 n. 8

'Laws of the Red Heifer'
    3: 4   188 n. 20

'Laws of (Ritual) Impurity of Foodstuffs'
    16: 8   144 n. 1, 189 n. 22, 190
    16: 9   188 n. 19
    16: 12   88, 92 n. 9, 189 n. 23, 203 n. 61, 244 n. 32

'Laws of Immersion Pools'
    1: 8   189 n. 27
    11: 12   **183–220**

Book of Damages (Torts)
'Laws of Robbery and Lost Property'
    11: 7   243 n. 27
    11: 17   243 n. 28

'Laws of Wounding and Damaging'
    4: 10   246

'Laws of Murder and the Preservation of Life'
    4: 10   237 n. 6
    4: 11   237 n. 6
    4: 12   237 n. 6
    13: 4   243 n. 29
    13: 13   241 n. 22
    13: 14   **221–34**

Book of Acquisition
'Laws of Sales'
    12: 12   244 n. 32

'Laws of Neighbours'
    14: 5   244 n. 32

'Laws of Slaves'
    1: 6   237 n. 8
    5: 4   262 n. 74
    8: 12   237 n. 6
    9: 7   245 n. 36
    9: 8   64 n. 97, 107 n. 4, 226 n. 15, **235–66**

Book of Civil Laws
'Laws of Hiring'
    7: 7   244 n. 32

'Laws of Creditor and Debtor'
    22: 16   241 n. 21

'Laws of Inheritance'
    6: 11   244 n. 32
    11: 5   267 n. 4
    11: 12   **267–76**

Book of Judges
'Laws of the Sanhedrin'
    13: 3   137 n. 37

Index of Citations

'Laws of Mourning'
    14: 2   64 n. 98

'Laws of Kings and their Wars'
    5   299 n. 74
    5: 9   244 n. 32
    5: 9–12   5 n. 12
    6: 4   140 n. 48
    8: 9   138 n. 39
    8: 11   33 n. 72, 43 n. 8, 58 n. 71, 141 n. 52, 141 n. 55, 149 n. 18
    9   148 n. 13
    9: 1   43 n. 9, 55 n. 56, 58 n. 71, 237 n. 6
    10: 12   13 n. 38, 79 n. 19, 250 n. 50
    11–12   277–301
    11: 1   77 n. 12, 188 n. 21, 189 n. 22, 198 n. 52
    11: 3   77 n. 12
    12: 1   291 n. 50
    12: 2   80 n. 26, 278 n. 3
    12: 4   186 n. 11
    12: 5   281

Commentary on the Mishnah

Introduction   111, 136 n. 35, 199, 200 n. 56, 202, 249 n. 44

Betsah
    3: 4   241 n. 22

Megilah
    2: 1   77 n. 11
    2: 4   77 n. 11

Ḥagigah
    2: 1   17 n. 20, 21, 21 n. 39, 99 n. 32, 206 n. 67

Sotah
    1: 1   85 n. 11
    3: 3   92 n. 9

Kidushin
    1: 10   149 n. 18

Sanhedrin
    10: 1 ('Introduction to Perek ḥelek')   3 n. 4, 19 n. 29, 20 n. 32, 60 n. 77, 137 n. 36, 149 n. 18, 231 n. 35, 248 n. 42, 278 n. 3, 282, 284, 293 n. 58, 294 n. 60

Makot
    3: 17   149 n. 18

Eight Chapters (introduction to commentary on Mishnah avot)

    4   44 n. 16, 66 n. 110, 90 n. 3, 119, 175 n. 5, 179 n. 19, 216 n. 98, 318 n. 30
    5   98 n. 27
    6   100, 154 n. 32
    7   168 n. 73

Avot
    1: 2   162 n. 55, 216
    1: 18   216 n. 98
    4: 4   271 n. 24
    4: 7   126 n. 63

Zevaḥim
Introduction   10 n. 31, 200

Menaḥot
    13: 11   199 n. 53

Ḥulin
    7: 6   58 n. 70

Kelim
Introduction   200

Book of the Commandments

Introduction   92 n. 8, 157 n. 40, 241 n. 21, 252, 257

Positive Commandments
    1   37
    2   37
    3   10 n. 30, 26 n. 51, 28–34, 36, 39, 158 n. 49, 302
    7   115
    8   240 n. 19, 255 n. 60
    9   122 n. 52
    109   226 n. 14
    147   94 n. 14
    206   15 n. 6

Positive Commandments (*cont.*):
    215   59 n. 73
    223   84 n. 9

Negative Commandments
    40–5   151 n. 24
    125–53   110 n. 18
    172–206   110 n. 18
    365   77 n. 12

Guide of the Perplexed
Introduction to Part I 2 n. 3, 10, 10 n. 30, 17 n. 20, 20 n. 32, 100, 213 n. 92, 213 n. 93, 213 n. 94, 295 n. 62
    i. 1–2   279 n. 6
    i. 2   184 n. 2, 207 n. 72
    i. 7   209 n. 79
    i. 14   207 n. 71
    i. 16   63 n. 88, 64 n. 89
    i. 34   23 n. 41, 99 n. 32, 152 n. 26, 206 n. 67, 322 n. 5
    i. 36   211 n. 84
    i. 39   34 n. 78
    i. 50   212
    i. 54   63 n. 88, 119 n. 40, 124 n. 59, 168 n. 73, 308, 309 n. 13, 309 n. 14, 322 n. 8
    i. 55   158 n. 47
    i. 59   151 n. 23, 211 n. 84, 213
    i. 60   211 n. 84
    i. 61   65 n. 107, 274 n. 34, 274 n. 35
    i. 61–4   274 n. 33
    i. 62   99 n. 32
    i. 63   274 n. 36, 275 n. 37, 275 n. 38, 306 n. 2
    i. 64   212 n. 88
    i. 67   71 n. 127
    i. 69   163 n. 58
    i. 70   268 n. 6, 270 n. 19, 273 n. 29, 273 n. 31
    i. 71   24 n. 47, 42 n. 4, 71 n. 130, 206 n. 70, 273
    i. 72   205 n. 65, 326 n. 33, 328 n. 44, 334 n. 59
    ii. 4   323 n. 11, 325 n. 20, 325 n. 22
    ii. 5   212
    ii. 6   11 n. 35, 325 n. 20, 325 n. 22
    ii. 7   329 n. 45
    ii. 8   212 n. 86
    ii. 9   336
    ii. 9–10   130 n. 7
    ii. 10   326 n. 25
    ii. 12   187 n. 14, 187 n. 15, 257, 324 n. 19, 326 n. 26
    ii. 13   65 n. 105
    ii. 21   326 n. 31
    ii. 23   51 n. 43
    ii. 24   11 n. 32, 165 n. 64, 166 n. 68, 167 n. 71, 323 n. 13
    ii. 25   7 n. 17, 71 n. 130
    ii. 28   44 n. 12, 44 n. 13
    ii. 29   76 n. 10, 255 n. 61, 284 n. 24
    ii. 31   71 n. 128
    ii. 36–7   326 n. 28
    ii. 39   30 n. 61, 32 n. 67, 67 n. 112, 98 n. 27
    ii. 45   52 n. 45, 166 n. 67

Introduction to Part III 153 n. 27
    iii. 8   44 n. 14
    iii. 8–9   57 n. 68, 205 n. 66
    iii. 9   44 n. 14, 149 n. 18, 327 n. 40
    iii. 11   66 n. 111, 86, 297
    iii. 12   46 n. 24, 64 n. 90, 256, 327 n. 39
    iii. 13   249 n. 44, 261 n. 70, 326 n. 34, 327 n. 36
    iii. 14   327 n. 37
    iii. 17   64 n. 91, 64 n. 92, 250 n. 48
    iii. 18   217 n. 100
    iii. 22   207 n. 74, 248 n. 41
    iii. 24   53 n. 48, 64 n. 93, 67 n. 113, 67 n. 114
    iii. 25   125 n. 62
    iii. 26   150 n. 20, 153 n. 28, 153 n. 29, 154 n. 32, 160 n. 51
    iii. 27   45 n. 18, 96 n. 21, 98 n. 28, 99 n. 32, 160 n. 52, 179 n. 20, 327 n. 41
    iii. 28   35 n. 80, 66 n. 109, 153 n. 30, 310 n. 18, 310 n. 19
    iii. 29   32 n. 67, 65 n. 102, 151 n. 25

iii. 31	97 n. 25, 148 n. 14, 148 n. 15, 160 n. 50, 265 n. 78		102 n. 40, 142 n. 59, 161 n. 53, 161 n. 54, 171 n. 80, 213 n. 90, 216 n. 98, 230 n. 29
iii. 32	71 n. 129, 99 n. 34, 150 n. 19, 151 n. 23, 213, 289 n. 44, 299 n. 75, 306, 307 n. 5, 307 n. 6, 331 n. 52	iii. 51–2	170
		iii. 52	35 n. 84, 67 n. 113, 98 n. 26, 171 n. 81, 171 n. 82, 180 n. 26, 180 n. 27
iii. 33	45 n. 17, 48 n. 31, 56 n. 62, 57 n. 66, 91 n. 5, 92 n. 9, 251 n. 54	iii. 53	64 n. 94, 69 n. 120, 108 n. 6, 245 n. 34, 245 n. 35
iii. 34	4 n. 7, 4 n. 8	iii. 54	4 n. 5, 27, 66 n. 108, 66 n. 110, 98 n. 29, 99 n. 31, 99 n. 32, 209 n. 79, 237 n. 6, 258 n. 67, 258 n. 68, 271 n. 20, 279 n. 7, 298, 308 n. 11, 328 n. 42
iii. 35	15 n. 5, 83 n. 3, 88 n. 26, 90 n. 2, 115 n. 30, 115 n. 31, 190		
iii. 36	15 n. 4, 16 n. 7, 115 n. 32, 195 n. 43		
iii. 39	129 n. 3, 268 n. 12		
iii. 40	150 n. 20		
iii. 43	71 n. 128, 164 n. 60, 185 n. 5		
iii. 45	73, 144 n. 3, 195 n. 45		
iii. 46	60 n. 77, 150 n. 20, 176 n. 6, 192 n. 36, 195 n. 42		
iii. 47	92 n. 7, 144 n. 2, 150 n. 20, 155 n. 36, 183 n. 1, 189 n. 23, 189 n. 24, 189 n. 28, 190, 190 n. 30, 330 n. 48		
iii. 48	150 n. 20		
iii. 49	42 n. 6, 43 n. 10, 44 n. 15, 45 n. 20, 46 n. 21, 49 n. 34, 63 n. 87, 164 n. 62, 165 n. 66, 251 n. 52, 252 n. 55		
iii. 50	16 n. 8		
iii. 50–2	316 n. 27		
iii. 51	5 n. 9, 10 n. 30, 16 n. 8, 28 n. 57, 35 n. 81, 35 n. 83, 37 n. 85, 68 n. 117, 97 n. 26,		

Letters

Epistle to Yemen 5, 77 n. 12, 140 n. 48, 278 n. 5, 285 n. 27, 297 n. 71
To Ibn Tibbon 215 n. 95
To Joseph Ibn Jabbir 59 n. 74
To Obadiah the Proselyte 46, 46 n. 22, 139 n. 47, 226 n. 16, 251
To Pinhas of Alexandria 111 n. 21
To R. Hisdai of Alexandria 30 n. 61
To R. Joseph concerning the dispute with the head of the academy 5 n. 11
To the rabbis of Montpelier on astrology 334 n. 61
Treatise on Resurrection 289, 297 n. 71

Responsa

On the importance of astronomy 26 n. 51
On the ink used in Torah scrolls 136 n. 35
On the status of *minim* (sectarians) 227 n. 20

Index of Subjects

A
Abraham:
  alacrity of regarding God's commandments 67–9
  in *Book of Knowledge* 52–4
  in *Book of Love* regarding circumcision 40–72, 262
  converts identifying as descendants of 47, 137
  discovery of God by 52–4, 66–8, 139–42, 223–4, 226–7, 233, 261, 265, 300–2, 305, 317–19
  God of Aristotle vs. God of the patriarchs 27, 272 n. 28
  love of God of 14, 18, 19 n. 24, 21, 25, 29–33, 36–9, 53–4
  mercy as common trait of children of 242, 251–3, 256
  as model of Maimonides 306–11
  moral and intellectual legacy of 52–4, 178, 261, 263, 265–6
  name of God of 125 n. 60
  obligations of the descendants of 230, 232–3, 236, 280, 313
  and observance of the commandments 30 n. 61, 50, 224 n. 7
  pairing with Moses in Maimonides' works 40–72, 306–11
  as patron of *Book of Love* 54–5
  as philosopher 267–76
  as pillar of the world 31–2, 51–62, 140
  rebellion of against idolatry 31–2
  righteousness as coming from 176–8
Abraham ben David (Rabad) 140 n. 48, 289
Abraham ben Maimonides 30 n. 61, 292 n. 54
Abrahamic model:
  covenant of 49, 60, 69, 72, 262–3, 302
  as God's original intent in the Torah 280, 308, 310–11, 319
  Levi as faithful to 68–9
  love as value of 54–5, 69, 72, 262, 302
  messianic world as closest thing to 280, 308, 310
  Mishneh torah expressive of 308, 311, 318–19
  monotheism as part of 2, 306, 308
  Mosaic law as embodying 53–4, 61, 66, 68–70, 72, 319
  spirit of discovery in 71, 263, 309, 319
  as taking precedence over Mosaic model 263, 302
  tension between Mosaic model and 262, 305–6
  universalism of 2, 51–3, 55, 57–8, 61, 67, 262, 266, 300–1, 305, 308 n. 10, 311–12
Abravanel, Isaac:
  on God's second intention 307 n. 7
  on knowledge of God's existence as foundation of everything 23–5
  on Maimonides' thirteen principles 131 n. 12, 232 n. 39
  Principles of Faith 23–4
  on Torah and science 23, 25
  on universalism of the Mishnah 135 n. 31
accommodation, divine 308
accommodation in Judaism 262–4
acquired intellect 22 n. 41, 43, 181 n. 28, 232, 328
Adam 58 n. 71, 137, 142 n. 59, 206–7
agent intellect:
  Book of Purity corresponding to 203–4, 219, 260
  in study of physics and metaphysics 214, 216
  tenth angel as 203, 325, 336

agent intellect (cont.):
  turning away from matter towards 203–4, 206, 208–11, 219, 260, 314–15, 326 n. 28, 328, 336
  see also *ishim*
aggadah 7 n. 20, 136, 266, 294
agnosticism 196
akedah 52, 53 n. 50, 67 n. 114
Akiva, R. 87, 107 n. 5, 288–9
al-amr al-ilahi 103
Al hanisim, commandment to recite on Hanukah and Purim 73, 79–81
Aleinu 290 n. 46
Alfarabi 167 n. 70, 204, 324, 326 n. 34, 336
al-Fayyumi, Netanel ibn 293 n. 57
al-Ghazali 108
'all who come into the world' (*kol ba'ei olam*) 9, 129–40, 142
allegories 68 n. 118, 291
almsgiving, *see* charity
al-Qadi al-Fadil 28 n. 57
Amalek 299 n. 74
Amidah 79
amor Dei intellectualis (intellectual love of God) 22, 27, 60, 67–8, 329, 331
angels:
  de'ot as 178 n. 15
  fear of the shofar 133
  free choice of 44 n. 15, 329
  Gabriel wanting to save Abraham 32 n. 69
  God as beyond comprehension of 308, 328
  hierarchy of 71, 167, 187, 198, 203–4, 206, 214, 321, 325–30, 335–7
  ma'aseh merkavah as being about 18 n. 20
  see also separate intellects
animals, prioritizing slaves and 246–7
anthropomorphism 71 n. 127
aravot 268–73, 275, 316
archetype, Adam as 206–7
Aristotelianism:
  God as First Cause of existence 32 n. 71
  on intellectual and moral virtue 15, 93, 176, 300
  in Kellner's writings 6
  on knowing as becoming 63
  in *Mishneh torah* 321
  model of the universe 11 n. 35, 167, 322, 324
  on nature below the moon 166
  on the potential becoming actual 326 n. 28
Aristotle:
  Abraham as anticipator of 272–6
  on aesthetic perfection 309 n. 15
  four causes of and reasons for the commandments 163–5
  God of vs. God of the patriarchs 27, 272 n. 28
  on intellectual and moral virtue 322
  love of God of 38
  model of the universe 11 n. 35, 322 n. 11
  name of God of 125 n. 60
  on spheres 212 n. 86, 322 n. 11, 324
Ark of the Covenant 136, 145
astrology 102–3, 334
Averroes 33
Avicenna 204, 324

B
ba'alei teshuvah, *see* repentance
Babylonian exile 248 n. 41
Bahya Ibn Pakuda, R. 16 n. 12, 230–1
Balaam (Bilam) 285, 287
Bar Kokhba 288–9
Baris, Michael 29 n. 58
Berlin, Isaiah 296
Bible, books of:
  Prophets 40, 76, 225
  Writings 76, 225
Bienenfeld, R. Jeffrey 296 n. 69
Bilam (Balaam) 285, 287
blessings:
  in *Book of Love* 21, 40–1, 51 n. 41, 213
  on circumcision of converts and slaves 51 n. 41
  imitation of the middle path as resulting in 261
  as material things 257
  performance of commandments to obtain the Torah's 18, 285

Index of Subjects

priestly 21, 40
Blidstein, Gerald (Ya'akov) 30 n. 61, 79 n. 18
Book of Acquisition:
  Book of Civil Laws as continuation of 267
  as continuation of *Book of Damages* 234
  mercy as *imitatio Dei* in 107, 259–60, 304, 316
  middle/straight path mentioned at the end of 318 n. 28
  pursuing knowledge of God and immortality in 260–1, 265–6
  slavery vs. universal humanity in 13, 234–66, 304, 313, 331
  summary of contents of 235
The Book of Acquisition (Klein) 1 n. 1
Book of Agriculture:
  'all who come into the world', meaning of in 129–34
  attitudes to possessions in 109, 129, 315, 330
  Book of Temple Service as continuation of 143
  as countercurrent to *Book of Asseverations* 127
  Levites as model for God-seekers in 109
  middle/straight path mentioned at the end of 318 n. 28
  sanctifying all human beings in 127, 129–43, 303
  summary of contents of 129
Book of Asseverations:
  clash of values in 112–13
  consecration as oath in 107, 112, 115–16, 118–19, 121, 123, 128, 303
  as continuation of *Book of Holiness* 114–16, 123, 127–8, 303
  meaning of *hafla'ah* in 113–16, 128
  middle/straight path mentioned at the end of 120, 128
  Mishneh torah's structure as guide to meaning of 121–3
  restraint of appetites in 90 n. 1, 107, 110, 120–1, 315, 330
  social responsibility and sanctifying God's name in 106–28
  summary of contents of 106
  unifying concept of 109–12
Book of Civil Laws 111, 267–76, 305, 316–17, 331
The Book of Civil Laws (Rabinowitz) 1 n. 1
Book of the Commandments:
  achieving holiness in 91, 92 n. 8
  arrangement of laws in *Mishneh torah* vs. 115, 130
  belief in God (positive commandment 1) in 37
  circumcision (positive commandment 215) in 59, 252
  on the criteria of commandments 241 n. 21, 252
  equality in 226 n. 14
  imitation of God (positive commandment 8) in 255 n. 60
  on the language of *Mishneh torah* 257
  love of God (positive commandment 3) in 10 n. 30, 14, 26 n. 51, 28–34, 36, 39, 302
  paganism in 151
  restraint of appetites in 110
  the *sotah* in 84
  unity of God (positive commandment 2) in 37
Book of Damages (Torts) 221–34, 260–1, 304, 316, 331
Book of Holiness:
  Book of Asseverations as continuation of 114–16, 123, 127–8, 303
  commandments as instruments in 90–105, 122, 149, 303, 313, 315, 333
  holiness as negative in 82 n. 1, 123
  middle/straight path mentioned at the end of 318 n. 28
  restraint of appetites in 90–1, 110, 112, 114, 119, 122, 127–8, 149, 303, 315, 330, 333
  summary of contents of 90
Book of Judges:
  as continuation of *Book of Civil Laws* 276, 317
  messianic universalism in 277–301, 305
  naturalistic messianism in 284, 286, 288–9, 293, 331–2

Book of Judges (cont.):
  pacific nature of messianism in
    298–301
  as reflection of *Book of Knowledge* 277,
    280, 316
  roles of Christianity and Islam in 284–5,
    289–91, 299
  separation of messiah and resurrection
    in 289
  summary of contents of 277
  universal adoption of true religion (*dat
    ha'emet*) in 291–3
Book of Knowledge:
  Abraham in 52–4, 70–2
  Book of Love as continuation of 17, 20,
    36, 38, 40, 70–1, 213, 330–1, 334
  commandments as instruments in 102
    n. 41
  as conceptual driver of subsequent books
    14, 23, 53, 116, 187, 314, 332, 334
  connection between beginning and end
    of *Mishneh torah* and 279–80, 302,
    312, 316–17
  connection with books of *Temple Service*
    and *Offerings* 181, 194, 220
  dietary advice in 110
  doctrine of the mean in 109
  emanation in 304, 332–3
  equality in 38
  esotericism in 17
  fear of God in 56
  God of Aristotle in 272
  idolatry in 82 n. 1
  knowledge as love in 14–39, 70–2, 302,
    316
  'Laws of Repentance', ch. 10 18–21, 280,
    302
  'Laws of the Foundations of the Torah',
    1: 1 and 2: 1–2 22–8
  messianism in 16, 198
  morality in 54, 56, 181, 298 n. 73, 312
  pattern of God, self, study, repentance in
    208–12, 316
  repentance in 82 n. 1, 208–12, 316
  summary of contents of 14–17
  as top of the hierarchy of enlightenment
    198, 213, 330–1
  universal structure of intellect in 211,
    304, 314, 332
  universalist message in 39, 42, 53, 312
Book of Love:
  Abraham as patron of 54–5, 69–72, 302
  Book of Seasons as continuation of 71, 73,
    84
  circumcision in *Guide* vs. 48–50, 315
  connection between circumcision and
    the sabbath in 71
  connection between *Book of Temple
    Service* and 314–15
  as continuation of *Book of Knowledge* 17,
    20, 36, 38, 40, 70–1, 213, 330–1, 334
  covenants of Abraham vs. Moses and
    circumcision in 40–72, 262, 302, 314
  love as actions in 333
  prayer in 55, 57, 79, 213
  purpose of the commandments in 57,
    60, 69, 72, 82 n. 1, 314, 330, 334
  restraint of appetites in 315
  summary of contents of 40–3
  universalist message in 42, 48, 55, 72
Book of Offerings:
  Book of Purity as continuation of 219
  commandment performance as respect
    for God in 105 n. 49
  connections with books of *Purity* and
    Temple Service 88 n. 27, 144, 175,
    181–3, 188, 193, 208, 219, 304
  as continuation of *Book of Temple Service*
    219
  co-ordination of *Mishneh torah* with
    orientations of the human psyche 204
  ending of as antithesis to ending of *Book
    of Temple Service* 193–4, 202–4
  individual sacrifices in 201, 202 n. 58,
    203, 211
  middle/straight path mentioned at the
    end of 318 n. 28
  morality of the commandments in
    173–82, 193, 304
  objective and subjective in 88 n. 27

Index of Subjects 367

  parable created by the ending and
    context of 194–7
  rearrangement of mishnaic material in
    202
  reasons for the commandments in 172,
    178, 180, 182, 193, 312
  summary of contents of 173
  universal structure of intellect in 211
Book of Purity:
  as based on Order *Tohorot* 185
  Book of Temple Service as preparation for
    156, 182
  connection with *Book of Agriculture* 315
  connection with *Book of Women* 88
    n. 27, 314–15
  connections with books of *Offerings* and
    Temple Service 88 n. 27, 144, 175,
    181–3, 188, 193, 208, 219, 304
  as continuation of *Book of Offerings* 219
  co-ordination of *Mishneh torah* with
    orientations of the human psyche 204
  ending of as synthesis 193–4, 202–4
  ending of summing up books 1–10 of
    Mishneh torah 187, 203, 219, 304
  intellectual and moral purity in 183–220
  as last of books concerning *mitsvot bein*
    adam lamakom 185, 187 n. 12, 219, 221
  objective and subjective in 88 n. 27
  parable created by the ending and
    context of 194–7
  as parallel to agent intellect (*ishim*) 203,
    219, 260, 304, 315, 330 n. 48
  rearrangement of mishnaic material in
    219
  return as theme of 210, 219, 315
  as second-longest book in *Mishneh torah*
    73
  statutes in 191, 193
  summary of contents of 183–4
  universal structure of intellect in 211
  universalist message in 183, 186
  water as metaphor for intellect in 185–8,
    192–3, 296 n. 69
Book of Seasons:
  commandments in as physical and
    contingent 82 n. 1, 330

  connection between *Book of Women* and
    84–5, 88 n. 27, 315
  as continuation of *Book of Love* 71, 73, 84
  marital and universal peace in 78, 84–6,
    302, 314–15, 317 n. 28
  middle/straight path mentioned at the
    end of 317 n. 28
  reconfiguration of Hanukah and Purim
    in 73–81, 302
  sotah in 84, 86 n. 17, 315
  summary of contents of 73
  time-bound prohibitions in 110
Book of Temple Service:
  Book of Offerings as continuation of 219
  commandment performance as respect
    for God in 105 n. 49, 169, 171
  commandment to build the Temple in
    332
  commandments as parables 194–7
  communal sacrifices in 173, 201, 202
    n. 58, 203
  connection with *Book of Love* 314
  connection with *Book of Women* 88 n. 27
  connections with books of *Offerings* and
    Purity 88 n. 27, 144, 175, 181–3, 188,
    193, 208, 219, 304
  consecration as oath in 106
  as continuation of *Book of Agriculture* 143
  co-ordination of *Mishneh torah* with
    orientations of the human psyche 204
  divinity of the commandments in
    144–72
  equality in 143, 176
  love in the rituals of 218 n. 101
  messianic holiness in 143, 180
  middle/straight path mentioned at the
    end of 180, 318 n. 28
  morality in 304
  motto of 5 n. 12
  objective and subjective in 88 n. 27
  parable created by the ending and
    context of 194–7
  prohibition on impure people entering
    the Temple in 191
  rearrangement of mishnaic material in
    202

Book of Temple Service (cont.):
   sacrifices in 106, 150, 172, 197, 202, 332
   statutes in 148, 150, 174, 180, 193, 303–4
   summary of contents of 144–5
   universal structure of intellect in 211
   universalist message in 172, 182
Book of Women:
   as based on the body 82 n. 1, 330
   connection with *Book of Holiness* 90 n. 1
   connection with *Book of Purity* 88 n. 27, 314–15
   connection with *Book of Seasons* 84–5
   holiness in 90 n. 1, 264
   marital and universal peace in 82–9, 303, 315
   middle/straight path mentioned at the end of 317 n. 28
   pattern of loss and restoration in 82 n. 1, 314–15
   sotah in 314–15
   summary of contents of 82
Buchman, Asher Bentzion 271 n. 23

C

calf, R. Judah the Prince and 248–9
Canaan and Canaanites 32, 53, 235, 237, 299 n. 74
celestial hierarchy, emanation and 323–5
ceremonial commandments, see *mitsvot bein adam lamakom*
charity:
   Abraham as standing for 64, 176–8
   mercy as connected to 255
   morality through 176–8
   as not resulting in poverty 225
   prioritizing money received as 74
   righteousness as connected to 255
   sabbatical and jubilee laws relating to 129, 142, 331
   slave receiving 245
   as universal trait 177
chosen people, Jews as 2, 141, 233, 257, 293
Christianity:
   acceptance of Torah and commandments by 291 n. 48
   Francis of Assisi as representative of 108–9
   as idolatry 3, 291 n. 48
   and messianism 284–5, 289, 291–2, 299
   morality vs. philosophy in 300
   original sin in 132 n. 16
   proselytism in 3
   salvation in 3, 5 n. 13
   slave ownership in 236
circumcision:
   Abraham and Moses regarding 40–72, 262, 302
   in *Book of Love* vs. *Guide* 48–50
   as a comprehensive commandment 47–8, 54
   of converts 51 n. 41, 69–70, 138, 224 n. 7, 237 n. 6
   as essential for entrance into world to come 41, 43, 48–9, 60
   excluded from Noahide laws 43
   in *Guide* 43–50, 52–3, 57, 66–7, 70, 72, 315
   of the heart 55–7, 251–2, 290
   importance of 41–3, 50–1, 54, 66, 72
   laws of 21, 41–2, 58–61, 66, 72, 213, 251, 262, 302, 317
   Maimonides' sources regarding 50–1
   in messianic era 290
   as one of Abraham's ten trials 52–3, 68
   other nations lacking 41, 43, 48, 50, 236, 251–2, 256
   perfection and 41, 43–5, 47–50, 53, 62, 66–7, 72
   punishment for not performing 59–60, 62
   for reducing desire 44–5, 47–9, 57, 252, 315
   as ritual 306
   and the sabbath 70–2
   as a sign and reminder 41, 45–7, 49, 53, 55, 57, 60, 69, 71–2, 251, 315
   of slaves 51 n. 41, 237 n. 6
   Torah as amplification of 66
   universalism of 42 n. 5, 47–8, 57, 72, 262

Cohen, Hermann:
  on Maimonidean ethics 4, 132 n. 19
  on messianic era 282, 287 n. 38, 297, 300
commandments:
  Abraham's alacrity vs. Moses' reluctance in performance of 68–9
  Abraham's legacy restored through Moses via 52, 54, 58–61, 70, 72, 137, 141, 261, 266, 302, 306, 308–9, 319
  as all God has in this world 200 n. 56
  Aristotle's four causes applied to 163–5
  Avot as lacking 7, 278
  benevolence as goal of 13, 129, 176–7, 221, 237–8, 240–8, 250, 255–7, 259, 263, 265–9
  between man and God, see *mitsvot bein adam lamakom*
  between man and his fellow, see *mitsvot bein adam leḥavero*
  blessings as 41
  circumcision as one of 41–3, 45, 47–51, 54, 56–62, 66, 69–72, 251–2, 302
  classification of 10, 106, 110, 112, 114–15, 166, 190, 199–200, 202, 239 n. 16, 269, 311, 315
  conflict between, *see* conflict between commandments
  consecration of wealth as not one of 106–9, 112–13, 116, 118, 120–1, 126–8, 176, 240 n. 20
  contemplation of 27, 29–30, 33, 36–8, 152–3, 158, 161, 165–9, 214–15, 310–11
  converts performing 47, 137, 233, 237 n. 6
  cosmology and 6, 10, 98, 163, 274, 276, 305, 310, 321–35
  covenant of love vs. law 54, 58–62, 67, 69–70, 72, 262, 264, 302
  Decalogue 145, 307 n. 6
  as distinguishing Jewish people 122, 127, 149, 333
  divinity of, *see* divinity of the commandments
  esotericism of 100–2, 167, 311, 332
  fear of God as one of 25, 26 n. 51, 27–8, 67, 98, 169, 171, 180, 190–1, 205, 277, 322, 331
  foundational 332 n. 55
  free will as essential to observance of 15
  Gentiles and 4, 43, 104, 122, 137, 140–1, 147–50, 153, 154 n. 32, 155, 170, 176, 230–3, 237 n. 6, 238, 240–7, 251–2, 257, 263, 265–6, 291 n. 48, 292 n. 52, 303, 306
  good deeds vs. 222 n. 2
  Greeks forbidding observance of 75
  halakhah vs. meta-halakhah 8–10
  hierarchy of 13, 43, 167, 240, 329–31, 333–4
  as hints 143, 185, 192, 196
  ḥok (statute) as contradictory vs. unexplained 154–6
  holiday-related 76–7, 79–81, 314
  holiness as fulfilment of 91–2, 104–5, 122, 303
  imitation of God as one of 53, 56, 89, 118–19, 124, 126, 197, 238–40, 243, 245, 253–5, 258–9, 261–2, 266, 271, 305, 313, 316, 322
  as instilling fear of God 35
  as instruments 6, 8, 90–105, 278, 303, 318 n. 28
  Israel of the 229–30, 233
  knowledge of God as one of 6, 10–12, 14–15, 16 n. 12, 20 n. 36, 22 n. 41, 25, 26 n. 51, 27, 29–30, 34–7, 60, 66, 69, 122–3, 158, 163–4, 171, 182, 186–7, 216, 219, 256, 274–7, 302, 305–6, 310, 312–14, 316, 322, 329–31
  lifnim mishurat hadin 240–2
  love of God as one of 10, 20 n. 36, 21, 25, 26 n. 51, 27–40, 54, 56–7, 60, 62, 66–7, 69–70, 123, 149 n. 18, 150, 158, 163–4, 169, 180, 205, 277, 302, 310, 314, 322, 333
  Maimonides vs. Halevi regarding observance of 102–4, 158, 216–17
  marital peace as one of 84, 85 n. 15, 87, 89
  as means to a universal end 1, 11, 21, 97–8, 120, 148, 169, 171, 176, 186, 197 n. 50, 319

commandments (*cont.*):
  in messianic era 2, 6, 16, 147, 186, 188, 278, 281, 285–90, 292 n. 52, 293, 301
  metaphorical interpretation of 185–7, 192–3, 210, 219, 304
  as metaphysical accomplishments 98 n. 28, 102–3
  Mishneh torah's book endings as lacking 1, 6–10, 306, 333
  morality of 8–9, 38, 43, 47–8, 66, 72, 88 n. 26, 89, 96–7, 99, 102, 105, 121, 126–8, 148, 149 n. 18, 160, 170, 173–82, 185 n. 5, 190, 193, 203–4, 208, 211, 216, 219, 229, 233, 243, 253–4, 256, 258–60, 263, 265–6, 268, 285, 286 n. 32, 300, 304–5, 310, 312–14, 319, 322, 329 n. 47, 332–3
  motives for performing 18–19, 118, 122, 149 n. 18, 150, 158, 213, 286 n. 35
  as mystical prescriptions 102–3
  Noahide, *see* Noahides
  pagan explanations for 151, 155–6
  as parables 12, 102, 144, 194–7, 200, 214–15, 217–20
  patriarchs' fulfilment of 30 n. 61, 50, 224 n. 7
  perfection arising from observance of 2, 8, 37–8, 43, 45, 47–50, 52 n. 45, 62–3, 67, 72, 89, 96, 98, 104 n. 46, 105, 137, 162–5, 167 n. 70, 186, 216, 229, 233, 239, 253, 264, 285, 286 n. 32, 286 n. 35, 300, 304–5, 309, 319, 329, 332–3
  performing out of love 16, 18–20, 54, 62, 149 n. 18, 150, 331
  philosophical study as related to 33, 196–7, 306, 313, 319
  practicality of 71, 110, 161, 200, 202, 218, 332
  prophecy as basis for 16, 166, 168, 224, 329
  punishment for not performing 59–60, 62
  reasons for, *see ta'amei hamitsvot*
  reflecting laws of nature 2, 7, 63, 163–7, 181 n. 29, 216, 254–5, 304, 309–10, 329
  repentance as one of 15, 134, 140, 196
  respecting 105 n. 49, 122, 146, 169, 190, 288
  for restraint leading to the middle path 43, 45, 47–8, 56, 119–20, 122, 124, 149, 175–6, 179–80, 186, 193, 244–5, 252, 254, 315, 318, 330, 333
  sacrifices as 108, 120, 144, 147, 150–1, 155–62, 176, 194, 197–8, 201, 202 n. 58, 204, 211, 215–16, 332
  sanctification of 73, 82 n. 1, 90–105, 112, 114, 122, 146, 152, 154, 174–5, 182, 264–5, 303, 333
  self-awareness as one of 207, 216
  sheḥitah as one of 94, 168–9, 313
  in the Shema 40–1, 54, 56–7
  statutes vs. ordinances 146–62, 166, 168–70, 174, 183, 189, 193, 202–3, 213, 216, 219, 239–40 n. 16, 265, 303
  stepping away from to see the bigger picture 1–2, 6, 8, 10–11, 18 n. 20, 70, 72, 81, 116, 187, 260, 332
  Temple-related 120, 144–5, 147, 150, 153–60, 162, 169, 171, 176, 188–91, 194, 197–8, 201, 202 n. 58, 204, 211, 215–16, 331–2
  thirteen rules for derivation of 131
  as timeless yet historically contingent 73, 330, 332
  tripartite pattern of 259–60
  universalism of 1–2, 4–7, 9, 11–13, 21, 30, 39, 47–8, 70, 72, 104, 126, 144, 147–50, 152, 161, 166, 168–71, 176–7, 182–3, 186–8, 197, 210, 218, 239, 242, 248, 253, 256, 262–3, 266, 275, 286 n. 32, 300–1, 303–4, 308 n. 10, 311–13, 318–19, 333
  wisdom of God in 29 n. 59, 38, 123, 148–9, 160, 165, 191, 215 n. 95, 255–6, 259, 265, 310, 312
  world to come as reward for performing 16, 18, 43, 60, 141, 147, 149 n. 18, 150–1, 168–72, 180, 232, 285–6
Commentary on the Mishnah:
  arrangement differs from that of the Mishnah 111, 202

continuity between *Mishneh torah* and
   201
covenants of love vs. law in 58, 61
equality in 249 n. 44
esotericism in 17
honour of God in 21 n. 39
marital peace in 85
meaning of 'all who come into the world'
   in 137
messiah in 281–6, 301
on originality of classification of the
   Mishnah 199–202
on purpose in the world 200 n. 56
restraint of appetites in 90
virtue vs. self-discipline in 100
'commune with your own heart upon your
   bed, and be still' 212–15
conflict between commandments:
   consecration of wealth 112–13
   covenants of law vs. love 69–70, 262
   levirate marriage 155, 239–40
   particularist vs. universal 13, 126, 242,
      253, 262, 266, 304
   philosophers vs. sages 101
   positive vs. negative 240
   red heifer 155
   sabbath vs. preservation of life 239
   slavery 239–42, 262–3, 266
   statutes 155, 239 n. 16, 253
converts and conversion:
   before Sinai as impossible 224
   circumcision of 51, 69–70
   commandments as instruments of 105
   due to Abraham 52, 227
   equality of 46–7, 241
   identifying as descendant of Abraham
      47, 137
   inheriting the Land of Israel 47
   Israel of the commandments including
      229, 232–3
   in messianic era 292, 299
   mikveh immersion as part of 184
   nilvim as not 226–7, 230, 233, 304
   of proselytes 224 n. 7, 227
   of slaves 237 n. 6

cosmology and the cosmos:
   aravot 268–73, 275, 316
   of Aristotle 11 n. 35, 167, 322, 324
   and the commandments 6, 10, 98, 163,
      274, 276, 305, 310, 321–35
   emanation of 13, 304, 317, 321, 323–5,
      327
   in *Guide* 10 n. 30, 24, 167, 270–1, 273,
      322, 325 n. 20, 325 n. 22, 328, 334, 336
   as a hierarchy 13, 71, 167, 187, 198, 209,
      323–8, 330, 333–7
   human beings as microcosms of 6, 163,
      167, 197, 212, 308–10, 321–2, 327–9,
      333–5
   and knowledge of God 26 n. 52, 29, 36,
      204–6, 218, 310, 325–30, 336–7
   as a living organism 204–7, 213–14, 218,
      304, 323–9, 334, 336–7
   and love of God 26 n. 52, 29, 36, 204,
      206, 218, 310, 324–5, 327–9, 335–6
   of Maimonides 289 n. 43, 327, 336–7
   Mishneh torah as modelled on 6, 10–11,
      13, 143, 163, 166 n. 69, 197 n. 50, 310,
      321–2, 324, 331–2, 334–5
   morality of 203, 254, 322–3, 329
   as paradigm 6, 321–35
   as perfection 6, 24, 50–1, 163, 205, 213,
      317, 326, 328–9
   as proving existence of God 6, 22, 24,
      27, 29–31, 36, 42 n. 4, 54, 140, 163, 166
      n. 69, 167, 171, 204–5, 212, 270–1,
      273–4, 276, 305, 310, 322–3, 325,
      327–9, 336
   see also microcosm
covenant:
   ark of the 136, 145
   between Abraham and God 41–2, 46,
      49, 55, 59–62, 67–70, 72, 262–3, 302,
      317
   between Moses and God 42, 49, 55, 59,
      61–2, 68–70, 72, 262, 302
   between Noah and God 50 n. 35
   circumcision as 41–3, 45–6, 48–51, 55,
      59–62, 67–72, 262, 302, 317
   converts entering 224 n. 7
   during the Exodus 69, 224 n. 7

covenant (*cont.*):
  keeping God's 256, 314
  as land in Genesis 61
  of love vs. of law 58–62, 69–70, 72, 262, 264, 302
  in messianic era 131 n. 15, 222–3
  perfection and 49–50, 62–9
  sabbath as a 71
Creation:
  Abraham's belief in 32 n. 67, 51 n. 43, 64–7
  belief in as uniquely Jewish 11 n. 35, 197
  commandments preceding vs. following 51
  eternity of the world post- 43, 164 n. 61, 206
  humans as not glory of 327
  'Laws of the Foundations of the Torah' chs. 1–4 as philosophized retelling of story of 206
  Maimonides' belief in 11 n. 35, 26 n. 51, 42 n. 4
  Moses' belief in 51 n. 43, 168
  as product of *ḥesed* 255
  sea as *mikveh* in the story of 186 n. 9
  stories of in Genesis 17 n. 18, 206
  Torah preceding vs. following 51, 181 n. 29
  validity of Torah as dependent on doctrine of 7 n. 17
Crusades 282

D

Daniel 290
David, King:
  and equality 132, 142
  faith in God 150, 256
  fear of God 139
  and *ḥukim* 146, 153, 160–1, 168, 197
  love of God 25–6, 28
  messiah as descendant of 285–90
Day of Atonement 73, 135, 143, 145, 194
Decalogue 145, 307 n. 6
Deutscher, Isaac 297
dialectics:
  in endings of books of *Temple Service, Offerings*, and *Purity* 193–4, 202–4, 219, 259, 311, 313–14
  as moral and intellectual progress advancing each other 202–4, 219, 259, 298, 313–14
discovery, Abraham as exemplar of 66–8
Divine Name, *see* name of God
divine order 103
Divine Presence, *see shekhinah*
divinity of the commandments:
  enquiring into reasons for commandments despite 174, 182, 312
  in *Mishneh torah* generally 273 n. 30
  observance of commandments because of 144–72, 182, 219, 313
  social commandments as infused with 319
Dome of the Rock 287

E

Edom and Edomites 288 n. 39
Egypt:
  idolatry in 224
  Israelites going to 306
  Israelites in 224
  Israelites leaving 69, 150, 173, 224 n. 7, 307
  St Francis in 108
Egyptians 107, 224
Eight Chapters:
  commandments as road to middle path 66 n. 110, 119
  forbidden sexual relations as statute or ordinance 154 n. 32
  truth and peace as virtues 179 n. 19, 216 n. 98
  virtue vs. self-discipline 100
Elazar ben Azariah, R. 50, 108 n. 7
elected people, Jews as, *see* chosen people, Jews as
elements of matter, four:
  as components of sublunar entities 321, 323, 326–7, 331, 334, 336–7
  as *ma'aseh bereshit* 18 n. 20
  Mishneh torah books on *mitsvot bein adam leḥavero* as corresponding to 44, 316, 321, 330–1, 335

as universal 323
Elijah 80–1, 293
Elisha ben Abuyah 103
elitism 2–3, 159–62, 167, 233
emanation:
  from *Book of Knowledge* 332–3
  and heavenly hierarchy 71, 143, 187, 203–4, 206–11, 219, 260, 304, 317, 323–7, 332–3, 334 n. 59, 336–7
  Mishneh torah's form as representing 13, 62, 71, 143, 187, 203–4, 209, 219, 257, 260, 304, 317, 324–5, 328, 332–3, 334 n. 59
  of Mosaic covenant of law from Abrahamic covenant of love 62, 253, 258, 261, 304, 317
  water as metaphor for 187–8, 210–11, 219, 257, 304, 324
  see also hierarchy
Emden, R. 196 n. 47
ending of book as bridge to following book:
  Acquisition to *Civil Laws* 267
  Agriculture to *Temple Service* 143
  Civil Laws to *Judges* 276, 317
  Damages (Torts) to *Acquisition* 234
  Holiness to *Asseverations* 114–16, 123, 127–8, 303
  Knowledge to *Love* 17, 20, 36, 38, 40, 70–1, 213, 330–1, 334
  Love to *Seasons* 71, 73, 84
  Purity to *Damages (Torts)* 219–20
  Seasons to *Women* 84
  Temple Service to *Offerings* 219
  see also *Mishneh torah*, endings of books
Enosh 30, 206
epikoros and *epikoresut*:
  due to changing commandments 288
  due to disputing statutes 146, 149, 153, 168
  due to doubting foundations 231
  Maimonides' treatment of sacrifices as 196 n. 47
  place of in the Jewish community and world to come 227–8
Epistle to Yemen 5, 278 n. 5, 297 n. 71
erelim 325, 334, 337

Esau, Mount of 288 n. 39
esotericism:
  of the commandments 290
  ma'aseh bereshit and *ma'aseh merkavah* as 17, 167
  as means of communication 70 n. 125
  in *Mishneh torah* 12, 167, 217
  see also *ma'aseh bereshit* and *ma'aseh merkavah*
Esther 223 n. 5
ethics, *see* morality
Eve 142 n. 59, 206–7
Even-Shoshan, Abraham 65 n. 104, 114 n. 29
Exodus, the 69, 173, 258, 307
Ezekiel 2 n. 3

F
Feast of Tabernacles, *see* Sukkot
First Being (First Cause), *see* God
Flood, the 58
form:
  of action towards repentance 192 n. 36, 195–7, 203, 206–7, 209, 212, 219
  Adam as human 207
  God's visible vs. invisible 69, 165
  humans as equal in 47, 264
  intellect as highest 4, 86, 179, 203, 206–7, 209, 213, 215, 219–20, 237 n. 6, 264, 297, 310, 324, 326–7, 332, 336–7
  matter and 207, 324, 327
  Mishneh torah and humans as microcosmic 6, 13, 71, 163, 187, 197, 203, 206, 212, 308–10, 325, 329, 331–2
  Mishneh torah as universal 6–7, 12, 311
  in Plotinus 324, 332
  transcending covenant of law to reach covenant of love 62, 203, 206, 310
four causes, Aristotle's 163–5
Francis of Assisi, St 108–9, 127
freedom, human:
  in messianic era 293 n. 59, 295–6, 313
  political 283, 293 n. 59, 313
  repentance as form of 195
  serving God as form of 139, 142, 142–3 n. 60, 169, 184, 295–6, 313

freedom, human (cont.):
  vs. slavery 261 n. 70, 262–3
  of will 15, 44, 64, 131 n. 12, 139
Friedman, Mordechai Akiva 278 n. 5
fringes (*tsitsit*) 21, 41, 122

G
Gandz, Solomon 73
Garden of Eden 207, 280 n. 11
Gates, Bill 287 n. 36
Gentiles:
  Abraham as 142
  avoiding idolatry 122, 170, 237 n. 6
  avoiding martyrdom 122
  conversion of 224 n. 7, 237 n. 6, 241, 292
  discrimination against 4, 13, 238, 240–1, 259, 261, 266, 304, 313
  holiness of 93 n. 13, 105, 303
  Jewish 230, 233, 297, 304
  Levites as model for 109
  love of God of 16, 22, 30, 33, 38–9
  in messianic era 16, 147 n. 12, 159, 292
  nilvim as 226–7, 304
  no inherent distinction between Jews and 2, 138, 149 n. 18, 176, 229, 237 n. 6, 241, 258, 292, 300, 306
  Noahide commandments for 43, 147, 237 n. 6, 292 n. 52
  observance of commandments of 104–5, 147–50, 153, 176, 233, 252, 257
  prayers of 21 n. 37
  proselytism of 3
  purity of 186 n. 8
  recognition of God of 122
  righteous 141
  sanctification of 93 n. 13, 105, 139, 143, 303, 308
  science of 23–4, 28 n. 57, 30, 33, 38–9
  as slaves 13, 226, 235, 237 n. 6, 238, 240–1, 243–6, 250–1, 253–4, 258–9, 261–3, 265–6, 304, 313
  status of 28 n. 57, 147 n. 12
  statutes in the eyes of 3 n. 4, 146, 148–9, 153, 154 n. 32, 155–6, 159–60, 170, 265
  support of poor 250 n. 50
  as uncircumcised 43, 236, 251–2, 256
  understanding of the commandments by 3 n. 4, 265
  universalism of Jewish relations with 2, 4, 13, 79–80, 132 n. 19, 148, 170, 176, 223, 233, 255 n. 62, 259, 261–3, 266, 304, 319
  wars between Jews and 76
  as wicked 43, 251, 256
  in world to come 33 n. 72, 43, 141 n. 52, 149, 170, 229
Gersonides 3, 281
get 78
glory, inner virtue as God's 127
God:
  Abraham's alacrity vs. Moses' reluctance regarding commandments of 67–9
  agenda of 8
  anthropomorphization of 71 n. 127
  Aristotelian view of as First Cause 32 n. 71, 324
  belief in 4, 6 n. 15, 46–9, 52, 54, 227–8, 233, 251, 299, 315
  centrality of 4, 293
  charity as dependence on 107–9, 119–21, 127, 142, 177, 303
  commandments between man and, see *mitsvot bein adam lamakom*
  contemplation of 28–30, 33, 36–8, 43, 65, 67, 123, 151, 171, 212–16, 303, 308, 316, 325, 330
  cosmos as proof of existence of 6, 22, 24, 27, 29–31, 36, 42 n. 4, 54, 140, 163, 166 n. 69, 167, 171, 204–5, 212, 270–1, 273–4, 276, 305, 310, 322–3, 325, 327–9, 336
  covenant with 42, 45–6, 50, 58–62, 67–8, 224, 314
  as creator of the world 32 n. 67, 32 n. 71, 42 n. 4, 63–7, 69–70, 123, 140, 160, 163–4, 206, 208, 254–6, 259, 280 n. 9, 298, 306–7, 317, 323
  in Decalogue 307 n. 6
  emanation as starting from 13, 187, 198, 219, 257, 260, 304, 324–5, 327–8, 336

equality as from 47, 64, 133–4, 137, 140, 142, 143 n. 60, 176–7, 226, 236, 249–50, 254–6, 259, 263, 265–6, 300–1, 303, 308–9
false worship of 31
as father of orphans 269–73, 276, 316–17
fear of 18–19, 20 n. 34, 25, 26 n. 51, 27–8, 56, 67, 98 n. 26, 135, 169, 171, 180, 190–1, 205, 214, 277, 294, 322, 331
First Cause as principle of existence 22–3, 27, 63
in *Guide* 6, 10 n. 30, 27, 34–5, 37, 55 n. 55, 66–7, 72, 121, 123–4, 126, 128, 180, 255, 258, 260, 271, 274, 279–80, 308
honour of 21 n. 39, 120–1, 128
imitating, see *imitatio Dei*
incorporeality of 23, 54, 72, 93 n. 11, 208, 211 n. 84, 264, 302, 307 n. 4, 324, 330
knowledge of 6, 10–12, 14–15, 16 n. 12, 20, 22 n. 41, 23–40, 44, 49, 52, 57, 60, 64, 66, 69–70, 72, 86, 99, 108, 120–8, 131, 139–42, 158, 163–4, 169, 171, 179, 181–2, 186–7, 198, 203, 205, 207–9, 211, 213–14, 216–17, 219, 224, 234, 237 n. 9, 248, 250, 256–9, 264, 271, 274–7, 279–80, 295–6, 298–300, 302, 304–6, 309–10, 312–17, 322, 324–5, 327–31, 336
knowledge of First Cause as commandment 23, 25, 27
lessening human desire 57, 315, 327–8
love of 10, 14, 16–22, 25–40, 44–5, 48, 53–7, 60–2, 66–72, 98 n. 26, 123, 131 n. 15, 158, 163–4, 169, 171, 180, 205, 209, 223–4, 272, 277, 281, 293–4, 302, 305, 310, 314, 318, 322, 325, 327, 329–31, 333, 335
loyalty to 55
Maimonidean view of as First Cause 324, 336–7
man created in the image of 2, 38, 142, 181, 295 n. 67, 300, 327
mercy as from 107, 119, 126, 185, 225, 240, 246–7, 249–50, 253–6, 258–9, 316
in messianic era 16, 37, 280, 283, 287, 288 n. 39, 290–3, 299–301, 305
middle/straight path as way of 53, 104, 119, 124, 131, 139, 142, 181, 243, 261, 308, 317–18
morality of humans as coming from 54, 56, 66–7, 72, 88–9, 97, 120–1, 126–8, 176, 181, 216, 243, 254, 260, 266, 285, 303–5, 314, 323, 327, 329, 333
name of, see name of God
negative attributes of 54
in parables 194, 220
peace between Israel and 81, 88–9
people 'joined' to besides Jews (*nilvim*) 46, 222, 224, 226–8, 233, 304
perfection of 26, 44, 47, 49–50, 63–5, 67–8, 70, 89, 124, 128, 163, 205, 213–14, 239, 255, 258, 262, 271, 279, 285, 304–5, 308–9
of philosophers distinguished from God of patriarchs 24, 27–8, 30, 32, 37–9, 68, 125 n. 60, 267–76
praise to 73, 204–5, 212–14
presence of, see *shekhinah*
punishment from 59–60, 146, 282 n. 19
and repentance 185, 208–12, 219, 314, 316
reverence for 88, 94, 105 n. 49, 169
as rock 31, 44, 47, 62–5, 67, 165, 275
as saviour 75
and self 204–5, 207–14, 216, 219, 304, 314–15
service of 18–19, 20 n. 34, 32, 33 n. 72, 36–7, 43, 49–50, 53–4, 56, 58, 60–2, 68, 95, 105 n. 49, 117, 119, 122, 139, 141 n. 52, 151, 155, 160, 162, 171, 180, 207 n. 74, 214, 216, 220, 231 n. 34, 234, 252, 290–2, 299, 307, 316, 331
as subject of *ma'aseh merkavah* 18 n. 20, 54, 95, 100, 102, 166 n. 69, 214, 270, 272, 310–11
Temple as house for 145, 160, 171, 176 n. 6, 191, 212, 223

God (cont.):
  Torah and commandments as from 26
    n. 51, 97–8, 100, 136–7, 154, 157,
    160–4, 166 n. 69, 167–9, 171, 197, 200
    n. 56, 202–4, 214, 215 n. 95, 216, 224,
    239, 252, 265, 274, 276, 285, 303, 305,
    307
  transcendence of 6, 271, 273, 275–6,
    305, 317
  turning away from 55 n. 54, 135, 146,
    169, 224, 282 n. 19, 284–5, 290, 307
  unity of 17, 22–3, 31–2, 40, 45–9, 52,
    54–5, 66, 70, 122, 124, 140, 158, 182,
    208, 213, 226, 251, 258, 263, 277, 299,
    315
  will of 30, 69, 153, 160, 215 n. 95,
    253–60, 303, 311
  wisdom of 25, 28, 29 n. 59, 33–5, 38, 66,
    69, 99, 123, 148–9, 160, 165, 169, 185,
    191, 205, 215 n. 95, 253–60, 265,
    310–12
  world to come as reward for serving
    18–19, 33 n. 72, 43, 49, 60, 95, 141
    n. 52, 171, 231 n. 34, 234, 299
Gog 80, 293
Golden Calf 307
Grace After Meals 79
Great Assembly 151, 215
Green, Kenneth Hart 25 n. 50, 167 n. 72
Guide of the Perplexed:
  Abraham in 52–3, 63–4, 66–7, 72
  allegory in 280 n. 11
  binding of Isaac in 53 n. 50
  circumcision in 43–50, 52–3, 57, 66–7,
    70, 72, 315
  classification of commandments in 111,
    114–15, 121, 123
  as coming full circle 279, 280 n. 12, 308
  considered a forgery 196 n. 47
  cosmos in 10 n. 30, 24, 167, 270–1, 273,
    322, 325 n. 20, 325 n. 22, 328, 334, 336
  equality in 129, 142 n. 59, 149, 249, 250
    nn. 48 & 49, 256, 261 n. 70
  eternity of the world in 42 n. 4, 206–7
  ethical stance of Maimonides in 109
    n. 12

Gentiles and the commandments in
    48–50, 147–50
  God as object of worship and imitation in
    6, 121, 123, 128, 255, 258, 260, 271,
    279, 308
  on graduation from obedience to
    discovery 302
  hierarchy of enlightenment in 197–8,
    330 n. 48
  idolatry in 64, 159, 237 n. 6
  intellect as bond between man and God
    180, 258
  intellect vs. matter 44 n. 14, 213
  Job's spiritual journey in 248
  Joseph ben Judah as addressee of 5
  knowledge of God in 34–5, 37, 66, 126,
    280
  knowledge of truth and good in 181
    n. 29, 182, 212
  laws in Decalogue 307 n. 6
  legalistic study of vs. science of law 295
    n. 62
  love of God in 27, 34–5, 37, 55 n. 55,
    66–7, 72
  Maimonides the Jew vs. philosopher in
    281, 298
  messiah in 16 n. 8, 66 n. 111, 86, 279
    n. 7, 280 n. 11, 284 n. 24, 289 n. 44,
    297–9, 301, 308 n. 11
  microcosm theory in 328, 334
  Mishneh torah as preface to 280
  morality in 15 n. 5, 66–7, 88 n. 26, 99
    n. 32, 111, 126, 160, 176 n. 6, 179,
    184 n. 2, 185 n. 5, 216 n. 98, 237 n. 6,
    245 n. 35
  Moses in 52–3, 63–4, 67, 72
  motto of 317
  names of God in 124, 126, 128, 274
  nation of Israel in 217
  nazir in 110, 114
  parables in 10 n. 30, 28 n. 57, 37, 67,
    100, 192 n. 36, 194, 196, 207, 214, 217,
    219–20, 230 n. 29
  poetry in 23 n. 42, 185 n. 5, 279 n. 7, 297,
    308 n. 11, 318
  purity in 144, 183 n. 1, 189–92, 214,
    218–19, 304, 330 n. 48

reasons for the commandments in 10
  n. 30, 98 n. 26, 98 nn. 28 & 29, 100–1,
  121, 123, 130, 150–3, 155, 159–62,
  164–5, 167, 170, 172, 179–80, 182,
  190–1, 196–7, 218–19, 251, 268,
  304, 306, 314–16, 331
repentance in 16, 219
restraint of desire in 45, 47–8, 56–7, 83
  n. 3, 90, 111, 315
rock defined in 63–4, 67
sacrifices in 150–2, 155, 156 n. 39,
  159–62, 164, 172, 182, 196–9, 214,
  218, 220, 289 n. 44, 306
science of the Torah in 2 n. 3, 10, 20
  n. 32, 54, 167, 218 n. 103
statutes in 150–3, 155, 159–60, 162, 172,
  219
time-bound commandments in 73
Torah's validity as dependent on Creation
  7 n. 17
universalism of 11, 48, 52, 91 n. 4, 148,
  150, 152, 197, 218, 308
water as metaphor for emanation in 187,
  211, 257, 324 n. 19
on welfare of body and soul in the Torah
  95, 113, 164, 179, 191, 314
as written after *Mishneh torah* 248 n. 42
guides to holiness, commandments as
  104–5

H

Habad Judaism 293 n. 58
Hacohen, Aviad 83 n. 4
hafla'ah, meaning of 113–16
ḥakham, *see* wisdom
ḥakhel 173
halakhah, *see* commandments
Halakhic Man 9 n. 23
Halbertal, Moshe 275
Halevi, Judah:
  on born Jews vs. converts 45 n. 19, 47,
    53, 241, 272–3, 300
  contrasted with Maimonides 102–4,
    158, 216–17, 319
  on elevation of prayer 99 n. 33
  on observance of the commandments
    102–4, 158, 216–17

parable of the physician's dispensary
  102
on religious pluralism 293 n. 57
on sacrifices 157–8
on Temple rituals 157–8, 217
Hallel 75
Haman 223 n. 5
Hanukah 73–81, 302
Har hamoriyah (Shatz) 181 n. 29
Haran 29, 36, 52, 306
Hartman, David 132 n. 19
Harvey, Warren (Zev) 231 n. 33, 297
ḥasidut:
  consideration as part of 119, 242, 244,
    258
  deliberate poverty as not synonymous
    with 106–7, 118–19, 125–6
  imitation of God as part of 46, 88, 119,
    227, 251, 253–5, 258, 266, 333
  immortality as reward for 2
  kindness as part of 255
  legalism balanced against 12
  Noahides as example of 58
  purity as part of 88, 92, 203
  separation as part of 88, 92, 203, 333
  Torah study as not synonymous with
    126–7
  treatment of slaves 13, 235, 238, 242–5,
    253, 258, 266
  and vows 118–20
  and wisdom 242–5, 253, 258, 266
  see also *ḥesed*
ḥayot 325, 337
Heidegger, Martin 28 n. 57, 300
Heller, Hayim 22–3 n. 41
heretics and heresy, *see epikoros* and
  epikoresut
Herford, Robert Travers 7
Herzl, Theodor 138 n. 41
Heschel, Abraham Joshua 289 n. 44
ḥesed (loving-kindness):
  Abraham as standing for 64, 66
  as beneficence 108, 255
  commandments as imbued with 269
  as dissolving social differences 255 n. 62
  as God's mode in creation 255

ḥesed (cont.):
  imitation of God's 36, 124, 126, 254, 260, 271, 279–80, 305, 308
  Jews as prone to 264
  succouring widows as 271 n. 23
  towards animals and the poor 250
  as will of God 258
  world standing upon 151, 162, 215–16
hierarchy:
  of books of *Mishneh torah* 13, 71, 167, 187, 198, 209, 213, 304, 329–31, 333–5
  of the commandments 263, 266, 304, 329–31, 333
  of cosmos 13, 71, 167, 187, 198, 209, 323–8, 330, 333–7
  in *Guide* 197–8, 330 n. 48
  of pagan gods vs. human worshippers 215 n. 95
  see also emanation
High Holidays 134
High Priest 75, 79, 143, 145, 161
holiness, *see* sanctification
Holy of Holies:
  Ark of the Covenant and Ten Commandments in 145
  laws of 143
  self-sanctification equal to 93 n. 13, 105, 109, 132, 138–9, 142–3, 279, 303, 308
  virtuous mind as 143, 214
  see also Temple, the
honour of God 21 n. 39, 120–1, 128
Horeb, Mount 42
ḥukim, *see* statutes
human beings and humanity:
  Adam as archetypal 206–7, 211
  as created in the image of God 2, 38, 142, 181, 295 n. 67, 300, 327
  distinction between Jews and the rest of 48, 50, 132, 134, 135 n. 31, 142 n. 59, 237 n. 6, 292–3
  freedom of, *see* freedom, human
  hierarchies of gods and 215 n. 95
  as intellectual beings 10, 12, 16 n. 11, 20, 22, 36–7, 67, 86, 102, 126–7, 149 n. 18, 153, 154 n. 32, 160, 167, 170, 172, 174, 179, 181–2, 184, 186–7, 192–5, 203–14,

217–19, 237 n. 6, 249, 260, 264, 271, 279, 281, 290, 295–7, 300, 302, 308, 314, 323, 327–30, 334
  in messianic era 2, 37, 198, 280 n. 11, 282 n. 19, 283, 284 n. 26, 286–7, 288 n. 39, 290, 292–3, 295–301, 305
  as microcosms 6, 163, 167, 197, 212, 308–10, 321–2, 327–9, 333–5
  nature of 186, 198, 295 n. 66, 300, 305
  not central in Maimonides' system 4, 249 n. 44, 327
  perfection of 3–6, 8, 16, 36, 38, 44–5, 47–8, 50, 63, 67, 72, 96, 98, 104–5, 118–19, 126–7, 163–4, 186, 195, 213–14, 215 n. 95, 255, 258, 266, 271, 279, 280 n. 11, 281, 283 n. 19, 295 nn. 66 & 67, 300–1, 308, 317, 319, 326, 328–9, 331
  pillars of 51, 54, 63, 67, 72, 166–7
  sanctification of all 93, 104–5, 129–43, 279, 303, 308
  sexual drive of 43–4, 47–8
  slavery vs. universal 235–66
  Torah as directed at all 3, 7, 9, 13, 22, 37–8, 47, 79–81, 89, 96, 99, 104–5, 129–43, 148, 153, 160, 163–4, 167, 172, 175–6, 178, 185–6, 193–5, 203–4, 208, 217, 220, 228–9, 232, 256, 263, 275, 280, 286, 299–300, 303–5, 308, 316, 319, 330
Hyamson, Moses 269 n. 14

I
Iamblichus 215 n. 95
Ibn Ezra, Abraham 136, 180, 223
Ibn Tibbon 215 n. 95, 257
idolatry:
  Abraham ridding the world of 31, 52, 54, 64, 68–9, 140, 226, 280 n. 9, 310
  breach of sabbath laws as equivalent to 314
  ceremonial commandments as counters to 170
  Christianity as a form of 3, 291 n. 48
  commandment to deny 14, 278
  destroying names of 77–8

eliminated in messianic era 284, 299
as error 169, 209
as ever-present threat 284
expunging for welfare of the soul 150
followed by repentance 82 n. 1, 210
Gentiles also avoiding 122, 148 n. 13, 237 n. 6
heathens as 79 n. 18, 237 n. 6, 251 n. 51
as immoral 177–8, 237 n. 6
as impure 184–5, 210
Israelites practising 224, 307
Maimonides reading works of 151 n. 25
not genuine 31 n. 64, 52, 125, 164
origin of 31, 125, 206, 209
sacrifices and 159
Torah as antidote to 284, 331
war against 64, 68, 299 n. 74, 310, 331
ikarei hadat 10 n. 30, 222, 227–33
 see also Thirteen Principles of Faith
image, *mikveh* as unifying 185–8
imitatio Dei:
 Abraham's discovery and teaching of 54, 253
 actualization of humanity as 4
 as commandment 15, 53, 56, 89, 118–19, 124, 126, 197, 238–40, 243, 245, 253–5, 258–9, 261–2, 266, 271, 305, 313, 316, 322
 creation as form of 254–5
 equality as form of 259, 266
 as goal 93, 303
 in *Guide* 6, 121, 123, 128, 255, 258, 260, 271, 279, 308
 holiness as form of 119, 265
 as imitation of God's ways in nature 63, 119, 254–6, 260, 263, 309, 313, 322
 as imitation of God's wisdom and his will 253–60
 justice as form of 67, 305
 kindness as form of 36, 271–2, 279–80, 305, 308
 knowledge of God preceding 214, 280, 305, 313, 327
 mercy as form of 13, 64, 79–80, 107, 119, 124, 126, 131, 185, 225, 236, 240–1, 246–50, 253–60, 262–4, 266, 304, 314, 316

mindset as form of 88–9, 119, 254, 255 n. 60, 258, 262–3, 292 n. 54, 313, 322
morality as form of 88–9, 93, 181, 243, 254, 258–9, 262, 266, 271 n. 22, 305, 327, 329 n. 47, 333
perfection as form of 50, 67, 89, 93, 214, 255, 258, 262, 266, 271, 279, 305, 308
righteousness as form of 36, 271, 279, 305, 308
self-governance as form of 254, 258–9, 328
as universal 259, 280
immersion, see *mikveh*
immortality:
 for all enlightened humans 2, 38, 139 n. 44, 149 n. 18, 151, 170, 182, 229, 234, 328
 for all pious Jews 2, 149 n. 18, 150, 170–2, 215
 as reward for performance of commandments 149 n. 18, 150–1, 170–2, 215
 see also world to come
inadvertence 145
inner virtue as God's glory 127
intellect and intellectual virtue:
 of Abraham 31 n. 65, 43, 52–3, 60, 64, 66, 68, 72, 178, 263
 agent, *see* agent intellect
 capacity of 153, 158, 160, 162, 165, 167, 323
 of the cosmos 204–7, 213–14, 218, 304, 323–9, 334, 336–7
 decline and extinction of 60, 143, 160, 169, 209, 237 n. 6
 equality of 47, 148, 149 n. 18, 229, 233, 237 n. 6, 249, 300, 305
 as honour of God 21 n. 39
 human 204–7, 209, 211, 213–14, 217–19, 237 n. 6, 249, 264, 281, 295 n. 66, 300, 305, 314, 323, 326 n. 28, 328, 334
 knowledge as within reach of any level of 95, 179
 knowledge gained by tradition vs. acquired 22 n. 41, 43, 181 n. 28, 232–3, 328

intellect and intellectual virtue (*cont.*):
  love of God as 22, 27, 60, 67–8, 329, 331
  matter as impediment to 44 n. 14, 203, 206–8
  in messianic era and world to come 77, 149 n. 18, 170, 172, 214, 229, 231 n. 34, 232, 279, 285, 295 n. 66, 296, 300–1, 305
  morality as prerequisite to 66, 89, 99 n. 32, 123–4, 126–8, 143, 170, 178–9, 183–220, 229, 258, 279, 298, 300–1, 319, 327
  of Moses 63–4, 68, 275
  opposition of matter and 44–6, 149 n. 18, 207, 210, 215 n. 95, 324, 327–8
  perfection of 3–4, 15, 21 n. 39, 28, 36–8, 44–5, 47–8, 53, 57, 60, 63, 72, 89, 92–3, 96, 99 n. 32, 165, 186, 205, 213–14, 229, 232, 258, 262, 271, 279, 281, 285, 286 n. 32, 286 n. 35, 295 n. 66, 300–1, 304–5, 308
  perversion of 121, 123–4, 126–8, 190, 329
  in Plotinus 210, 324, 328, 332
  purity of 183–220, 260, 304, 314, 330
  ritual as parable of 207, 214, 217–19
  separate 170, 187, 198, 211, 324–5, 336
  Torah as tool for improvement of 25, 66, 102, 148, 149 n. 18, 160, 161 n. 54, 162, 165, 167, 170–2, 180, 197–8, 203–4, 214, 219, 258, 260, 286 n. 32, 286 n. 35, 312, 319, 322, 330–3
  transcendent 6
  tripartite orientation of 208, 219, 259–60, 304, 313–16
  uncontrolled desire as impediment to 45, 47–9, 57, 210
  universal structure of 211
Isaac:
  binding of 52, 53 n. 50, 67 n. 114
  God of Aristotle vs. God of patriarchs 27, 272 n. 28
  as initiator of afternoon prayer 55
  learning and teaching the true path 32, 42, 54–5, 58 n. 71, 223
  name of God of 68, 125 n. 60
  obligations of descendants of 54, 230, 232–3
  observance of the commandments by 30 n. 61, 50, 224 n. 7
Isaiah 135, 279
ishim 203, 325–6, 334 n. 60, 336–7
  see also agent intellect
Ishmael, R. 50, 87
Islam:
  distinguished from Judaism 3, 292 n. 54
  emanation in 324
  and messianism 291, 299
  as a monotheistic religion 3
  morality vs. philosophy 28 n. 57, 300
  poverty as an ideal as controversial in 108
  proselytism in 3
  relationship between religion and philosophy in 11, 33
  slave ownership in 236, 238–9 n. 12
Israel, Land of:
  Abraham's descendants inheriting 61
  all Jews living in 189 n. 22
  convert's stake in 47
  impure food in 93 n. 10
  Israelites entering 164, 265, 287
  Levites not granted a share in 129, 131
  Maimonides' feeling towards 5
  in messianic era 282 n. 19, 283–4, 295
Israel, people of, *see* Jewish people

J

Jacob:
  God of Aristotle vs. God of patriarchs 27, 272 n. 28
  as initiator of evening prayer 55
  learning and teaching the true path 54–5, 58 n. 71, 131, 137, 223–4
  name of God of 68, 125 n. 60
  obligations of descendants of 54–5, 61, 137, 223–4, 230, 232–3
  observance of the commandments by 30 n. 61, 50, 224 n. 7
  prohibition originating with vs. commandment of Moses 58
Jastrow, Marcus 114 n. 28

Jerusalem:
  bringing sacrifices to 145, 287, 307
  in messianic era 282 n. 19, 287
  praying for peace of 5 n. 12, 218 n. 101
  Temple of 139, 145, 287, 307
Jesus 285 n. 29, 290
Jew, definition of 221–34
Jewish people 5, 7, 53, 94, 122, 127, 139 n. 44, 149–50, 157, 164, 176, 187 n. 22, 217, 228–33, 257–8, 272, 314, 333
Job:
  book of 84–5, 236, 245–8, 254
  identity of 247–8 nn. 41 & 42
  imitating God 236, 250
  spiritual journey of 248
Jobs, Steve 287 n. 36
Joseph ben Judah 5
Jospe, Raphael 293 n. 57
jubilee year 131 n. 15, 287
Judah the Prince, R. 7, 50, 248–50, 278, 306
judgements, *see* ordinances (*mishpatim*)

K
kabbalah 97 n. 24, 153, 289, 292 n. 54, 334 n. 59
Kafih, Joseph:
  on equality 222 n. 4, 241 n. 21, 242
  on God's creations 26 n. 51
  on morality 178 n. 14
  on Purim 77 n. 11
  on the sabbath 71 n. 126
  on world to come 149 n. 18
Kant, Immanuel 16, 104
karet 59–60
Karo, Joseph 83 n. 4, 95 n. 19
Kellner, Jolene S. 27
kiddush 76
Kimhi, David (Radak) 223
knowledge:
  acquisition of 22 n. 41, 29, 36, 69–70, 108, 121, 126, 128, 141, 166, 172, 205–9, 211, 214, 219, 250, 274, 327–8
  vs. belief 6 n. 15, 22 n. 41, 25
  of the cosmos 26 n. 52, 29, 36, 204–6, 218, 310, 325–30, 336–7

  of God 6, 10–12, 14–15, 16 n. 12, 20, 22 n. 41, 23–40, 44, 49, 52, 57, 60, 64, 66, 69–70, 72, 86, 99, 108, 120–8, 131, 139–42, 158, 163–4, 169, 171, 179, 181–2, 186–7, 198, 203, 205, 207–9, 211, 213–14, 216–17, 219, 224, 234, 237 n. 9, 248, 250, 256–9, 264, 271, 274–7, 279–80, 295–6, 298–300, 302, 304–6, 309–10, 312–17, 322, 324–5, 327–31, 336
  of good and evil 143 n. 60, 181 n. 29
  imitatio Dei as following 280
  immortality as dependent on 6, 149 n. 18, 186, 279, 286, 294 n. 60, 295, 298, 313
  as love 10, 14–39, 69–72, 208–9, 218, 280, 302, 325, 331
  matter as impediment to 205
  morality as following 66, 126, 128, 149 n. 18, 174, 178–9, 181–2, 214, 219, 296, 298 n. 73, 305, 310, 315, 317, 322, 327
  Moses' special 141, 166–8, 181 n. 29, 275
  parables as 100, 218
  perfection of the soul as 44–5, 63, 96, 186, 214, 279
  privation of 66 n. 111, 86, 94 n. 16, 95, 136, 153, 297–8, 325
  purity as following 185–7, 203, 207, 211, 214, 218–19, 304
  of scientific/philosophical truth 8, 12, 38, 123–4, 172, 197 n. 50, 210, 214, 218, 230 n. 29, 275, 303, 310–11, 313, 322
  as standing for Order *Tohorot* 185–6
  Torah as route to 9–10, 12, 14–15, 20, 25, 33, 37, 53, 66, 102–3, 140, 153, 155–6, 167, 210, 256, 310–11, 313, 315, 322, 329–31
  as universal 12, 20 n. 35, 30, 39, 168, 170, 182, 186–7, 210–11, 219, 234, 259, 263, 280, 291, 295 n. 67, 299, 301, 304, 311–12, 316, 319
kol ba'ei olam ('all who come into the world') 9, 129–40, 142
kosher laws 101, 146, 149, 173
Kraemer, Joel 23 n. 42
Kreisel, Howard 32 n. 71, 93 n. 11, 217 n. 99
Kuzari 45 n. 19, 241, 272, 293 n. 57

L

Lamm, Norman 29 n. 58, 232 n. 40
lamp, Hanukah vs. sabbath 73–6
law, *see* commandments
'Laws of Acquisition and Gifts' 235
'Laws of Agents and Partners' 235
'Laws of Blessings' 41
'Laws of Borrowing and Depositing' 267
'Laws of Circumcision':
   covenants of Abraham vs. Moses 41, 48–50, 51 n. 41, 53, 55, 57, 59–60, 62–3, 68, 70–2, 262
   on marital and universal peace 315
   on slavery 51 n. 41, 237 n. 6
   on universalism 55, 57
'Laws of Corpse Impurity' 183, 186 n. 8
'Laws of Creditor and Debtor' 241 n. 21, 267, 269
'Laws of Daily and Additional Offerings' 145
'Laws of the Day of Atonement' 145
'Laws of Diverse Kinds' 129
'Laws of Divorce' 82, 264
'Laws of Entrance into the Sanctuary' 145, 191
'Laws of *Eruvin*' 73
'Laws of Fasts' 73, 223, 225
'Laws of the Festal Offering' 108 n. 8, 173, 225
'Laws of First Fruits' 129
'Laws of Firstlings' 173
'Laws of Forbidden Foods' 90, 112, 114
'Laws of Forbidden Intercourse':
   on conversion 224 n. 7
   on equality 251 n. 51
   on levirate marriage 239 n. 16
   on restraint of desire 112, 114
   on slavery 237 n. 6, 251 n. 51
'Laws of the Foundations of the Torah':
   Adam as archetype in 206–7, 211
   on the cosmos 24, 211, 268 n. 6, 273, 310, 321, 322 n. 11, 327 n. 35, 332 n. 55, 336
   on the desecration of God's name 123, 125
   esotericism of 2 n. 3, 17, 18 n. 20, 20, 22 n. 41, 28, 95 n. 19, 208 n. 76
   eternal ideas of 82 n. 1
   on fear of God 22–8, 34, 67 n. 114, 169
   on the God of Aristotle 272, 309 n. 15
   on holiness 92 n. 9, 121–3
   humans as microcosms implied in 328 n. 44
   on the ideal person 244 n. 33
   on idolatry 237 n. 6, 278
   on imitation of God 181
   on knowledge of God 22–8, 34, 123, 169, 181, 208–9, 277, 280, 302, 310, 314, 324, 327 n. 35
   on love of God 10 n. 30, 17, 19 n. 24, 20–8, 29 n. 58, 30, 34, 38, 67 n. 114, 123, 169, 209, 277, 280, 302, 324, 327 n. 35, 333
   on morality 237 n. 6
   on prayer 17 n. 14
   on prophecy of Moses 52 n. 45
   on the sanctification of God's name 121–3, 125, 208, 241, 333
   as template for first ten books of the *Mishneh torah* 121, 128, 208, 260, 332
   on ten orders of angels 187, 321, 325 n. 22, 327 n. 35, 336
   on unity of God 213, 277, 324
   universal structure of intellect in 211
   on validity of the Torah 7
'Laws of Fringes' 41
'Laws of Gifts to the Poor':
   on charity 176, 225, 226 n. 12, 250 n. 46
   on equality 251 n. 51
   on proselytes 223
'Laws of Heave Offerings' 129, 189 n. 22
'Laws of Hiring' 267
'Laws of Idolatry':
   on covenants of Abraham vs. Moses and circumcision 52–4, 60–1, 63–4, 71, 140, 306, 309
   on the God of Aristotle 32 n. 71
   on love of God 25, 30
   on origin of idolatry 206, 208–9
   on proselytes 223, 226–7
   universal structure of intellect reflected by 211

'Laws of Immersion Pools':
  deliberate placement of 202, 219
  intellectual and moral purity in 184–6, 191–3, 210, 219
  objective and subjective in 88 n. 27
'Laws of Impurity of Foodstuffs' 88, 188, 189 nn. 22 & 23, 190, 203
'Laws of Impurity of Leprosy' 183–4
'Laws of Inheritance' 267, 271, 273
'Laws of Kings and their Wars':
  equality in 13 n. 38, 33 n. 72, 140 n. 48, 141, 149 n. 18, 170, 250 n. 50
  messianic universalism in 277, 278 n. 3, 281, 286–97
  on messianism 80, 189 n. 22, 198
  on origin of commandments 58 n. 71, 137
  on praying for Jerusalem 5 n. 12
'Laws of Leavened and Unleavened Bread' 73
'Laws of Levirate Marriage' 82, 264
'Laws of Lulav' 73
'Laws of Marriage' 82, 84, 264
'Laws of Megillah and Hanukah' 73, 77, 79
'Laws of Monetary Damage' 221
'Laws of Moral Qualities':
  on Abraham's ethics 54, 177–8, 252, 261, 266
  on bad dispositions 184 n. 2, 193, 268
  connection between *Book of Offerings* and 208, 211
  on deliberate poverty 116–18, 121, 125, 128
  on diet 110
  on equality 245, 266
  humans as microcosms reflected in 328 n. 44
  on imitation of God 15, 56, 124, 181, 238, 247 n. 39, 253, 255 n. 60, 258–9, 262, 266, 271 n. 24, 316, 322
  on knowledge of God 120–1
  on the middle path 53, 109, 119, 124–5, 175, 208, 243–4, 253
  on the self 314–15
'Laws of Mourning' 277, 280
'Laws of Murder and the Preservation of Life' 221, 237 n. 6

'Laws of Naziriteship' 106, 110, 116–17
'Laws of Neighbours' 235
'Laws of Oaths' 106, 111, 115, 121, 123
'Laws of Offerings for Transgressions Committed through Error' 173, 202 n. 58
'Laws of Offerings Rendered Unfit' 145
'Laws of Other Fathers of Impurity' 184
'Laws of the Passover Offering' 173
'Laws of Pleading' 267
'Laws of Prayer and the Priestly Blessing' 17 n. 14, 40, 55
'Laws of the Ram's Horn' 73
'Laws of the Rebellious Elders' 277
'Laws of the Recitation of the Shema' 17, 40, 54, 213
'Laws of the Red Heifer' 183
'Laws of Repentance':
  on atonement without repentance 195 n. 44
  commandments as instruments implied in 102 n. 41
  on equality 135
  on free will 44 n. 15, 131 n. 12, 139, 142 n. 60
  knowledge as love in *Book of Knowledge* 15–21, 25, 26 n. 52, 27, 36–8, 280, 302, 316
  on love of God 17–21, 25, 26 n. 52, 27, 36–8, 55–6
  on prayer 17 n. 14
  on prophecy of Moses 52 n. 45
  on repentance as permanent state of mind 208–9
  on theme of restoration and return 26 n. 52, 209, 315
  on ulterior motives 118 n. 39, 134
  universal structure of intellect 211
  on world to come 15–16, 228, 285, 294 n. 60, 295
'Laws of Repose on a Festival' 73, 223–4
'Laws of Repose on the Tenth of Tishrei' 73
'Laws of Ritual Impurity of Foods' 92
'Laws of Robbery and Lost Property' 221
'Laws of the Sabbath' 71, 73, 77 n. 14, 237 n. 6

'Laws of the Sabbatical Year and the Jubilee'
  8, 131–43, 303
'Laws of Sacrificial Procedures' 106, 111,
  145
'Laws of Sales' 235
'Laws of the Sanctification of the New
  Moon' 73, 322 n. 2
'Laws of the Sanhedrin' 137, 277
'Laws of the Second Tithe and the Fourth
  Year's Fruit' 129
'Laws of Shekel Dues' 73
'Laws of Slaughtering' 90, 94, 168
'Laws of Slaves':
  adaptation of rabbinic anecdotes in
    245–50
  din and lifnim mishurat hadin in 240–6,
    249, 252–5, 258, 262–3, 266
  doctrine of accommodation in 262–4,
    266
  on equality 226 n. 15, 240, 242–3, 246,
    249, 255 n. 60, 258, 266
  imitatio Dei in 239–40, 243, 258, 261–2,
    266
  slavery vs. universal humanity in 235–7,
    240, 242–4, 246, 249, 255 n. 60, 258,
    261–4, 266
'Laws of Substituted Offerings' 88–9 n. 27,
  173–5, 178–9, 181, 202
'Laws of Sukkah' 73
'Laws of Tefillin, Mezuzah, and Torah
  Scroll' 41, 136
'Laws of the Temple' 144, 190, 207 n. 73,
  239 n. 14
'Laws of Temple Utensils and Servers' 145
'Laws of Testimony' 277
'Laws of Theft' 221
'Laws of Things Forbidden for the Altar'
  145, 176 n. 6
'Laws of Those Who Render Couch and
  Seat Impure' 184
'Laws of Those Whose Atonement Is Not
  Complete' 173
'Laws of Tithes' 129
'Laws of Torah Study' 15, 126, 200 n. 56,
  208–11, 314

'Laws of Trespass':
  on commandments as instruments 102
    n. 41
  divinity of the commandments in
    145–6, 150, 154 n. 32, 156–61, 168–9,
    171
  objective and subjective in 88 n. 27
  position of different from in Mishnah
    202
  on statutes 146, 150, 154 n. 32, 156–61,
    168–9, 171, 174–5, 215–16, 303, 312
'Laws of Utensils' 184
'Laws of Valuation and Consecration':
  on deliberate poverty 112, 121, 125–7,
    240 n. 20
  social responsibility and sanctifying
    God's name in 106, 109, 111–12,
    120–1, 125–7
'Laws of the Virgin Maiden' 82
'Laws of Vows' 106, 110, 116–18, 120 n. 46
'Laws of the Wayward Wife' 82–4, 303, 314
'Laws of Wounding and Damaging' 221,
  246
Leibowitz, Yeshayahu 300
leprosy 150 n. 20, 184
'Letter to Obadiah the Proselyte' 46, 251
Levi 223
Levites:
  agricultural restrictions of 129, 131–2
  circumcision always performed by 69
  as head of Jacob's children 224
  in messianic era 294
  as model for seekers of God 109
  Moses as one of 68
  obligations towards 173
  as set apart for service of God 131–2, 145,
    318 n. 28
  songs of 214
Lewis, Bernard 236, 239 n. 12
life after death, see immortality; world to
  come
lifnim mishurat hadin 240–2
love:
  covenant of law vs. covenant of 54,
    58–62, 67, 69–70, 72, 262, 264, 302
  diminution of 57

of God 10, 14, 16–22, 25–40, 44–5, 48, 53–7, 60–2, 66–72, 98 n. 26, 123, 131 n. 15, 158, 163–4, 169, 171, 180, 205, 209, 223–4, 272, 277, 281, 293–4, 302, 305, 310, 314, 318, 322, 325, 327, 329–31, 333, 335
  induced by contemplation of the cosmos 26 n. 52, 29, 36, 205–6, 310, 327–9, 335
  of Israel 61 n. 80
  of Jerusalem 5 n. 12, 218 n. 101
  knowledge as 10, 14–39, 69–72, 208–9, 218, 280, 302, 325, 331
  of the messiah 285
  of moral and intellectual virtue 179 n. 19
  as motive force of the cosmos 204, 218, 324–5, 327
  of other people 15, 85, 231
  performing commandments out of 16, 18–20, 54, 62, 149 n. 18, 150, 331
  Song of Songs as about 19, 281
  tempered by fear 67, 205, 217–18
  as universal 21, 39, 262
loving-kindness, *see ḥesed*
Lubavitcher Rebbe (R. Menachem Mendel Schneersohn) 8, 278 n. 3, 293 n. 58
lulav 100

M

ma'aseh bereshit and *ma'aseh merkavah*:
  Abraham's knowledge of 309–11
  importance of studying 22 n. 41, 28, 124, 157, 206 n. 67, 210, 214, 310–11
  Maimonides' inclusion of in his works 6, 10, 17, 18 n. 20, 22 n. 41, 28 n. 57, 95, 98 n. 28, 99, 127, 187, 199, 204, 207, 209, 218, 230 n. 29, 309, 323, 332
  as physics and metaphysics 1, 2 n. 3, 17, 22 n. 41, 100, 272, 275. 298
  prophecy as elevated insight into 166, 168
  relationship between God and the universe 270–2, 275
  restrictions on teaching 17 n. 20
  Torah as universal discipline of 1, 6, 18 n. 20, 95, 100, 166 n. 69, 167, 182, 197, 208, 210, 218, 298, 302, 310–11, 332
  see also esotericism
Magog 80, 293
Makbili, Yohai 88, 295 n. 65, 295 n. 67
Malachi:
  book of 80–1, 293–4
  messianism according to 80–1, 285, 293–4
  prophecy of 80–1, 285, 293–4
Marah 307
marital peace 74, 76–89, 291, 299, 301, 303, 305, 314–15, 317 n. 28, 319
Mattathias son of Johanan 79
matter:
  four elements of, *see* elements of matter, four
  as impediment to knowledge 205
  opposition of intellect and 44–6, 149 n. 18, 207, 210, 215 n. 95, 324, 327–8
  in Plotinus 324, 328, 332
Megillah (book of Esther) 75–6, 77 n. 11
Meir, R. 87
Mendelssohn, Moses 132 n. 19
mercy:
  as common trait of Abraham's children 177, 225, 236, 242, 251–3, 256, 259, 264–5
  as imitation of God 13, 64, 79–80, 107, 119, 124, 126, 131, 185, 225, 236, 240–1, 246–50, 253–60, 262–4, 266, 304, 314, 316
  as indivisible 258–9
  as middle path 244
  poor people not shown special 107, 126, 240 n. 20
  of Raban Gamliel 249–50
  of Rabbi Yohanan 246
  showing towards slaves 13, 235–6, 238, 240–7, 250, 253–5, 262–4, 266, 304
messiah and messianism:
  abolition of part of the Torah in the days of 76, 289
  anticipation of forbidden 296
  as assisting attainment of world to come 16, 279, 284, 286, 289

messiah and messianism (*cont.*):
　belief in 285, 287
　as climax of *Mishneh torah* 7, 15–16, 143, 278, 281–6, 301, 305, 328
　as close to God's goal of Abrahamic faith 280, 301, 305, 308, 310
　in *Commentary on the Mishnah* 281–6
　denial of as apostasy 198, 287
　in *Guide* 16 n. 8, 66 n. 111, 86, 279 n. 7, 280 n. 11, 284 n. 24, 289 n. 44, 297–9, 301, 308 n. 11
　holiness as accessible to all 143
　human nature as unchanged in the days of 198, 283, 286, 288–91, 293, 301
　Jewish destiny culminating in 6, 37, 66 n. 111, 260–2, 266, 279, 284, 294 n. 60, 299, 301, 313
　keeping commandments in the days of 2, 147, 186, 284, 286
　knowledge of God in the days of 86, 186, 279, 298–9, 328, 331
　logic of 298–301
　as a means to a universal end 279, 282–3, 298–301
　naturalism of Maimonides' messianism 284, 287–8, 293
　peace in the days of 77, 79–81, 86, 186, 282–3, 291, 293, 296, 298–9, 301, 305
　as perfection 16, 186, 266, 280 n. 11, 295 n. 66, 300–1, 316, 331
　as a process 189 n. 22, 278 n. 5, 279, 281–3, 286–7, 291–2, 301
　prophecy of Moses as greater than 52 n. 45
　rebuilding the Temple in days of 143, 159, 183, 188, 189 n. 22, 286–7, 289, 332
　re-establishment of sabbatical and jubilee years in the days of 130, 131 n. 15, 287
　restorative rather than utopian 283, 287
　roles of Christianity and Islam in 291
　separate from resurrection 289
　social regeneration and 316–17
　universalism of 2, 6, 77, 80, 147, 186, 233, 276–301, 305, 308 n. 10

meta-halakhah vs. halakhah 8–10
metaphors:
　circumcision of the heart 252
　of foundations of the Torah 332 n. 55
　referring to world to come 291
　rock as origin of everything 63
　shofar as alarm 192–3
　water as emanation 187–8, 211
　water as knowledge/intellect 185–7, 192–3, 210, 214, 219, 296 n. 69, 304, 330 n. 48
metaphysics, see *ma'aseh bereshit* and *ma'aseh merkavah*
Methuselah 31
mezuzah 21, 41
microcosm:
　human beings as 6, 163, 167, 197, 212, 308–10, 321–2, 328–9, 333–5
　and macrocosm as a relational correspondence 333–5
　Mishneh torah as 6, 10, 13, 71, 187, 321–5
　Temple rites as 217 n. 99
middle path:
　circumcision as means of maintaining 43–5
　commandments' purpose as 66 n. 110, 94, 102, 104, 120, 175, 180, 193, 318 n. 28
　deliberate poverty as not 109, 125, 128
　examples of in *Mishneh torah*'s book endings 317–18
　going to extreme in order to regain 119, 175
　holiness as 119
　imitating God via 53, 119, 124–5, 243, 258, 261, 292 n. 54, 318
　for marital and universal peace 83, 87, 89 n. 27
　morality as 44–5, 66 n. 110, 125, 128, 174–6, 178, 180–2, 193, 219, 243, 258, 265, 304, 315
　in oaths and vows 116–21
　as outcome of self-understanding 208
　of the pious person 244
　restraint of appetites as 128
　sacrifices as 120
　of the wise person 244

Midrash vs. Maimonides regarding
  definition of a *ḥok* 152–7
mikveh:
  contrast with shofar 192–3
  as conversion rite 184, 224 n. 7, 237 n. 6
  laws of 184, 186, 188 n. 16, 189 n. 27
  for men 184
  as metaphor for intellect 185–8, 192–4,
    210, 214, 219, 260, 304, 330 n. 48
  as purification 89 n. 27, 184–6, 189,
    192, 213, 219, 330 n. 48
  as statute 89 n. 27, 184, 188–9, 193–4,
    213–14, 219, 330 n. 48
  as unifying image in *Mishneh torah*
    185–8
  see also purity and purification; water
Mishnah:
  arrangement of Maimonides' writings
    as different from 82, 110–11, 199,
    201–2
  as model for *Mishneh torah* 7–8, 278,
    306
  tractate *Avot* as judgement on 7, 278
Mishneh torah:
  arrangement differs from that of the
    Mishnah 82, 110–11, 199, 201–2
  commandments as instruments in
    90–105, 303
  correspondence to ten intellects (angels)
    325
  definition of a Jew in 221–34, 304
  divinity of the commandments 144–72,
    303–4
  endings of books of 1, 4–8, 11–12, 144,
    193–7, 202–4, 207, 214–15, 217,
    219–20, 259, 302–6, 308–9, 311–20,
    333
  equality in 13 n. 38, 33 n. 72, 38, 47, 64,
    129–43, 170, 176, 226 n. 15, 235–66,
    303–4
  first specifically Jewish commandment
    in 333
  Genesis 21: 33 as motto of 32 n. 67,
    64–5, 267, 276, 280 n. 9, 306, 317
  God of Aristotle and God of Abraham in
    267–76, 305

vs. *Guide* regarding Gentiles and
    commandments 147–50
  vs. *Guide* regarding sacrifices 150–2,
    197–9
  hierarchy of books of 13, 71, 167, 187,
    198, 209, 213, 304, 329–31, 333–5
  Maimonides' systemization of halakhah
    in 311
  messianic era in 7, 15–16, 143, 278,
    281–6, 301, 305, 328
  messianic universalism of 277–301, 305
  microcosmic structure of, *see* microcosm
  Mishnah as model for 7–8, 278, 306
  philosophical basis of 5–7
  place of final two chapters in 277–81
  sanctification of God's name in 106–28,
    303
  title of as term designating book of
    Deuteronomy 9 n. 26
  universalism of 1, 3–13, 21, 42, 48, 53, 72,
    91 n. 4, 127, 150, 152, 158, 172, 176, 181,
    186, 188, 218–19, 237–8, 242, 256,
    266, 276, 295 n. 67, 301–2, 305–6,
    308–9, 311–12, 318–19
  see also individual book titles
Mishneh torah, endings of books:
  argumentation in 312–13
  biblical citations in 311–12
  commandments lacking in 1, 6–10,
    306, 333
  as a genre 311–20
  messages of 302–6
  middle path, examples of in 317–18
  parable, creation of from book endings
    and contexts of *Temple Service*,
    Offerings, and *Purity* 144, 194–7, 207,
    214–15, 217, 219–20
  style and expression of 318–20
  see also ending of book as bridge to
    following book
mishpatim, *see* ordinances
mitsvot bein adam lamakom:
  in *Book of the Commandments* 115
  first ten *Mishneh torah* books as dealing
    with 130, 167, 185, 187 n. 12, 219, 221,
    264, 269 n. 15, 317, 321, 329, 332

mitsvot bein adam lamakom (cont.):
  significance of as moral correctives 168–70, 175, 186–7, 213, 219, 260, 305, 317, 319
  violations of considered intrinsically bad 101 n. 39
mitsvot bein adam leḥavero:
  corresponding to the four elements 321
  damage to property or people 260, 269
  God in 260, 319
  last four *Mishneh torah* books dealing with 130, 167 n. 70, 185, 187 n. 12, 221, 234, 260–1, 264, 267, 317, 321, 330
  treatment of slaves 264
Moab 42, 287 n. 39
Mohammed 290
Montag, Avram 280
moon, the:
  angel governing 321, 326
  Aristotle on existence beneath 164, 166, 323
  emanation of 325–6, 337
  Maimonides on existence beneath 321, 331
  New Moon 40
morality:
  of circumcision 43, 45, 47–9, 52–3, 57, 62, 66, 72, 302
  as coming from love 67, 322
  of the commandments 8–9, 38, 43, 47–8, 66, 72, 88 n. 26, 89, 96–7, 99, 102, 105, 121, 126–8, 148, 149 n. 18, 160, 170, 173–82, 185 n. 5, 190, 193, 203–4, 208, 211, 216, 219, 229, 233, 243, 253–4, 256, 258–60, 263, 265–6, 268, 285, 286 n. 32, 300, 304–5, 310, 312–14, 319, 322, 329 n. 47, 332–3
  connection between intellectual clarity and 4, 8, 15, 28 n. 57, 38, 53, 57, 62, 66, 72, 93, 99 n. 32, 105, 124, 126–8, 143, 148, 149 n. 18, 170, 178–9, 181, 187, 190, 203, 208, 210, 214, 219, 229, 237 n. 6, 258, 260, 262–3, 271 n. 22, 279, 283, 285, 286 n. 32, 296, 298, 300–1, 304, 310, 312, 317, 319, 322, 327, 331–3
  in the covenant between God and Abraham 46, 52–4, 60, 62, 66–7, 69, 71–2, 178, 256, 263, 265–6, 302, 308–10, 312
  decline of 60, 128, 179, 185 n. 5, 190, 237 n. 6
  de'ot as qualities of 15 n. 5, 88–9, 96–9, 107, 128, 148, 162, 170, 174, 176–81, 184 n. 2, 193, 203–4, 210–11, 214, 216, 243, 245, 258–60, 262, 265–6, 268, 303, 314–15, 317, 319, 322, 327, 329 n. 47, 333
  distinguished from asceticism 107, 111–13, 115–18, 120–1, 123, 125–6, 128, 303, 315, 327
  of Gentiles 28 n. 57, 38, 233, 237 n. 6, 300, 304
  and health 15, 48, 124, 303
  as holy 88, 93, 143, 182, 303, 333
  as *imitatio Dei* 88–9, 93, 181, 243, 254, 258–9, 262, 266, 271 n. 22, 305, 327, 329 n. 47, 333
  Jewish 177, 229, 266, 333
  Maimonides' vision of in the commandments 1, 3–4, 15, 56, 79 n. 19, 89, 93 n. 11, 105, 107, 109 n. 12, 118, 121, 127–8, 143, 149 n. 18, 170, 182, 195, 233, 237 n. 6, 263, 265–6, 268, 285, 304, 329 n. 47
  of the middle path 44–5, 66 n. 110, 125, 128, 174–6, 178, 180, 193, 219, 243, 258, 265, 304, 315
  Mishneh torah book endings as expressions of 1, 7–9, 268, 278, 306, 312, 314–15, 317
  as peace 84 n. 7, 85, 88–9, 179 n. 19, 216 n. 98, 298, 303, 314
  as perfection 4, 8, 15, 28 n. 57, 38, 43–5, 48, 53, 57, 62, 72, 89, 93, 98–9, 105, 128, 162, 216, 229, 233, 253, 262, 271 n. 22, 279, 285, 286 n. 32, 300, 304–5, 332
  as purity 88–9, 183–220
  of slavery 85, 254, 259, 262, 266
  of statutes and ordinances 148, 157, 160, 182, 253
  subjective 260

of Temple rituals 143, 176 n. 6, 181, 192, 195, 211
as truth 97, 178–80, 182, 187, 263, 296, 310
as universal 3–4, 9, 12, 47, 89, 143, 148, 176–8, 182, 237 n. 6, 256, 266, 286 n. 32, 304, 312
of the universe 203, 254, 322–3, 329
world as standing on 162, 216
world to come as reward for 57, 143, 180, 279, 283
see also perfection
Moriah, Mount 145
Mosaic model:
Abrahamic model as taking precedence over 263, 302
circumcision as a commandment of 61, 69, 72, 262, 302
commandments in 306, 308, 319
covenant of 49, 69, 72, 262
as institutionalizing Abrahamic teaching 53–4, 69, 72
in the messianic world 305
Mishneh torah as expressive of 308–9, 311, 319
Shema as vessel for love in 54
tension between Abrahamic model and 262, 305–6
universalism of 51–3, 58, 61, 70
Moses:
and circumcision 40–72
as messenger of God 135, 141, 166 n. 69, 180, 257 n. 65, 272, 274–5
in messianic era 301
as model of Maimonides 306–11
observance of commandments as beginning with 30 n. 61, 103
pairing with Abraham in Maimonides' works 40–72, 306–11
as pillar of the world 51–62
as prophet 7, 52 n. 45, 166, 168, 224, 257, 274, 285–6
reluctance of regarding God's commandments 67–9
special knowledge of 141, 166–8, 181 n. 29, 275

as teacher 42, 58, 61, 137, 141, 287, 332 n. 55
Torah as law of 14, 19, 30 n. 61, 49, 52–5, 58–64, 66–7, 69–70, 72, 87, 96, 137, 166, 253, 257, 266, 272, 283 n. 19, 294 n. 60, 302, 305–6, 308–9
wanting a religion of reason 300, 305
motto, Genesis 21:33 as Maimonides' and the *Mishneh torah*'s 32 n. 67, 64–5, 267, 276, 280 n. 9, 306, 317
mysticism 49, 97, 100–2, 162

N
Nahmanides:
'The Gate of Reward' 284 n. 26
on magic 189 n. 26
on sacrifices 157, 159, 307 n. 8
on standards of behaviour 241 n. 21
on world to come 284 n. 26, 289
name of God:
essence vs. actions as reflected in 65, 272–5
Maimonides' definition of 123–7, 273–4
sanctification of 120–5, 127, 241, 303, 333
and the *sotah* 74, 76–8, 315
unity of 227
nature:
commandments as not beyond 102, 164–6, 169, 181 n. 29, 216, 310, 313, 322, 329
as conducive to love 10, 26 n. 52, 37–8, 67, 70, 123, 158, 169, 310, 322
as contingent 164 n. 61, 320
God as separate from 260, 310
and God as the only two realities 158
imitating God's actions in 119, 254–6, 260, 263, 304, 309, 313, 322
messianic process as part of 282 n. 17, 283, 291
miracles as interruptions of 75 n. 7, 283
as model for perfection 2, 44–7, 53, 62–5, 67, 70, 96, 165, 167 n. 70, 304, 309, 329, 331
study of as leading to love of God 29 n. 58, 160, 310
sublunary vs. celestial 166, 167 n. 70, 249 n. 44, 331, 335

nature (*cont.*):
  Torah as reflection of 7, 10 n. 30, 63, 67, 70, 96, 165, 181 n. 29, 254, 309, 329 n. 46
  as unchanging 164 n. 61, 212, 304, 309
  understanding 2, 10–11, 26 n. 52, 37–8, 53, 63, 70–1, 119, 123–4, 158, 163–6, 169, 181 n. 29, 206, 212, 216, 260, 304, 309–10, 322
  as universal 7, 166, 169, 304, 320
Nazirites 82, 93 n. 10, 106, 110, 114–19
Neoplatonism:
  emanation and return in 13, 62, 187, 198, 209, 215 n. 95, 257, 324–5, 328, 332, 334 n. 59
  God of Aristotle in 27
  incorporation of into *Mishneh torah* 321
  nature in 166, 212
  purification in 210, 212, 214, 296 n. 69, 314, 328, 332
  sacrifices and worship in 215 n. 95
  sefirot as deriving from 334 n. 59
  structure of thought in 204
nilvim 131 n. 15, 222–7
  not converts 226–7, 230, 233, 304
  as Gentiles 226–7, 304
  as people 'joined' to God besides Jews 46, 222, 224, 226–8, 233, 304
  see also God: people 'joined' to
Noah:
  as originator of Noahide commandments 58, 137, 148 n. 13
  recognition of God by 31, 50 n. 35, 296 n. 68
Noahides:
  commandments of 43, 58, 137, 141, 147, 148 n. 13, 170, 237 n. 6, 292 n. 52
  recognition of God by 33 n. 72, 140, 141 n. 52, 237 n. 6, 292 n. 52
non-Jews, *see* Gentiles

O

oaths as sanctification of God's name 115, 121, 125
  see also vows
Obadiah the Proselyte 46, 226, 251

ofanim 325, 337
offerings, *see* sacrifices
olam, meaning of 64–6
olam haba, *see* world to come
olam hazeh ('this world'):
  achievement of intellectual perfection in 232
  benefits of statutes vs. ordinances in 146, 151, 162 n. 55, 170
  commandments as instruments in 97–8, 102
  as existing parallel in time to *olam haba* 284 n. 26
  God's care of people in 132, 139, 142, 257
  material blessings in 257
  messianism from point of view of 284, 286, 288–9, 296
  Torah as only in 284 n. 26
Oral Torah 9–10, 76, 289, 311–12
ordinances (*mishpatim*):
  definition of 146 n. 9, 147, 152–4
  as eternal 288, 307 n. 7
  as expression of God 50–1, 160, 236, 253, 256, 265
  learning and teaching 131, 137, 265
  for Noahides 137
  as not parables 100
  Torah's urging of observance of 56, 146–7
  as understandable 100, 146–8, 152–4, 157
  as universal 148
  world to come as reward for 147, 149, 151, 169–70, 180, 318 n. 28
orphans, God as father of 269–73, 276, 316–17
Orthodox Judaism 282 n. 17

P

paganism:
  hierarchies of gods and humans in 215 n. 95
  in messianic era 299–300
  purity in 189, 195

Index of Subjects

statutes in 146, 149–51, 153, 155–6, 160, 168, 215 n. 95, 307 n. 8

parable:
- in Proverbs 214
- commandments as 12, 102, 144, 194–7, 200, 214–15, 217–20
- creation of from book endings and contexts of *Temple Service*, *Offerings*, and *Purity* 144, 194–7, 207, 214–15, 217, 219–20
- God in 194, 220
- Judah Halevi's of the physician's dispensary 102
- of the palace 10 n. 30, 28 n. 57, 37, 230 n. 29
- purity as 144, 194, 214–15, 220
- of the scapegoat 192 n. 36, 194–6, 207, 217, 219
- silver and gold layers of wisdom in 11–12, 67, 100, 194–5, 197, 207, 214–15, 217–20
- vs. symbol 195 n. 44, 214
- Temple and sacrifices as 144, 194, 196–7, 200, 214–15, 217–20

pardes 1, 18 n. 20, 95, 208 n. 76, 302

particularism:
- of *Mishneh torah*'s content in relation to universalism 6, 42, 48, 53, 72, 91 n. 4, 158, 176, 186, 237–8, 242, 256, 276
- perceptions of Maimonides as exponent of 132 n. 19, 292
- vs. universal values 12–13, 53, 58, 91 n. 4, 126, 149, 170, 233, 237–8, 241–2, 251, 253, 256, 259, 262, 266, 276, 304, 320, 328, 333

Passover:
- counting for seven weeks after 145
- divine judgement on 133
- funerals and fasting forbidden on 224
- prohibition of leaven on as statute 307 n. 7
- prohibition of leaven on as time-bound commandment 110
- sacrifice before 173

patriarchs' observance of the commandments 30 n. 61, 50, 224 n. 7

patterns in Maimonides' books, *see* tripartite orientation of the intellect

peace:
- knowledge as 86, 186, 282, 298–9, 301, 319
- marital 74, 76–9, 81–9, 303, 314–15
- messianic era as time of 77, 79–81, 86, 186, 282–3, 291, 293, 296, 298–9, 301, 305
- morality as 84 n. 7, 85, 88–9, 179 n. 19, 216 n. 98, 298, 303, 314
- offerings 201, 225
- righteousness as 225, 270–1
- sabbath lamp as priority for 74, 76–7
- to those who love Jerusalem 5 n. 12, 218 n. 101
- as universal 74, 76–89, 291, 299, 301, 303, 305, 314, 317 n. 28, 319
- world as standing on 216 n. 98

Pentecost, *see* Shavuot

Perek ḥelek:
- on the messiah 278 n. 3, 282, 284, 293 n. 58, 294 n. 60
- on opposition of intellect and matter and world to come 149 n. 18
- on proposed book explaining *midrash* 248 n. 42
- on statutes (*ḥukim*) 3 n. 4

perfection:
- circumcision as 41, 43–5, 47–50, 53, 62, 66–7, 72
- commandments as 2, 8, 37–8, 43, 45, 47–50, 52 n. 45, 62–3, 67, 72, 89, 96, 98, 104 n. 46, 105, 137, 162–5, 167 n. 70, 186, 216, 229, 233, 239, 253, 264, 285, 286 n. 32, 286 n. 35, 300, 304–5, 309, 319, 329, 332–3
- cosmos as 6, 24, 50–1, 163, 205, 213, 317, 326, 328–9
- covenant and 49–50, 62–9
- as essential for entrance into world to come 38, 57, 143, 180, 229, 232, 279, 282–3 n. 19, 285, 286 n. 35
- as form of *imitatio Dei* 50, 67, 89, 93, 214, 255, 258, 262, 266, 271, 279, 305, 308

perfection (*cont.*):
  of God 26, 44, 47, 49–50, 63–5, 67–8, 70, 89, 124, 128, 163, 205, 213–14, 239, 255, 258, 262, 271, 279, 285, 304–5, 308–9
  and God as rock 31, 44, 47, 62–5, 67, 165, 275
  human 3–6, 8, 16, 36, 38, 44–5, 47–8, 50, 63, 67, 72, 96, 98, 104–5, 118–19, 126–7, 163–4, 186, 195, 213–14, 215 n. 95, 255, 258, 266, 271, 279, 280 n. 11, 281, 283 n. 19, 295 nn. 66 & 67, 300–1, 308, 317, 319, 326, 328–9, 331
  intellectual 3–4, 15, 21 n. 39, 28, 36–8, 44–5, 47–8, 53, 57, 60, 63, 72, 89, 92–3, 96, 99 n. 32, 165, 186, 205, 213–14, 229, 232, 258, 262, 271, 279, 281, 285, 286 n. 32, 286 n. 35, 295 n. 66, 300–1, 304–5, 308
  love of God as 16–17, 36, 68, 205
  material possessions as not 99
  in messianic era 16, 186, 266, 280 n. 11, 295 n. 66, 300–1, 316, 331
  moral 4, 8, 15, 28 n. 57, 38, 43–5, 48, 53, 57, 62, 72, 89, 93, 98–9, 105, 128, 162, 216, 229, 233, 253, 262, 271 n. 22, 279, 285, 286 n. 32, 286 n. 35, 300, 304–5, 332
  moral as a prerequisite for intellectual 4, 28 n. 57, 38, 89, 93, 229, 285, 286 n. 32, 286 n. 35, 300
  nature as 2, 44–7, 53, 62–5, 67, 70, 96, 165, 167 n. 70, 304, 309, 329, 331
  Song of Songs as about 281
  as universal 4–5, 38, 47, 67, 286 n. 32, 295 n. 67, 301, 308, 319
permanence vs. process 331–2
Persian empire 223 n. 5
persuasiveness of Maimonides' writings 46, 83 n. 6, 226 n. 12, 228, 318
Pharaoh 135–6, 140
Pharisees 88, 92
phylacteries, *see* tefillin
physics, *see* ma'aseh bereshit *and* ma'aseh merkavah
piety, *see* ḥasidut

pillar of the world:
  Abraham as 31, 32 n. 67, 51–62, 140
  God as 22–4, 27
  kind deeds as 151, 162, 215–16
  Moses as 51–62
  offerings as 147, 151, 161–2, 215–16
  peace as 216 n. 98
  prayer as 151
  Temple service as 151, 215–16
  Torah as 151, 215–16
Pines, Shlomo:
  on commandments 95 n. 20, 96 n. 22, 171
  on morality 15 n. 5
  and the names of God 272
  on righteousness 255
  on universalism 1
piyutim 133–4
planets:
  angels governing 321, 327
  emanation of 325–6
  as intellectual beings 204, 323
  movement of 24, 322 n. 11, 323, 327, 334
  no correspondence between humans and 334
  permanent nature of 326
  as proof of God's existence 24
Plato 68, 215 n. 95, 307
Plotinus 324
Popper, Karl 296
Porphyry 215 n. 95
poverty and the poor:
  avoiding 250
  benevolence towards 79, 129, 177, 226, 250, 268
  charity as not resulting in 225
  charity towards heathens 79, 177, 226
  as a contemporary virtue 108–9
  giving sacrifices to 173
  nazir as not necessarily one of 118 n. 37
  not synonymous with piety 107 n. 5, 108, 125–6, 128, 142, 240 n. 20
  obligations of 225
prayer:
  Al hanisim as added on Hanukah and Purim 79, 81

apprehensions of intellect in 213
and commandments as instruments 97,
    101
devaluation vs. elevation of 99 n. 33
on fast days 225
of Gentiles and proselytes 21 n. 37, 46
as inadequate praise of God 212–14
laws of 21
for the messiah to come 285, 296
for peace of Jerusalem 5 n. 12, 218 n. 101
placement of in hierarchy of worship
    215 n. 95
set services for 40, 55
Shema as foundation for 17 n. 14
sincerity of 161
tefillin worn during morning prayer 41
Temple as house of 131 n. 15, 223
for way of truth 139
world standing upon 151
priestly blessing 21, 40
Prime Existent, *see* God
principles of faith 131, 231–2, 273 n. 32,
    284, 296
Principles of Faith (Abravanel) 23–4
principles of Judaism 227–33
principles of religion, see *ikarei hadat*
process vs. permanence 331–2
prophets and prophecy:
    of Abraham 51, 52 n. 45, 58–9, 312
    against immoral people entering Temple
        192
    Amalekites' aspiration to 140 n. 48
    commandments as transmitted via 7,
        329
    of Daniel 290
    on deliberate poverty 107, 121
    of Elijah 80, 293
    emanation of from God to 187, 257
    false 31
    of Gentiles 38, 229, 241
    God as bestowing 208
    in *Guide* 10 n. 30, 16
    on imitating the middle path of God 124,
        139, 181
    as insight into physics and metaphysics
        166, 168

of Isaiah 279, 286, 291, 296 n. 68
Maimonides not a 289 n. 44
of Malachi 285
in and of messianic age 16, 278 n. 5,
    279, 283 n. 19, 285–8, 289 n. 44,
    290–1, 293–4, 296 n. 68
of Moses 7, 51, 52 n. 45, 58–9, 61, 68,
    166, 168, 224, 257, 274, 285–6, 329
Nazarites as equal to 117–18
parables as part of 100
scoffing at as sin without possibility for
    repentance 135, 139
serving God with ulterior motives not
    ranking with 18
as teacher of 61
and unity of God 22
as universal 7, 312
proselytes 15, 46, 222–7, 233, 251
providence:
    of the cosmos 164
    of God 64, 66, 171, 250, 258
    perfection leading to 38
    universalism of 229
punishment, *see* reward and punishment
Purim 73–81, 223, 302
purity and purification:
    after leprosy 150 n. 20, 184
    in *Commentary on the Mishnah* 200
    of food 88, 92, 93 n. 10, 184, 189, 203
    of Gentiles 186 n. 8
    of God 77, 80, 294, 314
    intellectual 183–220, 260, 304, 314, 330
    intentionality of 184–5, 189, 192, 210
    laws of as serving the individual 189–90
    marital 83–4, 86–9, 314
    materiality vs. 203, 211
    in *Mishneh torah* 9, 190–2, 207
    moral 88–9, 183–220
    as parable 144, 194, 214–15, 220
    of physical objects 183–4, 186 n. 8, 188
    ritual 89, 92–3, 106, 145, 183–220, 304,
        307
    of sacrifices and the Temple 75, 80,
        144–5, 156, 159, 162, 172–3, 183–4,
        188–94, 198, 203, 207, 211–15,
        218–20, 304, 307, 330

purity and purification (*cont.*):
  separation leading to 88, 92–3
  as statute 150 n. 20, 155–6, 159, 183–4,
    188, 190–4, 204, 213–15, 219, 330 n. 48
  see also *mikveh*

R
Raba 74 n. 5, 95
Rabad, *see* Abraham ben David
Rabinovich, Nachum 26 n. 51, 83 n. 4, 130 n. 9
Rabinowitz, Jacob J. 1 n. 1, 268
Radak (David Kimhi) 223
Rashi 82 n. 1, 179, 223, 241 n. 21, 250
Ravitzky, Aviezer 53 n. 50, 280 n. 11, 298 n. 73
reasons for the commandments, *see ta'amei hamitsvot*
red heifer:
  in messianic era 159
  Moses' knowledge of reason for 166 n. 69
  purification of 155, 159, 183, 193 n. 37
  similarities to paganism 155
  as statute 146, 150 n. 20, 155, 166 n. 69, 183
Reif, Stefan 79
repentance:
  after vow of consecration 174
  atoning without 195 n. 44
  as beginning of moral and social regeneration 317
  benevolence towards sinner in expectation of 222, 227, 316
  as commandment 15
  on Day of Atonement 135
  following idolatry in *Mishneh torah*'s structure 82 n. 1, 210
  free will as essential for 15, 139
  passion for 195, 207, 209, 219
  as purity 210
  sacrifices as encouragement for 195, 199, 219
  shofar as wake-up call for 192, 196
  sins without 135–6, 139–40, 228
  as state of mind 208–9
  and Torah study 209
  as universal 140
  world to come as a result of 228
resident alien 137, 141
reward and punishment:
  vs. actions for their own sake 19–20, 31 n. 64, 62
  capital 269 n. 14
  of commandments 19–20, 50, 60, 62, 78, 101, 157, 170, 172, 231–2, 285–6, 315
  free will as essential for 15, 64
  for morality and immorality 18 n. 23, 101
  perfection as love of God without regard for 16–17, 19–20, 60, 62
  revelation and reason 7, 13, 153 n. 27, 293 n. 57
  truth beyond 17
  without repentance 140
  in world to come 19, 60, 168–72, 231–2, 286
righteous Gentile 141
righteousness, *see tsadikut*
ritual purity and immersion, *see mikveh*; purity and purification
rock, God as 31, 44, 47, 62–5, 67, 165, 275
Rosenzweig, Franz 291
Rosh Hashanah 133–5, 192
Rubenstein, Shmuel Tanhum 26 n. 51

S
Sa'adyah Gaon, R.:
  Book of Beliefs and Opinions 230–1
  introducing systematic theology into Judaism 230
  on rational vs. revealed commandments 157
  recognition of God before 23
  version of *Al hanisim* 79
sabbath, the:
  circumcision and 50–1, 70–2
  as a dual-purpose commandment 314
  lamp 73–4, 76–7
  observance of 131 n. 15, 222–3, 239
  as one of the Torah's only intended original laws 307
  restrictions 73

sanctification of 74, 76
slaves working on 237 n. 6, 240
sabbatical year 131 n. 15, 173, 287
Sabian cult 164
sacrifices:
  communal vs. individual 145, 173, 200–4, 211
  as connection to God 157, 203, 207, 220
  as consecrations 106–8, 111, 120, 126
  on Day of Atonement 145
  demise of 10 n. 30, 161, 198, 200
  disqualifications for 145
  eating 145 n. 8, 173, 188–9, 215 n. 95
  as God's second intention 307, 331
  in *Guide* 150–2, 155, 156 n. 39, 159–62, 164, 172, 182, 196–9, 214, 218, 220, 289 n. 44, 306
  vs. intellect 259
  Isaac as 52, 53 n. 50, 68
  in Judaism as accommodation to pagan practice 150, 164, 195, 213, 263, 307 n. 8
  karet as punishment for failure to circumcise or make the paschal offering 60 n. 77
  lasting value of 198–9
  as lowest form of worship 151, 198, 213, 215 n. 95
  Maimonides' systematization of 201–2
  as means of influencing divinity 30–1, 102, 157–8
  in messianic era 131 n. 15, 159–60, 198, 224 n. 7, 286–7, 289 n. 44
  morality as coming from 176, 204, 304
  in Neoplatonism compared with Maimonides' system of 215 n. 95
  outside the Temple 117 n. 35
  as parable 144, 194, 196–7, 200, 214–15, 217–20
  as part of conversion 224 n. 7
  as a prompt to thought 150, 160, 164, 181, 195, 198–200, 204, 207, 211, 213–16, 220, 304
  as purification 173, 188–9
  as reflecting cosmic structures 204–8
  role of in repentance 145, 195, 199
  as sanctified 175
  self-perfection as ideal 215 n. 95, 304
  as statutes 99, 147, 150–1, 155–62, 169, 193 n. 37, 216, 307
  substitutions for 173–5, 181
  Temple as house for 131 n. 15, 145, 203, 223, 224 n. 7, 287, 307, 332
  Torah study as modern-day equivalent to 198
  as training for middle path 120
  as universal 31, 161, 169, 172, 176, 197, 259
  world stands on 147, 151, 161–2, 215–16
Samuel 247
sanctification:
  of the commandments 73, 82 n. 1, 90–105, 112, 114, 122, 146, 152, 154, 174–5, 182, 264–5, 303, 333
  for entrance into world to come 138–9, 143, 279
  of God's name 121–6, 241, 333
  morality leading to 88, 125, 333
  positive and negative aspects of 90 n. 1, 122–3
  purity leading to 88, 189–90
  of the sabbath 74, 76
  of sacrifices 175
  separation as 82 n. 1, 88, 90–3, 114, 122, 127–8, 303
  of the soul 88
  universal 93, 104–5, 129–43, 279, 303, 308
Sanhedrin 269 n. 14, 277 n. 1, 283 n. 20
Sarah 63, 306
Satan 87 n. 22, 154 n. 32
scapegoat:
  as parable 192 n. 36, 194–6, 207, 217, 219
  sacrifice of on Day of Atonement 145, 150 n. 20, 194
Schiller, Friedrich 12
Schneersohn, R. Menachem Mendel (Lubavitcher Rebbe) 8, 278 n. 3, 293 n. 58
Scholem, Gershom 283 n. 21
Schwarz, Michael 15 n. 5

Schwarzfuchs, Simon-Raymond 295 n. 65
Schwarzschild, Steven 230, 282, 297
science of the Torah 10–12, 23, 33, 162, 216, 322
Seeman, Don 29 nn. 58 & 59, 218 n. 103, 281 n. 14
Seeskin, Kenneth 284
sefirot 334 n. 59
Seir, Mount 288 n. 39
semikhah 283 n. 20
separate intellects 170, 187, 198, 211, 324–5, 336
  see also angels
separation:
  of angels from matter 203, 324
  of the covenants of law and love 61
  of God from the cosmos 32 n. 67, 65, 260, 270, 310, 317
  hafla'ah as 113–16, 127–8
  intellectual 93
  of the Jewish people 47, 91–2, 114, 149
  of means and ends of commandments in *Guide* 11
  as sanctification 82 n. 1, 88, 90–3, 114, 122, 127–8, 303
Septimus, Bernard 14 n. 4, 18 n. 21, 22–3 n. 41, 30–1 nn. 62 & 63, 223
Seth 287 n. 38
sha'atnez 101
Shailat, R. Isaac 8, 227, 295 n. 65
Shatz, M. Y. 181 n. 29
Shavuot 133, 145
shefa, *see* emanation
sheḥitah, *see* slaughter as an instrumental commandment
shekhinah:
  Gentiles sheltering under the wings of 224 n. 7, 226
  sacrifices causing Jews to dwell with 157
  sanctification of the soul leading to imitation of 88, 92–3, 203
  in the Temple 171
Shem 31
Shem Tov ben Joseph ibn Shem Tov 230 n. 29
Shem Tov ben Shem Tov ibn Shem Tov 96 n. 23

Shem Tov ibn Shem Tov 28 n. 57
Shema:
  vs. apprehensions of the intellect 213
  connection between Abraham and 54–5
  as a foundation for prayer 17 n. 14
  laws of reciting 21, 40, 57
  love of God in 17, 40, 54, 55 n. 55, 56–7
  mezuzah containing 41
  tefillin containing 41
  tsitsit mentioned in 41
  understanding 213 n. 90
Shimon ben Gamliel, R. 216 n. 98
shofar 133, 192–3, 196
Simon the Just 151, 161–2, 215–16
Sinai, Mount:
  idolatry at 307
  Judaism as starting at 58–9, 71, 224
  revelation at 7, 58, 141, 142 n. 59
Sinai wilderness 307
slaughter as an instrumental commandment 94–102
slaves and slavery:
  as accommodation to economic reality 262–4
  benevolence and mercy towards 13, 129, 224, 226, 235–66, 304, 313
  circumcision of 51 n. 41, 237 n. 6
  descendants of 294
  equality of 253–7
  social not racial 264–5
social commandments, *see mitsvot bein adam leḥavero*
Socrates 68 n. 118
Solomon, King:
  love of God of 19
  messiah as descendant of 285
  messiah as even greater than 282 n. 19, 286
  Torah before 100
  understanding of statutes of 150 n. 20, 174, 181 n. 29
Soloveitchik, R. Joseph B.:
  on commandments 97 n. 23, 104, 196–7
  The Halakhic Mind 197 n. 50
  on knowledge 22 n. 41
  on loving-kindness 255 n. 62

on *Mishneh torah* as halakhic 8–9
subjective correlative of Maimonides vs. 196–7
on time 65 n. 105
sotah 78, 84, 86 n. 17
soul according to Plotinus 210, 324, 328, 332
spheres:
  as beyond human comprehension 164–5
  as eternal 22, 24, 273, 326–7, 331
  God as in control of 22, 24, 30–1, 32 n. 67, 140, 163, 165, 218, 271, 273, 309–10, 327, 336
  hierarchy of 167, 321–7, 335–7
  as intellectual beings 44, 204–8, 211–14, 218, 323–5, 327, 329, 334, 336
  as *ma'aseh bereshit* 18 n. 20
  outermost 24, 268–73, 275, 316, 323, 325, 334
  worship of 31
Spinoza, Baruch 27, 34, 132 n. 19
stars:
  as eternal 24, 326–7, 334
  God as in control of 24, 30, 32 n. 67, 54
  hierarchy of 321, 323, 325, 327, 329, 334, 337
  as intellectual beings 204–8, 211, 323, 325, 327, 329
  worship of 30–1, 140
statutes (*ḥukim*):
  bestowal of by God 236, 253, 256, 265, 312
  as contradictory vs. unexplained 154–6
  as conveying esoteric message 157, 214–15
  definitions of ordinances vs. 146 n. 9, 147, 150, 152–7, 162, 166
  dispute of 146, 149, 153, 156, 168
  explanations for 3 n. 4, 150, 155
  as expression of God 160
  King David knowing reasons for 161, 168, 174
  levirate marriages as 155, 239 n. 16
  Maimonides' approach to as part of dialectic 193–4, 202, 219

Moses knowing reasons for 166 n. 69
necessity of keeping God's 56, 146–7, 156, 174, 193 n. 37
not a fixed category 155, 159, 169
not universal 149
opinion of by other nations 3 n. 4, 137, 148, 153, 155–6, 265
performance of as meriting life in world to come 147, 149, 151, 169–70, 172, 180, 215, 318 n. 28
purity laws as 150 n. 20, 155–6, 159, 183–4, 188, 190–4, 204, 213–15, 219, 330 n. 48
sacrifices as 147, 150, 155–7, 159, 161, 169, 193 n. 37, 216
as universal 144, 147–8, 158, 161, 166, 169–70, 172
value of 148
Stern, Josef 57 n. 67, 155 n. 33, 156
Strauss, Leo:
  on equality 132 n. 19
  on esotericism 167 n. 72
  Kenneth Hart Green on 25 n. 50
  on Maimonidean numerology 129
  on messianic enlightenment 282 n. 18
  and names of God 272
style and expression of *Mishneh torah*'s book endings 318–20
subjective correlative of Maimonides vs. Soloveitchik 196–7
Suhrawadi, Abu Hafs al- 108–9
Sukkot 100 n. 37, 133, 173, 224
sun, the:
  angel governing 321
  deification of 195
  emanation of 325, 336–7
  as metaphor for enlightenment 68 n. 118
  movements of 323
supererogatory behaviour 240–2
Syrians 75 n. 7, 80 n. 24

T
ta'amei hamitsvot:
  Aristotle's four causes and 163–5
  benevolence 129

ta'amei hamitsvot (cont.):
  contemplation of 29 nn. 58 & 59
  as education and habituation 66
  endings of books of *Temple Service, Offerings*, and *Purity* as 144, 147, 172, 175–6, 179, 182, 187, 193–4, 197, 202–4, 208, 211, 213, 216, 219, 303–4, 316
  as esoteric 167, 218
  in *Guide* 10 n. 30, 98 n. 26, 98 nn. 28 & 29, 100–1, 121, 123, 130, 150–3, 155, 159–62, 164–5, 167, 170, 172, 179–80, 182, 190–1, 196–7, 218–19, 251, 268, 304, 306, 314–16, 331
  as instruments 90–105
  looking for 158, 162, 164–5, 174
  love of God as one of 57
  in *Mishneh torah* 191–2, 196, 218, 301, 329
  negative 115
  opposing views on 157–8
  pagan practices as background to 150, 164, 195, 213, 263, 307 n. 8
  for restraint leading to the middle path 43, 45, 47–8, 56, 119–20, 122, 124, 149, 175–6, 179–80, 186, 193, 315, 318 n. 28, 330, 333
  separation of Jews from other nations 122
  statutes vs. ordinances 146–60, 162, 166, 168–70, 175, 183, 189, 193, 196, 202–3, 213, 215 n. 95, 216, 219, 239–40 n. 16, 265, 303
Tabernacle, the 78, 139, 201 n. 57, 307
tabernacles (sukkot) 100
Tabernacles, Feast of, *see* Sukkot
tefillin 21, 41, 122, 231 n. 33
Temple, the:
  actions as parables in ritual of 194, 196–7, 214, 217–20
  arrangement of laws of in *Mishneh torah* 194, 304
  avoiding over-familiarity with 190
  bringing first fruits to 47
  commandments compared to fabric and contents of 153

deriving personal benefit from 145
destruction of second 75, 183
donations to 175
ethical aspect of rituals 181
fabric of 173, 239, 332
First 145, 161
Greeks breaching 74–5
hakhel in 173
Hanukah miracle in 75, 80
as link between books of *Temple Service, Offerings*, and *Purity* 193, 201–4, 211, 214, 217, 219–20, 304, 330
moral value of rituals of 195, 214
as one of three things the world stands on 151, 215
paying for upkeep of 106, 110
philosophical notions of rituals of 143–72, 197, 207, 212–14, 217–20, 304
physical aspects of 145, 153
prayer in 55, 214
prohibition of devoting all of one's assets to 116
purity laws as serving 80, 144–5, 156, 159, 183–4, 188–93, 203, 207, 212–14, 219–20, 304, 330
purpose of rituals in 160
rebuilding and function of in the messianic age 143, 159, 183, 188, 189 n. 22, 198, 224 n. 7, 286–7, 289, 332
respect for 145, 169, 171, 176 n. 6, 190–1, 214, 218–19, 304, 307, 331
rituals of as statutes 156–61, 214, 330
sacrifices in 117 n. 35, 145, 156, 159–61, 173, 194, 198–9, 201–3, 207, 213–14, 220, 224 n. 7, 287, 307, 332
sanctification of the Holy of Holies in 138–9, 143
Second 75, 161, 183
service in 145, 151, 214
sotah test in 78, 85 n. 15
studying laws of 198–9
vandalism of 122
voluntary sacrifices in 111, 119
see also Holy of Holies
Ten Commandments, *see* Decalogue
Tepper, Aryeh 130

Tetragrammaton 23, 274
theurgy 158, 185 n. 5, 303, 305
Thirteen Principles of Faith 131, 231–2, 273 n. 32, 284, 296
  see also *ikarei hadat*
Torah, bestowal of 166 n. 69, 257–8
Torah scroll 21, 41, 136
Torah study:
  as equivalent to Temple offering 198
  as including physics and metaphysics (*pardes*) 1, 10, 33, 100, 208 n. 76, 210, 298
  motivation of 118 n. 39
  not synonymous with piety 126–7
  and repentance 209
  as waters of intellect 210–12
Touger, Eliyahu 132 n. 19
Tower of Babel 291
transcendence of God 6, 271, 273, 275–6, 305, 317
Treatise on the Art of Logic 130
Treatise on Resurrection 289, 297 n. 71
tripartite orientation of the intellect 208, 219, 259–60, 304, 313–16
truth, morality as 97, 178–80, 182, 187, 263, 296, 310
tsadikut (righteousness):
  in *aravot* 270–1
  charity as mark of 176–7, 225
  as coming from Abraham 176–8, 226–7, 236, 261, 318
  of the commandments 265
  of Gentiles 141, 265
  of God and as imitation of God 36, 124, 126, 131, 139, 222, 226–7, 236, 254 n. 60, 255–6, 258, 260–1, 271, 279, 305, 308, 318
  in messianic era 282–3 n. 19, 284
  moral virtue as 66, 258, 265
  motivation for 228
  of Noahides 141
  obligation to live in society that practises 125
  power of 80, 134, 143 n. 60
  and repentance 228
  on Rosh Hashanah 135
  statutes and ordinances as 147, 149, 151, 169–70, 180, 236, 256, 265, 318 n. 28
  world to come as reward for 141, 147, 149, 151, 169–70, 180, 228, 284, 318 n. 28
tsedakah, see charity
tsitsit, see fringes
tsora'at, see leprosy
Twersky, Isadore:
  on the arrangement of *Mishneh torah* 110
  on the foundations of law 11 n. 34, 312
  Introduction to Code of Maimonides 8
  on messianic era 278 n. 5, 308 n. 10
  'The *Mishneh Torah* of Maimonides' 278 n. 5
  on morality 178, 242, 252–3
  on the non-halakhic aspects of *Mishneh torah* 6, 8
  on statutes 148 n. 16, 151, 161 n. 54, 196 n. 49

U
Unetaneh tokef 133–4
Universal Declaration of Human Rights 262 n. 73
universalism:
  of the Abrahamic model 2, 51–3, 55, 57–8, 61, 67, 262, 266, 300–1, 305, 308 n. 10, 311–12
  in attitude towards slaves 13, 129, 224, 226, 235–66, 304, 313
  of charity 177
  of circumcision 42 n. 5, 47–8, 57, 72, 262
  of the commandments 1–2, 4–7, 9, 11–13, 21, 30, 39, 47–8, 70, 72, 104, 126, 144, 147–50, 152, 161, 166, 168–71, 176–7, 182–3, 186–8, 197, 210, 218, 239, 242, 248, 253, 256, 262–3, 266, 275, 286 n. 32, 300–1, 303–4, 308 n. 10, 311–13, 318–19, 333
  definition of 1–5
  elements of matter as 323
  and esotericism in the Torah 1, 6, 18 n. 20, 95, 100, 166 n. 69, 167, 182, 197, 208, 210, 218, 298, 302, 310–11, 332

universalism (cont.):
  of *Guide* 11, 48, 52, 91 n. 4, 148, 150, 152, 197, 218, 308
  imitatio Dei as 259, 280
  of Jewish relations with Gentiles 2, 4, 13, 79–80, 132 n. 19, 148, 170, 176, 223, 233, 255 n. 62, 259, 261–3, 266, 304, 319
  of knowledge 12, 20 n. 35, 30, 39, 168, 170, 182, 186–7, 210–11, 219, 234, 259, 263, 280, 291, 295 n. 67, 299, 301, 304, 311–12, 316, 319
  of love 21, 39, 262
  messianic 2, 6, 77, 80, 147, 186, 233, 276–301, 305, 308 n. 10
  of *Mishneh torah* 1, 3–13, 21, 42, 48, 53, 72, 91 n. 4, 127, 150, 152, 158, 172, 176, 181, 186, 188, 218–19, 237–8, 242, 256, 266, 276, 295 n. 67, 301–2, 305–6, 308–9, 311–12, 318–19
  of morality 3–4, 9, 12, 47, 89, 143, 148, 176–8, 182, 237 n. 6, 256, 266, 286 n. 32, 304, 312
  of the Mosaic model 51–3, 58, 61, 70
  of nature 7, 166, 169, 304, 320
  of ordinances 148
  vs. particularist values 12–13, 53, 58, 91 n. 4, 126, 149, 170, 233, 237–8, 241–2, 251, 253, 256, 259, 262, 266, 276, 304, 320, 328, 333
  of peace 74, 76–89, 291, 299, 301, 303, 305, 314, 317 n. 28, 319
  of perfection 4–5, 38, 47, 67, 286 n. 32, 295 n. 67, 301, 308, 319
  prophecy as 7, 312
  providence as 229
  repentance as 140
  sacrifices as 31, 161, 169, 172, 176, 197, 259
  sanctification as 93, 104–5, 129–43, 279, 303, 308
  statutes as 144, 147–8, 158, 161, 166, 169–70, 172
  of world to come 3, 48, 57, 138, 169–70, 182, 234, 305
universe, *see* cosmology and the cosmos

Ur of the Chaldees 31–2, 140

V

values, clash of, *see* conflict between commandments
virtue, poverty as a 108–9
virtue as God's glory, inner 127
visions in book of Ezekiel 2 n. 3, 17 n. 19, 153 n. 27, 167
vows:
  of abstinence 82 n. 1, 106, 113–19, 121
  annulling marital 111 n. 19
  of consecration 106–7, 110–13, 117–21
  motivation of 118
  oaths as sanctification of God's name 115, 121, 125
  and piety 118–20
  as restoratives of the middle path 116–21
  as separation 113–15
  and substituted offerings 174

W

water:
  as metaphor for emanation 187–8, 211, 219, 257, 260, 304, 324
  as metaphor for intellect and knowledge of God 86, 186, 219, 279, 296, 298–9, 304
  as metaphor for Torah 100, 210–12
  mixed with red heifer ashes 155, 183, 193 n. 37
  as one of four elements 321, 326, 337
  of the *sotah* 78
  see also mikveh
wisdom:
  analysing the world as interrelated parts 255
  of avoiding deliberate poverty 127
  of the commandments 29 n. 59, 149, 158, 160, 165, 191, 215 n. 95, 253, 265, 285–6, 312
  of creation 165, 255–6
  of Gentiles 141 n. 52
  glory of 99 n. 30, 271
  of God 25, 28, 29 n. 59, 33–5, 38, 66, 69, 99, 123, 148–9, 160, 165, 169, 185, 191, 205, 215 n. 95, 253–60, 265, 310–12

imitating God's 69, 253–60
as key to a share in world to come 283, 285–6, 295–6
in messianic era 282–3 n. 19, 284–6, 288, 295–6
and the middle path 119, 243–4, 318 n. 28
morality as means towards 283
of Noahides 141
in parables 11–12, 67, 100, 194–5, 197, 207, 214–15, 217–20
and piety 242–5, 253, 258, 266
of repentance 135
of statutes 137, 148–9, 158, 160, 253, 265
of the Torah 3 n. 4, 18, 20, 285–6, 295–6, 298
treatment towards slaves 235, 238, 242–4, 253
warning the wayward wife with 85–9
world to come:
Abraham and his followers achieving 33 n. 72, 43, 48–9, 141 n. 52, 232
circumcision as essential for achievement of 41, 43, 48–9, 57, 60
commandments as instruments for achievement of 172, 180, 285–6
as concurrent with this world 284 n. 26
as contemplation of God 43, 170
converts' share in 229, 232
era of Torah ending with 284 n. 26
Gentiles' share in 3, 33 n. 72, 43, 138–9, 141, 149, 229
heretics' place in 227–8, 231
messianic era's purpose as achievement of 16, 279, 282 n. 19, 283–6, 295–6
moral and intellectual perfection as essential for achievement of 38, 57, 143, 180, 229, 232, 279, 282–3 n. 19, 285, 286 n. 35, 295–6
motive for achieving 18–19
Nahmanides on 289
parallel verses in Genesis and Isaiah regarding 296 n. 68
as part of the laws of repentance 15, 18, 228
performance of statutes and ordinances as essential for achievement of 147, 149, 151, 162 n. 55, 169–70, 180, 318 n. 28
performing commandments out of love regardless of 16, 18–19
prophecies of Isaiah regarding 279, 286, 291, 296 n. 68
rewards in 168–71, 231 n. 34, 285–6
understanding and acceptance of the Torah as essential for achievement of 231–2, 285–6, 295–6
universalism of 3, 48, 57, 138, 169–70, 182, 234, 305
see also immortality
Written Torah 9, 138, 289, 311–12

Y

Yehudah, R. 118 n. 39
Yohanan ben Zakai, R. 155–6, 193 n. 37, 245–7
Yom Kippur, *see* Day of Atonement

Z

Zion, Mount 288 n. 39
Zionism 282 n. 17
Zohar 104 n. 46

www.ingramcontent.com/pod-product-compliance
Lightning Source LLC
Chambersburg PA
CBHW061421300426
44114CB00015B/2018